THE LONG WEEK-END

A Social History of Great Britain
1918–1939

ROBERT GRAVES was born in 1895 and educated at Charterhouse and St. John's College, Oxford. He came of age on the eve of World War I, and served in France with the Royal Welch Fusiliers. His autobiography, *Goodbye to All That,* which he wrote in 1929 and revised in 1957, stands as a monument to the overwhelming disillusionment that the war brought to his generation.

Graves has gained a distinguished reputation as a poet, as a novelist, and as a translator. His novel *I, Claudius* won the Hawthornden and James Tait Black Memorial Prizes for 1934. Among his outstanding translations is *The Golden Ass of Apuleius.* He was awarded the Gold Medal of the National Poetry Society of America in 1960, and was appointed Professor of Poetry at Oxford in 1961. He presently makes his home on Mallorca in the Balearic Islands.

ALAN HODGE was born in 1915 and educated at the Liverpool Collegiate School and Oriel College, Oxford. He was Assistant Private Secretary to the Minister of Information from 1941 to 1945 and then entered the publishing concern of Hamish Hamilton as editor of "The Novel Library." Since 1951 he has been joint editor with Peter Quennell of the magazine *History Today.*

Besides *The Long Week-end,* Alan Hodge has written *The Reader Over Your Shoulder* and *The Past We Share* (with Peter Quennell).

THE LONG WEEK-END

A Social History of Great Britain
1918-1939

by

ROBERT GRAVES

and

ALAN HODGE

The Norton Library
W · W · NORTON & COMPANY · INC ·
NEW YORK

First published in the Norton Library 1963

To

K.G.

in gratitude for much
hard work

SBN 393-00217-9

PRINTED IN THE UNITED STATES OF AMERICA

8 9 0

Note to First Edition

═══════

We have done what we could to verify the facts contained in this short history. A number of errors must still remain, if only because the sources that we chiefly rely on—memoirs and contemporary newspapers—are themselves far from trustworthy. For example, we have lately been interested to find widespread disagreement in the Press about even so recent and important an event as the German re-occupation of the Rhineland: according to a large body of opinion it took place in March 1934, not 1936. We cannot explain this.

There are also, no doubt, a great many more events and topics that could have been included, had we thought of them, and had time and paper been unlimited. Why, it may be asked, are silver-fox farms not mentioned? Or the novels of Mary Webb? Or the Antique Dealers' Exhibitions? Or the Duke of Gloucester's wedding? Or the Gordon Bennett Balloon Race? Or the Mannin Beg steeplechase for racing cars? Or infant welfare centres? Fill the gaps in for yourself, please, everybody! A score of books could be written on the same general lines as ours, each completely different from the rest.

A criticism that we feel like making ourselves is that events in London and its environs are here treated in disproportion to events elsewhere. But this could not be helped: the tendency was for things either to happen first in London or to be first noted there. We have no prejudice in favour of London—and, in fact, neither of us lived there for more than a year or two during the twenty-one-year period with which we deal.

5

Note to Second Edition

We were finishing *The Long Week-end* about the time of the Dunkirk evacuation and found it difficult to keep an equable attitude of mind when there was a grave risk that German might soon be spoken in Whitehall.

We were lucky to get the work done before research facilities ended and before our chief assistant, K. G., got interned as an enemy alien—later to join the Royal Navy under a new name but the same initials—before the Long Week-end, in fact, had really closed. There was still no shortage of tobacco or chocolate, the call-up had hardly begun to disrupt family life, fashion had not been frozen by rationing and purchase tax, and Neville Chamberlain was still a member of the Government. If a bomb killed a sheep in Yorkshire it was hot news, and the accounts we gave of the ceremonies and popular demonstrations in the historic streets and buildings of London had as yet no melancholy interest.

After getting our chapters in order we wrote the opening paragraph:

'The more newspapers people read, the shorter grows their historical memory; yet most people read little else. Any sudden overwhelming public event that engrosses the headlines for days or weeks is a sponge for all that immediately preceded it. And news heard on the radio is forgotten even sooner. In the indignant outcry against the Russians, in November 1939, when the Finns resisted their demands for a strategical frontier that would put Leningrad out of range of modern guns and the Russians set up a "Red Puppet Government", one thing was universally forgotten. This was that whatever were the rights and wrongs of the case,

6

Britain had twenty years before formed a legion of Red Finns, whose existence was now denied, against General Mannerheim, their White oppressor, an ally of the Germans, who was now accepted without question as the saviour of his country. (Soon that indignant outcry too will doubtless be forgotten.)'

Indeed, by the time that the edition was exhausted, about a year later, there had been another sudden political change and a friend of our was sighing: 'Oh what a fool I was! Why did I go rushing round to my old St. Moritz friends persuading them to send their ski-ing outfits to those lousy Finns?' Now here we are in 1949 and in these days of smaller newspapers Finland has temporarily disappeared from the news so completely that not one ordinary person in a thousand could say off-hand on which side of the Iron Curtain it lies, and whether he ought to frown or smile if he happened to meet a Finn in the Strand, wearing a pair of gift ski-boots.

Dunkirk is an event already gilded with something of the glamour of Agincourt or Waterloo, and anything that happened before belongs to the legendary golden age when everyone could go where he pleased and do as he pleased when he got there, and income-tax was only a shilling or two in the £, and a man could get drunk on beer without drowning first, and a pint-kettle could be boiled on the pages of a single issue of the *Daily Telegraph*, and Britain (then called England) was still a first-class power. Re-reading *The Long Week-end* is a little embarrassing. It is like untying a bundle of your youthful love-letters or accounts of cricket matches written home from school. 'Was this really yourselves?' you will ask. And was this the same Ernest Bevin? The same Bertrand Russell? The same Bebe Daniels? It is also a salutary reminder that the years between the two wars were not at all so golden and that, whatever you may say of the dullness and restrictiveness of the present, Britain is at any rate well rid of its nastier internal dissensions and its neurotic sense of imminent catastrophe. You feel that the worst has now happened, that it was deserved, that the British as a whole have since behaved better than at any period of their history, and that though it is hard to decide whether one should view the cutting-away of so much national top-hamper with admiration or resentment, they may even, after all, have a future.

AUTHORS' NOTE

We regret that because the type of our book had to be melted during the war, it has been necessary to reprint the original text by a photographic process, which has prevented us from either making corrections or adding footnotes. It would have been fun, for example, to compare the progress of demobilization, de-rationing and re-housing after World War I with the same after World War II, and give brief accounts of the subsequent careers of such key-characters as the Duchess of Windsor, C. E. M. Joad, P. G. Wodehouse, Amy Johnson, Sir Oswald Mosley, Madame Lupescu, King Zog, and the Russell Baby.

One day, perhaps . . .

R.G.
A.H.

Contents

CONTENTS

CHAPTER ONE

Armistice, 1918

This book is intended to serve as a reliable record of what took place, of a forgettable sort, during the twenty-one year interval between two great European wars.

The more newspapers people read, the shorter grows their historical memory; yet most people read little else. Any sudden overwhelming public event—such as the outbreak of war, the coming of peace, a general election, a large-scale strike, a ruinous financial crisis—that engrosses the headlines for days or weeks, is a sponge for all that immediately preceded it. The cheapening in the price of newspapers and their immediate circulation to remote villages in the kingdom has even broken down the traditionally long memory of the countryman. And news heard on the radio is forgotten even sooner. In the indignant outcry against the Russians, in November 1939, when the Finns resisted their demands for a strategical frontier that would put Leningrad out of range of modern guns and the Russians set up a 'Red Puppet Government', one thing was universally forgotten. This was that whatever were the rights and wrongs of the case, Britain had twenty years before formed a legion of Red Finns, whose existence was now denied, against General Mannerheim, their White oppressor, an ally of the Germans, who was now accepted without question as the saviour of his country. (Soon that indignant outcry too will doubtless be forgotten.)

The 'Great War', which broke out on the 28th July 1914, with an attack by the Austrian Empire on Servia, ended on the 11th November 1918 with an armistice signed between the opposing Army High Commands. The countries which had been drawn into the fight on the side of Servia—the name being then spelt Serbia in the Press to remove the servile suggestion —were the British, French, Belgian, Italian, Portuguese, Russian and Japanese Empires, Greece, Montenegro, China, Rumania, the United States and several Latin American Republics; on the Austrian side, the German and Turkish Empires and Bulgaria. Peace was not to be signed for another seven months. Though by far the greater part of the world was belligerent, the heaviest incidence of the War had been in Europe. Japan, China, and the Latin American Republics had contented themselves chiefly with despoiling what seemed to them the losing side, of ships and other property, and selling war material to what seemed the winning side. The United States had entered the war late, and though they sent an expeditionary force of two million men to France their casualties were fortunately slight in proportion to their population—about one-fiftieth of the British proportionate losses, which in turn were about half the French and less than one-third of the German. Materially they were richer than before, while the British and French were impoverished, the Germans bankrupt, the Austrians destitute. The Americans now regarded themselves as the leading nation in the world, with most of the world's royal metal in their safe-deposit vaults as a proof of this, and with the indisputable glory of having decided the issue of the war, not so much by what they did as by what they threatened to do. Their national exuberance and the lead they gave in all social fashions, while withdrawing politically from co-operation in 'restoring world-order', is a leading factor in the 1918–39 period.

The effect on other nations of escape from the full incidence of war must also be noted: a self-satisfaction among the Scandinavian peoples as paladins of neutrality, who spent their public money on social services rather than on wasteful armaments; a sense of invincible power among the Japanese, which sent them marching into Manchuria and China; a fatal sense among the Spanish that they had escaped the war only by accident (their military rulers having in general favoured the Germans, while their industrialists supported the French) and that they would one day have to pay for their neutrality, which had been at the expense of national honour.

The Germans were beaten, though not in the spectacular military way that the Bulgarians had been beaten at Salonica, the Turks in Palestine and the Austrians on the Piave. The famous Hindenburg Line had been breached, but the Germans were retiring in good order to other defence works. The decisive element was the British blockade and mutiny behind the lines. The very severe terms imposed at the Armistice were a recognition that the game was up. At the expense of a few thousand more men the German armies could soon have been driven back into their own territory, because of the breakdown of their supply system. Pershing, the American army commander, would have preferred this to an armistice. Perhaps he was right: a complete German rout would have ruled out the later Nazi legend of an invincible German army that had its glories signed away by traitors.

Most European wars in the past two hundred years have ended in what is now derogatorily called a 'patched-up peace', that is to say a peace in which the loser is forced to cede colonies or pay an indemnity but retains national sovereignty throughout its territories—and is allowed to gather its forces for a revenge if it wishes. Our four gentlemanly wars with France in the eighteenth century, for example, had been of that nature. But this war was different: the Germans, it was said, had fought it on the novel principle of deliberately disregarding the accepted rules of European warfare. It was true that while individual French, British, Austrian, Turkish and other soldiers had done numerous atrocious deeds in the course of the fighting, usually in revenge for real or alleged atrocities by the enemy, the philosophy of 'total war', that a war can best be won by complete ruthlessness, was of German origin and did not seem decently applicable to European warfare. The torpedoing of hospital-ships, the sinking of unarmed neutral vessels without provision for the crews' safety, and the use of flame-throwers and poison-gas were German introductions that genuinely shocked British opinion; victory had therefore been looked forward to by the British generally as a justification by force of civilized manners. It was felt that a really severe peace must be imposed on the Germans (throwing the sword into the scales with a *vae victis*) in punishment for all the damage to property, the loss of life and the outrage to sensibilities that they had caused to

Europe. The Victory Medal, issued soon after the war ended, officially approved the view by styling the War 'The Great War for Civilization'.

It must here be emphasized that by the end of 1918 there were two distinct Britains: but not the two Britains of governing and governed classes, as in peace time, since the common fear of war had temporarily relaxed and almost eliminated the old rigid class distinctions. For example, a woman of aristocratic family might now without question marry not only into the merchant class but even into the labouring class, so long as the man she chose had a good military or naval record—John Galsworthy based a one-act play on this phenomenon. The two Britains were: the Fighting Forces, meaning literally the soldiers and sailors who had fought, as opposed to garrison and line-of-communication troops, and the Rest, including the Government. They talked such different languages that men home on leave after months on active service felt like visitors to a foreign country and often expressed great relief to be back on duty with their units. The reiterated conviction of the Rest, whether genuinely felt or not, was that the Fighting Forces were heroes and had a prior claim to anything good obtainable, in recompense for their extraordinary sufferings and exertions; and the Fighting Forces accepted this as their due, understanding that the gratitude would continue when victory was won, and that the world would be their football as soon as they were demobilized.

The official propaganda machine, under Lord Northcliffe's direction, had been busy spreading atrocity stories against the Germans which it did not take the trouble to verify, or to contradict if found untrue. Very many of these—such as the one about the Germans extracting fat and other raw materials from human corpses, and about the crucified Canadian, and about picked German soldiers being sent back on leave to inseminate war-widows and other husbandless women—were as false as they were plausible, and accepted without question by the Rest. But the partial or dishonest war-communiques and over-cheerful despatches from the field by special correspondents shocked the Fighting Forces, who knew the facts, and undermined their simple faith in the printed word. In the end, the disasters of war taught them a gradual disgust for the 'muddle-through' politicians who spoke in the name of Britain; bitter anger against the General Staff, who from safe billets behind the Line condemned hundreds and thousands of men to useless butchery; and a contempt, mixed with envy, for all fit males of military age, even technicians in key-industries, who had escaped their share of front-line service. Into the last class fell all young ministers of religion, except Roman Catholic chaplains, who were admired as always at hand to give extreme unction to the dying, and the exceptional Dissenting or Anglican 'Woodbine Willies' who lent the stretcher-bearers a hand on bad days, but were regarded as 'comic turns' rather than heroes. The B.E.F. were in general irreligious: they had reduced morality to the single virtue of loyalty. The Seven Deadly Sins of Pride, Envy, Lust, Avarice, Intemperance, Anger and Sloth were venial, so long as a man was courageous and a reasonably trustworthy comrade. God as an all-wise Providence was dead; blind Chance succeeded to the Throne.

This view naturally induced a perverse sympathy for the German fighting men opposite; and the simple sentiment was tediously reiterated that if the Kaiser, the Crown Prince, Hindenburg and Company were put into one trench and the British Government were put into another and both parties forced to throw bombs at each other, peace would be signed within three minutes. It was, of course, admitted that the German Government was malignant, while the British Government was just criminally stupid. The trend of feeling was thus towards 'ideal anarchism' and the consoling *après-la-guerre-finie* hopes of the serving soldier included two principal items: first a crushing of the German Government, by a defeat of the German Army, and next a clean sweep in Britain of all oppressors, cheats, cowards, skrimshankers, reactionaries and liars who had plagued and betrayed him during his service. The mood is most clearly and forcibly presented in *Counter Attack*, a book of poems by an infantry officer, Siegfried Sassoon, published before the war ended. The Lower Deck had much the same feelings, though the sailor's respect for the Germans against whom he fought was lower than that of the soldier, especially after the scuttling of the German Fleet at Scapa Flow. This anarchic mood was not constructive. Few wished to 'build a new world', as the politicians promised; the general intention was merely to cleanse the old one. The average man thought fondly of stepping back into civvies and resuming his original job, with the sole difference that he would no longer be 'b——d' about by people in authority. And the emancipated women war-workers, some millions of them, thought the same.

The popular newspapers during the latter part of the war always referred to the Germans as 'Huns'. The shortness of the term recommended it to caption writers, and it had a historical reference: the Kaiser in sending off the German contingent to the relief of the Foreign Legations at Pekin in 1900 had exhorted them to show themselves as ruthless and terrible to the Chinese as had the Huns. The implication was that the policy of barbarity in modern war had been initiated by the Kaiser on this occasion. This was not quite fair. There had always been a tacit understanding that a different code might be used by European nations against savages who would not appreciate the civilized courtesies of war; and the Chinese Boxers had indeed put themselves into the uncivilized category by their obscene mutilation of British marines. The British had taken this line in most of their colonial wars, and in 1914 the German professional officers were shocked to find that British officers were breaking the Hague Convention by carelessly using revolver bullets of the soft-nosed sort that had been necessary for 'stopping' the fanatical Dervishes. Few soldiers in the War used the word 'Hun'; the common terms for 'German' being 'Fritz', 'Jerry', 'Heinie', 'Squarehead', and 'Boche', the last borrowed from the French, short for 'Caboche' or 'cabbage-head'. Horatio Bottomley's *John Bull*, the widest-read weekly paper, tried to popularize the clumsy form 'Germ-Huns', but without success.

The propaganda campaign had been remarkably successful. The Rest of Britain, not feeling the freedom, which active service overseas alone conferred, to question or criticize the official voices, had been whipped into a blind hatred of all things German. Rudyard Kipling did some of the whipping. He wrote a popular short story about an English spinster who allowed a German airman to die before her eyes without giving him even a drink of water; and conveyed his approval of her attitude. He also wrote a poem: 'When the English Began to Hate'. 'The English' meant the Rest, not the Fighting Forces. This hatred was almost the only emotional luxury allowed them; but they had taken to church-going and to cultivating virtues at which the Fighting Forces mocked, such as High Endeavour, Humility, Thrift, Prudence, Sobriety. In schools there had been a return, under 'dug-out' masters, to an almost monastic discipline; imposed by an appeal to the boys to 'prove yourselves worthy of your brothers, who are now making the supreme sacrifice'.

These two disparate Britains were slowly and confusedly to unite in the period that came to be called, in a wistful or disparaging tone, 'The Careless Twenties'.

At the Armistice, the sudden cessation of the artillery fire which had continued ceaselessly on the Western Front for more than four years had an almost frightening effect on the troops. It was as if the kitchen clock had stopped at eleven o'clock in the morning and the household was uncertain as to when the potatoes should be put on to boil, if at all. 'When the guns stop' had been a synonym for 'when the war is over'. Yet was it over? The men were warned that they could expect no more than a temporary lull, and sternly forbidden to fraternize with the enemy. It was only very gradually that the realization came that the war was indeed over. The Army was thus in a sense cheated of a manifestation: for by the time that the official victory celebrations were held, the story was already nine months stale and had begun to stink a little. A few young officers who could get local leave from their units did immediately celebrate what was known as a 'beano' in the nearest French town; but there were no scenes in the trenches even remotely resembling those that took place at home. There the lighter-hearted part of the population ran mad, the lead being taken by Dominion soldiers and airmen with their women friends. The constabulary in many towns had orders not to intervene in any scene of disorder whatever, unless fire or loss of life threatened. There were extraordinary scenes of joviality. Guns captured in battle were pulled in procession round the towns to which they had been officially presented and pushed off bridges or quays. Sexual affairs between perfect strangers took place promiscuously in parks, shop entrances and alleyways. In the Cornmarket, Oxford, a woman paraded up and down the street waving a flag, with her skirts kilted up to her naked middle, and was cheered as a sort of presiding Venus by the Army and Air cadets quartered in the colleges. At Cambridge the cadets attacked and smashed up the office of the *Cambridge Magazine*, the only literary periodical that had been pacifist in policy.

The first night was everywhere haphazardly celebrated, but given a dignity, in London, by the appearance of King George and Queen Mary on the balcony of Buckingham Palace to bow acknowledgements to the wildly cheering crowd. Trafalgar Square was the focus of disorder. Here a party of Dominion soldiers tore down a watchman's hut to make a Victory Bonfire at the base of Nelson's Column. The pediment, the usual stand for speakers at Sunday demonstrations, is scarred to this day. The second night was 'pretty thick'—base plans having been concocted for taking advantage of the general licence. On the third night the police put on the brake, and some arrests were made.

CHAPTER TWO

Revolution Averted, 1919

The problem that now faced the Government, local authorities, and what were conveniently known as 'vested interests', was how to smother the threat of social revolution which the Fighting Forces constituted. The time-honoured solution was to soothe them with handsome promises until they were safely demobilized, meanwhile depicting the dangers and penalties of revolt in the most horrid colours. The first step, therefore, was for the Government to 'go to the country' for a vote of confidence in themselves as the men who had won the war and would now win the peace. The snap General Election that December was later called the Khaki Election on the analogy of the Boer War election of 1900. Actually, the vote of the Fighting Forces was largely annulled by this hurried manœuvre, because the new voters, though allowed to vote by proxy, had not yet been put on the registers. Besides, the Opposition to the Coalition Government had not had time to raise its head from the dust into which the Defence of the Realm Act had crushed it; so that in most constituencies no alternative candidate was offered to the Lloyd George nominee.

The election went off quietly, even apathetically. Barely half the electorate in the London Boroughs voted; and in the provinces the proportion was not much higher. Demobilization had been undertaken so cautiously that only a few of the first category in the order of precedence—schoolmasters and other harmless specialists—had been able to get home for the poll.

The Rest of Britain looked upon Lloyd George, 'The Wizard

of Wales', with fascinated reverence, and expected him to build the new world order with a wave of his wand, while they relaxed. It was to them that the political catchwords 'Hang the Kaiser' and 'Make Germany Pay' were addressed. To the Fighting Forces, Lloyd George made promises which he was unable to fulfil and which eventually discredited him: the chief one being that slums would soon be swept away from the face of Britain and 'homes fit for heroes' constructed in their place. The result of the election was an enormous Coalition majority, consisting of highly amenable members, few of whom had previous parliamentary experience. Such a majority has always been dangerous as tempting a government to override, either in idleness or over-busyness, all criticism from both inside and outside the House. The Liberal Party that had been so securely in power before the war was divided against itself: most candidates received a 'Coalition coupon' as followers of Lloyd George, and of those who remained true to Asquith (whom Lloyd George had ousted from office in 1916 as a result of popular clamour largely instigated by the *Daily Mail*) only twenty-seven got elected—they were known as the 'Wee Frees'. Sixty-two Labour members brought the forces of the Opposition up to eighty-nine; the Coalition securing 516 seats. The disparity would have been less grotesque had the seventy-three Irish Nationalists, then called Sinn Feiners, taken their seats. The Irish vote had traditionally been the sliding make-weight between the two elder parties. But the Sinn Feiners unanimously refused to take the Oath of Allegiance, and consequently could not sit. Among them was the Countess Markiewicz (née Gore-Booth), who had won an infamous notoriety for shooting a wounded British policeman during the Troubles.

The Countess was the only woman elected to Parliament: a generally disappointing result of the new law by which, as a reward for their war services, women were for the first time allowed both to vote and to become members of Parliament. It was not, however, full adult suffrage that had been granted them, as to the men: though women over twenty-one were allowed to stand for election, only women over thirty were allowed to vote. It was expected that these elder women, uninfected with the revolutionary mood that possessed the younger ones—who had done the hardest and most thankless war-work

—would be an asset to 'the party of law and order' with which the Coalition now identified themselves. It was also calculated that few women in the early thirties would care to register as voters, for fear of revealing their age: in those days excessive delicacy was still observed in the matter of mentioning a woman's age. The 'safeness' of women voters was emphasized in the Press: a woman writer in the *Daily Mail* was encouraged to observe, for example, that 'we women think that the things in life that really matter will count for more, and that the squabbles of the "in's and out's" will count for less, because of the women's vote'. The violent heroines of the pre-War Suffragette movement, who had disfigured putting-greens with vitriol and chained themselves to railings, and screamed, were almost forgotten. This granting of the vote to the elder women created far less excitement than the subsequent enfranchisement of women of twenty-one—the so-called Flapper's Vote—which was held by most Conservatives to be a gratuitous present to the forces of revolution.

Though the Great War was over, so far as the fighting was concerned, the blockade against Germany was being relentlessly enforced until the disarmament terms of the Armistice should be fulfilled and Peace duly signed. Several smaller wars too were still in progress. British troops co-operating with the White generals, Koltchak and Denikin, against the U.S.S.R.—sent partly to secure British investments in Russia, partly to identify the British Army with an anti-revolutionary cause—were not withdrawn before 1920. The war against the Sinn Fein guerillas in Ireland continued until 1922; the Turkish-Greek dispute until the Treaty of Lausanne in 1923. War had been almost the sole topic of conversation for four and a half years, and it was puzzling at first for the newspapers to find any peace topic sufficiently captivating to replace war news. At the end of 1918, when the country, owing to its tremendous shipping losses and the necessity of still maintaining an army of some millions, continued under severe restrictions in food, clothing, coal, and other necessities, and German prisoners of war, with coloured patches sewn on their clothes to prevent their escape, were still working on the land, it was natural that the papers should go on printing war-pictures. The *Illustrated London News* in November and December was publishing photographs and detailed imaginative drawings of the Austrian, Bulgarian, and German surrenders; of the German Fleet approaching Scapa Flow; of the secrets of the Q-ships; of the Allied armies on guard in Cologne. For a full year more the *Daily Mail* continued to call itself 'The Soldier's Paper'. But, in general, though people were willing to read epilogue news of the war which they had won, they showed little interest in the highly coloured reports of the victorious progress of the White Russian armies, or blood-curdling stories of Red atrocities. A letter-writer to *The Times* remarked on the public indifference to the murder of Tsar Nicholas, and himself made a sober comment in a Latin elegiac couplet:

'Sir, if the story told in *The Times* a few weeks ago of the Bolsheviks' murder of the Tsar Nicholas II and his Consort and their family was as true as *The Times* seemed to think it, it was as execrable a crime of its sort as history records. Yet no comment upon it of any sort has followed, so far as I have seen. It occurred to me to write an epitaph suggested by Dido's dying cry for retribution:

> *Virtutis humani nos praeda jacemus; at ultor*
> *Ossibus e nostris exoriare aliquis!'*

Death was still extremely active that winter: but with pestilence, not shot, shell, and gas. For the first two years of the war the opposing armies had been remarkably free of infectious disease, despite mud and lice. But then came a new epidemic called Spanish or septic influenza: gathering force in 1917 and reaching its height in the winter of 1918–19. It killed twenty-seven million people, throughout the world—twice as many as the war itself—with the heaviest mortality in the territories least affected by the fighting. Nearly the whole populations of certain areas of Asia and Africa·were swept away by it: 8,500,000 died in India alone. In Germany influenza had contributed very largely to the Revolution, the British blockade having weakened physical resistance to it; and even in the United Kingdom, where the population was comparatively well fed and clothed, over 200,000 deaths were recorded. New Zealand and Australian troops fell particularly easy victims, as extensive graveyards on Salisbury Plain and elsewhere still remind us. In

England entire households, and even streets of households, were often dangerously ill in bed at the same time with nobody to look after them. A severe coal shortage aggravated matters. To Hun-haters it was some consolation that the mortality was twice as great in Germany. In the summer of 1919 there was a recurrence of the epidemic, but its victims were fewer. In church, trains, and other public places people wore antiseptic masks of flesh-coloured gauze over nose and mouth.

The general mood of weary relief at the end of the war was reflected in advertisements. 'Army Club' cigarettes showed a girl and a man in uniform, with this dialogue:

She: 'Thank goodness it's all over—now, Jack, we can settle down to peace and plenty.'

He: 'Rather, dear old thing, give me plenty of Army Club cigs and I'm at peace with the whole bally world.'

Yet in an advertisement for Beecham's Pills there was a sense of foreboding that peace might not be everything that it had been expected. A girl with cards, gazing into a crystal—for fortune-telling was enjoying a huge popularity among people who had lost relatives in the war, or who were beginning life afresh—was saying: 'Yes, there's a bright future before you—if you take Beecham's Pills.'

Serious voices were, of course, emphasizing the grave peacetime problems confronting the country and the necessity of united national effort: the 'high endeavour' note was sounded by statesmen, the Church, and a few newspapers. About this time, for example, the Conservative and sedate *Country Life* condemned a new volume of W. H. Davies's poems, as 'a number of lascivious little love poems, very much out of keeping with the time'. And the reviewer went on to say, 'Equally unworthy of the spirit of the age is the song:

> They're taxing Ale again, I hear,
> A penny more the can:
> They're taxing poor old Ale again,
> The only honest man.'

The radical *New Statesman* similarly deplored the frivolousness of people's reaction to their release from the strain of war. From a January 1919 article on 'Village Topics': 'Meanwhile, round about, "shoots" are going on. Hounds are killing or drawing blank. Estimates are being prepared for the refitting of yachts. The merits of rival designs for new motor-cars are being discussed, and dodges for enticing young women into domestic service. Plans are being made for world-wide travel. The wines of the future, the price of season-tickets and of suits and millinery, the decline of the poetry-boom, the fullness of restaurants, the prospects of the theatre—these furnish topics of animated conversation. And the necessity of a bathroom for each guest-room in the after-war house is frankly admitted. It is almost astonishing: it is wildly funny, having regard to the fact that millions of people are starving in Europe. . . .'

But it was hard work to organize peace-time pleasures, even in the country. Gardening, for example, had suffered a tremendous setback since 1916 by the gradual destruction of ornamental shrubs and trees to make room for potatoes and cabbages. The extremely cold winter of 1917–18 had killed many survivors and the lack of fuel for greenhouses had allowed some of the rarer varieties to die out altogether. Game birds had been neglected; and as for horses, few of the hunters that had been bought up for the Army had returned in condition. The breeding of dogs and other pets had also been so discouraged by the war that pedigree puppies were almost unobtainable. To make matters worse a widespread outbreak of rabies, the first for a great many years, made an order necessary for the compulsory muzzling of dogs. Muzzling was a problem, because the huge number of muzzles required could not be supplied in a hurry, and many dogs, especially short-nosed kinds, such as Pekinese, were exceedingly difficult to fit. The outbreak was due to the evasion of the usual quarantine at British ports by R.A.F. officers in France, who flew their pets over. The most fashionable dogs of the moment were Alsatians, which had been used in the Belgian and French armies as watch-dogs in outposts and as *chiens sanitaires* for ministering to the wounded. Their striking appearance and the legend of their wolfish ancestry well suited the new sporting scene. They were at first called variously, 'Police dogs', 'Continental (or German) sheepdogs', 'Chiens loups', 'Malinois', and 'Loups de Lorraine': until an 'Alsatian Wolf-Dog Club' was formed, with Lieut.-Col. Moore-Brabazon, the pioneer motorist and airman, as secretary. The club set itself to popularize these dogs, noted for their 'vigilance, fidelity, and suspiciousness towards strangers', and to see to it that the patriotic Allied name 'Alsatian' should be universally observed. In the following year *The Times* declared: 'To-day it is about as easy to buy an Alsatian as to rent a house or a flat in London. A good specimen can be sold for £300, and any sort of pedigree puppy cannot be bought for less than sixty guineas.'

As for metropolitan pleasures, a sprightly writer for *The Bystander* complained: 'Even the least observant must rub their eyes at the wild metamorphosis of London from war to peace. . '. . Those forgotten aeons when, at certain times of the day, anyway, there were seats and to spare in the tubes and buses. Or when cars actually "plied" for hire. Or, when at restaurants you could get a quite good dinner for a mere £1, without any insolence from waiter people and with *vin ordinaire* a lot less than 6s. or 7s. a bottle. And when, even at Christmas time, shop-assistants remembered that but for US they wouldn't cut much ice.'

Indeed, there was more money than goods about. Production had to be readjusted to peace-time conditions, and during the interval prices were high, and some goods had still to be rationed. Christmas had been the favourite date, every year, by which the war was confidently expected to end; but for this first peace-time Christmas practically no toys could be bought at any price, and the glass bottles in the confectioners' shops stood as empty as they had for the last two Christmases.

The 'But for US' theme was fretfully reiterated meanwhile in every camp and barrack at home and overseas where troops waited for relief or demobilization. The volunteer soldier was desperately home-sick, and now that the war was over, except in name, saw no reason why he should not go home—and get back his peace-time job before someone else took it. He had only enlisted 'for the duration'. But Army discipline, instead of being relaxed, was intensified, and the only relief from 'spit-and-polish' parades was educational lectures on subjects that seemed to him very remote. There were protests, strikes, and even mutinies among the troops left in France. Lord Byng was sent to Calais, in January 1919, to deal with an ugly situation: a 'Soviet' had been established among two thousand infantry, and the Army Service and Royal Army Ordnance Corps men were on strike. All were dissatisfied with bad food, worse accommodation and delays in demobilization. Lord Byng settled the mutiny without bloodshed; but it was allowed to remain publicly unrecorded for some years. A similar mutiny of about two thousand details of the five Guards regiments stationed at Shoreham camp, in Sussex, broke out two months later. They marched into Brighton, amid friendly cheers from the crowds along the roads, to lodge a protest with the Mayor, who received them so graciously that they returned to camp feeling that something had been done. Their immediate grievances were indeed attended to by a sympathetic emissary from London, and the exemplary sentences that awaited the ring-leaders were not promulgated for some time, when the danger of further disturbance had disappeared.

Books and newspaper articles about the war grew unfashionable as demobilization gathered momentum. Already, in January 1919, Ralph Strauss wrote in a literary column: 'War books have suddenly become "dud". I can think of no better word. Yet I imagine that a volume devoted to those secret things of war which have not yet been explained should have a success quite out of the ordinary.' For the public was not interested in the official histories of battles and of regiments which were beginning to appear, nor in the memoirs of generals and admirals; though the names of French and Jellicoe on the cover automatically sold a few thousand copies. No historian yet had the courage to give the facts truthfully, even if he had the inclination. The propaganda habit of suppressing disgraceful events persisted, the Defence of the Realm Act being still in force in many of its articles. Conversation about the war died down even before the Peace Celebrations. Among regular soldiers it soon came to be regarded as bad form, especially since the senior officers and N.C.O.s of the reorganized battalions had in most cases seen little regimental service—having either been employed on staff duties or spent most of the war in German or Turkish prison camps. Civilians were only too glad to suppress all memory of the nightmare from which they had just awakened, and the only intelligent audience for the reminiscences of ex-servicemen being their fellow ex-servicemen, the topic of 'this rag-time f——g peace' succeeded that of 'this bloody f——g war'. (The habit of continuous obscene language, which a long and miserable war has always induced, persisted for four or five years more and had even spread to the younger women.)

The revolutionary tendency among the Fighting Forces had been idealistic rather than practical: one reason being that everyone who had served in the trenches for as much as five months, or who had been under two or three rolling artillery barrages, was an invalid. 'Shell-shock', from which all suffered to a greater or less degree, was a condition of alternate moods of apathy and high excitement, with very quick reaction to sudden emergencies but no capacity for concentrated thinking. It was credibly explained as a morbid condition of the blood, due to the stimulation of the thyroid gland by noise and fear. Shell-shock, which brought distressing nightmares with it, often affected its victims with day-visions and warped their critical sense. Its effects passed off very gradually. In most cases the blood was not running pure again for four or five years; and in numerous cases men who had managed to avoid a nervous breakdown during the war collapsed badly in 1921 or 1922. Many officers and N.C.O.s, especially in 'shock-divisions' and the Royal Air Force, had also become confirmed whisky and rum addicts. The problem of the re-absorption of these men into civil life was complicated by their unfitness for any work that needed reliable judgement and steady application. They had been led to believe that the fact of having served honourably at the Front would be a safe coupon for employment; whereas, on the contrary, the more exhausting their service had been, the smaller was the peace-time demand for them. A million men found that their old jobs had either disappeared or were held by someone else—usually a woman, or a man who had escaped conscription.

To keep them quiet until the expected Peace Boom started, the Government gave every member of the Fighting Forces below commissioned rank a free Unemployment Insurance policy, which entitled him to benefit while he was seeking work. No steps were taken at first to provide for munition-workers, or other civilians who had been employed in war-work. A similar scheme, however, was hurriedly devised to cover them, and in 1920 their position was regulated by extending the original Unemployment Insurance provisions of 1911 to cover all classes of manual workers, except agricultural labourers and domestic servants. Unemployment was not allowed to depress the wage-rates of those who continued in work, for the Wages Act of 1918 stabilized the wages then in force.

No provision was made for ex-officers, on the assumption that they had either private means or useful connections. For many of these the problem of employment was acute. Some enlisted in the ranks and were sent to Cologne to the Army of Occupation; some, the wilder spirits, joined the special police force in Ireland, nicknamed the Black and Tans, and there showed remarkable savagery—for to them the Irish were traitors who had stabbed England in the back in the Easter Week rebellion of 1916, and deserved no mercy. Many used their savings, wound-gratuities and the customary Victory bounty (proportioned to pay) to set up in independent businesses, causing a great demand for small offices—and extortionate rents. Most of these businesses failed soon after they had started, and their owners drifted into the employment of large commercial and industrial firms. Younger officers crowded back to the Universities on Government scholarships to complete their interrupted education. Colonels, majors, and captains were plentiful among these aged undergraduates. They showed condescension rather than respect to the dons, and made it clear that they would stand for no nonsense—the word 'Soviet' was heard again at Oxford when the undergraduates at St. John's College took united action against what they considered tyranny in the catering department and successfully demanded reform and representation. On the whole, the absorption of soldiers into civil life went on fairly smoothly: by November 1920 the unemployment figure had dropped to half a million.

Until the Germans had signed on the dotted line, and for some little time afterwards, even the unemployed were still officially 'heroes'. They were entreated to have patience with the unavoidable confusion caused by the switch-over from war to peace: and especially to do nothing to embarrass those of their rulers who had gone in January to Versailles to remodel the map of the world. Most soldiers on their return found conditions, however difficult, such a vast improvement on active service in the field that they did not at first grumble. To be able to sleep all night on a spring mattress, to have the company of women and children, to be done with mud and trench-rats or tropical heat and flies, to be given something else to eat than bully-beef, biscuit, and plum-and-apple jam, and above all to be absolute masters of their spare time—such relief made them care very little what was going on in the public way. And all seemed to be going pretty well. The Government was indeed interesting itself actively in reconstruction. In February 1919 Lloyd George summoned a National Industrial Conference, and appealed to it for assistance in preserving national unity. The Conference recommended that a maximum working-week of forty-eight hours and minimum rates of pay should be made universal. Meanwhile, throughout 1919 Whitley Councils and Trade Boards were being formed in most industries. These were named after the chairman, J. H. Whitley, of the commission that had recommended their formation—he later became Speaker of the House of Commons. Their purpose was to enable employers and workers to co-operate in settling trade disputes.

The Peace Conference news roused little popular interest by comparison with events of a more happily 'pre-war' flavour, such as the resumption of racing and prospects of seaside holidays. The popular Press was obliged to recognize this need for distraction. Only a few newspapers, of small circulation, described the task before the Peace Conference as 'enough to sober the thoughts of every serious person', and held that the Allies were creating the machinery for a safe civilization and a better-ordered world. If the machinery could not be created, or if it proved defective, they declared, the immediate future might be even worse than the immediate past. They kept up this note for several months, occasionally glancing aside to reprove the ambitions of Poland, Rumania, and Italy; but were generally unheeded.

The Government did not stint the public of parades. In March, the Guards Division marched from Buckingham Palace to the City, through densely crowded streets. The dominant note of the spectators, so the newspapers said, was one of pride and thankfulness: for they were 'neither weary of military spectacles, nor ungrateful for sacrifices rendered, nor unmindful of glory gained'. After this the Australians had their day, and then the Canadians. And at the end of May there were mild celebrations at the signing of Peace. As usual, crowds gathered outside Buckingham Palace and cheered the King and Queen and the

Royal Family. At Downing Street, Lloyd George was prevailed upon to address a crowd from his windows, and in the House of Commons he was cheered—the Members rose and sang the National Anthem in unison. Then, as though Armistice Day and Peace Day had not been enough, the people were promised an official Victory Day for July 9th. The only newspaper that took the line 'Now they are ringing the bells, soon they will be wringing their hands', on the grounds that the Peace terms were intolerably severe and an unjust enslavement of the German people for generations to come, was the almost unread *Daily Herald*.

The war had now to be solidly commemorated by public subscription. Plans were made for the organization of vast war cemeteries in France, and in every village in England the problem of the local war memorial was raging—where should it be placed? What form should it take—statue, obelisk, or cross? Could the names of all the dead be inscribed on it? Or would it not be more sensible to use the money collected for a recreation ground and engrave the names on an inexpensive plaque in the church? So great was the demand for war-memorial designs and so puzzled were committees as to where they should go for them that the Medici Society inserted a full-page disclaimer in the weekly journals: 'In view of the daily enquiries for price-lists, catalogues, etc. of War Memorials, the Medici Society begs to repeat that it does *not* supply "stock designs", *nor* issue price-lists or catalogues of Memorials.' Funds were also collected to buy out of 'Continental slavery' the faithful British transport horses that had been left behind in France and Belgium. And the Royal Society for the Prevention of Cruelty to Animals launched a £20,000 Soldiers' Dog Fund, describing as a tragedy of peace the fact that Tommy and his 'pal' must say good-bye on the other side of the water unless the public intervened with their usual generosity. The public, of course, did.

Meanwhile Great Britain was slowly recovering its peace-time appearance. Khaki had disappeared from the streets, naked lights were permitted at night, munition works had closed down or switched over to peace-time production, newspaper placards ceased to be overprinted on old newspapers, the spy-fever ended. Tobacco restrictions were removed in January 1919, food-coupons were abolished in May and bread-rationing in August; but sugar-rationing went on until November 1920, and licensing restrictions were only very slightly relaxed for the rest of the period.

On Victory Day a great Allied Parade was held. That night there were numerous parties. In the Berkeley Hotel all diners were given crackers and trumpets, dolls and golliwogs. When the trumpets sounded, an officer of the 19th Hussars jumped up and proposed a toast to 'The Fox-Hunt'; and all joined riotously in singing 'John Peel'. In Hyde Park, at the same time, there was a public display of fireworks.

Peace-making was not yet over. *The Bystander* reminded its readers that, though peace had been made with Germany, Britain was still playing the policeman in Fiume, Constantinople, Palestine, Mesopotamia (which had in the mouths of the Little Englanders become 'Mespot'), India, Siberia, Hong Kong and Singapore. The public, however, was unperturbed. Germany at least was beaten and these minor problems of the peace did not concern them much. The League of Nations was suspect, as an instrument for keeping Britain tied to the troubles of Europe; still, it seemed only fair to give the thing a trial, and some even had profound faith in it. *Punch*, on the first anniversary of Armistice Day, awarded a kindly cartoon to Viscount Cecil, who was starting his campaign to make the aims of the League better understood.

Germany was not yet, of course, included in the League, but regarded officially as a moral outcast. Nothing known to be of German origin could be sold in the shops and even the war-time ban on German classical music remained in force for some time. The popular Press continued to refer to the Germans as Huns even so late as 1920; nor was any faith given to the complaint of Germans during the Armistice period that they were starving —as many of them were. In January 1919 *The Times* proved to its own satisfaction that this complaint was 'the latest, but not the last proof of a mean and lying and greedy spirit': northwestern Germany, *The Times* maintained, was amply supplied with provisions—in fact, raw food was even seen going to waste. *Punch*, in February, produced a cartoon of the German Criminal saying to the Allied Policeman: 'Stop, you're hurting me,' and then aside: 'If I only whine enough I may be able to wriggle out of this yet.' *Punch* continued to reflect this official view of German baseness with cartoons, in May, entitled 'Germany draws the pen and keeps it rattling' and 'Honour satisfied'. The text to the latter was, 'German Delegate: "Sign? I'd sooner die." Aside: "Give me the pen." ' And in September, with a note of alarm, came a cartoon: 'The New German offensive', representing the German commercial traveller about to invade Britain.

Liberal papers, on the other hand, took the view that, now that the Hohenzollerns were dethroned, no cause for fear remained. Germany would be democratic, though perhaps a little more authoritative (the word 'authoritarian' had not yet come in) than other democratic countries. The German people, it was felt, would never again let their fate pass out of their own hands. And the daring *New Statesman* poked fun at the hue-and-cry after the Kaiser: 'Looking through the newspapers the other day I found Mr. Tillett calling for his ex-Majesty's removal from earth, Sir Gilbert Parker demanding his internment in some distant island, and Lady Byron supplementing a plan for a judicial investigation with the palpably biased remark that, should the defendant not be condemned to the gallows or the guillotine, then the foulest deed must be applauded and floral tributes laid on the shrine of Satan.'

Even the soldiers who had expressed a fellow-feeling for their fellow-unfortunates on the other side of no-man's-land could not now spare much pity or thought for German ex-servicemen and their families; though generosity was shown by the Army of Occupation to German civilians in distress. It was not as if food was either plentiful or cheap in England: and, after all, who had started the war—and who had lost it? Besides, there was a great housing shortage, and recently married men were wondering for how many more months, or years, they would have to live with their wives' parents or their own. For five years the building trade had been at a standstill—few repairs, even, had been done. The number of skilled builders had been halved during the war, because the trade had no chance to recruit apprentices. What skilled labour there was had more repair work in hand than it could manage. *The Sphere* in September 1919 observed that all over London the work of painting and repairing walls, windows and railings was in progress; Downing Street by then was only just refurbished. To make matters worse, streets and roads had been neglected during the war, and throughout 1919 gangs of roadmakers were busy in all London's thoroughfares. Nearly the whole of Oxford Street was dug up and relaid in a single operation.

At first, very few new houses were built. Even in 1921, the British census showed 750,000 more families than separate dwellings. This was remarkable, because just before the war it had been reckoned that there were more unoccupied houses in London than occupied houses in Paris. Owing to the scarcity of materials the cost of building rose enormously: it was impossible to put up houses which could be let at the prevailing controlled rents. A Director-General of Housing was appointed in 1919 to help local authorities and private builders with subsidies; but these were not sufficiently attractive to start a housing boom. In 1920 a Ministry of Health house of a working-class type cost £900 to erect, even though indifferent materials were used—unseasoned wood and uncohesive plaster; and wages were lagging behind the rise in prices. In consequence, many respectable families went to live in old houses that had been awkwardly cut up into flats, in mews, in army huts, wooden and metal, roughly adapted to civil life, and even in old railway carriages, and converted coal barges and lighters.

Yet, despite everything, people were determined to enjoy themselves. Professional cricket was revived, yachting at Cowes, and polo and hunt-balls—though there was still a great shortage at these of male partners. The Derby was a record one: since the beginning of the year everyone had been talking in a most extravagant way of the favourite, Sir Alec Black's 'The Panther', as the greatest horse of the age. The first big disappointment of the peace was when The Panther came in fourth; Lord Glanely's Grand Parade being the winner at 33–1. Opera enjoyed a great social season; Dame Melba was at the height of her popularity. Russian Ballet was in fashion, with 'La Boutique Fantasque', 'Petrouschka', and 'The Three-Cornered Hat' as the most popular pieces—and Massine, Karsavina, and Lopokova to dance them. One consolation for the Russian Revolution was that it had released the Imperial Ballet school for service abroad. At Wimbledon Mlle Suzanne Lenglen began her long domination of the British lawn-tennis courts by defeating Mrs. Lambert Chambers. At Henley the regatta was held again, and the victory of an Australian eight over Oxford in one of the events assisted the prevailing sentiment of Imperial goodwill. In the course of a military tournament at Olympia real tanks charged obstructions in the arena, and sent bricks and mortar flying splendidly. And between parades and sporting events there was always some social happening to engross the attention. The smartest was the wedding of Lady Diana Manners, the reigning beauty of the day, to young Alfred Duff Cooper—the last social wedding that crowds and crowds of factory girls talked about and turned out to see. Later in the Twenties it was only film stars that could attract such crowds. Lady Diana was fortunate; at the moment when glamour was turning from peers to stars, she was both an actress (the Nun in *The Miracle*) and a duke's daughter.

In August came the great holiday scramble. Thousands of people set off for the sea on their first holiday for five years. The seaside towns were overwhelmed. Fifty thousand people went to Yarmouth from London alone. Clacton received thirty-five thousand more people than it could accommodate. Sofas in living-rooms and temporary beds in bathrooms were snapped up. Blackpool had more than three hundred thousand visitors. Hundreds were obliged to return home after a fruitless search for lodgings; hundreds walked the streets all night, or slept on sand-hills and cliff-tops. The police, in some cases, allowed women and children to occupy cells at police stations. The beaches were black with crowds; queues waited outside bathing-machines and dressing-tents for their turn to swim. The London County Council thoughtfully provided, for the children of those who could not get away, heaps of specially refined sand in St. James's Park, railed off in play-corners. But bereaved wives and parents who could afford to do so went on personally conducted tours to the 'Devastated Regions' and ate picnics in the trenches with old ammunition-boxes as makeshift tables. Towards the end of the year Continental holidays became possible again. St. Moritz was popular for skating and skiing—as yet expertness in skating was more common than in skiing among society people. The illustrated weeklies during the winter of 1919–20 were full of photographs of Lord So-and-So's party on skates. The Riviera too was packed, thousands of people going south in spite of the acute coal-shortage in France. On the trains, sleeping berths to Cannes and Nice were booked up months ahead of time.

But popular satisfaction with the winning of the war subsided somewhat as the winter drew on. A reaction of mild doubt set in: 'Is this the Peace we were promised? Are these the homes fit for heroes? Will Germany really be made to pay?'

The Bystander of October 1919 printed an account of a holiday-maker returning to a chaotic London—war rations, dim lights, high prices, and strikes. There had been a nine-day railway stoppage, which the newspapers had treated as if it had been the threatened Revolution, urging patriotic citizens to volunteer as amateur train-drivers, and using such war-time terms as 'doing one's bit', and 'seeing it through'. The strike was finally settled by granting the railwaymen a sliding scale of pay, which was to vary according to the official cost-of-living index figure. There had also been a police strike, which greatly alarmed the Law-and-Order party; if even the police proved unreliable, what was left to stem the tide of revolt? The *Spectator* in an August issue denounced this police strike: 'An ugly feature was the secrecy with which it had been planned for the eve of the holidays. Had the Union order been obeyed, great cities would all have shared the fate of Liverpool, where the mob had command of the central shopping district and looted and destroyed property to the value of £200,000 before it was dispersed by rifle-fire. It is to be noted, also, that the *Daily Herald*, the organ of the extreme Socialist faction, allowed itself to be used for purposes of announcing the mutiny and grossly exaggerated the number of policemen who deserted.'

The words 'mutiny' and 'deserted' were used to identify the Government more securely with the nation. That the police were ex-servicemen almost to a man, and that they had won great popular sympathy for their strike, was suppressed.

CHAPTER THREE

Women

The B.E.F. were unfortunate in being quartered during the war among the *gens du Nord*, who were a byword in France for their grasping ways; this had soured them a little, but British comradeship with France was still by no means a fiction. Suspicions of the United States were far stronger. To begin with, American participation in the war, though officially welcomed, had never touched the British heart; and the Americans were accused of exaggerating their eleventh-hour services in France at the expense of those who had borne the heat and burden of the day. Certainly in a huge Victory Anthology of poems, written by excited American civilians, though the French and Foch as Generalissimo—'Focus of Freedom: Foch!'—were given occasional bouquets, there was hardly a mention of their British allies, and the minor engagements in which the American army took part became Austerlitzes and Waterloos. In the United States it was also currently believed that Britain had been prostrated by her war effort and would never again recover her former proud position. She was described as a mangy lion licking her sores, and it was confidently prophesied that before long England would be a pastoral country without dependencies and with much the same political significance as Denmark. Americans would then visit it in much the same spirit as the Romans of the early Empire went to the ancestral ruins of Troy. Britain's effeteness seemed to be borne out in the next few years by her inability in the realms of sport—tennis, boxing, golf, yachting, athletics—to make any sort of showing against Americans.

This American attitude was much resented by the British. There was general disgust too with the way in which Americans, enriched by the woes of Europe, were buying up books and art treasures—it seemed with more acquisitiveness than real taste. £175,000 was paid for the Duke of Westminster's 'Blue Boy' by Gainsborough, and the Christie-Miller Library, most of which went to America, fetched £500,000. They even bought up ancient mansions, such as Great Lodge in Essex and Agecroft Hall in Lancashire, and transported them for re-erection, stone by stone, in the States. They engrossed the grouse shooting in Scotland, being ready to pay up to £7,000 for three months—as late as 1925 £750,000 went north in this way. 'Good American money' was heartily cursed by the New Poor—especially by those with nothing to sell in exchange for it. Pussyfootism was another American trait that did not please. The American women's clubs, a powerful organization with no British counter-part, had taken advantage of the earnest wartime mood to impose teetotalism on the United States. This excited British derision and 'Pussyfoot' Johnson, who came to England to preach the cause, was so roughly handled by undergraduates that he lost the sight of an eye. 'Pussyfoot' became a general term of reproach for all milk-and-water idealists.

The problem of the immense war-debts owed by Britain to the U.S.A. had not yet become acute enough to embitter feelings still more between the two countries. But the United States Government was criticized in Great Britain for 'baulking its responsibilities in Europe', and much sympathy was felt for Woodrow Wilson, the Democratic President: he had been per-suaded or (the Americans said) 'bulldozed' by Lloyd George and 'Tiger' Clemenceau of France into signing their draft of the Versailles Treaty, which was not at all in keeping with his own Liberal views. The United States Senate, like most individual Americans, considered the terms over-severe, and likely to in-volve them in costly entanglements. Why, they were even expected to undertake a mandate for Armenia—where the heck *was* Armenia anyway?—in order to keep the Turks from massacring alleged Christians! The American armies were with-drawn from the Rhine, and American participation in the League of Nations was withheld. *Punch* published a cartoon, 'Home from Home', which showed President Wilson sailing back to Europe, saying: 'Time I was getting back to a hemisphere where I am really appreciated.'

Yet the British gladly welcomed gay American fashions in dress, music, dancing and fun, having temporarily lost their own inventive power. Syncopated music had been denounced as barbarous and blatant in 1912 when it first came to England, despite the magnificent dancing of the Castles; and the more extravagant 'rag-time' dances had not been socially approved. 'Rag-time' was an adjective of reproach; a rag-time regiment was a disorderly and untrustworthy one. But after the war the new fantastic development of Jazz music and the steps that went with it, became, in the contemporary phrase, 'all the rage'. Cocktails were also accepted, though they went directly against British upper-class tradition, the chief ingredients being gin and vermouth. Gin had for two centuries been considered a very lower-class drink indeed, and vermouth, like absinthe, was dangerously Parisian. Only wines or 'fruit cups' had been drunk on social occasions before the war; with whisky reserved for sporting uses. *Punch* printed many a joke against cocktails, but cocktail parties even in 1920 were not yet popular enough to rouse the anger of clergymen. American slang was still barred as vulgar. A revue, in which Noel Coward appeared as a youthful actor, had to have its original title 'Oh Boy!' changed to 'Oh Joy!' lest it caused offence.

In January 1919 *The Bystander* reported that there was morning dancing in country houses and town mansions; for the 'newest jazzes and the latest rags' had to be learnt without delay. But it did seem a little odd that a negro jazz-band could earn more in a season than the Prime Minister did in the course of a whole year. The *Daily Mail* in February described 'This Jazz Age': 'People are dancing as they have never danced before, in a happy rebound from the austerities of war. . . . But the dancing is not quite as it was in the dim old years before 1914. The "Tango", "Maxixe" and "Boston" have gone with the "Turkey Trot" and "Bunny Hug". . . . The "Baleta" and "Maxina" are revivals of these under new names, and it is even said that the "Lancers" is being privately practised, so that the programme will no longer be limited to the "Fox-trot", "One-step" and "Hesitation-waltz". . . . Dancing without gloves has become the mode, because the cost of gloves has risen to impossible figures, and smoking was never so common when sitting out.'

There were plenty of Americans about to show how these dances should be properly performed. The influx into Europe of wealthy tourists from the States began as soon as the Armistice was signed. Most Americans spent the greater part of their stay in France—the American predilection for things French having continued ever since the Revolution as a sign of their complete independence of Britain—or in touring Italy; but a visit to Britain was almost always included in the itinerary. They brought unfamiliar fashions along, among them lipstick, rouge, eyebrow and eyelash colouring Hitherto unashamed use of facial pigment in Britain had not gone very far along the usual course that daring female fashions had always taken— white silk stockings, by the way, had just accomplished the run —and even with American encouragement it did not reach its goal for another ten years. The course was: from brothel to stage, then on to Bohemia, to Society, to Society's maids, to the mill-girl, and lastly to the suburban woman. Openly attended 'beauty-parlours', rare even in America at this time, were unknown in Britain. But face cream and powder were already used, and fast young women powdered their noses in public. American example also persuaded the ordinary Englishwoman to give up permanently her old-fashioned stiff whale-bone corsets that she had been forced to wear even as a schoolgirl of thirteen. (Women war-workers had already abandoned theirs.) As an American girl observed in London: 'Men won't dance with you if you're all laced up.' The new dances certainly demanded a freedom of movement which was not possible in old-fashioned corsets. American chewing-gum was now sold in the streets as a novelty, and given full-page advertisements in the newspapers; but never became fashionable, except among schoolboys as a permissible alternative to smoking.

Women in the United States were famous for enjoying far less social restraint than Englishwomen. This characteristic had first been noted during the American War of Independence, when the women had carried on in the absence of their men-folk in the army; in the Civil War they had done the same again. The Great War similarly freed the Englishwoman.

Short hair and short skirts were the outward sign of 'This Freedom' (the theme and title of a best-selling novel by the most popular novelist of the day, A. S. M. Hutchinson, author of *If Winter Comes*). Short hair had been introduced into London just before the war by 'the crop-haired crew' at the Slade Art School; they got it from Paris. It was then gratefully adopted by women land-workers, who had to get up at unearthly hours to milk cows and had no time for the toilet that long hair entailed. Munition workers followed suit. The use of short skirts, which had already been adopted in tennis, was widely extended during the war; the saving of material recommending it as a national economy. But a skirt was then considered short if it came well above the ankle: the swell of the calf was still hidden. Women land-workers wore gaiters, breeches and overalls, which for a while excited surprise and disgust among the country people: but they were encouraged by Lee White's song 'Good-bye, Madam Fashion, Come again some day', in which it was asserted that:

> Dainty skirts and delicate blouses
> Aren't much use for pigs and cows-es.

The solution was 'overalls and trousiz'. But when Madam Fashion came back she did not remove the trousers from the many women who still continued to work on the land, mostly as smallholders. And before long she popularized trousers for women that were indistinguishable, except in the matter of fly-buttons, from men's. This was in revenge for her pre-war rebuff in the matter of the split skirt, which had been laughed out of existence with the phrase 'Not in these Trousiz'. The phrase, which came from a song in which a young man refuses to take his girl to the races so dressed, had even displaced 'Archibald, Certainly Not' as a complete general negative.

Women's fashions in 1919 were already setting the standard to which they adhered throughout the Twenties. Men's dress had not yet noticeably changed—narrow trousers, high-buttoning jackets and stiff collars were still universally worn, though the hard black bowler and the tall silk hat were yielding to the soft coloured Homburg, originally introduced by King Edward VII. (King George V, by the way, had only two sartorial peculiarities: a taste for single-breasted jackets and a habit of creasing his trousers down the sides, like pyjamas, instead of down the front. The first caught on, but not the second.) There was no sign that the short skirt would ever be abandoned, though one's legs got very cold in winter time, especially when woollen stockings went out of fashion. Stockings were of all colours now, black ones tending to disappear altogether, and white giving place to flesh colour. The rayon industry was in its infancy and stockings were still mostly of wool or cotton: only well-dressed women wore silk, and even the upper half of their stockings was often of cotton or wool. High heels, which had hitherto always been associated with the Stage, Paris, and Immorality, now came into more general use: though elder women could not accustom themselves to them and the medical profession condemned them as causing uteral displacement and being a threat to the birth-rate. The tubular look of women in the 1920 fashion plates was completed by the new sack-like blouses and jumpers. The *Sunday Express* protested that the cut of many of these was so startlingly low as 'surely not to be welcomed in ordinary business offices'; though the flat-chested fashion considerably lessened the allure.

The Bystander in March 1919 began a long series of jokes about the scantiness of women's dresses with the remark that, though evening gowns were once more permissible, it seemed as if there was a conspiracy among women to leave as much of the spinal column uncovered as was compatible with a scanty bodice—the age should be called 'The Dorsal Period'. During the Peace celebrations, which began in May and were described as a Jazz Season, shorter and shorter skirts were worn, all very gay. Sleeves, too, were shorter, receding now far above the elbows. Hats were inclined to floppiness, for the well-known cloche or 'extinguisher' shape had scarcely yet come in. The cloche-hat was designed for short hair, and in 1919, despite thousands of bobbed heads, long hair was still the prevailing fashion. Newspapers advertised means of 'preserving women's crowning glory', and the International Hairdressers' Competition of 1920 was won by an elaborate, monumental pile, surmounted by a large Spanish comb. But short hair had become so fixed a symbol of female independence that pig-tailed schoolgirls, who had once looked forward ecstatically to the day when they would put their hair up, now felt an equal longing for the day when they would cut it off.

The free mixing of men and women was commemorated in

the woollen jumper—hitherto only worn by sailors and little boys, who called it a jersey. Most women in 1919 were wearing jumpers, knitted by themselves as a relief from 'socks for soldiers'; and soon afterwards men, too, began to adopt them under the name of 'pull-over'. The pull-over, in the form of a white open-necked 'sweater' with club colours, had long been in sports use; but the new garment, of subfusc colouring and worn by daring young men over a soft-collared shirt, with a coloured tie and no tie-pin, was for more general wear. It was the first garment that could be used interchangeably by men and women.

Towards the end of 1919 many new dance clubs and dance halls were opened. In the newspapers there were columns of advertisements for tea dances, practice dances, subscription dances, and Victory dances. Innumerable young women offered to help Win the Peace at the many dances held in aid of Ex-Servicemen, Serbian Relief, Rumanian Relief, etc. by teaching tangoes, fox-trots, hesitation-waltzes, one-steps, and the brand-new Ki-ki-kari, described as a 'fascinating variation on the one-step'. By the beginning of 1920 jazz had become universal—in fact, as a headline put it, the shimmy was 'shaking Suburbia'. The 'shimmy' or 'shimmy-shake' had, as its name suggests, begun life in the American 'sporting-houses'. There were, of course, many protests against these dances even when they were already accepted by the most refined hostesses. One clergyman wrote at the end of 1919: 'if these up-to-date dances, described as the "latest craze", are within a hundred miles of all I hear about them, I should say that the morals of a pig-sty would be respectable in comparison'. However, by this time the new waltz (in which one no longer merely spun round and round but tacked and veered and trotted), and the tango, were 'ever so much more *it*' in Society.

The shameless abandon with which the new free woman danced, allowing her partner a near-sexual closeness of embrace, her immodest dress and coiffure and her profane looseness of language, were by no means the only charges against her. A letter to the *Spectator*, in 1919, complained that young women were learning to frequent public houses. It followed up this complaint with a suggestion that was not put into practice until the Thirties: that there should be soda-fountains, as in America, where non-intoxicating drinks could be obtained at all hours. Women were also smoking in public, and this innovation had a mixed reception. It was reported in the *New Statesman* that a young lady in a small restaurant had a cigarette knocked out of her mouth by an irate elderly waiter. The writer observed that bourgeois restaurants were stricter in preserving the old proprieties than more fashionable eating-houses; and that while women could smoke without exciting interest in the restaurant-car of a train, it was still improper for them to smoke on the tops of buses. They tended to smoke Egyptian and Turkish cigarettes. Virginian cigarettes were a little vulgar even for men: there was a transitional stage in the early Twenties, before the general adoption of Virginians, when in offering a cigarette-case one would say, 'I hope you don't mind: it's only a Virgin' or, more familiarly, 'Excuse stinkers!'

The chattier journals accepted women's new habits without criticism. According to the *Sphere*, one realized that a revolution had taken place in social customs when one saw girls in the débutante stage not only dispensing with chaperones, but actually giving dances of their own without even a presiding mamma in the offing, and issuing invitations in their own names. To some extent the 'modern girl' was still the popular heroine that she had become when working on munitions in factories. She was known as 'the flapper', yet this was not a term of reproach. Flapper in the Nineties had meant a very young prostitute, scarcely past the age of consent, but the word had improved just before the war to mean any girl in her teens with a boyish figure. The craze for the flapper had begun in Germany (where they called her a *backfisch*) as a sexual reaction against the over-fed under-exercised monumental woman, and as a compromise between pederasty and normal sex. It reached England about 1912. In the war, the shortage of sugar and butter and the popularization of hockey and tennis greatly reduced women's weight; and when they were freed of their tight corsets the popular 'hour-glass figure' gave place to the neatly cylindrical. To the post-war eye, Italian prima donnas and old postcard portraits of Edwardian stage favourites had an irresistibly comic look.

'Flapper' was now a term for a comradely, sporting, active young woman, who would ride pillion on the 'flapper-bracket' of a motor-cycle. It did not become a term of reproach again, with a connotation of complete irresponsibility, until 1927 when *Punch* noted: 'Flapper is the popular press catchword for an adult woman worker aged 21 to 30, when it is a question of giving her a vote under the same conditions as men of the same age.' There was a British film in 1919 called 'The Irresistible Flapper'; the heroine was a high-spirited girl who shocked her old-fashioned parents with her free behaviour and boyish slimness, yet was in truth a 'brick'. This flapper went to stay with her married sister, whose secret affair with a matinée-idol threatened to wreck her life. The flapper took things into her own hands, impersonated her sister, made love to the matinée-idol and spoilt his schemes. At first she was suspected by everyone of philandering, but eventually her sister confessed, thanked her for saving her from disgrace; and all was well.

But the flapper already had many enemies and not only among Church people. Before the war, it was enough to say of her in the words of the 'Dapper Flapper' song: 'She is oh, so tender, Figure so slender, She loves chocolate creams and me.' But now the air of competence which young women had assumed from doing a 'man's job' during the war was widely resented by advocates of 'femininity'—which included sweet inconsequence, childishness, and submissiveness. Girls were blamed for being cocksure and ill-tempered and even brazen in their advances to men. The brazenness they had learned as flag-sellers. By the end of the war there were about as many flag-days every year as there had been Church holidays in the Middle Ages. The flags or flowers or other lapel-decorations that everyone bought, or was expected to buy, when accosted by a pretty girl in the street, were sold for every conceivable cause—the blind, the limbless, the toothless, and the refugee—and Peace did not end the practice by any means.

The women who only a year or so earlier had been acclaimed as patriots, giving up easy lives at home to work for their Country in her hour of need, were now represented as vampires who deprived men of their rightful jobs. By Trade Union pressure they were dismissed from engineering, printing, and transport work, though cheap and efficient workers, and from the factories where they had worked on munitions. No Unemployment Benefit scheme was arranged for them. They were expected instead to become domestic servants, for whom there was an always unsatisfied demand. But any girl who had earned good wages in factories, and had come to like the regular hours, the society of other workers, and the strict but impersonal discipline, was reluctant to put herself under the personal domination of 'some old cat' who would expect her not only to work long hours for little money, but show complete subservience and dispense with all former friendships or amusements. The servant shortage remained a problem for years, though in fact most families that had once kept servants could no longer afford to do so, and facilities for housewives to run their homes themselves with a minimum of effort were fast being introduced from the United States, where the same reluctance for domestic service had always existed. 'Labour-saving' devices in cooking, washing up, cleaning, laundering, a far wider choice of tinned and bottled fruit, refrigerators, mass-produced clothes, invisible-mending services: all these were offered and taken up readily.

Most demobilized young women therefore turned to the obvious profession of marriage; but women had slightly out-numbered men in England even before the war killed off one eligible man in every seven and seriously injured another, so that the problem of the 'surplus woman' was much debated. However, women assistants continued to be employed in shops and offices to a far greater extent than before the war—there being no male Trade Union strong enough to exclude them from these trades—and many who had experience in munition factories got engaged in the new electrical and wireless industries. There they were paid, on the whole, only about two-thirds of the wages that male employees received. Among the middle classes after the war, daughters were expected to take up business careers, or at least do *something*. Some, of course, regarded their business life as an interval between school and marriage, and this naturally debarred them from jobs in which continuity of work was of more advantage to the employer than cheap labour. Doing *something* often meant pretending to take up music or art. Music was the harder and sterner profession, so art schools had a tremendous membership, which did not sensibly decrease throughout the Peace. By 1939, it was calculated that there were at least 200,000 self-styled artists in England, of whom the great majority were women, but fewer than 200, mostly men, lived wholly by their art.

More and more women were going to universities. Oxford admitted them to full membership in 1919. Though many dons felt that this would destroy the purely intellectual life of the colleges, the Bishop of London, at a special service for Oxford women students, blessed the movement for higher education among women. At the same time he pointed out that they were '*all* destined to become the wives of some good man' —he meant *each*. (This sort of grammatical carelessness, due to thinking in rigid blocks of words rather than in well-articulated sentences, became more and more common in public speaking as the years went on. Asquith was the last politician whose speeches could be printed as decent examples of English prose.) The Cambridge Senate refused to admit women to university membership, but in 1921 passed 'Graces' which granted degree titles to women graduates. While the proposal was being debated the undergraduates behaved with the same archaic ungallantry towards the women's colleges that hecklers had shown at pre-war Suffragette meetings. Oxford was virtuously shocked.

The Sex Disqualification (Removal) Act of 1919 admitted women to many professions, including the Bar. The first woman barrister was called to the Bar in 1921, and in the following year thirty more were called. The newspapers concentrated public interest on cases conducted by 'our new Portias', much to the embarrassment of the more sedate judges. These were also embarrassed by women-jurymen, provided for by an Act of 1918: when the case happened to be one in which violence, especially sexual violence, or any distressing pathological incident figured, and a woman-juryman was in the box, a judge would cough warningly. If the cough failed to rouse her sense of modesty, he would suggest that she should retire. She usually did retire—more out of pity at his embarrassment than out of real squeamishness. But *The Common Cause*, the organ of the combined societies for the freedom of women, constantly protested that women jurors should stick it out, especially where men jurors would be likely to mitigate the severity due for criminal assault upon children. The 'Votes for Women!' cry now gave place to that of 'Equal Pay for Equal Work!' But the industrial magnates and the Trade Union leaders proved to have harder hearts than the politicians: and the discrimination against women continued throughout the period. Even the solitary woman who remained a departmental head at the B.B.C. was paid at a lower rate than her male colleagues.

The first woman to sit in Parliament was the busy, American-born Prohibitionist and Christian Scientist, Lady Astor, who was returned in 1919 for the Sutton division of Plymouth, at a by-election caused by Lord Astor's elevation to the peerage. She was a Coalition candidate and was ceremoniously introduced to a respectful house by Lloyd George and A. J. Balfour. Shortly after her introduction she was reported to be sitting on a joint committee dealing with 'serious moral issues'. It was two years before she was joined in the House by other women members. In 1921 Mrs. Wintringham, the widow of a former Liberal member, was elected for Louth; and the Conservative Mrs. Hilton Philipson (the popular actress, Mabel Russell), also the widow of a former member, for Berwick. Mrs. Wintringham was warmly welcomed by the earnest women's-freedom societies; but Mrs. Philipson was considered a traitor to their cause, as being submissively pro-male in any question affecting the relations of the sexes. The number of women members remained extremely small throughout the period, because no party would give a woman a safe seat to contest except for such special reasons as the death of a husband who had occupied it, or other very strong local interest.

Various fresh measures of emancipation were introduced. The Chancellor of the Exchequer was persuaded to tax a married woman's income separately from that of her husband, on the ground that it was unjust for a woman's right to own property to be respected by the Commissioners of Inland Revenue if she were unmarried, but not if she were married. The Chancellor agreed that 'it has always been an intolerable anomaly that, so far as taxation is concerned, it is cheaper to live with a woman not one's wife than with a woman who is'. As a matter of fact, so far as taxation was concerned, it continued cheaper at certain levels of income, until the end of the period.

Other legal anomalies were also amended. In 1920 the section of the Larceny Act was abolished which assumed that a woman living with her husband could not steal from him. In 1923 the Matrimonial Causes Act provided that adultery of either spouse should be sufficient reason for divorce—previously, a woman bringing a petition had also to prove cruelty or desertion. And in 1925 the Criminal Justice Act did away with the presumption that a woman who committed a crime in her husband's presence did so under his coercion. Women were thus at last legally recognized as morally responsible persons. Even the Church agreed to this recognition, for in the report of the Lambeth Conference of 1920 the bishops stated: 'The Church must frankly acknowledge that it has undervalued and neglected the gifts of women and has too thanklessly used their work.' They firmly repudiated the argument that women were ceremonially unclean; and concluded that the ministry would be strengthened if freer use was made of women's spiritual gifts. The humblest of Holy Orders—the diaconate—was thrown open to them: women could thereafter preach and conduct church services, but not bestow the Blessing or perform any sacrament.

It must not be thought that the consciously 'free' women were more than a small minority: conservatively feminine women, who wished things to be as they had always been, were frequent. However, the large betwixt-and-between class soon swung over to the new fashions in dress and behaviour because of the success that they obviously had with the marrying sort of men; and the feminine women had to follow suit for fear of seeming dowdy.

Nor were all fashions, even in dancing and music, American. To those who still thought the Negro-Jewish-American importations blatant, strident and unlovely, other modern alternatives were offered. There was, for a start, Eurythmics, an adaptation of gymnastics to rhythm. This was a system invented by Jacques Dalcroze of Geneva; its devotees improvised movements in different musical times, their ears, brains and muscles working in close co-ordination. A demonstration was given in the Queen's Hall which attracted much attention. Newspapers for a year and more afterwards published photographs of girls in Greekish costumes, casting themselves into the air, sometimes in Regent's Park, sometimes in Kensington studios. But Eurythmics, which was described as an 'expression of time-values in bodily movement' and a 'plastic realization of music', soon lost its general popularity and became relegated to advanced girls-schools.

If a more English sort of dancing was wanted, to correspond with the intensely cultivated Englishness of *Georgian Poetry*,

48

there was the revived folk dance. The English Folk Dance Society, founded by Cecil Sharpe a few years before, had made numerous converts, especially in country villages, where the Elizabethan morris-dance had become practically extinct. Young men in cricket flannels and young women in short white skirts jigged about to the fiddle, or piano, in the long-forgotten steps of 'Gathering Pease-cods', 'Rufty Tufty', 'Black Nag', 'Sellenger's Round', and the rest. Folk dancing enjoyed a great popularity for about ten years, chiefly under Church patronage; and one or two well-attended conventions were held at the Albert Hall. But Tin Pan Alley', the New York music factory, killed it in the end. For there could be no new composers of folk dances, and each dance had only one tune, and there were only a limited number of dances. Even in the country a constant refreshment of tunes was demanded, as soon as a wireless set was installed in every home. Tunes, like clothes, were now expected to wear our after very short use.

These folk dancers, and the readers of *Georgian Poetry* and the *London Mercury*, were loosely affiliated with what came to be known as the Arty-and-Crafty (as distinguished from the merely Arty) Lot. The Arty-and-Crafty Lot were in turn mingled with the 'Back-to-the-Landers'. They had small holdings in picturesque villages; kept chickens and goats; spun, wove and dyed cloth; ran communal hand-presses; did lino-cuts; bottled fruit and home-made wines; wore 'peasant' dress, sandals, and bright smiles; serenaded one another in summer evenings with folk songs and Elizabethan lutanist love-songs with fiddle accompaniment. The men usually affected beards, until the sudden craze for 'Beaver' made them return to the razor. Two or more people walking down a street would play a twenty-point game of beaver-counting. The first to cry 'Beaver' at the sight of a beard won a point, but white beards (known as 'polar beavers') and other distinguished sorts had higher values. When the growing scarcity of beavers ended the game in 1924 King George, distinguished foreigners, and a few Chelsea pensioners were for some years almost the only bearded men left in Great Britain. Beards came in again, chiefly among the Leftists, in the middle Thirties.

CHAPTER FOUR

Reading Matter

What did people read, besides newspapers, in the period immediately following the war? The low-brow public ('low-brow' and
'high-brow' were American terms first popularized in England
by H. G. Wells) read monthly story-magazines and 'pulp' fiction
—that is to say, the light amorous and melodramatic sort,
printed on wood-pulp paper, like newspapers, and not intended
to last. Most of these novelettes were written by hacks and sold by
the title and cover-design rather than by the pull of the author's
name, But one name was outstanding—Nat Gould, whose
numerous racing novelettes had all had practically the same
plot for the last twenty years or more: the right horse always
won in the end and in spite of every possible mishap. Gould died
in July 1919, but his books continued in favour for ten years
longer. William Le Queux turned out mystery and spy stories
with loose and improbable plots, and such scandalous revelations as *Love Affairs of the Kaiser's Sons*; he went on writing until
1927. Sax Rohmer's Chinese romances were also to the fore: in
1919 his *The Golden Scorpion* was advertised widely as a thrilling
'shocker'. (The terms 'thriller' and 'shocker', with the semi-
literate type of fiction that they covered, had been in use since
the Eighties—an early by-product of mass-education.) The
adventures of Dr. Fu-Man-Chu were soon to be filmed as a
serial, which people flocked to see week after week. Detective-
novel writing was not yet an industry; Sherlock Holmes stood
alone. Indeed, the pre-war gentleman-cracksman, initiated by
Arsène Lupin and Raffles, was still a more popular type than

the professional detective. J. S. Fletcher's *Middle Temple Murder*, published in April 1919, was an early example of the coming fashion in which the amateur detective ran away with the honours. There was also a growing vogue in pseudo-scientific fiction, especially for boys: this followed uninventively along the course set by Jules Verne's *Twenty Thousand Leagues under the Sea*, and *The Moon Voyage*, and H. G. Wells's *The War of the Worlds*, *The Food of the Gods*, and *The Island of Dr. Moreau*. But the more modern death-rays, robots, invisible men, and helicopters also figured in these stories; and such advanced boys' magazines as the *Champion* and the *Wizard* challenged the established *Gem* and *Magnet*, which remained true to old-fashioned themes of school-bullies and heroes. The school-settings of the *Gem* and the *Magnet* were a romanticized public-school of about 1910, the characters never altering their vocabulary or jolly, pugnacious behaviour; there was no female interest in them. Their chief readers were secondary schoolboys, errand and shop-boys, and a large number of elderly, sentimental stamp collectors who had been reading this sort of fiction for fifty years or more. Frank Richards (not to be confused with his namesake, the Old Soldier) wrote Billy Bunter stories for the *Magnet* for thirty years, never flagging.

The American short story with a whip-crack ending on the O. Henry model had now been adopted by British magazine writers, for there had been an O. Henry boom half-way through the war. American natural-history writers, such as Ernest Thompson Seton and Gene Stratton Porter, had already set a fashion in writing about harmless wild animals in a highly personal way; and this fashion persisted. Then along came another American, Edgar Rice Burroughs, to write pulp melo-dramas of the jungle. 'Tarzan of the Apes' was the most popular fictional character among the low-brow public of the Twenties; though the passionate Sheikh of Araby, as portrayed by E. M. Hull and her many imitators, ran him pretty close. Tarzan was a glorified Mowgli, from Kipling's *Jungle Tales*, who wrestled with lions and beat upon his breast like an orang-outang. He was unaware that he was the lost child of a distinguished ex-plorer and his wife; and when he fell in love with a girl whom he saved from the fangs of savage beasts, a delicate scruple pre-vented him from marrying her. She could not fathom the reason. Then it came out: ' "My mother was an ape," he said simply!'

Edgar Rice Burroughs later developed an H. G. Wells theme of an invasion of the Earth by Martians: his was an expedition to Mars by Earth-dwellers. His hero married a Martian maiden. The *Times Literary Supplement* expressed astonishment at his successful discovery and exploitation of *The Land of Tosh*: it was admirably nonsensical stuff. As the Twenties lapsed into the Thirties, it may here be noted, the low-brow public in Great Britain gradually grew up. The sharpening of its critical sense by slicker cinema-pictures sharpened its literary judgement too: the annals of the Land of Tosh no longer carried wide conviction and the mezzo-brow 'Book of the Month' choice of the dailies became (through the Twopenny Libraries) the shop-girls' reading too—or such of them as did not sweep all modern fiction aside as 'capitalistic dope'. Even Elinor Glynn's passionate novels then appeared a little grotesque, with their tiger-skin and orchid settings; and, aware of the growing influence of famous book-reviewers on the semi-literate public, she ceased to send out review-copies of her new books. But in these early days, though not read by the more discriminating, Elinor Glyn was the reigning queen of popular love literature and considered 'very hot stuff'. P. G. Wodehouse was still rather a low-brow writer. He had not yet perfected his purely humorous style, but mixed the realistic and sentimental with the farcical in the manner of Jerome K. Jerome. He had been a writer of public-school stories before he became a journalist in New York. His Jeeves and Bertie Wooster were inspired by the American notions of the English dude and butler; but they were sartorially and socially irreproachable and his lyrical-ludicrous style, combining American slickness with English sensibility, eventually made him the most generally appreciated contemporary writer.

Comforting rather than oppressive religious books were much read, and works on spiritualism—especially Sir Oliver Lodge's *Raymond, or Life After Death*, as being written by a distinguished scientist. 'Gift verse' was immensely popular among the low-brows—an appealing mixture of love-themes, religion and optimism. John Oxenham (*Bees in Amber*) sold by the hundred thousand, and Ella Wheeler Wilcox, an American (*Poems of Pleasure, Poems of Passion*, etc.), was even more successful. Mrs. Wilcox's work had begun to appear in Britain during the war in small pocket volumes, bound in violet or green suede. They had been conventional gifts from soldiers of the lower middle classes to those they left behind. The coming of Peace did not immediately end Mrs. Wilcox's popularity, but it had long been the fashion to sneer at her, as at Hall Caine, Marie Corelli, and Charles Garvice. The *Daily Mail* took a knock at her in 1919: 'Early this year Mrs. Ella Wheeler Wilcox came to London from France, complaining bitterly that she had not been able to get hot baths there. Evidently the flow of the lady's verse was not checked by her limited ablutions, for she has now published a little volume of it called *Hello, Boys*, which was mostly written 'over there', and which exhibits all the qualities that have gained for her a wide public, especially, I have read and can well believe, "among society people, many of whom order special editions in extravagant bindings stamped with their monograms". They would.'

Among higher-brows the boom in poetry had begun in 1915 with Rupert Brooke's death. He had been an aesthete and a 'Swan' at Cambridge before the war, and his early poems, many of them purposely intended to shock, had been roughly handled by the reviewers. When he died of sunstroke in the Mediterranean, before seeing any actual fighting but after writing some stirring sonnets about war and death, the *Morning Post*, which had been his leading detractor, made a sort of 'Balder Dead' of him. Charles Sorley, a truer poet, though only twenty years old, wrote in May 1915 with disgust against the application to poetry of such irrelevant criterions as the subsequent heroic death in action of the poet. But a 'soldier-poet' was a new and fascinating phenomenon and when Sorley himself was killed in action five months later he also was among the immortals. Rupert Brooke's former comrades in Edward Marsh's anthology *Georgian Poetry*—Lascelles Abercrombie, W. H. Davies, Wilfred Gibson, Gordon Bottomley, Walter de la Mare, and the rest— were all for some reason unfit for active service (they were referred to as 'Eddie Marsh's spavined crew'). But they benefited by their association with his illustrious name, and new soldier poets such as Siegfried Sassoon, W. J. Turner, and Robert Nichols came into the picture and were included in the subsequent editions of *Georgian Poetry*, which was a best-seller.

When the war ended, the sharp contrast, whether expressed or implied, between the horrors of war and dimly remembered rural joys, did not long remain topical. Edward Marsh had the good sense to discontinue his series after a single post-war number, resigning the care of the poets he had fostered to J. C. Squire, the popular *New Statesman* satirist, who founded the *London Mercury*, a new literary monthly, in 1919. Like most such magazines in their first number, the *Mercury*, which believed in 'the birth of a lyrical age', proclaimed that it would follow no one theory, and represent no one school. 'The more intense the troubles of society,' Squire wrote in his editorial, 'the more uncertain and dark the future, the more obvious is the necessity for periodicals which hand on the torch of culture and creative activity. . . . The *Mercury* will concern itself with none of those issues which are the field of political controversy, save only such —the teaching of English, the fostering of the arts, the preservation of ancient monuments are examples—as impinge directly upon the main sphere of its interests.' Thus the character was already set for the more ephemeral literature of the Twenties: it was not to deal with the pressing questions of the day, but with the eternal problems of 'art'. The *Mercury* lasted almost to the end of The Peace, though in the Thirties it was practically 'on the dole'; it stood for the bland Liberal tradition of English Literature, which on the one hand had no use for the outworn literary language still employed by most elder writers, but on the other discouraged the 'avant-garde experimentalists' who tried to popularize Franco-American 'free verse' and 'Imagism' and discovered great foreign poets for translation. Making an exception in the case of the scholarly Arthur Waley's translations from the Chinese, the editor wrote: 'There are those to whom any foreigner, writing in some mysterious wonderful language, like French, or Polish, or Spanish-American, is a portent; but we are not among them.'

The *Mercury* was on the dull side, but the opposition to what was known as the 'Squire-archy', which dominated the literary world for the next five years and which such well-known elder poets as Thomas Hardy, W. B. Yeats, Hilaire Belloc, Rudyard Kipling, and Robert Bridges were pleased to acknowledge, was only feeble. Its self-appointed leaders were Edith, Osbert, and Sacheverell Sitwell. Edith edited an annual anthology *Wheels* with futuristic cover designs by Severini; the *Mercury* dismissed it as mere fireworks. Among other struggling 'Literary Bolshies' were T. S. Eliot, James Joyce, and Wyndham Lewis: the last-named, who was at once poet, critic, painter, and novelist, had started the whole 'avant-garde' movement just before the war with his magazine *Blast*. Joyce, who had not yet completed *Ulysses*, the outstanding period-book of the Twenties, was known chiefly for his charming pre-war *Dubliners*, on account of which Edward Marsh had successfully recommended him for a British Civil List pension as a deserving and indigent writer. Eliot was a young expatriate, polymath American, working in a bank, and known for a few slight, bitter *vers de société*. He was not yet renowned as a Shakespearean critic and editor of the learned *Criterion*, the literary quarterly which was to break the power of the *Mercury* before foundering itself shortly afterwards under the weight of its own guns and armour.

For established writers the *Mercury* had great respect. It held Joseph Conrad, H. G. Wells, and Arnold Bennett to be the three finest novelists still writing—Hardy now wrote only poems and George Moore was rather unhealthy, though a skilful craftsman. Good things were to be found in Rose Macaulay and Clemence Dane; Joseph Hergesheimer's bright American novels struck a new manner which would have a great effect on subsequent English fiction. (It is difficult to remember now what enormous respect was paid to Conrad at this time: a Pole who chose mainly seafaring themes, and wrote the language of his adoption almost too well. His *Almayer's Folly* appeared in 1920.) The *Mercury*, mentioning Yeats, Masefield, Kipling, and Bridges together as the best living 'exponents of verse' (a phrase which conveys the contemporary view of poetry as a fine art rather than as an embodiment of thought) remarked that it did not now 'expect the unexpected' from them. The *Mercury* was, indeed, against the unexpected.

By far the most important literary periodical at the beginning of the Peace, and throughout it, was the *Times Literary Supplement*, under the unobtrusive editorship of Bruce Richmond. It pursued a policy of impartiality, on the whole with remarkable success. It was not a mere appendage to *The Times* and won its independence during the short period when Lord Northcliffe took *The Times* over from the Walter family. Lord Northcliffe, it was said, consented not to 'axe' the *T.L.S.* only if Richmond could within a stipulated time raise its circulation to what

seemed an impossible figure; Richmond was given a more or less
free hand and he succeeded. His policy was to list every new
book as it appeared and to cover as many as possible, in long,
closely printed reviews—the only other paper to attempt this
formidable task had been the old-established *Athenaeum*—and to
keep a long list of sober and trustworthy experts ready to deal
with every conceivable subject that was likely to come up.
Reviews in other weekly papers were usually signed; this had
once been favoured as more to the interest of literature than
anonymous reviewing, because it prevented secret back-biting
and log-rolling. But Richmond kept his reviewers anonymous,
knowing that they would thus be less likely to forget their commission—which was to give some notion of the contents and
quality of the book entrusted to them—in the temptation to
show off their own personalities with side-comments on things
in general. In other papers, as the post-war years went on, more
and more reviewers who signed their names tried to make
columnists of themselves, and were not discouraged by their
editors.

The Times held an unchallenged position as the best-informed
and most independent journal in England, and was accepted as
gospel. Its typical readers were Government servants and their
families. The lay-out was old-fashioned, such ancient spelling
conventions as 'aera', 'oeconomy', and 'restiff' had only recently
been abandoned, and the title was still printed in Gothic type.
The first three pages, and the last three, were crammed with
small advertisements. The middle was chiefly occupied with
political news in closely printed columns. Some space was given
to books, plays, and fashions, but not much. Sport had its page,
with preferential emphasis on such social events as the Eton-
Harrow cricket match, the University boat race, the 'Classic'
horse-races, but little mention of professional football and other
plebeian sports. When in the Thirties *The Times* became a semi-
official journal, the British daily treated with the greatest confidence abroad was the Liberal *Manchester Guardian*. The lay-out
of the *Morning Post*, the typical readers of which were envisaged
as the retired senior officer and his family (King George V
was a typical *Morning Post* reader), resembled that of *The
Times*, but its treatment of news was odd—in some ways
more radical, in others more reactionary. It was at times curi-

ously far-sighted in matters of social welfare, yet admitted its contributors to express an anti-Jewish bias and accepted without question the authenticity of the famous 'Protocols of Zion', a supposed international Jewish agreement for the secret domination of the world—after *The Times* had conclusively proved the document a forgery. Usually the *Morning Post* was more die-hard than the Government: it warmly supported intervention in Russia and published lurid details of alleged Red massacres. Jews were here again the villains of the piece. When the Labour Ministry, some years later, recognized the Soviet Government, the *Morning Post* protested more vehemently than any other paper, opened a fund for the support of the persecuted Russian Church and begged its readers to subscribe to a petition condemning the Government's action. Readers responded in large numbers, and for several weeks whole pages were given over to anti-Soviet extracts from their letters. The *Morning Post* also took up the cause of General Dyer, who, in 1919, lost his head during a seditious mass-meeting of unarmed Indians at Amritsar in the Punjab and allowed his troops to open fire, killing large numbers of them. General Dyer was retired, but *Morning Post* readers of the Shoot-'Em-Down brigade rallied to his support: he was pleased to accept the sum of £26,000 subscribed by them as a testimonial.

The *Daily Telegraph* modelled itself on *The Times*, but was rather the business-man's paper. It had the largest advertising columns of any paper—one could boil a pint kettle on a single issue of it.

It was a sign of gentility to take in at least one of these three select papers, all of which were Conservative: attempts to found a Liberal paper on the same solid lines had always failed. Among the 'penny papers', which were printed on cheaper paper than the twopennies and threepennies, and did not carry nearly so many advertisements, the Liberal *Daily News* supported Lloyd George and the Coalition, but, being owned independently of politics by the Cadbury family, who were Quakers, was often impartial in its criticism of the Government. The secondary material—not news, but book reviews, theatre and film reviews, fashion and cookery notes—was superior to that of any other paper: as a guide to what middle-class people were talking about in the early Twenties the files of the *Daily News* are unrivalled. The *Daily Chronicle*, Wee Free Liberal, was inclined to sensationalism, allotting more space to murders and divorces. The Conservative *Daily Express* at the end of the war was a poor thing; but an enterprising Canadian, Lord Beaverbrook, had just saved it from failure by acquiring a controlling interest in it for a paltry £17,500. In 1918 its circulation was only 350,000, not much greater than the expensive and advertisement-rich *Daily Telegraph*. In 1920 it had risen to half a million and by 1922 was approaching one million. This increase was due to an imitation and enlargement of *Daily Mail* methods, at a time when the *Daily Mail* under Lord Northcliffe had achieved the same ascendancy in the popular Press as *The Times* enjoyed over the select Press.

Lord Northcliffe, a hard-working Irishman, was the man who first 'gave the public what they wanted' by introducing into England the American 'Yellow Press' methods of journalism, with which the name of Hearst is inevitably associated. The *Daily Mail* had outgrown the reputation for inaccuracy that it had unluckily won by a premature report of the massacre of the Foreign Legations at Pekin in 1900 and its newsboys no longer hawked it under the genial nickname of 'Daily Liar'. It was regarded with popular affection. Lord Northcliffe himself, according to Tom Clarke's *My Northcliffe Diary*, defined what he considered to be the function of newspapers and how they should treat the news: 'News is surprise—an unexpected happening; if a dog bites a man it is not news, but if a man bites a dog it is news. . . . There are two main divisions of news: one, actualities; two, talking points. The first is news in its narrowest and best sense—reports of happenings, political resignations, strikes, crimes, deaths of famous people, wrecks and railway smashes, weather, storms, sporting results and so on. The second is getting the topics people are discussing and developing them, or stimulating a topic oneself, such as "The Truth about the Night Clubs", "Government Waste", "Are our Motor Traffic Regulations Obsolete?", "Women's Fashion Changes", "The Riddle of Spiritualism". . . . There are some who say it is the second sort of news, these "features" and "talking points", that sells the newspapers. I do not agree. It is *hard news* that catches readers. Features hold them.' The wise-crack about man and dog is usually attributed to Hearst, and *hard news* is also an American usage—like 'hard drink' for spirits and 'hard money' for specie.

From Lord Northcliffe's list of important features some per-manent lines of the *Daily Mail*, and consequently of middle-class thought, can be construed. The *Daily Mail* was always on the look-out for Government waste and delay: two bureaucratic figures with tall top-hats, labelled 'Dilly' and 'Dally', figured prominently in the cartoons signed 'Poy'. It also followed atten-tively the progress of new inventions, such as aircraft, motor-boats, and wireless. Spiritualism, the question of whether re-ligion was decaying, the question of what moral attitude to adopt toward bottle-parties, night-clubs, revues and chorus girls, and all problems involving women: those were its leading features. Northcliffe, indeed, advised his editors always to have a woman's story in the headlines. He had been, even before the war, the first newspaper owner to abandon the convention that news was only what men talked about in clubs. He knew it to be also what people talked about in kitchen, parlour, drawing-room, and over the garden wall; namely, other people—their failures and successes, their joys and sorrows, their money and their food, their peccadilloes. The *Daily Mail* was thus the first to cater for women readers, and for children too—Folkard's 'Teddy Tail' was the first children's feature in the popular Press. This technique was soon adopted and extended by other news-papers. Northcliffe, however, was against sensationalism for its own sake. His advice was: 'Be bright, but dignified. . . . People who genuinely mistake brightness for sensationalism are to be pitied.'

The process of brightening the news had not yet been taken very far. The *Daily Mail* in 1920 was less sensational than the *Daily Telegraph* became fifteen years later. The news was closely and badly printed; headlines were in comparatively small type, and had not achieved the compressed, suggestive qualities of the American tabloids. Crime was not dwelt on at such loving length as in the popular Sunday papers.

It would be a mistake to think of the *Daily Mail*, or any other popular newspaper of those years, as intended for the working class as such to read. The only paper of that sort was the Socialist *Daily Herald*, founded by George Lansbury immediately after the war. It was more clumsily written than most of its contemporaries, because it could not afford to pay high salaries to the best available journalists. It contained fewer features, had a sneering underdog tone, and gave the purely Labour view of any news-item—to a circulation of only 100,000. Its position in the early Twenties was similar to that of the *Daily Worker* in the middle Thirties, except that, whereas the *Daily Herald* appealed almost solely to the Socialist working class, the *Daily Worker's* public always included a large number of Left Wing intellectuals. There were very few of these in the Twenties. Any middle-class person subscribing to the *Daily Herald* was suspected and shunned by his neighbours; though the London clubs usually had a copy on their files for information—the *Daily Herald* printed a good deal of news that other papers would not touch.

It was to the middle and lower-middle classes that the *Daily Mail* appealed. Following up his assumption that the things people talked about were news, and that they talked most about personages and personalities, Northcliffe advised: 'Get more names in the paper—the more aristocratic the better, if there is a news story round them. . . . Everyone likes reading about people in better circumstances than his or her own. . . . Write and seek news with at least the £1,000 a year man in mind.'

Northcliffe was famous for his dodges (by this time called 'stunts') even before the war: for a bet, it is said, he had undertaken to change the daily food of the nation within six months, and did indeed persuade practically everyone to abandon bleached white bread, temporarily, in favour of Standard Bread. This was a whole-meal loaf of an unappetizing grey colour that was said to contain 'both the germ of the wheat and the semolina'. The monster *Daily Mail* sweet-pea competition had also been a great success and the prize bloom, entered by a clergyman, was much admired. Then there were prizes for Aerial Flights, and the Paper Bag Cookery Campaign. The war had interrupted these enterprises, but in the summer of 1920 the *Daily Mail* ran a sand-competition for children: £1,000 was offered in prizes for whoever could make the best sand-design advertising the *Daily Mail*, on the seashore. The Boy Scouts' Jamboree of that year was also heavily featured in order to attract the juvenile reader. Northcliffe even occasionally attempted a political stunt that took him beyond his usual position on the left wing of the Conservative Party. For instance, in January 1920 there was a strike of clerks in the Pearl Insurance Company; they were asking for minimum-wage regulations. North-cliffe supported them, hoping thereby to gain the confidence of the black-coated Labour movement. When the Pearl Insurance Company sent him an advertisement, he refused to publish it while the clerks' demands were unsatisfied. Instead, he gave £500 out of his own pocket to the strikers' fund.

The *Daily Mail* hat, a compromise between the bowler and the Homburg, was launched in December 1920, and described as the perfect headgear for every man. One or two M.P.s were persuaded to wear it, and so was ex-King Manoel of Portugal, whose name was never difficult to obtain for advertising pur-poses. A model was sent to Winston Churchill, famous for his catholicity in hats, but he was never seen wearing it in public. In fact, this was one of the few *Daily Mail* stunts that failed—even the staff of the paper, except very lowly members who hoped to catch the Chief's eye, could not be persuaded to adopt it for everyday use.

The *Daily Mail* was laughed at, usually pleasantly, sometimes unpleasantly, and taken with little seriousness; but people were always interested to know what in the world it would take up next. It was this popular confidence that enabled it to spend a great deal of money in financing its stunts and become the public clearing-house of every amusing 'nothing of the day'. Northcliffe died in 1922 and his brother Lord Rothermere succeeded him. Lord Rothermere did not keep the stunts going so assiduously as did Lord Northcliffe. One odd cause in which he tried to interest the *Daily Mail* readers was the injustice done to Hungary at Versailles, when Transylvania and several dis-tricts which had never formed part of that principality were ceded to Rumania. He urged that the treaties be revised. The *Daily Mail* public was puzzled—it did not know Transylvania from Pennsylvania—and a rumour went around that Lord Rothermere was angling for the Hungarian throne.

Shortly after the war ended, Sir Max Pemberton founded the London School of Journalism, first of the big correspondence courses that flooded an ever-growing free-lance market with writers of short stories, articles, and news-features. Thousands took the course but few succeeded in earning anything ap-proaching the fabulous 'spare-time' incomes that were promised in the prospectuses of the many 'schools' to anyone with a knowledge of English grammar and a little diligence. The advertisements were weighted with the testimonials of former pupils, most of whom, after 'paying for the whole course out of earnings resulting from the first lesson', claimed to have gone on to earn between £10 and £20 per week entirely in their spare time. These schools of journalism were not a 'racket', for they did teach their pupils certain journalistic formalities which had to be observed if they were to get anything published at all. By the middle Twenties the boom in writing was well started, and it became the ambition of hundreds of young men and women to 'go into a publisher's' or to 'go into Fleet Street'. The cachet of a literary calling was cried up not only by the schools of journalism and by foundering publishers who were glad to take in rich 'apprentices', but also by large numbers of experienced but unsuccessful journalists who took personal classes of private pupils.

A feature of post-war newspapers was the increased space given to gossip; of which, however, Lord Northcliffe at first disapproved on the grounds that it was bad news-writing. News of what 'society' was doing, he felt, should be given without the snobbish personal touch of 'I met Lady C., who was wearing . . .' or 'Lord K. told me . . . his brother-in-law the Hon. P. C. is a well-known . . .' etc. But this was before the penetration of higher journalism into the elder universities, which became the training ground for many of the best correspondents and brightest feature-writers of the day. The recruits that newspapers needed were no longer drudges trained from the age of fourteen in a newspaper office, but university men with a superficial knowledge of many things, full of 'ideas', and with a snappy way of expressing them. These Oxford and Cambridge could provide—but especially Oxford. Charles Graves, Beverley Nichols, Margaret Lane, 'Peterborough', and 'William Hickey' all began their journalistic careers at Oxford.

Even members of the aristocracy were induced to become gossip-writers and boldly sign their names instead of using pseudonyms. Lord Castlerosse first began to write 'The Londoner's Log' for the *Sunday Express* in 1926; but the gossip-writer was by now a 'columnist' and provided a critical and authoritative commentary on life in general rather than humble gossip about the private life of his social betters. Shortly afterwards,

Lady Eleanor Smith (Lord Birkenhead's daughter) began to write for the *Weekly Dispatch*, but soon retired from her 'Window in Vanity Fair', preferring to write novels exploiting her passion for gipsies. Then another Irish peer, Lord Donegall, was engaged by the *Sunday News*. Towards the end of the Twenties *The Times*, which employed no columnist: sponsored an agitation against the practice of columnism; letters appeared signed by 'London Hostess', deploring this 'new and dangerous tendency in social life , and condemning the 'sneak-guest' as an unprincipled cad. But the columnist could not be suppressed. He was the most feared and courted member of Society and was welcomed by head-waiters, masters of ceremonies, seaside mayors, golf-club secretaries and the like as if he were visiting royalty. The best known columnists by the end of the Peace were, like their American counterparts, earning far more than the managing editors of the papers for which they wrote—and this did not include the perquisites of their envied office.

CHAPTER FIVE

Post-War Politics

In spite of the Bolshevik bogey that they manipulated it was correctly assumed by the newspapers that the country was 'sound at heart'. The elder members of the working class for the most part resented the identification of their Trade Unions with Socialism. They favoured one or other of the two elder parties, and continued in their traditional loyalty to the Crown and the Peerage, and their unabashed respect for the Squire or Owner. They 'knew their place'. The younger members were Socialistically inclined, but even the few who had picked up the Marxian catchwords had no real ambition to overthrow and displace the Capitalist class. A more usual ambition was to rise into the substantial grade above the artisan, by becoming a foreman or skilled technician, and so rank socially with clerks and independent tradesmen. Foremen, clerks, and small tradesmen similarly wished to rise from the black-coated class into the middle class of manufacturers and wholesale merchants. It was for such ambitions that the highly popular Pelmanism was designed, which advertised in every newspaper and periodical of the time. This was a method of memory training, and its argument was that human energy and will-power could be systematically developed: each person could make the most of his natural gifts by intensive training. Pelmanism set out to train people how to practise self-analysis and self-drill, in order to eliminate mind-wandering and promote concentration. The headlines of its advertisements were: 'How to overcome brain-fag', 'How to originate ideas', 'Self-expression develops ability',

'The hygiene of study', etc. It was a simple commercial version of the work which psychologists were then doing—in fact, the first form in which psychology reached the wider public. Instead of undertaking to correct unfortunate aberrations in character, as the psycho-therapists did, it emphasized the success side of living. Everyone had abilities, and all that anyone needed was training in order to get to the top of the ladder. 'There is plenty of room at the top' was the catchword. Once the revolutionary crowd-spirit had thus been canalized into a million streams of individual ambition, the representatives of Law and Order could be easy at heart; and the more pleasantly they lived, the greater the incentive of those below to rise socially and enjoy the same honour and security.

The simple annals of the unambitious poor were simple indeed in these days: few could afford to get drunk and street-fighting therefore declined, there was as yet no B.B.C., religion had lost both its terrors and its consolations. The men's chief interest was betting on horse-races (most of them seldom or never saw a race-horse), watching professional football, and cultivating their allotments. The women had the traditional women's interests of children, the household, and making ends meet; and the new weekly cinema-going habit was sufficient entertainment. If in the lower and lower-middle classes some movement or novelty of an interesting kind had occurred, it would surely not have escaped some *Daily Mail* reporter's keen eye for news. But they were too closely occupied now with the struggle for existence to produce any newsworthy item except an occasional crime of violence. It was this, rather than the snobbery imputed by the *Daily Herald*, that kept them out of the news at the expense of 'Society', one of whose main functions had come to be providing active topicality.

What was Society now? The former 'ruling class', whose sons had gone into Parliament and the services as a matter of course, was now forced more and more into business; because of increased taxation, the rise in the cost of living, and the reduction of Army and Navy establishments. The old upper-middle classes with fixed incomes of about £5,000 a year were obliged to cut down their social expenditure. Their town mansions were converted into flats, and their political power lived on only in so far as they became influential in business. Politics and business were thus becoming openly the occupation of the same class. The aristocracy, for the most part, lived a quiet life, trying hard to preserve what it could of its old estates. 'Society' had ceased to have any strict meaning. Already in Edwardian times this process had gone far, the King himself having admitted the Jewish plutocracy, leading actresses, and such self-made merchants as Sir Thomas Lipton, to his intimate acquaintance. But whereas, in Edwardian times, poverty and divorce were failings equally fatal to social ambition, by the Twenties the light-hearted American view of divorce, as rather a joke than a misfortune, had come into fashion, and 'The New Poor' positively boasted of their penuriousness. No surprise was caused when Mayfair women opened dress-shops in Bond Street, or started Social Bureaux for supplying guides to American visitors. 'Society', it was generally assumed, had to earn its living like any other class; so 'Society' came to mean 'people worthy of a columnist's respectful mention'. As the period advanced the 'Mayfair accent' changed remarkably from an over-sweet rather French lisp to a rasping tone that had traces in it of Cockney, American, and Midland provincial.

Times were felt to be hard: everyone who counted was to some extent the victim of the disgusting war-profiteer, and it now began to be realized that there could be peace-profiteers as well. In January 1920 *The Tatler* remarked that 'perfectly hair-raising stories were going about of the huge and horrible fortunes made by profiteers out of a war-worn people'. Prices of even the simplest necessities had got beyond the joke-stage, and people were beginning to ask themselves why. Life was in such a whirl of confusion, however, that few paused for an answer. *The Tatler*, after raising the question, went on to complain hotly that hundreds of thousands of pounds were being collected to feed 'Hun babies', and that railway porters were earning £3 a week, while British ex-officers were walking the streets, looking for jobs. The moneyless ex-officer was a new social phenomenon in England. For, whatever one's birth or antecedents, a commission automatically made one a gentleman—as did a degree at an elder university or Holy Orders in the Anglican Church. Before the war, gentlemen without money were usually soon found in ditches with sporting rifles beside them; or were exported by their wealthy connections to distant parts of the

Empire. But, towards the end of the war, commissions had been granted to men (known as 'temporary gentlemen') who had greater military talent than claims to gentility. After the war they were entitled to keep honorary military rank, but if they happened to become beggars—with no rich relatives to support or export them—did not feel the dignified necessity of suicide.

Milk and bread prices are a convenient indication of the cost of living at any period. In October 1919 the price of a quartern loaf rose from 9½d. to 1s. 4d.; it did not fall again to normal until 1922. Milk, in the winter of 1920–1, rose to 11d. a quart, and did not come down to the normal 5d. until April—and this was ordinary milk, left at the doorstep in unsealed cans, for the practice of grading and bottling had not yet begun. This sudden rise in prices to levels not even reached during the war was caused by the rapid reduction in unemployment and by a consequent sharp advance in wages. It was essentially a price-boom, rather than a boom in industrial production. People were now willing to pay for a great number of goods and services which for the last five years they had been unable to get. Demand was so great and so sudden that the resulting shortage induced a sharp rise in prices, which in turn induced a feverish attempt to re-equip industries—not always wisely. The cotton industry of Lancashire, for instance, was re-equipped at such expense, in the hope of a permanently large demand for its goods, that it was crippled for the next twenty years.

Even during this short-lived boom there were constant complaints against the Lloyd George Government. It was remembered that England was supposed to be a democratic country; and business men felt that war-time 'authoritative' habits of government ought to be relinquished as soon as possible, and private enterprise given its head once more. In spite of the disorganization of the railways, caused by war-time wear and tear and the transfer to France of railway equipment, wide dismay was caused by the Government's proposal to create a Ministry of Ways and Communications. The Ministry was to enjoy almost unlimited control over roads, railways, canals, harbours and docks, with the power to acquire any means or instrument of transport by simple Order in Council. Such far-reaching authority was held only justifiable in time of war; and Lloyd George was remembered by Conservative back-benchers as the pre-war introducer of the atrocious Land Tax, the meddling National Health Insurance, and other Liberal legislation which logically could only end in State Socialism and the nationalization of mines and industry in general.

It was also feared that the Ministry would spend too much money in helping the railways to rehabilitate themselves—when it was already clear that lorries, buses and cars were reliable, economical and more direct means of transport. 'The future of British industry,' the Press agreed, 'lies on the roads.' Lord Montagu, a pioneer of the sport of motoring, wrote to *The Times* in January 1919 to praise the smooth running of motor transport behind the lines in France during the war, and to suggest that the War Office should lend some of its transport experts to help reorganize road traffic at home. At that time speed-limits and traffic regulations were by no means uniform in England.

The motor manufacturers joined in the outcry against the Government: they held that there had been unnecessary delay in transforming the productive capacity of the country to meet peace-time needs. They now had neither enough factories nor enough material to cope with the number of orders received. American competition could therefore not be met, and they were indignant that the Government should have imposed a duty of only $33\frac{1}{3}$ per cent on the importation of foreign cars. Great Britain seemed an almost virgin market for cars to the American exporter: in the United States in 1921 one person in every fourteen was a car owner, but in Great Britain only one in every one hundred and sixty-eight.

Although most manufacturers were working energetically, despite the extraordinarily high prices of labour and materials, to restart their industries, there were numerous prophets of disaster. These pointed out the dangers of an unfavourable balance of trade, caused by the enormous increase of imports in 1919 and to the comparatively slow growth of exports; and spoke of the 'vicious spiral' of high prices and high wages, followed by higher prices and higher wages. The Labour Party was attacked in the Conservative Press for 'lending a too-ready ear to unscrupulous opportunists', who wished to dislocate public services and hamper private enterprise by causing unnecessary strikes; but the Government was at the same time accused of wilfully prolonging the rate of public expenditure which had been necessary during the war, and of launching out into its housing, land and road schemes in 'an orgy of extravagant finance'.

The break of this industrial boom came in 1921, when industries were beginning to work normally again and the first peacetime reaction of extravagant spending had died down. A trade depression was revealed in the growing unemployment-rate and in the frequent strikes. The ex-Serviceman who lost his temporary employment was no longer a hero but a good-for-nothing living on public charity. The Government began to divest itself of embarrassing responsibilities. There was much talk of 'retrenchment', and of 'wielding the axe'. It was the task of Sir Eric Geddes, then Minister of Transport and a former railway manager, to wield this axe, and he and it figured prominently in cartoons and newspaper comments of the time. The projects of the National Industrial Conference were abandoned. The Government became more cautious in its housing schemes and gave up its war-time control of the railways, having kept it only long enough to assist in the grouping of the various lines into four large systems: L.M.S., L.N.E.R., G.W.R., and Southern.

Government control of the coal industry during the war had worked fairly smoothly, and in 1918 the miners had demanded nationalization of the mines. The commission appointed in 1919, under the chairmanship of Mr. Justice Sankey, to enquire into the coal industry, actually endorsed this demand and recommended the raising of wages. Wages were raised and, after a twelve-day strike in October 1920, slightly raised again. In March 1921, however, when it seemed clear that the boom in manufactures was ending, and that the demand for coal would decrease, Government control was withdrawn. The mine-owners then wished to revert to wage-rates that would vary from district to district, on the ground that some mines were more expensive to run than others and so could not afford the prevailing high rate. The miners put forward an alternative scheme: a uniform wage to be paid out of a national pool of profits, which would enable the poorer districts to be supported by the richer. The mine-owners could not agree among themselves to accept this, and on 1st April 1921 the miners came out on strike. The railwaymen and transport workers usually supported the miners in what was known as the Triple Alliance, but this time they were restrained by their leaders, J. H. Thomas and Frank

Hodges; and when the Government proclaimed a state of emergency, the miners prudently called off the strike. They knew that the demand for coal was diminishing for a number of reasons, and would continue to diminish. Many shipping companies were installing oil-burning engines in their ships. The use of electricity for domestic and industrial purposes was increasing. Railways would need less coal because of the competition of lorry traffic on the roads. What was worse, Germany, having no specie, was being made to pay for the war in kind. Coal exported to fulfil the Allies' 'Reparations' demand was competing with the home industry, and any stoppage by British mines meant so many customers lost to Germany. The retail price of coal was slowly falling—in 1920 it had been 8os. a ton, and by 1923 it was to be only 50s.

The miners had been handicapped by their lack of unanimity in agreeing on any positive policy: they aimed merely at resisting change and compelling concessions. Nor could they count on the support of other unions, each of which was autonomous. None either desired or had made any preparation for a prolonged industrial struggle. The day on which the miners went back to work and district rates were reintroduced was called 'Black Friday'. To soften the blow, however, the Government agreed to grant the industry a yearly subsidy of £10,000,000 to offset the fall of wages in poorer districts. This subsidy was continued until 1925, when its withdrawal precipitated fresh troubles. The humiliating defeat of the miners was largely responsible for a nearly two-million drop in general Trade-Union membership.

The slump of 1921 made it clear that recovery from the effects of war could not be achieved by the individual action of any one nation. Britain was dependent upon foreign trade, and to stimulate such trade the world had first to be set in better order. To begin with, enormous sums of money were still being spent, and many lives lost, in garrisoning the conquered Turkish territories of Palestine, Transjordania, and Mesopotamia. The popular Press was girding at the Government to clear out and cut its losses: 'Mesopotamia' and 'Mess-up-at-home-here' were twin anti-Government catchwords. The Press had a powerful ally in Colonel T. E. Lawrence, who had been the chief instrument in detaching the Arab inhabitants of these countries from their allegiance to the Turks, and who regarded the imposition of British or French rule over them as not only economically and militarily unwise but a flagrant breach of faith to allies. Since he held the key to the situation, so far as the British side was concerned, the Government capitulated, and asked him to draft a settlement which the Arabs would accept and which would safeguard British interests as far as possible. He consented, and in the name of Winston Churchill a satisfactory arrangement was made for a gradual withdrawal.

In a draft preface to his *Seven Pillars of Wisdom* Lawrence wrote: 'In 1919 powerful elements in the British Government were seeking to evade their war-time obligations to the Arabs. That stage ended in March 1921, when Mr. Winston Churchill took charge of the Middle East. He set honesty before expedience in order to fulfil our promises in the letter and in the spirit. He executed the whole McMahon undertaking (called a treaty by some who have not seen it) for Palestine, for Transjordania, and for Arabia. In Mesopotamia he went far beyond its provisions, giving to the Arabs more, and reserving for us much less, than Sir Henry McMahon had thought fit. In the affairs of French Syria he was not able to interfere, and the Sherif of Mecca can fairly complain that the settlement there is not yet in accordance with the Anglo-French agreement of 1916, or with our word to him. I say "not yet" advisedly, since the McMahon proposals (being based on racial and economic reasons) were to have imposed themselves eventually, even if Mr. Churchill's progressive British military withdrawal from Mesopotamia had not come to prejudge the future of all the Arab areas. . . . England is out of the Arab affair with clean hands.'

By implication the French (who did not decide to cut their Near Eastern losses until 1936) had dirty hands. Their military hold on Syria was the real argument against relinquishing British conquests in the Middle East. And in the Turko-Greek dispute they backed the winning side, the wa.like Turks, while in the interests of trade the British backed the mercantile Greeks—who were ignominiously thrown out of Smyrna. The Entente was beginning to crack.

In the interests of trade, too, the British Government helped the League of Nations to restore the financial stability of Austria and Hungary. And it was clear that another important preliminary to general European recovery was the industrial reconstruction of Germany. But here again the British Government met with opposition from France. France was largely an agricultural nation and French industry was not so dependent as British on the prosperity of the rest of Europe. French statesmen were thinking politically rather than economically. They were resolved to keep Germany down.

This same divergence of opinion made itself felt in the tangled Reparations problem. Conference after conference had been called to settle it; but no agreement could be reached. The French wished to make reparations and war debts cancel each other, so that Germany would be paying France's debts to Britain and to the United States. They also encouraged their client states to take advantage of Germany's weakness. For example, Briand, the French Premier, approved the Polish filibustering expedition into Silesia under Korfanty. But Lloyd George strongly condemned this raid: he did not wish Germany to become too weak, and considered that she should pay only for damage done during the war. The price was not to exceed what experts calculated to be her paying capacity. At the Genoa Conference of 1922, it was decided that the Allies should take over control of German finances in order to determine this capacity—but how to control them was a point on which no decision could be reached. In January 1923, with the excuse that the Germans were wilfully behindhand in their stipulated payments of coal to France, the French Army occupied the Ruhr territory; and there tried to foment a Rhineland separatist movement. They were met with passive resistance by the Germans, who refused to have any dealings with the Allies until the Ruhr was evacuated. The British plainly dissociated themselves from the French action. The origin of the war was now forgotten, the Germans forgiven, and France openly accused of trying to impose security on Europe by brute force.

By this time the slump and the international tangle had already brought about the fall of Lloyd George. He was accused of being the man who had nearly lost the war and who had effectively lost the peace. It was said on the one hand that he had abandoned Ireland to the Sinn Feiners, and on the other that he was responsible for the Black and Tan 'atrocities'. In the opinion of the die-hard Conservatives he had been too lenient with Germany, and in that of the more liberal-minded he seemed to be yielding to France's efforts to dominate Europe. He had promised a land fit for heroes, but all that the country had enjoyed was at first high prices, and then a slump. He had promised reconstruction, but all that he had done, apparently, was to waste public money on houses, education, and schemes for roads, which private enterprise could have carried out more cheaply and efficiently. He was the victim of his own enthusiastic promises of 1918, and of the public wish to find a scapegoat for the unpleasant truth that peace did not automatically bring prosperity.

The Conservative Party, which had not exercised independent office for sixteen years, saw its opportunity. It was thought safe, now that the Army and Navy were again wholly professionalized, to dispense with the Liberal buffer that had interposed between the forces of Law and Order and the war-time revolutionaries. 'The country is sound at heart'—and this meant Conservatized. Bonar Law, the leader of the party, emerged from retirement and approved the Conservative withdrawal from the Coalition. Since the Liberals themselves were sharply divided in allegiance between Lloyd George and Asquith, the Conservatives now came swimming into power. But in May Bonar Law himself resigned, owing to ill-health. He died in the same year and was buried in Westminster Abbey; as a reward less for his ministerial services than for having broken, it was hoped for ever, the spells of the 'Wizard of Wales'.

Stanley Baldwin, who succeeded him, was also little known. Although he had been Chancellor of the Exchequer for nearly a year, no-one had been impressed by any obvious qualities of leadership in him: indeed, he had earned very bad marks in the Press by his handling of the war-debts problem. Max Beerbohm expressed the general astonishment at his elevation by a cartoon which showed the schoolboy Baldwin looking at the grown-up Baldwin and exclaiming: 'Good Lord! *You*, Prime Minister!'

The war-debts problem was briefly this: Britain owed the United States more than nine hundred million pounds, but was owed by other countries over two thousand million pounds. At first Britain and France proposed that all war debts should be cancelled, but the United States naturally refused to give up their advantageous position as the greatest creditor nation. Balfour, the former Conservative leader, then Lord President of the Council, thereupon presented the debtor countries with a note writing off their debts to Britain except for such a sum as would enable her to pay the United States; thus putting on the Americans the odium of playing the dun in a street of beggars. Some Americans realized that the Allies could only pay in goods, and that quantities of foreign goods dumped in the United States would upset domestic economy and mean stepping up the tariffs on imports still further. The majority, however, took up the uncompromising attitude that American help had saved the Allies from losing a bungled war, and that this help should be paid for: it was not the fault of the United States if the Allies had bungled the peace too—for Congress had refused to ratify the Versailles Treaty. This combination of moral righteousness with what seemed the spirit of usury infuriated the British, and Baldwin's mission to the United States in 1923, to settle the war-debt problem, was therefore highly unpopular at home. The generous Baldwin actually agreed that Britain should pay £33,000,000 annually between 1923 and 1932, and afterwards £38,000,000 annually until 1984; his intention was to maintain Britain's reputation for financial stability. But once the Americans had this settlement signed, they allowed far more favourable agreements to other debtor nations. Throughout the Twenties, the *Daily Mail* and *Daily Express*, whenever they fell out with Baldwin on any point of policy, never failed to bring up this debt settlement against him.

A General Election was due in 1923, and Baldwin chose to put forward a tariff policy, which delighted Big Business, consisting of a tax on manufactured imports, a preferential rate being allowed for Empire products. But elsewhere it raised an outcry against the prospect of 'dear food'—though, to the disgust of the farmers, foreign meat and wheat were exempted from taxation—and served to unite the Asquith and Lloyd George factions of the Liberals. Baldwin was staggeringly frank even in those days: after the election he confessed that he would not have risked a tariff policy had he thought that 'there was a bed wide enough in the United Kingdom to hold both Asquith and Lloyd George'. But in his election speeches he made much of being a 'plain man' and an 'ordinary person'. As such he was cartooned by the Opposition Press: the rising young Australian-born cartoonist David Low showed him shrinking into a very plain and ordinary tadpole. The election on the Liberal side was fought with spirit. Lloyd George referred to the Tories as 'tinned crabs' and 'tinned salmon'—those foods being supposedly what the public would have to subsist on if tariffs were introduced. The *Daily News* provided several electioneering songs, which were actually sung at political meetings. One ran:

> 'No, we won't have Protection,
> We won't have Protection to-day.
> 'Twould rush up the prices
> And squeeze us like vices
> And we'd have to pay, pay, pay . . .'

a parody of the American song 'Yes, we have no bananas', which was then the rage. On the other hand the Liberal main plank, Free Trade, which had always previously secured them a majority whenever Tariff Reform came up, was seen to be tenable only while Britain maintained undisputed mastery of world markets—and it was obvious that this was no longer the case.

The odd result of this election was that neither side won. Baldwin had underestimated the effect of his tariff policy on the Labour vote. It was not enough for his supporters to drown the 'No Bananas' melody with 'Vote, vote, vote for Stanley Baldwin, Roll old Asquith in the mud.' For the slump had given ex-Servicemen of the working classes, now on the voting registers, plenty of leisure for remembering their rebellious war-time moods. If Lloyd George had failed them, they could have no better hopes from Bonar Law—or Baldwin. They were not Socialists and they hated 'Socialistic clap-trap'; but they would punish the two elder parties for letting them down. 'Them Socialists can't make no bigger bloody box-up nor the old lot didn't', was the current opinion of the back-streets. Thus, though the Conservatives remained the largest party in the House of Commons with 258 seats, they were outnumbered by the combined Liberal and Labour parties together, who held 158 and 191 respectively. This was the first time in Parliamentary history that the old sham-fight between the two elder parties had been disturbed by a third party of such alarming dimensions. The Conservatives expected Asquith to do the decent thing: forget past injuries and keep the 'Wild Men' out by co-operation with themselves. But Asquith did not want to do anything that might seem an invitation to a class war; and most of his party agreed with him that the more sensible course would be to support the Labour Party, if they would take office, and make them instruments of Liberal policy. Labour, of course, would have been politic to refrain from taking office, and instead put the Liberals into servitude on their behalf; but the temptation was too strong. Ramsay MacDonald became Premier.

The Liberals were strongly criticized for their decision and described as 'the patient oxen'—dragging Labour through Parliament and fated at the end to be slaughtered by Labour opponents in by-elections. And it was true that from a party point of view, Asquith had made a grave tactical mistake. He should have forced the Conservatives, as the biggest party, to take office and be answerable to him that they did nothing to injure Liberal interests. In three-cornered contests thereafter it was decided by property owners who had been taught to fear the nationalization under Socialism, of 'everything, including women', that a vote for the Liberals was a vote for Labour. Asquith had been brought up in a Britain where the word 'compromise' had an attractive ring, and he intended his to be the compromise party. But as soon as Labour grew strong enough to challenge Capital, political feeling began to run so high that 'compromise' had an odious connotation of weakness and treachery. Except in a few Scottish and Welsh strongholds the Liberal cause was lost, and the party remained an almost pathetic minority for the rest of the period.

Disillusion at the fall of a great man, whose war-time popularity had rivalled even Lloyd George's, was another reason for the swing-over to Socialism. This was Horatio Bottomley, the last of the demagogues. He was of humble origin and educated in an orphanage. Persistent rumour made him the illegitimate child of Annie Besant and Bradlaugh the equally famous atheist, whom he strangely resembled in features. Bottomley was amused by the story and did not deny it—he was, however, the son of a distressed tailor's foreman. He was a plausible lay-lawyer and had amassed a large fortune by promoting a number of tricky financial schemes, chiefly lotteries and monster competitions. These were advertised in his weekly, *John Bull*, which specialized in 'spicy' reports of murders and divorces and in the merciless showing up of vice and graft—and most of the prizes were won by imaginary competitors, or members of Bottomley's entourage. He was a genial rascal and took the line that people who were fools enough to be duped by his swindles deserved all they got. On one occasion a trembling office-boy was hauled up before him by the head clerk, having been caught red-handed stealing a very small postal-order from a competitor's entry to a 'Bullets' competition. Bottomley glared at the boy for a few moments. Then his features relaxed and he said apologetically to the head clerk: 'Well, damn it all, it's only sixpence, I know, but I suppose he has to begin *somewhere*.'

In 1906 he had been elected Independent M.P. for South Hackney, a seat that he held for six years until he had to resign because of bankruptcy. Having extraordinary persuasive powers, he was able to pose in his *John Bull* editorials as the champion of the underdog and the enemy of humbug. The war provided him with his great opportunity. He proved himself the patriot of patriots and the ablest recruiting agent in the country. At mass meetings, under the banner of 'Fight for King and Country', he was a more popular draw than any Cabinet Minister except Lloyd George himself. But he did not give his services free: he made £27,000 out of these recruiting meetings. When a Zeppelin bomb nearly destroyed his office premises, *John Bull* made it appear that the Germ-Huns were trying to assassinate their Horatio because of the will to victory with which he inspired the Boys in the Trenches. The boys in the trenches were certainly devoted readers of his cheerful pages. At the end of the war he was able to apply for his discharge as a bankrupt, and to resume his seat in Parliament for South Hackney.

He was then launching new prize schemes—the Premium Bond Scheme of 1918, for example, to which his readers subscribed £90,000. Out of this he had agreed to pay £10,000 in prizes; the rest he paid into his private account. He did not hoard his winnings, but spent lavishly on champagne (of which he was the largest drinker in the country), women, and the races. The champagne led him, in his betting, to a total disregard of the

77

real odds. He backed his own horse, Aynsley, for £40,000 in the Manchester Cup of 1919. It lost, but he immediately lodged a protest that the winning horse, By Jingo, had been wrongly entered—the owner's name was Depledge, and by mistake it had been entered as De Pledge. His protest was overruled, and the Turf thereafter considered him a very poor sportsman. The House of Commons similarly took offence when Bottomley, in *John Bull*, described Lady Astor, who had been pressing her teetotal convictions on the House of Commons, as a 'hypocrite of the first water'. On his next appearance in the House, Bottomley was greeted with a storm of boos; it was an unwritten law that members should not make personal attacks on one another in the Press. Bottomley's nerve was unshaken: he felt himself secure in the hearts of the greater part of his countrymen.

Already, however, he was being accused of swindling. A pamphlet headed 'Horatio Bottomley Exposed' which had been sold in the streets at intervals since the earliest days of the war, was damaging him a good deal. Bottomley set in motion his usual procedure for getting out of such difficulties. He asked his friend Rueben Bigland, a Birmingham printer known in sporting circles as 'Telephone Jack', to find some needy fellow-printer who would undertake for a fee of £100 to reprint the pamphlet and be successfully sued for libel. That would prevent the repetition of similar statements. Everything went according to plan. Bottomley, as usual, conducted his case in person and gave Greaney, his sham opponent, such a dressing-down in the witness-box that the jury awarded him £500 damages—which, of course, Greaney did not pay.

Thus triumphantly vindicated, Bottomley launched out on his Victory Bond Scheme. The Government had issued a Victory Loan, to which the smallest amount that anyone might subscribe was £5. Bottomley represented this as unjust to the small investor and promised that any reader of *John Bull* who subscribed £1 would be given a fifth share in a Government £5 bond. The bonds bought by these subscriptions were to be handed over to trustees: big prizes would then be paid out of the accruing interest. Bottomley's intention was perhaps to embezzle only a part of the capital, as he had done so often before, by inventing imaginary prize-winners. But when nearly three hundred thousand people took the bait, and the total sum subscribed was more than £650,000, his office staff were unable to cope with the sackloads of correspondence. Counterfoils could not be filled in, no person of repute would consent to act as trustee, and Bottomley found it impossible to carry out his proposed scheme. Meanwhile the cost of living had risen so steeply that to keep up his luxurious style he was obliged to draw on the subscriptions. He had been foolish enough to quarrel with Bigland, who now began to harass him with pamphlets exposing his swindles. He silenced criticism for awhile by publicly handing over £5 for a single £1 Victory Bond certificate. This gesture, however, brought him hundreds of requests from other subscribers to repeat it; and he was obliged to employ a band of pugilists to protect him from them.

When he had spent so much of the money subscribed that he could not hope to repay it, he determined to crush Bigland. He charged him with trying to obtain money by menaces. The case was tried at Bow Street and, when Bottomley drove up to the court, he was received with vociferous cries of 'Three cheers for Mr. Bottomley'. He had previously arranged for a claque of demonstrators, at the rate of five shillings each, to stir up a crowd that was naturally eager for his name to be cleared. Bottomley, however, fumbled the case: he made the mistake of calling a witness who, under cross-examination, admitted that terms of apology for Bigland had already been written out. 'By whom?' asked the magistrate. 'By Mr. Bottomley,' was the answer. This revealed to the magistrate that the charge was framed: he dismissed the case.

Bottomley then brought a second action against Bigland at Shrewsbury, but when the evidence was called it became obvious that it was no longer Bigland, but Bottomley who was on trial. Bigland's assertions could not be disproved, for Bottomley dared not produce his books. The case was again dismissed and Bottomley was now ruined—thousands of demands were pouring in for the repayment of Victory Bond subscriptions. *The Times* devoted a leader to exposing him, and the *Daily News* charged him with 'quite unconceivable obliquity and hypocrisy'. Nevertheless, he tried to explain himself in his own newspaper, the *Sunday Illustrated*. When this failed to restore confidence, he resolved on a bluff. He wrote to the Director of Public Prosecutions, inviting him to take possession of all his books; after destroying every damaging document that he could find. The next day a summons was served; his affairs were examined at Bow Street in March 1922, and he was committed for trial at the Old Bailey. The trial was in May, and he pleaded 'most decidedly not guilty'. The concluding speech for the prosecution was held over by the intervention of a week-end. Bottomley tried to brazen things out: he went on Saturday to a boxing contest at the Crystal Palace and spent Sunday drinking champagne. On Monday the jury found him guilty and he was sentenced to seven years' penal servitude. The House of Commons immediately expelled him.

When he was freed in 1927, he tried desperately to regain his old position, first by writing up his prison experiences for the newspapers under the title: 'I Have Paid, But——'. These included a poem, in imitation of Oscar Wilde, 'The Ballad of Maidstone Gaol'. He next tried to start a rival to *John Bull* called *John Blunt*, but it failed within a year. Finally he was reduced to shambling on to the stages of cheap music-halls and telling a few bad jokes in a scarcely audible voice for a wretched wage. He died in 1933, having made the headlines again a short time before with a buoyant interview granted to the *Daily Mail's* star reporter Margaret Lane, in which he babbled about his old-age pension.

A great deal of political lying and deception was practised on the British public—and with far more dangerous results—in the later Thirties; but the large-scale personal despoliation of poor people's savings was not tried again throughout the Peace.

CHAPTER SIX

Various Conquests

Shortly before the Great War, there was a feeling current among people of ideas—it was most emotionally expressed by E. M. Forster in a Utopian short story 'The Machine Stops —that Man had at last with the help of machines conquered the forces of Nature, and that it was a dangerous conquest. Now that he could, if he wished, easily provide sufficient food, clothing, and shelter for every member of his species throughout the world, and store up a surplus against difficult times, and control birth, and cure most diseases, and navigate the stormiest oceans, and even fly: what world was left for him to conquer? Would he not slothfully rest upon his laurels and grow fat and out of condition? Well, the war certainly had sweated off a few pounds of Man's surplus fat, and war damage provided his machines with plenty of repair work: thus putting off the miserably perfect millennium for another decade or two.

Meanwhile, there were still several conquests to complete, and even some fresh ones to make. The nineteenth century had been the great age of exploration; but even the more recent American discovery of the North Pole and the Norwegian discovery of the South Pole had not ended geographical romance. There still remained the South Polar Continent to survey and other enormous unexplored territories in Greenland, Siberia, the Arctic, New Guinea, Central America, Brazil; also the 'forbidden city' of Lhas in Tibet (visited but not explored by Sir Francis Younghusband before the war) and the lost city of Sheba in Hadramut, and the secret city of the Senussi in the African deserts.

And there were many still unclimbed mountains—among these Mount Everest, the highest in the world. Even in England there were hundreds of miles of underground caverns, in Derbyshire especially, where the foot of man had not trodden since Neolithic times, if ever—and a few hazardous precipices unscaled on Snowdon and in the Lake District.

To the few whose thirst for rough living and adventure had not been quenched by the war, these mopping-up operations were extremely attractive, and the publicity value of success would amply cover expenses. The assistance of the Press to discovery was no novelty: the Stanley Expedition to Africa in search of Dr. Livingstone had been sent out by the *New York Herald*. Britain scored a number of successes—Dr. McGovern was first into Lhasa after painfully disguising his blue eyes with lemon juice, Mrs. Rosita Forbes (escorted by a young Egyptian diplomat, whom she rather pushed into the background on her return) first into the Senussi capital, and an official British surveying party made an end-to-end journey through the hinterland of New Guinea, despite the opposition of several hitherto unrecorded tribes of British subjects.

Britain was anxious to add the South Polar Continent to her list of trophies, for the nearest inhabited land, South Georgia, was under the British flag, a lonely customs-officer being posted there permanently for the convenience of whalers. In 1921 a Polar expedition sailed under Sir Ernest Shackleton in *The Quest*; they were provided with a number of new devices for exploration, including an aeroplane. Thousands of visitors inspected *The Quest* as she lay at anchor in the Thames, but the new methods of journalism concentrated public interest less on the object of the expedition—for fantastic geographical expectations had been disappointed in 1911 when the South Pole was reached by Roald Amundsen—than on the drama of the Ideal Scout. There was a last-minute vacancy for a handy boy in the expedition and it was to be reserved for the toughest, smartest, and manliest boy scout who volunteered; after several days' suspense the scout selected of the many thousands who offered proved to be Scout Marr, a Scot. The anticlimax came when, on arrival at South Georgia, Shackleton died of influenza, and his men, abandoning the proposed raid on the South Pole, made less hazardous explorations along the fringes of Antarctica.

Mount Everest defied every British attempt to reach the summit. A reconnaissance was made in the spring of 1921, when a height of 23,000 feet was attained, and a serious attempt in 1922. By pushing up supply camps to increasing altitudes, and using oxygen apparatus, four members of the expedition attained 25,000 feet; and two of these pressed on to 27,300 feet—only some 1,700 from the summit. The monsoon then broke, seven Tibetan porters were swept away, and the attempt was abandoned. General Bruce, the organizer of the expedition, tried again in 1924; the hardships were more severe than ever, the monsoon threatened to break early and the oxygen supply began to fail. Two of the party, Mallory a veteran climber and a young fellow named Irvine, may have reached the summit. They were going strong up the final easy slope when last seen and photographed through a telephoto lens; but they failed to return to camp. Mallory was a public-schoolmaster with three children. Though a fanatic in his feeling for mountains, his rational excuse for attempting the climb was to gain a reputation that would secure him a teaching appointment under the new Oxford Extension scheme. He had originally taken to climbing to correct a weak heart.

These expeditions seemed like extra events in the Olympic Games series, and brought out the same unsporting instincts in patriotic sportsmen. It was a matter of great regret, for instance, that a German, poaching on what the British considered their territory, bagged Sheba; and of small regret when a German climbing expedition, intruding on the British Himalayan attempts, had no better success and more numerous casualties.

The Derbyshire caves were gradually explored and charted, the adventurers crawling through tiny holes, swimming through lakes, even doing interior mountaineering. Rock-climbing became a popular sport, and a new technique was introduced from America of climbing in rubber-soled 'sneakers'. This was regarded as rather effeminate by the hob-nailed veterans of the perpendicular school; but sneaker-wearers were able to score unexpected successes, by scaling smooth two-in-three gradients on which the nailed boot had found no purchase.

It was generally considered, however, that the glory of crawling up or down into inaccessible parts of the world's surface was inferior to that of flying over it. The attempts on Mount Everest were eventually abandoned, because of the shortness of the climbing season, but it was felt that a full revenge would be taken on the jealous Goddess of the Mountain by flying over her. An expedition for this purpose was financed by the cranky and ultra-English Lady (Fanny) Houston. A weighted British flag was successfully dropped on the summit, photographs taken, and no lives lost.

Lawrence of Arabia, the only first-rate strategist, tactician, and story-book hero whom the war turned up, considered the conquest of the air as the most important task of his generation. So did the *Daily Mail*, which offered large money prizes to adventurous airmen. Aeroplanes had improved in speed and stability during the last years of the war, though still resembling flying crates; and great hopes were entertained for the future of civilian flying, now that designers did not need to consider problems of armament and high manœuvrability. *The Spectator* reported in January 1919 that the R.A.F. soon expected to open a Cape-to-Cairo service, and added that 'London and provincial centres may be linked up for newspaper delivery and carriage of copy and photographs. Adam Smith's "waggon way through the air" is about to be realized.' In that year a regular mail-service was started between London and Paris.

What most caught the popular imagination were the various attempts to fly the Atlantic. In April 1919 Major Wood and Captain Wyllie tried it from east to west. Before starting, their machine was blessed by an R.A.F. chaplain; but came down disappointingly in the Irish Sea. In May, Harry George Hawker, who was employed by the Sopwith Company as a test pilot, and Commander Kenneth Mackenzie-Grieve, who had been navigator of an aeroplane base-ship during the war, made a west-to-east flight in a machine equipped with a collapsible boat. Anxiety and grief greeted their non-arrival in Ireland, but the *Daily Mail* would not abandon hope. Intense relief was felt some days later when the placards proclaimed HAWKER SAFE. The plane had flown for fourteen and a half hours, and then come down in the Atlantic. The intrepid aviators, after an hour and a half in their collapsible boat, were picked up by the *Mary*, a Danish steamer unequipped with wireless. HAWKER SAFE seemed of immeasurably more significance than the Versailles Treaty, which was just being signed, and all England thrilled to read that the vicar of Hook, where Hawker had his home, preached a sermon on the text: 'For this my son was dead and is alive again; he was lost and is found.' Triumphal honours were prepared. Hawker and Mackenzie-Grieve were transferred from the *Mary* to a destroyer and taken to Scapa Flow, where they spent the night on board the battleship *Revenge*; next they were put on board another destroyer, which took them to Thurso, from where they came south by train. At every stop along the line great crowds gathered to greet them, and the jubilation at King's Cross on their arrival recalled scenes at Victoria when the first trainloads of lightly wounded came in from the 'Somme Victory' of July 1916.

Meanwhile, six United States airmen in the seaplane N.C.4 had left Newfoundland shortly after Hawker and Grieve. They reached the Azores safely, having covered 1,381 miles. Two other machines of the squadron were forced down, and their crews rescued. Commander Read of the N.C.4 was later given an official welcome at Plymouth, and hailed as a descendant of the *Mayflower* emigrants. Two R.A.F. fliers, Captain Alcock and Lieutenant Brown, made the first successful flight between America and northern Europe, starting from Newfoundland. This was on the 21st June 1919, and they used a Vickers-Vimy with twin Rolls-Royce engines; they flew 1,880 miles in 15 hours and 57 minutes and on arrival in Ireland had to make a forced landing, their machine sinking into a bog up to the axles, and tipping up, nose down, tail in the air. Their wireless had been out of action during the flight, so that they could not give notice of where they were. As soon as they had managed to telephone their whereabouts from the nearest Irish village, an enthusiastic welcome was prepared for them. But it had not been a Press-organized flight; so though the heroes were knighted and shared a *Daily Mail* £10,000 prize for the feat, the exploit was not a 'drama', and easily forgotten. (Sir John Alcock unhappily lost his life in the following year—an aeroplane accident in northern France.) When the American 'Flying Fool' Charles Lindbergh made his 'epic solo west-to-east flight' in 1927, it was generally assumed even in Britain that this was the first time that the Atlantic had been flown by a heavier-than-air machine.

The general opinion about Atlantic flights, in spite of public enthusiasm for the fliers themselves, was that they had more scientific than commercial value, and more sporting value than scientific. No freight could be carried, it was pointed out, in such small aircraft, and the strain of such long distances was bound to exhaust the pilots. A great deal of organization and much mechanical improvement were needed before Atlantic flights could become commercially practicable. It was some years before anyone else 'made the hop'.

Similar doubts were held about airship travel. Early in 1919 the Admiralty built two new hydrogen-filled airships on the German model, with which to attempt an east-to-west Atlantic flight. These were the R33 and R34, and both made successful trial trips over Britain. On July 5th the newspapers reported that the R34 had left her hangar in preparation for a voyage to New York: she was expected to make the crossing in forty-eight hours. The R33, meanwhile, flew over London and impressed people more with her elegance than her size. The R34 did indeed reach Long Island safely and landed at Roosevelt Field. The first man to arrive in America from Britain by air was Major Pritchard, who leaped out of the airship in a parachute, in order to give landing instructions to the ground-crew. A stowaway, found in the gas bags, provided the human drama. The trip was considered glorious as a sporting achievement, useful in stimulating good feeling between Britain and the United States, but disappointing from a commercial point of view. The airship, which arrived with no more than one hour's supply of petrol left, had taken 108 hours to make the crossing, and twice, over Newfoundland and Nova Scotia, had been badly buffeted and blown out of her course by thunderstorms too high to affect ocean-going liners. General Maitland, her commander, revealed in his log that the dangers of the voyage had been greatly underestimated. Not until weather conditions over the Atlantic were more closely investigated could airships compete with liners: as yet they were neither safe nor speedy. The regular aerial ferry to New York remained a pipe-dream for another twenty years.

The most remarkable flight of all, but one that strangely enough was almost uncelebrated in the Press, was that of M'Intosh and Parer from England to Melbourne. These were two Australian lieutenants who determined, when the war ended, to go home by air in a condemned D.H.9, bought for a few pounds. Almost every part of the machine was defective, including the petrol-pump and magneto, bolts kept working loose from the engine and propeller, the struts were unsound, the instruments faulty. They started on the 8th January 1920, had vexatious delays in France, climbed up to 14,000 feet to avoid a storm over the Apennines and then as they were about to cross the Adriatic went on fire at 3,000 feet, but extinguished the flames with a steep dive. They reached Cairo, by way of Athens and Crete, after forty-four days; the usual flying time for this distance was forty hours. Everyone there thought the two men crazy to persist in their journey, but they patched up the machine and flew on east. They had to come down in the central Arabian desert because of engine trouble, M'Intosh keeping Arab marauders off with Mills bombs and a revolver, while Parer tinkered with the plane. He got her off just in time. They reached Baghdad—the first time that the flight from Egypt had been made—changed a broken propeller, and flew on over Baluchistan to India. Parer remarked, 'We'll fly this bloody crate till it falls to bits at our feet.' He did so, and more. When the engine failed over the Irawaddy jungle they made a lucky forced landing; but soon afterwards a crash at Moulmein wrecked the undercarriage, smashed the radiator, and damaged the compass. For six weeks they worked in the jungle at fitting together the bits and pieces and then took off again. They crashed twice more, but somehow managed to cross the most dangerous obstacle of all, the Timor Sea, where they lost their bearings and flew blind, reaching Australia with only a single pint of petrol left in the tank. Their last crash was at Culcairn, close to their goal: there was practically nothing left unbroken of the D.H.9, but the two airmen escaped unharmed. The fragments of the machine were reassembled for exhibition in the Sydney Museum; Parer and M'Intosh were decorated by the Australian Prime Minister and given a purse of £1,000 to defray their expenses. They had already paid part of these by trick-flying and scattering handbills over the cities passed in their flight. M'Intosh died soon afterwards in a plane accident; Parer later operated a self-supporting unsubsidized air-line in New Guinea between the coast and the goldfields in the interior.

Experiments in controlling aircraft by wireless from the ground were still unsuccessful, but ordinary commercial flying developed rapidly. In 1922 aeroplanes began to be used for sky-advertising: plans were made for using luminous smoke by night and coloured smoke by day. On Derby Day, shortly before the main race, a small machine appeared over the course two miles up in the sky and traced the words *Daily Mail* in smoke-letters half a mile high. Aeroplanes were also employed to fly low with advertisement streamers—usually for such commodities as Bile Beans.

In 1922 flying had not yet become popular among business men who travelled to and from the Continent. They complained that the converted war-machines then in use were not sufficiently comfortable; and when more luxurious 'air-expresses' were introduced, they complained of the time lost on motor connections between the airports and the cities. The volume of air-mail passing between London and Paris was also at first disappointing. The speed of aeroplanes—then only one hundred miles an hour—did not allow much time to be saved over so short a distance. Passenger air-traffic was therefore seasonal; summer vacations, when a large number of American tourists used the air, were the most profitable time.

By 1923 many improvements had been introduced. The new steel aircraft inspired far more confidence than the early wood-and-wire contraptions. Air-expresses were flying in all kinds of weather, except thick fogs, and experiments were made in night flying—until then direction-finding equipment had only served for day flying. In 1924 a unified system of radio communication was put into force throughout Europe, to assist in direction finding. Further technical improvements, such as slotted wings to reduce landing speed, and three-engined planes, were adopted. In 1923 the Government approved plans for a commercial airship service to Egypt, which it was hoped would eventually extend to India and Australia. Experiments were also made in the production of gliders with small accessory motors; a prelude, it was hoped, to cheap, popular flying.

Another still incomplete conquest was 'the air' in the other sense: wireless telegraphy. The drama of wireless had engrossed the headlines several times before the war: there had been Philips of Godalming, the heroic wireless operator of the sinking *Titanic*, and the arrest at sea by means of wireless of the murderer Crippen as he was escaping to Quebec in disguise with his accomplice Miss Le Neve. During the war wireless had been of immense service in naval warfare, particularly in the rounding up of German commerce-raiders. But as yet the American development of popular broadcast news and entertainment had not reached Great Britain. This came with the Peace and at first was carried on in a haphazard manner by amateurs. The game was so fascinating that soon mechanically minded youths were everywhere busy in their home workshops building 'crystal' receiving sets, and transmitters too, from electrical odds and ends. The range of even the best sets was limited and it was generally thought that the curvature of the earth would prevent direct communication between its distant parts. In 1919 large-scale transmission was undertaken by the Marconi Company from Writtel, near Chelmsford. Weather reports and time signals were at first the only regular features broadcast by the company—the term 'broadcast' had just been imported from the United States; and the eight thousand wireless amateurs in England found it hard to convince the Postmaster-General that a weekly half-hour concert broadcast would not interfere with the reception of commercial messages by official stations. Only a vigorous agitation secured them permission for this to be arranged. Their appetite had been whetted by a special concert sponsored by the *Daily Mail*, at which Dame Nellie Melba sang —'Dame', by the way, still had a slightly comic sound, titles for women having been a war-measure. In 1922, after further pressure, the Postmaster-General permitted the formation of a broadcasting company, which would give regular programmes of entertainment from several stations. So began the British Broadcasting Company—it was not elevated to the dignity of a corporation for another four years. Wireless manufacturers were to organize it, the Postmaster-General undertaking in return to stop the importation of foreign sets for two years, and to pass on five shillings of the yearly ten-shilling licence fee for the upkeep of the stations. Any manufacturer could join the B.B.C. on taking out a £1 share. Since the state-socialistic Lloyd George Government was still in power, the B.B.C. was given the same sort of monopoly of the 'aether' as the Post Office enjoyed on the earth. The step was justified on the grounds that the aether in America was in such a confusion from the cut-throat jamming of one another by rival stations, that it would be wise to keep British aether under a single control before rival commercial interests began a war in it.

Stations were set up in London, Cardiff, Birmingham, Glasgow, Newcastle, Bournemouth, and Aberdeen. Simultaneous broadcasting was tried, and it was proved that programmes on different wave-lengths did not interfere with one another. In the early days of the B.B.C. the big London stores set up loudspeakers whenever there was a special concert, and large crowds of shoppers gathered around them. Sometimes the concerts failed to come through. There is a story that on one of these occasions the younger Mr. Selfridge promptly relayed gramophone records to the crowd in his store, which was completely taken in. A triumph over the other less resourceful stores, where the crowds complained bitterly of hearing nothing. The most successful broadcast items were excerpts from operas, performed by the National Opera Company. Thousands more heard Dame Nellie Melba. The managers of concert halls, however, were so suspicious of broadcasting that Chappell's, for instance, declared war on wireless and refused to allow any of its artistes to broadcast. At the same time, newspapers denounced the B.B.C. news reports as farcical résumés of newspaper work. Some papers rather mischievously started a campaign for the broadcasting of the proceedings of the House of Commons, and spoke of a 'wireless Hansard', and of the beneficial effects it would have upon electors to hear their representatives speak. The House wisely refrained from adopting the suggestion: debate in 1922 did not reach a very high oratorical level and, besides, Parliamentary procedure involved long pauses, confused noises, and formal divagations which would have given an impression of muddle and wasted time.

The B.B.C., with its headquarters at Savoy Hill, Strand, was a lively and informal company: it had not begun to take on the serious and stifling air of a Government department. The voices of announcers often came over queerly, not only because transmission and reception were still very uncertain and every 's' was a whistle, but because there was as yet no system of tests to standardize announcers' voices within a certain register. Nor was there yet anything like so strict a surveillance as ten years later either of the performers' scripts or of the private morals of B.B.C. employees. The Bishop of London was the victim of one of the very frequent mistakes that occurred at the microphone. He was understood to end a very solemn address with the ironical aside 'I *don't* think!'; but he had merely been cut off while remarking 'I *don't* think that was too long, do you?'

By 1923 wireless began to enjoy a boom of which notice was taken by advertisers, though the American system of advertising directly by wireless was forbidden in the B.B.C.'s charter. Rinso, for instance, used the slogan 'Rinso washes while you listen in', and showed a housewife sitting in an arm-chair by the fireside wearing earphones, while a tub of washing soaked in a corner. But the B.B.C. was having trouble with its revenue. The Post Office proposed that wireless sets should be taxed according to their type. Only *bona-fide* experimenters were to be exempt from the tax. Most listeners bought the parts of their sets and assembled them at home, regarding themselves as *bona-fide* experimenters. The cost of keeping up the B.B.C. thus fell upon the wireless manufacturers, who naturally complained. People were, in fact, more attracted by the fun of putting sets together and trying to make them work than by the prospect of actually listening. Professor A. M. Low, the scientist, considered that this hobby might have considerable educational value, especially for women. He urged women to buy for thirty shillings the parts of a crystal set and a booklet on how to put them together; it would amuse them in their homes and teach them handicraft.

Even in 1924 broadcast programmes were still short and lacking in variety; but great excitement was aroused in August of that year by apparently serious attempts to pick up messages from Mars. The tests were made with twenty-four-valve sets, the largest and most powerful yet constructed. The chief object was to test the practicability of multi-valve sets, but it was also decided to try to pick up again the mysterious signals which Signor Marconi had heard three years before, and which were popularly supposed to come from Mars. No signals from Mars were heard, but much was found out about the uses of valves. To have a set with a large number of valves became a suburban snobbery, like the number of cylinders in pre-war motoring.

Science had gradually become the faith of numerous cold-blooded people who had no use for revealed religion: their creed was limited to: 'I believe in things only in so far as they conform predictably to the known laws of the universe.' They also had a morality: to judge nothing on insufficient evidence, not to make evidence conform to preconceived ideas, and to pursue knowledge only for the sake of knowledge, not for such ulterior ends as excitement, fame, commercial advantage or discovery beneficial to mankind—letting nothing stand in the way. The 'Martyr to Science' who inoculated himself with some rare disease in order to keep a progressive watch on its symptoms, did not act for humanitarian reasons, nor were the psychologist who induced nervous breakdowns in rats by frustration of their habits, and the zoologist who removed the sensory apparatus of bats and then set them loose in a room full of wires, simple sadists.

Professor W. H. R. Rivers, the eminent ethnologist, psychologist and neurologist, confessed that science practised in this sense by himself and others was indistinguishable from any other morbid compulsion. He greatly deprecated the Himalayan expeditions, saying that Mount Everest could wait another thousand years: meanwhile this spare money and energy should be spent on further ethnological field-work among fast-disappearing primitive peoples, of the sort that he had himself done among the Todas of Melanesia. Thereupon, ethnological field-work came into fashion: the explorer and (usually) his wife camping in tents near some primitive community in Africa, South America, or Oceania and taking intimate clinical notes of rituals and taboos. Sometimes they were such poor scientists that they became very friendly with their subjects of study. The true scientist was not supposed to fraternize with his guinea-pig, for fear that he might influence its emotional behaviour. And sometimes they could not disguise their bawdy relish in the sexual habits of primitives, and their reports were published rather as refined erotic reading than as stern works of research. The ordinary research worker was content to clear up some thoroughly unimportant corner of science, without any thought of its possible utility or significance. Almost his only relaxation was the invention of new terms for phenomena: a painstaking zoologist won a newspaper mention for a new worm, which he discovered in the course of a round of golf with his colleague Professor McIntosh—he named it *Golfingia McIntoshii*.

The general public had no patience with these formalists of science: they liked a man who invented amusing or useful things rather than one who merely expanded the corpus of heavy knowledge. The newspapers knew this and gave no mention at

all to fresh zoological classifications, fresh mathematical for-
mulae, fresh unutilizable chemical compounds. But medical
discoveries, especially for the treatment of supposedly incurable
diseases, were front-page news. The use of X-rays in cancer—it
was reported that 80 per cent of cancer cases responded in early
stages to such treatment—and the insulin treatment of diabetes,
seemed more important than whole departments of ordinary
science. X-rays added considerably to the thrills of boot-buying
when West End stores used them in their footwear departments
to ensure the perfect fit. The sort of scientific invention, however, that made the most popular reading was a wireless receiver
that could be fitted inside a hat, so that people could listen-in
while walking the streets, or a submarine sledge, fitted with
rudders and connected with a motor-boat, in which, it was
claimed, divers could glide about on the ocean bed, independent
of air-pipes, to investigate ancient wrecks. An amusing invention in 1921 was the Lookatmeter, a dramatic exposition of the
dull scientific fact that the human eye radiated an appreciable
amount of energy: even a casual glance would deflect the sensitive plate.

Most of these inventions, all described as 'epoch-making',
were never heard of again after the first news-thrill; and so-
called scientific expeditions—to Panama, for example, to prove
or disprove the legend of the lost Continent of Atlantis—never
started, or if they got there never found anything, or if they
found anything never found anything newsworthy. Generally
it was the most useless inventions or stunts that attracted the
most attention. There was a magnificent Press for Dr. Flettner's
rotor ship, which was propelled by huge cylinders on deck
rotated by the wind. The ship sailed all right, but its use was
altogether uneconomic.

In 1924 reports appeared in the Press that experimental work
was being done on a death-ray, and in more than one laboratory. An inventor named T. F. Wall of Sheffield claimed to have
produced a ray that would set fire to anything inflammable,
wreck aircraft, and destroy life. It could only be of use in warfare. Later, however, Mr. Wall modified his machine and used
it in an attempt to split the atom. This seemed more dangerous
still. People were terrified at the prospect of a successful splitting
of the atom; they feared that it might set up a process in neigh-

bouring atoms that would blow up the world. (American scientists fortunately proved that fear groundless, a few years later.)
At the same time one Grindell-Matthews invented a different
death-ray, which he claimed could also be used therapeutically,
and was granted interviews with the Air Ministry to explain its
potentialities. The British Government, however, did not make
him an attractive enough offer and he therefore hurried off by
plane to sell the ray in France. His associates, who claimed a
52 per cent share in the ownership of the invention, obtained
an interim injunction to restrain him; but arrived at Croydon
airport just too late to serve it. Questions were asked in the
House of Commons about the advisability of allowing such a
valuable weapon to pass out of the country. The Under-
Secretary for Air replied that his experts considered it of doubtful
value. The Grindell-Matthews death-ray was occasional news
throughout the period and when at the end of the Thirties a
new war with Germany threatened, many found great consolation in the belief that the East Coast of England was securely
girdled by pylons carrying an unbreakable band of death.

It was partly this popular disinterest in the more abstruse
departments of science that had no obvious application to life,
and partly the embarrassment of admitting that a German-
speaking scientist could possibly have found anything of real
interest, that kept the public unaware until 1921 of the genuinely
epoch-making researches of Albert Einstein. Though only half
a dozen British mathematicians could follow Einstein's deductions from observed phenomena, all agreed that there was no
mistake in his formula. The plain English of their deductions
from his deductions was that light did not travel in a straight
line, and that Euclid's geometry in so far as it claimed practical
demonstrability for its theorems was disprovable: because of the
curvilinear nature of the universe two parallel straight lines
would eventually meet at a point. The interpreters of Einstein
were gracious enough to admit that Euclid's conclusions were
'untrue only in the universal sense': as the geometry of straight
lines in another sort of universe, which might perhaps exist, they
were irreproachable. This was a terrible blow for elderly mathematics masters and mistresses and for all who had held fast to Euc-
lidean truth as the one practical certainty in a weltering world.

There was worse to come. Philosophers had for centuries played with paradoxical theories of existence—such as the non-reality of the seeming real—but nobody took the philosophers seriously. One could bang one's fist on an oak table to prove its obvious solidity and echo Dr. Johnson's manly words: '*Thus* I refute him!' On the other hand, astronomers and mathematicians were respected and trusted implicitly, and a gasp went up when Professor Eddington lectured in the summer of 1921 to a crowded audience at the British Association Hall on the physical implications of Einstein's work. He declared that distance was not a constant gap, nor was space finite, but both were variable relatives.

There was no serious attempt to disprove these conclusions: the uselessness of defending any exploded universal theory had been too often shown. ('What a knock the anti-evolutionaries had taken! Well, well, so the crazy philosophers hadn't been so wrong after all! The old materialistic theories of physics were dead. Solidity being merely a subjective sensation, the reality of matter was annulled, and energy alone remained—if energy was the right word for what was usually stabilized in material form and had only an abstract existence apart from matter. People, then, were no longer people but merely peripatetic points of view. This also disposed of Time as a constant. What a joke!')

The theoretical dismissal of Time as a constant was followed by a method of practically demonstrating its variability through a case-record of one's dreams. The inventor of this method was J. W. Dunne, a mathematician and engineer, well known as having in 1906–7 designed and built the first British military aeroplane. Towards the end of the Thirties, J. B. Priestley, the novelist and publicist, clearly summed up the conclusions of Dunne's *Experiment with Time*, first published in 1927:

'Dunne believes that each of us is a series of observers existing in a series of Times. To Observer One, our ordinary fully awake sharp selves, the fourth dimension appears as Time. To Observer Two, which is the self we know in dreams when the first observer is not functioning, the fifth dimension would appear as Time. This second observer has a four-dimensional outlook, and this fact explains the fantastic scenery and action characteristic of dreams. Dunne says this is because we try to interpret in our ordinary three-dimensional fashion these strange images gathered by our four-dimensional selves, who have to work during sleep without the sharp focus and business-like attention of the first observer. Remembering dreams on waking, we feel as if we had been plunged into another kind of existence . . . and there is often lingering in our minds a feeling that somehow they were oddly significant. Now Dunne holds that the dreaming self, now moving in Time Two, has a wide length of Time One, the fourth dimension, stretched before it, and so contrives to telescope into the fantastic narratives of dream both images from the past and *images from the future*.

'It was this interpretation of dreams, forced upon him by his own experience, that opened these dizzy vistas to Dunne. Over a period of years he remembered and analysed many of his dreams, made elaborate notes, and then discovered that they ransacked the future as well as the past. You dream that you see three elephants walking round a pond. On waking you remember that the pond is one you knew as a child. But you have never seen three elephants walking in that particular fashion. Yet perhaps, years hence, you will one day see three elephants not walking round a pond, but moving in the same way as they did in your dream. You arrive at that point in the track of Time One which you, as Observer Two, to whom Time One is not real Time, caught a glimpse of, years before, in the dream. You will then be haunted by that strange feeling of familiarity of having seen all this before. There are several explanations for it, ranging from reincarnation to a supposed occasional time-lag between the two halves of the brain. Dunne's seems not only the most fascinating, but also the most satisfying. And his theory of dreams went further than all others in accounting for the queer scenery and personages and actions of these dramas of the night.

'Out of this Serialism of Dunne's came a theory of immortality. . . . According to Dunne we catch a confused glimpse, immensely confused and chaotic because we try to interpret what we experience in terms that lack a necessary dimension, of this more complicated existence in our dreams. As a series of observers with our attention for ever moving across new fields of Time that are really added dimensions, we must, in Dunne's view, be immortal, or at least, the ultimate observer in us must be immortal. We are engaged, according to him, in the process of learning how to live. On this theory, the tragic brevity of Life is immeasurably expanded and is no longer tragic.'

This was more comforting than any conceivable form of the traditional life-after-death. Whatever happened, one was always *somewhere*, looking attentively at oneself.

The word 'relativity' now came to be commonly used, out of the context of Einstein's theory, to mean that a thing was only so if you cared to assume the hypothesis that made it so. Truth likewise was not absolute: 'beautiful results' could be obtained by mathematicians from consistent systems based on the hypothesis, for example, that one could slide a left hand into a rigid right-hand glove—or simultaneously into a pair of rigid right-hand gloves. What an amusing conquest of man's this was! He had freed himself for ever from the slavish and constraining superstition that two and two necessarily made four! Later, when the revolutionary Bohr theory of atomic construction was published, it was accepted without demur by the experts as a logical deduction from the known facts: despite the slight difficulty that a certain atomic element, in order to cross a certain space in no time at all, must temporarily cease to exist. That was victorious news too—discontinuity was proved! And no joke was made of the fact that the strain of working out this theory had put Nils Bohr into an asylum for the insane.

What was better still, man need have none of the crouching feeling of insignificance that had been enjoined on him by the Church as soon as the Copernican system had been officially recognized. He was aware of the incredibly vast astral distances and the absurdly large size of such stars as Betelgeux by comparison with the Sun: now, with the improvement in microscopy, a new universe was opening. The microcosm was as extensive in its way as the macrocosm and organized apparently according to the same formula. Man now felt balanced comfortably midway between these two unthinkables. As a poet of the Twenties wrote:

'Between insufferable monstrosities
And exiguities insufferable,
Midway is Man's convenience. We no longer
Need either hang our heads or lift them high
But for the fortunes of finance or love.

97

VARIOUS CONQUESTS

We have no truck either with the forebeings
Of Betelgeux or with the atom's git.
Our world steadies: untrembling we renew
Old fears of earthquakes, adders, floods, mad dogs
And all such wholesomes. Nothing that we do
Concerns the infinities of either scale.
Clocks tick with our consent to our time-tables,
Trains run between our buffers; Time and Space
Do not amuse us with their rough-house turn,
Their hard head-on collison in the tunnel.
A dying superstition smiles and hums
"Abide with me"—God's evening prayer, not ours.
So history still is written and is read:
The Eternities of divine commonplace.

CHAPTER SEVEN

Sex

======

Only highly trained specialists in mathematics and physics could hope to understand Einstein, Bohr, or others of their kind, and the mass of the people were therefore rather in the position of church-goers in the Middle Ages, who, even if they understood enough Latin to follow the Mass, which was seldom, had no training in ecclesiastical philosophy. They had to take the priest's word for the accuracy of the dogma. Einstein, who became a popular figure because of his fine head of hair, his fiddle-scraping, and an unsuccessful argument with a Viennese tram-conductor over the simple arithmetic of small change, deprecated all attempts to over-simplify his theory. He told an American woman who asked him to explain it in a few words: 'My dear lady: a blind man was walking with a friend down a hot and dusty road. His friend said: "O for a nice drink of milk!" "Drink I know," said the blind man, "but what is this milk you speak of?" "A white liquid." "Liquid I know, but what is white?" "White is the colour of a swan's feathers." "Feathers I know, but what is a swan?" "A bird with a crooked neck." "Neck I know, but what is crooked?" The exasperated friend seized the blind man's arm and stretched it at full length. "*That* is straight," he exclaimed, and then, bending it at the elbow, "*this* is crooked." "Ah," cried the delighted blind man, "*now* I understand what milk is!" '

Yet no warning of Einstein's against popular misinterpretation of his theory could hope to be effective. The implications had already been clarified by Eddington, and now Professor

Wildon Carr of London University observed: 'The religious importance of the Einstein theory is enormous. It is going to produce a revolution in religious thought. . . . In fact, I should go so far as to say that relativity can only be interpreted in terms of an immanent God—a reality which in its very nature is life and consciousness. If you are going to get a concrete basis for the reality of the universe, you cannot separate the minds of those who are observing from that which they observe. . . . Materialism as a world-view is left in the air.' This was a not very scientific conclusion; for, scientifically speaking, God was not an axiom but an unproved hypothesis, or group of conflicting hypotheses. The fact was, the popularizers of science found it difficult to slough off the habit of religious thinking and usually remained at least broad-churchmen, as had Darwin. Professor Jeans, for example, who was then contemplating the 'mysterious universe' and who published his reflections some years later, did not find his patriarchal conception of the Deity inconsistent with the fantastic figures-to-the-power-of-letters in which he dealt. As for materialism, that was soon to reappear sturdily: for though solidity might in a philosophical sense be only an illusion, yet if one bumped one's head on a low lintel it still hurt; and though two parallel straight lines might ultimately meet at a point, nobody would ever live long enough, however fast he travelled, to observe that phenomenon. Meanwhile the blessed word 'relativity' was applied by the revolutionaries whom the war had made to moral and ethical contexts and with no consideration at all for Divine Immanence.

The study of comparative religion and the overseas observations of soldiers and sailors had long popularized the notion that while nearly all ethical systems claimed final truth, they contradicted one another, and that there were good and bad people in all ethical systems. Two possible conclusions could be drawn: either that it did not really matter what one did, though it was more comfortable to conform to the reigning system of ethics in the country to which one belonged, or that it mattered a great deal, though virtue lay less in the truth of an ethical system than in the sincerity and loving-kindness with which private lives were lived. But whichever of these two conclusions was reached, it seemed desirable that the ethical system should become looser in some articles and stricter in others. Samuel ('Erewhon')

Butler, a prophet before his time, had suggested in his *Note Books* that any sexual practice in vogue among 'nice people' at any remove of space and time could not be reprehensible. The Greeks and Polynesians he thought nice people, and was perhaps making a covert plea for both sentimental homosexuality and pre-marital promiscuity. Samuel Butler was widely read in the Twenties.

Homosexuality had been on the increase among the upper classes for a couple of generations, though almost unknown among working people. The upper-class boarding-school system of keeping boy and girl away from any contact with each other was responsible. In most cases the adolescent homosexual became sexually normal on leaving school; but a large minority of the more emotional young people could not shake off the fascination of perversity. In post-war university circles, where Oscar Wilde was considered both a great poet and a martyr to the spirit of intolerance, homosexuality no longer seemed a sign of continued adolescence. Shakespeare, Caesar, Socrates, and Michelangelo were quoted in justification of the male practice; Sappho, Christina of Sweden, and the painter, Rosa Bonheur, of the female. True, Christianity condemned it, but Relativity dismissed Christianity as a take-it-or-leave-it hypothesis. So long as one acted consistently in accordance with one's personal hypothesis, and was not ashamed of what one did, all was well. Thus homosexuals spent a great deal of their time preaching the aesthetic virtues of the habit, and made more and more converts. Their text-books were *The Intermediate Sex*, a bright little volume by Edward Carpenter, and Havelock Ellis's massive *The Psychology of Sex*. The Lesbians were more quiet about their aberrations at first; but, if pressed, they justified themselves more practically than the men by pointing out that there were not enough men to go round in a monogamous system, and that though the Act of 1886 penalized sodomy there was no definite illegality in the female practice if not performed to the public scandal.

When anti-French feeling in 1922 had caused a revulsion in favour of the poor downtrodden Germans, the more openly practised homosexuality of Berlin seemed brave and honest: in certain Berlin dancing-halls, it was pointed out, women danced only with women and men with men. Germany land of the free!

The Lesbians took heart and followed suit, first in Chelsea and St. John's Wood and then in the less exotic suburbs of London.

Havelock Ellis had been a pioneer in the study of sexual psychology, but much more work on the subject had been done in Germany and Austria than in Britain. The name of Sigmund Freud was first popularly heard about 1920, though his methods were in repute during the war. They were used by the psychologists confided with the task of treating shell-shocked patients in such special hospitals as Maghull near Liverpool and Craiglockhart near Edinburgh; there Freud's conception of the mechanism of dream imagery was used as a means of finding out what suppressed fear or criminal pre-occupation, intensified by war-strain, was preying on the patient's mind. When this was discovered it could often be dispersed by practical advice or reassurance; the dreams ceased and the patient, who was encouraged to take up some practical hobby, gradually recovered. These psychologists were the 'straighteners' prophesied in Samuel Butler's *Erewhon*. But few reputable practitioners would go all the way with Freud, who had complicated his simple thesis, of the disguised emergence in dreams of feelings suppressed in waking life, with a most fantastic one. He held that, besides particular adult suppressions, there were general ones which dated from earliest infancy and had a strong sexual colour: particularly what he called the Oedipus Complex, which made a male child want to kill his father and enjoy his mother. This 'psycho-analysis'—the non-elision of the *o* in *psycho* before *analysis* was noted by purists as a ready instance of the scientists' increasing disregard of the humanities—consisted in dredging up from the oozy depths of the mind childish memories of thwarted inclinations which would account for later aberrancies, and indeed for almost every ruling motive in life. To be encouraged by a doctor to talk about oneself in the most prattling detail, and to be listened to with serious interest, was a new and grand experience, especially for moneyed and lonely women who had had 'nervous break-downs'. Followers of Dr. Ernest Jones, who had been psycho-analysed by Dr. Freud himself, set up as psycho-therapists and made very handsome incomes. To them, men and women were not thinking beings of independent judgement, but behaviouristic animals whose natural modes of behaviour had been interfered with by superstitious moral codes.

'The first requirement for mental health is an uninhibited sex-life. To be well and happy, one must obey one's sexual urge. As Oscar Wilde wisely counselled: "Never resist temptation!" '

Such was the Freudian gospel as it filtered down into people's minds, through translations, interpretations, glosses, popularizations, and general loose discussion. 'Intriguing' new technicalities were bandied across the tea-cups or the Mah-Jong table: 'inferiority complex', 'sadism', 'masochism', 'agoraphobia', 'sublimination' (which got mixed up with 'sublimation'), 'id', 'ego', 'libido'. A woman in Mecklenburgh Square committed suicide when under psycho-analytic treatment. The inquest came before Mr. Ingleby Oddie, the Westminster coroner. When he heard the technical evidence, 'I am not a scientific person,' he said, 'but it sounds to me like jargon.' The Press in general agreed. Though, as the *Daily Mail* put it, 'real good has been done in cases of nervous breakdown and paralysis by letting the bottled-up emotions have free vent—unconscious inhibitions often bring about a general weakening of mind and body', one could have too much of a good thing. At the end of 1922 the *Daily News* commented on a book by Isadore Coriat, *Repressed Emotions*: 'We are all psycho-analysts now, and know that apparently innocent dreams are the infallible signs of the most horrible neuroses; and so we suppress our nightly divagations as feverishly as a murderer tries to remove blood from his shirt-front.' The reviewer concluded by bidding his readers beware of a morbid interest in their primal instincts.

Ecclesiastical comment was still stronger. Dr. Orchard, speaking in 1922 on 'Religion and Psycho-analysis' at St. Paul's, Covent Garden, pronounced psycho-analysis to be 'dogmatic and obsessed with sex'. Its attitude to religion was 'dangerous and confused', and it gave 'unbridled licence to free sex-expression'. He believed in self-control and counselled that the 'dustbin of the mind' should be left undisturbed. Psychology did, however, in his opinion, recognize the valuable gospel of sublimation, through which the sex-instinct could be turned to higher things—such as art, politics and religion. But Dr. Orchard and other earnest self-controllers were warned with equal earnestness by the Freudians how dangerous self-control was to mental health; and the effect of mental health on physical health was a commonplace—even the women's columns in newspapers freely suggested that dyspepsia was as much due to worry as to actual disorder of the digestive organs.

Psycho-analysis figured on the agenda of the Conference of the Educational Association in 1921. Children, it was there admitted, were given to fantasies. They were often liars, sensation-mongers, and swaggerers, but this did not mean that they were deliberately sinful. These propensities should be recognized and carefully directed. Teachers would greatly benefit in their dealings with children from courses in psycho-analysis. Children only told lies and swaggered in order to gain the lime-light. They should be trained to enjoy a moderate amount of limelight—otherwise they developed inhibitions which made them incapable of leading a happy adult life. Lady Betty Balfour, who spoke at one of the Conference meetings, advised parents to abandon the moral attitude in dealing with children. She declared she was 'not sure that the moral attitude was not responsible for all the crime in the world': but explained that by the moral attitude she meant one that treated every peccadillo committed by a child as a serious sin. Courses in psycho-analysis certainly led to very unusual pedagogical practices. A woman practitioner explained in a book on the subject of children's libidos that she had discovered 'Case H., aged six years', a furtive unhappy little boy, lifting up the chintz skirts of an easy-chair and looking underneath. 'Why are you doing that?' she asked. 'Isn't it really that you want to lift up my skirts and see what I look like?' Case H. responded to the suggestion; she gratified his curiosity and thereby saved him from a miserable and haunted adolescence.

Freud, though the best known psycho-analytic prophet, was by no means the only one. Dr. Jung ran him close, having an equally remarkable theory of racial psychology, with its phobias, suppressions, and popular fantasies. Jung did not agree with Freud on every point, and the modernists were divided up into opposing parties, Freudians and Jungites, in much the same way as they were divided some years later into Stalinites and Trotskyists.

The most popularly compelling fiction of the day was sex-problem fiction. The philosophical promiscuity of Aldous Huxley's, the gallant degeneracy of Michael Arlen's, and the earnest mysticism of D. H. Lawrence's sex-ridden men and women were weighed and compared even in Suburbia. A new character was introduced into the English novel: the tragic female Don Juan with her fatal lust for boxers, bull-fighters and such.

Sexual liberty was made easier by the newer contraceptives. Hitherto contraception had been practised as if it were a sort of secret vice, but now it came into open discussion as having hygienic advantages over the old leave-it-to-chance system. Its former advocacy by the atheist Bradlaugh and the Neo-Malthusian League, and its association with the pornographic literature of rubber-shops, had to be lived down. A prophet was found to conduct this difficult campaign with religious fervour, no sense of humour and complete integrity—Dr. Marie Stopes. She was not, as one might suppose, a doctor of medicine, but of science, being a leading expert on coal; and was fervently assisted by her husband, the well-known aeroplane designer, A. V. Roe.

In 1922 she hired the Queen's Hall for a meeting to advocate the use of birth-control as a cure for racial disease. Her platform was honoured by the presence of the Medical Officer of Health for Leicester, and the hall crowded by a queer, attentive, and rather fanatical audience. She wore a picture hat. There were no interruptions. But she soon encountered great opposition throughout the country. To the Catholics, the use of contraceptives, which discouraged souls from birth, was only one degree less heinous than abortion, which forcibly restrained them and was a lesser form of infanticide. Dr. Stopes's reply to this view was that by the use of birth-control one got fewer but healthier souls. She was not against procreation; on the contrary. The Anglican attitude, expressed by the Bishop of Woolwich at Oxford in 1923, was that 'the purpose of contraceptives is to make possible the exercise of a spiritual faculty for the satisfaction of a physical desire only, and to prevent the spiritual consequences for which the faculty was given by God.' Dr. Stopes replied in her monthly news-sheet that married love was a sacrament and that one could not divorce the physical from the spiritual. The Bishop of Exeter opposed birth-control on racial grounds: he said that the French practised it and that as a result their population was on the decline and they had to import

Italian and Polish workmen. But a Royal Physician, Lord Dawson of Penn, came in on Dr. Stopes's side, and defended her thesis not only on medical but on economic grounds.

Dr. Stopes later pointed out in her book, *Mother England*, that though maternal mortality and infant welfare were being gravely discussed by the doctors, very little of practical use was being done about them: doctors often told a woman that to have another child would mean death, but never told her how to avoid having more children, except by abstinence. It was to remedy this sort of thing that she had inaugurated her birth-control clinic in the East End. There she received in three months more than twenty thousand requests for procuring abortions, mostly from over-worked and sick mothers who were unaware that abortion was criminal. Needless to say, she did not comply with these requests, but instead advised women on the correct use of contraceptives. In 1926, when she wrote *Mother England*, prosecutions of drug-sellers who claimed that their wares produced abortions were averaging one a fortnight.

In 1923 the Catholics gathered their forces against her and she had to bring a libel action against a writer who suggested that she was profiteering by the sale of contraceptives to working women. In point of fact the clinic made no profits, and the profits from her book *Married Love*, which went into ten editions, were devoted to the upkeep of the clinic and to the Constructive Birth-Control Society. In the course of this libel action Dr. Stopes stated that she believed herself to be a channel of divine inspiration, and that the 'art of contraception' had been revealed to her in a message which she had received 'beneath the old yews' at her house at Leatherhead. This drew a scornful attack from the defending K.C.: 'Dr. Marie Stopes will have you believe that God sent down this beastly, filthy message!' She lost her action; the words complained of were found defamatory, but true in substance and in fact. As a result of this unfortunate publicity a proposal to place the Oxford Union Hall at her disposal was withdrawn at the request of the Union Committee. However, A. V. Roe came in her stead to address the leading undergraduate society. On being asked a searching question by an Indian graduate, he evaded it with the counter-question: 'Tell me, do you think that birth-control is from God or from the devil?' The Indian remarked: 'I think that is the most ingenuous question I have ever been asked in all my twelve years at this university.'

In the next year the Cambridge Union carried a motion in favour of birth-control and by the late Twenties the battle was won. The Anglican clergy then generally came round to approve of the contraceptive device recommended by Dr. Stopes after consultation with leading gynaecologists. She was careful to reassure them that it was only intended for genuine married people: it could not be fitted to a virgin. A large and successful Birth-Control Ball was held at the Hammersmith Palais de Danse, and to show that it was a philoprogenitive movement, rather than otherwise, a leading woman novelist attended it in an advanced stage of pregnancy. Doctors, too, with the example of Lord Dawson to encourage them, overcame their professional embarrassment and gave birth-control information when it was demanded by patients. Most of them, however, got it more explicitly from Dr. Stopes's books, which were on sale in every decent bookshop and prominently displayed in the rubber-shops also, side by side with *The Masterpiece of Aristotle, The Heptameron,* Paul de Kock's erotic novels, and *The Merry Order of St. Bridget,* with other books on flagellancy.

Partly as the result of the widespread use of birth-control, there had been changes in the prostitute's profession. In certain cities during the war—Nottingham was the most famous—the enthusiastic amateur had swept away all professional opposition. There were a number of aerodromes and a large machine-gun school in the neighbourhood of Nottingham, and any soldier or airman, it was said, could always get free sexual accommodation from the local factory girls. The convention was supper with the girl and her parents, who after a time politely retired to bed, and then, for appearances' sake, a loud good-bye and a slamming of the front door—with the visitor still inside. But not every city was so kind, and the number of prostitutes in the country as a whole is believed to have increased; the figure in 1922 is put as high as 75,000. Prices, of course, varied immensely: the underground folklore of the 'dirty story'—it had attained extraordinary dimensions by now and was freely communicated to respectable women whose only stipulation was that a story should be really funny, not merely dirty—included one that throws light on this point. Three sisters decided to be in the fashion and take to free love. Being members of the New Poor they decided that it would be foolish not to capitalize their experiences. They set out after dark and agreed to meet in their Kensington flat in the early morning. The eldest returned home at midnight, the middle sister at two o'clock. They compared notes. The eldest had been to Bond Street: 'How much is six times two guineas?' The middle one had been in the Marble Arch district: 'How much is seventeen times seven-and-sixpence?' They had to wait until breakfast time for the youngest, who had gone down to Whitechapel: 'How much is a hundred and forty-four times tenpence-halfpenny?' The economical style of this story should be noted: humour was getting streamlined, like everything else.

That so many professional prostitutes were still about suggests that there was a phenomenal increase in sexuality; for the enthusiastic amateur was as enthusiastic as ever. A young man who had to pay for his pleasures would consider himself not much of a hero, even if for the moment he had no regular woman friend. The 'living together' of young people who could not afford to marry was socially recognized by now as 'companionate marriage' and considered even as a 'higher' form of relationship than legal marriage.

> 'Come, girl, and embrace, and ask no more I wed thee.
> Why reck of churchling and priest. . . ?'

The young author of these popular lines did, as a matter of fact, in the end marry the girl to whom they were addressed: for he became a farmer, and had to conform with the county, which was still rather old-fashioned in such matters. The poor girl of Victorian legend who was betrayed by a wicked squire, cast off by her parents, and forced to 'go away to London for to hide her sin and shame' was now a joking reference only. It was extremely rare for an Englishwoman in the Twenties to be forced on the streets by sheer necessity or the brutality of parents.

Prostitutes, plying chiefly for the benefit of elder men, had to alter their ways. They became smarter and quieter in their dress; solicited with tact. There was a steadily diminishing number of prosecutions for annoyance and indecent behaviour. The common prostitute had a far longer career now than before the war; she took greater care of her health, drank less, attended the hospital clinics fairly regularly—syphilis could at last be cured if caught in an early stage, and gonorrhea, though more dangerous to a woman than a man, was not nearly so fatal and disfiguring as syphilis. Yet venereal disease was still a tabooed subject in the Press, and a doctor to whom an infected married woman came for treatment seldom dared tell her in so many words what was wrong: for to accuse anyone of having venereal disease was a highly slanderous act. Besides, a doctor did 'not want to cause trouble in the home'. Consequently a great many children were born blind or half-witted who should never have been born at all. This medical inhibition continued throughout the period, but the general taboo against mention of venereal disease weakened. Sufferers went to qualified physicians rather than to quacks and developed a social conscience against spreading the disease. Moreover, blindness due to venereal infection in the process of birth was after a time antiseptically provided against in all lying-in hospitals.

The remarkable change in the sexual code also showed itself in a different attitude to divorce. The American view was adopted: marriage was regarded as a social habit, rather than as a sacrament. Where one had made a mistake it could be rectified by divorce, a bright smile, and remarriage; though the process was not so easy in England as in most of the United States. To bear resentment against one's partner in such a mistake was ungentlemanly or unladylike. Noel Coward, in his autobiography, describes how at Ivor Novello's parties in 1921 'divorced couples hob-nobbed with each other, and with each other's co-respondents'. Divorce, however, still carried a slight social stigma in old-fashioned circles, especially where the woman was the offending party; to oblige their guilty wives, therefore, most men were gentlemanly enough to go through the farce of adultery with a woman unknown' and thus give their wives grounds for divorcing them. Divorce lawyers, winking at this collusive irregularity, were usually able to fix the husband up with a professional 'woman unknown' and with chambermaids' evidence at some Brighton hotel.

In 1918 there were more divorces than ever before; in 1919 there were half as many again. This increase was at first explained as due to the interruption in family life caused by the war, to hasty war-marriages, and to the fact that during the war many people for geographical reasons had not been able to obtain divorces. Nevertheless, the divorce-rate continued to increase steadily. In 1923 Lord Birkenhead, the Lord Chancellor, was complaining of congestion in the divorce-courts. The Matrimonial Causes Act of 1923 established complete equality between the sexes in regard to grounds for divorce, and also, by extending jurisdiction over divorce to the Court of Assizes, lessened the cost of divorce to the poor. The number of divorces then again increased: in 1928 more than four thousand decrees *nisi* were made absolute. Eighty per cent of divorces each year were undefended, and in only one case out of fifty was the husband ordered to pay alimony: the American 'gold-digging' trick of marrying a rich man, goading him into infidelity, and then 'soaking' him, did not catch on in England.

The chief obstacles in the way of intended divorces were fear of causing offence to religious relatives, the spiteful refusal of the partner in marriage to sue, and the fear of sordid newspaper publicity. Whether or not one got sordid publicity was a matter of luck. Sometimes the Press treatment of a case was by no means damaging to the parties concerned. The *Daily Mail* gave prominence to the following charming dialogue between a theatrical couple who had 'come to the parting of the ways'.

Husband (cross-examining wife): 'How did we live?'
Wife: 'Well, we owed everybody.' (Laughter.)
Husband: 'You struck me across the head with a sunshade.'
Wife: 'A sunshade! Why, it was night-time.' (Laughter.)
Husband: 'Well, you were always eccentric in your dress.' (More laughter.)

But, in general, what the public wanted was sexual detail of as intimate a sort as was printable; and rather than lose circulation to less scrupulous rivals, each popular paper began sailing as near the wind as possible, especially where the Church or the nobility were concerned.

The famous Archdeacon Wakeford case in 1921 was not a divorce case—for the wife firmly believed in her husband's innocence—but one of Church discipline, and heard before an Ecclesiastical Court. The Archdeacon was accused of committing adultery at the Bull Hotel, Peterborough. He appealed from the decision of the Consistory Court and briefed Sir Edward

Carson to appear for him: the appeal was heard at Downing Street at a Judicial Committee of the Privy Council. The protracted hearing was enriched with sensational bedroom evidence by chambermaids. Until the end it seemed doubtful what the verdict would be, for who and where the woman in the case was never appeared; and the chief witness for the prosecution mentioned pyjamas, whereas the Archdeacon asserted that he had never in his life worn anything but nightgowns. Carson, defending, accused Wakeford's brother-in-law and one Moore of rigging a frame-up in order to discredit him. Excitement was caused in court when, at the mention of a girl with no wedding ring who was said to have been in the company of the Archdeacon, the poet Edmur Blunden's wife fainted. Mrs. Blunden had been giving evidence of having, with her husband, seen the Archdeacon dining unaccompanied in the Bull Hotel on the fateful day. She suggested that the wedding-ring incident was a confused recollection of the waitress. She herself from feministic principle was not wearing a wedding ring—why should she, if her husband didn't?

The Archdeacon's appeal was dismissed, and a large anxious crowd of women, who had gathered outside the court, cried out sorrowfully, 'Oh, oh, there must be some mistake!' They had known him as the hard-working and popular vicar of a low-church slum-parish, from which he had been translated to the high-church close of an East Anglian cathedral town. Cathedral society preferred to believe him guilty if only because of his shocking manners: when greeted by his Bishop on Easter morning with the ancient salutation 'Christ is Risen' he had boorishly withheld the expected response, 'He is Risen Indeed', and said instead: 'Yes, Sir!'

The unfortunate Archdeacon was ruined financially, professionally, and in health. He soon died, after a pathetic lecture-tour on which, accompanied by his wife, he attempted to prove the verdict an unjust one. The lecture was supported with moving-pictures, to bring out especially the point about the pyjamas and nightgown.

This was a comparatively clean case. The climax in sex-reporting came with a High Society divorce embodying a number of dramatic features, all of which were jam to the salacious public. It appeared that the defendant, a spirited woman, had refused either to have a child or to use contraceptives. Though the balked husband was thus denied ordinary sexual intercourse, a child was born—as a result, she claimed, of his 'Hunnish practices'. The husband denied paternity and cited several co-respondents. Eventually she proved her case, because the co-respondents could not be produced, and medical evidence was submitted that her hymen was still unbroken. The House of Lords, to whom the appeal was referred, upheld the verdict which, the judges remarked, concerned them nearly: for the child (who, by the way, closely resembled the father) could in the course of time expect to take a seat in that august House. This conclusion pleased everyone, and the wife set up a Mayfair shop which no-one who was anyone failed to visit.

The publicity given to cases like this was not welcomed by the legal profession, and eminent K.C.s found in them also an opportunity for protesting against the employment of women jurors. Sir Edward Marshall-Hall was reported to have said that he felt 'at a great disadvantage in dealing with cases of that kind before women as well as men. There are certain sexual matters which one cannot possibly discuss, except with one's wife.' The Press had certainly gone a little too far on this occasion. Not long after, the combined forces of Law and Church, exercised on the Press through the Home Secretary, made newspaper proprietors agree together on a self-denying ordinance: they would omit all intimate sexual details from their reports, so far as was consistent with their mission of publicly branding vice wherever it appeared. A number of old-fashioned readers, too, had written to protest that their children's minds were being corrupted by accidental contact with this beastliness. Indeed, the Press got cleaner and cleaner as the period advanced, and as the sex-obsession waned.

CHAPTER EIGHT

Amusements

The country was now in the full sunshine of Peace. The two former Britains, of the Governing Rich and the Governed Poor, had returned, though not nearly so distinctly as before. People no longer spoke to one another in trains as a matter of course without introduction. Pedestrians no longer counted it their right to stop lorries and private cars on the road and demand 'joy-rides'. There were few pre-war habits that had not securely re-established themselves, though in modified or extended forms: the conventional religious habit among these. Yet the regular communicants of the Church of England, with women in a great majority, gradually sank in numbers until in the Thirties they only just exceeded the Roman Catholic figure, the well-to-do classes, especially in the country, still regarded themselves as socially bound to the Church by whose rites they were christened, confirmed, married, and buried. But no more than socially: and Puritanism languished except in a few Dissenting congregations, and among the elderly. The Rev. Samuel Chadwick, a Westminster preacher, was quoted by the Press in 1921 as declaring that 'Multitudes have no interest in the things for which the Churches stand. . . . Thousands of young people are being brought up without religious instruction and without religious examples. . . . Woman's rebound from conventional virtue is as daring as her attire.' The Press used Church comment as a convenient measuring stick for popular tendencies. It was news if a bishop denounced the modern girl, and equally news if an advanced vicar gave select cinema-shows in his

113

vestry; but the scales were always slightly weighted in favour of 'modernism'.

'Modernism', losing its eighteenth- and nineteenth-century connotation of something to be disparaged because new, had become synonymous with lively progress. Councillor Clark, of a South Coast town, who thought seaside liberty in dress and behaviour disgusting, was taken up by the Press with mock-seriousness, and became a popular figure of fun, a sort of male counterpart to 'DORA'. DORA (the initials of the Defence of the Realm Act) was the official spoilsport personified. Then Sir Herbert Nield, at a meeting of the Lord's Day Observance Society in 1921, complained, 'We have gone recreation-mad.' There had been a deterioration in the conduct of the people, he said—parental control was diminishing—the Press had been affected by American yellow journalism—more and more people were cheating the railways by travelling first class on third-class tickets—Hampstead Heath was crowded from 7 p.m. until mid-night by young men and girls who had much better not have been there at all—crime was no longer felt to be a disgrace—and Sunday had become the greatest casualty of the law. This last observation started a long controversy.

It is true that the habit of Sunday picnics in cars was now emptying the city churches. So was the 'rambling' habit: for those who could not afford cars held that the country could only be properly enjoyed on foot. Though 'hiking' had not yet been imported from the United States, nor the Youth Hostel system from Germany, many office-workers were forming themselves into week-end 'rambling clubs', and going out by the new suburban bus-routes to starting-points for long country walks. In 1923 the London Underground, wishing to popularize 'Metroland' and the new Tube-extensions that were about to be opened, published two guide-books to the north and south of the Thames. These contained 'twenty-three photographs of typical beauty spots and twenty-three specially drawn maps, which will simplify the rambler's journey by field path from point to point'. The Press made out that large numbers of these ramblers attended country services; and printed letters from readers to the effect that man came closer to God in the Cathedral of the Woods than in a dull dogmatic church. Soon instructions for particular rambles were given weekly in two or three dailies.

In 1924 the Rev. H. L. C. V. de Candole of St. John's, West-minster, defended the Churches against the charge of being dull. His sermon was summarized under the title, 'Why Are the Churches Empty? Craze for Exciting Pleasures.' 'If the services are dull,' he said, 'it is because people are not there to put life into them. If the preaching is bad, it is because nothing takes the heart out of an earnest man so much as preaching to empty pews. As for the charge that church-going people are no better than their neighbours, let Thomas Carlyle answer—"As to the people, I say the best class of all are the religious people." '

London was quite ready to welcome religious revivalists, if they were sufficiently good showmen. There was, for instance, Gipsy Smith, the Methodist, whose meetings in the Albert Hall at first attracted as many as ten thousand people. His style was colloquial and he would occasionally burst into song about birds and the love of flowers. Photographs appeared in the Press, showing him standing on one foot, hands poised, as if conducting an orchestra. When a collection was held at his meetings he would often talk in this style: 'Not a cent of your money will come to me; so that I can hit you as hard as I like. Some of you say: "How are you paid?" Do not ask rude questions! I am paid by the committee from another source. Hands up those who are glad to see me here! Now put them in your pockets!' He would say that when a mother cared more for jazz than for mothering her baby, it was time someone spoke out. In modern cities the Devil was at large. There was no real faith, and London life was a 'social swindle'. For his part, he would burn all Church creeds, for they served only to keep people apart. If Britain was to hold her own she must tighten her grip upon the Lord's Day. (At this point there were usually cheers from the audience.) A Christian, in his opinion, was a good sport, an open-air man, one who refused to tell or listen to dirty stories, a teetotaller—or, at least, a very moderate drinker—a humorist, a mother-lover. Smith appealed mostly to the middle classes, and castigated them for drinking too much: 'Your back-bone is made of cotton-wool.' They loved such accusations. When at the end of one of his meetings he invited 'all who needed more of God' to stand up, all but ten did. He asked these ten if they considered themselves good enough. They, too, then stood up. But like most revivalists who have tried to work independently of the Churches, Gipsy

Smith did not succeed in building up a permanent follow-ing. By the end of 1924 he had ceased to be news, though gramophone records of his salvationist hymns had a wide sale for some years.

The Church, in a belated endeavour to recover the souls that it had lost by its opposition to Darwin, now signed a sort of concordat with the scientists, or rather with the popular scien-tists. Canon Barnes, later Bishop of Birmingham, preached a sermon at Westminster Abbey in 1921, in which he came out strongly in favour of scientific modernism. He considered that man was not originally endowed with a soul, but had gained it by a process of evolution. Religion therefore dealt with the Ascent and not the Fall of Man. 'The immergence of the soul in man,' he said, 'is the last stage—as far as man can know. . . . Evolution was designed to produce spiritual beings who can survive bodily death, and enjoy eternal communion with God if they accept Christ's doctrine of the immortality of the soul.' The Canon warned his congregation, however, that acceptance of such biological views in no way implied approval of spiritualis-tic doctrines. 'In Christian teaching', he said, 'there is no con-firmation of the pretended revelation of modern spiritualists, that after death the spirit enjoys an existence which is to some extent a counterpart of earthly life, with spiritual clothes and even spiritual cigars.' But here he was not on firm theological ground. As Charles Wesley had long before pointed out, to dis-believe in ghosts was to deny the truth of the Bible—had not the Witch of Endor summoned the ghost of Samuel to an interview with Saul? Spiritualism continued to divert many worshippers and a great deal of money from the still too materially minded Church.

Leading Church-people did their utmost to prevent any ex-tension of public pleasures. Temperance societies, for instance, protested in 1922 against the installation of 'listening-in sets' in public-houses, on the ground that this would make them too popular. Local clergymen supported these protests, and in godly Nottingham several publicans were refused wireless licences. The Bishop of London declared that he would die on the doorstep of the House of Lords rather than allow the passage of a Bill permitting an extension of the closing-hour to 11 p.m. through-out London. Largely owing to his energetic opposition the Bill was defeated; but this neither decreased the amount of drinking, nor increased public affection for the Church.

At the Church Congress of 1922 the Bishop of Birmingham denounced bridge-playing as a waste of time and deplored the immorality of betting, and Dr. E. B. Turner declared that soldiers who had found opportunities for promiscuity overseas expected to carry on in the same way when they came home, and that morality had been deteriorating ever since the beginning of the neo-Malthusian campaign forty years before.

Nevertheless many clergymen and their wives and daughters rejected the merely negative policy of frowning on lay pleasures: they wished to start a 'brighter religion' campaign. At the same Congress, the Rev. Kenneth Hunt, an ex-international footballer, defended the watching of football matches. He said that soccer was clean, and the occurrence of deliberate fouls was greatly exaggerated. For most of the poor, watching football matches was the only alternative to sitting in pubs. An appeal was also made for a revival of religious drama. Miss Lena Ashfield, who had been a prominent organizer of concert parties for the troops during the war, said: 'The theatre to-day is in a state entirely divorced from real emotion. Its roots are superficial, instead of being deep in the real springs of the religious life of the world.' The wife of the Bishop of Chester proposed that the naves of churches should be used for religious drama. But, though the proposal was sympathetically heard, it was easier to pass motions in favour of religious drama than to find dramatists to write it.

Sir Herbert Nield's criticism of the country as recreation-mad was not unjust, if he meant the part of the country that had money and was therefore in the news. A prime recreation of the poorer part of the country, of course, was reading about the recreations of their betters. The Press had learned from the United States the art of witty headlining: already in 1921 it had publicized Relativity with the jocular HUN PROFESSOR CATCHES LIGHT BENDING. ('My word, if I catch you bending' was still a popular phrase.) News editors were finding out by sales tests what sort of news whetted the appetite for more news. There were three main condiments, crime, sex, and folly, but they must be served with the potatoes and meat of respectability. Simple crime performed in a sordid way by an habitual criminal was not news, even if it was murder; conviction of prostitutes was not news unless someone of note were involved; and folly in the provinces had to be extremely original to win a mention in the Metropolitan papers. Yet it was wonderful, once they had learned the trick, how journalists could conjure a mountain of news out of a molehill of fact. In 1922 a few well-dressed young missionaries and a Bishop of the Mormon Church in Utah came to London to make converts of both sexes. A wild agitation was started against this 'Religion of Lust'. The *Daily Mail* proclaimed that Mormonism was founded on fraud, and that the only antidote to the insidious poison that the missionaries were spreading was to banish them from England. An editorial announced: 'We believe that the Mormon quest for girl converts in this country sins against our best instincts. . . . Mormonism is a disgusting attempt to sanctify sensualism under the garb of religion. Its purpose is the luring of innocent girls to a life of misery. What Mormonism proffers to its simple-minded victims is not honest marriage. We believe that this Mormon quest for girl-victims nauseates every decent-minded person in the country. The presence of the missionaries is a moral offence; it should be regarded as a legal offence. Every Mormon missionary should be sent out of the country.' Bishop Savage of the Mormon Church, in an interview with a *Daily Mail* reporter, said in reply to this attack: 'If the Government tells us to quit, we shall quit.' Nobody said 'quit', however, because the Government knew as well as the newspapers themselves that Mormonism, despite its successful social undertakings in Utah, was a dying, dated faith, which might attract a few cranky adherents of either sex, but had long since abandoned its practice of polygamy, which alone would make it news.

Dancing was still the chief contemporary pastime. Journalists wrote, pretending to be scandalized, of 'Nights in the Jazz Jungle'. Jazz in the early Twenties meant heavily punctuated, relentless rhythm, with drums, rattles, bells, whistles, hooters, and twanging banjoes. The wild melancholy saxophone and trumpet had not yet come to England. A *Daily Mail* feature-writer described the atmosphere of 'Jazzmania': 'Women dressed as men, men as women; youth in bathing drawers and kimonos. Matrons moving about lumpily and breathing hard. Bald, obese, perspiring men. Everybody terribly serious; not a single laugh, or the palest ghost of a smile. Frantic noises and occasional cries of ecstasy came from half a dozen negro players. Dim lights, drowsy odours and futurist drawings on the walls and ceiling.'

Protests from eminent persons filled the newspapers. Bishop Weldon declared in 1920: 'The use of dances as a means of raising money for war-memorials is little less than a national humiliation.' An anonymous surgeon exposed 'the great degradation and demoralization of these wild dances'. Leyton Urban District Council, in letting their municipal hall for dances, prohibited the one-step and all forms of jazz. Analogies were drawn between the disorder of jazz-music and that of jazz-minds; and girls who sacrificed their nerves and beauty to the fox-trot were warned that old age would claim them early.

Dance-steps were changing all the time: there was the 'Twinkle', the 'Jog Trot', the 'Vampire', the 'Missouri Walk', the 'Elfreda', the 'Camel Walk', and the more famous 'Shimmy'. These were all jerky steps; and though the quieter 'Blues' came in late 1923, dancing did not long remain quiet, for the 'Charleston' and later the 'Black Bottom' brought back the jerks. At first people danced mostly at dance-clubs, but the larger restaurants were beginning to introduce dance-floors. The Savoy was the first to popularize dancing with meals. Such attractions made fashionable the habit of dining out, which few Englishwomen until then had practised.

Not until some of the DORA restrictions were removed in 1921 did restaurant-life really begin. The Licensing Act of 1921 was later much reviled, but at the time it was welcomed as an encouraging concession to gaiety. People submitted willingly to ordering unwanted sandwiches with their drinks after 11 p.m., and to having their glasses removed at 12.30. Solemn warnings were meanwhile being delivered by physicians on the drinking habits of the younger generation. The *Practitioner* declared drink a repressant, not a stimulant, and particularly deplored the effects of drink on the young—they 'lost their power of manly self-control'. As for cocktail drinking, it was 'the most reprehensible form of alcoholic abuse'. Although the restrictions of the Licensing Act were denounced by the moneyed and the young as absurdly Victorian, the authorities continued to thwart all efforts to make London gay. The first introduction of cabaret on a large scale—'The Midnight Follies' at the Metropole—was banned by the L.C.C. A 'Brighter London Society' was formed in 1922 beneath an array of names which included Lord Curzon, the famous Foreign Secretary, and Gordon Selfridge; but it achieved nothing and DORA remained.

One effect of the law was to stimulate the rapid growth of night-clubs: some highly respectable—the 'Night Light' had two princesses and four peers on its committee—some vicious and squalid, all well attended and all very expensive.

A few so-called night-clubs were as punctilious in the removal of bottles and drinks from the tables at the legal hour as in the collecting of their heavy subscriptions. But with scores of night-clubs proper the only concession to the law was an attempt at legalizing their club status by 'signing on' new members at the door—the secretary generally proposing, and the negro-drummer, or head waiter, seconding. This was not, however, good enough for the police, who raided them with methodical persistence. Time and time again well-known establishments were closed down and their proprietors fined or sent to prison; time and time again the self-same establishments reopened, their owners simply writing off the amount of the fine, or the business losses involved in the prison sentence, against the enormous profits made during the successive short spells of existence. The police made no distinction between the respectable and the vicious, so that every club had to be carefully guarded against intruders by bolted doors and wickets; police raids were often made by way of skylights. A raid on the famous and fashionable Kit-Kat Club on the night following a visit by the Prince of Wales, and the conviction of the manager of 'Chez Victor', which had been the centre of night-life for some months, thoroughly frightened fashionable night-club-goers, including a number of débutantes. The *Sunday Express* reported in 1929 that Victor had opened a new club in Paris, and that he had written to Sir William Joynson-Hicks, the Home Secretary, who was responsible for his deportation, asking him to patronize his club whenever he was in Paris. 'Jix' replied on Home Office notepaper, expressing pleasure that he was succeeding so well and promising to call when next in Paris. In spite of such gentlemanly exchanges the 'clean-up' was accelerated and the penalties made still heavier. Lord Byng, the Commissioner of

Police, was soon able to boast that London night-life was dead.

Victor had shared with Mrs. Kate Meyrick the sovereignty of the night-life of London. In 1921 she had founded the famous '43'—at 43 Gerrard Street, where Dryden once lived. In her memoirs, *Secrets of the 43 Club* (1933), Mrs. Meyrick wrote: 'I could picture the old poet so clearly sitting at his desk, with sheets of paper strewn around him and more lying about on the floor, his hand clasping his brow in the effort of thought. I could follow the shifting expressions of his long, mobile face with its noble forehead, its neat little Vandyke beard, and its frame of silky hair, once light brown, now transmuted by age into silver.' Her visitors' list was distinguished, for the times—Augustus John, Jacob Epstein, Joseph Conrad, J. B. Priestley, 'June', the actress, Carpentier, the boxer, and Jimmy White, the Lancashire millionaire, who one night brought six Daimlers full of show-girls and ran a champagne party that cost £400. 'Brilliant' Chang's dope-gang operated there—Chang himself was a member, and had a restaurant opposite. Mrs. Meyrick claims to have tried to stop Chang peddling in her clubs, but remained on friendly terms with him. The '43' was first raided in 1923, when she was fined £300 but allowed to pay in instalments.

In 1924 Mrs. Meyrick was sentenced to six months' imprisonment and served it in Holloway: winning great sympathy from her distinguished clients, who now included the Crown Prince of Sweden, Prince Nicholas of Rumania, Tallulah Bankhead, Edna Best, Herbert Marshall, Jack Buchanan, and Michael Arlen. In 1925 she opened the 'Manhattan'; securing the custom of Gordon Richards, the jockey, Sophie Tucker, the American 'Red Hot Mammy', and Rudolf Valentino. Paul Whiteman, the American King of Jazz, occasionally played there after his theatre shows. King Carol went—he was then in exile, and not so dissipated as people said he was, Mrs. Meyrick observed. In 1927 came the grandest place of all, the 'Silver Slipper' in Regent Street. The walls were painted with Italian scenes, the dance-floor made of glass. Prince Nicholas, executing a particularly boisterous caper, broke a small pane of it. Teddy Brown played there, and Brenda Dean Paul was a visitor—someone said of her: 'She wakes each morning with a song on her lips just like a bird'—she had not yet become a famous Society drug-addict. More raids and fines. In 1928 Mrs. Meyrick was implicated in the Goddard case: he wás a police-sergeant accused of taking bribes from night-club owners and of passing false money. She unluckily had some of the money and was sentenced to fifteen months' imprisonment. 'Colonel Barker' was in prison with her at the same time—a fantastic British Fascist who had turned out to be a woman. Mrs. Meyrick came out of prison in 1930, did a Continental tour, and then carried on with the '43': adding Jim Mollison, the airman, and Primo Carnera, the boxer, to her roll of honour, but taking no risks with the police. She had long since adopted the practice of running several clubs at the same time, so that if one were raided and closed down, the others could carry on—even when she was in prison. Of the dance-hostesses in her clubs, she wrote that nearly all of them married happily. Three of her daughters, who stood by her throughout her troubles, married into the peerage, by way of the '43'. May married Lord Kinnoull, the racing motorist; Dorothy, Lord de Clifford; Gwendoline, the Earl of Craven.

Among the smart people, fancy-dress parties had been fashionable since the war ended. There was, for instance, a Russian party at which a negro band played and·for which a whole house was specially redecorated *à la russe*—Imperial Russian, of course, for the U.S.S.R. was not yet fashionable. There followed a swimming party, held at St. George's Baths. This was considered very daring and aroused indignation among newspaper readers because of the conjunction of a negro band with white girls in bathing costumes. And yet the costumes worn were still very modest—men's and women's both had skirts, the legs came well down the thigh, and the sleeves reached just above the elbow. Then there was a Mozart party, held to the strains of Mozart's music with appropriate dances, the guests wearing period costume—photographs of them, posed at Piccadilly Circus with the workers who were engaged in mending the road, appeared in the illustrated weeklies. And another party to which people came as their own ancestors.

Oxford and Cambridge were two main hubs of advanced recreational fashion: they were not merely suburbs of London, as they afterwards became. Such novelties as the canary-yellow hunting waistcoat, green velveteen trousers, suède shoes, were initiated there. The famous wide-bottomed trousers, 'Oxford bags', which superseded the conventional peg-top variety in

1924 and set a fashion for the whole world, are said to have started at Cambridge two years previously. The elaborate type of hoax was another Oxford borrowing from Cambridge. For example, a number of dons attended Dr. Emil Busch's well-advertised psychological lecture and many were impressed by his foreign accent, stimulating argument, and complicated vocabulary. He was an undergraduate in a false beard. Then there was the duel in November 1923 at Godstow near Fair Rosamund's Tower between cloaked figures armed with pistols. After the first exchange one duellist fell bleeding, and doctors ran up to bandage him. The subject of the duel was reported in the London Press to be an 'undergraduette of Somerville', and great excitement was aroused. But no names came out; and the blood was only red ink after all.

There was a fashion at both universities for eccentric clubs. In 1921 there was an Oxford University Hide-and-Seek Club that had one very successful meet on Boar's Hill, in and out of the gardens of the professors and prominent literary people who had made it the most distinguished hill in England. At Cambridge, on the other hand, there was a University Pavement Club, whose members united in agreeing that there was too much rush in modern life. One Saturday, at midday, members of the club sat for an hour on the pavements in King's Parade, passing the time with tiddley-winks, noughts and crosses, marbles and nap, reading and even knitting. While they were so engaged, a Proctor passed and they had to break the rules of the club in order to stand in his presence while he took their names; he was so sympathetic that after he had gone the club unanimously elected him their president. They then bound themselves to sit for another hour next week and carried a resolution that lunch-baskets should be brought. All passers-by were invited to join in, 'in order to secure that unanimity which is essential to pavement life'. Then there was the Oxford Railway Club, formed to popularize the pleasure of drinking on trains at night. A party of a dozen young men in full evening dress would board the Penzance–Aberdeen express at Oxford and travel on it as far as Leicester; they would return at once by the Aberdeen–Penzance express. On the outward journey they would dine, and on the way back make speeches. Both universities had climbing clubs, the members of which did a number of extraordinarily dangerous night-climbing feats on colleges, libraries, and museums, causing much damage to ancient roofs. Almost every year at Oxford someone performed the classic climb up the Martyrs' Memorial to stick a chamber-pot on top. Usually the police shot it down with a rook-rifle, but if it was enamel they had to rig up scaffolding, at great expense.

Those were still the days of the long-standing war between the hearty and the aesthete—the hearty being the man who was up chiefly in the hope of getting a Blue, and the aesthete being a literary fop. At Oxford on Election Night, 1923, a prominent aesthete in evening dress (who had introduced side-burns into Oxford, carried about a pet monkey on his shoulder, and persuaded Gertrude Stein to lecture to an undergraduate society) was mobbed by a crowd of drunken hearties; in self-defence he felled a Rugger Blue with a loaded stick. Hitherto aesthetes had been expected to undergo debagging and having their rooms wrecked without protest or compensation—and to like it. This same aesthete resented the invasion of his room by drunken hearties after a 'binge' so sincerely that he drew a sword and cut off a thumb of one of the invaders.

In younger London Society neither the literary aesthete nor the hearty came much into the picture. The correct thing to do, for intelligent young people with a fixed income and no particular vocation, was to call themselves 'artists' and live in Chelsea studios. There they gave 'amusing' parties and played at being Bohemian. Bohemianism was understood to mean a gay disorderliness of life, cheerful bad manners, and no fixed hours or sexual standards. One sign of the perfect Bohemian was to use implements for unconventional purposes: for instance, to spread butter with a cut-throat razor, drink tea out of a brandy glass, or use a dish-swab as a hair net. These people pretended to paint but had little or nothing to show for their pretensions, and their chief influence on art was to make the rents of studios rise so high that real artists could no longer afford them. Pseudo-studios were chiefly furnished with brightly coloured cushions, strewn about the floor or on divan beds—chairs were out of fashion. The *Daily Dispatch* hit off this kind of life, under the headline 'Not Artists at all, but Arty People', with: 'They just talk about drawing and painting and their studios are only used for dressing-up for parties and for dances—"do's", they call them.'

Real painters were going abroad to work—at first to Mont-parnasse in Paris, until the arty people followed them there and raised rents and forced them south to Cassis and Cagnes, or west to Brittany. When these places had also been invaded, they went as far as Spain and Portugal, or back again to some country part of England. If they gave up the struggle and consented to become London social parasites, there were always Mayfair hostesses who would delight to show them off at mixed parties, along with actors and musicians, as 'latest discoveries'. Indeed, artists who did not cultivate such connections had a difficult time; for in Mayfair, the best market for contemporary art, people had uncertain standards of value and bought the paintings of impressive young men whom they had met at parties, rather than paintings they really liked. In general, the more intolerably assured, ill-tempered, and tyrannical a painter seemed to be, the higher the prices he could command. The same was perhaps also true of architects and interior decorators.

Mayfair was now a sort of informal university: with hostesses for heads of colleges and a constantly changing never-completed syllabus. The 'Bright Young People' provided the sports, which were harmless and playful. They first became news in 1924, when the *Daily Mail* prominently featured one of their activities: 'A New Society Game. Chasing Clues. Midnight Chase in London.' This was the birth of the treasure-hunt. People were given lists of most dissimilar objects to find, sent off in cars to find them, and told to rally again, usually at 2 a.m., at some central place such as Piccadilly Circus or Charing Cross. They also held a party to which all came dressed as very young children, and behaved in character.

The discovery at Luxor early in 1923 by the British School of Archæology of the unrifled tomb of the Pharaoh Tutankhamen was given typical Twentyish publicity. Ancient Egypt suddenly became the vogue—in March the veteran Professor Flinders Petrie lectured on Egypt to an entranced Mayfair gathering. Replicas of the jewellery found in the Tomb, and hieroglyphic embroideries copied from its walls, were worn on dresses; lotus-flower, serpent, and scarab ornaments in vivid colours appeared on hats. Sandy tints were popular, and gowns began to fall stiffly in the Egyptian style. Even the new model Singer sewing-machine of that year went Pharaonic, and it was seriously proposed that the Underground extension from Morden to Edg-ware, then under construction, should be called Tootancamden, because it passed through Tooting and Camden Town. Cambridge students staged an Egyptian rag, raising from the dead Phineas, the purloined mascot of University College, and awarding him an honorary Blue. A secret tomb (a subterranean public lavatory), was prepared in Market Square, and undergraduates appeared at the appointed hour, wearing towels like Egyptian slaves. At the cry of 'Tut-and-Kum-in', the dead Phineas arose. The lost tribes of Cleopatra then appeared and performed the 'Cam-Cam'.

But that was not all: a month after the principal discoveries Lord Carnarvon, the leader of the expedition, suddenly died. A mosquito had bitten him, near the entrance to the tomb, and the bite turned poisonous. Almost everyone agreed that his death was due to the Pharaoh's anger at having his rest disturbed. A well-known Egyptologist declared that a curse was un-doubtedly responsible, though tough Howard Carter, the deputy leader, laughed at the idea and continued to excavate. Conan Doyle, the creator of Sherlock Holmes, who was well-known as a spiritualist, was asked for his opinion by reporters on board the *Olympic* at New York. He observed mysteriously: 'An evil elemental may have caused Lord Carnarvon's fatal illness. One does not know what elementals existed in those days, nor what their power might be. The Egyptians knew a great deal more about those things than we do.' During the next few years, several other members of Lord Carnarvon's expedition died, from natural causes, and each time the rumours of Pharaoh's Curse were revived.

Serious archaeologists were surprised that so much popular interest greeted this discovery, which had done no more than fill up a small gap in comparatively recent Egyptian history, while so little could be beaten up for far more interesting, ancient and beautiful discoveries in the Mesopotamian cities of Ur, Nineveh and Carchemish, and in the Indus valley. The fact was that Tutankhamen, who had succeeded his revolutionary father-in-law the Pharaoh Akhenaton, seemed somehow to embody the modernist spirit; whereas the Mesopotamians were boringly ancient. Even Sir Leonard Woolley's discovery at Ur of evidence for the local truth of the Flood Legend did not hold anything like the overwhelming significance that it would have held for the Victorians. Bible-reading was out of fashion.

Recreation now became increasingly hard work, as late hours, mixed drinks and too much percussion wore out the 'poor little rich girl' of Noel Coward's song, and her partners. The new keyword was Disillusion—not the Byronic melancholy and the Sorrows of Werther which had been in fashion after the Napoleonic Wars, but a hard, cynical, gay disillusion. It needed a poet for its expression, and there was T. S. Eliot waiting. His 'Love-Song of J. Alfred Prufrock' and 'Preludes' struck just the right note:

> 'For I have known them all already, known them all——
> Have known the evenings, mornings, afternoons,
> I have measured out my life with coffee-spoons.'

And

> 'Wipe your hand across your mouth—and laugh!
> The worlds revolve like ancient women
> Gathering fuel in vacant lots.'

His 'Waste Land', which first appeared in the *Criterion* in 1922, was read by the side-burned aesthete to a large gathering at Oxford in Eights Week in the following year: through a megaphone.

'Man has conquered', was the wearied recreationalist's view, 'but he has also failed. The old barriers are down, but the road that now lies open for him is no longer enchanting. Man has flung away his chains, but misses their comforting clank. It is all very well for the working man who has his job and his struggle for existence to distract him from such questions, but for the leisured modernist what remains?'

This was the opportunity for the Catholic Church to make converts. In a relative world the Catholic point of view seemed far wiser than most, because it had been developed throughout the centuries until logically unassailable—granted the original hypotheses, which were no more fantastic than most. As soon as the surrender was made, all problems were over: one was not allowed to think for oneself. A great many university aesthetes, Mayfair people, and middle-aged cynics were now jocularly reported by their friends to have 'embraced the Scarlet Woman':

Evelyn Waugh, the Oxford and Mayfair arch-playboy and most gifted novelist of the new Disillusion (*Vile Bodies, A Handful of Dust*, etc.); G. K. Chesterton, the elephantine paradoxist; the Hon. Evan Morgan, a leader and inspiration of the Bright Young People. The same report was constantly being made of T. S. Eliot himself, but he clung with a poet's conscience to a modicum of liberty for thought, and would go no further than Anglo-Catholicism: it was he who eventually supplied, in *The Rock* and *Murder in the Cathedral*, the spiritual plays for cathedral performance which the 1922 Church Congress had demanded.

Modern woman was held by psychological novelists to be ripe for the same sort of surrender. *Gifts of Sheba* by W. L. George, a typical advanced novel of 1925, had for its hero Hallam, a sadistic sensualist who got a kick out of making Isabel, an earnest feminist, happy by destroying her ideals, after first coolly murdering her earnest invalid husband. For Isabel he was 'a sort of vice, something unpleasantly seductive and forbidden, slightly nauseous but the only man who had ever aroused her curiosity'. He looked contentedly at her, in the last chapter. 'By Jove, life has made something of her. Taken the sociology out of her, smashed up a few of her ideas and made her what she ought to be—a woman to be enjoyed by a connoisseur.' He told her: 'You're a modern woman. You can't love properly as the beasts do, and they're the only creatures that know. You can't live with strong men, because you're damned if you're going to be ruled; and you can't live with weak men because you're damned if you're going to be bothered to manage them. . . . The only kind of man the modern woman can live with is the kind that doesn't care a damn for them.' He yawningly declared that he didn't care a damn for her; and she fell into his embrace. Of course, Hallams to whom weary feminists could surrender were few, but when 'Feminism is not Enough' became the right thing to say, there was neo-Victorianism to play at, and Leftism.

Meanwhile the denunciation of modern youth was a permanent Press feature. The *Daily Express* came out in 1925 with a bitter attack on 'The Modern Girl's Brother'. He was said to be weary, anaemic, feminine, bloodless, dolled up like a girl and an exquisite without masculinity; he resembled a silken-coated lap-dog, but 'it is not suggested that he is sexually depraved.' The Prince of Wales, however, was held up to this poor wretch as a shihing example of manly behaviour. His activities as 'the travelling salesman of Empire' filled a very great number of columns in these years. After the war, he had gone in turn to the United States, Canada, Australia, and New Zealand. Photographs of his tour and of his life on the battleship *Renown* filled the picture papers. The public came to look upon him as the hope of the future—though perhaps a somewhat enigmatic one. His speeches at banquets, with their diffident, humorous touches, were fully reported. When he was thrown at a steeplechase and broke his collar bone, it was sporting news and letters were written to the Press, asking whether his riding should not· be stopped 'in the national interest'; when he wore shorts at a Norfolk beagles meeting it was fashion news; when he walked under an arch of artificial silk stockings during a visit to a factory, it was really democratic news. He became a symbol of industrious, go-ahead youth, fully acquainted with all the world's problems; having, it is true, no plan by which to solve them, but at least a determination to tackle them and to struggle through, and thoroughly entitled to whatever harmless recreation came along. He occasionally danced at the Kit-Kat night club, and that was forgiven him: thirty peers were known to be members.

County Cricket never aroused such popular interest as League Football: it was wearisome to watch, rain frequently stopped play, the wicket was too far away and the ball too small and fast for spectators to catch the finer points of the game. Nevertheless in the summer months the Press had to rely largely on cricket to provide drama for the Silly Season. In 1925, for instance, there was the drama of Jack Hobbs the Surrey veteran: would he beat W. G. Grace's long-standing record of one hundred and twenty-six centuries in first-class cricket? He made 266 at Scarborough in a Gentlemen-versus-Players match; 215 at Birmingham, playing for Surrey against Warwick; and other centuries followed until he had notched one hundred and twenty-five in all. Then in late July and August came a lull in his scoring: match after match was played and no more centuries made. But at last on August 17th, at Taunton in a match against Somerset, Hobbs began to score again. During the match newspapers carried excited headlines: 'Will Hobbs Do It?', 'Within

9 of that 100', and finally 'Bravo Hobbs!' as he reached his 101. In the second innings he made a second 101, so passing Grace's record. The King sent him a congratulatory letter. Altogether that season he made 3,000 runs, including sixteen centuries.

But fine journalistic drama was provided by the Test Matches. ENGLAND IN PERIL and CAN WE AVOID DISASTER? were usual headlines. Even non-cricketers felt themselves personally involved in the fortunes of their country.

Social columnists gave considerable space to the crazes which, in the early Twenties, swept not only Society but the wider public, too. There was first the motor-scooter, spelt in American by one firm of manufacturers: 'Motoscoota'. With this vehicle, it was prophesied, 'the birth of an entirely new era in locomotion is about to take place'. In the future, scooter-ways would be constructed on either side of roads. The motor-scooter, however, was expensive to run and unreliable in performance: its doom was sealed when Sir Philip Sassoon took a bad toss by confusing stop-lever with accelerator. Shortly afterwards Sir Philip bought an aeroplane and took to hedge-hopping.

Then there was the pogo-stick. This was a pole with a crosspiece at the bottom on which to put one's feet; the upper part of the pole was grasped with both hands; at the bottom was a strong spring which enabled one to progress by jumping. It was described in the autumn of 1921 as a 'new French toy'. Newspapers came out with headlines and pictures of a 'Stars' Pogo Race'—Mona Vivian and Reginald Sharland having raced each other down the streets on pogo-sticks outside the Hippodrome Theatre. The *Daily News*—then running a children's feature of which the hero was a spectacled boy named Japhet—inaugurated a pogo-stick championship for members of the Japhet Club. It was won by a boy from Cliftonville who did 1,600 hops in fifteen minutes, and covered six hundred yards in eight minutes.

A less strenuous craze was Mah-Jong, a Chinese game which, like ginger and the Pekinese, had once been a prerogative of exalted rank. It was played with chips and domino-like counters and had a terminology full of quaint chinoiseries. People excitedly called 'Pung', 'Ching', and 'Bong' when they completed particular sets, and talked mysteriously of the 'East Wind', the 'Noth Wind' and the 'Red and Green Dragons'. Mah-Jong came from the United States in 1923; by Christmas the West End stores were full of expensive sets, and several Mah-Jong handbooks were published. Instruction in the newspapers consisted of such advice as: 'Don't forget to say "mah-jong" very quietly and with a restrained air. The moral effect is doubled.' And: 'Don't either lie or speak the truth consistently.'

Then crossword puzzles. This craze was noted in the United States in 1923, the puzzles appearing at first in books. At the end of 1924 very easy ones, under the name of 'crossword squares', began to be printed in the British Sunday newspapers. Soon afterwards the dailies followed suit. From the woman's chat page in *The Bystander* for December 1924: 'A quite fairly 'citing life after all—more especially since you don't know when you're going to be cat-burglared next. Or be asked to solve one of those crossword puzzles that're making life such a miserable burden for us all.' (Cat-burglars did not force ground-floor doors or windows, like ordinary burglars or policemen, but, like policemen raiding night-clubs, scaled waterpipes, ran along roofs, appeared suddenly through skylights. They greatly brightened crime.) *Punch* commented in the same year: 'The allure of Epstein and Oxford trouserings has been for the few; the Crossword Puzzle captivated the many.' (Jacob Epstein was a modernist English sculptor who by 1925 had been forgiven his unglorious military career, and was commissioned to execute a memorial to W. H. Hudson, the novelist-naturalist. In May 1925 Stanley Baldwin unveiled this: on the plaque was a flight of odd-looking birds and in their midst a female figure, Rima, the wild genius of the forest from Hudson's *Green Mansions*. 'Rima' was declared unworthy to commemorate Hudson's memory, and unworthy to be exhibited in a public park. Attacks on her were made not merely in the newspapers; periodically during the middle Twenties gangs of unclever young men attempted to tar and feather her or smother her in green paint. An old portraitist, the Hon. John Collier, in a speech at the Authors' Club described Rima as a 'bestial figure', and Sir Frank Dicksee, R.A., registered a formal protest.)

A simple type of crossword prevailed at first; as it grew popular, immense prizes were offered for solutions and for new puzzles. The odds against winning the prizes were higher than they seemed, for the puzzles were so constructed that alternative words could be used in many cases, and only the arbitrary combination selected by the editor won. Possibly the craze would have died out in Britain, as it did in the United States, had not serious weeklies and academic journals borrowed the daily crossword and crossed it with the old-fashioned acrostic—making use of literary allusions, anagrams, puns, and every kind of indirect reference. Thus started a stream of 'different' crosswords, which ran parallel to the daily stream and helped to keep it flowing. For three or four years the weeklies kept the 'different' puzzle going, and when the reader of the dailies became bored with filling in spaces with obvious words, the dailies took it over in all its tortuousness. Mr. and Mrs. Everyman were found equal to it. Crosswords held their own throughout the Peace because people had become genuinely interested in words: solving the puzzles was an amusing way of improving one's education—jigsaw puzzles and Patience had led nowhere. Now everyone knew that ERNE meant a sea-eagle, that RA was an Egyptian God, and that ACNESTIS was the part of one's back which one can't easily reach to scratch.

In 1922 the craze was for a simple gambling device known as 'Put and Take'. It was a small six-sided top which players, after putting money into a pool, each spun in turn; and then acted according to the order printed on the side that lay uppermost when it fell—put one more coin to the pool, or two or three; or took one or two; or took all. People spun their tops on luncheon table, on the bars of pubs, on the covers of magazines in railway carriages. For a few months scarcely a home was without its top, then suddenly the game entirely ceased. The simpler the craze, the more universal its scope, and the swifter its end.

CHAPTER NINE

Screen and Stage

Cinema development had been remarkably slow between 1900, when Moving Pictures were merely a novel side-show at the Crystal Palace, and 1910. The pictures, popularly known as the 'shakies', moved all right, but so spasmodically that even a two-reel show would give most people a headache. And as an American writer drily remarked: 'There's no Art for Art's sake in the movies': they were made on the cheap and, apart from one or two news-films of processions and crowd-scenes, dealt only in the crudest farce and melodrama. But a little before the war pictures grew less jumpy, though the cracking of the celluloid film after half a dozen showings still made them look as if they had been acted in pouring rain; and the first big pictures— Griffiths' 'The Birth of a Nation' (starring the sylph-like Lilian Gish), and his episodic 'Intolerance', showed the possibilities of screen drama. A boom then started in British picture-houses, but public interest was intermittent: most of the smaller ones were continually passing under new management for lack of patronage, and many reverted to their original status of church hall, gymnasium, concert-room, or shop.

The turn came in the spring of 1915, a very gloomy stage of the war, when Charlie Chaplin was introduced to Britain as 'the greatest laughter-maker of our time'. Though the Press reported with disgust that he was a young Englishman who was not 'doing his bit', he soon won enormous popularity among the troops at 'camp-kinemas' with his custard-pie comedies. They sang of him on route-marches:

'Oh, the moon shines bright on Charlie Chaplin!
His shoes are cracking
For want of blacking,
And his little baggy trousers they'll need mending
Before we send him
To the Dardanelles.'

His anti-German 'Shoulder Arms' restored him to official favour, and he was the main cause why half the population of Britain in 1919 went to the pictures twice a week. His female counterpart in glory was the 'world's sweetheart', Mary Pickford. The weather had no effect upon attendance at the picture palaces: even during the hottest summer evenings of this Year of Victory queues formed as early as 6 p.m.—most shows started at eight o'clock, like theatres.

Newspaper readers were soon pleased to learn that picture-going had become the settled habit not only of the working classes but of respectable theatre-goers: West End cinemas were visited by scores of the nobility and many members of Parliament, and the venerable Queen Alexandra frequently gave exhibitions at Marlborough House. On the 12th August 1919 a moving picture was exhibited in the House of Commons to nearly two hundred members. It was an American exposure of the evils of Bolshevism, projected from the first portable machine to be used in England.

The new dramas, which formed the bulk of cinema programmes, were admittedly 'not much class'; but to see photographs really moving about on a screen was still such a novelty that audiences were uncritical. Clara Kimball Young appeared as a Tarzan girl in 'The Savage Woman'—found by a French explorer in Africa, brought to Paris, and introduced to European ways. In the end she fled back to the jungle, dissatisfied with being regarded merely as a curiosity and not loved for herself. Then there was 'Riders of the Purple Sage'. William Farnum, as the star, rode out to find his married sister, who had been kidnapped by the Mormons and hidden in the wilds of Mormondy. By the time he arrived, however, she was dead. Undisconcerted by this disaster, he fell in love with a Mormon girl and adopted a Mormon orphan. Together the three escaped, but not to civilization: they shut themselves in a secluded, primitive valley, where they were left to live happily ever after.

Improvements in photographic technique encouraged greater care in the details of interior and the beauties of exterior, scenes. The public enjoyed the new travel pictures, their knowledge of geography having already been broadened by the war. These often took the form of 'travelogues'—lectures illustrated by moving pictures, such as Lowell Thomas's 'With Lawrence in Arabia and Allenby in Palestine', which was given before vast crowds at Covent Garden and initiated the great Lawrence legend which was to last for another fifteen years. (Lawrence, by the way, insisted that Lowell Thomas had not spent more than ten days or a fortnight in Arabia during the war: and even those at the Akaba base.) Many semi-religious and instructional films were also made, to encourage those who had hitherto looked upon going to the cinema as sinful.

Even the stickiest British families seemed ready to abandon their mistrust of the cinema, if the vulgar American scene could only be replaced by a wholesome British one. The *London Mercury* held that: 'The cinematograph drama might become genuine art, because one can look through the generality of the photograph into the human imaginative synthesis.' The highbrow attitude had for some time been one of disdain: photography was compared with painting, to its obvious disadvantage. When painting was taking on highly dynamic forms, photography, even motion photography, seemed to offer a very impoverished reality. But the macabre German Ufa films of the early Twenties—'The Cabinet of Doctor Caligari', 'Warning Shadows', 'Doctor Mabuse'—and the charming silhouette picture 'Prince Achmed', removed the prejudice. A highbrow Film Society was founded in 1926 for Sunday performances at the New Gallery Cinema.

The full technical development of the cinema had clearly not been reached with the silent film. Already in March 1919 the *Spectator* had reported an invention which would 'supply the human voice simultaneously with the spectacle of human beings in dramatic action.' It was not the old plan of synchronizing a gramophone record with the film: that had been proved ineffective. The new invention consisted in recording the human voice on a sound-track attached to the film. 'We cannot foresee', observed the *Spectator*, peering uneasily into the future, 'the effects upon the methods of the film-star. If the appeal is not to be only to the eye, there will be a slump in the value of facial contortion.' The hit was a just one: the early film-star usually grimaced at his audience like someone trying to convey news of terrific importance to a stone-deaf and half-witted child.

It was at first thought that there was a great future for British films. In 1919 a British production company with £1,000,000 capital was launched, and it was confidently asserted that the great fight between British and American films was about to begin. In 1920 Britain produced over two hundred pictures—and though at the same time American production was running into thousands annually, Hollywood had just celebrated the twenty-fifth anniversary of the film industry by declaring in favour of fewer and better pictures. British critics took this for a sign that the sources of American film plots were drying up: that would never happen here. And once the technical side had improved with the help of all this money, British audiences would respond with proper enthusiasm to comedies in which trains were familiar British trains, without negro waiters or cow-catchers, and in which policemen did not wear hats like busmen or swing clubs about. Many of the new British pictures would be semi-factual reconstructions of war themes, on heroic lines, dealing with the battles of Mons, Coronel, and the Falkland Islands, the blocking of Zeebrugge and the exploits of Q-ships. The Americans could not compete here!

These bright hopes for the British film industry, however, had begun to fade in 1922: the picture palaces were still crowded, but American producers had taken to selling their pictures to European exhibitors in blocks—if one good or grandiose picture was wanted, many indifferent ones had to be bought at the same time. The one good picture was beyond the scope of British producers; picture palaces were already booked up with indifferent American ones; and British producers could no longer find enough exhibitors to justify their attempting anything grandiose—after making a picture they often had to wait two years before recovering production costs. Meanwhile American film companies were buying up the cinema-houses and tightening their hold still more. Several British producers went out of business—even the bold expedient of bringing over American stars to work for them failed. Questions were then asked in

Parliament and it was agreed that something should be done to stem the tide of American pictures. In November 1923 the Prince of Wales inaugurated what were called 'British Film Weeks', in which British films were to have the preference on British screens; but the American producers forestalled this move by flooding the market beforehand.

The Germans were held up as models for British producers to imitate: during the war they had built up a successful film industry, protected from American competition, and since the war they had erected huge studios and were producing films that rivalled the American in technical excellence and cost far less to make. By 1924 they had got a firmer foothold in the British market than the British themselves. The German actor Emil Jannings became a world star. Several British firms went to Berlin to make films, but even this did not save them. The industry was dead again by the end of the year. Then American money drew to Hollywood most of what was new or active in Germany; and in Britain began replacing the old picture palaces, which had originally been designed for some other purpose than film shows, with functionally designed luxurious cinemas to seat several thousand people. Already cinema organs, at a cost of about £3,000 each, were being installed to supplement the orchestras. Even the poorest cinema at this time provided its own music: usually an ex-music-mistress who vamped a piano, hour after hour, and tried to suit the melody to the mood of the film. Entrance fees were higher where there was a fiddler as well.

In 1922 began the system of showing pictures at trade-shows, where cinema managers decided whether to book or not and where newspaper critics came to write reviews. Often a year elapsed between the trade-show and the general release, by which time people had forgotten what the film critics had written about the picture. The *Daily Mail* was the first paper to announce that it would no longer publish criticisms of trade-shows and thus give managers free guidance in their choice, but would review films that were actually showing and thus guide the public instead.

No remarkable experiments in film-technique were made in these years but there was a continuous improvement in production—gestures growing less jerky, settings less improbable, the connection between sequences smoother; and one no longer had to wait for a minute or two every time one reel was removed from the projector and another inserted. An unsolved difficulty was that of sub-titles—these were words flashed periodically on the screen between shots, or at the bottom of shots, to explain the immediate action. Different parts of the audiences read at different speeds; the quicker readers grew impatient with the slower, and the slowest of all never got to the last words before these vanished. In 1923 a film was shown that did without sub-titles; it pleased the film-critics but not the mass of film-goers, who could not make out what was supposed to be happening. Besides, sub-titles were great fun: audiences would read them aloud in an appreciative undertone. Such quaint Americanisms, for instance, as 'Beatrix Esmond goes nix on the love-stuff', when she registered haughtiness and stamped her foot, and 'You've dribbled a bibful, Baby' when some Keystone Baby had given her Sugar-Daddy useful advice, were widely quoted. Sub-title writers, even in Britain, were known as Came-the-Dawners, from the more romantic part of their calling.

The morals of the film story were at first under no control in the United States; but in 1920 the women's clubs and the Churches began a nation-wide drive against sexuality in films. The big American producers were forced to formulate the usual fourteen points—it had always been 'fourteen' since President Wilson's peace terms gave the number a mystic ring—covering the sort of pictures which they pledged themselves not to make. Two years later the Motion Picture Producers' and Distributors' Company was formed, with Will Hays, a former Postmaster-General, as President; its purpose was not only to look after the practical interests of the cinema industry but to exert moral control over the films released. In the same year the London County Council prepared the way for an official film-censorship by ruling that no children should be permitted to see films which did not bear a 'Universal' licence; for young criminals had a stock plea in court—'I saw it at the movies.' The movies were blamed for a great many disagreeable innovations, from the film-star behaviour of domestic servants to the lowering of white prestige in the East by American crook and sex-dramas. But Britain was less strictly treated by its censorship than the United States, where, for example, Middle Western influence insisted on a nonsensical sub-title to Chaplin's 'Woman of Paris': giving the heroine a legacy from an aunt to conceal the disgraceful fact that she was the kept mistress of the hero, Adolphe Menjou.

This was the golden age of pictures, between their first quaint beginnings and their eventual streamlining as Big Business. The public was developing a 'cinema-sense': now that the pictures were no longer a novelty, they began to learn the difference between good and bad. The boos which at first were reserved for the villain in the Western or crook drama were sometimes awarded to the dullness and stupidity of a block-booked film, made for American, not British, hicks. Audiences rather liked the short educational films introduced in 1921, the Goldwyn-Bray Pictographs, which showed the growth of plants, the behaviour of insects and so on, and even reproduced authentic life in north-west Canada and the wilder parts of Australia. In the following year short travel-films came in; consisting usually of a dull succession of only slightly moving views, interspersed with jocular or poetical comments. Later these merged into story-films with naturalistic settings: 'Nanook of the North' in 1924 showing life in an Eskimo community, then 'Trader Horn' with West African scenes, and in 1927 'Chang', over which the most serious journals grew lyrical. *The Spectator* declared: ' "Chang" is a magnificent film. The cinema has here brilliantly fulfilled a part for which it is better fitted than any other artistic medium. No book, painting, musical impression, or circus could give so adequate and vivid a picture of the jungle. And it is hardly a picture but a slice of the actual life of a Siamese tracker and his delightful family. They live in a log hut built on stilts, with a tame monkey, Bimbo, as the family jester. And around the solitary homestead leopards prowl, stealing by night the goats on whose milk Kiu's children depend, until the last goat is sacrificed as a bait to catch this ruthless marauder in a trap. There are snakes, ant-eaters, large scaly lizards, bears, tigers, and monkeys galore in this labyrinth of sinister-shaped trees and interwoven undergrowth. At one time a herd of elephants—some hundred I should think—are driven by fearless natives into a kraal. . . . The picture of this jungle life is not only conveyed by the film but also by the sounds of the different types of animal characters who appear, which have been recorded in the Zoological Gardens.'

The sexual attraction of an actor or actress was an increasing draw. Hysterical scenes took place when the most famous screen lover of the day, a smooth-faced young Italian, Rudolph Valentino, died. Half the female population seemed to be his widow. His romantic performances in the screen versions of E. M. Hull's *The Sheikh* and *The Son of the Sheikh* made the word 'sheikh', pronounced to rhyme with 'shriek', a synonym for the passionately conquering male. In 1927 a journalist wrote of an actor who was performing Nelson in 'The Divine Lady': 'With an arm missing and blind in one eye, he still managed to have sex-appeal.' 'Sex-appeal' was a new word with a tremendous vogue; it passed whole into most European languages. 'It' was another word of the same sort invented that year by the novelist Elinor Glyn: meaning the fascinating magnetic quality which her heroines, and Cleopatra—'and most cats'—and one or two of her cosmopolitan heroes possessed. 'It' meant being slinky and mysterious, for slinkiness was the leading erotic quality of the early post-war years: the 'Kirchner' flapper whose scantily draped limbs and kittenish face, cut from illustrated papers, had brightened nearly every dug-out in France, had set the slinky fashion, and the Vampire or 'vamp', Theda Bara, had confirmed it. In the Thirties 'It' gave place to 'Oomph', a more vigorous sex-appeal—Clara Bow, the temperamental red-haired comedienne, was really an 'Oomph', not an 'It', girl.

The most popular departure in the Twenties from ordinary film-technique was the animated cartoon. The adventures of 'Felix the Cat' were what the public really went to see, shouting out, to the accompaniment of the picture-palace piano, the famous ballad: 'Felix kept on walking, kept on walking still.' Felix was a black cat with a few touches of white who walked with his hands behind his back through nightmare landscapes and was totally indestructible. Even after calamities of dynamite, sharks, earthquakes, and lightning his scattered limbs always reassembled like mercury. He had a habit of detaching his tail and sending it off on adventures of its own. The limitless craziness of Felix, and of the manikin who came 'Out of the Inkwell' in a series combining realistic photographs with the cartoon, was popular education in that suspension of ordinary time-and-space values which the new physics had enjoined on scientists. Far more fantastic things happened to Felix than to his slick successors, the Bonzo dog and Mickey Mouse; and his departure from the scene about the time that short skirts reached their ebb-tide level and turned again marked the end of an age.

'Westerns' were the picture palaces' surest stand-by: they had hard-riding, tough-guy heroes like Hoot Gibson, William S. Hart, and Tom Mix with his wonderfully trained horse. Then there were ambitious romantic dramas, featuring the athletic and debonair Douglas Fairbanks ('The Thief of Baghdad', 'The Man in the Iron Mask', 'The Black Pirate', 'Robin Hood'), with duels, rescues, and hair-breadth escapes. There were personal love-dramas, too, with Gloria Swanson, the first film-actress to marry into the French nobility, and Bebe Daniels, who made screen history when she had her Hittite nose Grecianized by plastic surgery in the interests of her art. Everyone loved Lon Chaney, the master of disguise, whose most famous rôle was Quasimodo in 'The Hunchback of Notre Dame'. It was a joke, when one saw a black-beetle scuttling along the floor, to cry: 'Don't kill it; that may be Lon Chaney in disguise.' Everyone also loved 'The First Dog Star', the Alsatian Rin-Tin-Tin, who saved his master from a thousand deaths by super-doggish intelligence and a fine set of teeth. But the best that British producers could show was a not really successful costume-drama, 'The Glorious Adventure', staged at the court of King Charles II, and including one hundred and thirty principal players— among them Lady Diana Duff Cooper.

Next to Felix and the Westerns in popularity came the American slap-stick comedies—with the gross Fatty Arbuckle; the spectacled Harold Lloyd in comically appalling situations; the unsmiling Buster Keaton receiving jam-tarts plumb in his eye and tidily wiping away the jam; the Mack Sennett bathing beauties. But Chaplin remained 'The King of the Silver Screen': by far the most popular film in the Twenties was 'The Kid', a mixture of farce and sentiment, in which Chaplin as a lonely tramp found and brought up an orphan child, Jackie Coogan. The drama lay in their enforced separation and happy reunion. Enormous interest greeted Jackie Coogan when he visited London in 1924: the first child-wonder of the screen—'The hero of Nine who is Unspoilt'. He came as the representative of American children who had raised a million dollars for relief work in the Near East, and was greeted like a Crowned Head. Later

Chaplin himself came to London between films and was followed about by gigantic crowds. When he visited Sir Edwin Lutyens's studio in Appletree Yard, a cul-de-sac near St. James's Square, a corner tobacconist chalked up on his board 'Charlie is Down the Yard'. The streets for a quarter of a mile around were solid with sightseers. Chaplin was no longer merely the funny little man with the baggy trousers and the stick: 'The Kid' and 'The Gold Rush' had made him emblematic of the gay spirit of laughter in a cruel, crazy world. But the laughter grew more and more painful and satirical as the years went on and Chaplin had domestic troubles; and when the Marx Brothers came along with their irresponsible haywire comedy in the Thirties he seemed by contrast a rather seedy old Socialist with a message.

The theatres had come to believe that the cinema held no real threat for them: the human voice and the actor in the flesh would always prevail over dumb shadows. Theatre rents, owing to sub-letting of leases, were absurdly high at first, but even the falling-off in attendance at the beginning of 1921, when a coal-strike had made the theatres too cold for comfort, did not worry the managers; the autumn season was very successful. There were phenomenal runs. 'Paddy, the Next Best Thing', a sentimental Irish comedy, completed its third year, and 'Chu Chin Chow', a grandiose pseudo-Chinese drama, which had started during the war, ran for nearly five years, and achieved a since unapproached record of 2,238 performances. There were also crook-dramas such as 'Bulldog Drummond' and problem plays in the tradition of Brieux and Ibsen. The leading serious dramatists were pre-war favourites: earnest, puzzled John Galsworthy, and argumentative, always-right Bernard Shaw—Shaw's plays were the stand-by of the Hampstead Everyman Theatre, the only repertory theatre in London. And above all J. M. Barrie, whose annual 'Peter Pan' was the making of each young actress chosen to star in it, and whose 'Dear Brutus' and 'Marie Rose' transcended the logic of facts with the same briny-sweet whimsicality.

Theatre-going was now again a social obligation, like church-going, and revivals were the fashion. The extraordinary success of Gay's 'The Beggars' Opera', under Sir Nigel Playfair's direction, which had a more than three years' run at the Lyric, Hammersmith, encouraged the resurrection of a number of forgotten Elizabethan and Jacobean plays—Ford, Jonson, Beaumont and Fletcher—by the Phoenix Society. Oscar Wilde's comedies, the Gilbert and Sullivan operas, 'Box and Cox', and 'Charley's Aunt' were all brought out for an airing, to see what they looked like in a changed world. They looked very well. 'Charley's Aunt' provided a stunt in 1921 for raising money for ex-Servicemen. Two characters from it, Lawyer Spettigue and Lord Fancourt Babberley (disguised as Charley's Aunt) ran a race at the White City. In spite of bad weather a large crowd gathered to see it. The *Daily News* reported the event in full: 'Lord Fancourt Babberley's skirts tripped him up in the first twenty yards, and Mr. Lawyer Spettigue's valuable top-hat fell off. So a start was made again—to the tune, as before, of quite a hundred toy trumpets. On the runners now went, the skirts having been more tightly gripped and the top-hat pushed well down, and behind went the great crowd. In the Boxing Arena "Babs" was very nearly caught, his skirts being unmercifully tangled in the ropes; but the two strange figures ran on to the finish, where poor perspiring Spettigue lost by "five lengths" (official), and the honour of Charley's Aunt was completely vindicated. . . .'

There was no Shakespeare revival in the West End, but the Birmingham Repertory Theatre advertised a new fashion when it produced 'Cymbeline' in modern dress. The Britons wore evening dress at Court and in the daytime lounge suits; in the war scenes they were put into khaki. Cymbeline himself appeared as a field-marshal; the Queen and Imogen wore Paris frocks; the Romans, Italian uniform. Belarius in the cave-scenes was a modern sportsman with a shotgun. When the fighting started he and his two charges became Australian officers.

Many foreign plays and players arrived in 1923. The legendary Duse appeared in England for the first time for seventeen years. There was a Sacha Guitry *Grand Guignol* season; Carel Capek's 'R.U.R.', and Eugene O'Neill's daring 'Anna Christie' played by an American company. New British plays included Somerset Maugham's 'Our Betters', which the public found shocking and unpleasant.

The hit of 1924 was Shaw's 'Saint Joan', with Sybil Thorndike in the leading rôle. Dame Sybil came to identify herself so closely with the part that later, when she commissioned Jacob

Epstein to do a head of her, she is said to have annoyed him by assuming a Saint-Joan-like, heavenward look. When Shaw was asked why he had written the play he said that it was 'to save Joan of Arc from John Drinkwater'—an indefatigable historical playwright, and director of the Birmingham Repertory Theatre, whose 'Abraham Lincoln' had been one of the great stage successes in 1922. 'Saint Joan' won the Nobel Prize for Shaw that year; it had gone to W. B. Yeats in 1923 and was to be won by Galsworthy in 1932. The other play of this season was the rural novelist Eden Phillpotts' comedy 'The Farmer's Wife'. It was something simple and clean to take one's aunt or mother to, and was constantly revived for this purpose throughout the period.

Such younger dramatists as Frederick Lonsdale and Noel Coward found it difficult at first to get a hearing, for the easily offended stalls ruled the box-office. Coward's 'The Young Idea' had only a short run in 1922: and when 'The Vortex' was moved from the Everyman to the West End in the autumn of 1924, the drug-taking son and the immoral mother in the play seemed far too sympathetically presented. It aroused what was known as 'a storm of protest', but the publicity was useful and Coward helped things along by releasing a photograph of himself in bed, wearing a Chinese dressing-gown in a scarlet bedroom decorated with nudes, his expression being one of advanced degeneracy. He followed up the success of 'The Vortex' with 'Fallen Angels'. Its subject was attacked in the Press as vulgar and obscene, the *Daily Express* describing the women characters as 'suburban sluts'; Coward received a sackful of abusive letters. His 'Sirocco' caused another storm in 1926: from the stalls came cries of 'rotter', and from the gallery cat-calls and shrieks. Handsome Ivor Novello, author of 'Keep the Home Fires Burning', was playing in it and his film-fans were disappointed at seeing him in so unattractive a rôle. But Coward was now rapidly taking his place as the leading British dramatist: his light touch, perfect timing of laughs and quick anticipation of modern tendencies had been learned on the stage itself. He had been an actor since childhood and gained as shrewd a knowledge of the limitations of actors and audiences as Shaw himself. He could also write good lyrics, set them to catchy tunes and sing them pleasantly; and gave most of his plays a start by taking the lead himself—in 1927 he had four shows running simultaneously

Perhaps the most typical play of the middle Twenties was Miles Malleson's 'Fanatics', first published in volume form in 1924. So daring was it that no producer could be found for it until 1927, when it was put on at the Ambassador's. The *Observer's* verdict was: 'Mr. Malleson remains the undergraduate of dramatists, and when he writes a play we know we are in for one of these deep discussions of freedom with which men in their first year fill their evenings—"freedom" meaning looseness of behaviour accompanied by an entire lack of intelligence.' However, the play ran for nearly a year. James Agate summarized it fairly in the *Sunday Times*:

'The upshot of the argument is that Age cannot do right or Youth think wrong. . . . No doubt as to the author's bias in the matter. Mr. Freeman's dining-room is described as "middle-class but sumptuously so: he is rather short and rather round, a little red, a little bald. He continues to eat his fruit—there is no other sound". It is obvious that Freeman and the class for which he stands are in for a thin time.

'Young Freeman, the son, is revolted at the notion of £500 a year in wholesale ironmongery and a partnership when he marries. He has had five years [*sic*] in the trenches, realizes that there is something rotten in the state of post-war England, and deems it a cursed spite that he should be chained to his father's office when he has bright ideas for the regeneration of the world. John is a muddled thinker in whose airy book-keeping the fact that England is still England and not Germany is not even an entry. To war's debit he places not only the fact that stay-at-homes like his father prospered exceedingly, but also a number of things which cannot by any possibility be brought into the account. There's that old matter of monogamy. How can a fellow know that in one woman he will find both soul-mate and mistress? The remedy is trial marriage, with birth-control until the parties are satisfied that their attachment is lasting. Immoral? John sees nothing moral in a system whereby an epileptic woman in a slum can have twelve children by a confirmed drunkard, and thousands of babies roll about in filth. "Religion doesn't do anything, because it thinks birth-control wicked; Big Business doesn't do anything, because it wants cheap labour; the

Government doesn't do anything because they want soldiers for the next war." John has a sweetheart to whom marriage is largely a matter of window curtains and dinner parties. John, wanting assurances which are not forthcoming, takes a mistress. John also has a sister who is so far bitten by his doctrine that, having secured a lover who wants to marry her, she will not consent until she has made the experimental trip. The sister's young man has a friend who has made three such voyages, declares herself a famous sailor, and is all in favour of this particular ocean-going experiment. Huddled over John's gas-fire in the dead of night they talk each other and the audience blue in the face. In the middle of their abstractions and hypotheses is thrown a bombshell of accomplished fact—the housemaid is going to have a baby, and all through waiting at table and listening to their silly talk. The father is a married man and what are they all going to do about it? John stammers that he will help her financially. But as his father has thrown him out of the business, and his future income is dependent upon the sale of pamphlets on trial marriage, we do not quite see how.'

The Twenties did indeed temporarily raise the mental age of the average theatre-goer from fourteen to seventeen.

Frederick Lonsdale's 'Spring Cleaning' was another successfully abused 'shameless' play of the Careless Twenties; so were dramatizations of Michael Arlen's *The Green Hat*, with Tallulah Bankhead, and Anita Loos's *Gentlemen Prefer Blondes*. This was the time when any successful novel immediately became a stage success too. *Gentlemen Prefer Blondes* was a best-selling American story of two kept women and their gentlemen friends, told in artless pseudo-baby language; *The Green Hat* was about people committing suicide for purity's sake when devoured by sexual passion. Arlen was 'cynical, daring, and ruthless'. The *Weekly Dispatch* in May 1925 quoted from him in illustration of the perfect amusing style: 'Lady Surplice was relentless in her generosity and indomitable in her indiscretion', and 'Mrs. Amp was as mean with money as a Temperance Hotel with matches, but even so she could stay the stars in their courses, anyhow for at least five courses, and then make them sing and dance to her guests on top of it.'

Tallulah Bankhead, about whose private life as many fantastic stories were current as about Noel Coward's, was an American actress with an attractively husky voice and a large forehead. When she took the lead in 'The Green Hat' something new happened: in the old days there had been male matinée idols such as Forbes Robertson and Gerald du Maurier, whom school-girls raved about, just as there were female ones whom school-boys raved about. But the craze or *Schwärmerei* of women theatre-goers for an actress was something hitherto unknown in Britain and Tallulah soon had a bigger fan-mail from women than any male rival. The Press increased the vogue by featuring 'The Hysterical Gallery Girl'. Another 'Queen-bee' (the contem-porary American word for the object of such a craze) was Edna Best, heroine of Basil Dean's dramatization of *The Constant Nymph*. This was a novel by Margaret Kennedy, the great suc-cess of 1926, which described the doings of a musician named Sanger and his 'Bohemian' family: none of them with any moral sense except where instrumental music was concerned. The principal scenes were set in the Austrian mountains; and the heroine died just in time to avoid technical adultery. This play started a fashion for Austrian dresses and Austrian summer holidays, and finally reconciled the suburbs to 'Bohemia'.

Coward was the dramatist of disillusion, as Eliot was its tragic poet, Aldous Huxley its novelist, and James Joyce its prose epic-writer. They all had in common a sense of the unreality of time. The main theme of the revues that Coward wrote for C. B. Cochran was that one now knew a little too much for happiness; and that this was a 'period' period, without a style of its own any longer, but with full liberty to borrow from any wardrobe of the past. His songs 'World-Weary' and 'Dance, Dance, Dance Little Lady' were felt to reflect the mood of his time. A typical Cochran revue scene: the contrast between a Victorian and a neo-Georgian wedding night. In the first, the young bride, un-aware of the facts of life, howls miserably for her mamma, and the husband is embarrassed but stern; in the second, the couple feel the springs of the bed, pronounce them all right, and make it quite clear that this is by no means their first sexual encounter.

C. B. Cochran was the leading showman of the period and the best liked. He sometimes made large sums of money on his ven-tures, as often went broke by misjudging the British capacity for 'taking it', but would always find backers for something new. He was a chief link between the United States and Britain.

Cochran lost thousands on Russian ballets, brought Balieff's Chauve-Souris from Paris (not a success), introduced American cowboy 'rodeo' (crabbed by the Society for the Prevention of Cruelty to Animals), promoted a number of big prize fights, dropped £20,000 on a single revue, earned as much on others, introduced the many-ringed Circus at Olympia, made his 'Young Ladies' into the best revue-chorus of the day. Cabaret, straight plays, musical shows—there was nothing Cochran did not touch: only he shrank from what was dull and 'safe'. He had once been a struggling 'trouper', and the recklessness, generosity and good comradeship of the Stage distinguished him from most of his fellow showmen, whose chief interest was finance, not entertainment.

Edgar Wallace was by far the best-known and most widely read low-brow writer, and a successful dramatist too. He had been a journalist before the war and even when he became a popular novelist did not lose touch with Fleet Street. In 1926 he was editing the *Sunday News* and writing topical weekly articles. In 1927 he was racing correspondent for the *Star*—as a result the *Star's* circulation rose considerably—and in 1930 he was dramatic critic for the *Morning Post*. His pre-war novels had been set in Africa; but after the war he settled down to producing ordinary home thrillers. He worked with notorious industry in a hot room, all windows shut, smoking cigarette after cigarette through an immensely long amber holder, drinking every half-hour a cup of sweet, weak tea, pacing about in a dressing-gown, dictating to his secretaries. In this way he was able to complete a book in four days; the plots were shaky, but the style vigorous. During the last six years of his life—he died in 1932—twenty-eight of his novels were published and it was a joke to ask at a bookstall for the 'midday Wallace'. At the same time he was writing plays. 1928 was an Edgar Wallace year in the theatre, three of his plays, 'The Man Who Changed His Name', 'The Squeaker', and 'The Flying Squad' being produced in the West End at the same time. In addition he did the book for a musical comedy, 'The Yellow Mask,' and put on a suburban production of 'The Lad'. All these plays were straight, old-fashioned melodramas—situation piled on situation, with increasing suspense, the dialogue racy but not clever.

Wallace's standard of living was about the same as Bottomley's had been. He kept a racing stable and a box at Ascot; betted frequently and not very wisely; played poker with less skill than imperturbability; gave parties of roast lamb, ice-cream, and champagne to the casts of his plays. In 1930 he decided to stand as Liberal candidate for the Aylesbury Division of Bucks, and began to open Liberal bazaars all over the constituency. He told his audiences that he wanted to enter the House of Commons because 'a writer of crook stories ought never to stop seeking new material'. Aylesbury was a Conservative constituency, however, and he did not make much progress; a year later he withdrew his candidature. In 1931 he went to Hollywood to take up scenario-writing, his ambition being to become a film-director. But already he was suffering from diabetes and in 1932 he died of double pneumonia. The film 'King Kong', on which he had been working, was finished after his death.

The healthy, light American musical comedy was popular in the Twenties: 'No, No, Nanette' in 1925 was followed by 'Tip Toes' and 'Lady Be Good', distinguished by the dancing of the Astaires—Adele had not yet married into the peerage, nor had Fred become No. 1 World-Hoofer on the films. The heavily romantic, improbable, low-brow spectacular play still drew enormous crowds; as did its cinema counterpart. 'The Desert Song' in 1927, starring Edith Day, was the most famous of these; it was the 'Sheikh' period and the scene was therefore Morocco, where a French general lived in a palace fitted out like the most luxurious of Turkish baths. His son was considered a good-for-nothing and had failed in love; to escape from this failure he became the mysterious Sheikh of the Riff Arabs, 'The Red Shadow'. The 'Shadow' abducted Miss Day, gave her a Paris frock in the Riff mountains, forced back her head on an ultramarine cushion, kissed her. Complicated adventures followed, the 'Shadow' being torn between love for Miss Day, loyalty to the Riffs, and loyalty to his father and to France. In the end everything came right, with the help of an American war-correspondent, who supplied comic relief, and the wives of the Foreign Legionaries, who all wore Paris frocks and hats.

CHAPTER TEN

Revolution Again Averted, 1926

The rise of the Labour Party to respectability was an important feature of the immediate post-war period. At the Khaki, or Coupon, Election of December 1918, the party slogans had been: 'Peace of Reconciliation', 'Hands off Democracy', 'Land for the Workers', 'A Million Good Houses', 'A Levy on Capital', 'Nationalization of Railways, Mines, Shipping, Electric Power'. Even in that Hun-hating and Lloyd George-cheering year, the programme had a wide enough appeal to secure 57 seats and 2,250,000 votes. Labour was also winning municipal elections, where seats would often be unexpectedly snatched because of the apathy of Conservative and Liberal voters. In 1912 there had been only 46 Labour councillors in the London boroughs; by 1919 there were 572, with a clear majority in twelve boroughs.

At first the question of Russia divided the Labour Party. A 1919 conference could not easily decide whether to support or oppose British intervention on the side of the Whites. The British working-man tended to think of the Russians as foreigners rather than fellow working-men. Philip Snowden, of the Fabian League, denounced the Reds as 'wanton revolutionaries' and Colonel John Ward, 'the Navvies' M.P.', who had himself served at Murmansk, supported him with tales of Red atrocities. But it was clear that no good could be done, and much harm, by identifying Britain with the Tsarist cause, and the conference finally voted against intervention. In 1920 London dockers refused to load the freighter *Jolly George* with munitions for the use of Poland, which had been invaded by the Russians, and

Labour came out solidly in their support. Later, the *Jolly George* incident was often cited by Left extremists as an example of how the action of the workers could thwart the aggressive designs of the Capitalists against the U.S.S.R.; but it had made no real difference to the result of the Russo-Polish War—the Russians found that, unaccountably, the Polish proletariat did not rise to welcome the Red Army, and the Polish forces, recovering bravely from a first setback, defeated them.

In 1920 the Transport Union, the General Workers' Union, the National Union of General and Municipal Workers, and the Amalgamated Engineering Union, each absorbed several small craft-unions; which greatly aided united Labour action. The policy of that year was given in a manifesto: 'We of the Labour Party ... recognize, in the present world catastrophe, if not the death, in Europe, of civilization itself, at any rate the culmination and collapse of a distinctive industrial civilization, which the workers will not seek to reconstruct. . . . The industrialist system of capitalist production ... with the monstrous inequality of circumstances which it produces and the degradation and brutalization, both moral and spiritual, resulting therefrom, may, we hope, indeed have received a death-blow. . . .'

This difficultly worded prophecy of woe, to which were added methodistic hopes for a righteous and equalitarian future, had little effect on the working class until the slump of 1921 recalled it. Meanwhile, the indefatigable Socialist historians, Beatrice and Sidney Webb, were trying to persuade intellectuals and manual workers alike, in *Labour and the New Social Order*, and numerous other books and pamphlets, that the war really had brought about the end of the old era, but that only the Labour Party on a Fabian, no-class-war programme could decently inaugurate the new.

The Labour Party made a virtue of refusing affiliation to the Communist Party of Great Britain, which was formed in 1920 by the union of three 'ginger' groups—the British Socialist Party, the Socialist Labour Party and the South Wales Socialist Society. They accused the Communists of taking their orders from Moscow and plotting to stab Labour in the back—though, in fact, the Communist Party at that time was too small to be dignified with such notice, and showed no signs of getting any larger. The social gap between the British governing and governed classes had narrowed greatly since Karl Marx's day, and nobody could think of the class-war that he had prophesied except as a figure of speech. Yet the class-war as it had been waged in Russia was real, and the Bolshevists were undeniably Socialists; and for Labour to be in any way associated in the popular mind with a massacre of the nobility and gentry was most damaging to its cause. In the upper classes anyone who merely visited Russia, such as Claire Sheridan the sculptor (whose *Russian Portraits*, published in 1921, was not at all pro-Bolshevist), was socially ruined; a Balliol undergraduate and ex-officer, who went there for his vacation, was asked to leave the college on his return. Two other undergraduates were subsequently rusticated for 'Russian Communism'. For, according to the Conservative Press, the Bolshevists were not only murderers and ruffians and enemies of private property: they were also active atheists and had 'nationalized women for sexual purposes'.

In 1921 Labour showed its heroic side. The Poplar Borough Council, with a Labour majority, withheld payments due to the London County Council, as a protest against the saddling of impoverished local bodies with the whole burden of poor relief. Most of the council, among them George Lansbury of the *Daily Herald*, were then imprisoned for contempt of court. They declared themselves 'Guilty—and proud of it'. They were, however, soon released: it was realized that their protest was justified, and legislation was rushed through to distribute the incidence of relief more evenly among the rich and the poor boroughs. The Poplar Councillors' victory was an important one, since nearly all the half-million people then drawing relief—quite a distinct payment from the national 'dole'—lived in a few poor boroughs, which consequently found their revenues grossly overstrained.

Early in 1922, with the object of further underlining Labour's repudiation of all things Russian, J. H. Thomas, the leader of the railwaymen, sued the editor of an obscure paper, *The Communist*, for libel: *The Communist* had accused him of betraying the miners' interests in the strike of that year. The court proceedings were hilarious. Thomas and the officers of the Law together enjoyed themselves at the expense equally of parliamentary procedure and of Bolshevist behaviour. The *Daily News* reported these extracts from the Court dialogue:

Mr. Thomas: 'No two Parliamentarians use the same words to convey the same meaning.' (Laughter.)

Serjeant Sullivan (defending): 'That is, my Lord, what is called finding a formula.' (Laughter.)

His Lordship: 'I think it perfectly priceless.'

Mr. Thomas: '. . . My complaint is that I am not accused of being a traitor to the Communists, but of being a traitor to the Trade Unionists.'

His Lordship: 'Am I to understand that *The Communist* is kept going by the capitalist?' (Laughter.)

Mr. Thomas: 'I have no hesitation in saying that Russian money at the moment is subsidizing the Communist movement.'

Serjeant Sullivan: 'The rouble is extremely depreciated.'

Mr. Thomas: 'But the jewels have gone up in value.' (Laughter.)

This was the time when the Russian Government was hastily raising funds by selling abroad confiscated jewels and works of art. The case, which Thomas won, was a great reassurance to those who had been encouraged to believe that Labour intended Red ruin and despoliation.

Later in the year, Ramsay MacDonald was elected leader of the Labour Party. He had been in disgrace during the war as a pacifist, and even forced to resign from his local golf club; but by 1922 this was counted rather a feather in his cap. At the Party Conference in the following year he and Sidney Webb came out firmly in favour of 'the inevitability of gradualness', 'the futility of violence', and 'the spirit of fellowship preached by William Morris'. This moderate line won them enough seats at the General Election of 1923 to undertake a government—with Liberal support, as has been described. A Labour government was a great joke for the popular Press: what, for a start, would the Cabinet Ministers wear at Royal levées? The King obligingly relaxed the rule that they should wear black knee-breeches and white silk stockings. A great wave of delighted relief was felt. So a Labour Prime Minister could kiss the King's hand upon taking up office, without the need for a revolution—a man too who had come up from the very bottom, and was not even born in wedlock! All was well, after all. And Sidney Webb had consented to become Lord Passfield—what a joke! and, richer still, his wife had refused to be Lady Passfield, out of combined feminist and socialistic conviction, and remained Mrs.

Webb—how funny that would look when they registered at hotels! Soon J. H. Thomas, who had spent many years as an engine-driver, became a well-loved figure of fun as Colonial Secretary, because of his undisguised love of evening dress and cigars: Low saluted him as 'The Rt. Hon. Dress-Shirt'.

Thomas had for private secretary the art-and-poetry-loving Edward Marsh, a 'famous first-nighter', who had previously served, in turn, Campbell-Bannerman, Asquith, and Winston Churchill. Eddie and Jimmie were said to have struck up a warm friendship. It pleased the Press to find that there were touches about the new Ministers, such as MacDonald's long moustaches, which could be made as endearing as Joe Chamberlain's monocle and orchid, Baldwin's pipe, or Churchill's hats. Better still, the new hostess of 10 Downing Street was the Prime Minister's daughter, Ishbel MacDonald, then aged twenty. Reporters were sent to find out whether she was a typical example of the 'modern girl'. She described No. 10 as 'a nice place, but awfully complicated', and said that she was studying at the Domestic Science College. Reporters tried to draw her out, to see if they could represent her as a less serious girl than this suggested. She admitted a fondness for music, hockey, and golf, and for 'a really thrilling tragedy like *The Mill on the Floss*'. 'I've never been centred in a whirlpool of jazz and I do not intend to be,' she announced. This comforted many readers. So did Snowden's budget, which omitted to impose the dreaded Capital Levy and did nothing more newsworthy than provide a 'Free Breakfast Table' by reducing the import duties on tea, coffee, sugar, and chicory.

The fact was that Labour had only been able to count on Liberal support if, in Asquith's phrase, 'its claws were cut'; it cut its own claws by including in the Cabinet the former Liberal War Minister Lord Haldane, and Lord Chelmsford, an ex-Colonial governor. But it had by no means an easy time. Strikes continued: one among the transport-workers in London and one among the builders of the forthcoming British Empire Exhibition at Wembley. Ramsay MacDonald had to invoke the Emergency Powers Act, that 'sinister instrument of Capitalist tyranny', as the *Daily Herald* had called it, to deal with the situation; J. R. Clynes, as Home Secretary, declared in a speech at Wembley that Labour had been 'converted from its former grooves to the wider view'. The 'wider view' meant, of course, behaving like any other Ministry. When, for instance, Arthur Henderson dared to speak of revising the Versailles Treaty, MacDonald at once repudiated him. In foreign, as in domestic policy, Mac-Donald was obliged by his Civil Servants, if not by his own inclination, to follow a Conservative line, especially in his severe dealings with nationalistic movements in British possessions and dependencies overseas.

When MacDonald boldly denounced the French for endangering the peace of Europe by their occupation of the Ruhr, he was expressing the general trend of British public opinion. It was recalled that at the Washington Naval Conference of 1921 the French had, for prudential reasons, refused to agree to the abolition of submarines and of military aircraft. In the popular Press the French, rather than the Germans, were now the villains of Europe: accused of exploiting the Allied victory to their own advantage. Lord Birkenhead, the famous barrister, politician, and Orangeman, even went so far as to suggest that the French were preparing for war against Britain; nor was this view thought fantastic—France was Britain's hereditary enemy, and had twice nearly been at war with her over the near-Eastern question within living memory.

Certainly the French were exploiting the victory. For while the British (who, unlike the French, had not had their country invaded twice in the last fifty years) decided to further their own trade by magnanimously helping in the reconstruction of Germany, the French feared that economic reconstruction might also bring about the revival of German ambitions. The Hitler-Ludendorff 'putsch' at Munich in 1923, though a fiasco, showed that the Germans had not yet been reduced to complete docility. This revolt was provoked by the catastrophic fall of the German mark, when the occupation of the Ruhr put a lien on Germany's chief remaining wealth. By the winter of that year the mark was quoted at fifteen million to the £ sterling, and its fall shook the franc down from sixty-seven to ninety to the £. The British then grew worried. A *Daily News* special reporter, sent to Bavaria to investigate the causes of unrest, poured scorn on the Hitler movement, but went on to say: 'Hitler, the tub-thumping patriot, may be heard from again some day. It is not generally known that this man, who is an Austrian by birth and a sign-painter by profession, was badly gassed on the British front. Previously he had been badly wounded, but after he recovered from the gas-attack he stated he had seen a vision and received a message. He had been summoned as the Saviour of Germany!'

In 1924 the French had a change of government; and of mind, if not of heart. Obviously, Germany's capacity to pay would be reduced to nothing if her currency continued so fantastically inflated: for all industry and trade would cease. Collaboration was essential, even from the strict point of view of 'making Germany pay'. The Radical Herriot, who replaced Poincaré as Premier, found himself in close sympathy with MacDonald. In August 1924 the Ruhr was evacuated and a period of collaboration between the Allies and the moderate Germany of Stresemann seemed about to begin.

It was ironical that what brought about the end of Labour-Liberal co-operation was the Anglo-Soviet Treaty, by which Britain first recognized the U.S.S.R. Labour meant this only as a formalization of the commercial amity already existing between the two countries. For in 1921, despite the question of the repudiated Tsarist debts to Britain, Sir Robert Horne, on behalf of the Coalition Government, had signed a trade agreement with the Soviet representative Krassin; and a Soviet trading office, Centrosoylus, had been opened in England. Russia was a promising customer for British goods, and it was considered wise to 'cut our losses' before the Germans captured the market. The Labour leaders were therefore surprised at the self-righteous Liberal opposition to the Treaty, which had been recommended in the interest of trade and industry by permanent officials of the Civil Service, and had no 'ideological' significance. They were no more 'shaking hands with murder' than the Liberals themselves in 1921; and now that Russia seemed on the way to becoming a great power once more, it was in the oldest British tradition to recognize the fact diplomatically. Besides, if it came to that, the U.S.S.R. was at least the equal, morally, of pre-war Turkey—or Tsarist Russia. But the Liberals were resolved to escape the odium of having 'thrown Britain into the arms of Russia'. They withdrew their support from Labour in the House and another General Election followed—at which Labour was stabbed in the back not by the Communist Party, but by hands unknown.

On 21st October, only eight days before the polling date, the Foreign Office issued to the Press an intercepted letter purporting to have been written by Zinoviev, the President of the Third International. It was addressed to the Communist Party of Great Britain, whom it urged to stir up the masses, sow propaganda among the troops, and keep a careful watch on Labour leaders—who tended to betray their class by straying into the folds of the bourgoisie. The Russian Treaty, the letter asserted, would help to revolutionize the proletariat as much as a successful military rising.

This letter, which the *Daily Herald* at once proved by internal evidence to be a clumsy forgery, put MacDonald into a cleft stick. He doubted its genuineness himself, but dared not prevent the Foreign Office, who pretended to believe in it, from lodging an immediate official protest with the Soviet Charge d'Affaires: for to do so would be represented as a condonation of treason. The Russian Government passed on the protest to the Third International, a quite separate organization, which naturally repudiated the letter. MacDonald had enormously underestimated the damage that the publication of the letter would do him in the popular Press. He saw only that it associated him and his colleagues with the forces of Law and Order and might therefore be expected to do more good than harm. But the *Daily Mail* played it up as irrefutable evidence of the Red Menace of which the Labour leaders were being made the dupes; and the rest of the Conservative Press unanimously maintained that a vote for the Liberals was a vote for Labour, and a vote for Labour was a vote for the Communist Party. This appeal to the passions overrode all considerations of fact or probability—the Communist Party in England was still neither more powerful, numerous nor rich, than the Geoplanarian Society whose members were bound together in the staunch belief that the earth was really flat, or the Plymouth Brethren, or the Mormon Church. Yet the middle-class electorate, forgetting how reassuringly J. H. Thomas had joked about Bolshevist jewels, how charming a hostess Ishbel MacDonald had been, how gentlemanly had been the parliamentary behaviour of even the wildest of the Wild Men, rushed to the defence of the National Liberties. As a result the Conservatives, who had wisely dropped tariffs from their programme, came to power with 415 seats. Labour polled a million more votes than in the previous year, but chiefly in constituencies where these were wasted. They could secure no more than 152 seats. The combined Liberals were the real losers: they kept only forty-two. There was one Communist member, Saklatvala of Battersea, whose election indicated the seriousness of housing conditions in that depressed borough rather than any Marxian convictions among the electors.

It was a glorious victory for the Tories—too glorious indeed for parliamentary health: never had the House been so full of inexperienced members. Baldwin was again Prime Minister. Winston Churchill was Chancellor of the Exchequer—reconverted from Liberalism to Conservatism, after having for the past two years tried unsuccessfully to form his own Centre Party out of Asquithian Liberals and advanced Conservatives. His Budget in 1925 was a model of orthodox finance. The Treasury had decided to reaffirm British financial stability by a return to the Gold Standard at pre-war parity. Though this meant an overvaluation of the post-war purchasing power of the £, it was useful at the time in re-establishing Britain's commercial position, which had been affected by the recent slump. The low rates at which France and Belgium would stabilize their currencies, as a threat to British trade, were not then foreseen.

This Budget was publicized as 'The Silk Stocking Budget' because of the tax it imposed on raw and artificial silk. There had been an extraordinary increase in the production of artificial silk in Britain. The first artificial silk process was Hilarie de Chardonnet's in 1883, launched commercially by the Société d'Exploitation de Soie Artificielle at Besançon. The results were unsatisfactory and thirty years passed before improved British processes took the squeak out of the new material and gave it the desired soft frou-frou. And it was not until after the war that the British output of artificial silk showed a sudden increase: in 1919 it amounted to 35,000,000 lb.; in 1922 to 80,000,000 lb.; in 1926 to 235,000,000 lb.; and in 1928 to 341,000,000 lb.

The Bolshevist bogey, that had brought the Government into power, was kept alive by frequent exercise. Sir William Joynson-Hicks, the Home Secretary, denounced Red Gold as the insidious instrument by which the National Minority Movement of Tom Mann and Harry Pollitt worked to corrupt trade unions from the inside. A boycott was in force among many M.P.s against Saklatvala: he was to accompany a delegation to the Inter-Parliamentary Union Conference in the United States in August 1925, but three M.P.s refused to be delegates if he were included, declaring that they loathed and detested his utterances. At the last minute the United States Government cancelled his visa, and all was well.

A leading occupation of this rather hysterical time was making forecasts. In 1924 J. B. S. Haldane inaugurated the famous 'To-day and To-morrow' series of booklets published by Kegan Paul with his *Daedalus, or the Future of Science*. A good idea of what 1925 was really like can be deduced by an analysis of its *Futures*. A typical orthodox one, for the next twenty-five years, was Sir Sidney Low's article in the *Daily Mail Year Book*. As a Conservative journalist he felt it his duty to emphasize the peril of Bolshevism: Russia might choose before long to repeat the menace of Genghiz Khan and pour its Asiatic hordes upon Europe. But in Central Europe there would be peace: the French and Germans were now showing hopeful signs of collaboration.

Sir Sidney prophesied great changes within the British Empire. Ireland would become an independent republic; Canada would be absorbed into the United States—merely out of unwillingness to be mingled in European affairs. India would be a loose federation, governed more by independent princes than Bengal orators, and the British would have withdrawn to the coastal towns, as in the early days of the East India Company. Britain itself would have contracted its interests, and would no longer be a great world-trading power. He also prophesied that within the next twenty-five years there would be 'tele-pictures' as well as wireless (nobody had yet coined the equally mongrel word 'television'). People would be able to fly by aerial saloons to New York in twenty hours, and spend weekends in Tunis and Tangier as easily as in Torquay. The open fire and the smoking chimney would be abolished. 'Everyone' would be using electric heaters, electric baths, electric cleaners, and electric cookers. (By 'everyone' he probably meant 'everyone who matters socially'; this being the abbreviation used in the popular Press throughout the period.) Wireless transmitters would be carried in people's pockets like cigarette-cases, and medical research would have prolonged the normal span of life to a hundred years. At the same time, Sir Sidney reflected sombrely that in the next twenty-five years some new Alexander, Caesar, Napoleon, or Lenin might arise to make a new Europe and shatter all that was left of the old one. Optimists believed that the Powers would agree to disarmament, and that disputes could be settled by the League, but realists would expect a few more wars—though not a world war like the last. These wars would be terrible but short; no longer would millions of infantrymen sit in trenches for years—the fighting forces would consist of small bodies of highly trained airmen, engineers, chemists, and mechanized artillerymen. Movements would be rapid, and a campaign might last no more than a few weeks. A limited number of professional combatants, like the standing armies of the past, would replace the nation-at-arms.

In this concluding item, which did not square very well with his 'Russian hordes' fantasy, he was making a resumé of the views of the *Morning Post* military correspondent, Captain Liddell Hart, who had written in September 1924: 'Pure numbers, as military history teaches us, do not constitute an effective army, and the more the means of war develop, the more does this truth hold good. . . . The tank is not so much a weapon as a rapid and cross-country means of moving weapons. Since we have centuries ago replaced man's arms by mechanized arms—rifles, machine-guns, and guns—it seems but the logical course of evolution to replace his legs by a mechanical means of movement. . . . With the development of long-range artillery and bombing aircraft it is difficult to see how long, slow-moving columns of infantry could continue.' Captain Liddell Hart, as military correspondent successively to the *Morning Post*, *Daily Telegraph*, and *The Times*, continued for the next fifteen years to plug his message: 'Mechanize everything. Not to increase our tank force in order to keep cavalry and infantry is a suicidal policy.' The reception given to his views was quite warm at first. An early convert, General Sir George Milne, Chief of the Imperial General Staff, in an address to the officers of the newly formed Experimental Mechanized Force at Tidworth (September 1927) promised whole armoured divisions and remarked: 'Crowds of men are out of place on the battlefield, when you have low-flying aeroplanes against them. Think of their communications and supplies!'

The popular Press was pleased with the idea of mechanization: it was possible now to save £4,500,000 a year on the Army estimates. Nevertheless, it seemed almost unnecessary to argue about the Army and its weapons: they would surely never be needed again in the era that was now dawning. For in December 1925 the Locarno Pact had been signed between Germany, Italy, France, and Britain. Briand, the French Prime Minister, had said: 'We are now only Europeans', and Sir Austen Chamberlain, then Foreign Secretary: 'These treaties are the real dividing line between the war years and those of peace.'

The stage being thus cleared for former belligerents to fight the war again in friendly debate, the *Daily Express* published an article by the German Admiral von Tirpitz, who claimed that the Battle of Jutland had been a German tactical success. The German ships were superior, von Tirpitz said, and the training of their men perhaps a little better. The prolongation of the war, he concluded, was due to the failure of British seamanship to force a victory. Lord Jellicoe defended himself against this charge by accusing the Germans of withdrawing before he could make his superior numbers felt; in any case the German Fleet had never again tried conclusions with the British. Then Admiral Mark Kerr declared—a little irrelevantly—that the Germans had suffered many more casualties than the British, because the action had taken place at night. The United States semi-official naval historian was invoked to prove that the British failure to win a complete victory had allowed the Germans to keep their submarine routes open, and so contributed to the U-boat campaign of 1917 which almost won them the war. Finally the Finnish attaché to the British Fleet gave his opinion: German ships and guns were qualitatively superior.

At this point the editor of the *Daily Express* stepped in to call for an inquiry: 'These statements cannot go unchallenged or unheeded. The truth is infinitely more important than naval reputations. If the British Fleet could have forced a decision, let us know. If our strategy was at fault, let the public be told.' This was rather the *Daily Mail* line than that of the *Daily Express*, which was described by the judicious Lord Morley as 'that huge engine for keeping discussion at a low level'.

Various experts sent their views to the *Express*. Commander Kenworthy (later Lord Strabolgi) asserted that the British Fleet had been, and still was, defective in its air-arm. Admiral Sir Reginald Bacon in reply disparaged the usefulness of aircraft to battleships. Vice-Admiral Sir Cecil Lambert held that von Tirpitz's statements were on the whole justified: British ships had been inadequately armoured against German naval shells The editor then again intervened, demanding whether errors in armament had now been made good. Nobody answered him, however, and the controversy faded into discussions of whether aircraft could sink battleships, and 'Is the Battleship Doomed?' This was the beginning of the 'debunking' era: the word 'debunk' being shortly afterwards introduced from the United States, meaning 'to remove the false glory from famous reputations'—especially war-time ones.

As international news brightened, domestic affairs took a turn for the worse. The movement which resulted in the General Strike of 1926 had been maturing for some time. Labour was irritated by the prospect of five years of Conservative rule, won by what seemed a dirty trick. The *Daily Herald*, which had not yet become the respectable organ of the T.U.C., had recently increased its circulation by railing against injustice, sneering at the dignified follies of the Law-and-Order party, and cheering on every strike in Great Britain and every 'fight for freedom' by the oppressed masses of the rest of the world. It never preached or countenanced violence, but was read earnestly by the more thoughtful and emotional worker and was largely responsible for a feeling that 'everyone' should, in the Utopia promised by science, literally mean everyone.

The housing shortage was still severe, the unemployment figures were high, and so was the cost of living. Then in July 1925 the Government subsidy to the coal industry came to an end. The mine-owners, in view of the continued low price of coal, gave notice that they intended to reduce wages, abolish the minimum-wage principle, and enforce longer hours. The Miners' Union and the T.U.C. took this as a challenge to declare the class-war that they had now heard so much loose talk about, chiefly from Conservative papers. They threatened a coal and railway strike if the mine-owners carried out their intentions. The Government thereupon appointed a commission under Mr. Justice Sankey to investigate industrial conditions; and meanwhile continued the subsidy. The Sankey Commission condemned subsidies, recommended that hours should be left as they were but that wages should be reduced, and proposed the collective selling of output and the closing of pits which did not pay their way. The mine-owners were constrained to accept this report. The miners rejected it with the slogan 'Not a minute on the day, not a penny off the pay', and were supported by a great number of other unions. The general feeling among working men was that Labour ought to show its gigantic combined power, for once: not to punish, or destroy, but just as a warning that there were certain things that it would not tolerate.

The Government then prepared to face the threatened general strike. An 'Organization for the Maintenance of Supplies' was formed, and volunteers were enlisted from the middle and upper classes. The Labour Party could not make up its mind what to do. Its official policy had been explained in a pamphlet, 'The I.L.P. and the Nation', published at the end of 1925: 'The Labour Party pursues a co-ordinated policy of National Reconstruction and reform which seeks, by Parliamentary means and progressive stages . . . to develop the material and mental resources of the nation.' And Ramsay MacDonald had declared that 'Socialism is the idea of the political state acting more and more in co-operation with the industrial state.' But this general strike thoroughly alarmed the Labour Party. Though it sympathized with the miners and, in fact, represented them in Parliament, yet to support them in a movement that might lead to the overthrow of parliamentary government seemed suicidal.

On April 26th the miners ceased work. Though the General Council of the T.U.C. declared that it would give them the fullest support, J. H. Thomas pleaded for moderation. 'To talk at this stage,' he said, 'as if in a few days all the workers of the country were to be called out, is . . . letting loose passions that might be difficult to control. . . . Instead of organizing, mobilizing and encouraging the feeling that war is inevitable, let them concentrate on finding a solution honourable and satisfactory to all sides.'

The Government, having completed its warlike preparations, rejected the last-minute offers of the miners' delegates. To start negotiations at this stage would seem like yielding to intimidation. The T.U.C. then announced a general strike for May 3rd, to include all workers except those engaged in public health services. The day was awaited like a prophesied End of the World.

It came. In London extraordinary things happened. All union labour went on strike. The Stock Exchange was feverish. Hyde Park was closed to the public and used as a milk depot. Troops were stationed in Whitehall, and employed in convoying food. Public transport ceased completely—trains, omnibuses, trams, even taxis. But non-union business carried on, and thousands of office workers who could not cycle, or get a lift in the crammed private cars, walked fifteen and twenty miles a day to and from suburbs. Many firms engaged rooms for their staffs in neighbouring hotels. The power plants were taken over by the Government, but illuminated signs were prohibited in order to conserve electricity supplies. Fog added to the confusion. Soon amateur train, tram, and bus drivers inaugurated a skeleton service. The material damage was considerable: it was not only that the strikers broke the windows of the 'scab' vehicles, but that the amateur drivers mishandled the engines from ignorance.

These were days of wild rumours, for the newspaper printers had come out on strike—even those of the *Daily Herald*. It was perhaps a tactical error on the part of the T.U.C. to allow the *Daily Herald* printers to come out, because the small daily sheet that they published themselves, *The British Worker*, could not compete against the news service of the Law-and-Order party. This included a Government broad-sheet, *The British Gazette*, run by Winston Churchill; the *Daily Mail*, which was now printed in Paris and flown over to England; other newspapers in very small format; and above all the B.B.C. The *Daily Herald* rummaged around for volunteer printers and managed to get out a daily quarter-sheet. The same news items, however, kept on appearing day after day. The headlines were: 'Justice for the Miners: Labour's one Aim'. 'If it be War, so be it'. 'Blame rests on Government'. 'Beware of the Wireless! The Government controls it!' And: 'Bishops call for Justice, Mercy and Humanity' —the Bishops of Winchester and Southwark had called for a further subsidy to the coal industry, because it was 'the very backbone of the body industrial'. Christian principles, they said, demanded further negotiations and not open strife. Unfortunately, for lack of space, the *Herald's* leading articles often broke off in the middle of sentences. The Bishops' appeal, for example, faded out with: 'from the human point of view. . . .'

The *Daily Mail* represented the extreme middle-class reaction to the strike. On May 3rd it came out with headlines: 'The Pistol at the Nation's Head', 'Great Menace to Free Press'. The editorial, headed 'For King and Country' (the *Daily Mail's* slogan), declared that 'A general strike is not an industrial dispute. It is a revolutionary movement intended to inflict suffering upon the great mass of innocent persons in the community and thereby to put possible constraint on the government. . . . This being so, it cannot be tolerated by any civilized government, and must be dealt with by every resource at the disposal of the community. . . . We do not wish to say anything hard about the miners. As to their leaders, all we need say at the moment is that some of them are (and have openly declared themselves) under the influence of people who mean no good to this country.' This last phrase was aimed particularly at the Miners' Union secretary, A. J. Cook, who was popularly supposed to be the reddest of Reds.

On March 5th, in a leader headed 'No Fumbling', the *Daily Mail* quoted Wordsworth:

> 'We must be free or die, who speak the tongue
> That Shakespeare spake: the faith and morals hold
> Which Milton held.'

And again, on March 6th:

> 'Tis well! from this day forward we shall know
> That in ourselves our safety must be sought:
> That by our own right hand it must be wrought,
> That we must stand unpropped or be laid low.
> O dastard, whom such foretaste doth not cheer!'

The well-to-do and the un-unionized lower-middle classes stood 'unpropped' fairly comfortably, with the help of emergency transport organizations, for the nine days that the strike lasted. They rallied to volunteer services as they had rallied during the war; for the B.B.C., which by now had about 2,000,000 regular listeners, and the Law-and-Order Press, were persuading them to stand firm and to 'do their bit'.

On May 8th Sir John Simon, former Attorney-General and

Home Secretary, then out of office, ventured to declare the General Strike illegal, on the ground that it was not covered by the Act of 1906 which rendered trade union funds immune from claims for damage caused by industrial disputes. Although Simon's declaration was immediately contested by some legal authorities, it startled and worried many trade union leaders. The unions had, at the start, been by no means united in agreement on their general policy, and MacDonald and Thomas had both declared themselves against the principle of a general strike. A rift was growing between the Miners' Union and the T.U.C. The miners had authorized the T.U.C. to act on their behalf only so long as it refused to consider wage reductions; but the T.U.C. was, in fact, already negotiating with the Government's unofficial representative, Sir Herbert Samuel, about wage reductions. When A. J. Cook, for the miners, demanded guarantees that the Government would carry out any agreement reached by Sir Herbert and the T.U.C., J. H. Thomas was reported as saying: 'You may not trust my word, but will you not accept the word of a British gentleman who has been Governor of Palestine?'

The Government was dealing successfully enough with the disorganization caused by the strike, the Labour leaders were wavering, the Samuel proposals seemed promising; the T.U.C. therefore called off the strike on May 13th. Nevertheless the dockers, printers, and transport workers remained out, in disgust, for five more days, and the miners for another six months. The *Daily Mail* headlined the end of the strike: 'Surrender of the Revolutionaries', 'A Triumph for the People', and declared more boldly than plausibly that Zinoviev had planned the strike in 1918 and that five hundred Soviet agents had fomented it. 'Dissolve the T.U.C.' 'Clear out the Soviets', the *Daily Mail* urged.

It was a great relief to get back to normal life, without bloodshed or starvation; but people in general wore a rather sheepish look, wondering what it had really all been about, for bus and tram conductors on their return were as polite and unwarlike as ever and even *Daily Mail* reporters had discovered no secret revolutionary arsenals.

The miners came off the worst. That summer many of them were reduced to a diet of home-grown lettuce and stolen mutton from the hills. The coming of winter gradually forced them back to work; groups of them sued separately for peace with the mine-owners. Numerous poorer pits closed down for good, and unemployment among miners was so widespread that during the next few years the population of South Wales alone decreased by 250,000: the more vigorous workers migrating to industries in other parts of the country, or to the Dominions.

The Trade Unions philosophically recognized that they had taken a beating; and their view was 'Never again!' They did not raise any strong objection when a new Trade Disputes Act, passed in 1927, illegalized the General Strike. They decided instead on a policy of co-operation with industrialists, and in September 1927 held parleys with a group headed by Lord Melchett, who directed the important new chemical industry. As a result, a National Industrial Council was formed, with a joint standing committee composed of Trade Union leaders and nominees of the Federation of British Industries and the National Conference of Employers. A great number of workers, however, remained discontented and suspicious. They believed that the Labour leaders had been bought and that the Unions would now be used as instruments not for protecting the workers but for dragooning them. A number of political idealists in the middle and upper classes were also disgusted with the way in which the Law-and-Order party had muddied the waters. The miners' case had been a strong one and the Conservatives seemed to be using a fiction of class-warfare to goad a decent and loyal people into insurrection. 'Talk about hanging the Kaiser! Parliament is full of little unhanged Kaisers!' This was how 'The Left' started: as a generous reaction against ungenerous reaction. But before long it came to include every sort of minority opinion in the country—the muddled, foolish and ill-conditioned as well as the young, healthy and hopeful.

The Left soon became internationally minded. The first cause that genuinely stirred their emotions was, strangely enough, not a 'European but an American one—the Sacco-Vanzetti affair of July—August 1927. These two men, 'Red' Italian immigrants, had in 1921 been sentenced to death for murder by a Massachusetts court. They were then allowed to live on from reprieve to reprieve, because it was generally realized that there had been a miscarriage of justice; yet the State Government did not wish to acknowledge its error, and Governor Fuller, who detested Reds, finally decided that no further appeal should be allowed. The drama of their fate was prolonged. The case was reviewed, the State Supreme Court denied the petitions; a new appeal, with the undertaking to provide fresh evidence, was rejected; the prisoners were removed to the death house in Charlestown prison. Liberal feeling in America was deeply stirred, the more so as Charlestown prison stood within the Bunker's Hill battle-field, sacred to the cause of popular freedom. An application was made to the Federal Supreme Court for a stay of execution; the men were taken out of the death house until the application should be considered. The Federal Supreme Court refused the stay of execution. 'Back to the Death House'. 'Final Appeal to President Coolidge'.

Meanwhile, in most countries of the world, agitation against this 'judicial murder' was being worked up. The Communist International first protested to the United States Government. There were demonstrations in Copenhagen, Berlin, Leipzig, Zurich, Rouen, Paris, Nice, Basle, Geneva, Athens, Tokyo, Helsinki, and many other cities, often with the use of bombs and revolvers, the United States Consulate or Embassy being the usual goal of the hostile crowds. In Britain the first protest was made by the Bristol branch of the Communist Party; but early in August the Independent Labour Party also took up the cause and addressed a telegram of appeal to the President. On August 8th the Communists demonstrated in Trafalgar Square and marched in procession to the United States Embassy. The police dispersed them, made arrests, and secured exemplary prosecutions. Finally, the Trades Union Congress also roused itself and sent a stern telegram to Governor Fuller. Demonstrations were held in every important city and town in Britain. The largest took place in Hyde Park on August 22nd. Perhaps 200,000 people attended and speeches were made from several platforms. The Park was thick with mounted police waiting amongst the trees to charge down on the unarmed crowds should they attempt any breach of the peace. However, the general mood was one of sympathetic agony, not bellicose ardour.

President Coolidge rejected the appeal and the men were executed on August 23rd. The physical shock of horror that the news brought to millions of anxious homes cannot be readily conveyed. There was nothing like it throughout the period. On the evening after the execution a Memorial gathering was held in Hyde Park. The mounted police had orders to take action at the slightest sign of disorder in the crowd, which was large, sorrowful, and orderly. Vanzetti's noble message of farewell drew sobs and groans when it was read out.

The *Daily Express* reported next morning that twenty people, including four women, were injured. 'At the close of the proceedings the crowds were dispersing after the meeting when somebody suddenly started singing the 'Red Flag'. Hundreds of people cheered and joined in, while uttering threats against the police. The police charged and split up the crowd.' The *Daily Express* felt itself bound to disregard the matter editorially, for the police action was generally felt to have been wantonly aggressive. But the *New Statesman* commented:

'Hundreds of thousands of people all over the world must have greeted the news of the actual deaths of Sacco and Vanzetti with a deep sigh of relief. We can at least be sure that, innocent or guilty, their seven years of suffering and suspense are now ended. The whole episode has been barbarous from beginning to end. It is impossible to imagine its having happened in any fully civilized country—in any country, that is to say, in which civilization is more than skin-deep. They ought, at the very least—to have been granted a fresh trial. So much justice, indeed, they might confidently have expected in, say, Moscow, or Belgrade, or Constantinople. In all respects the behaviour of the Massachusetts Court has been abominable and inexcusable. Their system of justice is their own affair, but if their methods lead to trouble in London, we are certainly entitled to complain. There is grotesque irony in the fact that the killing of these two Italians involved in the U.S. a display of armed force such as no American citizen has ever before seen, and in every European country a police mobilization costing huge sums of money.'

Further grotesque irony lay in the close agreement of the Communist Party, the I.L.P., the T.U.C., and the Radicals on this and other foreign issues, but seldom or never on domestic ones. The most unfortunate result of the affair was that the United States, already regarded with suspicion and jealousy, as having 'enriched itself at the expense of Europe', and with contempt for its toleration of gangsters and non-enforcement of Prohibition, became the object of popular execration in Britain as 'the new home of tyranny'. This ill-feeling did not subside until the Roosevelt administration, and was constantly fomented by fresh accounts of 'American barbarity'—the Mooney case, the Scottsboro' case, Southern lynchings, and bloody strike-breakings in Pennsylvania and West Virginia.

CHAPTER ELEVEN

Domestic Life

By 1923 building materials had cheapened and the Government subsidies granted to Urban and Rural District Councils
were tempting enough to set the housing boom gradually in
motion. This boom, which kept a great many trades occupied
and benefited the workers themselves by giving them comfortable homes to live in, took another five years to get well under
way; but was a great steadying factor in national life. Builders
of houses had to conform to certain specifications of size, airiness
and convenience before they could earn the subsidy, and the
sites had to be approved by the district surveyor; the result was
a great improvement in the general health of the nation, a
remarkable decrease in infant mortality, and the elevation of
slum-dwellers to lower-middle class rank by virtue of such
amenities as gas, electricity, bathroom, and water-closet. The
Conservative papers joked at first about the uses to which these
unfamiliar baths would be put, but on the whole the filthy
habits of the slums were left behind with the foul air and bugs
and the communal earth-closet. Ruffianism in crowded trains
and buses, at places of public entertainment, and in public-
houses, grew most exceptional and if ever it occurred was likely
to be put down at once by some strong-armed champion of
popular opinion—usually an ex-Serviceman. For the habits of
discipline and cleanliness learned in the Army and Navy had
contributed largely to this improvement in public behaviour.
Another main cause was a new-found pride of the younger
women, who wished everything to conform in cleanliness and
respectability to their new domestic standards.

Since London clay, unlike Manhattan Island rock, would not support skyscrapers, a limit was set by the L.C.C. to the height of buildings (it is said that it was first imposed to placate Queen Victoria's fury at having her view of Westminster blocked by the erection of Queen Anne's Mansions). London expanded outwards rather than upwards. In any case, a suburban detached or semi-detached house, with the front door on ground level, and a bit of garden, was what the working classes generally preferred to tenement-flats in the city. Huge housing estates were developed, and new 'dormitory suburbs' created by the extension of the Underground and Metropolitan railway systems. The first large extension was in the autumn of 1923, when the Hampstead line was continued from Golders Green as far as Hendon. Sir Philip Lloyd-Graeme, afterwards Lord Swinton, President of the Board of Trade, officially opened the new line by switching on the current with a golden key. His ten-year-old son, wearing a bowler hat, drove the first train, which contained only transport officials, through to Hendon. In 1926 the *Daily Express* headlined the question: 'What will London be like in 1930? How soon will the population reach the ten-million mark?' The Morden Underground extension was to be opened that midsummer, and the Southern Railway had recently electrified more local lines. In Morden it was calculated that there was room for eight thousand houses and twenty-five thousand people. Land that three or four years earlier had been sold at £380 an acre was now worth £1,500.

There were similar developments at Edgware. The Underground advertised: 'Stake your Claim at Edgware. Omar Khayyam's recipe for turning the wilderness into paradise hardly fits an English climate, but provision has been made at Edgware of an alternative recipe which at least will convert pleasant, undulating fields into happy homes. The loaf of bread, the jug of wine and the book of verse may be got there cheaply and easily, and, apart from what is said by the illustration, a shelter which comprises all the latest labour-saving and sanitary conveniences. We moderns ask much more before we are content than the ancients, and Edgware is designed to give us that much more.'

The loaf of bread, the jug of wine and the book of verse were to be obtained from multiple stores which purchased the new shops erected on these estates. These shops were designed to have plenty of depth, though not the cosy back parlours which small traders liked; they were bought up by W. H. Smith's the newsagents, International Stores and Sainsbury's the grocers, Dewhurst's the butchers, The Victoria Wine Company, Lord Leverhulme's immense fish-retailing system, Mac Fisheries, the Express and United Dairy Companies, Burton's and Meaker's the ready-made tailors, the Times Furnishing Company, the Co-operatives, Woolworth's, Marks & Spencer's, the British Home Stores. There was usually a bank and occasionally a branch of one of the Building Societies (which advanced money to the middle classes to buy these estate houses and would also help them to buy and recondition approved old houses), seldom a church or chapel. The roads on the new estates were furnished by the builders: when first made, they looked all that roads should be, but by the time that the houses had been built, and the local Councils took them over, they were usually full of holes and ruts.

Most of the houses put up were of red brick, and the prospective tenants thought the designs 'ever so pretty'. The problem of the architect was how on a limited expenditure he could give what was called 'individuality' or 'personality' to a house. People did not care to live in oblong boxes, like the old yellow-brick slum houses, and wanted something 'different from the ordinary', with pebbledash, half-timbering, ridge-tiling and unexpected minor features. The houses they were given were not quite so grotesque as the French seaside villas built at the same time—the French likewise wanted personality or 'cachet'. There was no bright blue paint, no Moorish arabesques and coloured tiles: but a tendency to mock-Tudor exteriors. Yet the cost of houses still had to be kept down to estimate: so on a suburban road one could often pass sixteen or seventeen new £1,000 dwellings, each not bad in itself but all precisely alike in their difference from the ordinary—the same unexpected feature of round stair-window, finacled porch, or rough-elm-boarded garage appearing in 'Rosslyn', 'The Elms', 'Mon Abri', 'Waratah', 'Orillia', 'Haytor', 'Treen','Bryn Newydd', and all the rest. These were the houses of people with incomes of £5–£10 a week.

At a later stage the customers of the speculative builder insisted on their houses being not merely distinctive but unlike those of their immediate neighbours. The best contemporary studies of architecture are Osbert Lancaster's *Progress at Pelvis Bay*, a satiric account of the architectural degeneration of a seaside town, and his *Pillar to Post, the Pocket Lamp of Architecture*, both illustrated by himself. In the latter, after giving the characteristics and social explanation of a variety of modern styles, he comes to 'By-Pass Variegated'.

'As one passes by, one can amuse one's self by classifying the various contributions which past styles have made to this infernal amalgam; here are some quaint gables culled from Art Nouveau surmounting a façade that is plainly Modernistic in inspiration; there the twisted beams and leaded panes of Stockbroker's Tudor are happily contrasted with bright green tiles of obviously Pseudish origin; next door some terra-cotta plaques, Pont Street Dutch in character, enliven a white wood Wimbledon Transitional porch, making it a splendid foil to a red-brick garage that is vaguely Romanesque in feeling. But while he is heavily indebted to history for the majority of his decorative and structural details (in almost every case the worst features of the style from which they were filched), in the planning and disposition of his erections the speculative builder displays a genius that is all his own. Notice the skill with which the houses are disposed, that insures that the largest possible area of countryside is ruined with the minimum of expense; see how carefully each householder is provided with a clear view into the most private offices of his next-door neighbour and with what studied disregard of the sun's aspect the principal rooms are planned.

'It is sad to reflect that so much ingenuity should have been wasted on streets and estates which will inevitably become the slums of the future. That is, if a fearful and more sudden fate does not obliterate them prematurely; an eventuality that does much to reconcile one to the prospect of aerial bombardment.'

The poorer classes were given less fanciness in the Council houses; and the new barrack-like tenements built in the cities under the slum-clearance schemes were spared the 'gorblimey' trimmings of Portland stone which decorated the middle-class and luxury flats. Lancaster remarked: 'They look like pickle factories, but quite good pickle factories.' One great blessing of the tenements was that they were provided with wide paved courts where the children could safely play; and another was that, unlike the luxury flats, they were built away from the main streams of traffic and were peaceful enough. Curious class-distinctions were observed in the nomenclature of these new buildings. Working-class flats formed 'tenements', and were usually named 'So-and-So Buildings'; whereas middle-class and luxury flats formed 'blocks', and were usually 'So-and-So Court' or 'House' or 'Close'. Neither type, however, could compare in comfort with the new German or Austrian flats: there were few balconies, and these too small for family use, and little storage room on the ground floors, even for prams and bicycles. The classes were, indeed, being increasingly separated by the lay-outs of new estates. The Town-Planning Act of 1932 perpetuated this cleavage. Until mid-Victorian days there had been a mixed development of new houses, but now there was 'zoning'—whole districts were to be developed at the scale of one house to the acre, eight to the acre, or twelve to the acre, thus inevitably segregating families according to their incomes.

The most remarkable outward change of the Twenties was in the looks of women in the towns. The prematurely aged wife was coming to be the exception rather than the rule. Children were fewer and healthier and gave less trouble; labour-saving devices were introduced, especially for washing, cleaning, and cooking —the introduction of stainless plate and cutlery saved an appreciable amount of time daily and this was only one of a hundred such innovations. Provisioning also had become very much easier. The advertising of branded goods was simplifying shopping problems. Housewives came to count on certain brands of goods, which advertisers never allowed them to forget. The manufacturers' motto was: 'Swear not by the moon, the inconstant moon, but swear by constant advertising.' They made things very easy for the housewives by selling their foods in the nearest possible stage to table-readiness: the complicated processes of making custard, caramel, blanc-mange, jelly, and other puddings and sweets, were reduced to a single short operation by the use of prepared powders. Porridge had once been the almost universal middle-class breakfast food. It now no longer took twenty minutes to cook, Quick Quaker Oats reducing the time to two; but even so, cereals in the American style, eaten with milk, began to challenge porridge and bacon and eggs in prosperous homes, and the bread and margarine eaten by the poor. At first the only choice was Force and Grape-Nuts; but soon there was a bewildering variety of different 'flakes'; and grains of rice, wheat and barley 'puffed' by being fired at high velocity from a sort of airgun. Bottled and tinned goods grew more and more various and plentiful. When the war ended the only choice was soup, salmon, corned beef, Californian fruits, and potted meat; but by the Thirties almost every kind of domestic and foreign fruit, meat, game, fish, vegetable could be bought, even in country groceries. Foodstuffs that needed no tin-opener were also gradually standardized: eggs, milk, and butter were graded and guaranteed and greengrocers began selling branded oranges and bananas. Housewives could send or ring up for goods without inspecting them, more and more shops called daily or weekly for orders and delivered free of charge, as light commercial vans displaced the horse and cart. The fish-van brought fresh fish to the door even in inland towns and villages. The cleanest and neatest shops secured the best custom; flies and wasps disappeared from grocers' counters, finding no open pots of treacle or boxes of sugar to attract them, and the butchers began keeping their carcases in refrigerators out of sight, not suspended bleeding from hooks in the full glare of the sun. By the Thirties cellophane, a cheap wood-pulp product, was coming into general use for keeping dry groceries and cigarettes fresh and clean, and soon also covered baskets of strawberries, lumps of dates, and even kippers and other cured fish.

Woolworth's stores were the great cheap providers of household utensils and materials. There had been a few '6½d. Bazaars' before the war, but the Woolworth system was altogether new. It worked by small profits and quick returns in a huge variety of classified and displayed cut-price goods; some, such as excellent glass and hardware, were even sold below cost price to attract custom. The *Daily Herald* reported in 1924 that the T.U.C. was reviewing complaints about working conditions in Woolworth's—'the well-known bazaar-owners'—and that this was the more serious because the stores were patronized chiefly by the working class. But the firm never had any difficulty in engaging unskilled sales-girls at a low wage; for 'the local Woolworth's' was increasingly the focus of popular life in most small towns. And the name of Woolworth was a blessed one to the general public; wherever a new branch was opened, the prices of ironmongers, drapers, and household furnishers in the neighbourhood would drop twopence in the shilling. The middle class at first affected to despise Woolworth's goods, but they soon caught the working-class habit and would exclaim brightly among themselves: 'My dear—guess where I got this amazing object—threepence at Maison Woolworth! I don't know *how* they do it.'

Woolworth's, the Building Societies, and the Instalment System made it financially possible for people of small means to take over new houses. The instalment or 'never-never' system was being applied to all major household purchases, such as furniture, sewing-machines, vacuum-cleaners, gas-ovens, wireless sets. A *Punch* illustration showed a young mother, watching her husband writing out the monthly cheque to pay off the maternity-home debt: 'Darling, only one more instalment and Baby will be *ours*.'

The *Daily Mail* greatly assisted in the general improvement of living by its succession of Ideal Home Exhibitions. The British Empire Exhibition of 1924 at Wembley did the same thing in a more grandiose way; it was intended as much for enlarging the domestic market as for encouraging the export trade. The exhibition was advertised as 'deriving its interest from its intense realism'. The public found, in the first weeks after its official opening by the King, that the roads between the pavilions— named by Rudyard Kipling 'Anson's Way', 'Drake's Way', 'Commonwealth Way', and so on—were as muddy as country lanes. Kiwi Boot Polish patriotically advertised: 'Wembley Mud Exaggerated. A little dirt is certainly not going to deter Britishers from seeing this epoch-making exhibition—use Kiwi.' As entertainment the exhibition was a great success. The Queen's Doll's House, full of miniature wonders, all done to exact scale, brought in £20,000 for charity. It greatly endeared the Queen to the country, and the King too, who was reported to have roared with laughter at a tiny tin of Colman's mustard on the pantry shelf. Also there was a complete Gold Coast village set up, on the model of the 'Assuan' and 'Hairy Ainu' villages at the old Earl's Court permanent exhibition. The Empire Pageant, depicting life in different parts of the Empire, past and present, sometimes drew 25,000 people at a time. The military tattoo included a reproduction of the Battle of Balaclava, and air-raids started conflagrations that efficient firemen immediately put out. The Amusement Park proprietors did very well—the Great Dipper was the steepest switch-back railway ever seen in England, and there were flip-flaps, a cake-walk, or rocking-platform, and all the latest American Luna Park thrills. But financially the exhibition was a heavy failure, as almost every such national exhibition had been since Prince Albert's successful Great Exhibition of 1851.

The great change in women's clothes in the Twenties was mainly due to the development of the artificial silk industry. Rayon (as it was first officially called in 1927) was light, warm and cheap, and took bright colours well. By its use, the weight of clothes that a woman carried was reduced from pounds to ounces and the amount of material for a complete costume from nineteen yards to seven. Underclothes, blouses, dresses, stockings, scarves—all were soon rayon.

Since rayon was not very durable, new clothes were bought more frequently; which shortened the time-lag in fashions between their sale to the well-to-do and their adoption by the poor. It was now at last possible to mistake working girls for titled ladies, if one judged by dress; and since educated speech was a valuable asset in business, and the B.B.C. taught it free, as time went on one could not always judge even by the voice. The American habit of buying cheap mass-produced goods for short use was a novel one to the British: it was gradually extended from clothes to shoes, handbags, and household goods. If the old-fashioned shop assistants still mumbled 'I can guarantee this—it will last a lifetime', the modern come-back was 'Then for goodness' sake show me something else!'

The general outline of women's dress did not change much in these years, though there was constant variation of trimmings and draperies attached to blouses and skirts; sometimes blouses had square necks instead of pointed ones, and there were fashions in waistcoats and 'different' jackets. Each season brought in a 'new colour', meaning a new name for a hitherto unfashionable shade. The Twenties showed great bravado in names—'Yes, modom, we stock it in all the new shades: Mud, Nigger, Rust, Gunmetal, Old Boots, Dust, and Self.'

By 1925 the skirt, after a temporary drop in 1922–3 to just above the ankles, had receded to just below the knees even for women of sixty and seventy, and in 1926 the knee-caps were often free and there was a glint of knickers. Yet bathing-dresses remained modest, with high necks and long sleeves, and after bathing one either wore a wrap or got dressed again. To play tennis without stockings was considered immodest; and as late as 1923 the Underground refused advertisement-space to a French film showing girls wearing backless evening-dresses. In the following year the employers of Birmingham waitresses started a 'morality crusade', forbidding their staff to wear short skirts at all.

Short hair did not come into fashion among the well-to-do until 1923, when it was reported that 'many men are wearing their hair long and permed at Deauville while women are almost all "shingled", as the Americans call the new, very ugly bobbed and shaved haircut.' Newspapers mistook this for a passing fashion only and came out with comments such as 'Bobbed Hair and Bobbed Love', 'Shingle's Blow to Marriage'. But the 'bob', 'shingle', and 'bingle' were succeeded in 1926 by the boyish 'Eton crop'. Heavy make-up was not yet practised. In 1922 the first Elizabeth Arden advertisements appeared, but they were only for powder and eye-lash dye.

Men's fashions changed far more slowly. Most men still wore shirts with detachable hard collars; the soft collar was only sported by motor-salesmen and similarly advanced business men. Flannel trousers and plus-fours—loose golfing knicker-bockers first recorded in 1920 at Oxford—were only for holiday wear. But the heat-wave of 1923 popularized tussore and other light materials and M.P.s dared to appear in the House in something less stuffy than their official black and grey. Mr. John Hodge made Parliamentary history by turning up in a lemon-coloured shantung suit, cream socks, and a panama hat.

The immediately post-war interior of a well-to-do sitting-room was something of this sort. Walls of soft bluish-grey distemper—wallpaper had gone out during the war-time paper short-age, and had not yet returned—with, above, a low white picture-rail and a dado of faintly blurred lilacs in their natural colours of white and mauve, white woodwork and mantelpiece, a fireplace with pale green tiles and a curb of polished steel, a pale green carpet, lilac-patterned cretonne chair-covers, curtains of lilac-coloured silk, and on the walls water-colours framed in dull silver. The furniture was pseudo-Jacobean. This cool effect was disturbed in 1919 with cushions and hangings in startling 'jazz' patterns—influenced by Russian Ballet décor—'futuristic' lamp shades, huge ridiculous ornaments to make guests laugh, and a general clutter of 'souvenirs'. In 1922 came a swing back to sobriety: the mantelpieces and walls grew less encumbered, and jazz-colours were succeeded by pale apple-greens, lemon-yellows, and soft blues. The 'arty people' were proving their artistic seriousness by designing their own cushion-covers and curtains, usually using balloon-silk remaindered after the war. They dyed it by the Javanese batik method, which was to cover with melted wax the parts of the silk not intended to take the dye. 'Good batik is a joy,' the *Daily Mail* approved. In 1923 came the magpie school of decoration—white walls and woodwork, black curtains, black-and-white squared carpet. Then a coloured-check period; after which it is difficult to trace any period at all, because 'interior decoration' had been discovered as an art. This meant the exercise of ingenuity in a combination of unusual woods, paints, fabrics, and bric-à-brac to express the personality of the owner of the room or the purpose for which it was intended: on the lines of the Continental painting fashion of *collage*—sticking odds and ends to the canvases to enhance an atmosphere. Numbers of interior decorators made large incomes by collecting odd and useless junk from antique shops and giving it a new life in modernistic sitting-rooms in combination with stainless steel, white paint, and plaster imitations of serpentine or malachite. Then 'everyone' became his own interior decorator.

This was the age of disguise. Since large houses had given way to flats, space had to be greatly economized and furniture now had a trick of folding away into nothing—or revealing unexpected secondary uses. It was not only a sofa that turned into a bed, but a shelf-full of standard poets was also a telephone-container, an easy-chair incorporated a cocktail-bar, a decorative screen opened out into a bridge table. 'You never could have guessed if I hadn't shown you.' Old period pieces were 'vandalized', as the antique dealers called it, by being converted to modern uses: a William-and-Mary commode would be gutted to house a gramophone and records; a Georgian sewing-box repartitioned for cigarettes. In 'Stockbroker's Tudor' houses, as Osbert Lancaster noted, exceptional ingenuity was displayed in olde-worlde disguise for interior fittings: 'Electrically produced heat warmed the hands of those who clustered round the yule-logs burning so prettily in the vast hearth; the light that showed so cosily from the old horn-lantern was obtained from the grid; from the depths of some old iron chest were audible the dulcet tones of Mr. Bing Crosby.'

To save tablecloths, polished tables and mats were used. White painted wooden twin-beds replaced the old mahogany or brass double-bed for married couples. It was the time of glass-topped dressing-tables: buoyant imitation-leather chairs; chromium-plate and glass bathroom appliances; miraculously organized kitchen-cupboards with white enamel fittings; lamps and lamp-shades of degenerately seductive style.

The British motor-car industry had been stimulated by the import duties on American cars and by the system of taxing car-licences according to horse-power—for American cars were in general more powerfully engined than the new British models. The British were suspicious of speed and quick acceleration. In fact, a recurring newspaper theme throughout the early Twenties was an attack on motorists as 'road-hogs'. Roads in some parts of England were indeed thoroughly unsafe for motor traffic—narrow places, banks and hedges concealing turnings, bottle-necks, restive horses, unattended railway crossings.

The Austin advertisements of 1919 had been headed with the word *Distinction*! 'Everything about the new Austin 20 is distinctive and high-class, the graceful streamline from the radiator to the back of the body, unbroken by a flapping, bulging hood, is a feature not to be found in any other car.' For the aeronautical word 'streamline' was already applied early in the Twenties to other objects than planes and airship-gondolas—in this case to open cars. The use of streamlining as a modern style in domestic objects such as electric irons, floor-polishers, and prams, followed in the middle Thirties. The Ford 'Tin Lizzie' was the greatest rival to the popular British family four-seater: even with the tax it was still the least expensive, and though much derided on account of its undistinctive shape—box-like body and diminutive bonnet—was recognized, by country drivers especially, as the most serviceable. It was now manufactured in England, seventy per cent of the parts being shipped over from what were termed 'mammoth factories' in the United States and Canada. But by 1923 British manufacturers were also using mass-production methods, and though music-hall jokes of the Harry Tate 'Motoring' type were still as popular as ever, the performance of cars was becoming reasonably trustworthy: one seldom saw a car drawn up at the side of the road with the boots of the driver sticking out from underneath as he tinkered away with screwdriver and spanner. Soon the Morris-Cowley and Morris-Oxford family cars ousted the Ford. In 1923 cord-fabric was first used as a component of tyres, prolonging their lives by five thousand miles. Four-wheel brakes were also introduced, and superchargers to improve acceleration. By 1924 the increasing use of cars by week-enders brought the Baby Car into the market. The 'Austin Seven' cost £165. It was described as 'The Mighty Miniature', but the popular name was 'The Bed Pan'. Then came the solid-tyred Trojan four-seater at £125, and the Morris Minor.

The many small firms among which British motor-production had been divided were now beginning to amalgamate. Humber, Hillman and Commer, for example, amalgamated in 1929, with Rootes as their distributing agents. This grouping tendency, and the disappearance of many small firms, such as Cubitt's, AC, and Angus-Sanderson, were due to the pressure of mass-production. It was not only the lower price of the mass-produced car that recommended it, but the readiness with which spare parts could be supplied—a car of obscure make which met with a slight accident in some distant country spot might have to wait days and even weeks before the appropriate spare part could be found and fitted. Technical improvements in bodies and engines meanwhile continued, but in small, barely perceptible ways, as in film production. The 1913 25-h.p. Talbot, the first to exceed one hundred miles an hour, was still considered a wonder of engineering, for a recently constructed 300-h.p. Fiat had failed to reach two hundred miles an hour, although its engine was twelve times more powerful. The gearless car and other equally revolutionary productions were constantly prophesied, but never arrived.

Scores of thousands of new drivers, who were given no preliminary tests, brought road accidents into the news. There was hopeful talk of great new road-planning schemes; but for a long time the authorities concentrated on widening and rectifying old roads rather than building new. The Automobile Association and the Royal Automobile Club co-operated by putting up numerous warning signs and providing 'scouts' as extra traffic-policemen on difficult cross-roads. Country people grew to hate cars, for their noise, smell, danger, and the unconcerned bearing of the drivers, and often encouraged children to pelt them with stones and line the road with glass and upturned tacks to cause punctures. A new division of Britain took place: Motorists and Pedestrians. In most country places the magistrates were at first pedestrians, and imposed heavy fines for the slightest offences. Their view was that motoring was still not so much a means of transport, as a dangerous form of sport. Motor-traps, of police-men with stopwatches, were laid on long, straight, clear roads where motorists might be tempted to exceed the local speed-limit; and, since the limit in some districts was fifteen and even ten miles an hour, the courts were crowded. Godalming Bench was the most notoriously pedestrian-minded of all.

Parking was a great problem—there were not enough car-parks in any of the big cities—and traffic jams were another. These often lasted twenty minutes and sometimes half an hour; for there was no central control, and a complicated crossing like Piccadilly Circus was managed by several policemen at once. Point-duty and a watch on motorists' offences were engrossing the attention of the constabulary almost to the exclusion of all other social services. Though hundreds of policemen were em-ployed on the Derby course and its approaches in 1928, the forty thousand cars that appeared caused jams that took hours to sort out. 'Safety First' campaigns started in the Press. Pedes-trians were advised not to cross roads between meeting trams, not to stoop to pick up parcels in the streets, and not to read newspapers when crossing roads. But the only new traffic regu-lation adopted in the cities was to limit side-streets in busy areas to one-way traffic.

Buses began to run on new traffic routes: as London and other cities spread out, so the local buses extended their itineraries. Covered-in buses were now the rule; fresh-air lovers complained, forgetting the misery of an upper deck on a cold, rainy, windy day. Pneumatic tyres were also replacing solid ones. A new sort of bus-service began—the long-distance charabanc which chal-lenged the railway for speed and comfort, and even made night journeys from the north and west of England to London. It was the charabanc that opened up rural districts of the Midlands and East Anglia which were still almost inaccessible by rail. This new development greatly vexed the railways; and also the local authorities through whose districts the charabancs pounded their non-stop way—because the cost of keeping the roads in repair fell less on the charabanc companies than on ratepayers who did not directly benefit by the service.

The public soon realized that old-established omnibus companies were only private concerns after all. The scarlet of the London General Omnibuses, which suggested pillar-boxes, Post Office vans, Guards uniforms, and other unchallengeable public institutions, did not protect them from competition by small bus companies and even one-man-one-bus concerns. Not only did private buses—some scarlet, some green, some blue—start competing with 'Generals' over the same routes, but they also reduced fares. There was a startling case of 'General versus Admiral'. An 'Admiral' bus from Southgate to Wood Green was approaching its terminus at Garage Road, when a 'General' inspector on the far side of the road gave a signal, and a 'General' bus shot out from a concealed turning. A collision was narrowly avoided by the good driving of both drivers. The passengers on board the 'Admiral' felt strongly enough about the rights of private buses to call the police and take action. At court the defendant driver was charged by the 'Admirals' with being an 'extra turn': especially employed to chase 'Admirals' and get to the bus-stops before them. He was cautioned and fined £10 for dangerous driving, the magistrate observing that the fault lay not with him but with those 'Generals' who gave the inspector orders to signal him on.

The cheap car and the new bus-services brought about a development of the housing industry: ribbon-building. This meant stringing houses along main roads instead of building them in compact village-like masses. For the tenants, the advantage was obvious: they had direct access to the road, and they got an uninterrupted country view from their back windows. But it spoilt the roads for travellers, who saw only the houses and, in gaps between houses, advertisements of Desirable Building Sites, and of Petrol and Motor Oil. Stanley Baldwin in a speech at Winchester in July 1928 warned: 'It is no exaggeration to say that in fifty years at the rate so-called improvements are being made, the destruction of all the beauty and charm with which our ancestors enhanced their towns and villages will be complete.' Yet steps were already being taken to avoid the worst outrages. The National Trust was buying estates in different parts of the country, in order to save them for the nation, and several special bodies, such as the Oxford Preservation Trust, came into existence. Even local councils sometimes discovered a conscience: in 1928, for instance, the Mid-Surrey Town-Planning Council saved the commons in the Dorking-Reigate region from being sacrificed to road-makers and speculative builders. And the larger petrol firms, such as Shell and B.P., won public applause and saved themselves a great deal of money by agreeing to support the 'preservation of the countryside' movement: they took down most of their competitive roadside hoardings.

The countryside was going through a difficult time. Some farmers had made a great deal of money during the war by selling fodder to the Army during a fodder shortage, and potatoes during a potato shortage, and recklessly ploughing up pastures which should never have been disturbed. They used cheap female labour, and neglected ditching and draining. Extravagant stories went around of farmers wintering in 1919 on the French Riviera: actually, most of those that did not bank their savings against bad seasons ahead were tenant-farmers who were now forced to buy their holdings—the landlords were selling up because of the heavy land-tax—if they did not wish to leave them altogether. Many raised part of their purchase money by mortgages, and when after the slump of 1921 farms hugely depreciated in value, the interest on mortgages still had to be paid. Also, the prices of farm-produce fell seriously twice: in 1921 and in 1929. Farmers were also complaining of the extra cost of labour, caused by the minimum wage regulations, and the scarcity of good men. This burden would have been offset by the various Government reliefs and subsidies had British farmers been quicker at learning new ways; but many of them were better ploughmen or veterinarians than accountants or chemists, and slow to combine together for co-operative buying and marketing—as the Irish and Danes had done so successfully—and slower still to develop new markets. The situation was complicated by large numbers of 'slut farmers'—men with sufficient private means not to worry about making their farms pay. They left their fields to get full of thistles and even thorn-bushes, which provided cover for game; and found rough shooting far more fun than uneconomic farmwork. However, the Government did what it could to teach those who wished to learn, the B.B.C. being of great assistance; and toward the end of the Twenties, tractors, which had been tried during the war but largely abandoned because of their mechanical defects, came in again with better models. A few farms in East Anglia and in Hampshire were wholly mechanized and produced cereals at a very low cost—even by comparison with the farms of Canada and Australia.

The general tendency was away from arable farming. Between 1919 and 1939 more than three million acres passed out of cultivation, in spite of the great increase in sugar-beet growing, which was encouraged by Government subsidy. Farmers went in for livestock, instead, chiefly because they were unable to compete with cheap Australian and Canadian wheat. The largest demand for British wheat was for biscuit-making, for which it was particularly suitable. Market gardening also increased, to meet the needs of the canning industry. Before the war most tinned vegetables and fruits came from America, but by the end of the Thirties the greater part of the trade—except for citrus fruits, pineapples, and peaches—was British. Peas became the most important vegetable crop, and raspberries, loganberries, strawberries, and plums the chief fruits. A great deal of market gardening was done on small holdings. Sixteen thousand of these were created after the war, and twenty-four thousand ex-Servicemen settled on them. By 1926 a quarter of these had left. Small holdings really were uneconomic, but the system was kept alive by the willingness of the holders to pay for their independence by long hours of hard labour. By the end of the period agricultural workers had decreased by 250,000.

Another trouble which beset British farming was the spread of foot-and-mouth disease from the Continent. This was especially serious at a time when more and more farmers were taking up livestock farming. Outbreaks of foot-and-mouth occurred in 1922, 1923, 1924, and 1926, and cost the country over £3,000,000 paid in compensation for the compulsory slaughter of the infected cattle. The compensation did not differentiate between pedigree and ordinary stock, so that the loss in actual wealth was even greater than this. In 1926 importations of livestock from the Continent were temporarily forbidden, and thereafter strictly controlled. In spite of much research, practical means of relief remained undiscovered: slaughter of the sick beasts, quarantine of the rest, orders against the conveyance of infected straw and fodder were the only palliatives known.

In the areas around towns and cities, especially London, much farming land was being used up by the extension of housing estates. The problem of housing agricultural workers was everywhere a difficult one. Old cottages were being condemned by sanitary authorities, very few new ones being built, and the agricultural labourer on his meagre pay—only 30s. in some parts of East Anglia—could not compete with the week-ender from town for the possession of any cottage that fell empty. Cottage rents before the war had varied from half a crown weekly to five shillings: by the middle Twenties a cottage at even ten shillings a week was a rarity, unless in a district where company water, sewerage, gas, and electricity had not yet penetrated.

There was strangely little difference between the food of the lower-grade industrial and agricultural workers: the main meal in either case was supper, consisting of strong tea, bread and margarine, tinned salmon or sardines—if this could be afforded —otherwise, fish and meat pastes. The bread was bleached white bread, which lacked the hearty consistence of the old stone-ground whole-meal loaf that had been the traditional food of the British labouring classes. In the country, as a rule, only one hot midday meal was cooked a week, on Sundays: otherwise it was bread and cheese, with pickles. This was partly due to the high price of coal in many country districts and to a lack of wood. The poor man seldom had scraps enough to fatten a pig; and if he happened to have enough, he first had to get permission from the sanitary inspector to erect a pig-stye; which, for sanitary reasons, was only granted when there were no neighbours to complain of the smell, noise, etc.—besides, the building of an 'approved' pig-stye was no cheap matter. Compulsory education also kept his children from herding geese along the roadsides. Cottagers tended to grow flowers in their small gardens rather than vegetables, and wild salads such as dandelion and watercress were no longer gathered, nor country wines bottled. Sir William Beach Thomas, writing in the *Spectator* in July 1927, reported the complaints of a farmer against the mania for tinned food: ' "Two-thirds of our people," he maintained, "consume not fresh but tinned milk, as well as much other tinned food (as you could infer ocularly from the village dump)". He would prohibit or heavily tax this tinned milk for the sake of national health, not less than for the good of the farming community. A taste for fresh home-grown food is essential for the physical welfare of our people.'

This farmer had evidently been reading about vitamins which, though discovered by C. Funk in 1912, were not taken up popularly until the early Twenties. Before this, people in general had known a little about such food constituents as proteins and carbo-hydrates. And 'calories' as a measure of the energy-results of food were as old as the Boer War—the *Westminster Gazette* had calculated in 1901 that soldiers must have at least 3,500 calories daily in their ration. The *Daily Herald* in its protest in 1921 against the diet to which dockers were reduced still reckoned in terms of calories. But when vitamins came into fashion, they ousted all these elder terms; and since the scientists could not pretend to know exactly what they were, chemically speaking, but had established that their absence caused deficiency diseases, a number of health foods were launched which claimed to contain them. There had been health-addicts for many years—even Eustace Miles–Bernard Shaw vegetarianism was as old as Shelley's day—but the special Health Food Shops which flourished between 1923 and 1934 and sold exotic nuts, dried fruits, herb-teas, breakfast cereals, tonic wines, grated carrots, vegetable cooking-fats, and so on, were something new. They were connected with Theosophy, New Thought, and other esoteric philosophies, and with the Coué-ists, who used to repeat a hundred times a day to themselves under their breath the formula they had learned from Professor Coué, the French psychologist: 'Every day, in every way, I am getting better and better.' (Coué believed that auto-suggestion could cure many ailments, including nervous dyspepsia; the *Sunday Express* reported in June 1922 that the Foreign Secretary, Lord Curzon, who was suffering from a persistent attack of insomnia, had sent for him from Paris in the hope of obtaining some relief. Under Coué's influence Lord Curzon made a distinct improvement for some days, but soon relapsed into his usual sleeplessness. In the following year, however, Coué had more success: he was able to cure a number of sea-sick passengers on the liner *Majestic*, which was fighting its way through a severe Atlantic gale, by first converting the stewardesses.)

Vitamins were the great stand-by of the Health Shops. They sold a special 'Vitamine Cream' and a bread which was advertised: 'The secret of its nourishment is the wonderful vitamine it contains: without this, health cannot be maintained.'

Patent medicines, all of which had 'gained the highest medical approval' and offered a wide curative scope, were advertised more widely than ever in the Press; and the Press politely abstained every year from making news of the official analytic Register of Patent Medicines, which gave away the pitiful secrets of pills, wines, ointments, salves, and cure-alls. The vitamins sold in patent-food form and at patent-medicine prices could have been absorbed just as easily and far more cheaply by chewing a few blades of grass. Bovril disdained such trickery. It had taken its name originally from the vitalizing fluid 'Vril' in Bulwer Lytton's Utopian novel *The Coming Race* of 1871: and anyhow was not a food—it had been exempt from the burdensome ration restrictions that fresh meat extracts, such as Brand's Essence of Beef, had undergone in the war—it was still a vitalizing fluid. Bovril now used historical references in its advertisements. One ran: 'Napoleon's Secret. The secret of Napoleon's power was his immense vitality. The same is true of most great men—Julius Caesar, Michelangelo, Gladstone, Cecil Rhodes—they were successful because they were never tired. Don't get tired, drink Bovril.' This was accompanied with a large arresting portrait of Napoleon in one of his more truculent moods, and with smaller portraits of the other 'vital' men.

The fashion for slimming was not widespread until 1927, when it set off the Eton crop; in the full tide of the Twenties advertisements were rather for Skinny People who wished to 'gain two and a half stone of sound healthy flesh in six weeks', than for the Plump who wished to slough off the same amount. But vitamins were all-weather favourites: they nourished the slimmer, as well as the person in search of sound healthy flesh; and before the end of the Thirties were lettered from A to E in the hearts of even the most backward villager. Everyone then talked Diet and read Diet, especially 'the balanced Diet'. In 1927 the *Lancet* introduced the idea of 'roughage'—it was, apparently, useless to eat nothing but vitamins, proteins, and carbo-hydrates —these needed something fibrous and banal to introduce them to the intestines. 'Roughage' was the last term to enter the popular dietetic vocabulary: it was interpreted to mean something scratchy like bran, the peel that one had hitherto removed from stringy celery, and the stalky ends of asparagus—anything to give the vitamins full play. There immediately appeared 'roughage' breakfast foods, such as bran, to supply this need. All was well again: bran taken out of the flour, in order to give white bread the bleached appearance that people liked, was now being sold back to them in nice-looking packets, at the price of three small loaves.

CHAPTER TWELVE

Art, Literature, Religion

The general history of painting goes something like this: first painters painted things as they saw them emotionally; then they painted conventional religious or poetical fancies; then they painted things as they intellectually saw them, with an increasing attention to detail; then they painted according to rules derived from the work of the more intelligent painters. This last stage was called Academicism. In France, in the eighteen-eighties, appeared Impressionism—a way of painting things as one saw them at first glance without consideration of details. This was followed early in the twentieth century by Post-Impressionism, which was to paint things with a conscious disregard of how one intellectually knew them to be, for the purpose of emphasizing their emotional significance. In 1908 came Cubism, in which designs were based on the prism as the spectral source of colour appearance. Futurism, the only new Continental fashion which was Italian, not French, began in the same year: it represented the painter's dynamic private emotions as they were affected by vision. Then came Expressionism, which had its inspiration in Bergsonian psychology and was supposed to be a yielding to the 'violent storms of emotion beating up from the unconscious mind'. After an interval of Dadaism, which was art's scornful denial of art, Surrealism supervened. This went back several steps and then took a step in another direction. The idea of the Surrealists was to express anti-conventional fancies with realistic ardour: to produce a *frisson*, or shudder—a naked foot dog's-earing a book with the toes, candles rising like sandworms from a seashore, the blue sea washing into a drawing-room, a beautiful nude with hands where her breasts should be. The Surrealists in Paris, like the Futurists, Dadaists, and Expressionists, were not merely painters and sculptors, they were also writers, interior decorators, dramatists, and amateur philosophers. They flourished in the middle Twenties. In 1927 they held a conference on sex and published the results of their inquiries: they applauded the *frissons* derivable from the seduction of nuns and of women who never washed, from *outré* sexual positions, from homosexual eccentricity. All these art-movements in turn came to London from Paris: but British *avant-garde* painting and criticism was always two or three steps behind French fashion, and British popular taste two or three steps behind the *avant-garde* painters and critics.

In London, when the war ended, the Academicians were the dominant group, especially the Royal Academicians; but a number of Impressionists had also attained respectability—even the *British Journal of Photography* would no longer dare refer to 'the hideous plague of Impressionistic smudges'. Their literary champion was one of themselves, Roger Fry, whose *Vision and Design* became a text-book and whose Omega Workshops produced simple furniture painted in all manner of confused colours: 'like a Dragon's miscarriage', as a more academic painter impressionistically put it. Post-Impressionists were also on their way to respectability. The educated classes were ready not only to indulge them but even to pay good money for their work; on the recommendation of such serious critics as Clive Bell, whose *Since Cézanne* appeared in 1922. But they found Vorticism (a British blend of Futurism, Cubism, and Expressionism, sponsored by the painter-novelist Wyndham Lewis) too speculative a market as yet.

The *Observer* had commented during the war: 'The reviled Post-Impressionists, Cubists, Futurists, Expressionists, Vorticists of to-day may be the honoured masters of to-morrow.' The more popular Press was aware of this too, but knew that the average time-lag in art-fashions between France and educated England was about twelve years, and between educated England and the masses another twelve at least. They therefore felt it their duty not to hurry things on too fast, but to take their artistic stand between the old Academicians, who religiously painted each leaf of a tree the appropriate brown or green, and the Post-Impressionists, who were quite likely to paint the whole foliage in a series of red scrawls and make the trunk not only bright blue but discontinuous. The *Daily Mail* in 1924, in fact, stood about where the *Studio* stood in 1912, and would not catch up with the *Studio* of 1924 until 1936. The 'celebrated' painters of the popular Press in the early Twenties were therefore Augustus John, William Orpen, Ambrose McEvoy, and the prime flatterer, Philip de László; and the populace was rather encouraged than otherwise in its active opposition to Jacob Epstein. As late as October 1929 'Rima' was again assaulted, with tar and a few feathers; and when in the same year Epstein's new work 'Night' was unveiled over the entrance to the Underground headquarters in Broadway, Westminster, four young men, two in plus-fours, attempted to throw glass tar-containers at it. They were frustrated by the police, and drove away hurriedly in a car. Epstein, when interviewed by reporters upon these attacks, declared that he was in the historical tradition: Michelangelo, for instance, had been obliged to put bars around his statue 'David' at Florence in order to prevent the mob from mutilating it. An Epstein exhibition in 1931 included a large marble statue, 'Genesis'. It attracted record crowds to the Leicester Galleries, and had the usual man-handling from the popular Press. The *Sunday Express* described it as 'so gross, obscene and horrible that no newspaper has even published a full picture of it. As dinner-table decorations in ice-cream these atrocities would at least be gone by next morning!'

The painter who organized and led the painting *avant-garde* throughout the period was the restless Ben Nicholson, whose self-imposed task it was continuously to shorten the time-lag between Paris and London, and especially to help people catch up with each new 'period' of the inventive Catalan painter Pablo Picasso, who set the Paris fashions year after year. Nicholson started a succession of new groups and in each case broke away with a minority when the group seemed no longer up to date. There was *Group X*, and then the *Seven and Five*, and then *Unit One*, and so on. In 1926 the *Seven and Five* Exhibition was headlined in the *Daily Express*: 'Weird Puzzles in Paint'. The tone was ironic: 'The pictures and sculptures confirm the artists' ability to express what they feel; they proclaim also that it is unnecessary to express these feelings in their present state to a wider circle than the society itself provides.' Claude Flight's prismatically painted 'Street Singers', which would have been regarded in Paris in 1912 as rather *vieux jeu*, was dismissed as 'desperately clever'. And: 'Mr. Ben Nicholson has three muddy nudes against wishy-washy backgrounds. It is obvious that the figures are not meant to be anatomically probable—one woman's ankles are three times the width of her neck; one wonders simply why he had to paint them.' This sort of criticism continued in the popular Press until almost the end of the Peace. Even the old master, El Greco, whose 'Agony' had been bought for the National Gallery in 1919, was, for some years more, popularly regarded as unworthy of inclusion there. Stewart Dick, the Academician, described it in his *Half-hours in the National Gallery* as 'on the borderline of sanity'; but the more charitable theory was elsewhere advanced that El Greco had suffered from some optical malady.

The *avante-garde* spoke of the Academicians with cold contempt as *Les Pompiers*. Some of them even tried reprisals against the tar-and-feather brigade: in 1928 Sir George Frampton's sentimental Peter Pan statue in Kensington Gardens narrowly escaped mutilation. The public meanwhile was slowly being educated into seeing things in an Impressionistic or Post-Impressionistic way; and not by attending picture galleries, but by fashion sketches and advertisements. The lively Underground posters by McKnight Kauffer, Albert Rutherston, and Paul Nash were not torn down by irate strap-hangers or even disparaged by contrast with the dignified advertising work that such English *pompiers* as Frank Brangwyn consented to do for the Empire Marketing Board. In 1925 Sir George Frampton, R.A., described as 'splendid' the 'movement for decorating our streets with posters designed by some of our best artists; and it is the wish and hope of many that this really live movement should extend to permanent decorations, illustrating the history of our great Empire, and placed not only on the walls of public buildings, but also on those of our elementary schools, especially in slum districts.' But the 'best artists' did not possess the vitality that the advertising business, which was almost wholly American in spirit and direction, demanded; their ideal woman was still the slow, unathletic, big-bosomed Juno with the clinging draperies, that she had been before the war, and quite hopeless as a salesgirl.

The chief theme of R. H. Wilenski's influential *Modern Art*, which was published in 1927 and ran into several editions, was that photography had relieved artists of the job of naturalistic portraiture and landscape: they could now concentrate on enlarging experience by the grouping and colouring of abstract shapes in the classical manner. The public was by then relativity-minded enough not to care very much what convention the artists adopted, or what terms the critics used, so long as the result was neither dull nor demanded esoteric effort from them. They persistently refused to accept 'abstractions' as objects of study, though as decorative trimmings they were all very well. The respectable *Queen* in 1921 praised the novelty of 'quaint futuristic or jazz embroidery' and the *Observer* in 1927, 'ladies' coats displaying cubistic ideas, amusing to study in detail.'

People in general had been so well accustomed to deliberate distortion by the cinema cartoon, by caricatures, by fashion plates elongating women to a prescribed 150 per cent of their natural proportions, and by streamlined modernistic car-mascots and such, that their only objection to Post-Impressionism and Expressionism was when the distortion was heavy and repellent in effect—as with Epstein, and the imitators of Picasso's Gertrude Stein period, and the morose Wyndham Lewis ('The Enemy', as he called himself). They rather liked Stanley Spencer, of whom the *Sphere* wrote that he had the 'stark realism of inner vision'. His paintings, though modernistically simplified, did at least recognizably represent people. Besides, he painted 'problem pictures', as they were called. The newspapers every year featured a problem picture in the Royal Academy exhibition. There was one, for instance, showing a middle-aged professional man sitting on a chair gazing stonily in front of him: weeping on the floor with her head on his knee sat a pretty young woman. It was called 'The Fallen Idol'. The problem was: 'Which of the two has fallen—has he, presumably the husband, owned up to forgery, or she, presumably the wife, owned up to adultery?' But that was the distinguished painter's secret, which he roguishly refused to give away to reporters. Stanley Spencer's 'Resurrection', which showed cubistical souls rising from their graves on Judgement Day, was not a 'weird puzzle in paint': it was a journalizable problem: 'Where are the waiting angels? Are these the souls of the saved or the souls of the damned?'

'A running horse has twenty legs' was the old revolutionary Post-Impressionist formula, and it was possible now to advertise petrol by a galloping horse with twenty flickering legs, illustrating 'quick startability'. The full force of popular derision was turned rather on the academically heroic horse given Lord Haig to ride in his commemorative public statue by Alfred Hardiman—Lord Haig, who not long before his death had opposed Army mechanization with: 'As time goes on you will find just as much use for the horse, the well-bred horse, as you have ever done in the past.'

Hardiman kept tinkering away at his work in face of hostile criticism from Lord Haig's widow and horse-loving friends: the Academical-heroic was out of fashion in the depiction of men and horses. Alfred Munnings had set a standard of veterinary realism in his equestrian portraits that no sculptor could afford to flout. The statue was finally unveiled on Armistice Day 1937 —by which time Haig's military reputation had slumped nearly to zero: Liddell Hart's account of the 'Passchendaele bloodbath', ordered by Haig against all military common sense, had been widely read and could not be contradicted. *The Times*, however, reported on the dispirited final version of the Memorial Statue: 'The work as now is a compromise: the head of Haig is not in the same degree of stylization as the charger and cloak, but having regard to all circumstances, a successful compromise. . . . Mr. Hardiman is to be congratulated as much upon the patience as the skill with which he has modified his first conception in response to criticisms, expert from the military and veterinary points of view, but not so with regard to sculpture.'

That Academicism was losing ground rapidly was shown in the frightful fall in the values of Victorian paintings from thousands of guineas to a few shillings, and the compensating rise in the works of Manet, Cézanne, Van Gogh, the *douanier* Rousseau, and other safely dead French masters.

These movements in art had their literary equivalents. Paris became a centre of verbal experimentalism with James Joyce and Gertrude Stein as the two main exemplars, and with several magazines and one or two English presses to canalize production. It was at Paris that British and American literary *avant-gardistes* fraternized or came to blows. But though in the States an advanced writer or painter had first to go to Paris before he was accepted as arrived, in Britain the case was not so serious: there was an established *avant-garde* colony centred at Bloomsbury around the Hogarth Press—Leonard and Virginia Woolf, Duncan Grant, and Vanessa Bell—and the Sitwells, symbols of ultra-modernism in the popular Press, had close affiliations with Paris but resided in London. Aldous Huxley, who with James Joyce and D. H. Lawrence made up the outstanding trio of 'modernistic novelists', preferred living in Italy: and D. H. Lawrence lived all over the place.

Aldous Huxley had no eccentric history like James Joyce—Jesuit-trained, Irish ex-singer—or like D. H. Lawrence, brilliant consumptive, son of a working-class family in a midland industrial town: he came from a well-known English intellectual family. What he had in common with these other two was that he had read too much and wished to make some sort of synthesis of his reading, but could not face the task: when he finally made his testament in 1938 in *Ends and Means* the reading was still undigested. Meanwhile he wrote a number of critical essays, novels, and short stories which, until Evelyn Waugh in 1928 rose to dispute his position, made him 'the brightest of our younger writers'. The *Times Literary Supplement* said in 1922 of *Crome Yellow*: 'Mr. Huxley ticks off the present world and its vagaries—social, scientific, literary, artistic, sexual, occult, clerical, amorous, what-not—with the lightest and gayest of pens.' He was the novelist of intellectual sexuality, as was D. H. Lawrence of emotional sexuality.

Lawrence preached the Sun as a procreative deity; urged women that happiness for them lay only in yielding submissively to the dark sexual urge of strong-loined men; and mixed up for himself a confused private religion of the theosophical incoherences of Madame Blavatsky, the yoga writings of an obscure prophet named Pryse, the philosophical view of Heraclitus, Bacon and Bergson that all is flux, Jeans' interpretation of Einstein, the anthropology of Sir James Fraser (whose *Golden Bough* was a key book of the period) and others, Mexican legend, and the whole literature of Freudian, Jungian and Adlerian psychology. Lawrence was without either Huxley's wit, or

Joyce's playboy humour: he lived an anguished, bathetic life, and had a huge, anguished, bathetic following. His nearest approach to happiness was when in his last days at Taos, New Mexico, he bought a cow called Susan and used to milk her with mystic devotion. 'The queer cowy mystery of her is her changeless cowy desirableness.' He died in 1930, and a lesser Lawrence legend started when several of his friends wrote biographies of him, each contradicting the other.

James Joyce introduced into literature the 'stream of consciousness' technique with *Ulysses*, the most famous novel of the period, which reconstructed in over a thousand pages, written in a variety of real and parodied styles, a single day in Edwardian Dublin. It was banned as obscene in Britain, but was referred to appreciatively in the literary Press, even in leaders of the *Times Literary Supplement*, which, however, would not venture to review it. The 'stream of consciousness' was a method of writing in which the thoughts and feelings of characters were more important than action or dialogue. The method was also adopted by Virginia Woolf, daughter of a Victorian man-of-letters, in her novel *To The Lighthouse*, and others. Like E. M. Forster, she wrote with her nervous sensibilities, so that her readers shrank sympathetically at each painfully composed paragraph. She was married to Leonard Woolf, author of *The Jungle*, a competent novel about Ceylon, founder of the Hogarth Press (with money won in a Calcutta Sweep), and the man responsible for the working system of the International Labour Office at Geneva—which was the most practically successful of the League's undertakings.

The Sitwells, Osbert, Edith and Sacheverell, were brothers and sister of an eccentric county family. Osbert was the showman, knockabout rhymester, novelist, satirist; Sacheverell the rambling, romantic poet who was also an authority on Baroque architecture; Edith a sincere, irritable, very limited poet with a considerable knowledge of advanced French art and literature, who in such lines as:

> 'Jane, Jane,
> Tall as a crane,
> The morning light creaks down again'

was trying to make French Expressionism at home in an English nursery-rhyme world. Together they launched a number of fashions, chiefly in music, pictures and interior decoration; they always had a wide, if not a good, Press for their exploits; and were chiefly known for their popularization of early Victorian period furnishings—until then the Regency was the most recent of admired epochs. In the Thirties they instituted an annual mock prize which they conferred on the person who seemed to them the dreariest of those in semi-fashionable favour, and thus set themselves up as arbiters of literary elegance. Osbert became a Sunday columnist for awhile.

The *London Mercury* continued to represent the traditional stream of poetry: the chief younger writers being Edmund Blunden, whose pastoral poems had, according to the *Times Literary Supplement*, 'the savour which English literature has always loved', and Victoria Sackville-West, whose *The Land*, a long aristocratic poem about country joys, was the last notable 'Georgian' poem to appear. There was also a busy Jewish civil servant, Humbert Wolfe, whose duty at the Ministry of Labour was to interview strikers deputations and send them away charmed and hopeful. His poems, beginning with *Kensington Gardens*, had a huge vogue in the middle Twenties. They expressed easy sentiment in apparently advanced metaphors and the capital letters were modernistically lower-cased at the beginning of lines. *The Times* was shrewd enough to remark that, in spite of the 'certainty and delicacy of touch of a master musician', there was a lack of susbtance in his verse.

Gertrude Stein, who was the chief literary link between the British and American *avant-garde* writers, musicians and painters, and the French, was an American who had been the psychologist William James's favourite pupil. At John Hopkins University she had studied fatigue reactions. She had been living in Paris for some years now, doing research in the English language to test its capacity for the conveyance of sense when grammatic and syntactical usage was relaxed—on the technical analogy of Impressionism and Post-Impressionism. There was an undeniably comic side to the results of this research, however serious the intention, and since her publication of *Tender Buttons*, some years before the war, she had been a stock joke in British journalism. She persisted in her work, which somehow got published even in London: the Hogarth Press published her short and easy *Composition as Explanation* in 1926 and the Seizin Press her difficult *Acquaintance with Description* in 1927. She presided pontifically in Paris over the *avant-gardistes*. Her rich collection of early Picasso paintings proved that she had authority to give her blessing to any new generation of experimentalists—who always came to demand it—in music, art, or literature. There was a low-brow American Limerick current in the Twenties:

> 'I don't like the family Stein!
> There is Gert, their is Ep, there is Ein.
> Gert's writings are punk,
> Ep's statues are junk,
> Nor can anyone understand Ein.

It was in 1927 that Laura Riding, a young American who had recently come to Europe, first published her poems and critical work in England. Wiping her slate clean of literary and domestic affiliations with America, she became for the next twelve years the best of 'good Europeans'; the Americans only knew her as 'the highest apple on the British intellectual tree'. In England she was assailed as a 'leg-puller', 'crossword puzzle setter', 'Futurist', 'tiresome intellectualist', and so on: none of her books sold more than a few dozen copies, nor did she ever (as Gertrude Stein did after the Wall Street crash, in her chatty *Autobiography of Alice B. Toklas* and during her American lecture tour), consent to give the larger public what it really wanted. She was the one poet of the time who spun, like Arachne, from her own vitals without any discoverable philosophical or literary derivations: and the only one who achieved an unshakable synthesis. Unshakable, that is, if the premiss of her unique personal authority were granted, and another more startling one—that historic Time had effectively come to an end. In her *Preliminaries* to *Epilogue I* she wrote:

'All the Chinese bandits having chopped off all the foreign ears, we have time to consider not only the subject *Atrocity*, but the subject *Bandits*, and the subject *Missionaries*, and the subject *Foreigners*, and the subject *Chinese*. All the politicians who are going to be elected have been elected; and all the artificial excitement in events which no one really regards as either very important or very interesting has been exhausted. All the historical events have happened.'

This left the poets the pleasant if arduous duty of reporting 'the single event possible after everything has happened: a determination of values'. The literary *avant-gardistes* could do nothing with her: she was interested in value, not in post-temporal fashion, she had a better head than any of them and a better heart than most, she was accessible but not clubbable, and she resented the constant unacknowledged borrowing from her work by the ambitious and insincere. This made everyone uncomfortable: they would have liked to make a Great Woman of her, but to do so would have meant changing their own unsynthesized habits. They did their best to ignore her. Laura Riding was remarkable as being in the period but not of the period, and the only woman who spoke with authority in the name of Woman (as so many men in the name of Man) without either deference to the male tradition or feministic equalitarianism: a perfect original. At the very end of the period she returned to the United States, surprisingly rediscovered her American self, and wiped the slate clean again.

Many poets who took themselves seriously but lacked perfect self-sufficiency turned to the East for inspiration at some time or other. W. B. Yeats did so in his old age, collaborating with an Indian pundit in a translation of the Upanishads—after first abandoning his Celtic-Twilight for a brushed-up neo-American style, and then dabbling in spiritualism. T. S. Eliot, too, introduced the Buddhist keywords, 'Give, sympathize, control', into *The Waste Land*, the most famous poem of the period, and concluded the poem with 'Shantih, shantih, shantih', the formal ending to a Upanishad, meaning 'The Peace that passeth understanding'.

There had been Mrs. Annie Besant and Madame Blavatsky, European students of Indian esoteric thought. There was now Krishnamurti, an Indian student of these European students of Indian thought. He had a large following in Germany and Britain in the Twenties and was reckoned the most distinguished foreigner in Holland after the ex-Kaiser—thousands went from England to his holiday preaching-camps. Then Yoga was introduced into Britain by a few civil servants and soldiers who had served in India. Major-General Fuller, who was one of those responsible for developing the theory of tank warfare, and later a Fascist candidate at a London Borough election, wrote on it at length. He defined Yoga as a means of deliverance from worldly illusions. The Yogi's maxim was: 'Stop thinking and get beyond or behind consciousness and you will discover the meaning of Reality in super-consciousness.' The practice of the Yogi consisted in diverting his organs of sense from everyday objects and concentrating them on his inner self, in which was to be found a world of unity and rest. In this way the illusions of the various and changing world were avoided. Sensual pleasures, including those of sex, were to be denied. 'As for women,' Major-General Fuller remarked in a footnote, 'they are considered beyond the possibility of redemption, for in the order of reincarnation they are placed seven stages below a man, three below a camel, and one below a pig.' Gerald Heard, a writer on scientific subjects, concluded a book at the end of the Thirties, *Pain, Sex and Time*, with an explanation of how Yoga could help Western men to reach peace within their inner selves; and Aldous Huxley was another student of the subject. The advantage of Yoga over the Catholic Church, for men at least, was that not only did it forbid the devotee to think, but he remained his own confessor, Pope, and Deity.

C. E. M. Joad, a popular philosopher, who throughout the Twenties was the typical anti-ideal Realist, published in 1933 *Counter Attack from the East*, in which he surprisingly expounded the philosophy of the Indian Professor S. Radhakrishnan, of Oxford University. He began by defining the contemporary situation in Europe in the words of one of the characters in Bernard Shaw's *Too True to be Good*: 'I stand mid-way between youth and age like a man who has missed his train: too late for the last one and too early for the next. . . . I have no Bible, no creed: the war has shot both out of my hands. . . . I am ignorant: I have lost my nerve and am intimidated; all I know is that I must find the way of life for myself and all of us, or we shall surely perish. . . .' Europe's ruin, he continued, would surely be brought about either by another war or by the collapse of the economic system, which was unable to distribute equitably what it produced. European nations ought to take a leaf out of the book of the East and, instead of perpetually acting, learn to sit back and feel. European activity led nowhere. In writing and in the arts 'the flowing river of inspiration seems to have trickled away into the backwaters of formlessness, discord and experimentation for its own sake.' Philosophy was out of touch with life. Science could provide the means of satisfying people's desires, but it assumed no responsibility for distinguishing between good and bad desires. People were hostile to established religion, and yet in need of faith, for the hedonism of the early Twenties had been proved unsatisfying.

As a remedy, Joad proposed the 'intuitive approach', by which he meant the thorough investigation and control of feelings. This had always been the teaching of Eastern philosophers, and Joad claimed that Radhakrishnan could carry out the function of a liaison-officer between the traditional inner tranquility of the East and the materialistic energy of the West. The work of liaison was already being rather ineffectively carried out by a magazine, the *Aryan Path*, founded in 1930 in order to bring together the traditions of East and West. Indian doctrines could never make much headway in England, however, where among the governing class the prejudice against Indians as 'lesser breeds within the law' had persisted since Kipling's time; though they were popular among the working class, which found them generous and gentlemanly.

In the same class with Joad as a popular prophet was J. Middleton Murry, who began the Peace as the editor of the *Athenaeum*, then turned for relief from barren intellectualism to the rich mysticism taught by the Russian Ouspensky, and the semi-monastic group-life of Gudjieff's Institute at Fontainebleau. Shortly after his wife, Katherine Mansfield, the most gifted and careful short-story writer of the Twenties—in the Russian, not American, style—died at the Institute of consumption, he recanted much of his modernistic mysticism, rediscovered Christ, founded the earnest, popular, *New Adelphi*, and began to hail his spiritual affinities among the English poets, especially Keats, Blake, and Shakespeare. He interpreted Blake, for example, as teaching that the stifling grip of intellectualized life had to be defeated by a revolution of uninhibited feeling, before a just balance between feeling and thinking could be established. Murry saw a materialistic counterpart to this in Communism, and urged that real, or Christian, Communism would combine political revolution with revolution within people's individual selves. He continued his lay preaching throughout the period: growing more and more ecclesiastical in touch, and with an increasingly woolly following. He ended as a prominent pacifist.

Not only Indian and Russian, but Chinese thought was stirring the British mind. Confucius and Lao-tse were no longer names of reference, but were seriously studied; the Cambridge critic, I. A. Richards, wrote on Mencius. The attraction of the Chinese was their sensitivity of feeling, their moral criticality, their detachment from contemporary events. These qualities were most easily assimilable from the Chinese poems, translated immediately after the war by Arthur Waley into firm and unpretentious English. There was even a solid appreciation of Taoism, which preached the virtue of bowing before every storm, running away from every enemy or argument and cultivating the domestic virtues. It fitted in well with the anti-war talk of the late Twenties and early Thirties.

The only notable revival of simple Christianity in the period was known as the 'Oxford Group' movement. This had been founded in the early Twenties by Frank Buchman, an American minister of religion, who ran it on American advertising lines. The name 'Oxford Group' was a stroke of advertising genius: it provided a respectable academic ring and recalled the serious Oxford Movement of mid-Victorian times. In point of fact, Oxford University had no more to do with the movement than the Eiffel Tower with the well-advertised Eiffel Tower Lemonade. A smart, not to say disingenuous, method of propaganda was for its members to write privately to leading politicians and other public men, asking them whether they agreed with certain simple religious formulas; their favourable replies were then used as active endorsements of the Oxford Group. The movement was slow to gather momentum until 1931, but had by that time gained the support of a number of earnest Anglican clergymen, who saw it as a means of infusing life into the ritual-ridden Church.

By 1932 it had begun to attract newspaper attention. The *Daily Express* published a series of articles by young men on the revival of religious feeling. H. W. ('Bunny') Austin, the tennis champion, wrote: 'I believe that Christ was neither meek nor mild, nor frail, but a man magnificently built, tall and strong, and that His mind was even stronger than His body. . . . By the quickness and the keenness of His brain all those who argued with Him were outwitted and subdued.' This was an improvement on the 'Muscular Christianity' theory of the late nineteenth century. Austin's lead was followed by Godfrey Winn, ex-actor and sentimental columnist, who described how he had re-learnt the value of prayer. Never before, he said, had he had the courage to confess even to his most intimate friends that he believed in God. He concluded with: 'The dull routine of our daily job takes on a new significance, assumes a beauty and importance undreamt of before, if we consider it from the angle of service to God.' Preachers had been saying this for nearly two thousand years, but it was a new thing for a star columnist to say so. James Douglas, the calvinistic editor of the *Sunday Express*, found in these articles signs of 'the dawn of a new day breaking'.

The *Daily Express* then devoted an article to 'The Buchmanites Come to Town', in which their first group in London was described. The *Express* reporter found them 'healthy, hearty, athletic young men'. A fuller picture of Group activities was given in a book by A. J. Russell, *For Sinners Only*, which was selling widely in 1932. As one of the Groupist songs put it:

'It's not an institution,
It's not a point of view,
It starts a revolution
By starting it in you!'

Russell said that, in Coleridge's words, the Group was out to restore commonplace truths to their first uncommon lustre by translating them into action. Its members were to live Christianity, and emphasize practice more than preaching. One of their practices was to 'share' confessions of their sins; this was supposed to provide a healthy, common-sense way of solving personal problems by discussion. Their central belief was that God had a guiding plan for everyone's life. One of their sayings was: 'There is always from God concrete, adequate, accurate information on any subject at any time.' When people spoilt God's plan by sinning, He was always ready with a new one. In the early mornings Group members held 'Quiet Times', in which they 'listened-in to God', made petitions, and waited for guidance. By submitting their will to God every morning, they hoped to build up a real co-ordinated life for each day. The

Group recommended that its members should keep a 'guidance book', in which to record the thoughts that arose while listening-in to God.

The aim of the Group was to 'change' people's lives, on the theory that world-problems could only be settled by the personal reform of everybody. When people were 'changed', 'shared' their problems, and listened-in to God for 'guidance', problems disappeared; the desire for sexual sin no longer existed if the will was in God's charge, but like all other psychological errors could be richly sublimated. Money troubles, too, could be solved: Russell quoted several instances of 'changed' people who had prayed hard to God for a cheque by the next post, and had actually got it.

Frank Buchman, the Groupist Fuehrer, was described in Harold Begbie's *Life-Changers* as a 'young-looking man of middle life, tall, upright, stoutish, clean-shaven, with that mien of scrupulous shampooed and almost medical cleanliness or freshness, which is so characteristic of the hygienic American'. Begbie went on to tell how Group members looked upon him. 'I am tempted to think that if Mr. Pickwick had given birth to a son [*sic*] and that son had emigrated to America he would have been not unlike this amiable and friendly surgeon of souls. Fuller acquaintance of "F.B." brings to one's mind the knowledge that in spite of his boyish cheerfulness he is one of the house and lineage of all true mystics from Plotinus to Tolstoy.'

The Group directed its main drive against the upper-middle classes. For a time it enjoyed a vogue at the universities— ironically enough, chiefly at Oxford. Its success among titled people was advertised, just as with cosmetics. Special Group week-ends were held in the country, and only those who could afford to go away for week-ends attended. Though Buchman had plans for starting groups in factories, his movement scarcely affected working-class people. It appealed to those with an uneasy intellectual background, precisely because it was not an intellectual movement, but one of earnest, gentlemanly and restful comradeship.

A bid in Britain for the religious support of the less prosperous classes, from which, in the United States, she derived her chief support, was made by the American evangelist Aimée Semple McPherson, who arrived in 1928 with a large company

of 'Angels' and rented the Albert Hall for a meeting of her Four
Square Gospel Alliance. She and the angels were beautifully
garbed; but the Albert Hall, which was only half full, did not
yield the same theatrical effect of glory as her Temple at Los
Angeles. She retold Bible stories in the American vernacular
which the cinema had trained her audience to understand, and
persuaded them to sing:

> 'Thou, the rose of Sharon,
> Let thy praises roll!
> Lily of the valley,
> Flower of my soul.'

All those for whom Jesus was the lily of the valley were asked to
raise their yellow hymn books in the air when they came to the
last line of the song. All did. Then they sang:

> 'I've been "listening-in" to Heaven,
> And I've had a glorious time,
> I have heard such wondrous singing,
> And the music it was fine.'

But the show was not quite good enough to compensate for the
empty seats, and she omitted the note of Hell and Damnation
which an evangelist must use in such circumstances; besides, the
Anglican Church did not support her. She went home unsuccessful.

Religious people in England in 1927 and 1928 were concerned
with the controversy over the revised Prayer Book. A Royal
Commission on Ecclesiastical Discipline had been appointed in
1901 to inquire into the divergent 'High' and 'Low' Church
practices in ceremonial. It found in favour of bringing the
Prayer Book, by revision, into closer relation both with modern
needs and with the advances in liturgical scholarship which had
revealed deficiencies in the existing Prayer Book from the point
of view of traditional Christian worship. 'Letters of Business'
were then granted to Convocation by the Government to proceed with revision. The war interrupted the Bishops' labours, but
in 1927 a revised Prayer Book was finally produced. What it did
was to undo the drastic 1552 Protestant revision of the 1549
edition. Immediately, however, the Low-Church part of the
community protested against the 'Romeward' tendency of the

Church of England. The new Prayer Book was assailed as Anglo-Catholic for introducing Mass vestments, the wafer at Communion services, the eastward position and the mixed chalice, and for encouraging Mariolatry by giving special collects, epistles and gospels for three additional festivals of the Virgin. The House of Lords accepted the new Book, but the Commons rejected it, chiefly by the vote of its Northern Irish and Scottish members.

That either House had the right to decide on the matter was strange: for although, among the Lords, Anglicans predominated, there were a number of Catholic peers; and in the Commons a great many Dissenters, Catholics, Jews, and infidels. But Protestantism was the State religion and there were therefore remarkably few abstentions from voting, even though it was a non-party measure: the members had their duty to their constituents to consider. In 1928 a modified version was drafted, which the Lords again accepted; but in the Commons the Home Secretary, Sir William Joynson-Hicks, led the attack against it. He was an ardent Low Churchman, and had already written a book against revision, *The Prayer Book Crisis*. Largely because of his attacks, the new Prayer Book was again rejected by the Commons. There was nothing then for the Bishops to do but to give permission if they chose, each in his own diocese, for certain parts of the book to be used. The Church had been saved from officially taking a 'Romeward' step, but that did not prevent incumbents from conducting services as they wished. The old principle of compromise had been re-established in the State religion at least: Anglicanism was all things to all men, and if congregations objected to processions and candles and incense and other medieval revivals, they could always take car or bus to a neighbouring church where services were so low as to suggest a perpetual Good Friday. But the institutions or private people in whose gift the livings were, usually took pains to keep a parish at the level of Churchdom which its parochial council demanded.

CHAPTER THIRTEEN

Education and Ethics

The failure of the Churches to hold younger and more progres-sive-minded people even in weekly lip-service to the notion of Christendom; the knocking away by Einstein and his popularists of the lynch-pin of geometric absoluteness which held the con-ventional universe together; the loss of any sense of the immedi-ate present in the gap between the 'Futures of', which were pouring from the Press, and the encyclopedic popular 'Histories of' in monthly parts—all this was thoroughly unsettling. 'You are all a lost generation,' Gertrude Stein had said pertinently to the younger survivors of the war, who included such diverse characters as the Prince of Wales and Lawrence of Arabia. Those of the lost generation who had children were determined that these must not suffer as they themselves had from their upbringing, but must have as healthy and happy a childhood as possible and be encouraged from the first to become indus-trious and responsible citizens of the world. As a hopeful start, 'mothercraft' had recently been raised to an exact science by the meticulous Dr. Truby King. It was generally felt that the muddle into which the world had got itself could not be straightened out 'in our time', so that the chief hope lay in the next generation.

The Twenties were therefore a great time for children—never before had such attention been lavished on them nor parental control been so light. It was also a great time for educationalists, especially for psychologically minded ones who had learned from the case-books what terrible consequences might follow an early thwarting of a libido. Conventional British education before the war had been exceedingly repressive in all varieties of school, except the Froebel kindergarten, and school subjects were taught in a way that bored and repelled.

The new school movement, which was an extension of Froebel's theories and Madame Montessori's system for correcting defective and delinquent children, had three main features—co-education, encouragement to children to express their natural feelings and abilities, no punishments. A great many parents who looked back on their own schooldays with loathing and could afford the high fees that new schools were forced to demand sent their children to them. Even if they learned nothing they would at least be happy there and given the right number of calories and vitamins by a modern catering staff. This competition was soon felt by the more conventional preparatory schools, which now improved food, lightened discipline, rationalized clothes, and reformed in so many ways that the child no longer wept miserably on each return to school after the holidays. They could not break away altogether from school subjects, since they had to accommodate themselves to the demands of the universities. But some compromised, by providing conventional classes only for children who had eventually to matriculate or pass other examinations, and some substituted farmwork for the usual cricket and football.

Thus, as with the Churches, there was remarkable variation in scholastic ritual between neighbouring establishments. A few continued to give their pupils heavy Victorian food to eat and heavy Victorian clothes and hats to wear; teach them little but the Classics, mathematics, Scripture, and a little French; make crimes of small offences; and rout them out of bed early with the clang of the school bell for long and listless prayers. At the other end of the scale there were Libertarian schools where 'problem children' did just what they liked and when they liked (the teachers merely making suggestions and taking notes), even to the point of breaking windows, writing up dirty words on the walls, running about naked. The problem children were those who had started with a conventional education, but had 'reacted to it unco-operatively'. Usually they were the children of problem parents. A. S. Neill's school, Summerhill, specialized in children of this kind. At one time it was full of thieves and truants who went there because it was the only place that would accept them. Neill had himself cherished a resentment against his own repressive Scottish education: he had come to abominate the Classics, suspecting anyone who had any liking for them, and used to strop his razor on a leather-bound family Bible, not altogether from thriftiness. As he wrote in 1937 in his book, *That Dreadful School*, he wished to make Summerhill fit the children and not the children the school. He was a kindly and generous man and gave everyone at Summerhill equal rights, no matter what age they might be. All were free and undisciplined and expressed their natures to the full. He counted as his greatest discovery the fact that children were born sincere, and remained so unless warped by conventional education. Some turned out sincerely good, a few stayed sincerely bad. Everything got broken.

The Hon. Bertrand Russell, mathematician, Einstein expositor, advocate of complete sexual freedom—another man with a grudge against his education—and his Libertarian wife Dora Russell ran another famous 'free' school: it did not go quite so far as Summerhill and contained fewer delinquents. The Russells considered that the true object of education was not to instil certain beliefs into children, but to stimulate in them the power of independent judgement. Instruction was not so important as the development of 'personality'; children could always pick up book-knowledge later. Dora Russell's *In Defence of Children*, published in 1932, maintained that a child's education was best advanced by the observation of real things: plants, flowers, animals, chemicals, food, colours, its own body. It should be allowed to express its feelings freely about these things, so that when it became an adult it would be a 'whole person', not the conventional type whose emotional forces were repressed. She wrote: 'We need to start with male and female children together in nursery schools that are absolutely frank about sexual differences; then to let the children go on growing up together, providing for each one opportunities as an individual without neglecting the difference of sexual interest.'

The chief defect of these free schools was that the child did not stay there permanently, but went home on holiday for some five months of the year and immediately came into conflict with repressive social discipline, at the hands of neighbours and relatives, if not of its parents. It reacted sharply, caused a deal of trouble; and sometimes wept each time it left school for home.

Before the war the British educational system had been one of the clearest expressions of the class-structure of society. There were elementary schools, religious or secular, for the poor; dame-schools and grammar or cathedral schools for the trading classes; and preparatory and public schools for the governing classes. The usual leaving-age of the elementary school was fourteen; of the grammar school, sixteen or seventeen; of the public school, eighteen. Above these were the universities: Oxford, Cambridge and Dublin in one grade and 'the rest' in another. These social gradings were altered at the outset of the period by the extension of State-aided education. H. A. L. Fisher, the historian, was President of the Board of Education in 1918, and the Acts which he sponsored made it compulsory for local education authorities to provide their areas with secondary schools corresponding to grammar schools, and technical schools; many new ones were built. It was not every elementary school-child who could be transferred at the age of eleven to a secondary school or go on after the age of fouteen to a technical school, but quite a number of scholarships and 'free places' were annually awarded to the more intelligent ones, and the extension of the bus-services made regular attendance possible even in the deepest country.

Some grammar schools were now content to remain in their original social grade and admit the infiltration of the working class child; others moved up into the public-school category, by bringing themselves into the definition of public schools made in 1899 by the historian of Winchester College: 'Boarding Academies for young gentlemen, drawn from all parts of the country'. If they had no boarders before, they usually installed a few and became officially eligible to the title of 'public school' by substituting Officers Training Corps for the old Cadet Corps companies; or their headmasters were elected to sit on the national Headmasters' Conference, an honour which automatically carried with it public-school dignity, whether there were boarders or no. The eight original public schools—Eton, Harrow, Winchester, Rugby, Westminster, Charterhouse, Wellington, and Shrewsbury—had swelled to hundreds, and only a technical difference existed between the tail of this column and the head formed by the new secondary and technical schools. The excuse for the public school, where the teaching even on the 'Modern Side' was in general so formal and dispiriting as to encourage most boys to concentrate all their energies on games or out-of-school interests, was that it taught 'character'. The dormitory houses were, on the whole, self-governing republics of boys, who regarded the masters as strangers unfit for any confidences; and painfully inoculated each new generation with the Spartan virtues of modesty, reticence, endurance, courage, generosity, loyalty, personal cleanliness, and general decency—general decency meant not taking unfair advantage of a superior position. With the Spartan virtues went the Spartan prejudice against all things artistic, eccentric, abstract, poetic, studious, foreign, or feminine.

High schools for girls had the same social choice to make as the grammar schools: whether to raise fees and admit only ladies, or come under the secondary school system and get Government support. Social distinctions began to blur, in both girls' and boys' schools: for 'war-profiteers' sent their children to rub shoulders with the children of the aristocracy, and working-class children succeeded not only in winning scholarships and free places at secondary schools but in being elected to university scholarships.

The pre-war Board of Education had been in the hands of progressive and devoted men, who had made the funds allowed them by the Treasury go as far as possible. The result was a marked improvement in the teaching system at provincial universities and secondary schools—more marked than in the privileged elder universities and public schools—and consequently in the quality of elementary and secondary school teachers. After the war teachers were on the whole better paid, and the profession attracted more intelligent people. Part-time education was also being extended, by means of evening classes in technical colleges run by local authorities, and by adult education movements. In 1934 more than two million students were enrolled in England and Wales at part-time classes.

Most educationalists agreed that a school-leaving age of fifteen would make secondary education possible for all, whereas a leaving age of fourteen did not. The Hadow Report on Education, in 1927, recommended the universal extension of the school-leaving age. This was designed to give every child an education divided into two parts: primary up to the age of eleven, and secondary from eleven to fifteen. When a School-leaving Age Act was finally passed in 1936, however, it allowed local authorities to grant exemptions to children of fourteen who could take up 'beneficial employment', or whose parents were so poor as to be dependent on their earnings. The Act therefore had little effect in distressed areas especially. One of the recommendations of the Hadow Report, which was adopted locally, was that nursery schools should be established. These were to start good social habits in children from the earliest age, particularly in those whose mothers were too busy to look after them. Private nursery schools already existed, but now enterprising local authorities attached some to girls' secondary schools. This was supposed to train elder girls in mother-craft.

Other experiments in education included the use of broadcasting and films as a means of teaching. Of all the activities of the B.B.C., broadcasting to schools was the least criticized and the most generally welcomed. Miss Mary Somerville, who ran this department throughout the period, did not wish to put any ordinary school teachers out of jobs by competitive teaching of school subjects, but rather to supplement the ordinary curriculum with special talks by experts on this and that.

Education authorities as time went on gave not only permission for broadcasts to be incorporated in the schools curriculum, but also grants for the purchase of receivers, licences, and the B.B.C. pamphlets. By the end of the period some 11,000 elementary and secondary schools in England, Wales, and Scotland were listening-in. The talks were looked forward to as treats, as were the educational films to which schools were admitted in morning showings at local cinemas. Some schools were buying their own projectors and holding weekly shows in the school hall. One of the main activities of the British Film Institute, founded in 1933, was to encourage educational films. Some of the best of these were made by Gaumont British Instructional, dealing with such natural-history subjects as 'Tawny Owl' and 'Rock Pools'. The first British instructional film on history was directed by J. B. Holmes for this company in 1935. It was called 'Mediaeval Village', and showed pictorially the mediaeval system of land tenure and the rotation of crops, as they still survived in a remote Nottinghamshire village. Instructional films on Imperial subjects were also rented out by the Empire Film

Library. Most of them had been made for the Empire Marketing Board.

The formation of O.T.C. companies by grammar schools as a means of social elevation had its ironical side, because it was concurrent with a widespread anti-militarist movement. This began with the Labour Party, who were not only against the class-war but against 'Imperialistic wars' conducted by the privileged classes; and in industrial districts where they controlled local government the Labour men could back up their private opinions by overt acts. In 1927 the pacifist Housing Committee of Sheffield City Council refused to grant permission for a squadron of the Queen's Own Yorkshire Dragoons to drill on Sunday mornings on the Langley Housing Estate. This council had already abolished the O.T.C. company attached to the local King Edward VII School, and set going a general attack on O.T.C.s as fostering militarism in the young. The schools that were not forced to abolish theirs sent increasingly thinner detachments to the annual summer camps at Aldershot and on Salisbury Plain. War memorials and war trophies also grew unpopular: bands of ex-Servicemen were reported to be throwing German gun relics into rivers at night, and a move was made in 1928 to demilitarize Armistice Day. The Rev. H. Dunnico, M.P., said that fewer ex-Servicemen attended the celebrations each year, because they felt cynical about the prospects of peace. He suggested that a World Fellowship Day should be held instead. General Sir Ian Hamilton, who had commanded the British Expedition to Gallipoli, urged that Armistice Day should continue, but only in order to remind people, as they paused in the nation-wide Two Minutes' Silence, how disastrous the war had been, and to reinforce their determination that it should never occur again. There was a similar tendency in France, where the rising tide of Socialism was damping the military spirit. The *Sunday Express* greeted as a notable step towards appeasement the news that the French police had forbidden the use of the word *boche* in French films—*allemand* was to be substituted.

The disarmament question was canvassed in 1927, when an Anglo-American naval conference was held. It failed because Britain—on Churchill's advice, it is said—was unwilling to concede mathematical parity to the Americans. Thereupon Viscount Cecil resigned from the Government: he was the chief British advocate of disarmament and of co-operation between countries by means of the League of Nations. The public was nevertheless encouraged to feel that the era of perpetual peace was at hand when the Kellogg Pact was signed in 1928. The *Daily News* observed: 'A move to outlaw war throughout the world is the hopeful note on which the New Year opened. The draft of a treaty for the outlawry of war between the U.S. and France . . . contains a provision that it shall be open to other powers to add their signatures. . . . The intention is that the treaty should be only the first step towards a world-wide prohibition of war as a means of settling international differences.' Britain added its signature to this pact, and so did most other countries; but the statesmen who signed it were perhaps more aware than the public of the uselessness of denunciations of war, unaccompanied by any practical safeguard against it.

War-books suddenly came back into fashion in 1928–9: but to 'debunk' rather than glorify. The fashion started in Germany with Erich Maria Remarque's unbalanced *All Quiet on the Western Front* and Stephen Zweig's *The Case of Sergeant Grischa*. *All Quiet* took second place in German best-selling records after the Bible, but was later displaced by Hitler's *Mein Kampf*. As soon as *All Quiet* and *Sergeant Grischa*, in both of which soldiers were shown not as heroes but as uncomplaining victims of universal disaster, had been serialized in the British Sunday papers, the public was ready to read the same sort of story from the British side, and to see it dramatized on the stage. The greatest stage success of 1929 was R. C. Sherriff's *Journey's End*, a realistic study of the reactions of several men in a dug-out to war conditions; there were no women in the cast. A number of British 'war-books' became best-sellers. Richard Aldington's strident *Death of a Hero* denounced love-cant and war-cant with the necessary Continental fierceness, but Edmund Blunden's restrained *Undertones of War* and Siegfried Sassoon's wistful *Memoirs of a Fox-Hunting Man* had a strong literary flavour. Robert Graves' *Good-bye to All That*, another best-seller of the time, was neither a war-book nor literary, but a reckless autobiography in which the war figured, written with small consideration for anyone's feelings.

These four writers were all in the first place poets. Aldington practised 'Imagism', an American free-verse fashion which avoided the abstract, mystical and conventionally poetic by limiting itself in Chinese style to clear pictorial images. Siegfried Sassoon, whose *Counter Attack* has already been mentioned, had settled down to a dormant bachelor life, with eruptions of satiric pebbles and ash, but no longer the old lava. Blunden had risen to be the most commended nature poet of the period, but sacrificed the initial advantage that he derived from his country breeding by becoming a professor of English literature, first at Tokyo and then at Oxford, and not keeping his poems separate from his literary studies. Graves had been a 'Georgian' and later in his *Poetic Unreason* and other critical essays had set a fashion in psychological analysis of the effect on readers of various poetic devices. He was now declaring his intention of becoming a poet in a more responsible sense: considering the intrinsic truth of his statements rather than their probable appeal to anthology readers.

A more famous 'war-book' than any of these was T. E. Lawrence's *Seven Pillars of Wisdom*, a personal history of the Arab Revolt against the Turks, which he had largely directed. It appeared in a shortened trade version in 1936 to cover the expense of the full, illustrated limited edition published in the next year. The full edition was issued at £30 a copy to subscribers—but copies were soon selling at £600. Lawrence had written the book straight off in 400,000 words immediately after the war, painfully rewritten it when the manuscript was stolen, and then for years tinkered away at it, trying to convert a workmanlike and highly exciting story into a literary monument. Lawrence had been an archaeologist before the war, had refused an O.M. and an earldom for his war services, and then, after seeing justice done to the Arabs in the matter of Iraq and Transjordan, found his mind 'revving' at an uncomfortably high speed. He enlisted in 1922 under the name of Shaw in the Royal Air Force: as a means of curing himself by enforced discipline—'as one might go into a lay monastery'. After a time an officer recognized him and sold the news-story to the *Daily Express* for £30: questions were asked in Parliament as to what he was doing in the R.A.F. under an assumed name, and he was forced to quit after six months' service. He enlisted under the name of Ross in the Royal Tank Corps, but was quietly permitted to return to the R.A.F. two years later. He remained in the ranks until his discharge in 1935: where his mechanical genius revolutionized the design of motor torpedo-boats, his powers of organization made a brilliant success of the Schneider Trophy meet in 1931, and his influence with Air Marshals righted a good many wrongs of his fellow-aircraftmen. Lawrence was a man of extraordinary powers and with a constant temptation to use them for experimentally. He both despised and loved the legend that surrounded him, could not be constant either to his friends or himself. He wrote of himself what the man tormented with devils told Jesus: 'My name is Legion, for we are many.' His long self-humiliation in the R.A.F. made him forget after a time that he was a fellow of All Soul's and the son of an Irish baronet. It tempted him to reject deliberately the first-rate in literature and art in favour of the second and third rate, as too 'inside' and aristocratic. He began to idealize 'the little man', in the sense of the lower-middle class John Citizens of whom R.A.F. mechanics were largely made, and who in Germany and Italy were the backbone of the Fascist and Nazi revolutions; even played with the idea of himself becoming a dictator. If he had not been killed in a road-accident shortly after his discharge he would have found the temptation to strong political action almost irresistible.

The minds of the two Lawrences, D. H. and T. E., were representative of much that was happening in this confused epoch of thought and feeling. Both felt absolute liberty to range in their mental emotions wherever they pleased; but as soon as they returned to themselves were disappointed to find nobody at home but a little naked manikin. T. E. was no less content during his last R.A.F. years with his mechanic's 'bits and pieces' than D. H. in New Mexico with Susan the cow's teats, but it was a makeshift contentment in both cases. What secretly irked them was the question of Woman—whom they could neither do with nor without. Woman seemed to interfere with their freedom of spirit; yet this freedom they felt exhausting and terrifying. Where was the particular woman to reassure them that they were not frauds, that all male aspirations and conquests were not fraudulent? Yet if that woman had appeared and subsequently told them that very thing, they would have called her a liar. T. E. sent Robert Graves an obituary notice on himself just before his death, in which he remarked, with some satisfaction, that being a mechanic cut him off from all real communication with women—there were no women in the machines, in any machine—no woman could understand a mechanic's happiness in serving his bits and pieces. He added that 'all this reads like a paragraph of D. H. L., my step-namesake'. The chief difference between the two Lawrences was that T. E. had a healthy mind and body and deliberately fell short of the best from a proud Irish scruple against perfection; D. H. was not only unhealthy but spiritually blind and tried to overawe the best in others by vulgar menaces.

T. E. Lawrence's abandonment of literary and artistic perfectionism, and his self-dedication to the machine was as if to say 'we are getting too far from our base and straining our communications. Let us consolidate here and wait for the main body to come up. One thing at a time. This is the machine-age. Let us perfect the machines, and honour the mechanics who are the real nation, and who should count more than the scouts and outriders of the spirit'. This was a close interpretation of the national mood, as the Twenties waned. The chief aim was agreed to be a general spread of social contentment by organizing industry to increase the standard of living of the common people—so far at least as this was consistent with the capitalistic system, which had to support a large rentier class.

To begin with, there was a feeling that the human cogs of the machine should be overhauled—T. E. Lawrence had written of himself, in the same obituary letter, as a cog in the machine, and added that one of the benefits of being a part of the machine was to learn that one didn't oneself matter. The National Institute of Industrial Psychology was founded in 1921, to determine what kind of factory conditions would promote healthier and happier minds in workers, and to urge their adoption by factory owners. The aim was to consider the worker, the machine, and the task as one unit: not only to discover how to improve the worker's health and his enjoyment of work, but at the same time to increase his output. Industrialists became patriarchal, rather in the sense that feudal landowners had been, and set out to provide their workers with treats, benefits, bonuses, sports clubs and even 'tied' houses out of their business profits. This avoided strikes, kept up a high level of skilled work, and appeased their own consciences. It was found that the most economic method of business was to 'plough in' excess profits by investing money in the workers. Experiments in patriarchalism had been made even before the war by Cadbury's the Quaker chocolate makers; they were carried on by Lever's the soap-boilers, Huntley & Palmer's the biscuit makers, and Lyons' the tea-shop proprietors; and had a great success in almost every instance. The most notable setback was to Lord Leverhulme: when he tried benevolent industrialization in the primitive Scottish Isle of Lewis, the inhabitants refused to co-operate.

The General Strike of 1926 had two salutary results that offset the ill effects of the artificial division of political thought into 'Left' and 'Right': in the first place it abashed the governing classes, as its leaders had intended, by graphic demonstration of their dependence on the workers, in the second it abashed the working classes by a graphic demonstration of their incapacity for combined action even of a negative sort. The result was encouraging to the industrial patriarch, and his example spread. It became bad form to grind the faces of the poor, and if any particularly glaring instance of face-grinding came to public attention, the big business man would find himself shunned at his country-club or by his golfing acquaintances. A large number of his kind had been educated at public schools, if not also at universities, and so brought up in the *noblesse oblige* ethics of the governing class, not in the 'all's fair in business' ethics of the small trader. If he had not had a gentleman's education, he would secretly regret this as a business liability, and be the more scrupulous in his gentility.

So it was that the 'wicked capitalist' of Third International dogma, who had been only too common in Karl Marx's time, began to die out: in a great many industries he could not compete with the benevolent sort. Where he survived he was in general less wicked than unfortunate: he could not make his business pay well enough to satisfy both his shareholders and his work-people. He usually felt himself under a stronger obligation to his shareholders, whose money he had borrowed and some of whom had no means of livelihood but the dividends he paid, than to the work-people, who at least could find other work if they did not want their faces ground in his mine or factory. He felt no stronger moral obligation to them, in fact, than to private tradesmen and taxi-drivers, who also sold him their labour services in the open market. The *Daily Herald* in the early Twenties made Wicked Capitalists of a number of landowners who drew royalties from mines and rents from the dilapidated houses of the miners. This attack overlooked the divided allegiance of these landowners to the miners, their agricultural tenants, and their heirs. The agricultural side of the estates was their earliest obligation, and because of land-tax, death-duties, and a falling market for coal and agricultural produce, they saw themselves on the way to ruin. Death-duties were 50 per cent of the value of property, and if, as happened to some noble families, three heads of the house died in rapid succession, very little of the estate could remain unsold. Many peers had, however, converted their estates into limited liability companies soon after death-duties were first imposed: among them the Earl of Moray, Viscount Novar, and the Duke of Buccleuch.

These companies were given power to trade in farming, fishing, shooting, mining, oil and shale works, quarrying, forestry. (The quest for oil in England had already begun in 1919. Reports were published in the *Daily Mail* that oil had been struck in Derbyshire, and that soon it would be produced in marketable quantities. Well-boring continued for the next twenty years, but without profit.) In some cases the peers concerned continued to direct their affairs personally, but many, disgusted with democracy, left them in the hands of lawyers, who could be counted on not to err greatly on the side of generosity. One profitable source of income for northern landowners dried up in 1930 when the Wall Street crash ruined the American sportsmen who had annually taken over grouse-moors at extravagant rents: they ceased to come and by 1932 sporting-gun manufacturers were faced with ruin.

The *Daily Herald* had also frequently assailed the Ecclesiastical Commissioners as supervisors of slum property who had a cynical disregard of the poor. The Ecclesiastical Commissioners were estate agents who handled Church property, the rents of which went largely to the upkeep of churches and cathedrals and the payment of small stipends to struggling clergy. Their first duty was, they felt, to the owners of the property, not to the tenants who chose to hire it.

It cannot be pretended that business ethics were irreproachable. A good deal of business was done by personal contact at bars and over luncheon tables, and on the golf course between rounds, the conclusions being later confirmed by secretaries' letters. This made the atmosphere friendly and natural, but also gave large scope to poker-play technique and exercise of personality. An intelligent and forceful person who could persuade another into a one-sided deal was called 'a good business man': so long as he avoided committing his misrepresentations in black and white.

There were two serious financial crashes at the end of the Twenties; both the men concerned were 'good business men'. James White was a self-made man, having started as a poor boy from Rochdale. He worked with Beecham's, the pill and patent-medicine manufacturers, and came to have a controlling interest in the Beecham Trust—which controlled Dunlop's, the rubber firm. He financed prize fights, bought a yacht for £30,000, and owned a racing establishment—his horses won at different times the Royal Hunt Cup, the Cesarewitch, the Manchester Cup, and the Lincoln. He ran secret cock-fights; worked at an opulent desk with gold and silver fittings; always had his chef prepare lunch for twelve—though usually he had far fewer guests —and tried his hand as a theatrical producer. He rented a West End theatre for a season, where he used to attend rehearsals and interfere with advice given grotesquely in a Lancashire accent. On one occasion he hired a special train to take himself and one friend to Manchester for the opening of a play that he had financed. At midnight he distributed £5 notes to the station staff. In 1925, however, he was hit by the return to the gold standard; he continued his extravagances, but could not recover his financial position. In 1927 he committed suicide by means of chloroform, leaving debts of £610,000. In a last letter he wrote, 'I have been guilty of folly, but never refused a pal . . . the world is nothing but a human cauldron of greed. . . . It is one dark day after another. My soul is sickened by the homage paid to wealth.'

In 1929 came the crash of the Hatry group. Clarence Hatry was not a picturesque figure like White, and so newspapers blamed him more readily, though his crash affected comparatively few people. He declared that his job was 'to harmonize opposing personalities', for 'business is not only a matter of finance but also of personal relations'—perhaps the first time business had been admitted to be such in court. He was convicted for having recorded fictitious and valueless securities, and, with his four associates, condemned to a long term of penal servitude. He was not a dishonest man, but failed to get away with one of his deals, and so crashed. If he had got away with it, no one would have known about his interim juggling with figures, and no one would have suffered. On his emergence from prison, a number of his former associates raised a subscription for him and showed him by every means in their power that though he had broken the law, he had not offended business ethics—except in being caught out.

Bureaucratic ethics were altogether different. Bureaucrats proceeded by filled-in forms, inter-departmental minutes, and formal committee meetings. There was less personal contact, less smartness. Bureaucratic work consisted not in closing favourable deals but in doing things in orderly routine fashion. The good bureaucrat did not need to have a conversationally powerful personality. He needed to be punctilious in seeing that the proper forms were filled up, the proper people notified and consulted: that, in fact, the proper channels and formalities were used. The business conception of 'good-will', kept up by lunches, gifts, privileges—extras that had the same effect as bribes but were not given or taken as bribes—scarcely existed in bureaucracy, which was supposed to be impersonal. Since courtesy-favours, except of the subtlest sort were ruled out, real bribery was occasionally used and to more scandalous effect than any similar persuasion in business.

None the less, the bureaucratic system was elastic: influence could be exerted by departmental heads in particular instances. There is an eighteenth-century story of one noble member of the privileged classes coming to another in the Ministry and asking that, when candidates applied for a certain clerkship, a nominee of his own should, *ceteris paribus*, be chosen. '*Ceteris paribus* be damned,' the offended Minister cried, insulted. 'I have the gift of this appointment.' That spirit was dead; but if one knew a departmental head, or 'someone high up', one could very often have a personal note sent down by the Great Man to the underling concerned that, *ceteris paribus*, this or that action was recommended. The sort of action would be granting a work-permit to a deserving alien, withholding the criminal prosecution of an attempted suicide, ear-marking a military cadet for a regiment with which he had family connections, overriding a local government decision where amenities were threatened. Only, no *quid pro quo* might be accepted: the bureaucrat had to be scrupulously honest, and honesty was a formalized honesty. In business it varied greatly between one market and another, and even in different departments of the same market. Advertising firms, for example, had three standards of honesty—a high standard in their dealings with the business firms whose 'accounts' they managed, a lower standard in stealing 'accounts' from rival firms, and a still lower one in 'putting over' advertised goods on the public by misrepresentation.

The sharp difference between modern business morality and that of the established gentry caused some confusion in country districts where successful merchants took over the estates of impoverished land-owners and turned them into limited liability companies. The retainers were at first willing to transfer their allegiance to the new families, but resented the impersonal touch, the reluctance for a long chat, the circular letters, the raising of rents to an economic level, and especially the private investigations by secretaries and agents, which they regarded as 'ungentlemanly spying'. It was no comfort to them that 'the third generation makes the gentleman'. They had ceased to think in such long terms as these.

CHAPTER FOURTEEN

Sport and Controversy

London's extraordinary prosperity, as the Twenties drew to their close, was illustrated by the expansion of the restaurant trade: fashionable restaurants could afford to spend £50,000 on redecorating every few years, and £12,000 yearly on dancebands. When the first boom in dancing began to die down in the middle Twenties, cabaret came in, at a cost of anything up to £1,000 a week. The success of these restaurants led to a change in London's clubland. Since most young men worked by day, they counted on the society of women for the evening; consequently more and more men's clubs came to provide rooms where women could be entertained. Young men also wanted squashcourts and swimming baths, as well as conversation and good wine; the elder clubs had to modernize or die out. Original club-rules were relaxed in nearly every case, in order to keep up membership. Married men were allowed to join the Bachelors' on payment of a small fine, and the Travellers', for which the qualification had originally been that every member must have travelled one thousand miles in a direct line from London, came to admit many who had never been farther than Paris. Political clubs loosened their party ties, and cocktail bars were introduced into such strongholds as White's and the St. James's. Park Lane changed even more remarkably than Pall Mall: it ceased to be a street of large private houses for the nobility. Vast hotels on the American model went up in their place and seldom had empty rooms.

As has been related, the police had 'cracked down hard' on

the London night-clubs in the late Twenties, but nothing could shake the determination of visitors and residents to drink out of hours, or the eagerness of the night-club world to profit from it. Something else had to be thought of, and very soon the first 'private bottle parties' began to appear. It had been discovered that the law had no authority to interfere with the consumption of liquor or the provision of dancing, music and other entertainment at a privately convened party. So long as the organizer of such a party was a 'host', and his customers 'guests' and every drop of liquor on the premises had been ordered within licensing hours from a wine merchant by the 'host', the police were powerless. Bottle parties were conducted at first with great strictness and discretion. To 'gate-crash' without a printed 'invitation' was absolutely impossible—impossible, too, to secure a drink unless the order for it had been personally placed for the guest by the host many hours before his arrival. Naturally enough, the host's benevolence stopped far short of gratuitous hospitality, and 'feeling obliged to ask for some little help to meet his expenses over the pleasure at welcoming so many friends' he collected such help at the rate of 25s. for a bottle of whisky, 35s. to 55s. for inferior champagne, and 5s. for two rashers of bacon and an egg.

The early bottle-parties were provided with first-class dance-bands, irreproachably behaved waiters, and most luxurious premises. They rarely opened before midnight, and rarely closed before six or seven in the morning, when the last 'guests' were helped into waiting taxi-cabs. Soon, however, establishments appeared without pretensions either to luxury, decency, or good service. Since the Lord Chamberlain could exercise no authority over 'private' entertainment, the semi-nude cabaret appeared, accompanied by the frankly lewd song. Certain bottle-party establishments gave free invitations to Soho negroes; for well-to-do roisterers would pay huge sums for the excitement of sharing a dance-band with these simply sensual people. Bottle-parties were generally beyond the means of younger society. Their clientèle seemed largely made up of the sort of business men who preferred bank-rolls to cheque-books—bookmakers, pools-promoters, Soho vice kings, manufacturers from the provinces making whoopee away from their families—also amateur and professional prostitutes, and simple adventurers in search of London's night life, including a number of Army and Navy officers and Colonial officials on leave. By the time the new war broke out, bottle-parties in the West End of London numbered some hundreds.

In fashion there was now a tendency to vary the sack-like tubular figure of the early Twenties by accentuating the shoulder angles and spreading out sleeves and skirts. In 1926 pleats were rediscovered, but simple sports dresses were still so popular that even 'sports evening gowns' were sold. Every possible kind of material was being used in shoes: snake-skin, lizard, crocodile, sea-leopard, ostrich, zebra, dolphin, walrus, Siberian pony, and unclipped calf-skin. General fashion changes included the introduction of sun-glasses and deep-peaked eye shades for bathing, driving and tennis; and silk Japanese sunshades—stumpy in shape, like the fashionable umbrella. Raincoats were no longer drab, but made in bright colours, with checked and dotted patterns. Long Russian boots were worn, but chiefly by business girls to keep their stockings from being splashed by passing cars —'Russian Boot Rosie, Her feet are so cosy!' Beauty treatment became more and more common, and the Press was debating the morality of having faces lifted and eyebrows plucked.

Interior decoration was now geometrical: the fashion came from Paris, where the neglected beauties of Byzantine art had been rediscovered. Curves were soon held as vulgar in furniture as in the human figure. The Jacobean barley-sugar twist was therefore abandoned, even by the hire-purchase firms, in favour of unturned legs. Modern chests-of-drawers, chairs, tables, beds, appeared in walnut and light oak with provocatively obtuse instead of right angles, looking as if bits had been chopped off them; even such fixtures as lavatory basins, grates, and overmantels went geometrical too. This neo-Byzantine style suited the unlovable 'New Age' architecture—the steel and concrete and Portland stone of Bush House and the rebuilt Regent Street —better than debased Renaissance. Steel tubular furniture came from Paris in 1929, and before the end of the Peace provided a brightly impersonal touch to all up-to-date offices and consulting-rooms.

The same influence was affecting window-dressing: goods were draped stiffly over cylinders and triangles, and the old realistic wax-figures were being replaced in the advanced stores by flat papier-maché ones, painted in silver, gilt, grey, black, and orange. Window-dressing had become an art: smart shops no longer tried to stuff as much as possible into their windows, but concentrated on showing off effectively a few well-chosen things. Even sweetshops succumbed to this fashion. Now, flattening one's nose against the window where once lollipops, sugared almonds, caramels, and chocolate-creams had been paraded in serried ranks of jars, one saw a mediaeval Chinese vase, full of expensive chrysanthemums, a wisp of Persian embroidery and (following the composition line of the design, as taught by professors of the Fine Arts) the eye travelled eagerly to a very small closed carton on an antique silver salver, containing presumably some extraordinary delectable pralines. But one had learned that even this carton was a dummy—it would destroy the freshness and delicacy of the pralines to be exposed to sunlight.

In 1927 the 'refeminizing' tendency in women's fashions became more marked. At Ascot—a disastrously wet one—at garden-parties, and at theatres, long, frilled crinoline skirts were worn, made of yards and yards of tulle. Everyone laughed and gasped to see women going about in long skirts again: it seemed almost indecent. But for ordinary wear 'masculine' styles still prevailed—sleeveless waistcoats and cardigans, for instance, that matched the wearer's suit—and skirts remained short, though they had advanced two inches from the ebb-tide mark of 1926. Geometrical designs, in the form of applique pieces and insets, were displacing floral patterns. Suits in varying tones of the same colour were worn, and this fashion was also affecting interior decoration: walls were painted or distempered in a *dégradé* style, starting palely in one shade at the top and growing deeper and darker toward the bottom, and ceilings likewise were painted in colours. Women began to wear ankle-socks with gaily coloured tops, for the most part not on bare legs but over stockings. Hair was showing signs of becoming longer, the shingle beginning to curl up at the back. Hat fashion was on the move: at one time it was for wide-brimmed floppy hats, at another for close-fitting helmet-like ones, named 'Crusader', 'Aviator', or 'Lindbergh'—for Charles Lindbergh had just flown from New York to Paris.

Flying was very popular with both sexes, now that there was so high a standard of airworthiness in design and maintenance of planes that crashes were the exception rather than the rule. The Continental airways were regularly used by business men. There was also a great increase in private flying, due to the development of light aeroplanes and the founding of amateur flying clubs.

A new age of record-breaking began. Alan Cobham flew to Capetown and back in May 1926, and to Australia and back in October. After the Australian flight his seaplane alighted on the Thames by the Houses of Parliament, and he was officially welcomed by a group of members headed by the Speaker. The hysterical excitement caused in the United States and the American colony in Paris by Lindbergh's transatlantic flight was somehow communicated to Britain: this flight was accepted unquestionably as the greatest feat of a hundred years—it is difficult to see why. Counting airship crews, over a hundred persons had flown the Atlantic before, though not solo; and far more spectacularly foolhardy feats than Lindbergh's had been performed in America—Blondel's tightrope walk over the Niagara Falls is an easy instance. The first woman to fly the Atlantic solo was an American, Amelia ('Lady Lindy') Earhart in 1928. All speed records were beaten by Flight-Lieutenant Webster in his Schneider Contest plane that won the International Trophy for Britain in 1927. It was won outright in 1931. Great record-breaking hopes were also held out for the new airships, the R100 and R101, which were being built in 1928 at Cardington.

Britain was anxious to gain and retain the 'Triple Crown', for the fastest speed on sea, on land, and in the air. The land record had been won in 1926 by Parry Thomas, whose racing car did 178 m.p.h. on Pendine Sands, Carmarthenshire. He was later killed on the same sands, the chain of his car flying loose and strangling him. In 1927 Henry Segrave and Malcolm Campbell were both trying to be the first to reach 200 m.p.h. and in one attempt Campbell's car, the 'Bluebird', nearly sank in the quicksands at Pendine. Segrave was the most popular motorist of the day. His first experiments in mechanics were with model railways: he built a special house to contain an elaborate railway system with everything perfectly to scale. Then he became famous by winning the Grand Prix de France in 1923. Later he made attempts on the world speed records, both on land and water: he won the first in 1929 with his ice-cooled 1,000 horse-power 'Golden Arrow' on Daytona Beach, Florida, by doing 231 miles an hour. Some days later he also beat Gar Wood's speedboat record. (Gar Wood was an American speedster who had earned the execration of British sportsmen by sinking with his backwash a British competitor in a race —it seemed deliberately. That there was no written rule against the trick made it the more heinous: the greater ingenuity of American sportsmen in keeping within the letter of the sporting code while infringing what the British held to be the spirit was a great grievance. But we shall soon come to the ironical sequel to this in the 'Body Line' controversy in cricket.) It was when attempting to put up a new speedboat record that Segrave— who, like Cobham and Campbell was knighted for his feats— met his death on Friday, 13th June 1930. He took out his boat 'Miss England II' on Lake Windermere; on his first run he did 96 miles an hour and on his second 101 miles an hour. On the third run, however, 'Miss England II' shot up into the air, then sank: the propeller-blades had caught some small drifting object and snapped. Segrave was rescued, but with several ribs smashed. He had just strength enough to ask 'Did we do it?' and saw his rescuers nod in reply, before he died.

The hot summer of 1928 popularized sunbathing. Bathing-dresses therefore became much shorter, with low, sun-tan backs. Most of them still had a little overskirt; the separated two-piece suit had not yet come in. For use over bathing dresses brightly coloured, oilcloth beach-coats lined with towelling were worn; and women's beach-pyjamas, also, of loose-fitting crêpe-de-chine—the first publicly accepted form of sports-trousers for women. 1929 brought Mexican straw hats with wide brims, and sun-tan oil to keep the skin from blistering. It was fashionable to be sunburnt over as much of the body as possible—though their piebald appearance in the nude secretly troubled most women. They extended the tanned area by wearing no stockings on informal occasions, though a suggestion that competitors in the Wimbledon Tennis tournament might do the same caused a minor sensation.

Captain Webb had swum the Channel in mid-Victorian days, but in the Twenties it was thought necessary to prove that this feat was far less remarkable than it seemed, especially if one studied the currents and the weather, and greased oneself all over, and kept a boat handy to supply artificial stimulants. Between 1923 and 1926 several men swam the Channel, knocking hours off Webb's time. In 1926 Miss Gertrude Ederle knocked two hours off the best male record. Then six more women swam across, and by 1928 the thing had become rather a bore, to be made fun of in the Cochran-Coward revue, 'This Year of Grace'. What ended it was a heavy-handed joke by a Scottish woman doctor who brought public attention to the fact that no official control was kept on these records—by swimming a mile out to sea, then climbing into a boat and allowing herself to be rowed across for all but the spectacular last lap. This hoax upset everyone, especially Miss Ederle, who felt her honour impugned: however, she performed a feat that even Captain Webb had not attempted—she swam the Straits of Gibraltar, and under strict supervision too, careless of possible sharks.

The sun-bathing habit had a brightening effect on men's clothing. Coloured sports shirts and beach shirts came in, worn with open necks and no ties. Flannel and linen trousers appeared in many colours, besides the staid and universal grey. These innovations were at first limited to the few—chiefly to those who spent their holidays at French resorts.

Slimming was now a cult. Tablets and potions of all kinds were being sold as weight-reducers. Mechanical zoos appeared, with electric camels, horses and chairs, which bounced the patient about to irregular rhythms. Courses in physical training were given, and many people adopted the habit of doing early morning physical jerks. Women began to roll themselves with rubber rollers that had little studs all over them and were supposed to remove superfluous flesh. Fruit was being boosted as a slimming agent by an 'Eat More Fruit' campaign: the *Daily Chronicle* in March 1927 recommended orange-juice with a dash of gin. The *Sunday Times* suggested that the slimming effect could be given by piping at the hips of skirts. The *Daily Mail* printed numerous warnings by prominent doctors of the dangers to health of reckless slimming. But the cult continued in full vigour until at least 1932.

Several other novelties made their appearance in these years, such as fireproof glass dishes and casseroles for cooking. Potato crisps were a popular new food. These had originally been imported from France, but were now made in England and over a million packets were sold in 1928. People found them invaluable for impromptu parties and rush-meals. For a short time there were Photomatons in all the big stores: at a cost of one shilling they produced in a few minutes a strip of developed photographs of a sitter taken from various angles. Rubber soles and heels for shoes had been in popular use for years, but had been considered ungentlemanly—like celluloid collars. They could now be worn by the 'best people', as being more watertight, longer-lasting, and quieter to walk on than leather. Luggage was getting lighter and lighter: suitcases and hatboxes being made of 'fibre' and other light composite materials—salesmen delighted in jumping hard on the suitcases to show prospective customers how strong they were.

Almost all sports but archery, bowls, and croquet gained in popularity during this period, the greatest advances being in swimming and Association football. Before the war, practically no lower-middle or working-class people, except in sea-coast towns, could swim; now covered and open-air swimming baths, to which elementary school-children were taken, and cheap excursions by road and rail to the sea made the non-swimmer feel behind the times. Football had been brought by ex-Servicemen into country districts where it was unknown: a network of amateur football leagues spread all over Great Britain, and the Saturday afternoon matches were the chief event of the week in most villages: these were the 'junior leagues', the senior league teams being provided by towns not rich enough to pay for professionals. Teams from banks, factories, and public utility companies competed in another extensive league network.

Between the Football Association, which controlled professional football, and the Amateur Football Association, which had broken away from it many years before the war, there was a polite truce. The well-to-do classes had a strong prejudice against professional Association football as mercenary, venial and unsporting, and the Select Press published only the briefest reports of even First Division League matches with gates of hundreds of thousands. This was old-fashioned, for F.A. football was now at least as clean as the amateur variety—the crowds execrated any dirty play, the integrity of referees was beyond suspicion, and hard training had raised the level of professional skill to a point where even the best amateur team could not seriously compete. Every year the Corinthians, a club drawn from public-school footballers, entered for the Football Cup; but their kick and rush tactics and shoulder-charges, though disconcerting, never succeeded against the close passing and well-drilled manœuvres of the professional teams which they met. The amateur's chief scorn was for the end of season sale of players.

Rugby was the most honoured football game at the universities and among the upper-middle classes: it had escaped the 'taint of professionalism' everywhere except in parts of the north of England. The depressed and revolutionary South Wales, oddly enough, preferred this rougher but gentlemanly game to Association, and played it in a perfect amateur spirit, though generous expenses allowances semi-professionalized a few clubs.

Lawn tennis also became enormously popular, not only among the well-to-do, who had been prejudiced against it as a less manly game than cricket, but among the middle classes, who had not hitherto had any facilities for playing. Its social advantages were obvious. Now that women had added thirty points to their game by rationalizing their dress and adopting the overarm service, mixed doubles were no longer a nuisance to be gallantly borne with, but a real pleasure. And in half an hour's tennis one could get quicker and better exercise than in three hours of club cricket. Wimbledon tennis tournaments were attended by thousands instead of hundreds, new clubs sprang up everywhere, local authorities provided public courts in parks, and the *Daily Express* offered a trophy for a knock-out competition between representatives of London suburban clubs.

Most popular of indoor games was auction bridge: by 1929 it had completely ousted billiards from most large houses. Bridge was an upper-class and upper-middle class game. The lower-middle class continued to play the less skilful whist—from which 'auction' had developed in 1902 by way of Russian whist or dummy bridge—long after it had died out in the London clubs. Whist-drives for charity were a regular form of amusement in church and chapel circles throughout the period. In 1929 'Auction' began to be succeeded by the American variety of 'Contract'. Card games were becoming less and less a form of gambling. Although people played for small stakes 'to steady their game', their chief interest was now the game itself; the succession of improvements on the original whist having always had the same tendency—to make a good player increasingly superior to chance, by enabling him to limit the damage of bad hands. The *Observer* in November 1929 noted: 'Contract has been boomed in a way that Auction never was.' That was the year that Ely Culbertson and his wife, the American Contract experts, brought over a team which defeated two crack British ones. The publicity given to these matches was so great that international contests were played between Britain, Austria, Germany, and Holland. In 1933 twenty-seven thousand people attended a match at Selfridge's lasting for several days, between an American and a British team for the International Schwab Trophy. In that year over three hundred bridge clubs in London alone were affiliated to the newly formed British Bridge League. A good deal of poker was also played in the part of Society that had gone American, and among business men in the advertising trade and on the Stock Exchange: but it never reached the suburbs, as Contract did.

Two new spectacular sports were successfully tried in the later Twenties, both with the advantage over horse racing and football that they could be played under cover and by artificial light: these were dirt-track racing for motor-bicycles, an American novelty, and greyhound racing with the help of a mechanical hare. Dirt-track racing was very popular among the hero-worshipping younger men and women; but it did not take on so remarkably as dog racing, because it did not give so speculative a betting market. Greyhound and whippet coursing for live hares had long been a popular sport, particularly in mining districts, and the Waterloo Cup, an annual event, was patronized by the highest sporting society. The necessary elements for the new form of greyhound racing were therefore already to hand when in 1925 rumours of the electric hare first went round; but experts were almost unanimous in their view that dogs would never be so foolish as to chase a dummy hare more than once. Nevertheless the newly formed Greyhound Racing Association equipped the Belle Vue track at Manchester, and the first race-meeting was held on the 24th July 1926, under the shadow of the General Strike. Three thousand people came and the dogs proved as gullible as the promoters had hoped. Although Lancashire had been badly hit by the strike, and people had little money to spend, attendance slowly increased, and by the end of the season ten thousand was a small gate. The re-opening night in spring 1927 attracted a crowd of twenty-five thousand. More tracks were opened at Edinburgh, at the White City, at the Wembley Stadium, and finally all over the country. In 1927 sixty-two greyhound-racing companies were registered in different parts of Britain, with a total capital of £7,000,000. Greyhound racing supplied many of the thrills of horse racing, and was much cheaper both for the owners and the public. Dogs achieved celebrity far surpassing that of Waterloo Cup winners: the names of Charlie Cranston, the 1927 Champion of England, and his successor Mick the Miller (stuffed and preserved for posterity) were as honoured as those of Felix the Cat, the Agha Khan's famous racehorse Mumtaz Mahal, and even Tishy, the comic horse who twisted its legs, immortalized by Tom Webster, the *Daily Mail* sporting cartoonist.

In 1929 film-goers were bowled over by the talking pictures. 'The Singing Fool', with Al Jolson, at the newly opened Regal Cinema at Marble Arch prompted a competitor in the *Evening Standard* Film Criticism Contest to write: 'I have just seen my first talking picture—"The Singing Fool"—and was impressed with the tremendous possibilities of this new form of entertainment. It is uncanny the way almost a soul is breathed into the characters portrayed.' After this, silent films, except Chaplin's, fell into disrepute and soon all but the unpretentious provincial picture-houses had to close down for two or three months while they were being 'wired for Sound'. But Hollywood found great drawbacks to its new success: very few of its silent stars, though admirable as mimes and mannequins, had any training in elocution. Most of them had to be discarded; London and New York were raided for effective substitutes, at great cost. The same *Evening Standard* competitor confessed that he had felt 'a bitter disillusionment to hear the half-mumbled elocution of the otherwise beautiful women' in 'The Singing Fool'. And though the American accent in comedy was charming, it spoilt the theatrical illusion for British filmgoers to hear Mary Queen of Scots or Richard Coeur de Lion, in a historical drama, speaking with a Southern drawl, a Yankee twang, or the incisive accent of the Middle West.

The *Evening Standard* films editor commented on the critical

acuity of modern filmgoers: '. . . True, they are indulgent to
weaknesses in a film; but they *notice* them all the same. They
never fail to respond to the "high spots" of greatness. And they
forgive much that is poor for a flash or two of genius. Here are
no "hicks" or "rubes", but an educated, cultured, responsive,
sensitive people, eager to hail the work of the masters of the
studios.' The 'masters of the studios' had little to offer in the
way of smash-hits after Al Jolson had sonny-boyed the Talkies
into fame: they decided to forgo the obvious advantages of the
cinema in showing action beyond the technical resources of the
theatre, and used their newly recruited players to transfer stage
successes to the screen with little change of technique.

Paul Rotha, a professional cinema-critic, was one of the many
who regretted what had happened. In his *The Film of To-day*,
published in 1931, he sighed for the old silent days, when films
were not 'bolstered up with variety turns and orchestral interludes, as well as by the erection of vast palaces of luxury and
atrocious vulgarity. . . . Since talking films have occupied the
attention of studios, the pictorial value of the screen has greatly
deteriorated. The films of the last year of the silent period were
far more pleasing from a pictorial point of view. The public has
tired of its craze for simply hearing speech and seeing moving
pictures of the speakers. Audiences in 1930 failed to maintain
the big business created by the talking boom of 1929. Attend-
ances dropped to pre-dialogue level. The season of 1930–1
showed that box-office receipts had fallen 30 per cent in comparison with a year ago.' British film companies took advantage
of the confusion to try documentary films without much story
interest: John Grierson's 'Drifters' was the first short film of this
kind made in England. The most famous was 'Man of Aran' by
Robert O'Flaherty, which documented primitive life in the Irish
islands off Galway. The sequence showing how Tiger King, a
stalwart islander, killed a basking shark was regarded as the
chief screen event of 1933.

The coming of the Talkies hit another class of cinema worker
as hard as it did the 'dumb' silent star: the cinema musician. The
picture-houses, at the same time as they 'wired for Sound', dismissed their orchestras and replaced them with cinema organists
and their Wurlitzers. These orchestras had played unceasingly
throughout sessions in order to drown the click of the projector,

to breach the gap between reels, and to make it seem reasonable that one could not hear what the actors were saying. They had played chiefly Classical music—bits of the 'Tannhäuser Overture', of Schubert's 'Unfinished Symphony', of Gounod's 'Faust' and Verdi's 'Aïda' and Chopin's 'Nocturnes', but letting one melody flow into another as the mood of the picture seemed to require. All this ended as suddenly as sub-titles; for the talkies provided their own musical setting, hashed up by Hollywood musicians.

The provision of popular musical classics was left to the B.B.C. By this time wireless reception had so greatly improved that, except on occasions of really bad atmospherics, to switch on the wireless at home was almost as good as attending the Queen's Hall, and far cheaper and more comfortable. The B.B.C. now provided dance music: plenty of the humorous and sentimental kind—Jack Payne and Henry Hall, for instance— very occasionally the really hot stuff, straight from America. It gave light, tuneful tea-time music, and loud, stirring brass-band music; ballad concerts; and German *lieder* concerts. There were also such series as the 'Foundations of Music', which introduced the public to little-known, early works. By taking over the Promenade Concerts, the B.B.C. was able not only to produce the traditionally 'classical' symphonies but also to help in the Mozart and Haydn revival, and sponsor contemporary music. Music had been making developments analogous to those in modernistic art and writing: the octave was varied with quarter tones and eighth tones; twelve-tone scales were used and rhythms no longer based on the constant time-value of the musical bar; sound combinations that had hitherto been disallowed as dis- cords were exploited. The B.B.C. always kept decorously in arrear of the very latest experiments, but shortened the time-lag between the composer and the general public most remarkably: it put on the air a great deal of Stravinsky, Hindemith, Schön- berg, Sibelius, Bartok, of the Parisian experimentalists, 'Les Six', and such British composers as Sir Arnold Bax, Frederick Delius, Constant Lambert and William Walton, who otherwise would have had to wait years rather than months for a hearing. One advantage of the air was that usually meal-time and evening hours could be allocated to the low-brow or general public, the mornings to housewives, and mid-afternoon and late-night hours to the leisured.

People were no longer much interested in the technical progress of 'radio'—as it was now beginning to be called. Instead
they were acquiring a radio sense to match their cinema sense
and were becoming highly critical of programmes. There was
not enough jazz; there was too much jazz; the drama was too
exciting; the talks were too dull; there was not enough light
comedy; there was too much symphonic music. Everyone who
wrote in had his own opinion about what programmes the
public wanted. All seemed to agree, however, that the programmes were not sufficiently varied.

In 1926 the B.B.C. responded to the demand for brighter programmes with a lively experiment conducted by Ronald Knox
(brother of E. V. Knox, the *Punch* poet), who from being a witty
critic of the Roman Church, had become Father Ronald Knox,
a witty Catholic missionary. He broadcast a talk which took the
form of a circumstantial account of a revolution in England.
This was treading on delicate ground, for it was the year of the
General Strike. The *Daily Express* protested strongly, under the
headlines: 'A Blunder by B.B.C. Revolution Hoax by Wireless.
People Alarmed all Week-End.' A clear warning had been given
before the talk that the incidents described were imaginary, yet
people took seriously Father Knox's account of the blowing up
of the Houses of Parliament and of butchery in St. James's Park.
Sir Leo Chiozza Money, the financial journalist, said: 'The item
was utterly humourless,' and the Lord Mayor of Newcastle
complained indignantly that his wife had been seriously upset,
and that he had had to telephone to a neighbouring mayor for
reassurance. The B.B.C. defended itself by pointing out that,
since people complained that the dramas were too exciting and
the talks too dull and the programmes not sufficiently varied, it
had done what it could to oblige; and claimed to have received
many more letters in appreciation of this talk than of protest.

The newspapers kept up a running fire of criticism against the
B.B.C., the chief marksman being Collie Knox, the *Daily Mail*
wireless editor. The voices of announcers were a permanent
offence: they were 'too refaned' and it was considered prepos-
terous to stabilize what was called 'The Oxford Accent' as the
representative intonation of the whole vigorous people. In 1928
the trouble was censorship. L. J. Maxse, editor of the *National
Review*, and Handley Page, of aeroplane fame, were to take part

in a debate on 'Is Flying a Fraud?' which had been arranged for the benefit of King Edward's Hospital Fund. Their scripts were censored, however, because they not only attacked the Air Ministry but made propaganda on behalf of British flying. They indignantly pointed out that the B.B.C. had just allowed Emil Ludwig, the popular biographer, to make German propaganda in a talk on Bismarck. The controversy grew more bitter when Bernard Shaw was refused permission to broadcast on his seventieth birthday, because he would not guarantee not to be provocative. But any stick was good enough to beat the B.B.C. with and keep it from getting too powerful or self-important. When it refused to produce Reginald Berkeley's play, *Machines*, on the grounds of its being 'without interest', the Press most inconsistently accused it of banning the play, which dealt realistically with divorce and murder, for fear of stirring up a controversy like the one over Father Knox! There was more trouble in 1928 when the B.B.C., which had become a public corporation in 1927, proposed to bring out a literary weekly, the *Listener*, which was to reprint broadcast talks, give book-reviews, and publish some original articles. The newspapers strongly attacked this 'undesirable incursion' by the Corporation. They asked indignantly whether it was also proposed to publish a B.B.C. *Times* and a B.B.C. *Daily Mail*. The *Listener*, however, came into existence on the understanding that no more than 10 per cent of its material should be original: the rest would be reprints of broadcast talks. The *Listener*, though it had to remember its low-brow public, contrived to give more space and fairer reviews to advanced artistic and literary work than its most intellectually ambitious rivals. Its illustrations were the best to be found in any British popular magazine; and it published not only news-photographs but photographs of works in art galleries and museums.

The theatres also took part in these attacks against the B.B.C. When in October 1929 James Agate gave a series of broadcast talks on the drama for the B.B.C., several theatres sent him the usual critic's invitation card, with the curious conditions: 'The invitation is intended to meet the convenience of legitimate journalism, exclusive of broadcasting.' For theatre managers were beginning to regard the B.B.C. as a rival.

Controversy was the keyword of these years; and on the stage the controversial 'play of ideas' was coming back into favour. Shaw's 'The Apple Cart' was produced in 1929, and hailed as a 'wonderful achievement for a man of seventy-three'. It was a political extravaganza, making up in 'provocative thought' for what it lacked in dramatic unity. It showed Shaw's transition from orthodox Socialism to his personal brand of Leftism. He wrote of the play: 'The conflict is not really between royalty and democracy. It is between both and plutocracy, which, having destroyed the royal power by frank force under democratic pretexts, has bought and swallowed democracy. Money talks; money prints; money broadcasts; money reigns; and kings and labour leaders alike have to register its decrees, and even, by a staggering paradox, to finance its enterprises and guarantee its profits.... From the moment when the Socialists attain to what is with unintentional irony called 'power' (meaning the drudgery of carrying on for the plutocrats) they no longer dare even to talk of nationalizing any industry, however socially vital, that has a farthing of profit for plutocracy still left in it, and that can be made to yield a farthing for it by subsidies.'

Shaw was never an original thinker, but always daringly anticipated what intelligent people were on the point of all saying together. Nearly the whole of the Leftism of the Thirties is contained in 'The Apple Cart'.

The Press knew that sex was a subject that its public was increasingly interested in, yet knew also that straight pornography did not pay in a family newspaper. It solved the question by a Clean-the-Stage campaign, attacks on obscene books which the public would not otherwise have heard of, and attacks on the police for their handling of sexual offences. It featured the London Public Morality Council, not as Mrs. Grundy spoilsports, which would have been the attitude six or seven years before, but as crusaders for purity.

The Bishop of London was a prominent clean-the-stager. He presided at one meeting in Caxton Hall where objections were made to 'Scotch Mist', a play by Sir Patrick Hastings, K.C., who had been Attorney General in the Labour Government. One speaker remarked: 'For instance, in "Scotch Mist" a character tells his wife, "You are bad, aren't you?" The answer is, "I hope I am." That is merely nonsense. But then there are plays that take the name of God in vain. We claim that we have the right to ask the Censor to stop this.' Large numbers of Londoners, it was said, earned their living by various forms of vice, and plays such as this played into their hands. However, Sir William Joynson-Hicks, the Home Secretary, refused the recommendations of the London Public Morality Council, which had sponsored the Caxton Hall meeting. He declared that the Censor was doing his work properly, and suggested that the Council should turn its attention to obscene books.

The most controversial play of 1928 was a sex-play in a school setting, 'Young Woodley' by John Van Druten. 'Young Woodley' succeeded in passing the Censorship only after the Lord Chamberlain himself had seen it at a private production by the Arts theatre and decided that it was artistic rather than pornographic—like the gauze-draped 'Living Statuary' that was the nearest that revues dared go to complete stage-nudity. The *Daily Telegraph* said of it in 1929: 'Woodley continues to be, as he always was, perhaps the most exquisite study in existence of a boy's awakening to love; the young Romeo of our own times, with Mallowhurst for his Verona. "Adolescent" is a word that usually has rather sinister associations. Mr. van Druten clears away the ugly spots from the word; he causes us to hear, instead, the first rustling of leaves in a still forest. The shot-silk texture of the boy's innocence of life and his knowledge of life during his last term at school are subtly blended.'

Controversy over obscene books did not arise until the appearance in 1928 of *The Well of Loneliness*, the mannish Radclyffe Hall's emotional protest against the world's cruel misunderstanding of Lesbian love. Indignation was stirred up against it by James Douglas. He declared in the *Sunday Express*: 'I would rather give a healthy boy or girl a phial of prussic acid than this novel.' As a result of this and other protests, the book was banned. Like Norah James's banned *Sleeveless Errand* and James Joyce's *Ulysses*, it went into several editions in Paris. In the serious Press the banning of books was debated at length. Correspondents wrote to ask whether Customs officers had a secret index of banned books, and added that, if so, this was disgraceful in a free country. One letter to the *New Statesman* came from a member of the Reform Club, who had written to the Contact Editions Press, Paris, to ask the prices of two books, after having read excellent reviews of them in the *Criterion* and *Outlook*. For two months he got no reply; then he received back his original letter, together with a statement from Sir Archibald Bodkin himself (the Director of Public Prosecutions)—to the effect that all letters to Contact Editions were automatically searched, that the books, whose prices he had in all innocence inquired, were 'grossly obscene', and that he had made himself liable to prosecution under Section 63 of the Post Office Act, 1908. The writer protested against this unnotified confiscation of his mail and questioned his contravention of the Section of the Act mentioned, with which he was professionally familiar. The incident closed with his being again threatened with penalties under the Act— which provided for a maximum punishment of one year's imprisonment with hard labour—and told that the matter was duly recorded in the Department. This letter brought forth many complaints of the difficulty of obtaining James Joyce's *Ulysses*. It also brought the member of the Reform Club sixty-four offers of safe ways and means of obtaining the books he wanted.

The police were in trouble that same year over the Savidge Case. Miss Savidge was charged by the police with indecency in Hyde Park; her partner in the alleged indecency was a distinguished old knight who had assisted the Labour Government in 1924 as Chairman of the Committee on Withheld Pay for Naval Officers. The case was dismissed by the magistrate who heard it. But then Sir Archibald Bodkin authorized two police officers to make inquiries in order to rebut any charges of perjury against the police witnesses in the case. Miss Savidge was fetched from the business where she worked, and interrogated for a long time at Scotland Yard. Questions were asked in the House of Commons about the legality of such arbitrary interrogations, and the Home Secretary had to appoint a tribunal to inquire into the matter. The tribunal recommended that interrogations should only take place after preliminary information had been logded, and under conditions that protected the persons interrogated. This led to a parliamentary debate on the need for discretion on the part of the police.

Lord Birkenhead defended the police. He said about the Savidge Case: 'It is not my habit to frequent the park at disputable hours. . . . If there took place some caress, of a kind that was distinguished by the young lady herself in the evidence as being a kiss but not a kiss of passion, have they very great grounds for complaint if a policeman forty or fifty yards away misinterpreted the precise nature of the caress? . . . You must really range yourself definitely either on the side of the constitutional authority or amongst those who are willing, perhaps for quite inadequate reasons, not to do so.'

This view was attacked as militaristic—and it was thought significant that the Commissioner of Metropolitan Police was Viscount Byng of Vimy, a famous general. Lord Balfour of Burleigh complained that 'what the country wants in its police is that they should be the guardians of law and order, and not, as there is a tendency now for them to have to try to be, censors of public morals'.

Controversy was continued in letters to the Press, especially to the weekly Press. The following letter was published in the *New Statesman*: 'Did you know that it was a criminal offence to ask a girl to go for a walk? I didn't. An old gentleman did it last week in Hyde Park and the girl, instead of saying "No, thank you," like a little lady, called a policeman. The magistrate called the old gentleman a disgusting scoundrel, fined him several pounds, and told him he was sorry he could not send him to prison; but the girl he publicly congratulated on her courage for daring to be a housemaid and daring to call a policeman. Personally, I should have thought the old gentleman deserved a gold watch for his courage in daring to go into Hyde Park at all after recent events. But anyhow, did you know that it was a criminal offence to ask a girl to go for a walk? Perhaps because the gentleman was an old gentleman? If so, at what age does it become a crime to ask a girl to go for a walk? . . .'

These questions were never officially answered, and still from time to time police activities in Hyde Park made front-page news.

The Savidge Case was followed by the *Royal Oak* incident. Rear-Admiral Collard had a disagreement with two of his junior officers, Captain Dewar and Commander Daniel, as to which side of the battleship *Royal Oak* he should disembark from. When he came aboard the next day he insulted officers at the salute by walking straight past them. This irregularity was succeeded by another. One evening the band was playing on the quarter-deck, and dancing was in progress, when Rear-Admiral Collard suddenly summoned the bandmaster, Percy

Barnacle, to speak to him. The Rear-Admiral was alleged to have said, 'Come here, you b——. Do you call yourself a flag-ship bandmaster? I'll have you sent home. I've never heard such a bloody noise in all my life. It's like a dirge. No one could dance to it. Can't you play dance-music? In any case I will report you. Go and see if you can't do better!' Barnacle complained that these words were discouraging to band-work and detrimental to band-discipline. On the next day the Chaplain told the Admiral that he should not refer to people as b——s in front of guests. Dewar and Daniel were soon court-martialled at Gib-raltar for reading publicly in the wardroom remarks calculated to bring him into contempt, and which were subversive to naval discipline. They were found guilty. The Admiralty, however, reviewed the sentences and decided to place the Admiral on the retired list. The other two officers were 'not to be precluded from further employment when vacancies occur'. Captain Dewar was given another ship, but Commander Daniel pre-ferred to join the staff of the *Daily Mail*.

This incident led to jocularly indiscreet newspaper debate as to what name the Admiral had called the Bandmaster. A writer to the *New Statesman* observed that 'if it is the word which (I am sure) we all have in mind, it is fair to the Admiral and to the Bandmaster to recall that in Johnson's Dictionary the secondary meaning of that word is: "a term of endearment among sailors. . . ."' Another writer pointed out 'that the word was not the one which we have all in mind, but one which will be found applied by Shakespeare to Philip Faulconbridge in *King John*. Even this, pronounced with a short "a", might not have hurt the bandmaster's sensibility. But, pronounced with a long "a", it is apparently, even "among sailors", a deadly insult.'

A first-class newspaper story was the visit to London in March 1928 of King Amanullah of Afghanistan and his Queen. Pre-liminary reports described the Queen as being as chic as a Parisienne, and told how proud the king was of his European culture: much to the disgust of his Moslem followers, he was even wearing a top hat. In London the Afghan monarchs stayed at Claridge's Hotel, where, so the *Daily News* reported, 'British Empire elegance, with no attempt at pseudo-oriental splendours, is the keynote of the three suites.' Amanullah himself provided all the necessary Eastern colour. On his arrival he wore a long cloak of sage-green, a tunic of azure slashed with gold and decorated with jewelled brocade and glittering medals, trousers of geranium-scarlet. His black and red helmet was crowned with a white cockade. He attended banquets, where he drank toasts in lemonade; rode in a tank on Salisbury Plain; went to see *The Desert Song*; toured the B.S.A. works and there tried out a machine-gun, his eyes sparkling when he hit the mark. The newspapers rose to the occasion by going 'Eastern'. A member of Amanullah's suite was reported by the *Daily News* to have said: 'Look you, your English maidens are divinely beautiful. They are as fair as the pale moon which shines so gloriously in your western sky; their eyes are as bright as the eastern stars; and their complexion is just like the exquisite rose of Afghanistan.' When, on his return to Afghanistan, Amanullah lost his throne to an old-fashioned bandit, this was another good story. The Press generously attributed his fall rather to the backwardness of his people in accepting Western reforms, than to his own incompetence in putting them across.

Still another story blew up out of this. T. E. Lawrence, or '338171 Aircraftman Shaw', had got himself transferred to India to avoid the publicity of *Revolt in the Desert*, the shortened version of *Seven Pillars of Wisdom*. He was sent to the North-West Frontier. His literary agent sold the film rights of the story to an American company, the publicity agents of which planted on the American Press a nonsensical story of Lawrence, the Secret Service Master-Mind, organizing anti-Red spying from his headquarters at Benares, in impenetrable Indian disguise. This story was taken up by the British Press too, and Ernest Thurtle, a Labour member, asked a series of questions in the House about it. The suggestion was that Lawrence had stirred up the revolt against Amanullah, who had become too friendly with the Russians for British convenience. This baseless story became so embarrassing that, at the request of the British Minister at Kabul, Lawrence was recalled to England. Thereafter in mass trials in Russia—notably at the Donetz Valley sabotage trial—the spies who pleaded guilty often confessed to having had illicit commerce with Colonel Lawrence, the Super Spy, as well as with that other bogey-man of the Communists, Sir Henry Deterding, the Anglo-Dutch oil magnate.

CHAPTER FIFTEEN

The Depression, 1930

In the spring of 1929 the second Labour Government came quietly into office, as a natural election swing-over in two-party government. It held 289 seats, against the Conservatives' 260; however, the Liberals held the scales balanced with their 58. That women workers above the age of twenty-one were allowed to vote, under the Act of 1928, aroused little comment during the election; though the Flapper Vote outcry in the *Daily Mail* in the spring of that year had been extremely violent. The Labour ministers were no longer accused of being almost Bolshevists: indeed, the Bolshevists themselves had become respectable. *Punch*, in February 1929, published a cartoon which showed John Bull saying: 'This impossible Bolshie,' and the Bolshie: 'This impossible bourgeois,' and then both: 'Well, my friend, what about business?'

At first the Labour Government was popular. Philip Snowden, the Chancellor of the Exchequer, took a firm stand over the problem of French war debts to Britain, which made him a national hero. British upper-class resentment against the get-rich-quick habits of French hotel-keepers and the '*service, monsieur, service, monsieur*' of attendants at French theatres had been growing for some years. The beaten French fulminated against Snowden's 'terrible accountancy'; and the Select Press doubted whether the mere million or two of pounds sterling in question were worth the loss of good feeling between the two countries. Another popular act of the Labour Government was the withdrawal of the last British troops from the Rhine, authorized by

Arthur Henderson, the Foreign Secretary. The international outlook at the time was hopeful; Briand had produced a plan for the United States of Europe, which, though opposed by isolationists in England, was generally welcomed as a promise of peaceful times to come. J. H. Thomas toured Canada to show Labour's concern for the Empire. Ramsay MacDonald visited the United States, drove through showers of ticker-tape at New York, and was saluted with sirens from all the ships in the harbour. He and President Hoover sat together on a log over a creek on the President's estate, discussing the weather, fishing, and the prospects of a continued world peace.

At the end of October came the sudden end of the Hoover prosperity boom in the United States, when the whole of Wall Street stock-market, not merely a section of it, collapsed. The American public, encouraged by the Republican slogan 'a car in every garage and a chicken in every pot', had been interesting itself in the stock-market and plunging with enthusiastic ignorance. Financiers took advantage of this bullish tendency to drive up the nominal value of stocks to the highest figure possible, in order to unload on the amateur speculators to the very best advantage. They were too successful. When they baled out and allowed the market to find its own level, it crashed disastrously. Hundreds of thousands of Americans lost all their spare cash and then rushed to the banks to be sure at least of their capital: the rush broke the smaller banks by the hundred, and they dragged down many of the larger banks; though no real loss of wealth had taken place, millions of people were ruined and thrown out of employment.

Great Britain at first was not much affected, and it was hoped, for the sake of world trade, that the American market would recover its stability. But it gradually became clear that the financiers had buried themselves in the ruins of the market and that in America the Careless Twenties must give way to what Groucho Marx the comedian afterwards called the Threadbare Thirties. The Stock Exchange became very gloomy; but the general public had never played at speculation except in betting on sport. Great Britain was also far slower than the United States to catch fire in either panic or enthusiasm, and the British financial system had been protected against local panics by the federation of nearly all small banks into the Big Five, and the close co-operation between these. In Britain the Thirties were to be merely the 'Troubled Thirties'. Repercussions from Wall Street broke few windows in the City.

Nevertheless, there was a sharp rise in unemployment, due to the decrease in American orders and the general disorganization of world markets; and now emigration to Australia—a stock remedy in crises of this sort—was suspended by the Australian Parliament until the industrial slump should have ended. J. H. Thomas, who as Lord Privy Seal in 1929–30 was charged with the task of dealing with unemployment, brought forward road and railway development schemes. These were criticized as inadequate, and he pleaded for more time; which people at first were ready to grant him, for the matter did not seem so urgent. The Careless Twenties ended on no note of alarm or despondency.

John Buchan, the Scottish novelist, historian, publisher, politician, who became Moderator of the Church of Scotland and later, as Lord Tweedsmuir, Governor-General of Canada, summed up the decade in an article for the *Morning Post* on the last day of December 1929. His view is interesting as embodying the sanest Conservative opinion of the time. He held that there had been a widespread decline of parliamentary institutions, but the old self-conscious nationalism was discredited, and so was the sentimental internationalism of 1919. Dogmas were being broken down—social, philosophical, scientific, and literary, as well as political. Marxian Socialism, proved barren by the practice of Russia, had fewer adherents than ever. 'But for the bold experiment of Fascism the decade has not been fruitful in constructive statesmanship.' Only in Italy had new men with new ideas arisen. Nevertheless, owing to the patient work of the ordinary man, 'civilization has been saved, and, on the whole, the nations are once more a stable society'.

The Fascist revolution had been given a mixed reception in Britain: the Radical and Labour Press had furiously assailed it for the gangster methods of the Blackshirt partymen against Socialists and Radicals—'the rule of the rubber truncheon and the castor-oil bottle'—growing especially hot about the murder of Matteoti. But the Conservative Press saw Mussolini as an energetic saviour of Italy from Red revolution, loyal to his Monarchy; and travellers came back from Rome and Florence with enthu-

siastic praises for the new Italian spirit, which, at last, had succeeded in making railway trains run to time. That Fascism
could possibly grow into a menace to the British Empire was
considered fantastic: because of the inglorious military history
of Italy ever since she became a nation. Fascism in Britain had
not yet appeared as such, but Fascist behaviour was already
manifesting itself. Fascism in Italy, as National Socialism in
Germany, was opposed to Communism in being nationalistic
rather than internationalistic in character, anti-Trust rather
than anti-Capitalistic, and supported by the dissident lower-
middle class rather than the proletarian working class.

When the news had originally reached Britain of the Fascist
march on Rome (28th October 1922) the *Spectator*, which represented moderate Conservative opinion, noted editorially: 'There
were not many conflicts and the revolution was carried through
almost without bloodshed. The King sent for Signor Mussolini,
the Leader of the Fascists. . . . We must add one picturesque
touch very characteristic of an Italian revolution. The new
Ministers asked their chief as to the clothes they should wear
when kissing hands. 'Top hats and black coats,' was the laconic
order of the Prime Minister, though he had to send out one of
his colleagues in a hurry to buy him the necessary top hat.
Apparently the silken cylinder is to be the symbol of the new
Government's policy. Witness Signor Mussolini's excellent telegram to Mr. Bonar Law and M. Poincaré. 'We accept the omen.'
Mussolini's telegram to Bonar Law had run: 'I am confident
that in accomplishing the duties committed to me I shall be
able to safeguard the supreme interests of the country, which
are in accordance with the interests of peace and civilization,
and that the solidarity of the Allied nations which I regard as
indispensable for the effectiveness of their political action will be
assured.' (The *Daily Mail* carried no leader on Italian events: it
was too busy assailing 'Bolshevist' Arthur Henderson and his
associates: 'Labour *threatens every man's house and furniture, and
every woman's clothes and jewellery*, as was done in Russia. . . .
[*Daily Mail* italics]. Until now a cardinal principle of progressive politics in liberty-loving Britain has been "*No Taxation
Without Representation*". The slogan which the Labour executive
have emblazoned upon their red banner is "*Representation Without
Taxation*".')

In the summer of 1924 the *Spectator* further reported in an article 'The Nemisis of Communism': 'Less than two years ago the Fascists combined together in order to help to make the law prevail over anarchy. They have ended by overriding all law and asserting that they are the State. The Fascists are ultra-patriots, but what sort of attitude they will adopt towards other nations we do not know. We do not like their fury, but we cannot believe that they really have light enough hearts to upset the Peace, to try to filch away Italians from Switzerland, to reopen the Jugo-Slav question, to close the Adriatic Sea, to try to seize Malta and to win for Italy the hegemony of the Mediterranean. The reports which attribute such intentions to the Fascists are probably mad rumours.'

The *Daily Mail* subsequently gave its blessing to Fascism, and to National Socialism as soon as it came into power. Newspaper circulations tended to zoning according to the intelligence of subscribers. The *Daily Mail* could claim a higher coverage of the upper income group than the *Daily Express*, but the more progressive and independent-minded readers of both upper-middle and lower-middle classes were in the Beaverbrook zone—Fascism with its insistence on mass-thinking did not appeal to them.

The most spectacular British example of Fascist behaviour in the early Thirties, though it passed at the time for Red Socialism, was the seizure of the Mace on the 18th July 1930. That evening in the House of Commons the members were voting on an unimportant Bill, and when the tellers returned from the lobby they lined up to advance to the table. Among them was a Labour member, John Beckett, who was not long afterwards to help Sir Oswald Mosley to found the British Union of Fascists. Suddenly, according to *The Times* report, he struck a truculent attitude, failed to bow to the Speaker as was customary, and exclaimed: 'I don't know what you think, Mr. Speaker, but it's a damned disgrace.' He was referring to the Home Secretary's refusal to interfere with a sentence passed by a bench of magistrates, which condemned an eight-year-old boy to four strokes of the birch—Beckett had just described this as a 'monstrous outrage'. He then seized the Mace from its bracket on the table and hurried with it to the doors. Nobody had done such a thing since the days of Oliver Cromwell. When he reached the bar of the House a crowd held him up, and attendants recovered the

Mace, which was calmly brought back to the table by the Serjeant-at-Arms. Beckett, meanwhile, continued to lounge about in the gangway, his hands in his pockets, shouting insults at the protesting members. The Speaker then asked for the division to be withdrawn, and 'named' Beckett for disorderly conduct. By this time Beckett had left the House. The Prime Minister moved his suspension; which was carried by a division in which Beckett received only six favourable votes. Later he apologized to the House, and his suspension was revoked.

In 1930 the Conservative popular Press of London, conscious of its increasing political power, especially in combination, put this to a practical test. It would run by-election candidates independent of the party organization. First, Lord Beaverbrook, as a Canadian, complained in the *Daily Express* that in the 1929 election no one had mentioned the Empire. In the *Sunday Express* he published the challenge: 'Who is for Empire? The answer is all men and no one. For while all men are willing to register the sentiment of goodwill toward the Empire, the practical side of Imperial development has been forgotten.' He started an Empire Free Trade Crusade, which was to weld the Empire into a closer economic unit, by putting a tariff on all goods imported into Britain, with a special preference for Imperial products. He declared that the movement would support any party which took over its programme. The *Daily Express* began to print a small crusader, in red, on the front page of every issue. In leaders and cartoons it attacked Cobdenism and Free Trade, characterizing them as out-of-date Victorian ideas. Meanwhile, Lord Rothermere in the *Daily Mail* had also come out strongly for taxing imported food—a turn of events which the *Daily Express* described as a 'bombshell'. Lords Beaverbrook and Rothermere then co-operated in founding a United Empire Party. A quarter of a million of their readers subscribed £100,000 to party funds. In a by-election at Twickenham, Sir John Ferguson, the Conservative candidate, was persuaded to adopt the ticket of Empire Free Trade; and though officially disowned by his party was returned to Parliament. Another Empire Free Trader was returned for West Fulham.

Baldwin and Beaverbrook were now negotiating, but could agree on no common policy. Baldwin declared publicly that protection for agriculture was impossible in urban England, and at a Caxton Hall meeting attacked the Press Barons' attempts to dictate Conservative policy, and accused them of 'queering the pitch'. The Empire movement was supported, however, by a Bankers' Resolution, published in July 1930. It stated: 'Great Britain must retain her open market for all Empire products, while being prepared to impose duties on imports from all other countries.' This resolution was said to have been signed by four of the Big Five Bank chairmen and two of the Bank of England's directors; but no signatures were made public and the resolution seems to have been entirely unofficial.

The Beaverbrook-Rothermere collaboration was an uneasy one. Rothermere's readers could be roused by such low-brow diehard cries as 'Break with Moscow', and 'No Surrender in India', which did not suit Beaverbrook's public. Beaverbrook therefore withdrew from the United Empire Party, and returned his part of the funds to subscribers.

At the South Paddington by-election in October Beaverbrook and Rothermere candidates ran against each other. There was also an official Conservative candidate, Sir Herbert Liddiard, who at first accepted Empire Free Trade, but rejected it again upon receiving a reprimand from his Central Office. Lord Beaverbrook's Empire Crusaders put up Vice-Admiral Taylor as candidate and Lord Rothermere's United Empire Party appealed to the 'flapper vote' with Mrs. Stewart Richardson. A Labour candidate was also in the field, but no Liberal. Lord Rothermere, disliking the look of things, withdrew his support from Mrs. Stewart Richardson, and explained why in a letter to her chairman: 'The reference in one of my telegrams to the impossibility of Mrs. Stewart Richardson's winning the seat was based on the very firm conviction which I held that, in Conservative ranks, high titles are much more sought after than in any other of the political parties, and that apart from her own merits no woman candidate seeking to secure Conservative votes would have any chance of success unless, like the Duchess of Atholl or Viscountess Astor, she had a high title. . . .' This was true enough; and the *Daily Mail* by spot-lighting the peerage at the same time as it had deprecated the intrusion of women into politics was very largely responsible.

But Mrs. Stewart Richardson, who spoke in favour of higher wages, lower prices, fewer taxes, and more jobs for everyone, did not retire; and her supporters declared that Lord Rothermere's withdrawal had freed the United Empire Party of its greatest burden. They accused the Press Barons of selling out to the new Conservative group in Parliament, which was led by a former Chancellor of the Exchequer, Sir Robert Horne. Vice-Admiral Taylor was meanwhile electioneering with the help of many vans and loudspeakers. He breezily described the Government as having sentenced the Empire to be shot at dawn—for three years the Empire had been treated as if it were populated by foreigners; and had knocked in vain at the gates of the Mother-land. Sir Herbert Liddiard, the official Conservative, took an anti-Labour rather than an anti-Beaverbrook line. 'Just fancy South Paddington,' he said, '—nice, decent, respectable district that we are—represented by a Labour member!' He remarked of the Press Barons: 'They blame Mr. Baldwin for being obstinate. By Heaven, he seems to me to have been most accommodating.' The Labour candidate concentrated on attacking the Capitalist system, which in a meeting held in a public baths he held responsible for the new rise in unemployment. Most of all he blamed the Liberals: the Labour Government depended on their vote in the House of Commons, but they stood squarely in the way of social reform. Out of this extraordinary confusion the Vice-Admiral emerged as victor by 941 votes; and another Empire Crusader was elected for East Islington.

By now the effects of the Wall Street crash were being felt severely. The Conservatives had accepted the need for Protection and Imperial Preference, and Beaverbrook agreed to put up no more candidates of his own. In December 1930 J. M. Keynes the economist wrote: 'We have magneto trouble. How, then, can we start up again?' The Labour Government by itself seemed incapable of starting up again, and in the same month the Liberal weekly, *The Nation*, declared that 'there is a sense of crisis in the air, a sense of national emergency', and called for a National Government. A feeler had already appeared in *The Times*—a letter from General Seely, a Liberal War Minister from 1912 to 1924 and later Lord Mottistone, to the effect that 'Britain is confronted with a grave emergency', and 'it is equally clear that an election on party lines will not help to meet it'. He accused Labour of 'failing to cure unemployment or grapple with abuses of the dole'. Then Baldwin, as leader of the Opposition, attacked Labour in the House of Commons with: 'The enthusiasm is running out of your party all over the country, because you have lost faith in Socialism.' Several Labour members cheered this statement and shouted: 'Come over here, Stanley!' J. H. Thomas admitted that he had no programme of reconstruction, and jokingly confessed that he was breaking all records in the number of unemployed.

It was widely felt that mere coalition was not enough to counteract the Depression. That same year a new party was formed by two changeable, dissatisfied young men, Sir Oswald Mosely and John Strachey, both originally Conservatives, and a few Labour M.P.s. Its manifesto pledged itself to 'Action', the immediate action being, as with the Empire Crusaders, the introduction of a tariff in order to stimulate home-production and raise wages. The New Party was commonly regarded as Left-wing—Mosley himself had been Labour Chancellor of the Duchy of Lancaster in 1929. It was at first supported and given intellectual standing by such literary men as Osbert Sitwell and Harold Nicolson. But it was never numerous, and gradually lost its Labour supporters: what remained turned Fascist.

By 1931 George Lansbury, the most generally beloved of the Labour leaders, was invoking Christian principles to solve industrial troubles. Sir William Joynson-Hicks, who had by this time been raised to the peerage as Lord Brentford, rose to the bait. 'For God's sake don't let us mix politics with religion. He who shall not work shall not eat. There's nothing in the Bible about a seven-and-a-half hours day. Religion is an individual matter.' Bernard Shaw intervened in the argument. He praised George Lansbury as an out-and-out Christian after Christ's own heart, and jeered at the limitations of English gentility which restrained Lord Brentford from similar perfection. From George Lansbury's point of view, Shaw said, Lord Brentford might just as well not be a Christian at all, but an Antichrist.

The problem, however, was not one that could be solved even by the religious unanimity of every Christian in the country: it was an international crisis. All over the world, prices were falling; this was leading to an increase in the burden of national debts, and to several cases of national default. World trade was declining, markets shrinking, interest from investments drying up, foreign exchanges wobbling. Financial crashes became frequent—the Hatry case was followed by the crash of the British shipowner, Lord Kylsant, and by the failure and suicide of the Swedish match-king, Kreuger. Early in 1931, one of the chief links in the European banking system snapped—the Austrian Kredit Anstalt. A loan from the Bank of England and a guarantee from the newly established Bank of International Settlements helped to keep Austria solvent, but business men lost confidence in Central Europe. Foreign funds were withdrawn from Germany; which made the general financial situation still more precarious. Italy and Belgium both had Budget deficits, and nearly all countries were starting serious economy campaigns. President Hoover then put forward a proposal for a moratorium on the interest and principal of all inter-governmental debts. Had this been acted upon immediately it might have eased the situation, but the French objected on the grounds that they would lose most and the Germans gain most. The financial drain on Germany, in the form of reparation payments under the Young Plan therefore continued and German banks began to fail. A conference was called in London to deal with the German situation. Only the French were in a position to grant long-term loans, but they wanted political guarantees before they would do so. A deadlock followed. The effect upon many Germans was to convince them that only a policy of national self-sufficiency would rid them of the danger of complete financial and industrial collapse. This feeling the rising Nazi movement was able to exploit.

The Macmillan Report on Finance and Industry revealed the dangerous condition of British national economy, and the Report of the May Committee on National Expenditure forecast a Budget deficit of £120 million. This led to the withdrawal of foreign funds from Britain and the depreciation of Government securities. Loans had to be obtained quickly from Paris and New York. The situation was so serious that on the 23rd August 1931 a National Government was formed which included Conservative, Liberal, and Labour members. The bulk of the Labour Party, however, and many Liberals, refused to follow their leaders, whom they accused of having been stampeded by the Conservatives into betraying their party principles. On September 9th, the new Government brought in an Economy

Bill, involving a 10 per cent cut in the money available for Government wages. In the Navy the mistake was made of taking a flat shilling a day from the pay of all ranks, from admirals down to ordinary seamen. This shilling was a serious matter to the Lower Deck and there was a strike among ratings of the Fleet at Invergordon. They refused to put to sea. The Government soon capitulated, for the strike had been decently and respectfully managed, like the famous 'Mutiny at Spithead' in the eighteenth century: the cuts were revised on a percentage basis. The Admiralty felt obliged to make an example of twenty-four ratings, who had been unwise enough to appear as ring-leaders, by dismissing them from the Service. The further mistake was made of hushing up the story of the strike, distorted news of which reached the foreign Press. It was there represented as an ugly mutiny. Britain seemed to be on the verge of a social revolution, and more foreign funds were hurriedly withdrawn. In order to stop the export of gold, the gold standard was suspended; and the pound sterling found its true level at 70 per cent of its gold value.

On October 6th, a General Election was held on the plea that the National Government needed a 'doctor's mandate' from the people. The Opposition Socialists made use of the Invergordon strike in their electioneering. Posters were published with an illustration of the Battle of Jutland, and the caption: 'The British Navy at Jutland in 1916 beat the ex-Kaiser, and at Invergordon in 1931 it beat Mr. Montague Norman.' Montague Norman was the Governor of the Bank of England. The posters caused concern among those who still did not wish the public to know that there had been a strike at all. Admiral Dewar, however, late of the *Royal Oak* and now a Labour candidate for North Portsmouth, told reporters that the posters merely stated facts. They were said to have been published by the Co-operative Movement, although A. V. Alexander, the Labour ex-First Lord of the Admiralty and one of the leaders of the Co-operative Movement, denied any knowledge of the matter. Then the popular Conservative Press, which often attacked the Co-operative Movement in the interests of private tradesmen and merchants, came out with headlines such as 'Co-operators' Insult to the Navy'. In the election nearly all prominent Labour and Liberal leaders were on the National side, and joined in a strong appeal to the country for 'united action'. The National Government gained 554 seats, and the Labour opposition, led by Arthur Henderson and George Lansbury, only 52. The Liberal opposition sank to a mere 16. MacDonald remained Prime Minister, and in his Cabinet Baldwin served as Lord President of the Council and Sir John Simon, as Liberal leader, Foreign Secretary.

Among the economies immediately introduced by the National Government were cuts in unemployment benefit. These were effected by the Means Test, which reduced what was known as transitional benefit by withdrawing it from people who could be proved to have savings to fall back on, or moneyed relatives to support them. The popular name for unemployment benefit since June 1919, when the *Daily Mail* first coined it, had been 'the dole'. This was conveniently brief for headlines and general use but carried the invidious sense of an idle city mob living on the charity of the governing classes. The Press with almost the sole exception of the *Daily Herald* and the Liberal newspapers represented the unemployed as people too idle to seek work, and 'the dole' as a comfortable wage. An article in *Good Housekeeping*, an American-style monthly magazine for prosperous housewives, brightly referred in July 1926 to 'Profiteers, dole-drawers, music-hall artists—in fact the only people who have money to-day'. The truth was that most working people had a strong aversion to public relief and at first would have preferred to work for less than the pittance that they drew in the form of unemployment benefit, if there had been work to do. But as unemployment increased, and the Government could do nothing to remedy it, there came to be 'distressed areas' where whole villages were on the dole, and all scruples against accepting Government money faded. The weekly payment was enough to keep the people alive but not enough to keep them in good enough physical condition to undertake any work that unexpectedly offered. In such villages they lived a down-at-heels, aimless life, eking out their payment with a little vegetable growing, poaching, and such casual labour as would not affect their right to continue as pensioners. Unemployed in the towns were far worse off, with nothing to do but hang about at street corners or mope at home.

The Means Test aroused fierce anger among the unemployed

against MacDonald and the old Labour leaders, who were accused of 'betraying their class'. A party of unemployed Welsh miners marched to put their case before the T.U.C., which was meeting at Bristol. Demonstrations were held in Parliament Square, London, and the crowds were charged by the police. The National Unemployed Workers' Movement organized Sunday afternoon meetings in Trafalgar Square. Civil Servants held a meeting at the Albert Hall. In Birkenhead fighting went on for three days between demonstrators and police: bottles were thrown at police officers, the spikes of park railings knocked off and used as missiles, and the windows of Conservative Town Councillors' houses smashed. In retaliation the police carried out raids on working-class tenements and made indiscriminate arrests.

At the same time a National Hunger March was organized from the provinces to London. There had been hunger-marchers in the middle Twenties, but by scores rather than hundreds, as now. Two thousand five hundred marchers bore a petition signed by a million people, demanding for the abolition of the Means Test. They were welcomed by crowds of workers in Hyde Park, but the police charged them with batons. A violent skirmish took place in which one hundred people were injured and fifty arrests made. Most newspapers attacked the marchers as being instigated by the Reds, observing Bolshevik discipline, and wilfully baiting the police. The petition was never delivered to Parliament. It is said that the leaders of the marchers put the unwieldy document for safety in an Underground railway cloakroom, and accepted a receipt as guarantee of its safety; they did not lose the ticket, but the cloakroom most unaccountably lost the document. Another uncomfortable scene, as at the presentation of the Chartist petition in 1848, was thus avoided in the House, and the Press spared the necessity of declaring, as on that occasion, that two-thirds of the signatures were forgeries. However, the authorities were alarmed into granting extra relief in most parts of England.

The general unrest was accompanied by a growth in Left feeling. Now that the Government was behaving in an apparently reactionary manner, the dissatisfied elements in the working class were joined by equally dissatisfied elements in the middle and upper classes. University undergraduates and, in general, the children of prosperous families felt their conscience disturbed by hunger-marchers and the Means Test and their own comfortable existence. They no longer felt obliged, as during the General Strike, to rally to the support of the Government against a supposed revolution of the proletariat. The presence of Labour leaders in the Government broadened the issue to one of human justice. Anti-Governmental Labour clubs at the universities greatly increased in membership and by 1931 students were not only welcoming hunger-marchers but even marching with them. A few went to the extreme of calling themselves Communists—especially at the elder universities, where the test of being 'advanced' was no longer whether one understood modernist poems, but whether one understood Marxism. A magazine founded at Cambridge in 1932, *Cambridge Left*, published Marxian analyses of literature and poems about the class-struggle. The Communists, the party of the militant unemployed, had in 1930 been able to collect enough support from moneyed people to start a new daily paper, the *Daily Worker*.

The intellectual Left was demanding a clear-cut Labour policy to set against Ramsay MacDonaldism. 'Ginger-groups' appeared, such as the Socialist League founded by Sir Stafford Cripps and H. N. Brailsford. John Clynes, the former Home Secretary, who was one of the few Labour Ministers not to join the National Government, declared that Socialism had never been tried. He welcomed the new Labour policy of nationalization, by which the Bank of England and the joint-stock banks were to be publicly owned, and key-industries, such as those supplying transport, electricity and gas, were to be managed by public utility corporations. Lansbury gave his opinion that Capitalism had collapsed, as Marx had said it would, but that Socialism had not come into being, because Socialist teaching was not widely enough spread. To remedy this, the New Fabian Research Bureau, and other kindred organizations, began to pour out Socialist pamphlets. G. D. H. Cole's *Intelligent Man's Guide Through World Chaos*, 1932, had a big sale. Cole pointed out how essential it was for everyone to know something of economics: 'I believe that the understanding of present-day economic problems is not really so hard a matter as it is often made out to be. . . . The General Election of 1931 turned largely on such economic issues as the "balance of trade", the dangers of "inflation", the effects of going off the "gold standard", and the case for and against "tariffs". Everyone had to have views about these questions—or to act as if he had views about them. In every country the world slump has forced the questions into the forefront of political controversy.' Cole set himself to explain economic problems from a Socialist standpoint, and followed up his book with several others.

Newspapers in the Thirties discouraged the general desire to study economic and political problems. The popular Press provided brighter and brighter 'story' news, but never any helpful analyses of the world situation. It occasionally made news-stories of the latest economic panaceas: for instance in January 1933 the *Daily Mail* printed an article by Professor Soddy on the theory of Technocracy, which had been running wild in the United States for several months. The theory Technocracy was that, since this was the Machine Age, national governments should be run by technicians. It resembled Italian Fascism in that the chief industrial technicians—employers and employees —were to regulate each industry, and the central government was to regulate them. Technocracy also stood for abolishing the price-and-wages system: people were not to be paid in money but in energy-certificates for work done, entitling them to share in the general abundance which machines made possible. Pamphlets on Technocracy were added to the huge politico-economic literature which was challenging the works of Edgar Wallace, Elinor Glyn, and Edgar Rice Burroughs as the chief reading of the people.

The National Government, meanwhile, was pursuing a policy of financial 'retrenchment'. Neville Chamberlain, the Chancellor of the Exchequer, believed in increased taxation and increased saving. Interest on the War Loan was dropped from 5 per cent to 3½ per cent. An Exchange Equalization Account was set up in order to counteract short-term speculation and regulate foreign balances. German reparation payments, after the Dawes plan had been succeeded in 1929 by the still milder Young plan, were abolished in 1932, and England applied to the United States for the cancellation of war debts also. The United States, feeling the financial pinch more and more, though most of the world's gold supply had flowed there since the war, refused, and Britain thereupon paid in gold. France defaulted, and, the next year, encouraged by her example, Britain made a token-payment only. American public opinion was inflamed and in the following year after that the United States refused to accept token-payments. The British Government thereupon made no further payment of any sort, and ingenious articles were published in extenuation of this default to show that indirectly America had in effect been paid the whole of the war debt, and more. But public relations between the two countries remained strained for some years.

In February 1932 tariffs, which had caused so much controversy in the past ten years, were at last introduced. An Import Duties Act imposed a 10 per cent duty on all imports except wheat and meat. This was greeted in the popular Conservative Press as the long wished for funeral of Free Trade. Philip Snowden, however, who had now been made a viscount, attacked Protection as criminal, and accused the Government of 'gambling with the vital interests of the country'. When the Ottawa Agreements, establishing Imperial Preference, were signed, Lord Snowden and two Liberal leaders, Sir Herbert Samuel and Sir Archibald Sinclair, resigned from the Government. Lord Snowden had declared in 1930, on the failure of the Imperial Conference, that the Dominions wanted Britain to make all the sacrifices, and J. H. Thomas had called the Canadian offer of preference 'humbug'. In 1932, Lord Snowden, at least, had not changed his mind. Neville Chamberlain, however, spoke for the National Government, and for most people in the country, when he declared that Ottawa was 'the crowning achievement in a year wonderful in endeavour'. England was now committed to a policy of planning commerce by bilateral treaties with other countries. The Ottawa Agreements were followed by special, 'most-favoured-nation' trade treaties with the Argentine and the Scandinavian countries.

The Wheat Quota scheme was an instance of the new system of openly regulated economic production. It laid down that a fixed percentage of the total amount of wheat consumed in Britain should be British wheat. This was intended to guarantee the sale of British farmers' crops. Marketing Boards were also set up to control the sale and distribution of milk, potatoes, hops, and pigs. State-control was, in fact, everywhere being extended. Already there were public utility services, such as the B.B.C.

and the Central Electricity Board. To these was added the London Passenger Transport Board, which took over control of all London buses and tubes from the various private companies. Traffic Commissioners were also appointed to regulate the transport of goods in Britain, and to modify the competition between road and rail. The gradual tendency towards socialization was inescapable.

This extension of State control was soon challenged, but not at first by the Left, which had not yet come to fear that by these means Democracy might be quietly converted into Fascism. The challenges came from the lawyers. Lord Hewart, the Lord Chief Justice, wrote *The New Despotism* in 1930: in it he criticized the powers that Ministers, and the boards set up by them, were acquiring to issue orders that had the force of law. The orders were always meant to apply to special subjects and Lord Hewart did not attack them as unnecessary. What he did deplore was that most of them were neither examined nor given particular sanction by Parliament, and that there was thus no constitutional check on the law-making activities of Government departments and local bodies. A similar book, *Bureaucracy Triumphant* by C. K. Allen, published in 1931, pointed out that judicial as well as legislative powers were being delegated to local and departmental bodies. Special tribunals were now allowed to settle legal questions of right and wrong, as well as purely administrative matters, nor was there any appeal from these tribunals to any ordinary court of law. The Law was no longer kept strictly independent of the Administration, as democratic theory held it should be in order to preserve its judicial impartiality.

No steps were taken to prevent the growth of an all-powerful bureaucracy, though complaints against it continued to be made. In 1936, Sir Ernest Benn the publisher, in his book *Modern Government as a Busybody on Other Men's Matters*, wrote that it had become almost sacrilege to suggest that anything could be outside the scope of Government; and that the view that all private resources, intellectual and material, were governmentally controlled was all too readily accepted.

The future of India was another serious problem in the early Thirties. A commission under Sir John Simon had been sent out to India in 1927 to report on the situation. The Indian Congress was at that time demanding independence and following a policy of 'civil disobedience'. In 1930, Mahatma Gandhi was conducting a movement for the boycott of British goods, especially of cotton. In April, accompanied by eighty-four followers, he undertook a march of two hundred miles from Ahmedabad to Dandi as a protest against the new tax on salt. When they reached Dandi, a small town on the shores of the Arabian Sea, Gandhi retired to meditate; then he addressed his followers, and afterwards set them to work on the shore with buckets and spades to dig for salt. In his speech Gandhi said: 'Resist the confiscation of salt from your midst with all your might till blood is spilt. All women and children should also resist interference. Let us see whether the police dare touch our women. If they do, and if the sons and daughters of India are not so emasculated as to take such an insult lying down, the whole country will be ablaze.' Although digging for salt was a punishable offence under the new Salt Law, the police did not interfere. The few ounces of salt that Gandhi himself dug up were sold for £32.

Riots followed in the chief towns, where tramcars were burned, and raids on Government arsenals were made. In one such raid at Chittagong the sentries on duty were shot. The British Press described this as an outrage and called for an 'Iron Hand'. The Government, however, did not want to exasperate Indian opinion. The Simon Commission had just made its report and a Round Table Conference was to be called to work out a federal Constitution.

The Conference began its deliberations in November 1930. The popular Press published many photographs of Indian princes in their picturesque robes and contrasted their protestations of loyalty with the 'seditious' declarations of Congress. In 1931, Gandhi himself came to England to attend the Conference. His emaciated body and his loin-cloth earned much publicity. Unfortunately, he failed to establish any personal contact with the Prime Minister. He fell among Left-wing people, and so alienated himself from the Government, which had at first been in favour of negotiating directly with him. At the Conference he often contradicted himself, and always seemed tired. The *Sunday Express*, in September 1931, reported that his friends confessed him to be out of his depth in England, and to be doing nothing to help solve the many questions with which the Conference was dealing. He returned to India with some loss of prestige.

The Conference continued its sittings until 1932, and its conclusions were published in a White Paper in the following year. A Federal Constitution was proposed which would give autonomy to the provinces. Burma was to be completely separated from India, as Ceylon had been in 1931, and given semi-Dominion status. The Federal Constitution was intended to reconcile the divergent claims of Hindus and Moslems, the Princes and Congress. In 1934 a Bill embodying it was hotly attacked by Winston Churchill, who was not a member of the National Government, as a surrender to incompetent extremists; but it finally passed both Houses. Provincial autonomy was soon afterwards introduced in India; but Federation was delayed by the apparently irreconcilable claims of different sects and parties, and by the natural unwillingness of the Indian Civil Service to relinquish its functions.

CHAPTER SIXTEEN

Pacifism, Nudism, Hiking

The effect of the war-book revival of 1928–31 was to refresh public memory of the horrors of the Great War, and to increase anti-war feeling everywhere. The Press capitalized this tendency: the *Sunday Express*, for instance, in 1931 with a leading article, 'They Must Not Fight'. The writer observed that nearly three-quarters of a million more boys than girls had been born in post-war England; and that this might be Nature's way of repairing the loss of nearly a million men in the war. Yet the *Sunday Express* concluded optimistically that these boys had been born at a time when war was outlawed farther than ever before from civilized minds.

Germany had recently been admitted to the League of Nations—and the British Labour Government had agreed to the General Act for the Pacific Settlement of International Disputes, drawn up by the League of Nations Council at Geneva. To prove themselves in earnest the Government suspended the building of the Singapore naval dockyard. That year a new Naval Conference was held. Britain put forward a moderate estimate of its essential needs on the grounds of 'improved world relationships', and Britain, Japan, and the United States were able to come to an agreement—though not France and Italy. The Italians demanded parity with the French, but the French pointed out that this would amount to French inferiority in the Mediterranean, since units of their Fleet must be stationed in the East and in the Atlantic. The other powers could not end this deadlock, since all took the view that France's estimate of her essential needs was too high. Nevertheless, all five powers arrived at last at a formula which limited the number of submarines and of capital ships. This was the last positive achievement of the disarmament era.

Briand's new plan for an European Union was having a bad Press, because most countries feared that it would perpetuate French military predominance. At the Great Disarmament Conference in February 1932 the French, in accordance with Briand's ideas, put forward a plan for an international army to be controlled by the League of Nations. Sir John Simon replied to this on behalf of the British National Government by outlining a plan for qualitative disarmament, which would entirely forbid certain kinds of weapons. A proposal was then made to abolish all bombing from the air, but Sir John Simon could not agree to this, since air bombing of villages, after due warning, was the cheapest and most effective method of pacifying turbulent tribesmen on the North-West Frontier. A proposal to limit tanks to about eight tons was also rejected by the British delegation, who wanted it to be twenty tons—Britain had a new sixteen-ton tank undergoing trials. The French reduced the matter to absurdity by a further amendment, that tanks should be limited to seventy tons—they had been making experiments in siege-tanks of about sixty tons. (Of the British sixteen-ton tanks four only were in fact built; the development of the large fast tank was left to the Germans and the Russians.) Russia, in order to show up the insincerity of the Capitalistic powers, declared herself in favour of complete disarmament— it was clear that none of them would agree to it. Thereupon Mussolini, seeing that the Conference was making no progress, threatened to withdraw the Italian delegation. In Germany, meanwhile, a change of government had brought into power General von Schleicher, who took up a truculent attitude. Appearances were saved by the invention of a new formula, which combined the German claim for equality with the French claim for security. It was 'equality of rights in a system which will provide security for all nations'. New plans were produced for the supervision of armament manufacture in every country.

The Nazis then came into power. Not much notice was taken of the event in the British Press. On the very day that it happened, 30th January 1933, the *Daily Express* headline was

'Hitler baulked of Power'—there were rumours that von Papen was to be dictator. Later in the week, Strube, the *Daily Express* cartoonist, showed Hitler arriving, rather seedy-looking, at the palatial Dictators' Hotel. Further rumours were published of Army plots against Hitler, of a coming persecution of Communists and Jews, of Hitler's possibly repudiating the German war-debts. But more newsworthy at this time, especially in the popular Press, was the Moscow trial of Henry Thornton and three other Metropolitan-Vickers British engineers for alleged conspiracy to wreck Russian industrial plants, and the court-martial of Lieutenant Norman Baillie Stewart ('The prisoner in the Tower') for selling Army secrets for £90 to German agents through a mysterious girl-friend named Marie Louise.

The general impression derived from newspaper files of that time is that Hitler was not taken seriously, because of his fantastic demand that the one hundred million people of German race and culture scattered all over the world should be united within the Reich. His coming to power was regarded as a purely internal German affair, and it was not thought that he could last long. When in February the German Reichstag mysteriously caught fire, the photographs of the blaze were supported with letterpress giving the official Nazi version of the affair as a Communist arson plot. Several months later, during the trials of van der Lubbe and Dimitrov and their associates, the Communist theory that Goering himself had burned down the Reichstag was pooh-poohed in the official Liberal and Labour Press, though the Conservative Press was non-committal. The Conservatives were unwilling to brand the Nazis as gangsters, because if the fire had been arranged, as the evidence seemed to prove, this had been done in a good cause: just as the Zinoviev letter in 1923 (though perhaps not written by Zinoviev) had been published in a good cause.

When Hitler displaced von Schleicher as the German leader, the Disarmament Conference grew still less hopeful of results. At the same time Japan withdrew from the League of Nations— a dispute had broken out between China and Japan—and the Japanese occupied Manchuria. The League, of which both China and Japan were members, failed to bring its co-operative machinery into action against Japan. It awaited a lead from the British Foreign Secretary, Sir John Simon: but not wishing to arouse the hostility of Japan, he did nothing. Undeterred by this ominous failure, Ramsay MacDonald evolved a plan in March for limiting, by League agreement, the number of planes, ships, men, and guns allowed to each member state.

In Britain feeling against the inefficacy of the League was growing. On the pavement beside Boadicea's statue on the corner of Westminster Bridge was chalked in large letters: 'Gladstone, Palmerston, and Pitt guided the destinies of the British Empire from Westminster—not from Geneva'. And yet peace plans were still discussed. Mussolini produced one for a Four-Power Pact—between Britain, France, Germany, and Italy, to come into force after the Treaty of Versailles had been revised in Germany's favour at Poland's expense. The Poles protested, and so did the Little Entente. The plan, which appealed strongly to British Conservatives, as making an anti-Russian bloc, came to nothing. A deadlock also arose over the proposal that the period of military service in conscript armies should be shortened, because the Germans wanted longer service. For a while Hitler seemed conciliatory, and plans were discussed for the international supervision of army training. Suddenly, however, on October 14th, the German delegation received orders from Berlin to withdraw from the Disarmament Conference. Italy declared that to continue the Conference was useless. Yet negotiations went on—Britain leaning toward an acceptance of Hitler's demands, France set against them, until the Conference ended in smoke in May 1934.

A similar failure occurred in 1933: this was the World Economic Conference, which met to stabilize currency levels. The United States was immediately responsible for the failure, having just abandoned the gold standard: American bankers thought that stabilization would be unfavourable to them—they wanted the dollar to fall in value. While American delegates were proposing formulas at the Conference, and expressing the hope that stabilization would be attained, President Roosevelt suddenly sent a telegram repudiating them. That ended proceedings.

Anti-war feeling expressed itself in many contradictory ways. Already in 1929 the Labour Government had issued an order that Armistice Day should be demilitarized: fewer troops were present that year at the Cenotaph. And now the League of

Nations' Union and the Fellowship of Reconciliation were trying to abolish the annual Hendon Air Display, in order to prevent children from having their martial impulses stirred. In August 1932 an Anti-War Congress at Amsterdam was attended by two thousand men and women, who represented twenty-seven countries. Well-known writers were there, among them Henri Barbusse, author of *Sous Feu*, and well-known labour leaders, among them Tom Mann. Professor Einstein and Romain Rolland were prevented from attending only by ill-health. The Congress issued a manifesto branding the conflict of Imperialist ambitions as the real cause of war. The future of the human race, it declared, lay at the mercy of diplomatic disagreements, political crimes and frontier incidents. War might start at any moment. The manifesto put part of the blame for this situation on the Treaty of Versailles: the clause that saddled Germany with war guilt was 'a flagrant untruth which has been used by a trick of demagogic mysticism to contribute to the growth of Fascist reaction in Germany'. Yet the Congress used such slogans as: 'Stop the Transport of Munitions', 'Defend the Soviet Union', 'Stop the Brigandage of Japan', 'Break the Fascist Terror': as though pacifism were a militant power rather than a negative desire.

Beverley Nichols, an able journalist of the 'sob-brother' variety, to which Godfrey Winn also belonged, made a popular, non-political attack on war. His *Cry Havoc!* was dedicated to 'those mothers whose sons are still alive'. He objected to the use of the romantic and heroic word 'war' to describe modern warfare. A new word was wanted, 'not narrowed to the historical interpretation of armies in conflict, but which could be applied to the latest possibilities of blowing up babies in Baghdad by pressing a button in Birmingham'. Nichols went on to attack armament firms as promoters of war: he blamed them for supplying arms to hereditary enemies, such as Turkey and Greece. and thus encouraging them to make war on each other. (He was unaware that Turkey and Greece had recently become reconciled.) He also criticized scientists for saying that gas was ineffective, and dismissed with contempt the idea that gas-masks could be distributed to all civilians. He denounced O.T.C.s for their militaristic spirit—at the same time attacking their training as out-of-date. The League of Nations disappointed him; its talk of security he found to be only evidence of fear. Finally, he blamed newspapers and history books for putting a war-like emphasis on the facts of living. Nichols's book had a wide circulation, and was probably more effective in inculcating pacifism by its heart-to-heart unpolitical appeal than the carefully organized Left movements of the time.

Many political journalists surveyed Europe gloomily. Sisley Huddleston in *War Unless——*, published in 1933, accused the Press of concealing the dangers of a new war. He complained of the 'Balkanization' of Central Europe, and of the unwillingness of the victorious nations to consider essential treaty revisions; as for the League, its gestures were empty ones: despite its ritualistic proceedings and conventionally co-operative phraseology it had become the cockpit of contending nations.

The Government had to face criticism from the partisans of entirely opposed theories: accused on the one hand of disarming too rapidly, and on the other of not carrying out unilateral disarmament and thus setting an example to the rest of the world. Among those who took the military line was Lady Houston, the enormously wealthy widow of a shipowner. She published a letter protesting against the cuts in the defence forces, which the National Government had introduced, and sent a copy of it to Neville Chamberlain. She wrote: 'England is in deadly peril. When I read the terrible news that our forces of defence—already far, too far, below the safety mark—are again to be the victims of what only Socialists can call economy, every fibre of my being cried out against this further treachery. . . . To leave our homes and our children unprotected while every other country is feverishly arming is a Socialist invitation to our enemies to come and destroy us. . . . The British Lion, powerless to protect itself, is now like a toothless old lap-dog that can yap, but cannot bite.' She also sent a cheque for £200,000 to the Chancellor for the furtherance of rearmament, and had her expensive yacht illuminated all night with the legend 'Mac-Donald is a Traitor'. She bought the *Saturday Review* and filled it with extravagantly jingo articles, poems and news-items, a great many written by herself. 'Fanny' Houston was 'psychic', not to say 'slightly touched', and the uneducated extravagance of her style harmed the cause she defended by bringing it into public ridicule.

The phrase 'the next war' was used without any calculation as to who would be fighting whom. It was merely felt that competitive rearmament would automatically result in the guns going off, just for the thrill that the generals would get out of it. The only actual danger-spot seemed to be the Near and Middle East, where French, British, and Italian interests were in conflict. The *Sunday Express* in April 1933 published an article on what would happen in Br ain if war came again. On the first day a dictatorship would be established—a scheme for it was already being worked out by the higher Civil Servants. All enemy aliens would be interned; the most rigid rationing would be introduced; conscientious objectors who refused to do work of national importance would be given no ration-cards; wireless sets powerful enough to get foreign stations would be confiscated and the possession of transmitters would be forbidden.

Most war and anti-war talk was now a fanciful discussion of the horrors and glories of 'the next war'.

Many young men were feeling that war-talk was not just a newspaper stunt. A representative figure of the time was Lord Knebworth, who belonged to the generation that had been just too young to serve in the war. This generation felt itself misunderstood. It had come to manhood in a time of insecurity, after an education that presupposed security, and was made to feel inferior simply because it had not fought for King and Country. As an undergraduate in 1924, when the papers were publishing 'Ten Years Ago' pictures of the beginning of the war, he wrote to his father, Lord Lytton, who was later Chairman of the League Commission that reported on the Manchurian affair: 'My goodness, the war must have brought things really down to bed-rock—but then afterwards the world spends its time in rebuilding all the artificialities which it took centuries to conceive, and which those years of war shattered into a thousand fragments.' In October 1931, having just become M.P. for Hitchin, he wrote again to his father: 'The whole world is sitting on a bomb. It is even chances if it goes off or not. The world has hitherto existed on a form of slavery—depending upon having a large number of people poor and uneducated and content, while the affairs of the world were managed by a few people comparatively rich and educated and clever. This is no longer true and it is even chances what happens. The Capitalist system has temporarily failed. . . .' In the next two years Lord Knebworth was to find refuge from the 'pin-pricking, sickening, doubtful, depressing peace', in admiration for the orderliness of Italian Fascism, for the discipline of the Catholic Church, and for the healthy, school-like routine of the Royal Air Force.

The most remarkable circumstance of this 'next war' talk was that the military advisers to the Government did not suggest the obvious course of reducing the numbers of the Army in order to meet the public demand for disarmament and retrenchment, while at the same time increasing its actual fighting power. This course had been constantly recommended by the leading British military scientist, Captain Liddell Hart, at whose insistence, largely, the Experimental Mechanized force had been formed in 1927 as a new-styled mobile force to take the place of cavalry. There were still only four battalions in the infantry-supporting Royal Tank Corps, founded in 1923. Even by 1933 these had not been increased and were still equipped with a type of tanks in use ten years earlier—whereas eighteen horse-cavalry regiments and 136 infantry battalions were still being maintained. Liddell Hart had written in 1928 of an ideal strategy for tanks. 'The difference in mobility between an armoured force and a foot-marching force is so immense that it prompts the question: "Why should the former assault at all, even indirectly?". . . By constant "in and out" approaches over the widest possible area, the armoured force might reduce a vast infantry army to inertia. Once that happens, a moral rot is likely to set in among the hungry and helpless occupants of ineffective positions.' In 1933, as *Daily Telegraph* military correspondent, he strongly criticized the trifling sum devoted in Army estimates to tanks and other mechanized equipment—only £348,000, as against £520,000 in 1927. The new Commander of the Imperial General Staff, General Sir Archibald Montgomery-Massingberd, replied to this that there were critics who said that the Army should be organized for a war in Europe, but he ventured to say that the Army was not likely to be so used for many years to come. Duff Cooper, the Financial Secretary to the War Office, introduced the new Army estimates in March 1934, with the words: 'I have had occasion during the past year to study military affairs . . . and the more I study them, the more I am impressed—by the importance of cavalry in modern warfare.' He was supported by General Montgomery-Massingberd that November, when the Nazis had been in power in Germany for nearly two years: 'It is certain that if we do not go slowly with mechanization we shall land ourselves in difficulties. If we mechanize too much, an enormous tail is built up.' It is supposed that he meant a tail of supplies and replacements; but even this did not make sense—the tail of an unmechanized army was twenty times as long.

The fact was that these generals genuinely disbelieved in the likelihood of war and, this being so, were unwilling during their tenure of office to face the social implications of mechanization. For if some regiments of the Army must be sacrificed, to make room for the new armoured units, the obvious victims were the cavalry, whose rôle these units were to take over. But were the cavalry mechanized, cavalry officers with independent means who only held commissions from family habit and a love of horses, would refuse disgustedly to become 'garage-men' and resign. Most of these generals were cavalry men themselves, and also fox-hunters, and had for years been defending hunting against economic and humanitarian critics on the firm ground that it encouraged the breed of cavalry horses, trained young officers in cross-country work, and thus contributed to the defence of the country.

Pacifism had been introduced from Germany at the time of the Weimar Republic. So had three other libertarian fashions—sun-bathing, nudism, and hiking. Sun-bathing had originally been found useful in Germany to cure children of 'deficiency diseases' caused by the British blockade and by the severities of the post-war years. It had now become a general cure-all, in disregard of its stupefying effect on the minds of most of its addicts, and the warning of doctors that long exposure to the sun's rays weakened the resistance of the skin to infection.

Nudism was of psychological rather than medical origin. Though some of its more zealous supporters wished to abolish the consumption of meat, tobacco, and alcohol, as well as clothing, nudism proper had no such simple-life background. It was supposed to eradicate repressions by teaching people to take their bodies for granted, and to promote health by open-air life and exercises. A nudist society had to be extremely strict, in order to avoid all charges of immorality: prospective members must convince the secretary of their sincerity and, if they happened to be married or engaged, obtain the written consent of their husbands or wives or fiancés. The societies tried to keep the numbers of the two sexes equal, but men tended to predominate because a woman took greater social risks by becoming a member.

Nudism was not so popular in Britain as in Germany or the United States: it was not suited to the climate. At first nudists gathered in muddy and midge-ridden corners of solitary woods, but later built luxurious nature-camps, and in the winter held indoor meetings with sun-ray lamps. They adopted the Hellenistic Greek name 'Gymnosophists', and brought their children along with them. After a time most members found the routine of these camps monotonous, despite the earnest psychological and valetudinarian talk that went on in them. Women especially grew bored sitting about with no clothes, while attracting no erotic interest in the opposite sex, and being made wonderfully healthy by compulsory drill, and by lettuce and tinned-salmon teas. Far better to wear a bathing-dress on a beach and be conscious of its daringness, than to sit about with no clothes on and with everyone politely unconscious of it. At the superior nudist camps, a nice class distinction was made: the butlers and maids who brought along the refreshments were forced to admit their lower social standing by wearing loincloths and aprons respectively.

The Press attacked nudism as cranky and immoral. Indignant correspondents declared that no honourable person would strut about naked, and that on account of the nudist cult sexual crimes were becoming more and more frequent. Children should be brought up not to take an unhealthy interest in their bodies, but to consider them only as working apparatuses.

Hiking was the most popular of these health movements. The word came into popular use from the United States about 1927; when in an article in the *Daily Express* an official of the Camping Club wrote: 'We have 3,000 members. Most of these are solitary "hikers" who carry all their kit with them.' But the fashion was German: the '*wandervogel*' with his rucksack, Tyrolese costume, concertina (or beribboned mandoline) and singing girl-chum was the most popular figure in Republican Germany. In 1930 the Youth Hostel Association was founded to provide cheap country inns where young people on walking or cycling holidays could stay for a shilling a night, with breakfast for another shilling. The hostel-system, too, was German. Hiking was a more ambitious form of rambling: not a mere Sunday's jaunt in country near home, but a whole week or fortnight of tramping or cycling far afield.

Hiking began to enjoy a boom in 1931, though the weather that year was unfavourable. Many new clubs were formed to organize hiking parties. Provincial newspapers sponsored Hikers' Leagues, which soon had a large membership—especially in the industrial Midlands and in the North. There were communal hikes to the Aldershot Tattoo, the Portsmouth Navy Week, and similar events. Because hiking was cheap, many young people were able to take holidays in the country, which otherwise they could not have afforded. There were a few Labour and Liberal Hikers' Clubs, but in general the movement escaped the political and ecclesiastical regimentation to which the German *wandervogel* had been subjected after the first glorious days of post-war liberty.

Increasingly pressed by the competition of long-distance buses, the railways exploited the popularity of rambling and hiking. On the morning of Good Friday 1932 the Great Western Railway ran a 'Hikers' Mystery Express' from Paddington which was to take hikers out into the country, drop them for a hike—more properly a ramble—and bring them home again in the evening. It was amusing not to know one's destination; and enough adventurers turned up to fill two trains. Similar excursions were then provided by other companies. The Great Western followed up their success in brightening railway travel with a 'Kiddies' Express' from Paddington to Weston-super-Mare, by which only children were allowed to travel; during the journey they were entertained by clowns. 'Ramblers' Harvest-Moon Specials' were also run during the summer months along the Thames Valley. In July S. P. B. Mais, schoolmaster, journalist and publicist, conducted a Southern Railway Moonlight Walk over the South Downs to witness sunrise from Chanctonbury Ring on a Saturday night. There was a Special Supper and Breakfast Car Train, '*Experience the novel thrill of watching a summer dawn from the first streaks to the full sunrise!*' Forty people were expected; 1,440 turned up, and filled four trains. The moon had sunk below the horizon long before the passengers' arrival, and the sun refused to rise to order—Mais had some difficult explaining to do. But the Southern Railway thereafter made guided rambling a regular service. The L.M.S. started 'train-tours'; the trains, consisting of special carriages with large plate-glass windows, were driven very slowly through the Yorkshire dales and other 'beauty-spots'; and 'Romantic Specials' ran from Lancashire and other parts of the north to Gretna Green, where the blacksmith was supposedly waiting to marry eloping couples under Scottish law. (Immediate marriages could no longer be solemnized over the anvil, but Scottish law did at least make a romantic marriage more easily dissoluble than English.)

Hikers were adopting a special dress that was almost a uniform. The beret was an untasselled Basque tam-o'-shanter that the French tennis-champion Borotra had repopularized about 1927. It had been in vogue in 1901 on the northern grouse-moors, but for women only. Now both sexes wore it, above the same open-necked shirts, washable shorts, and waterproof ruck-sack. Those who wished to be independent of hostels carried, besides their change of clothing, aluminium cooking utensils, primus stoves, and oilskin tents. A complete hiker's outfit weighed about twelve pounds; the rucksack was usually built on a steel frame so that it did not slump against the back, but allowed a cool passage for air.

In 1934 the subject of hikers' dress came up in *The Times*. One correspondent deplored the 'spectacle of the country's youths and maidens in hideous uniforms'. Why did they all use potato-colour and khaki? Why not brighter colours? The experience of another correspondent was very different: in his part of the country most hikers wore disgustingly garish clothes, and dressed like pirates, with coloured handkerchiefs around their heads—he wished they would go in more for grey flannel—what could be nicer and neater than that? Another correspondent complained of the hikers' nakedness: why did they persist in revealing knobbly knees, fat legs, and broad hips? Bright colours served only to accentuate these deformities. The Bishop of Exeter then came to the defence of the hikers, most of whom, he said, had only one short holiday a year and were right to make it as colourful and interesting as possible. 'They strive to add colour to their lives by strange dresses and eccentric behaviour. They are dressing their parts, and if dress and demeanour raise a smile, it should also be a smile of welcome and encouragement.' Most readers of *The Times* endorsed this plea, and one wrote: 'When the Bishop of Exeter, belonging, as he reminds us, to a class that lives in beautiful homes and can take holidays in colourful countries, delights his flock by perambulating his diocese, at the age of seventy-one, on a bicycle of brilliant vermilion, surely we should have sympathy with the desire for colour of those whose different lives he so feelingly describes.'

Bright summer-wear of the sort hitherto only worn by smart visitors to the south of France was popularized by cheap cruises. This new form of holiday was provided by the shipping companies at the beginning of the Thirties when the Wall Street crash cut American tourist traffic alarmingly and they had to do something to keep their ships in commission. The advertised cruises suited middle-class people who could not afford Continental holidays because of the depreciation of sterling, but who wanted a change from the English seaside. The cruises ran to Norway, Spain and Portugal, Morocco, the Canaries, and the western Mediterranean. Ship's officers undertook to organize all kinds of entertainments—dances, swimming galas, deck sports, fancy-dress competitions, concerts, and cinema shows. They became as much compères of a prolonged variety show as working seamen. Cruises were one long party, with the added attraction of visits to foreign ports and sunny excursions in the hinterland. Many mothers took their daughters on cruises in the hope of finding them husbands; and the shipping companies advertised their success as 'Cupid's agents'. These girls spent most of their day in bathing-dresses or coloured linen beach-pyjamas and huge straw hats and if possible wore something excitingly different for every night of the trip.

Clothes in general were now becoming more cheerful in colour. To 'knock about in', men wore green and really blue (not merely navy-blue) trousers, and short-sleeved, coloured polo-shirts and coloured shorts in lemon, green, burgundy, and saxe. Gay cellular-woven shirts had come in by 1933 for the use of both sexes: their mesh of fine holes gave the skin the prescribed healthy ventilation. The increasing freedom of men's dress was expressed in the soft white evening shirt with a soft white collar, which was gradually replacing the starched shirt and collar with dinner jackets. Men's underwear, too, was changing: short cellular-woven pants with elastic tops instead of the old long, heavy, closely clinging woollen ones. Flannel trousers were becoming less uniform and more dignified, from the popularity of faint, wide-apart pin-stripes. With these trousers brown suède shoes were being worn—a fashion that, when first introduced at the elder universities a few years before, had marked the 'Pansy', or homosexual beauty.

Women's dress had become distinctly feminine. Skirts ceased to have a single all-day length, but were standardized in three lengths—to the knee for day wear, to the calf for formal afternoon wear, to the ankle for the evening. Women no longer tried to look boyish, but emphasized their difference from men by using cosmetics and enamelling their nails. The *Sunday Express* in 1931 remarked that one thousand five hundred lipsticks were being sold in London shops for every one sold ten years previously. All hairdressers, beauty parlours, large stores, chemists, and branches of Woolworth's now sold cosmetics and nail-enamel. The stage of imitating the health and vitality of youth had passed: cosmetics were used to make deliberate departures from nature. Blue nails, green eye-sockets, and orange lips enjoyed a short-lived popularity.

The neo-Victorian fashion started by the Sitwells had spread from interior decoration to dress. Leg-of-mutton sleeves and yards of seams, gores, and flares appeared. This tendency expressed the contemporary nostalgia for the secure social life of the Victorians, and was accompanied by a sudden fashion among well-to-do women for having as many children as they could afford: to be prolific had been vulgar in the Twenties. Flowing printed chiffon in all colours enlivened the summer of 1930, when hats were of layers of organdie and of lacquered straw. In 1931 the hats were even more ornate: first there was the feathered bowler, brought to London from Paris, worn tilted over the left eye. After the bowler came all kinds of Victorian hats, made to reveal coquettishly one side of the head. Victorian colours—plum, maroon, and violet—were in favour. Neo-Victorianism affected stockings too: pale beige shades, that had drawn attention to the legs, darkened to brown and mole.

In jewellery the bizarre and barbarous ornaments of the jazz-ridden Twenties were giving way to elaborately worked stones. Cameo and other Victorian jewellery came into fashion, and people went slumming in the Caledonian Market to find it. Jewelled brooches were worn on hats, corsages, gloves, and shoes. But, not to forget the *neo* of this Victorianism, bakelite and chromium-plate were used for accessory ornaments. The chromium-plate fashion lasted for several years: bracelets, rigid and chain-type necklaces, ear-rings, buckles, and brooches were made of it. At one time twelve or thirteen bracelets were worn on a single arm; at another one large handcuff, three or four inches wide. Bracelets worn above the elbow were called slave-bangles. Whatever the particular fashion, the general tendency in appearance of ornaments was toward the complex, the elaborate and the highly worked, so far as this was consistent with their function, which was to give the wearer pleasure without exertion. The elaborateness of Victorian women's dress was therefore copied, yet without taking over the disadvantages in weight and constriction. A whole complicated toilette could be rapidly removed, and without the help of a lady's maid, if one wished to get into shorts and a shirt for an evening set of tennis. This was made possible by a great simplification in dress-fastenings—elastic had superseded laces; and the press-stud, the hook and eye. Concealed press-studs often lay beneath a row of decorative but useless buttons. The metal zip-fastener, which about 1927 had spread from handbags and purses to airmen's and airwomen's uniforms and winter-sports clothes, could now be found on every sort of sports garment, including women's shorts.

The word 'functionalism' was first heard in 1930, applied to the sugar-cube architectural style imported from Germany. The *Observer* then wrote: 'This is what is called the architecture of functionalism. The architectural form arises purely out of the purpose of the building.' It was afterwards applied to a great number of manufactured goods. A functional pipe, for example, was one that burned tobacco coolly and slowly, cleaned easily, did not go out, and could be laid down on a flat surface without ash falling out. But functionally designed objects were usually ugly in shape. The whole fashion-sense of the Thirties was a compromise between what was 'amusing'—this adjective had succeeded the Victorian *chic* and the Edwardian 'smart' as a term of praise for any notably eccentric novelty—and·what was 'functional'.

Fashions in hairdressing had already broken away from the close-cropped Twenties' style. Rolls of curls were worn at the nape of the neck. The 'windswept' coiffure came over from Paris in 1931: in this the hair was cut short, brushed forward with a swirling movement, and plastered to the cheeks and forehead in ragged edges. Most women, if they could not afford the latest complications, at least had their hair cut so as to allow for an upward curl at the back and for generous waves on whichever side of the head was revealed the tilted hat.

As the Thirties drew on, fashions became more 'amusing' than ever. Day clothes in 1932 were made to suggest all kinds of male uniform, from Guardsmen's to 'bell-hops'. 'Guardee' overcoats were worn, with braided epaulettes, cord shoulder-straps, and rows of gleaming metal buttons. They were double-breasted and had huge lapels extending to the shoulders. The waists of these coats, and of all dresses, were well-defined and high—and went higher and higher until they began to look distinctly Third Empire. This fashion affected beach-dress, too. Floppy, glaring beach-pyjamas were going out; instead, tailored sailor trousers and vests, with slim hips and high waists, were worn. In 1933 the artificial emphasis fell still more heavily upon shoulders. Evening gowns and summer frocks had shelf-shoulders, with frills sticking out a foot or so, arranged in several tiers. Shops were full of boas, ruffles, and frills, all meant to accentuate shoulder-width. With wide shoulders went high throttle-necks, secured by bows and flounces. This flouncing tendency was also to be seen in swagger-coats. These were of three-quarter length; they hung loosely from the shoulders and fastened only underneath the chin. The emphasis on shoulders was heightened by a simplification of hats; and the fez came in. Most women wore them in the simple North African shape, but for the very smart there were tall, brimless models, named 'The Clown' and 'The Paper-Bag', and other crushed and folded, mediaeval-looking affairs.

CHAPTER SEVENTEEN

The Days of the Loch Ness Monster

Travelling at high speed through space was the first recreation of the age. T. E. Lawrence in a letter to Robert Graves in 1927 wrote enthusiastically about the 'lustfulness' of motor-bicycling across Salisbury Plain at 80 m.p.h., feeling the earth moulding herself under him, as if it was he who was 'piling up the hill, hollowing the valley, stretching out the level place'. But many unmechanically minded people felt the joy more romantic and acute when speed was not achieved with the help of electricity or the internal combustion engine. It was this that recommended ski-ing, tobogganing down long ice-runs on 'skeletons' in Switzerland, and surf-riding on the Atlantic rollers of the Cornish coast. Then there was gliding. There had been well-attended gliding contests on the Downs at Itford near Lewes as far back as 1923, but the new developments in 1930 were due to German improvements in glider design, and these in turn to the Versailles Treaty, which had put severe restrictions on German aeroplane-flying. By using air-currents skilfully, once a glider had been launched into the air down a run-way, the airman could often climb to a great height and remain aloft for hours. The *Daily Mail* encouraged British gliding by offering a £1,000 prize to the first person to glide across the Channel and back. It was soon won. The *Daily Mail* continued also to offer money-prizes for aeroplane flights to distant parts of the world.

Amy Johnson was a *Daily Mail* discovery. She was a young graduate of Sheffield University, who afterwards worked in a solicitor's office. She learned to fly in her spare time, became an excellent mechanic and pilot, and then suddenly achieved world-fame in 1930 by being the first woman to fly solo to Australia. She had prepared herself for this flight, which won her £10,000 from the *Daily Mail*, by careful meteorological study and by learning ju-jitsu and other defensive arts lest she fell among Arab sheikhs or Dyak head-hunters. She was greeted on her return to London, at a banquet organized by the *Daily Mail*, by leading representatives of women's achievement in sport, the arts, and the professions. Her speech pleased everyone by her ingenuous phrases and un-Mayfair accent. The *Daily Mail* then employed her for advertisement purposes on a flying tour of England. While she was following up her first success with other long-distance flights, J. A. Mollison, a former Royal Air Force pilot, was becoming famous in the same line of business. He shortened the London-Cape flight record by fifteen hours. On this journey he scarcely slept and was so fatigued on his arrival at Capetown that, dazzled by the lights of the airport, he crashed. However, he emerged unhurt and was welcomed by Amy Johnson, who happened to be there, with the words: 'I think you're wonderful, you hero!' Not long afterwards they were married.

Mollison, on his own candid confession, was a nervous, restless character and well aware that his wife was a better flyer than himself. Yet they were now 'the Mollisons' and he felt in duty bound to justify her change of name by showing himself at least her equal. He tried to break her records. This connubial rivalry amused the *Daily Mail* public. In 1933 the Mollisons tried a record-breaking Transatlantic flight together to the United States. At the last lap she handed the controls over to give him the honour of landing; but he pancaked, smashing the plane and injuring them both. After this, there were rumours of marital divergence, she continuing single-hearted towards him, he feeling himself unworthy of her and forming other attachments. The public heart was harrowed by sentimental forebodings for years before the marriage was dissolved in 1938, and Mollison married an actress.

The price that had to be paid, not only by the Mollisons but by all who came under the general category of 'public entertainers', was constant publicization of their private lives. 'Newshawks' in the American style were a new feature of British social life: they were trained to be completely unscrupulous in the matter of getting their news—bribing, lying, breaking confidences. Their loyalty was to their paper, and the paper's loyalty was to its news-hungry public. If the persons concerned in some newsworthy activity would make no intimate statement about themselves, there was always a neighbour anxious to earn money by telling what he knew. The newspapers paid well for 'beats', as 'scoops' were now called, and could pay for the best possible legal advice in protecting themselves against any mistakes made or any acts of trespass their reporters committed. The editors were as loyal to the reporters as the reporters to the editors— would never disown them in the style of a Government disowning its spies. It was next to impossible for a private person to get redress from a paper in the way of correction of, or apology for, factual mistatements. It was not that editors and proprietors did not regret any errors that were made, but that a paper would forfeit public confidence by any such retraction. The only test of libel was damage to reputation that could be assessed by a jury in terms of money. It was not libellous to suggest that two prominent young people were engaged, however incorrect and socially embarrassing this might be, unless one of the parties could prove, for example, that the report had led to the breaking off of an actual engagement to someone rich, and so caused him or her financial loss. But to sue for libel in such a case only led to still more damaging publicity; so the papers got away with it almost always. And since nearly everyone would give his or her ears to be the subject of even an incorrect mention in the Press, the public was on the whole very well served. Discretion in the matter of libel usually kept the papers from voicing popular indignation against known public enemies; only when a criminal conviction had been secured or when they were in possession of a cast-iron case could they comment freely.

The showing up of Yadil, a patent medicine, was a great event in 1924. Yadil seems to have started as a cure for the diseases of cows and hens, but it was soon enlarged into a cure-all for almost every human malady, including cancer and consumption. It was claimed that it contained oil of garlic. The *Daily Mail*, which had had a dispute with the Yadil Company over an advertising question, decided to expose the fact that an analysis of Yadil by Sir William Pope, Professor of Chemistry at

Cambridge, revealed that it contained no measurable quantity of oil of garlic: instead there was one per cent formaldehyde, which medical opinion regarded as a dangerous irritant if taken internally. The *Daily Mail* headlined this exposure; refusing to print Yadil's advertisements and warning the public against it. It also stressed Sir William's opinion that the garlicky smell of Yadil, which was its most noticeable characteristic, could be produced by an infinitesimal amount of chemical much cheaper than oil of garlic. Lord Horder, the King's Physician, joined in the attack, pointing out that poor people who suffered from consumption were being deluded into starving themselves of proper food in order to buy bottles of the mixture. The *Daily Mail* announced in a leader, 'Truth in Advertising': 'Yadil's impudence went even further. They declared that doctors who refused to prescribe Yadil were suppressing a cure for consumption lest they should lose money by the cure of their patients.' In reply the Yadil Company issued a writ for libel against the *Daily Mail*; they also applied for an injunction against further publication of the exposure, but this was rejected. The chemists' shops then ceased to stock Yadil, the ruined Yadil company never prepared its case, the action was dismissed, and the company was wound up. The *Daily Mail* exulted over Yadil's withdrawal from the market.

It is only fair to add that Yadil, whatever its chemical constituents, had proved effective in thousands of cases where a rise of temperature was a leading symptom, and was being ardently commended by hundreds of doctors. Also, that in homeopathic pills containing garlic or other drugs the amount would not be 'measurable'; that two of the Royal Princes employed homeopathic physicians; and that advanced bio-chemists were now proving the homeopathic case for minute quantities of drugs in trituration as against the allopathic practice of large, crude doses.

In the Thirties there was a hue and cry after Jacob Factor, the company promoter, who had an unfortunate record in financial transactions and was in England trying to find supporters for new schemes of doubtful security. He was successfully impeded in these. Moral indignation could also be roused against prominent foreigners who were in no position to bring libel actions. In 1926, when King Carol renounced the throne of Rumania, though some papers took the line 'Royal Romance', others knew their public well enough to title the story 'Carol the Cad'. His caddishness was assessed by the number of women in the case. If he had separated from Princess Helen because he wished to rejoin the morganatic wife whom he had been forced, for dynastic reasons, to abandon, it would have been a romance; actually, he went to live with a third person, Madame Lupescu. Public opinion now condoned a single change of heart, but not more: as the police-court ruling branded a woman who took more than a single lover as a common prostitute. This principle was applied in 1936 in the Mrs. Simpson case: she was a twice-divorced woman.

The Press derived a large part of its revenue from lurid crime stories—Mahon the Mumbles villa murderer, True the gentleman killer who managed to escape the rope by means of a plea of insanity, Armstrong the poisoner who put arsenic on tea-time sandwiches, Maltby the tailor who had failed to keep a suicide pact with his mistress and lived in a barricaded house for six months with her decomposing body in the bathroom, where he took his meals; Police Constable Gutteridge murdered by a car-bandit; No. 1 and No. 2 Trunk murderers. In crime cases the Press gave all possible assistance to the police in bringing the criminal to justice—with a single proviso: any new clue that a reporter unearthed, or that was communicated to an editorial office by a member of the public, should have its first appearance in print in that paper. British criminal law forbade the publication of evidence which might prejudice the jury against an accused person, but there were papers which often transgressed this rule in the spirit if not the letter. Judges on more than one occasion had to protest strongly against photographs appearing of people against whom a charge was likely to be made, lest this should assist witnesses in an identification parade, and even against the spiriting away of witnesses by newspaper men in order to reserve them for a dramatic statement at the moment most helpful to the paper to which they had sold it in advance.

True dialogue in 1928 in the reporters' room of a big London daily:

Small newsboy running in: 'Case of suicide. Worth half a crown, Guv'nor.'

Reporter, eagerly: 'Police told yet?'

Newsboy: 'No, 'course not.'

Reporter: 'Woman?'

Newsboy: 'Yep.'

Reporter: 'Young?'

Newsboy: 'Mother of five.'

Reporter: 'Oh. . . . Why did she do it?'

Newsboy: 'Booze.'

Reporter: 'Where?'

Newsboy: 'Down in Stepney, I came running right here.'

Reporter: 'Stepney—that's no good. Any last letter?'

Newsboy: 'No, she forgot.'

Reporter, disgusted: 'For God's sake, don't tell me she just put her blooming head in a gas oven?'

Newsboy: 'Sorry, Guv'nor, that's what she did. But it's worth half a dollar, honest, Guv'nor. And I brought it here straight away, same as they told us. It's my mother, Guv'nor.'

Reporter: 'O have it your way, then, blast you! It's not your fault, I suppose. Here's the blood money!'

Newspapermen devoted to their job had an entirely different set of values from other people. They had to be without hearts. What gave a news-editor the keenest satisfaction was the breaking of a big news-story at the exact right time for publication. Whether its human significance was alarming or cheerful made no odds to him at all. Romantic royal engagements, such as that of Princess Mary to Lord Lascelles, or of the Duke of York to the Lady Elizabeth Bowes-Lyon, or the birth in 1925 of Princess Elizabeth, were only more welcome than a colliery disaster if the story interest could be spread out over a longer period of time. When there was no news, news had to be made; and even an unexpected public disaster was a gift from the gods—the private tear had to be dashed away.

The greatest disaster of the period was the loss of the R101. As a story it broke at just the worst hour of the whole week. This airship had already made several trial flights: one over London in 1929, when the Press described it as 'large as the *Mauretania*'. Twice, in 1930, members of the Lords and Commons had been invited to take a short trip in it, but each time bad weather had prevented a start. R100, the sister ship, had made a successful flight to Canada, and it was hoped that R101, to which various structural alterations had been made, would prove even more successful. The airship left Cardington on a flight to India at 7 p.m. on Saturday, October 4th, carrying with it Lord Thomson, the Labour Air Minister, and almost all the airship experts of the Air Ministry. Radio messages reported its progress until nearly 2 a.m., when it was heard near Paris asking for its bearings. Then no more news came, and the Sunday papers 'went to bed'. Just too late to catch the news: the airship, buffeted by a heavy rainstorm, crashed near Beauvais. The hydrogen took fire and everyone aboard was burned to death but some men in part of a gondola that was torn off by a tree and fell clear. One of these, a wireless operator, escaped uninjured and telephoned the news to the Air Ministry from Beauvais. The Prime Minister was immediately informed at Chequers, the private country-house that had recently been presented to Parliament as a residence for successive Prime Ministers. Then the Sunday Press had to recall their worn-out and disgusted press-men to the office to get up special editions with full details of the crash; on any other day but a Sunday the afternoon papers would have been there to take over the story. Air-Marshal Sir John Salmond and his staff flew at once to Beauvais to examine the wreckage, special prayers were offered that evening in the churches, and France proclaimed a day of national mourning when the bodies were moved to England. Among the dead was Lord Thomson himself, who had insisted on the flight being made, against expert advice, because of his anxiety to get back from India to a conference as soon as possible.

Two days later a news-worthy sequel occurred at a séance held by Harry Price at his National Laboratory for Psychical Research. This laboratory had been founded in 1925 for an unbiased inquiry into the genuineness of psychical phenomena. On October 7th, Price was holding an investigation with a medium named Mrs. Garrett; in her trance, she began to deliver messages from Lieutenant Irwin, who had been in command of R101. These gave circumstantial details of defects in the airship, which were later corroborated at the official inquiry. Among other things, Lieutenant Irwin was said to have declared through Mrs. Garrett that the increased bulk of the airship since its reconstruction was too much for its engine capacity, that its gas-bags had been leaking, and that it had not had sufficient trials before setting out. (The conclusions of the inquiry into the loss, published in the following year, confirmed these revelations. It was found that the immediate cause of the disaster was the gradual loss of gas due to the wearing of holes in the gasbags.) The Air Ministry decided to stop the construction of airships; R100 was dismantled, and the airship station at Cardington closed down.

A gift from the gods in 1932 was the sensational and protracted trial of the Rev. Harold Davidson, rector of Stiffkey. The rector had begun his career as an actor, and, on becoming a clergyman, had served a small Norfolk parish for twenty-six years. He was brought up before the Norwich Consistory Court on charges concerning his moral conduct. These charges were substantiated by several girls, some of them prostitutes, in whom he claimed to have taken a purely fatherly interest. He was found guilty, unfrocked, and degraded. Davidson made use of his acting experience to pay for the cost of his defence: one of his stunts was a fast, performed in a barrel on Blackpool beach. While it was in progress the Blackpool police arrested him on a charge of attempting suicide by starvation. He was found not guilty, and brought a successful action for damages against the Blackpool Corporation. He was awarded £382. He continued to exploit his notoriety by public appearances: one of them on Hampstead Heath at a Bank-Holiday fair in the company of a dead whale. He next took up with a circus, and posed with lions in a cage. His end was eminently news-worthy. At a threepenny sideshow at Skegness in July 1937 a lion suddenly seized and mauled him; although a young woman lion-trainer gallantly pulled him out of the cage, he died of his injuries.

The great topic of 1933 was the Loch Ness Monster. The monster boom began with a series of circumstantial reports from residents and visitors to the loch. An A.A. scout claimed to have seen a serpent-like shape in the water; other reports suggested that the monster was a gigantic bearded eel. Yet when a big-game hunter went north to investigate, he found a spoor in the shingle by the side of the loch. Serpents and eels do not leave spoors; which discredited the local theories. The Natural History Museum then gave its opinion that the spoor resembled that of a hippopotamus. Sir Arthur Keith, the scientist, decided that the monster might be a legged reptile, but he suspected that it was an illusion and that the case was one for psychologists rather than zoologists. Others suspected a practical joke. Despite such doubts the monster's fame attracted thousands of summer tourists. The Catholic monks of Fort Augustus on the loch side had most of them seen the monster, and the Father Superior had been aware of its existence for some years. Theories multiplied, and so did efforts to trace the monster. A local ghilly declared that it was an old blind salmon. The most commonly accepted theory was that it was some sort of whale that had entered the loch when small and could not get back to the sea. But if so, on what would it subsist? Someone then tried to detect its presence with hydrophones; someone else reported having seen it cross the road with a sheep in its mouth. An old woman disappeared and her body was later discovered on the moors; she was said to have been carried off. Mutilated carcases of sheep were found on the shores of the loch, and the tooth-marks in them were pronounced to be the monster's. Someone said that it might be a walrus; but rather smudgy photographs which appeared in London newspapers bore out the whale theory. The Royal Scottish Museum suggested that it was a large tunny or shark come into the loch from the sea. A film was made, 'The Secret of the Loch', which showed occasional glimpses of dark shapes on the water's surface, but nothing to swear by; however, the proceeds of the film endowed a bed for divers at Greenwich Hospital. The monster was equally a gift to the foreign Press. A Japanese paper said that it was roaming over the great heaths where Macbeth saw the weird sisters. On April Fool's Day, 1936, the *Berliner Illustrierte Zeitung* announced that the monster had been captured and was now on exhibition at Edinburgh; and reproduced photographs of it by a 'famous Scottish zoologist, Professor MacKeenkool'. Yet the monster was not seen again, and interest in it gradually died down.

The Press exploited 'borderland' cases between science and mysticism, hard fact and prodigy. The usual line taken was to print the hard facts of a case but without spoiling the story for those who liked prodigies: Lieutenant-Commander F. Gould, author of *The Case for the Sea Serpent* and similar 'believe it or not' books, was the best-known journalist of this borderland. 'Dowsing' or water-divining with a hazel twig was a recognized profession, and the game of dowsing for metals was taken up seriously and often successfully in the Twenties by retired Army officers and such. The police were not too proud to call in the dowser to help them locate drowned bodies in the muddy beds of rivers; and one dowser found four such within a few months. There was also a vogue for diagnosing disease by the same methods of divination: the borderline, however, was generally considered to be overstepped when dowsers claimed that they could locate springs or buried minerals by using their wand over a map of the area of search; and when diagnosticians similarly claimed to be able to read disease symptoms merely from a ring or brooch worn by the patient. A famous borderland machine of the Twenties was 'Dr. Abram's Box'. This was an electrical instrument, not unlike a gramophone, which was supposed to diagnose diseases by detecting electrical radiations in a spot of the patient's blood or in a sample of his handwriting. The patient had to face west when preparing his sample for the machine. The Press reported that unscrupulous doctors made enormous sums from the box, though it had been proved a shameless fake by a group of eminent scientists. Yet many people remained convinced of its efficacy and held that the test had been unfairly conducted. As late as August 1939 the *Spectator* printed a letter from Lord Tavistock, inquiring whether 'in view of the large amount of money being spent annually on cancer research and treatment, it would not be a good plan to spend some on the exploitation of the late Dr. Abram's methods'.

The London Press was engaged in a bitter and exhausting circulation war. For some time the *Daily Express* had been competing with the *Daily Mail*, but real warfare did not start until 1930, when the amalgamation of the *Daily News* and the *Daily Chronicle* into the *News Chronicle*, and the reorganization of the *Daily Herald*, brought two more large dailies into the fray. The *Daily Herald* had been living a hand-to-mouth existence since its foundation, struggling on independently of both the Press Barons and the official Labour Party and constantly appealing for help to its readers. In 1930 it was no longer meeting expenses, and J. S. Elias (later Lord Southwood) of Odham's Press, which had also bought up *John Bull*, the *People*, and *Sporting Life*, at different times, acquired 51 per cent of the shares; the rest belonged to the Trade Unions. The deal contained a clause that Odham's and the T.U.C. were to be equally represented on the board of directors, with J. S. Elias as chairman, the *Daily Herald* was always to support Labour Party and T.U.C. policy. The *Daily Herald's* rôle as an organ of the extreme pro-Russian Left passed to the *Daily Worker*. The *Daily Herald* now came into line with the other big dailies in its reporting and feature news, and these felt the competition heavily; for a number of working people who would naturally have subscribed to the *Daily Herald* had found it too gloomy for everyday reading. In 1931, to retain the loyalty of its readers, the *Daily Mail* and its associated papers offered prizes for crosswords and other competitions which amounted to £125,000. The *Daily Herald* and the *News Chronicle* followed the same course, offering £50,000 each, exclusive of crossword prizes, in the course of the year. The *Daily Mail* was said to be spending £7,000 a week on house to house canvassing, the *Daily Express* and the *Daily Herald* £5,000 a week, and the *News Chronicle* £2,500. Enticement of subscribers to forsake one paper and embrace another now became the rule. This was not a criminal act, as was enticement of a servant to leave another's employment, or the alienation of a wife's affections. Free health and life insurance, with larger and larger awards, was another bait offered to catch readers. Competition became fantastic. Every time that one paper would add to its list some new accident or malady from which registered readers could benefit by certified death—tram-collision or diphtheria—a rival would add still another—ptomaine poisoning or a bursting household boiler. The aim of each newspaper-owner was to be the first to reach a daily circulation of two million. At the beginning of 1932 net sales stood roughly at 1,830,000 for the *Mail*, 1,650,000 for the *Express*, 1,440,000 for the *Herald*, and 1,200,000 for the *Chronicle*.

In the course of 1932 newspaper-owners agreed to stop the insurance war and offer more or less equally extensive policies. But warfare continued all the more determinedly by means of canvassing, prize competitions, and free gifts. Newspapers set up schools for canvassers, and newsagents had a difficult time because people continually changed their paper as each new bribe was offered. The free gifts were of all kinds: flannel trousers for husbands, mangles for wives, cameras, kettles, handbags, and tea-sets. In 1933 there was a momentary lull in the war, because the Government set up a Lotteries Commission to inquire into prize competitions; but afterwards newspapers came out with offers of valuable free books—encyclopedias, sets of Dickens and Shakespeare. A great many families were now subscribing to two or three papers—for the bribes, not for reading. The sales of the *Herald* and the *Express* both reached the two-million mark in July 1933. The *Express* reached it first, but at the same time exposed the 'sales racket' by proclaiming that it had spent £30,000 a week on the task and that each new reader had been bought at the cost of 8s. 3d. a head. It implied that from the newspaper-owners' and advertisers' point of view the new readers were not worth having. Upon this, open warfare ceased: but the *Daily Express* was left slightly in the lead. The *Daily Telegraph* took no part in this circulation war. Lord Camrose, who had bought and killed the *Daily Graphic* by merging it with the *Daily Sketch* in 1926, had taken over the *Daily Telegraph* from Lord Burnham in 1930. Camrose reduced its size, modernized its type, layout, and general appearance, rehoused it magnificently and gradually sent its circulation up from 140,000 to 540,000; in 1937 it swallowed up the *Morning Post*. But though now a penny paper—*The Times* still sold at twopence—it was still a select Press journal: the difference was in the treatment of news, as contemporary history rather than as drama, and in the greater space given to private, as opposed to commercial, advertisements.

A curious Victorian revival was that of Nonsense. The success of A'Beckett's forgotten *Comic History of England* was renewed in W. C. Sellar and R. J. Yeatman's *1066 and All That*, which proved so popular that it was even staged. These same authors repeated their success with *And Now All This*, which guyed golf, knitting, and other contemporary activities; and also *Horse Nonsense* and *Garden Rubbish*. There were several others in the field. The trend of nonsense was grotesquely violent rather than wistful in the Lewis Carroll, Edward Lear vein.

Soon nearly all the daily newspapers were running special nonsense-columns. They were written by advanced young men who drew on their expert knowledge of obscure corners of history and literature to make jokes so far above the heads of the ordinary reader as to pass for pure nonsense; though occasionally they descended to fields of allusion where advanced suburban readers could feel at home. The *Daily Mail* began it in the early Twenties with D. B. Wyndham Lewis, whose real interest was Provencal literature—apologizing profusely for his apparent craziness. (He also edited *The Stuffed Owl* in 1930; this was a humorously intended anthology of bad verse.) The *Daily Express* had a winner in J. B. Morton, who wrote under the name of Beachcomber, and whose literary, artistic, and social criticism under the cloak of nonsense was, like D. B. Wyndham Lewis's, far above the intellectual level of ordinary feature-writing for a daily. Of all humorous columnists of the period the most remarkable was Nathaniel Gubbins of the *Sunday Express*. His humour lay not in the bizarre or strained but in his dry presentation of damp humanity, and in his moral steadfastness, which seemed grotesque in the world of the Sunday newspaper.

Roller-skating had once more become a popular fashion in the middle Twenties after two previous crazes, in the 1880's and 1910's. Skating on artificial ice at Prince's had been only for the few, but in 1929 popular ice-rinks began to be opened in London and in several other cities, equipped with bands and snack-bars. In 1930 people who normally would have gone to tea-dances spent their Saturday afternoons at the large new rinks at Richmond, Golders Green, or Hammersmith, and there learned to waltz, tango, and cut the classical figures, and watched exhibition dancing from galleries when the ice was cleared.

Horse racing was helped in its struggle against the competition of greyhound racing by the introduction of the 'Tote', or Totalisator, which encouraged small betting. By 1930, most of the chief courses had installed these machines; partly because a betting tax had caused strikes among bookmakers in the later Twenties, and partly because bookmakers had a bad reputation both for giving unfair odds and for welshing. Welshing had been facilitated by the speed and startability of the small car. Like the electric hare in greyhound racing, the Tote was deplored by old racing men as a sign of the growing mechanization of sport.

Yet mechanization was unavoidable, as soon as sport became big business. To please the thousands who crowded to watch football matches and tennis and golf tournaments, players had to train as hard as professional acrobats or musicians; native genius or ability was useless if unimproved by joyless, mechanical training in strokes, shots or tackles, continuously speeded up by practice.

A charming craze which swept all round the world at this time was 'yo-yo'. It is said to have started in South America— 'yo-yo' being the Spanish equivalent of the English 'me! me!' when a child wants something. The yo-yo was a wheel wrapped round with a piece of string. By a flick of the wrist the string was made to unwind; the wheel ran down it, and then back again as the string rewound itself. It was not exploitable, as the diabolo craze of 1907 had been, for national and international competition, or, like Put and Take, for money-making; it was a very simple personal toy. Serious grown-up people wandering down the street would absently produce yo-yos from their pockets and jiggle them up and down.

Midget golf, which came from the United States, was complicated. It was a way of providing practice in difficult putting and approach shots within a limited space. At seaside resorts, outdoor midget courses with bunkers and roughs replaced the simple putting or clock-golf greens; but for the most part it was an indoor diversion. In 1930 Christmas present recommendations in the *Daily Telegraph* included 'An eighteen-hole midget golf-course complete'.

Cricket was one of the few largely attended sports that remained unmechanized; betting on cricket matches was not encouraged and the high direction of the game was in the hands of the unpaid and well-to-do sportsmen of the Marylebone Cricket Club. But professional cricketers, who, besides their weekly wage, were paid a bonus on outstanding performances, always looked out for some new way of taking wickets while keeping just within the code. They found one in 1932, and the English team which went to Australia that winter for the Test Matches gave it a trial. The idea was to pitch the ball fast and short on the leg side, so that it rose dangerously at the batsman, who, unlike the American baseball player, was unprotected above the thigh. The fieldsmen, meanwhile, were grouped together close on the leg side, waiting for catches if the batsman protected himself with his bat against this assault. The Australians called this novelty 'body-line bowling'; the British referred to it euphemistically as 'leg-theory'. Australian batsmen were constantly being struck and injured by the leg-theory balls of

Harold Larwood, and protested against them as 'preventable brutality'. No batsman, they said, who tried to score off Larwood could avoid injury. D. R. Jardine, the English captain, approved of leg-theory tactics, and was supported by most British writers on cricket, who claimed that there was nothing new in trying to cramp the batsman's range of strokes. The M.C.C. also deprecated the Australian suggestion of bad sportsmanship, and refused to make a ruling against leg theory. Feeling ran high in Australia, however—the Australians lost 'The Ashes' that time—and there was a threat to abandon Test Match tours altogether. J. H. Thomas, as Dominions Minister, then summoned members of the M.C.C. to Downing Street, and, it is believed, urged them not to strain Imperial relations any further. The chief sentimental link that bound the two countries together, after the Crown, was a common devotion to cricket. When, therefore, an Australian cricket eleven next came to England, Larwood was not included in the English Test match team selected to meet them.

Mechanization was spreading to all varieties of everyday things; there were moving stairs and ticket-and-change machines on the London Underground, and self-propelling luggage trucks for porters at terminal railway stations, and in the streets cigarette-machines, lunch and fruit-machines. A mechanized restaurant appeared, the American *cafeteria*: one queued up with a tray and passed between a rail and a chromium-plated counter to choose from an assortment of ready-to-eat standardized foods. Big stores and multiple shops, such as Woolworth's, installed *cafeterias* as conveniences for hurried customers; but they did not catch on popularly, as milk bars did. Milk bars had an equally mechanized appearance, with bright expanses of glass and chromium, high counters, high stools and machines for mixing tasty milk drinks with snappy American names. They were introduced into Britain during the 'Drink More Milk' campaign, and were a relief from the gloomily old-fashioned pub, or the depressing tea-shop, where one could seldom catch the overworked waitress's eye. At lunch-time, or in the evenings after a cinema show, it was convenient to drop into a milk bar, sit on a high stool for ten minutes and eat or drink something that looked and tasted wholesome. The design of the milk bar encouraged quick meals: it was usually open on the street side, and chilly, and its high stools were not comfortable enough to tempt anyone to stay long on them. Hearty young men visited them without shame, instead of showing their manliness by drinking beer. Before the war raw milk in any form had been drunk only by invalids and children; but milk-bars were American and modern—and what was ice-cream, anyway, which all the best people gobbled greedily in the form of nut or marsh-mallow sundaes, but dolled-up raw milk? Another competitor for the tea-shop and cheap restaurant trade was the snack bar, where hors d'œuvres, sandwiches, and tasty cold meats could be had at any moment of the day. It came in about 1930. The public-houses had for some time been doing what they could to keep their custom by combining a simple restaurant business with the sale of drinks; and began to find snack bars more profitable than the hot lunches of 'two vegetables and a cut off the joint'.

Since the Talkies were now specializing in spectacular musical shows, dependent on song or dance hits, the stage competed in the same line. London theatres were reconstructed with elaborate revolving stages, for the convenience of rapid scene-shifting. 'White Horse Inn' and 'Waltzes from Vienna' were the musical successes of 1931.

The Victorian revival was affecting the 'legitimate' stage. Not only Dumas's 'Lady with the Camellias' and Wilde's 'The Importance of Being Earnest' were successfully put on, but modern plays on Victorian subjects. One of the successes of 1931 was 'The Barretts of Wimpole Street', which dealt with the lives of Robert and Elizabeth Barrett Browning; and in 1933 a play about the Brontë family had a long run—in fact, three pseudo-historical plays about the Brontës were running at the same time. The costume play was not, however, limited to the Victorian: in 1933 came Gordon Daviot's 'Richard of Bordeaux' with John Gielgud as Richard II. The theme of an artistically-minded monarch, warped by the early death of his sympathetic young wife, and thwarted by barbarous philistine barons, had its greatest appeal to the Suburbs, which were still spiritually in the Twenties.

The most spectacular of all musical, historical, and costume shows was C. B. Cochran's production in 1932 of Noel Coward's 'Cavalcade', a variety show which evoked the sentimental charm, the belief in progress, and the patriotism of the Victorian age. Conservative playgoers, who had been accustomed to look upon Coward as a degenerate, were delighted to find their feelings so pleasantly stirred. And what a phenomenal piece of stage showmanship: a cast of four hundred impressively brought up to the stage from below by six hydraulic lifts! 'Cavalcade' was an immediate success because it appeared just when a stern national effort was being made to overcome the Depression. Coward himself rose to the occasion. In his speech on the opening night he said firmly and with real feeling: 'In spite of the troublous times we are living in, it is still a pretty exciting thing to be English.' The audience wholeheartedly agreed. The *Daily Mail* ran 'Cavalcade' as a serial.

The old music-halls, which had housed George Robey, Harry Lauder, Marie Lloyd, and Vesta Tilley were now nearly all gone, but variety made a come-back in the Thirties, especially by means of the radio. A ballot among listeners showed that variety was the most popular sort of entertainment broadcast by the B.B.C. The larger cinemas began to include short variety turns in their programmes—songs, dances, acrobatics, and conjuring acts. To compete with the cinemas, theatres then introduced fast, non-stop variety. Shows of this kind returned to the old team-principle: hard-working artistes and comedians sharing a common applause, rather than jealous stars lording it over miserable stop-gaps.

Only one variety star rose to national fame in the Thirties— Gracie Fields, the singer. A conservative writer, Major Rawdon Hoare, in his *This Our Country*, described her in 1934 as the only outstanding personality who was providing healthy entertainment for the multitude. 'In her own way she has done a tremendous amount of good. In the cinemas there is an absence of healthy amusement, there is too much sex-appeal: but in the performance of Gracie Fields we get a breath of fresh air and an opportunity for some real laughter. This all helps to keep the right spirit of England together—clean living, with a total absence of anything bordering on the unnatural.' Indeed, Gracie Fields's Lancashire accent and humorous, long-suffering but optimistic sentiment more truly represented contemporary England than slick Americanistic film comedies or heavily modern problem plays.

The Gracie Fields of literature was J. B. Priestley, whose *The Good Companions* and *Angel Pavement* dealt sympathetically and realistically with the homely aspects of English life. A. J. Cronin, a former doctor, published in 1931 his popular *Hatter's Castle*, a novel dealing with the family life of a tyrannical hatter in a Scottish town; and Louis Golding's *Magnolia Street* described the intimate lives of British city Jews. Realistic American novels were also being read: Sinclair Lewis's Main Street types, Ernest Hemingway's completely unmoral he-men, William Faulkner's hard-living, degenerate, poor Southern whites, and W. R. Burnett's pugs, gangsters and racketeers, had a large public. The prevalent feeling was against reading books merely for entertainment—the radio and cinema provided that: people read a novel to acquire factual knowledge pleasantly. It was expected of an historical novel, for example, that though certain romantic incidents and conversations must be invented, the framework of history should be sound and no major historical fact distorted.

While fiction was thus becoming more factual, factual books were being written in a fictional style. Lytton Strachey's *Queen Victoria*, which started the fashion, had been 'as good as a novel', and Philip Guedalla's coruscating biographies were 'as good as a modern novel'. In 1930, several publishers brought out series of short, lively critical biographies of famous men and women, commissioned from noted authors. At least two hundred such appeared, and sold very well. Their subjects ranged from Lord Byron to the Indian Emperor Akbar, and from Saint Paul to Mozart. This desire for readily assimilable factual truth was met in the department of science by simply written, rather sentimental books by Professors Jeans and Eddington on physics and astronomy, and by such encyclopedic compilations as *The Outline of Science* by H. G. Wells, and his biologist son, and Professor Julian Huxley the zoologist. There was still a great demand for scientific vistas of the future, especially the 'To-day and To-morrow' series of essays; and Aldous Huxley's *Brave New World* and H. G. Wells's *The Shape of Things to Come* were their fictional counterpart.

By 1933, however, political and economic facts were seeming more immediately important than scientific ones. The international situation was already disturbingly unsettled. It was clear that collective security was only a phrase, and that power politics had returned in full force. The success of the Coles's *Europe To-day*, Vera Brittain's *Testament of Youth*, Edgar Mowrer's *Germany Puts the Clock Back*, and Vernon Bartlett's *Nazi Germany Explained*, were not signs only of the growing danger of another war: they showed, too, that the public was anxious to learn how war situations developed, and how wars might therefore be prevented.

This new seriousness was reflected in the poems of the time. In the last few years poetical writing, finding no market as volumes of poetry, had overflowed into popular fiction. Francis Brett Young, for instance, a highly regarded novelist of the Twenties, had interpolated comedy and dialogue with this sort of high writing. The quotation is from his *Black Roses*: 'Under the swinging arc-lamps the live mass of tourists pullulated, their whitened faces turned backward toward the ship's bejewelled carcase. Ritchie stood by the rail, watching them disappear into the mass of darkness that marked the customs-house; he saw their cars swirl desperately down the sombre length of roadway that faced the dock where long trams went crawling and clanking past the unimaginable squalor of sailors' drinking-dens'.

But by the Thirties this sort of stuff was regarded as 'bourgeois decadent' or, in the American phrase that was being used, 'wet'. In 1932 *New Signatures* appeared: it was this anthology that first gave publicity to the work of W. H. Auden, Stephen Spender, and Cecil Day Lewis. Auden's *Poems* had appeared in 1930, and in 1932 *The Orators*, which was meant to study the contemporary situation in England. Spender's first poems were published in 1933, and Day Lewis was already publishing a volume of poems every year. Their work was preoccupied with the grave world situation, especially as it showed itself in depressed England and in Nazi Germany. Though only Day Lewis was an active Communist, all three believed that a violent revolution alone—or, at least, a violent change in British life—could save the country from becoming wholly degenerate and eventually going the brutal way of Nazi Germany. It was now believed that poets in the Twenties had taken refuge in 'ivory towers', there to conduct meaningless experiments with words that had no relation to real life; the duty of the poet of the Thirties was to get into touch with the masses and ally himself with working-class

299

movements. Auden was a synthetic writer and perhaps never wrote an original line: but modern literature was so extensive that his communistic use of contemporary work was not at first suspected. He wrote satirically of existing British society and rather vaguely drew the moral that only the teachings of Marx and Freud and Georg Groddeck could reform it; Spender wrote poor-little-rich-boy poems, full of genuine pity for the exploited poor, and for himself; and Day Lewis's sentiments were those of a simple-minded Red. When they were beginning to attract wider attention, a new periodical was founded, *New Verse*, which at first published the work of all three. *New Verse* advanced no political theory. Its policy was to publish poems that dealt with observations of real objects. The observations were in general listed impressionistically and tagged with the appropriate revolutionary feelings excited in the poet by them. *New Verse* made no theoretical claims for itself: it denounced the fancifulness of the experimental poets of the Twenties, and at the same time avoided aligning itself wholeheartedly with Communism, Surrealism, or any other contemporary doctrine. The work that appeared in it, though designed to represent actuality, made no evaluation of good and bad elements in actuality. The Thirties were like that: at least in their unacademic part.

Another serious periodical was *Scrutiny*, which was founded by a group of Cambridge dons in 1932. A manifesto in its first issue complained that: 'the general dissolution of standards is a commonplace. Many profess to believe (though fewer seem to care) that the end of Western civilization is in sight. . . . Those who are aware of the situation will be concerned to cultivate awareness, and will be actively concerned for standards.' *Scrutiny* proceeded to uphold and purify cultural standards by publishing learned articles on educational and scholarly subjects. It adopted a patronizing attitude to nearly all contemporary writers, and its circulation remained very small. The 'standards' of *Scrutiny* were critical in intention, but the moral or philosophical base to which they referred was left vague, for fear of conflict between the spirit of science and that of Christianity. The Thirties were like that, too: at least in their academic part.

Low-brow reading was now dominated by the detective novel. A large number of writers made comfortable incomes from this fashion, and a curious situation arose. In Great Britain, though a few score murders and acts of grand larceny took place every year, not more than two or three of these had features in the least interesting to the criminologist as regards either motive or method; nor, in any of these, did private detectives play any decisive part in bringing the culprits to justice—this was done by the competent routine procedure of the C.I.D. Yet from the middle Twenties onward some thousands of detective novels were annually published, all of them concerned with extra-ordinary and baffling crimes, and only a very small number gave the police the least credit for the solution. These books were designed not as realistic accounts of crime, but as puzzles to test the reader's acuteness in following up disguised clues. It is safe to say that not one in a hundred showed any first-hand knowledge of the elements that composed them—police organi-zation, the coroner's court, finger-prints, firearms, poison, the laws of evidence—and not one in a thousand had any verisimili-tude. The most fanciful and unprofessional stories (crimino-logically speaking) were the most popular. Detective novels, however, were no more intended to be judged by realistic standards than one would judge Watteau's shepherds and shep-herdesses in terms of contemporary sheep-farming. Of all the detective novelists of the period only one, the American Dashiell Hammett, happened to be both a first-rate writer and to have had a long experience of crime, in his capacity as a Pinkerton Agency manager. Yet even after his 'Thin Man' became a screen success, his *Red Harvest, The Glass Key, The Maltese Falcon, The Dain Curse*, and *The Thin Man* itself were practically unread in England.

The hard-boiled American manner, in which there was no moral dividing line between 'sleuth' and criminal was adopted by Peter Cheyney and others; and the terse graphic cinematic style by Graham Greene. Greene, an Oxonian, a Catholic and one of the most admired novelists of the Thirties, wrote in his *Journey Without Maps*, on returning to London from the West Coast of Africa: 'One was back or, if you will, one had advanced again, to the seedy level.' Arthur Calder Marshall, a critic from the Left, took the phrase up and characterized Greene's writing thus: 'The seedy level! That is the location of Greeneland. The sadist and the masochist, the impotent athlete, the incestuous brother and sister, the coward, the braggart, the man with the tic, the hare-lip, the spy-maniac, the torturer of spiders and the collector of small foreign coins, the diseased dentist in a foreign port, the one-legged military man managing a road-house, the rich Jew despised by aristocrats, the bullied chambermaid in an all-night hotel, the Major ordering whores by telephone ("a pig in a poke"), the lawyer who married beneath him lusting after typists who pass his window, the adulterous butcher; they are all different . . . but all seedy, the ingloriously vicious.'

Agatha Christie remained true in her detective novels to the romantic-cumbersome English style of the early Twenties. There were numberless other styles, including even the coldly scientific, in which microscopic examination of fluff in people's pockets yielded beautiful results. But the norm was the breathless, familiar, undistinguished, emotional style of Sunday newspaper special reporting. A detective story was considered well-written if the dénouement was a legitimate deduction from a small piece of evidence unobtrusively introduced in an early chapter, and if the suspicions successively cast on a number of persons in the story were plausible enough to divert attention from the criminal until the last moment. The reader felt cheated if the author gave either too much or too little away. In some hands the game grew more and more like a mathematic based on the supposition that infinity equals the square root of thirteen: the chain of reasoning was all that mattered. The geography and chronology of, say, 'The Scented Bath Crime' was such that it could have been committed only by someone with a knowledge of Chinese, in desperate need of money, who could persuade a left-handed negro dwarf to train a monkey to climb up a ventilator pipe and squirt a rare South American poison into the victim's hot bath—with a syringe through the keyhole—at the one short moment when the French maid's back was turned. . . . Therefore it could not have been A, who did not need money; or B, who had an aversion to negroes and dwarfs; or C, who did not know Chinese; but the only remaining character unaccounted for—D, who surprisingly enough was the maid herself, whose innocence had seemed established by a perfect alibi. Q.E.D.

For the cultured public, Dorothy Sayers topped the bill with her case-stories of 'Lord Peter Wimsey': he derived from the

Baroness Orczy's lackadaisical 'Sir Peter Blakeney' and out-classed all other detective heroes at least in the fantastic com-plications of his cases. Dorothy Sayers gave her lordling a love of rare books as an endearing foible (in this study, however, he was somewhat deficient) and made him the hook on which to hang incidental dissertations on art, music, the poets, and good food and drink. She was also an earnest publicist of the Anglican faith.

In spite of strong competition from amateurs who had 'learned to earn money in spare time', professional free-lance journalists in 1930 had a by no means precarious existence: many were earning upwards of £2,000 a year entirely from the sale of articles and short stories. A typical issue of the *Daily Express* in that year contained not only a short story, a leader page carry-ing three or four contributed articles, and a woman's page, but also a feature page containing as many as eight short articles written by free lances and signed by such titles as 'Pigeon Fancier', 'Woman Doctor', 'Psychologist', 'Nursery Expert', and 'Masseur'. The same sort of market was offered by the rest of the London popular Press and the provincial Press, too. Symposiums contributed by reader-writers provided the news-papers with whole pages of cheap copy, especially the even-ing papers, which had for some years been reduced from seven or eight to three—the Conservative *Evening News* and *Evening Standard* and the Liberal *Star*. (There was no evening Labour paper.) The *Evening News* invited people under forty to say what they thought of those over forty, later throwing open its columns to the over-forties to get their own back. Then followed sym-posiums of 'war stories' and Cockney humour; and readers were asked to tell of their most thrilling or romantic moments, to send in their most beautiful love-letters. A small fee was paid for everything printed, and a prize given for the best contribu-tion of the week. Later in the Thirties the *Evening Standard* devoted an entire page in its Lunch Edition to drawings, short stories, articles, and poems contributed by non-professional writers.

It had been generally agreed that the short story was good only for desultory holiday reading or for longish railway jour-neys. The oldest and most reliable popular fiction-monthly was the *Strand*. Its list of contributors changed little from year to year. Stacy Aumonier, E. Phillips Oppenheim, P. G. Wode-house, Dornford Yates, and the rest were names that smelt of the station-platform and restaurant car. The *Strand* had several imitators, but collections of short stories in book form were unpopular in the public libraries: 'Oh—it's only short stories!' In the Thirties the commercial short story, as taught by the schools of journalism, displaced the thriller feuilleton in the evening papers, and to some extent in the dailies. It was limited to fifteen hundred words, depended more on incident than on characterization or atmosphere, and was composed backwards, from the whip-crack ending as invented by O. Henry. This was a great free-lance field. One interesting limitation was that sexual immorality, while it could be glorified in seven-and-sixpenny novels, or in collections of short stories, could not even be condoned in the commercial short story. The popular Press found that its circulation contracted very sensitively when anything 'not for family reading' accidentally crept into its columns.

A characteristic of the Thirties in England was an attempt to be reasonable about the confusion into which the new theories of physics, astronomy, sex, and economics had plunged thinking people. Things were, it had proved, effectively the same as ever: foot-rules still measured accurately, the stars still twinkled mildly, the Wedding March still pealed out at church weddings, and in the words of Len Lye—the film director whose short colour films for commercial firms and the G.P.O. were the most original and diverting of the day—'money is like marriage: still in use'. Neo-Victorianism was a brave new façade to a house whose foundations had been shaken by heavy mechanized traffic. Inside there was a general consensus of opinion: never to do what the Russians had done and the Germans and Italians were doing—pull the house down and build up from new foundations—but to continue patching and revetting and bracing so long as it would stand. The country was still sound at heart; the British Empire still extended over one-quarter of the earth's surface; and the population of Great Britain was still slightly on the increase—though, to be sure, this was because the death-rate was declining faster than the birth-rate, and (if the statisticians were right) Britain in 1980 would be populated chiefly by elderly people.

CHAPTER EIGHTEEN

Recovery, 1935

England was recovering slowly from the Depression, which at its worst had thrown nearly three million people out of employment. The common conviction that a vigorous replanning of the democratic, capitalist system would bring about complete recovery was expressed by Sir Arthur Salter in his book *Recovery: the Second Effort*. Sir Arthur, who had been Chairman of the Allied Maritime Transport Executive during the war, and was now an Oxford professor of political theory, believed that planning could be made compatible with freedom; and that a planned society was essential, if the country were not to wheel round continuously in the familiar cycle of trade, from slump to recovery and back to slump again. Planning had to take all factors into account: economic, political, social, and personal. Human activities were now so closely interrelated that no one aspect of them could be separately treated: planning must therefore be on a world-wide scale. Had there been no special features in the Depression, Sir Arthur Salter considered, the world would already have recovered. But there were special features, and chief among them were the restrictions on the freedom of world trade, induced by the trend towards economic nationalism. The Depression had originally taken the form of a financial crisis. Whatever steps governments had taken to cope with it, their effects had been uniformly to reduce prices and incomes, cut down production and increase unemployment—generally, in fact, to lower the standard of living. Foreign trade was especially affected. Most governments had been trying to give their countries favourable trade balances—that is, to sell more than they bought. It was easier, however, to restrict buying than to extend selling, and so countries had actually tried to buy less than they sold. Their immediate aim was to save their currencies from depreciation and this they did chiefly by using tariffs to cut down imports. But it was the nature of international trade that if one country restricted imports, other countries had less money with which to buy its exports. Thus the circle of trade-relationships continually contracted; and with this failure in economic co-operation naturally went a decline of international goodwill in the political sense.

What Sir Arthur Salter was putting in economic terms, a very great number of people were putting in terms of common sense and elementary morality. However necessary restrictions might be, if the existing financial system were to be preserved, it was obviously iniquitous to reduce the amount of goods available, when millions of people lacked many of the barest necessities of life. General indignation was felt that food should go to waste merely because it could not be sold at a profit to producers. The Left, in particular, attacked restriction-schemes as a blatant instance of Capitalist greed and mismanagement. There was an outcry when the number of acres in Canada to be sown with wheat was limited, and another when thousands of tons of good Brazilian coffee were thrown into the sea, and still another when Roosevelt's Democratic administration paid farmers and cotton growers not to pile their produce into an already glutted market. These protests had an Old Testament prophetic ring, for there was a large Puritan element in the English Left; but more often they were phrased ironically, as if the crazy situation was beyond hope. H. N. Brailsford, for instance, in his book *Property or Peace* (1934), suggested that a new kind of Harvest Thanksgiving should be held: 'At our paradoxical harvest-home let us celebrate these phantom apples, this mermaids' coffee, this cotton that shall not ripen in the sun, and with them the dream cities they might have built. The old plan of inviting the ancestral ghosts to this festival has much to recommend it: we might entertain these guests with our potential wealth much as the Chinese burn paper-offerings to nourish them. . . . Let us honour the ruler who contrives that one ear of wheat shall grow where two grew before. . . . We may congratulate ourselves not merely on our potential wealth, but also on the steady diminution of the toil required to win it. It grows sensibly easier with every year that passes to brew coffee of an excellent flavour in the Atlantic Ocean, nor need one spend upon such tasks an excessive number of hours.' Such strong condemnation of the existing system was not confined to Socialists: indeed, Socialism gained few recruits merely by denouncing the effects of the Depression. It was rather international political events that now sent people to the Left, and for a solution of economic troubles they were attracted by more plausible remedies than a revolution of that unarmed and feeble minority, the British proletariat formerly called 'the Submerged Tenth'. Chief among these was Social Credit.

Major C. H. Douglas, a retired Royal Engineer, had been propounding his theory of Social Credit in a series of books and pamphlets for over ten years. In the Thirties a Social Credit party was formed; its members adopted the new political habit of wearing coloured shirts as uniforms, and chose green. The *Daily Mail* honoured the party with a mention in its Year Book for 1935. Serious economists criticized it in the serious weeklies, and T. S. Eliot, who had banking and commercial experience as well as literary eminence, welcomed it as a promising solution of the world's troubles. By 1935 the movement had spread to the Dominions. In Alberta, Canada, a Social Credit party was elected to the provincial legislature, pledged to distribute dollar bills periodically to the electorate. But like all economic plans, however sound in general theory, it could not be applied in a single isolated context, and many banking and business interests in Alberta took flight to other provinces of the Dominion; so that the Social Credit party, which was not even unanimous on practical policy, was starved into surrender.

The Social Credit plan was to distribute national dividends to everyone through the central banks. The basis of the value of these dividends was supposed to be the capital equipment and the energy possessed by the community. The present financial system, Major Douglas held, did not reflect the real credit of the community. To prove this, he developed a theory meant to show that some of the country's income was continuously lost by the interest charges of the banking system. 'Dividends for All' would remedy this by bringing a country's purchasing power up to the level of its productive power. Social Credit took for granted that modern science enabled productive power to be increased limitlessly, even to the point of luxury for all. From this followed the first step in its argument: that only a lack of purchasing power prevented the masses from enjoying the natural increase.

Serious people were glad to find a theory which seemed to provide a non-political solution for the world's troubles, the more so because the banks seemed the obvious scapegoats for the Depression. Not many people knew what was the function of banks, and the rest could easily be induced to look on them as concerns that exploited the public for the benefit of their directors. Major Douglas himself, however, pointed out that he regarded bankers not as dishonestly anti-social, but as victims of their own system. He wrote in 1934 of 'the necessity for exalting the individual over the group. I mean by that, the exact opposite of what is commonly called Socialism. The direct road to the emancipation of the individual from the domination of the group is, in my opinion, the substitution, to an increasing extent, of the dividend in place of the wage and the salary'. Such words were more than welcome to people who feared that their lives would be exactly regulated by Socialist or Totalitarian economics; but neither the orthodox nor the Socialist economists had any difficulty in pointing out the flaws in his argument. The Social Credit theory was never adopted by any influential political group in Great Britain. It merely provided another controversial topic.

That something was wrong somewhere, whether in the City or at Westminster, seemed obvious from the existence of Distressed Areas. These were parts of the country where heavy industries had been built up before the war, but where almost the whole population had now been thrown out of employment by the loss of foreign markets. The markets had been lost because of foreign tariffs; because production costs in England were high, compared with those of countries where the standard of living was lower; and because the out-of-date methods of the industries concerned could not be changed without great expense. There were four chief Distressed Areas: South Wales, where the coal industry was in difficulties and demand for tinplate had been reduced by the use of aluminium, glass, carton, and plastics; West Cumberland, also a coal area; Tyneside, where, besides the coal-mines troubles, many shipbuilding, engineering, and iron and steel plants were lying idle; and large parts of Scotland. The cotton area of Lancashire, though not officially classed as 'distressed', was also having difficulty in competing in Eastern markets with Japanese and Indian manufacturers. What could be done, in an increasingly troubled world, to help these districts to recover?

The National Government passed a Special Areas Act in 1934 —the euphemistic word 'Special' had been substituted for 'Distressed'. Among its enactments was one that workers should be transferred to more prosperous areas—to the motor industries in the Midlands and the new light industries in the south. Land-settlement schemes were to be tried again; waste land was to be planted with trees, marshes drained, and new industries set up in the Special Areas themselves. The Government set aside £2,000,000 to finance these schemes, and two Commissioners were appointed to carry them out, one for Scotland and one for England and Wales. The latter wrote a memorandum in 1935 on the first few months of his work. He complained that he was continually held up by the unwillingness of other Government departments to co-operate; each accused him of encroaching upon their territory. Eventually he found so much obstruction offered that he resigned.

The work of the Commissioners had no immediately beneficial effect, and what little improvement did occur in the Special Areas was not due wholly to their activities. They admitted in a report issued in 1937 that rearmament was responsible for the expansion of the coal, iron, steel, and shipbuilding industries. The increase in employment, however, did not equal the increase in output. The report also stated: 'It is a new thing for a Government to buy sites and build factories, in order to induce industry to go to an area where the percentage of unemployment is very high, yet already in Merthyr, Sunderland, and elsewhere, a beginning is being made.' Another example of intervention by the State in what had been regarded as the private field of business—as usual, neither on a large scale nor with notable success.

The most neglected Special Areas were in Scotland: the industrialized Lowlands were depressed and huge tracts in the Highlands extremely backward. The English had remained, on the whole, largely unaware of specifically Scottish problems, which did not lend themselves to journalistic controversy. Industrial problems on the Clydeside occasionally came up, but only when some drastic action called attention to them: strikes in the shipbuilding yards, or the arrival in London of hunger marchers from Glasgow. Workers in West Fife expressed their discontent in 1935 by electing a Communist M.P.—the only one in Parliament—and Glasgow became one of the strongest centres of Communism. The problems of the rest of Scotland, and especially of the Highlands, were completely ignored. The political world was astonished in 1935 when the traditionally Liberal Western Isles returned a Labour member to Parliament.

In the Highlands, agriculture and fishing were declining industries, and no new ones were taking their place. Bad road and railway services helped to perpetuate backward conditions, nor were the wild scenic beauties capitalized by any powerful tourist organization, as in Norway and Sweden. The old deer forests and grouse moors, which had employed numerous Highlanders as ghillies, were now being sold, because their owners found them too expensive to keep up. Most of this land was unfit for cultivation, and Government schemes for settling people on it were strongly criticized. Lady Astor ironically asked in the Commons whether the Minister sponsoring such schemes would care to live there as a crofter himself. In fact, almost the only employment open to most young Highlanders was in the fighting services. The Highlands remained, as they had been for two and half centuries, a fertile ground for recruiting.

New factories could not easily be established in the north of Scotland, but the Caledonian Power Scheme of 1936 contained a plan for producing calcium carbide by water power. This compound, used in the welding and cutting of metals, had so far been imported mostly from Norway. The House of Commons rejected the scheme in 1938 on the grounds that it was not essential to the rearmament programme. The member for Inverness led the opposition to the scheme in the House, on the ground that it would deplete the River Ness of water, to the detriment of the Inverness sewage system and of the salmon fishery. The Inverness Town Council supported him, declaring that tourists would be deterred from visiting the famous and beautiful glens if there were factories in them: the Loch Ness monster thus indirectly assisting in keeping away new industries from the Highlands.

Many Scots gave up hope of ever getting Parliament to listen to their grievances. A Scottish Nationalist Party had already been formed, under the leadership of the Duke of Montrose, to demand a separate parliament in Edinburgh to deal with Scottish affairs. It was largely a cultural movement and never succeeded in returning a member to Parliament, though its candidates frequently secured large polls. Scottish Nationalist delegations studied home rule in Northern Ireland and the Isle of Man, and made much in their reports of the lower rates of taxation which home rule brought. The Labour and Liberal parties also declared themselves in favour of some kind of devolutionary government for Scotland; but the Scottish Nationalist movement was never widely enough supported or militant enough to force any government to grant its wishes.

The minority demand for self-government also spread to Wales, but Welsh home rule was not so seriously canvassed: Welsh problems were hardly distinguishable from English ones and bilingual teaching in schools and the disestablishment of the Welsh Church had removed two principal grievances. Welsh Nationalists were chiefly university professors and students intent on reviving Bardic culture and only occasionally gave vent to political irritation. Toward the close of the period, for example, some Welsh university lecturers tried to set fire to an Air Force depot as a protest against the desecration of beauty spots. At their trial they stood by their Nationalist principles to the extent of refusing to plead in English.

In England a small but rowdy organization had begun to attract public attention: this was the British Union of Fascists. Its leader was Sir Oswald Mosley, who had been elected as Conservative member for Harrow at the age of twenty; married Lord Curzon's daughter; quarrelled with the party; gone over to Labour, quarrelled with Labour; helped to found the New Party, which disintegrated. He had now come to believe in 'Action'—of the kind that the Dictators practised; nevertheless, he derided the idea that he was aiming at a personal dictatorship. 'If a mandate be conferred upon us by the people at a general election, then this is a dictatorship by the will of the people, expressing for themselves what they want.' Mosley produced no plan for solving Britain's problems, and never secured his 'people's mandate'. His call for 'Action', however, attracted a number of tough young men, who seemed to enjoy strutting about in black shirts and behaving aggressively to Communists and to the poorer Jews. His Fascist Imperialism, and especially his call for the 'Strong Hand' in India won for him the temporary support of Lord Rothermere and the *Daily Mail*. Rothermere admired the apparent energy of dictators, and thought that Mosley could infuse the same energy into the lethargic people of Britain. Other newspapers then set themselves to expose the Blackshirts' deliberate imposture on Lord Rothermere. The *News Chronicle* published a letter sent by the Fascist leaders to all party branch officers. It urged them to write to the *Daily Mail* in seemingly disinterested approval of Fascism, to convince Rothermere that his support of Mosley was popular. The *Daily Mail* did print several such inspired letters, but when Rothermere realized what was happening he soon dropped the Blackshirts. Unfortunately for so strong an anti-Semite as Mosley, his wife (who retained her Socialistic convictions) was half-Jewish. However, she died and left him free to marry in 1937, secretly and with Hitler as his best man, a sister of the 'Perfect Aryan Beauty', Unity Mitford. Mosley was also a friend of Mussolini's and once appeared with him on a balcony, to be saluted by an Italian crowd.

The Blackshirts started their campaign with a meeting at Olympia in June 1934, and followed it up with a rally in Hyde Park in September. Their aggressiveness and use of knuckle-dusters against hecklers provoked the Left to make counter-demonstrations, which usually silenced the Blackshirt speakers. The danger that partisan warfare might break out in the streets led Parliament to pass a Public Order Act in 1936, which forbade the wearing of political uniforms at public meetings. Communists did not in fact wear red shirts, but only sang about the colour. The Act also gave the Chief of Police the power to ban political processions likely to cause a breach of the peace, and to place certain districts under an interdict. Another clause in the Act allowed the chairman of public meetings to summon constables to take the name and address of persons 'reasonably suspected to have behaved in a disorderly manner'. The offence of 'using insulting words and behaviour in public' was extended from London to the rest of England, and the penalties for it increased.

These clauses were primarily aimed at preventing Blackshirt disturbances, but they made the Left feel uneasy. Four other measures which seemed to threaten the rights of the citizen had already been passed, and the Left feared that the framework of a reactionary Fascist State was coming into existence in Britain. The Firearms Act of 1920—chiefly directed against armed bandits—had contained a clause empowering the Home Secretary to authorize the drilling and training of private citizens. The Left feared that this might now be used to authorize armed squads to indulge in unofficial Communist hunting. The Emergency Powers Act of 1920 allowed the Government to proclaim a state of emergency if essential social services were interfered with. This was an anti-strike measure, and was followed by the Trade Disputes Act of 1927, which made illegal all strikes calculated to coerce the Government. But what started the campaign against the infringement of civil liberties was the Incitement to Disaffection Act of 1934, popularly known as the Sedition Act. People feared that this Act would introduce Russian Ogpu or German Gestapo methods into Britain. As originally worded, it authorized police inspectors to search any place or person suspected of a treasonable offence and to seize anything suspected to be evidence. All that the police had to do first was to get a search-warrant from two local Justices of the Peace. This aroused strong protests, because local J.P.s would scarcely refuse anything to a police inspector; and the Act was altered so that the search-warrant had to be obtained from a High Court Judge. The Act aimed at preventing the dissemination of seditious literature among the armed forces, but it also rendered liable to prosecution anyone who had such literature in his possession, whether or not he had read it or tried to disseminate it.

In the light of the Sedition Act it was considered extremely sinister that Lord Trenchard, the Commissioner of Metropolitan Police and a former Air Marshal—the R.A.F. was suspected of Fascist leanings—should have introduced a new element into his organization, the 'gentleman-bobby'. The police had formerly been recruited from the lower-middle or working classes, and had been officered by men who had risen from the ranks.

Now young upper-class officers were to be trained in a sort of Sandhurst and allowed better chances of promotion than men who had been several years in the service. On the 31st May 1934 the Prince of Wales opened the Metropolitan Police College at Hendon—again the R.A.F connection! The object of the college was 'to enable men selected for their special qualifications to attain the highest police efficiency by a course of intensive training. Thus it is estimated that at the end of a course of fifteen months, followed by a year of actual police duties, a student will have acquired as much practical experience as if he had served in the force for ten years under the present system.' 'Special qualifications' meant a public school education and some knowledge of foreign languages. Students would wear the blue uniform of a probationary inspector. They would dine at 8 p.m. and would wear dinner jackets. When off duty they would be permitted to wear mufti. The complete course would occupy fifteen months, three of these being holidays. Ex-Servicemen would act as servants in the college and there would be one batman for every six students.

The Times the next day glossed over the class-question with these benignant phrases: 'The secret of the unique reputation enjoyed by the police in England is the mutual understanding between the citizen in uniform and the citizen in mufti. That understanding the new course of training is well calculated to preserve, because it will ensure that, while the policeman's professional skill is all his own, the life he lives and the ideals he cherishes will be those of the people from whose ranks he comes.'

The controversy raised by the Sedition Act led to the formation of a National Council for Civil Liberties, with E. M. Forster as President. The Council intended to preserve the citizen's rights by means of protests and agitation. One of the first activities it undertook was the defence of authors' rights. It protested, for instance, against the prosecution of James Hanley and his publishers on account of the homosexual passages in his book *Boy*. A policeman in Bury had happened to borrow a copy of this book from his local public library three years after it had been published. He judged it obscene and secured a conviction. The court imposed heavy fines upon the author and the publishers, and warned them that they were liable to prosecution for every copy of the book in circulation. The National Council

for Civil Liberties did not manage to get Hanley and his publishers reimbursed, nor did it achieve any notable alteration in
the laws. Like so many similar committees in the Thirties, however, its petty protests at least served as a guide to Parliament
upon public feeling.

However, 1934 was a quiet sort of year. The worst of the
Depression was over, and the series of international crises had
scarcely begun. The country was ready for some kind of national
celebration, which would assure people that existing political
troubles were of no great importance. The first public ceremony
to meet this need was the wedding of the King's fourth son,
Prince George, and Princess Marina of Greece. Their engagement was announced in September 1934—the newspapers describing it as the culmination of a 'holiday romance' in Slovenia.
Pictures and genealogies of all Princess Marina's relatives were
published, and much pleasant speculation was raised: what
royal dukedom would Prince George be given? where would he
and his bride live? what kind of wedding-gown would she wear?
Prince George, who became the Duke of Kent, was, like the
Prince of Wales, generally offered by the Press as a symbol of
ardent youth, although he was over thirty. The wedding took
place in December at Westminster Abbey with the usual State
pageantry. The illustrated weeklies issued special numbers, with
coloured photographs and coloured drawings of the wedding
ceremony, intended to be preserved as valuable mementoes. It
was a great many years since the Royal Family had been enriched by so stylish a bride. The shopping world celebrated the
occasion by naming fashions in hats, dresses, shoes, and stockings
after Princess Marina.

The splendours of the Kent wedding were far outdone by
those of the Silver Jubilee in the following year. Already in 1934
it began to be suggested that a celebration of the twenty-fifth
anniversary of King George V's accession to the throne might
be a fitting way of rejoicing that the Depression was over. The
King in a speech broadcast from Sandringham on Christmas
Day 1934, spoke of the happily surmounted trials of his reign:
'May I add very simply and sincerely that if I may be regarded
as in some true sense the head of this great and widespread
family, sharing its life and sustained by its affection, this will be
a full reward for the long and sometimes anxious labours of my

reign of well-nigh five-and-twenty years. As I sit in my own home I am thinking of the great multitudes who are listening to my voice, whether they be in British homes or far-off regions of the world. For you all, especially for your children, I wish a happy Christmas.' The King had been by no means popular when he first came to the throne. Many rumours had been current about his supposed secret marriage as a young man to an Admiral's daughter—he actually went into the witness-box in the Mylius libel case to deny this—and about his intemperance. But insensibly his homely virtues and loyalty to the Coronation oath had endeared him to the British public; until at the time of his illness in the winter of 1928–9, when he nearly died of pneumonia, a sincere national anxiety revealed how much he meant even to people who had laughed at him for a dullard or detested him as a 'parasite'. These fireside talks at Christmas, which he had now been giving for several years, stirred truly loyal sentiments. The country was quite willing to jubilate.

It is said that the Jubilee celebrations caused the King himself some misgiving; he feared that there was still enough unemployment and poverty about to make them a fiasco. As Jubilee Day approached, however, committees were spontaneously formed almost everywhere to organize local fêtes and hang out banners in the streets. The Office of Works arranged for London's historic buildings—the Houses of Parliament, Buckingham Palace, and St. Paul's—to be floodlit at night and covered with flowers. Local authorities put up elaborate decorations on lamp-posts, tram standards, and public buildings, and almost every household hung up its own flags and coloured streamers. (Only two houses in England defiantly flew the old republican colours, which had been used in the days of the Chartists: red, white, and green in horizontal stripes.) East End districts in London were enthusiastic and frank. A popular banner read: 'Lousy but Loyal'. In spite of some growling from the far Left, everyone decided to treat the Jubilee as a royal and popular fête—an extension of the 'Cavalcade' success—not as a celebration staged by the National Government.

Jubilee Day was on May 6th. The Royal Family drove in State procession to St. Paul's to attend a Thanksgiving Service. They were accompanied by all the Ministers of the Crown and

the representatives of foreign powers. The weather was perfect
—fortunately for the crowds, who had waited all night along the
route and slept on the pavements, wrapped up in newspapers.
London was crammed with visitors from abroad and from the
provinces—many of them amused Londoners by their fear of
such novelties as escalators. Hotels and rooms from which to
view the procession had been booked up long in advance. But
the atmosphere was so unusually gay that no one complained of
having nowhere to spend the night. In the evening of the 6th,
enormous crowds gathered outside Buckingham Palace and
cheered the King, until he came out with the Royal Family on
to the balcony to acknowledge their greeting. He is reported to
have said: 'I can't understand it. I'm really quite an ordinary
sort of chap.' But it was, indeed, a festival for every ordinary
good sort of chap, who had come through twenty-five difficult
years and who was still full of hope for the future. That night
ordinary chaps packed Trafalgar Square and Piccadilly Circus,
singing the songs of the Great War: 'Tipperary', 'There's a
Long Long Trail', and 'Keep the Home Fires Burning'. Although a large part of the crowd was made up of young people,
more recent songs were not sung—none of the 'Ain't it Grand
to be Blooming-well Dead!' which had helped people to endure
the Depression. Piccadilly itself resembled a drive in a public
park on Sunday afternoon: crowds strolled excitedly up and
down and motor traffic could scarcely get through. Even the
'intelligentsia' who had felt dismally that this was really 'going
to be a shame-making show' were surprised and touched by the
sincere and unaffected behaviour of the crowds.

The name 'Jubilee' was being given to every novelty of the
day, from a new sort of chocolate stick to the latest baby in the
Ape House at the Zoo. The Post Office broke the conservative
traditions of English philately by bringing out an issue of
Jubilee stamps. The King happened to be one of the keenest
philatelists in England—and about this time knighted the keeper
of his collections. There were also Jubilee dresses, Jubilee hats,
and even Jubilee finger-nails—these were painted on each index
finger in red, white, and blue with a small gold crown stencilled
on top. The Royal School of Needlework designed a Jubilee
sampler that everyone could make, decorated with pictures of
guns, palaces and yachts, and little verses such as:

'Prince of sportsmen, brilliant shot,
But happiest aboard his yacht.'

Jubilee celebrations continued mildly for several weeks after the memorable May 6th. Meanwhile, the National Government reshuffled itself before taking advantage of the popular enthusiasm to hold a General Election in the autumn. Ramsay MacDonald was still Prime Minister, but it was clear that he was becoming unfit for his duties. His public speeches were growing vaguer and vaguer. At first only Opposition newspapers noticed this: the *News Chronicle*, for instance, laughed at a speech delivered early in 1934 at Leeds Town Hall as part of the National Government propaganda campaign. In it MacDonald spoke of 'coming down to facts and facing them', of 'the sanctity of the firesides of the poor', and of the necessity of 'keeping in touch not only with progressive but also with retrograding movements in our advance'. He had a fatal facility for confused metaphors: a well-known one was, 'Ah, my friends, how easy it would be to listen to the milk of human kindness.' By 1935 many newspapers made cynical comments on reported statements of his, such as: 'Society goes on and on and on. It is the same with ideas.' In February *The Times* criticized him for 'lack of cohesion, lack of decision, and lack of calm' when he had excused himself in the House for not being able to answer a question about the Means Test. He explained that he had not been able to phone through to the right department to ask for information. In April, the *Observer* was significantly denying that he would retire before the Jubilee—nobody had yet officially suggested that he would. The Jubilee was in fact chosen as the right moment for him to be translated to the lesser dignity of Lord President of the Council. Baldwin then again became Prime Minister.

A General Election, though not due until the following year, was held in November 1935, because the National Government thought that the Jubilee had for a time quenched party feeling in loyalty and patriotism. They relied on Jubilee sentiment to put them back into power. The election, however, was by no means a quiet one. National Labour candidates were given a particularly rough time. Malcolm MacDonald was shouted down as a 'baby-starver' because of the Means Test; Ramsay MacDonald could scarcely get a hearing at his constituency of

Seaham; J. H. Thomas was driven to anger at one of his meet-ings, and called his audience cowards for not listening to the 'voice of truth'; his son Leslie Thomas, who was a candidate for Leek, was tripped up on his way out of a meeting and held down on the pavement. Nor did Conservative candidates have an easy time: a stone was thrown through the glass roof of the building in which Neville Chamberlain was speaking at Bir-mingham; Walter Elliott at Glasgow was attacked by rowdies and had to fight his way to the platform. Sir Austen Chamber-lain declared indignantly at Birmingham, where demonstrators continually interrupted him: 'You begin to see how a Socialist Government would treat you—free speech for them, but for no one else.' And Sir John Simon, the National Liberal leader, quavered out at Barnsley: 'I am facing the music, but you will not give me a chance.'

The result of the election strengthened the case for propor-tional representation in Parliamentary constituencies. The Con-servatives polled about ten million votes and the Socialists about eight million, yet the Conservatives held 238 seats and the Socialists only 151. The parliamentary strength of the National Liberal and National Labour parties was reduced, and that of the Opposition Liberals halved. In all, Opposition Labour had gained 92 seats, and the Conservatives lost 77. Ramsay Mac-Donald was defeated at Seaham by twenty thousand votes; but in the following year was smuggled into Parliament again as member for the Scottish Universities. He did not retire finally until 1937.

The King died at Sandringham in the New Year of 1936. Two days before, while public prayers were being offered for his recovery, the death of Rudyard Kipling had been announced. Someone wrote sentimentally to the *Daily Telegraph* on this coincidence that 'the King has sent his Trumpeter ahead'. The King's death took place at 11.55 on the night of January 20th after a succession of grave bulletins on the radio, the last of which at 9.25 in the golden voice of the chief announcer, Stuart Hibberd, told the country that 'the King's life is moving peace-fully towards its close'. The rumour ran about that the death had taken place some hours before, but that the announcement had been kept back until the last five minutes of the day to forestall the possible proclamation of a Stuart pretender before arrangements had been completed to proclaim the due accession to the throne of the Prince of Wales. At the death of Edward VII an embarrassing claim had been posted at the Palace Gates on behalf of Prince Rupprecht of Bavaria.

King George was sincerely mourned. The papers appeared with heavy black lines on the day of his death and on that of his funeral. All broadcasting programmes were cancelled and theatres and cinemas closed. On January 23rd the body was brought to London, where it lay in state at Westminster Hall, crowds filing past it every day, often at the rate of fifteen thousand an hour. The funeral was to take place on Tuesday the 28th, and on the night before, at midnight, the new King himself and his three brothers mounted guard for half an hour over their father's coffin. A day of National Mourning followed. The streets of London were sparingly but harmoniously draped in purple. The crowd, a large part of which had waited all night on the pavement, made quite a jolly affair of the funeral with lunch-baskets and camp-stools. 'Where's George?' someone cried gaily in Trafalgar Square; for the cortège from Westminster to Paddington Station, where it was to take train for the interment at St. George's Chapel, Windsor Castle, had failed to appear on time. The cry was taken up and a great roar of laughter arose. 'Where's George?' was a popular advertising catchword of Lyons' restaurants. Yet there was no disrespect in the laughter. 'He was a good little man and we'll miss him.' The new King, Edward VIII, walked behind the coffin with five other kings, and the representatives of numerous states, including Nazi Germany. According to the *Daily Worker*, General Goering had wished to come himself, but was warned by the Foreign Office that his personal safety could not be guaranteed in view of the hostility of Jewish refugees and others; Baron von Neurath and some generals came instead. The U.S.S.R. sent Marshal Tukachevsky and his wife. There were seven thousand casualties in the funeral crowds.

Two strange incidents were reported in the American Press: the first that the small golden cross fell off the Crown as it was being carried on a cushion at the funeral service. Omen or accident? The second was reported in Britain also, but only by the *Daily Worker*, on January 30th: 'It appears that King Carol, who does not often get among the lights of London, woke up on funeral morning feeling not too well. Resourceful attachés succeeded in securing the services of an able and energetic masseur of Rumanian origin, who worked hard on the King. Thinking that a last-minute work-over might do good, the masseur accompanied the King in his car—the lateness of Carol had already caused considerable confusion around Westminster Hall. The masseur, bewildered by marching troops, lost his head and, thinking escape impossible, lined up with the lesser diplomats, generals, and foreign attachés, and marched a considerable distance, clad in ordinary civilian clothes hastily put on over his masseur's dress and an ordinary felt hat on his head. Yesterday people tried to spot the masseur in newspaper pictures of the parade. Many of them pounced on the picture of a strange-looking man in white trousers and a brown trilby hat who was described vaguely in the newspapers as "a representative of Transylvania". Since there was no mention of such a person in the official list, many people thought that he really was the masseur.' The next day the *Daily Worker* reported: 'Yesterday's news about Carol created an uproarious sensation in London. There are further disclosures: the name of the "Marching Masseur" is Stoebs, and he is in fact the sturdy gentleman whose picture millions of people saw in the official photographs. He has been erroneously described as a Rumanian officer, a Balkan V.C., and a representative of Transylvania. At the moment everyone concerned is busily engaged in issuing denials of everything.'

There was, in fact, nothing in this exciting story. The supposed masseur was a member of the Rumanian delegation, a schoolmaster who had earned a V.C. in the war.

Thousands of schoolchildren were encouraged to send messages of sympathy to Queen Mary. Condolence came in from all over the world. The British public was touched to read messages from Nigerian chiefs and from the Tashi Lama of Tibet, where the monasteries spent the day in prayer. A graceful elegy by Edmund Blunden appeared in *The Times*, and John Masefield, the Poet Laureate, cabled a sonnet from Los Angeles, where he was staying. The first eight lines summed up the conventional Conservative theme of disaster overcome and Revolution averted:

'This man was King in England's direst need.
  In the black-battled years when hope was gone
  His courage was a flag men rallied on.
His steadfast spirit showed him King indeed.

And when the war was ended, when the thought
  Of revolution took its hideous place,
  His courage and his kindness and his grace
Scattered, or charmed, its ministers to naught.'

The laurel had greatly sobered Masefield. It was hard to
believe that this was the same poet of whom Max Beerbohm had
once written:

'A swear-word in a rustic slum
A simple swear-word is to some,
  To Masefield, something more.'

The new King was immensely popular, and the excitement at
his accession outweighed grief for the death of his predecessor.
'He won't stand no nonsense from Baldwin,' it was prophesied
in the pubs. And what a novelty in British history, a bachelor
King! The first since George III, and he had got married soon
afterwards. That was 1760. 'He'll have to marry now. What's
the betting it won't be a nice English girl for a change? He can
do as he pleases at last.' Every millgirl dreamed of herself as the
Cinderella of this exciting drama.

The select Press photographed him sitting pen in hand, and
a keen intent look on his face, in a severely furnished study.

CHAPTER NINETEEN

The Days of Non-Intervention

An international crisis was expected in 1935 when a plebiscite was to be held in the Saar district, where the French had been working the coalfields since 1919 as a means of exacting reparations. But the plebiscite passed off peacefully under the supervision of the League of Nations and of British, French, and Italian troops: the choice for the Saarlanders was between returning to Germany, remaining under a League mandate, or attaching themselves to France. Well coaxed and threatened by the Nazis, they voted overwhelmingly in favour of return to Germany. Already in 1934 the Germans had reintroduced conscription without drawing more than a mild protest from the other European powers. This and the Saar plebiscite were the first Nazi victories in international affairs. Europe took them quietly, for most politicians had long since abandoned the pretence of pinning Germany down to the letter of the Versailles Treaty. They were willing now to make 'gentlemen's agreements', conceding some of the German claims. But the Germans remembered that they had signed the Versailles Treaty under duress; the continuance of the British blockade for six months after the Armistice and the quartering of French colonial troops on their soil were memories that seemed to acquit them of all duty to act as 'gentlemen' in the Franco-British sense.

A crisis did arise in 1935: not from German but from Italian action. It began with Italian provocation of the Abyssinians on the undelimited frontier between Abyssinia and Italian Somaliland; both Governments lodged protests at Geneva. The League

323

set up its usual Commission to examine the problem. It seemed at first as though the Italians might not make war, if given a few concessions. When Pierre Laval, the French Prime Minister, had cordial talks with Mussolini in January 1935 the British Left Press interpreted them as a sinister move to dismember Abyssinia. (The Negus of Abyssinia was a popular figure among British newspaper readers: his barbaric Christian Coronation festivities in 1930, to which the Duke of Gloucester had gone as King George's representative, had enlivened the news for days.) The affair simmered for some months, rumours occasionally coming through of Italian military preparations. The Abyssinians again protested to the League in April 1935, this time against the recruitment of labourers in Egypt to work on military roads in the Italian East African colonies. The Italians, though they had themselves originally sponsored Abyssinia's candidacy for League membership, then announced that these uncivilized blackamoors had no right to chop logic with the new-born Roman Empire.

Opinion in England was decidedly pro-Abyssinian, though three leading newspapers, the *Morning Post*, the *Daily Mail*, and the *Observer*, supported the Italian case from the start. Moreover, a Peace Ballot had been held that year, and out of eleven and a half million voters, ten and a half million declared their faith in the League of Nations, and in the use of non-military sanctions against aggressor nations. But a large majority also favoured disarmament, and so it seemed obvious that the British people was not prepared for war with Italy. Besides, the heads of the Fighting Forces were uneasy. The Fleet was in fine condition, but the Italians had a powerful air force, and experts had been misled, by the recent report of how Dutch airmen had quelled a mutiny on an old battleship, into believing that a battle fleet was 'cold meat' to dive-bombers—especially to the Suicide Legion of Italian airmen. Moreover, the Royal Air Force was far inferior in numbers and modernity of aircraft to the Italian. This feeling of uneasiness filtered down to the masses. The question was: how far would the sanctions policy be carried if the Italians did invade Abyssinia? The French and British jointly held the key to the strategic situation by their control of the Suez Canal: but had no intention of turning it in the lock. For there was a canny reckoning in French and British Government circles that it would be no bad thing to let the Italians have a try at Abyssinia. If they succeeded, they would be kept busy for years trying to colonize that hopeless country; if they failed, they would be weaker still.

By September, Italian troops were sailing for East Africa, the Italian delegation had walked out of the League, and the Committee of Five, which was dealing with the Abyssinian dispute, had reached a deadlock. Early in October Mussolini declared that Italy had been 'provoked', and that 'the time had come'. On October 3rd Italian troops went into action and on October 6th they captured the town of Adowa. Since the Italians had now taken revenge for the humiliating defeat inflicted on them by the Abyssinians at Adowa in the Nineties, it was felt that a compromise might be reached. A plan drawn up by Sir Samuel Hoare, the Foreign Secretary, and Pierre Laval, for France, offered Italy territorial and economic concessions which would have virtually turned Abyssinia into an Italian protectorate. But before the plan had been officially approved by any government, news of it reached the Press and raised an outburst of indignation in both Britain and France: the Abyssinians were being let down, aggression was being condoned, League principles wilfully betrayed. Sir Samuel Hoare, made scapegoat, was compelled to resign.

Anthony Eden succeeded him: a popular figure—young, handsome, smartly dressed and with the reputation of being not only a good diplomat but honourable in the best British tradition. It was said that Stanley Baldwin regarded Eden as a sort of spiritual son. His own son, Oliver, was a violent Left. Eden persuaded the League Assembly to apply economic sanctions; that is, to forbid members of the League to supply Italy with war materials. Mussolini was thus able to whip up Italian feeling, which had not so far been particularly warlike, on the rhetorical grounds that the League was trying to starve Italy, and that only the possession of an empire in East Africa would forestall any such attempt in the future. Yet sanctions were never applied to oil and petrol, of which the Italians had insufficient stocks, and nothing therefore prevented Italian aeroplanes and tanks from coming into action against the ill-equipped Abyssinians. Feeling in England ran still higher against Italy. Atrocity stories were printed: the use of poison gas and the deliberate bombing of hospitals and ambulances. There was a call for the closing of the Suez Canal to Italian troopships. The Left in England held protest meetings, and formed committees to organize bazaars in aid of the Abyssinians. Even those who were aware of the formidable effect of air-attack combined with swift thrusts by a mechanized army, believed that the brave Abyssinians, under their mediaeval Rases and motley crew of European instructors, would keep the Italians busy for a long time to come by guerilla warfare. This time, it was said, Mussolini had bitten off more than he could chew. But when early in 1936 the Italians resumed their advance, having bribed several chiefs to desert to their side, the Abyssinian Army was unwise enough to engage them in a pitched battle and was handsomely defeated. The Negus then left his country, appealing to the remaining loyal chiefs to carry on guerilla warfare. The Government did not venture to override public opinion, which expressed deep sympathy for the Emperor and his countrymen, by recognizing the *de facto* Italian conquest of Abyssinia.

The Abyssinian crisis was the first to awaken people to the dangers of air-attack, though politicians had for some time been issuing warnings on air-raids, and planning to increase the R.A.F. Baldwin had said in the House in November 1932: 'I think it is well for the man in the street to realize that there is no power on earth that can prevent him from being bombed. Whatever people may tell him, the bomber will always get through. . . . The only defence is in offence, which means that you have to kill women and children more quickly than the enemy if you want to save yourselves.' At the time some newspapers—and not only the Opposition ones—accused Baldwin of being an alarmist, and of going back on his election promises. He had just pledged himself to a policy of disarmament and support of the League of Nations.

Yet some writers, even in Opposition papers, began to realize that aggressor nations might have to be stopped by force. Vernon Bartlett, the well-known political commentator, wrote for the *News Chronicle* in 1934 that the choice before Europe was one between order and anarchy: to prevent anarchy from supervening, aggression would sometime have to be countered. Bartlett wrote that he loathed war but would be willing to fight in a war

THE DAYS OF NON-INTERVENTION

against aggression. When air exercises were held over London in April 1934, the disquieting report was made that 70 per cent of the attacking planes reached their objectives. Baldwin made another of his calculated frank statements: 'Since the days of the air,' he said, 'the old frontiers are gone. When you think of the defence of England, you no longer think of the chalk cliffs of Dover, you think of the Rhine. That is where our frontier lies.' This speech was criticized in the ultra-Conservative Press as a provocative suggestion that Germany might be the enemy—on the contrary, the Germans were sincere workers for world peace. The Left Press declared that Capitalist politicians were again preparing to plunge Europe into an Imperialist war. Soon afterwards, it was announced that the Royal Air Force was to be doubled, that everyone would have gas-mask drill with firemen as instructors, and that black-outs were to be tried. Europe was beginning to split up into two camps. Socialists talked openly of the split as between workers and capitalists: Left and Right. Nobody felt quite certain, however, into which camp the National Government would go: the Government was, in fact, busily denying that there were two different camps. Anthony Eden made a speech at Fulham in May 1935, deploring the re-emergence of such meaningless phrases as 'pro-German' and 'pro-French': they belonged to a past epoch, and their use was dangerous because they might mislead foreign opinion as to the true attitude of Britain. 'The British are not anti any nation in Europe.' he said, but added warningly, 'but we should be, we must be, anti any who might seek by force to break the peace.'

In March 1936 the Nazi Government, having seen the failure of League action against Italy, reoccupied the demilitarized zone of the Rhineland. Their troops marched in without even being served out with ammunition, so certain was Hitler that France and Britain would not intervene. Nothing in effect happened. It was not as though Hitler had reoccupied Alsace-Lorraine, the British remarked. Besides, the French were safe enough—they had just signed a defensive pact with the U.S.S.R. And anyhow, the Germans weren't such bad people really, though they did have a mania about the Jews—those Olympic Winter Sports at Garmisch had been marvellously organized, and everyone had been so hospitable and polite.

The piling up of armaments, the politicians admitted, was a

useless and dangerous way of preserving the peace. But what else could be done? Baldwin confessed at the Lord Mayor's Banquet on the 9th November 1936, that rearmament made war more likely. Everyone knew, he said, that war would degrade the life of the people: 'I am prepared to devote all our efforts, whatever it may cost in men and money, to do what is necessary, but I am conscious all the time of the folly of all of us.' Neville Chamberlain, then Chancellor of the Exchequer, outlined at Birmingham in January 1937 the immense programme on which work was being started for the modernization of the country's defences. He, too, declared himself impressed by the 'incredible folly of civilization' which put such burdens on the shoulders of the nation. Again in April 1937, at a dinner of the British Bankers' Association, he was complaining of 'that fear of attack from somewhere else which is almost universal, but which may yet rest on nothing more solid than imagination'. Fewer and fewer people by 1937 were even so optimistic as Chamberlain. Yet Lloyd George was attacking the National Government as a 'Council of Despair'. 'Germany may never attack Belgium and France,' he said. 'I tell you, as one who has studied the whole situation, I don't think Hitler is a fool—he is not going to challenge the British Empire again by that act of folly.'

The combination of rearmament with admissions of its folly seemed to prove the pacifist case. People felt that if politicians could not stop war, they themselves should do so, by refusing to fight. A new pacifist organization, the Peace Pledge Union, was founded by Canon 'Dick' Sheppard. He was a public character: not only did his conversational sermons, strewn with amusing yarns, bring large congregations to his church of St. Martin's-in-the-Fields, but he became a sort of chaplain to the B.B.C. listeners. It was he who started the 'Ever-open-door' in the Crypt of St. Martin's, where the 'down-and-outs' could take shelter for the night. He had long been an active pacifist. When a Victory Ball was to be held in the Albert Hall on Armistice Night, 1925, he organized protests against it on the grounds that to commemorate a victory which had bred so much misery and hate would be blasphemous. Instead, Canon Sheppard held a service in the Hall, where he urged a congregation of many thousands to dedicate themselves anew to the peace cause. Nine years later, when the peace cause was in a bad way, he decided to revive it. In October 1934 he circulated a letter to the Press inviting men who would never support or sanction another war to send him a postcard saying so. He wrote: 'The idea behind this letter is not to form any fresh organization, nor to call pacifists together to abuse those who conscientiously are not able to agree with them, but to attempt to discover how strong the will to peace will be.' In June 1935 a meeting was held in the Albert Hall, attended by seven thousand of those who had signed the pledge. There the Peace Pledge Union was founded, and among its original supporters were Vera Brittain, Aldous Huxley, Rose Macaulay, Lord Ponsonby, and Brigadier-General F. P. Crozier, a sincerely penitent ex-fire-eater. By the autumn of 1935 eighty thousand people had renounced war, and by 1937 one hundred and thirty thousand.

The Union's aim was to spread pacifist feeling, and to form groups to study all threats to world peace: it held that a world conference could settle all problems by friendly discussion. One of these problems, in the Union's opinion, was colonies. Left-Wing people—and the pacifists were usually also Left-Wing—always considered that the colonial peoples were wickedly exploited. They seldom paused to study the particular difficulties of colonial administration and the best means of dealing with them. They relied on the vague formula of 'freeing the natives and allowing them to determine their own destiny': as when the Romans in the fifth century had withdrawn their garrison from Britain and left the prosperous demilitarized south as a prey to the wild tribes of the north and adventurers from overseas. The Peace Pledge Union also opened a book shop at Ludgate Hill and founded a journal, *Peace News*. Affiliated with the War Resisters' International, the P.P.U. took part in the International Peace Conference at Brussels in 1936. Its members refused to assist in any A.R.P. exercises.

Aldous Huxley, by now no longer a bright young satirist but an earnest student of world affairs, published through the Peace Pledge Union a pamphlet, *The Encyclopedia of Pacifism*. In it he criticized the Union for not going far enough; and defined pacifists as people whose job it was to see that desirable changes took place without discord. Communism was no remedy, because it was militaristic, nor was Social Credit—although it stressed one truth—that the present monetary system favoured certain groups of people and so fostered discord. The possession of colonies was another source of ill-will, because it created the unreal opposition of 'Have-not' to 'Have' powers (the 'Have's' and the 'Have-not's' was another classification of Europe's two camps). It was false to speak of the necessity for *Lebensraum* (German propaganda was already beginning to acclimatize this word in the English language), for if scientific agriculture were practised there would be plenty of room and food for everyone. Nationalism, too, was a dangerous doctrine: it assuaged the sense of individual inferiority by setting up the superiority of the totalitarian State instead. What was needed was a decentralization of government, so that people could live at peace in small self-governing groups.

Huxley's 'constructive pacifism' commended itself to those who felt that conscientious objection to war was too negative a view in the face of the growing menace of the totalitarian countries. Such ideas, however, could only be put into action by political means, and the existing political parties were enmeshed in the parliamentary game, and too powerful to permit the foundation of new parties. But the young, eager, and intelligent did not become disillusioned with politics: they were attracted to the only non-parliamentary political party—the Communists. Part of the allure of Communism lay in the sense it gave its adherents of being outside the ordinary political game, free to criticize it and free to speculate widely on new plans and ideas.

The Labour Party had long since ceased to be Left, and Left activities were without the sanction of Labour Party officials. Thus, the counter-demonstrations which met Mosley's British Union of Fascist marches were always staged by Communists and other groups of the Left outside. The Communist Party and the Independent Labour Party—now a very small group indeed, led by James Maxton—set up a Joint Committee in 1934 for Anti-Fascist action. Fascism had ceased to mean merely the form of government practised in Italy: it now covered all forms of totalitarian nationalism. As examples of Fascist aggression multiplied in the world, Left activity came to be more and more concerned with international politics. The Right was accused of trying to turn German ambitions in the direction of the Soviet Ukraine and the Left itself found reasons in Hitler's *Mein*

Kampf for thinking that this was where they would turn. Calls for anti-Fascist action were therefore always linked with calls for the defence of the Soviet Union, which was represented as the workers' paradise menaced by threats from the Capitalist inferno.

The Labour Party rejected persistent calls upon it to join in any united action either against Fascism or in favour of the Soviets. At the time, popular fronts of all the Left groups were being formed in France and Spain, and the extreme Left wanted a similar front in England. Only that way, they believed, could the National Government be defeated in an election. They talked of politics in military terms: there was a 'class-struggle', a 'front', many 'battles', and the prophesied 'victory of the working class'. Conservative newspapers were worried: *The Times*, for instance, observed that 'the spirit of 1926 which produced the General Strike is showing itself again'. It will be remembered that the idealistic revolutionary spirit among the rank and file of the fighting forces, at the conclusion of the Great War had been successfully appeased by promises, and broken by demobilization. It arose again as the early Twenties brought unemployment and disillusion and the Conservative Government of 1926 felt itself strong enough to ignore the recommendations of the official Sankey report on the nationalization of mines, but had again been broken. The Conservatives had for several parliamentary generations been called 'The Stupid Party', not only bitterly by its opponents but affectionately by its backbenchers. The National Government had been a stroke of political genius—a concentration of all that was lovably stupid of all three parties into a bloc, around the nucleus of the Stupid Party. All highly gifted politicians of the two elder parties, such as Lloyd George and Winston Churchill, the only two Members of Parliament who had any talent for incisive debate, were necessarily 'in the wilderness'. The official Opposition, the Labour Party, was also decidedly lacking in forceful speakers, and, perhaps for the first time since the Reform Act, the ordinary common-sense views of 'the intelligent man in the street' carried no political weight.

Labour had certain local successes. At the London County Council elections of 1934 its candidates gained a majority of seats over the Conservative Municipal Reformers. This majority was held for the rest of the period, thanks chiefly to the leadership of Herbert Morrison, the only contemporary Labour leader whose energy made any impression on the general public. The Labour L.C.C. had, on the whole, a good record—especially in matters of slum clearance and rehousing. Even the unofficial Left could find little to criticize in its actions. But the parliamentary Labour Party lacked fire: its dependence on the T.U.C., where routine qualities were those most prized, discouraged both brilliance and warmth of heart. To such a condition was the party reduced that Clynes, the former Home Secretary, could find no better way of stating Labour's case than to quote a compliment paid by Baldwin. 'The Labour Party as a whole,' Baldwin had said, 'has helped to keep the flag of parliamentary government flying in the world in the difficult periods through which we have passed.'

The unofficial Left, exasperated by the Means Test and wage-cuts, was out rather to tear down the parliamentary flag than keep it flying; a new means to this end, as Ramsay MacDonald might have put it in his failing years, was the sit-down strike. Strikes of this kind had already been practised in Poland, the United States, and France. The strikers took possession of the factories, mines, and sheds where they worked, and camped in them. Employers could not then attempt to carry on with black-leg labour but had either to use force to eject the trespassers, risking damage to the plant, or take immediate notice of the demands. The first strike of this kind in Britain was made by some Monmouthshire miners as a protest against the employment of non-Union men in the mine. They stayed down in the workings and refused to emerge until their demands were granted. The prospect of having men starving in their pits alarmed the mine-owners, and they gave way.

Another form of protest was the Hunger March, which had already been successfully tried three years before. The idea of unemployed men tramping across Britain, and relying for food and shelter on wayside charity, distressed the governing classes. A large march was organized in January 1934. Ramsay Mac-Donald, then Prime Minister, refused to see the marchers' delegates, but they were at least allowed to demonstrate without interference by the police. A still larger march followed in 1935. Official Labour then became impressed by this form of agitation. C. R. Attlee, the Labour leader, consented to speak from

THE DAYS OF NON INTERVENTION

the same platform as Wal Hannington, the organizer of the National Unemployed Workers' Movement, which sponsored the marches and which was generally considered to be under Communist influence. It seemed for a moment as though a United Front were about to be born; but when the Communists applied to be affiliated to the Labour Party in November that year, they were refused. Communist attention was thereafter diverted from hunger-marching to denunciations of Labour. Then came the Abyssinian and Spanish wars in rapid succession, and Communist energy found a new outlet—this time into anti-Fascist agitations.

The Communists still remained a small party—they had about seven thousand members at this time—but each member was an extremely active centre of agitation, and usually adept at giving a Marxist turn to every discussable topic. The *Daily Worker* had doubled its size and greatly increased its circulation. It now included a weekly book-page and criticism of plays, films, and art—all signs of the intellectualization of the party. Nevertheless, working-class supporters were provided for by a good deal of horse-racing, greyhound-racing, and boxing and football news. The *Daily Worker* was not the only literary means by which the Communists spread propaganda: between 1935 and 1937 nearly a million copies of their pamphlets and sheets were also sold. To belong to the party meant devoting one's time and money so whole-heartedly to the Cause and having one's political and social history so carefully investigated that very few sympathizers with the Communist position either desired to join the *corps d'élite* of the party or would have been accepted had they offered. But the Reds were so large a potential sales-public that Business, represented by Victor Gollancz the publisher, could not afford to neglect them.

The Left Book Club was founded in May 1936, on the model of the American 'Book of the Month Club' and 'Book Guild', which had been prodigiously successful in selling general literature. Left Book Club members paid a quarterly or yearly subscription and received in return one book each month, which had been commissioned by the selection committee: this committee was composed of Harold Laski, a Socialist professor of political theory, John Strachey, ex-Mosley supporter, now an able exponent of Marxist economics, and Victor Gollancz himself. It had an immediate success, and within a year forty thousand members had joined and four hundred local discussion circles had been formed. The books, bound first in yellow and then in orange paper, dealt with every aspect of the world about which it was possible to hold a Left opinion. Membership was maintained because, once the books started arriving by post each month, it was as difficult to break the habit as to stop paying instalments on an electric vacuum-cleaner or radio-set. Often, after the first enthusiasm had died down, they merely served to decorate bookshelves: glanced at, but never fully read, they were an armoury from which a weapon could be selected for argument on any conceivable subject. The Marxian twist to literature soon came to recall the monkish Christian twist of the Middle Ages. One picked up a supposedly scholarly book on the Conquests of Genghis Khan, the World of Hesiod, or the Court of Marie Antoinette, in ordinary brown, black, or grey binding and before one had read a dozen pages one was aware of the 'canting lay' of the professional Communist.

The existence of the club embittered the controversy between Labour and the extreme Left. Labour were invited to participate, but refused unless its point of view was adequately represented on the Selection Committee. The Left Book Club would not grant this. Although, therefore, a book by Attlee was among its early issues, the club chiefly published literature with a Marxian slant. Labour groups tried to counter this by setting up a Labour Book Club and a Socialist Book Club; the Diehard Conservatives already had their Right Book Club, and the Liberals were forming a Liberal Book Club. None of these rivals, however, was ever successful enough to challenge the supremacy of the Left. There was also a general book club: the Book Society, which never reached more than one-fifth of the membership of its American counterpart, but was much appreciated by overseas readers as a convenience for keeping in touch with contemporary literature. The safe quality of its choices can be judged from the names of some of its committee members—Miss Clemence Dane, Sir Hugh Walpole, Edmund Blunden, and George Gordon, the Merton Professor of English Literature at Oxford.

In July 1936 the Spanish 'Civil War' began. This three-year struggle moved not only the Left, but all intelligent people in Britain most strongly. The first news came through in the third week of July. It was reported that the progressive Spanish Government was arming the workers while the Foreign Legion and the insurgent regular army were marching on Madrid. It seemed at first as if the Spanish Government would soon be overcome, especially when it became known that the insurgents before they moved had come to an understanding with Italy and Germany. General Franco, who had assumed command of the insurgent armies on the accidental death of his superior San-jurjo, boasted that he had four columns marching on Madrid and a fifth inside the city, which would rise against the Government upon his approach. As it happened, Franco was halted outside Madrid by the hastily raised 'People's Army' of the Republican Government, the most dependable corps of which was the 'International Brigade' of non-Spanish anti-Fascist volunteers. The new word 'fifth-columnist' soon came into the English language, being particularly applied to certain political groups which seemed to be trying to bring Great Britain into the Fascist camp. Suspicion was attached to the lunches and week-end parties which Lady Astor held at her country house, Clive-den, in Buckinghamshire: the 'Cliveden Set' was whispered to be pro-Nazi, and at the bottom of all Fifth Column activity in England. Lady Astor herself vigorously denied these rumours, but she could not prevent the Left Press from always speaking of the 'Cliveden Set' and the 'Fifth Column' in the same breath.

The Spanish War soon developed into a standing European crisis. It could not be overlooked that the Italians and Germans were helping General Franco, and that, if he were to win, Britain and France would be threatened with an addition to the Italo-German 'Axis'. The Spanish Government, after appealing in vain to the League of Nations, decided to seek help from Russia. The Russians, who, like the Italians and Germans, wished to try their new weapons in actual combat, sent a certain amount of help, especially aircraft, pilots, and tanks, but not enough to compensate for the help that the Axis was ready to give to the other side. The Russian intervention decided the British and French Governments to remain neutral. It was feared by leading Conservatives that, if the Republican Government won, the Communists, who had been only a very small minority in Spain, would gain control of the country; that this would damage Anglo-French trade interests in Spain and put the Left into power first in France and then in Great Britain. The Spanish generals seemed to stand for the Law-and-Order party, whereas the Republicans were bitterly anti-Clerical and had killed a number of Spanish priests. The 'experts' advising the British Government believed that if Franco won, he could be detached from his new allies by a promise of financial assistance: the Axis powers were notoriously short of money. The pressure brought by these elements and the natural wish of the British and French to localize the war brought about the Non-Intervention scheme, according to which arms were not to be exported to either side. The Germans and Italians, who had agreed to the scheme, continued to support Franco not only with arms but with complete units of mechanized troops. The Republicans also continued to get outside help, but Dr. Negrin, the Premier, who allowed himself to depend on Communist advice, decided to buy arms only from Russia; though the Russian supplies were scanty, inferior, and slow in coming. Spain had a large hoard of gold in foreign banks, and armament firms in Czecho-Slovakia, Belgium, France, and the United States were quite willing to sell what he wanted, cash on delivery; they would find ways and means.

The Axis powers naturally exaggerated the help that the Russians were giving and minimized their own contribution. The British Press made the mistake of treating a military question as one of party politics. How sharply the Spanish question divided opinion in England can be seen from the attitudes of the newspapers. The *Morning Post, Daily Mail, Daily Sketch,* and *Observer* were decidedly in favour of Franco, and printed no Spanish news that did not discredit the cause and prospects of 'the Reds'. The *News Chronicle* was similarly one-sided in its support of the Republicans and pressed the British Government to 'end the farce of non-intervention' by raising the embargo on arms, even at the risk of starting a European war. The *Daily Herald* printed only Republican news but supported the party line of Non-Intervention. The *Daily Express* and *Daily Mirror* had Republican sympathies, but thought that nothing should be done to provoke the Axis powers. The *Daily Telegraph* and *The Times* set out to be impartial—the *Daily Telegraph* on the whole succeeding better than *The Times*; *The Times* decided that it was unwise to print articles written by its military correspondent, which pointed out the extreme danger to the British Empire of a Spain friendly to the Axis powers, and showed this as the first campaign in the coming World War. The National Government continued to put its faith in the power of gold to buy General Franco's friendship when the war was won. The Blum Government in France grew very restive and the Anglo-French Non-Intervention scheme could not have been maintained had not the British Government warned France that it would remain neutral if French action provoked a war with Germany. But there were strong pro-Axis elements in France too.

Never since the French Revolution had there been a foreign question that so divided intelligent British opinion as this. It could be seen in so many ways: as Fascism versus Communism, or Totalitarianism versus Democracy, or Italy and Germany versus England and France, or Force versus Liberty, or Rebels versus Constitutional Government, or Barbarism versus Culture, or Catholicism versus Atheism, or the Upper Classes versus the Lower, or Order versus Anarchy—however one's mind worked. But, though opinion was divided, the majority felt at least sympathy for the Republic. It was the Communists who organized the dispatch of the British companies of the International Brigade, before Non-Intervention came into force, and won increasing popular favour by so doing: of all the rallies organized by the Communist Party, the Help-for-Spain ones were the best attended. The Labour Party was bitterly criticized—this time not only by the extreme Left—for supporting Non-Intervention. Not only Left-wingers such as Professor Laski and Sir Stafford Cripps were attacking the party line, but even so staid a person as Sir Charles Trevelyan, who had been a Labour President of the Board of Education. He said: 'When the war that is looming comes and Japan and Germany crash in to destroy Soviet Russia, I hope the Labour Party will have some other policy to offer than sympathy, accompanied by bandages and cigarettes.' Individual Labour leaders, however, 'Clem' Attlee among them, went to Republican Spain and lectured on the situation when they returned. So did many other public figures, including the Conservative 'Red Duchess' of Atholl. Most people, in fact, who either held progressive views, or simply believed in 'decency', supported the Republican side, and many enthusiastic young men fought for it and were killed.

CHAPTER TWENTY

The Deepening Twilight of Barbarism

Being political had meant supporting one or other of the parliamentary parties; but people who prided themselves on their intelligence shrank more and more from contact with party affairs. Like the Church, Parliament seemed to them to have fallen into the hands of phrase-mongers and dead-heads. The two elder parties had now, they said, enticed Labour into the grand old party game, and it was idle to look to Westminster for reassurance as to the future of society. The Abyssinian and Spanish Wars, which destroyed those easy international ideals for which the League of Nations had stood, gave 'politics' a wider meaning: namely, thought for the defence of what was still sound in civilization. Some sort of non-party action seemed the readiest way out of a cramped and stupid situation. Political convictions in this sense were forced on well-known writers: if they continued at their ordinary tasks of writing for entertainment or general instruction they were derided as 'escapists living in ivory towers'. H. G. Wells in his *The Open Conspiracy, Blueprints for a Social Revolution*, and other writings, insisted on extra-parliamentary Radicalism as the cure for the times. A number of the brightest writers of the Twenties leant towards Fascism, including Wyndham Lewis, who wrote a book in admiration of Hitler (despite Hitler's detestation of modernist art, of which Lewis was a leading exponent), and Evelyn Waugh, who supported Italian action in Abyssinia and in Spain; and indeed old Bernard Shaw's new political religion was Fascist in trend. Siegfried Sassoon, Aldous Huxley, and Beverley Nichols

—his sidelines were gardening, God, and the glories of the English countryside—were bitter pacifists. The 'Bloomsbury set' was anti-Fascist, and E. M. Forster declared that if he were younger and bolder he would be a Communist.

It was thought incumbent on poets to 'get into touch with reality'. The three 'new poets'—Auden, Spender, and Day Lewis—were said to be achieving this by cultivating Left sympathies. With them was associated the cultural and donnish Louis MacNeice, who was realistic because he had written acidly descriptive poems on bourgeois subjects, such as lawn-mowing in Hampstead gardens. The theory of realism applied even more to imaginative prose than to verse, though the young Left prose-writers, with the exception of Christopher Isherwood, celebrant of life in Berlin under the Weimar Republic, had no public as yet. An annual, *New Writing,* was founded in 1936 to remedy this: it would print socio-realistic short stories and examples of descriptive reporting from various parts of the world. (Socio-realism seemed to provide just that new background to life for which young people in the Thirties were anxiously searching.) Bed-rock reality, it declared, lay in the life of the working class; books should deal with this from the hopeful point of view of the class struggle that was to improve working conditions. In order to get in touch with this sort of reality many young writers went to live or work in the slums; but produced neither memorable literature nor historically valuable reports of their experiences.

Socio-realism also invaded the theatre—an obvious territory for reform. The object of the new Unity Theatre was to make use of working-class dramatic talent and produce plays with a socialistic trend—or at least, plays which would appeal to intelligent and politically conscious working-class people. The most successful of the purely political melodramas which it staged was 'Waiting for Lefty', by an American playwright, Clifford Odets. The action was laid at a Trade Union meeting. The members were discussing a strike and waiting for a Communist leader to arrive. Several interludes gave domestic aspects of the strike. As the discussion at the meeting grew hotter, members of the theatre audience, primed beforehand, began to cry, 'We want Lefty.' An atmosphere of tense expectancy was worked up, but when Lefty did arrive, it was only to be promptly shot. This symbolized tragically the suppression of working-class activities by vested interests. Another successful play was by Herbert Hodge, a London taxi-driver; it was called 'Where's that Bomb?' and dealt with the struggles of a worker poet in his attempts to save himself from being sold to the symbolic figures of Money Power and British Patriot. In the end he was victorious: he refused adamantly to write verses to be printed on lavatory paper. This crude, sincere morality play thrilled working-class audiences in much the same way as the monkish Tudor morality plays, 'Magnificence', 'Everyman', and the rest, had thrilled their ancestors.

The upper-class Left poets also interested themselves in theatre reform: plays by Auden, Spender, and MacNeice were produced at the Westminster Theatre by a club called the Group Theatre. The Group also used the Unity stage but the Unity players themselves refused to produce Auden's work, considering it unreal and quite out-of-touch with working-class life. Auden's plays, 'The Dog Beneath the Skin', 'The Ascent of F 6', and 'On the Frontier' were written in collaboration with Christopher Isherwood. They were elaborate, farcical moralities with rambling plots and little characterization. Their chief ingredient was incidental satire in verse, usually spoken by masked choruses, directed against decaying suburban and capitalist life. MacNeice's single play was of much the same kind. Spender's bathetic 'Trial of a Judge' made no attempt to be amusing. It showed revolutionaries being shot and imprisoned when Fascists come into power. The Judge represented the average intelligent bourgeois, forced by events to support a political party whose methods were abhorrent to him; and in the end was imprisoned along with the revolutionaries. None of these plays was a popular success, but they were cried up as promises of a poetic revival in the theatre—and, in the case of Auden, as attempts to use fast-moving variety methods with a serious object.

Political literature and books of contemporary history began to encroach upon the sales of biography and fiction. Each new political event was celebrated by a huge number of explanatory volumes. At the Jubilee, for instance, there was John Buchan's *The King's Grace*, John Drinkwater's *The King's Reign*, Sir Philip Gibbs's *The King's Jubilee*, Arthur Bryant's *King George V*, and many more. The Abyssinian War yielded *Abyssinia on the Eve*, *Mussolini's Italy*, *Europe's Crisis*, *Mussolini's Roman Empire*, and so on. The long duration of the Spanish War permitted the publication of scores of books—including some by members of the International Brigade. Most of these were written from the Left viewpoint, with shrill warnings as to what would befall Europe if Franco were allowed to win; but a few from the Right, enlarging on the atrocities committed against the Catholic Church, commending the civilizing mission of General Franco, denouncing the 'Unholy Reds'. Particular crises merged into the General Crisis: this also evoked political interpretations, prophetic histories, personal records—John Gunther's *Inside Europe* and Madame Tabouis's *Blackmail or War*, Lilian Mowrer's *A Journalist's Wife*, and the like. At no time in English history had so much information on foreign affairs been available in lively popular form, nor so many conflicting views on policy and prospects. The result was less enlightenment than a permanent feeling of crisis, an expectancy of worse things to come, which grew blacker and blacker until its monstrous climax in September 1938.

The vogue for historical biography continued; it was now generally written in the American snappy style popularized by W. E. Woodward's *George Washington*, Phillips Russell's *Benjamin Franklin*, and similar 'debunkments'. In October 1935 a reviewer, asked by the *Observer* to notice a Gollancz biography, chose to make an example of it. The book was *Magnificent Hadrian* and Theodore Dreiser had written of it that it 'sets forth in detail and with patience—with beauty of words and beauty of understanding and sympathy—a story that the whole world should know and treasure.' This book, lavishly advertised, was typical of its class and period. The reviewer, after first calling attention to the bibliography of two hundred mixed titles, in which three of the five ordinary Classical historians of the period did not appear, contented himself with quotation and dry comment:

' "In A.D. 122 Hadrian entered Britain, the nearest of the Tin Isles, then the abode of blue-painted savages. . . . He watched the building of the Wall. He saw the rubble core being mixed with mortar and then faced with regular blocks of stone eight-and-a-half by ten-and-eleven-twelfths by twenty inches."

'The quickest way to criticize this passage is to rewrite it correctly:

'A.D. 120 is the accepted date of Hadrian's visit of inspection to Britain [or insert reasons for preferring A.D. 121 or 122], which had been a Roman province for seventy-four years. In Caledonia, to the North, lived certain wild tribes whose raids into civilized Britain Trajan hoped to restrain by a fortified wall of stone-faced rubble [never mind the eleven-twelfths, etc., but say from where the Wall started, and where it ended], held by a standing garrison. The Caledonians still tattooed themselves, a practice that the Britains had abandoned since becoming civilized. Tin, for which Britain had been known in early times, was no longer mined. [Here state the geographical problems raised by Greek and Latin references to the Tin Islands, which were probably a group of islands off the Galician coast, possibly the Scilly Islands, but certainly not Britain and Ireland.]

'Another quotation:

' "Lusius Quietus was a rampageous gentleman from Mauretania, country of Othello. During Trajan's Mesopotamian campaign he had led his cavalry."

'The quickest way to criticize this is to rewrite it soberly:

'Quintus Lusius Quietus was an independent Moorish chief, from a part of Mauretania not included in the Roman province, whose services to the Romans as a cavalry leader in Mesopotamia and elsewhere, under Trajan, recall those rendered by Othello, also a Moor, to the Venetians, in Cyprus and elsewhere. Spartianus represents him as hot-tempered and impulsive. [If Spartianus does.]

'Another quotation:

' "Quietus's eyes showed their whites when he heard of that appointment, his black brows and heavy lips took on a fiery, sullen gloom."

'The quickest way to criticize this is to rewrite it honestly:

'Quietus may have felt resentment, but he is not known to have expressed any.'

The *Observer* had the integrity to print the notice in full, but the reviewer was never again offered another such commission: business was business.

The Press was modelling itself more closely than ever on American lines: headlines shorter, news curter. The *Daily Mirror* imitated the American 'tabloids': it now consisted chiefly of photographs, bold headlines and sub-headlines, with only a small, brief core of news in column-form. The highly intelligent presentation of contemporary affairs which sold the American weekly *Time* to half a million readers was emulated in England by *Calvacade* and *News Review*—they even exactly copied *Time's* red and white cover. But neither journal had the financial or journalistic resources to make a *Time* of itself nor an editor of the quality of *Time's* Luce, and the racy American manner could not be copied without strain and absurdity. The sophisticated humour of the *New Yorker* was also imitated by a new weekly *Night and Day*; but the British public for this sort of writing was too small to sustain it long, and an unfortunate libel on little Shirley Temple's sex-appeal sank it suddenly. Even *Punch* learned the trick of streamlining its humour, but used this with restraint: for *Punch*, priding itself on being a national institution, knew native English humour to be as elaborate as it was leisurely. Daily and Sunday columnists adopted contemporary American methods without qualms. William Hickey's column in the *Daily Express* 'These Names Make News' (a title also borrowed from *Time*), was composed of snappy notes on anybody prominent in any walk of life: the scope of gossip was extended far beyond the old confines of Mayfair parties to deal indiscriminately with social, intellectual, artistic, political, and business topics.

At the same time there was a marked rise in the standard of advertisement 'copy'. Commercial firms no longer assumed their public to be wholly brainless and soulless. Gas companies advertised their stoves, fires, geysers, and refrigerators in short, clear sentences stressing the advantages that the friendly, Puck-like figure of Mr. Therm could bestow on the householder; Shell and Guinness used the brief, witty or humorous advertisement; radio manufacturers gave frank, man-to-man talks on the qualities of their sets; and most large stores had learned that the fewer and clearer the illustrations used in their catalogues the more likely was the eye to be caught.

Depression had driven many of the Hollywood film companies into liquidation. The industry was then rationalized by new directors, muddle and waste curtailed, and an attempt made to make films intelligent enough to attract an increasingly critical public. Stars now had to have more than mere sex-appeal: they had to work even harder than stage stars, and in return demanded reasonably sensible scripts. The old low-brow themes—the office-boy who became the power-boss, the shop-girl who met her Prince Charming at the glove-counter, were little used. Realistic crime dramas, usually with a newspaper-office setting, witty socialite comedies, 'haywire' fantasies, historical romances with some attempt at historical verisimilitude, were added to the song and dance spectacles. The greatest American film success of 1936 in Britain was the American 'Mr. Deeds Goes to Town', with Gary Cooper, the story of a young man who suddenly became a millionaire, and of the misfortunes that befell him when he tried to use his money for the public good. In 1935 Chaplin produced 'Modern Times', giving the pathetic and humorous side of the 'little man's' life under mechanization. These successes were followed by 'Dead End' and 'Winterset'—both stories set in the poverty of the New York slums, showing how young men were driven to crime. These films were not social tracts, but reflected the anxieties and discontents of the time without ceasing to be pleasantly dramatic entertainment. Sound was no longer an obstacle to the easy British acceptance of American films. Technical research had improved the reproduction of speech, and Hollywood was employing actors whose accents would not offend British ears and thus spoil a rich market.

British films, meanwhile, were making a great effort to stage a world come-back. It was still believed that they could do so if only they were given time; though they had already been given time, and money, and flattery. British studios were as well equipped as most, and to improve them further stars and technicians were imported from Hollywood. Yet there was only one popularly successful producer in Britain: Alexander Korda, a Hungarian. In 1935 he produced 'The Private Life of Henry VIII' with Charles Laughton: the first British film to score a success in the United States as well as in Great Britain. He gained powerful financial backing from the Prudential Insurance Company and followed 'Henry VIII' with further historical films, 'Catherine the Great', 'The Life of Rembrandt' —also starring Charles Laughton—and with 'The Ghost Goes West', a comedy directed by the Frenchman, René Clair. Clair's

'Sous les Toits de Paris' and 'Le Million' were two of the most popular films of the time at the 'different' cinemas, most of them in the London West End, where foreign and experimental work and revivals were shown. But the traditional deadness of British studios dispirited Clair; 'The Ghost Goes West' was flat, and none of Korda's later films, though workmanlike enough, managed to hold the market which 'Henry VIII' had opened.

The best individual achievement of British film-producers was in documentary work. The Government in 1936 had already sponsored forty short films by the General Post Office Film Unit and twenty by commercial companies, which illustrated departmental and industrial conditions. The Admiralty, the Air Ministry, and the War Office also separately sponsored feature-films, in which the work done in factories, trains, ships, and aircraft at home and in the Empire was presented directly and skilfully. Producers had learned from Russian film-methods how everyday life could be made interesting on the screen without fictitious drama or wise-cracking comment. The Post Office Unit was run by two of the innovators of documentary films—John Grierson and Alberto Cavalcanti. Grierson used commentaries as part of the pattern of his films, explaining only where explanation was necessary, as in 'Night Mail', instead of running on in a semi-facetious showman's patter. One of the Unit's most successful productions was Cavalcanti's 'North Sea', in 1938, which dealt with Aberdeen fishermen. Cavalcanti here improved on Grierson's methods by putting over his information entirely by dialogue without the help of commentary. Its popularity extended far outside Britain: at one time it was showing in twenty-five Paris cinemas.

The British, however, did not apply their documentary intelligence to the making of news-films in the style of 'March of Time'. 'March of Time', at first a radio feature, got behind day-to-day news and gave a perspective to events by tracing the causes which brought them about. It carried into the cinema *Time*'s tradition of free, lively comment on world affairs. A 'March of Time' film did not show, like ordinary news reels, a series of unrelated incidents, such as the launching of a ship, the opening of a bridge, a parade of soldiers. It treated one subject at a time in a connected way: the story of cancer research, the health of Britain, football pools, the payment of tithes, political problems in the Mediterranean, in the Far East, and inside Nazi Germany. It this way it gave real information and a point of view upon current problems.

Radio documentary, in the form of 'feature programmes', had been developing since the earliest days of the B.B.C. There was great excitement in the Twenties when, by scraping a fiddle, a B.B.C. naturalist persuaded a nightingale in the Surrey woods to sing into the microphone for the pleasure of millions of listeners. The technique of using sound to convey impression was slowly perfected. The B.B.C.'s mewing seagull that performed whenever a marine landscape was needed became something of a joke, but a good deal was done towards a practical 'bringing the world to the fireside' by accurate recording of British and foreign noises. The feature programme was now cried up as the purest expression and worthiest object of the whole broadcasting business—'a means of unifying the thought and understanding of the nation, showing the one half not only how the other half lived but what it meant'.

A new element introduced into films in the Thirties was colour. It was used, however, much as sound was at first—a lot of it and as strident as possible. Black-and-white films had slowly built up an expressive technique of shapes, shadows and shades, not to be found in colour films; indeed, so much colour was used that shapes were violently accentuated or completely obliterated, and successive images left only a confused impression.

The only really successful colour films at this time were cartoons, and especially the Silly Symphonies of Walt Disney. Disney's black-and-white Mickey Mouse cartoons had been popular with the public for some years. His Silly Symphonies proved even more popular. Their success was due partly to the technical reason that the colour photography of animated cartoons was a simple affair, compared with that of natural scenery; partly to Disney's sense of composition, design and characterization. The use of Mendelssohn's 'Spring Song' to illustrate a comically exuberant world of bursting flowers, hopping frogs, hunting herons, was shocking at first, but the ballet-effects were graceful, and the synchronization of music and colour-movement perfect. He made such simple things as clouds of gnats, whirling storms, schools of fish, hold the eye. With his animal characters—Mickey Mouse, Pluto the Hound, Donald Duck, the Three Little Pigs, and the Big Bad Wolf—he and his four hundred technicians created a fabulous world of childish imagery. Some Symphonies were founded on traditional fables —the Tortoise and the Hare, the Grasshopper and the Ants; others, particularly those in which the irritable hero Donald Duck featured, relied on the cruel misfortunes of slapstick comedy. Their appeal was to the eye, the ear, and the sense of comedy, no other popular films at the time succeeded so well in satisfying all these three senses. Children loved them, yet were secretly terrified by them, as their parents had been by the two Grimms' fairy stories and Shockheaded Peter.

There were no remarkable new developments in the commercial theatre of the Thirties. There were still crime dramas, such as 'Night Must Fall' by the young Welsh actor and playwright, Emlyn Williams; still Cochran reviews with a very high standard of dancing and Jessie Matthews as the acknowledged 'tops'; still Coward's satirical wit—less flamboyantly clever and more genuinely sentimental in 'Conversation Piece' and 'Tonight at 8.30'. Also dramas based on the problems of youth, as 'The Wind and the Rain', and romantic Bohemian plays, such as 'Escape Me Never', Margaret Kennedy's sequel to 'The Constant Nymph', which enjoyed a long run, chiefly because of the acting of the refugee actress, Elisabeth Bergner. J. B. Priestley had also turned to the stage and was attempting to enliven suburban interior scenes by experimenting with their time-sequence. And James Bridie, a Scottish doctor, wrote sinister character-studies, and modernized Bible stories. The nearest that the stage came to socio-realism was Seán O'Casey's unmoralistic 'Juno and the Paycock', and Walter Greenwood's 'Love on the Dole', which dealt humorously but pathetically with the life of the unemployed—the heroine saved herself and her family from starvation by becoming a bookmaker's mistress. Greenwood, who had published *Love on the Dole* as a novel in 1933, was one of the few socio-realists who wrote of distressed area conditions from unsought and appalling personal experience. He was from Salford, had only a board-school education, and wrote the book in the very circumstances described in it: it did not ramble, however, in the ordinary proletarian style but showed a disciplined literary sense.

British plays were generally well acted, often neatly written, sometimes amusing, seldom memorable. The most likely to last, T. E. Lawrence pronounced, were Coward's perfectly timed comedies—'Private Lives', 1930, was a good example. Films and the radio were now the chief forms of entertainment. They attracted more talent and gave rise to more enthusiasm—and to more controversy—than plays. There was, however, an enormous increase of amateur acting in the suburbs of the big cities. Since 1918 the number of provincial theatres had decreased and the provincial touring system had been curtailed For those who were not satisfied with mass cinema-going, amateur acting was a solution. It was a sociable, entertaining pastime. In 1936 there were nearly forty thousand amateur dramatic societies, and nearly one million amateur actors in Britain. About four thousand societies from every part of the country were affiliated to the British Drama League, founded in 1919 'to promote a right relation between drama and the life of the community'. The League organized an annual festival competition, with marks awarded to companies for acting, setting, costumes, and choice of play. The final stage of the competition was held in London, where the most successful companies had the thrill of appearing in a West End theatre. Even villages were taking up amateur acting; encouraged by the Women's Institutes, which held competitions of their own. The Churches had tacitly withdrawn their objections to the stage, and in many parishes the vicar himself organized amateur theatricals.

One form of entertainment in the Thirties which rapidly extended its popularity from highbrows downwards was ballet. Colonel de Basil's Russian Ballet first appeared at Covent Garden in 1934 with Léonide Massine as choreographer. De Basil had gathered his company at Monte Carlo, where they trained and performed for several years: it included several old hands from Diaghileff days and many young dancers from the ballet-schools of Paris. They performed the old Diaghileff ballets and a number of new ones: among these were two symphonic ballets, 'Les Présages', set to Tchaikowsky's Fifth Symphony, and 'Choreartium', set to Brahms' Fourth. Music-lovers disputed whether or not it was fitting to arrange dances and settings to symphonic music. Most musicians disliked the experiment; most ballet-lovers approved.

Between de Basil's, the most fashionable ballet company, and René Blum's there was bitter rivalry. Indeed, the ballet world was full of factions: there were threatened splits and law-suits within de Basil's company itself. There were also British companies, the Markova-Dolin and the Vic-Wells, and companies not in the Russian tradition, such as Trudi Schnoop's comic Swiss Ballet and the German-Dutch Expressionist Ballet Joos. Many books were written on ballet. The first and most successful of these was Arnold Haskell's *Balletomania*. Like most of its successors, it contained an historical account of ballet, an appreciation of famous dancers, summaries of the scenarios of different ballets, an explanation of the technical terms used in choreography, and an impressionistic description of how the writer was so entranced when he saw his first ballet that he became for ever afterwards a 'balletomane'—thus a new word was introduced into the English language. Few developments had taken place in ballet since Diaghileff days, but its new popularity coincided with the decline of grand opera, which to some extent it replaced as the great cultural event of London's summer season. Ballet had speed and complexity; grand opera lumbered.

Since the Twenties much private energy had gone into the application of art to industry—the intention being to give industrial products a cleaner look and neater lines. In the motor-car and domestic-heating industries and a few others this had been done most successfully. Cars now looked as if they had really been designed and not just assembled. British designers, however, never went so far as to clothe the anatomy of their machines with great, glossy, bulging curves and metal flutings in the American style. The gas companies' household models were very easy on the eye. White Ascot heaters, for example, replaced the old copper geysers with their inconvenient paraphernalia of pipes; cooking-stoves no longer looked like Victorian laboratory equipment; and pink, clean-looking waffle-shaped elements took the place of the old dirty-white, curly, spikey ones in gas fires. Telephones, too—nearly all now on automatic exchanges—were no longer upright and awkward, but compact and tolerably graceful. There were also improvements in lighting: opaque glass balls, directly attached to the ceiling or suspended from it by metal rods, compared favourably with the clumsily ornate electric chandeliers that went before; angle-poise reading-lamps that would swing and bend in any desired direction, though suggesting dentists' apparatus, were not vicious in appearance; and indirect, reflected lighting was used from several subsidiary points in a room. Where industrial design was at its worst was in any decorative effect intended to brighten up functional fittings. Lamp-shades and ash-trays were perhaps the most ornate, mean and fussy form of household decoration, though book-ends ran these very close. It was the period of the mock bronze finish to hardware and the artificial ageing of gilt and parchment. At the same time a great many famous old lines in household furnishing were either discontinued or debased. It was of melancholy interest to assemble, in series, successive variants of such outstanding products as the eighteenth-century Windsor chair, or the mid-Victorian 'Rose, Shamrock and Thistle' (mauve flowers encrusted on white) china breakfast service, or the small Regency picture-frame. The gradual deterioration of quality, design, workmanship was most remarkable. If one wanted an ordinary small brown-black teapot, a blue and white china beer-mug, or a simple-flowered small white china basin, one could only hope to find it in some old-fashioned village shop. New British lines in cheap china and glass combined the sordid with the flashy.

People who bought or rented unmodernized houses had great difficulty in buying suitable furniture and fittings for them. Unless one was rich enough to go to one of the very few shops that still employed their own craftsmen and catered for cultivated taste, the unappetizing choice was between the mass-produced mock-antique, the modernist 'gorblimey' or 'god-awful' in veneered walnut or bleached oak, tubular steel, light-coloured plywood. The only solution was to 'shop in the past' at country sales, street markets, or antique shops.

This break in tradition had an obviously depressing effect on the British Export Trade and in 1935 an 'Art in Industry' Exhibition was held at Burlington House to improve matters. One hundred thousand people attended, but the exhibits tended to reflect the dead academic taste of the old-fashioned polytechnic schools where the ghost of Ruskin still walked. The Government was then persuaded to sponsor a National Register of artists who could be recommended to manufacturers as persons of imagination, experience, and taste. The director of this extremely important venture, though starved of funds, did a great deal to improve designs in a number of industries; and made some surprising discoveries—such as that in the whole of Great Britain there was no school or art-class where one could learn the art of shoe-design—so that the very important shoe industry was dependent on France and America for new models.

In modern houses, cupboards and bookshelves were built into the walls to economize space. Windows were made of steel, and opened outwards: they let in more light and air than the old sliding sash. Walls and floors were sound-proofed. A new sort of window glass was introduced which admitted ultra-violet rays. Plate-glass was used for table-tops in homes as well as teashops. Yet, by the middle Thirties, neo-Victorianism was blending with functionalism. Curtains, bedcovers, and chaircovers no longer simulated wood, metal and concrete; losing their geometrics too, they grew delicately dotted, spotted, striped, and flowered. Even floral wallpapers came in again and Victorian knick-knacks were rescued from street-barrows for quaint effect.

It was odd that this geometric fashion in interior decoration should have passed just as the works of the Parisian 'abstract' artists of the Twenties, who had initiated it, were for the first time being put over on the British public. The leading British abstractionists now banded themselves together into a group, 'Unit One'. The sculptors were Barbara Hepworth and Henry Moore, the architects Wells Coates and Colin Lucas, and among the painters were Ben Nicholson, Edward Wadsworth, Tristram Hillier and Paul Nash. They set their faces, in a manifesto, against the 'unconscious school' (meaning Expressionism and its derivatives, which many of them had once embraced), declaring that it had completely broken away from the intellectual canons of abstract art. They offered themselves as a rallying point from which modern art, by its proved integrity, could influence modern life. A questionnaire was sent round to the members, asking what they felt (among other things) about Freud, Symbolism, and machinery. The answers revealed that Freud and Symbolism were no longer the dominating influences but that machinery had a strong attraction—stronger than that of natural scenery, because of its purposefully intricate design.

But the usual twelve-year time-lag having elapsed, there followed an importation of Surrealism from Paris. The first Surrealist Exhibition in England was held in 1936, and of course greeted in the Press with mockery and jeers. J. B. Priestley, who schooled himself as a new William Cobbett, tried to express the attitude of the average sturdy Englishman to the Surrealists: 'They stand for violence and neurotic unreason. They are truly decadent. You catch a glimpse behind them of the deepening twilight of barbarism that may soon blot out the sky, until at last humanity finds itself in another long night. . . . There are about too many effeminate or epicene young men, lisping and undulating. Too many young women without manners, balance, dignity—greedy and slobbering sensation-seekers. Too many people who are steadily lapsing into shaved and powdered barbarism. . . . Frequently they have strong sexual impulses that they soon contrive to misuse or pervert.' (This was rather like his dramatic experiments with Time: He was twelve years out of date with his remarks. But then, so were the newly made converts to Surrealism.) The attraction of Surrealism was twofold— its French connection with Communism and psycho-analysis, and the similarity between '*objets trouvés*', '*collages*', and 'constructions' and the neo-Victorian knick-knack collecting habit. The Surrealists, by the way, had made *grands maîtres* of Lewis Carroll and Edward Lear, the Victorian nonsense-writers.

Aesthetic judgements fall outside the scope of this history. However, it would be misleading to treat of painting in Britain during the period as wholly a matter of fashion, though complete commercial art was necessarily so, and since the livelihood of painters was precarious—in a B.B.C. dialogue between a layman and an art-expert it came out that not more than twelve good painters could be supported by the normal demand for their pictures—the competition for this market was intense, and regard for fashion naturally affected style. One must distinguish two sorts of fashion, to the first of which almost every painter had necessarily to make concessions—the fashion determined by the setting in which his pictures would be hung. Just as, with the decrease in the size of families and of ovens farmers had to reduce the size of the joints they offered the butchers, so pictures had to become smaller because of reduced wall-space in the houses of picture buyers. Sombre tones too, in the elder Rembrandt tradition, though they harmonized well enough with late Victorian furnishings, did not consort with neo-Georgian white walls. (Heavy gilt frames had also to be abandoned.) But the second sort of fashion, as irresponsible as the fashion in dress and similarly set in Paris, was felt by a number of British painters to be beneath their dignity.

A pleasant analogy is suggested by Savile Row. Throughout the period it set the world standard of men's tailoring as authoritatively as the Rue de la Paix set the *fashion* for women. In general the small Savile Row of British painters withstood the temptation to shelter themselves under the shield of the Royal Academy. James Pryde and William Nicholson, who as the 'Beggarstaff Brothers' before the war had first shown the possibilities of British poster-design, were the deans of the non-Academic school. Pryde continued to paint large thrillingly gloomy pictures for large houses; Nicholson turned his hand to portraiture, book-illustration, frescoes, décor for Cochran shows and anything else that came to hand, but was best known for his sedate and exquisite still-lives. Walter Greaves, in his last years as a Charterhouse Brother, also came into the period: with James Pryde, he was the last of the British Old Masters. He called himself a humble pupil of Whistler's and grossly underestimated his standing. Richard Sickert was of Savile Row too —he consented to enter the Royal Academic fold in 1934, but, like Augustus John, resigned soon afterwards because of disagreements with the hanging committee. His pictures were influenced by the late Impressionists, full of elegant shadow-work.

In the Twenties one painter of genius—in the most traditional sense of the word—appeared: young Christopher Wood. He lived a stormy life and put everything into his work. In 1927 he found his imagination 'revving' at too great a speed; he tried to keep pace by painting sixty pictures in a few weeks, then broke down. He threw himself under an express train at Salisbury station, leaving as explanation a few mysterious sentences on a slip of paper. He wrote that *living minds* were now at large on the earth—did they know who they were?

These aristocrats of painting felt committed to the task of making good pictures, not of being 'advanced' or testing theories of composition. Cedric Morris and John Aldridge were others. Morris's peculiar gift was for depicting the movements of animals and birds in delicate lines and colours. Aldridge was a landscape painter: he worked chiefly in a part of rural Essex that still retained a Tudor aspect. Then there were the Puritans, such as Paul and John Nash and Edward Bawden. They represented English provincial life and seem to have mistrusted, while admiring, the aristocracy; they had sufficient integrity to limit themselves to a narrow scrupulous vision—John Nash's engravings of poisonous plants, Bawden's cynical illustrations to Shakespeare's comedies, were in the Thomas Bewick tradition. Stanley Spencer was an abnormal case. He was a Puritan too, and seemed to regard oil-paint as somehow improper (as Milton was embarrassed by the Elizabethan tradition of poetry), but accepted the fuller gift of sight of which Bawden and the Nashes were shy; yet as a fellow-painter expressed it, 'being something of a gnome himself, he can't resist monstrosities, except in landscape'. There were also Duncan Grant and Vanessa Bell, much admired in Bloomsbury and strongly influenced by the careful but free style of Greek fresco and ceramics.

To use Army organization terms—painting is properly the I branch, intelligent reporting; poetry is properly the O branch, active decision. Both have connections with the Q branch, which covers the medium and the distributive system. The muddle into which poetry and the arts fell during the period was due to a general confusion of letters: ambitious artists, from the Futurists onwards, attempted to be O not I,; the poets of 'socio-realism' attempted to be I, not O; commercial art, literature, and music fell directly under the command of Q. Toward the end of the Thirties appeared John Piper, who abandoned the abstractionism with which he started for a truly realistic style, and the 'Euston Road' group, most of whom went back to start again from an Impressionist technique, showing that contemporary painting had solid foundations but was in no less confused a state than contemporary poetry.

Fashions in dress continued to exploit Victorian costume as a reminder to women that they were distinctly women, not mere emancipated modern creatures. Square shoulders were temporarily dropped in 1934; in some cases they were succeeded by sloping shoulders and wide necks, which gave a bottle-shaped effect. Wider and wider belts were emphasizing the increasing slenderness of waists. Sleeves were full, loose and bell-shaped, even bustle-like skirts began to appear for evening wear. The 1850's were fast creeping up on the 1890's. Jubilee Year brought even more fanciful trimmings: day skirts were gored and flared, and evening skirts lavishly draped and trained. More and more ornaments were worn: heavy jewelled belts, breast-plates of fine wire, and initial decorations in wood, leather, metal, and glass. The Chinese Exhibition was an excuse for new colours: duck-egg blue, pale green and black, scarlet and white. Hats were much influenced by the taste of the Duchess of Kent. At different times in Jubilee Year she wore a Homburg type, a Breton-sailor, a small toque-like straw with flower trimmings, a shovel-hat, and on Jubilee Day itself an immense picture-hat. All these had a wide following. It was the Duchess, too, who in 1936 popularized the fashion for eye-veils on hats, some of the finest mesh and some of coarse fish-net. In the winter of that year she was one of the first to wear the modish conical, pierrot-like caps. The death of King George V in January 1936 caused black and other sombre colours to be fashionable. These were only slightly relieved by touches of mauve and grey. Even in spring the court-mourning fashion persisted, though now mitigated by a revived enthusiasm for artificial flowers. These were worn everywhere: on hats, on lapels, on gloves, and on frocks, and tightly bunched up under the chin. Toward the end of the year, the coming Coronation began to influence colours. A new vivid blue was patriotically christened 'Royalist', a pinky mauve 'Regency', a deep crimson 'Coronation', and a more purpled crimson 'Durbar'.

For some years American film stars had set dress and hair fashions among British film-goers. In 1934, for the first time, a British picture had a similar effect: 'The Private Life of Henry VIII' started the vogue of looped, slashed, and padded sleeves, and one of the hat-crazes of the year—the Tudor halo style, usually carried out in velvet. Another spring hat was the shallow-crowned boater with streamers at the back, inspired by Katherine Hepburn in 'Little Women'. Films played a large part in the Victorian revival. The hair-dressing styles of the Eighties were introduced by 'The House of Rothschild' and by Anna Sten in 'Lady of the Boulevards'—her hair done like one of Manet's Parisian barmaids. 'The Great Ziegfield' in 1936 set a lush, romantic fashion that affected colours, materials, and designs. The film version of *Romeo and Juliet* produced the Juliet cap, the Juliet frock, long, demure and generally made of velvet, and the Juliet bob, in which the hair was parted in the middle and fell almost to the shoulders in long, heavy curls. These were put on the market before the film was released, as part of its publicity campaign. They were rapidly taken up: every shop now had to stock replicas of film-stars' hats and dresses and shoes. Upper-class women still looked to Paris for their fashions, but the working girl to Hollywood.

CHAPTER TWENTY-ONE

Three Kings in One Year

—————

There had been no entertaining news-stories in the Press for some time. The Talking Mongoose broke the spell. Reports had been published some years previously that the house of a farmer named Irving, in the Isle of Man, was visited by a talking mongoose. Harry Price, the psychic research expert, became interested in the case, and went there to investigate. With him went R. S. Lambert, editor of the *Listener*, who was an amateur student of psychic phenomena. The Irving family told these two that the mongoose had at first made meaningless noises, and developed the power of speech only after coaxing. It had then told them that its name was Gef and that it was of Eastern origin. It knew a smattering of foreign languages and used to sing nursery rhymes. Its greatest friend in the household was the Irvings' daughter, whom it used to accompany on rabbit hunts, but all the family claimed to have seen it from time to time and to have heard it talk. When Price and Lambert were present, however, the mongoose remained invisible; the Irvings explained that it had positively refused to appear in the presence of those who doubted its existence. Price and Lambert assured the shy animal that they did not doubt, but this did not tempt it to materialize; and they had to content themselves with examining the only evidence offered—a few blurred photographs, in which the animal was indistinguishable from the hillside, and some hairs and footprints, which were not unlike a dog's. On their return to London, Price and Lambert published, under the title of *The Haunting of Cashen's Gap*, a circumstantial account of the mongoose story. In it they discussed the possibility of poltergeist activity on the part of the Irvings' daughter, and suggested that a deliberately created family legend might have taken such hold that the family itself had come to believe in it; yet they did not entirely rule out the possibility of the Irvings' account being a true one.

The mongoose story was good enough to take from the book page and put into the secondary news columns; but it made the front page when it figured in a libel action brought by Lambert against Sir Cecil Levita. Sir Cecil was a member of the L.C.C. and of the committee which advised the Home Office on matters of Film Censorship. The action arose out of disagreements at the Film Institute, of which Lambert was a director, and in which Sir Cecil and his wife were interested. These disagreements led Sir Cecil to allege that Lambert was not a fit person to be a director; among other things he instanced Lambert's supposed credulity in the matter of the talking mongoose. The matter did not remain a private one, for Sir Cecil made contact with B.B.C. officials, and Lambert felt that his position as editor of the *Listener* was being endangered. The B.B.C. Council acted somewhat equivocally; at first it advised Lambert to settle the problem amicably, and then, when that proved out of the question, warned him that he was prejudicing his position with them by persisting in bringing an action. The B.B.C., in fact, felt the matter to be so important that Sir John Reith himself took a hand in the negotiations; however, Lambert could not be dissuaded from suing, won his case, and was awarded the enormous sum of £7,500 damages. He also kept his position on the *Listener*.

The newspapers made the most of the talking mongoose evidence in the case. After it was over an official inquiry was held into the conduct of the B.B.C., commemorated by Low with cartoons of 'Sir John Mongoose and the Trained Reiths' and 'The B.B.C. Haunted'. The Board of Inquiry apportioned the blame all round, but admonished the B.B.C. not to allow the personal freedom of its staff to be unduly limited by loyalty to the Corporation. For several years some of the B.B.C. staff had imagined that their private lives were being too much supervised, their letters opened, their movements watched, even their telephone lines tapped. Matters now improved.

B.B.C. programmes were still too serious for a large part of
the population; on Sundays they were gloomily puritanical and
almost everyone then switched across to Radio Luxemburg and
Radio Normandie, stations which gave light popular music and
variety turns, sponsored by advertisers. The B.B.C. could not
complain of an infringement of its monopoly: for the recordings,
though made in London, were transmitted from the Continent,
and any new British radio licenses taken out by fans of these
stations benefited only the B.B.C.; but it was hurt in its pride.
The Press felt hurt in its pockets: the Press Barons grudged
money spent on radio advertising that would normally have
been spent on newspaper advertising. The only newspaper
which had printed Radio Luxemburg programmes was the
Sunday Referee—one of the few papers independent of the big
Press combines. The Newspaper Proprietors' Association tried
to stop it from doing so in 1934, and when it refused expelled it
from membership. This meant that it could no longer benefit
from the co-operative distributing arrangements which the
Association ran. The *Referee* found it worth while to continue
its publication of Luxemburg programmes for the next three
years; but at last the sales-organization of the newspaper combines proved too strong. It found itself gradually losing its
advertisements and, abandoning Luxemburg, humbly pleaded
for readmission to the Association. The public never came to
know of the pressure and counter-pressure exercised in the
Luxemburg controversy. Newspapers now seldom washed their
dirty linen in public. But Radio Luxemburg was not closed
down until 1939.

In the spring of 1936, as it was said, there was 'mud on someone's dress-shirt'. The Budget of that year raised income-tax by
threepence and the tea-tax by twopence. Somehow news of
these increases leaked out just before Budget Day and there was
speculation in insurance against them on the Stock Exchange.
J. H. Thomas, then Lord Privy Seal, and his son, were strongly
rumoured to have been the channels of the leakage. Thomas
immediately asked for an official inquiry to be made. This was
granted, and after investigation the official tribunal reported,
despite the strong denials of all concerned, that there had been
an unauthorized disclosure by J. H. Thomas to Sir Alfred Butt,
the theatre magnate, and a colleague of his named Bates, who

had been spending the week-end with him. The tribunal found that they had made use of the information for 'private gain'. Thomas's son was completely exonerated, and Thomas himself excused on the grounds that his disclosure merely took the form of an indiscreet hint, and was not to be judged hardly. Though not prosecuted, he was compelled to retire into private life, with the condolences of all other Cabinet Ministers.

This was a big story for the Press, but there was another altogether too big for them to handle or even to hint at: King Edward VIII's friendship with Mrs. Wallis Simpson. For fifty years the Press had agreed not to attack Royalty or mention its foibles; Royalty was not fair game because, by etiquette, forbidden to reply. The last recorded offence was by a famous sporting sheet in the Nineties which headed its news column one week with the gratuitous statement that there was 'nothing whatever between the Prince of Wales and Lily Langtry' and the next week with the apparently unrelated remark: 'Not even a sheet.' The Press now chose to impose a censorship upon itself, for though the King wished the matter to be no secret from the public, the Cabinet was so embarrassed that it refused the Press official directions as to what line to take. Mrs. Simpson had occasionally been mentioned in Court Circulars, and one or two photographs of her in the company of the King and other friends had appeared at the time of his Mediterranean holiday on the yacht *Nahlin*, but she had not been publicized in any other way. Meanwhile, British subscribers to American magazines and readers of the Communist edited *The Week*, a postally distributed news-letter, were learning of her friendship with the King, of the King's intention to marry her, and of the constitutional crisis that was brewing. Speculators immediately began buying up the leases of houses on the fringe of Regent's Park near the Marylebone Road: Mrs Simpson was known to be installing herself there. The public at large knew nothing. When the *News Chronicle* in the autumn splashed the report that Mrs. Simpson was going to Ipswich to obtain a divorce, few of its readers knew what this implied, or troubled to inquire. The *Daily Telegraph* and other newspapers kept the news small. Ipswich and the Assize Judge himself were surprised by the crowds of American reporters, plain-clothes men, K.C.s, and by the general hugger-mugger at this undefended and unsensational case. A decree *nisi* was granted. An emergency Cabinet Meeting was called on 28th November 1936, but what it met to consider was not officially announced—in fact, hints were thrown out of a crisis in the Mediterranean.

The news broke from the pulpit. Dr. Blunt, Bishop of Bradford, attacked the King in a sermon, urging him to be more of a Christian, like his father. The Press seized the opportunity to reveal the whole story. The startled country was told that the King intended to marry a Mrs. Simpson, after having raised her to the peerage as Duchess of Lancaster. Yet what sort of person was this Mrs. Simpson? And who was Mr. Simpson? The Press did not commit itself to more than the barest biographical details.

The situation was complicated politically by the recent newspaper treatment of the King's visit to South Wales. During this visit he had expressed surprise and horror at the living conditions in the Special Areas and declared that 'something must be done' The *Daily Mail* thereupon made a contrast between the King's energy and the National Government's inactivity, and this view took a strong hold on the country. The semi-official *Times* on November 24th took the trouble to deny a rumour that the King's visit to Wales had been made against the advice of his Ministers.

Baldwin, meanwhile, had called a Cabinet Meeting to discuss the situation, and on November 26th told his colleagues that the King wished them to take legislative action which would permit him to marry Mrs. Simpson, but without making her his Queen, and resign all claims to the Throne on behalf of their putative issue. The Cabinet unanimously decided that such action would be unconstitutional. Next, the Dominion Governments were asked for their opinion, and their replies showed that in the Empire a doubly divorced woman was not considered a suitable Royal consort. Dominion feeling carried great weight because the person of the King was now the Empire's only remaining political link. But this feeling was not confined to the Dominions: *The Times* expressed it plainly, and it was a commonplace that what *The Times* was writing the Government was usually thinking.

On the night of December 1st a fiery omen was seen from Central London in the south-eastern sky. The word went round that the Crystal Palace was on fire. Everyone who could hurried there in buses, trains, and cars. The Crystal Palace, the Palladium of Victorianism, had been one of the sights of London ever since its original erection for the Great Exhibition in Hyde Park in 1851; but Sydenham was rather an inconvenient place to get at and the interior of the building was growing sadly dilapidated. Its principal uses now were as a hall for brass-band and choir competitions, dog and cat shows and the like—the grounds were chiefly devoted to football and November 5th fireworks. What to do with the Crystal Palace had long been a moot point. Sir Edwin Lutyens, the architect and President of the Royal Academy, drily suggested that it 'should be preserved in a glass case for posterity'. The fire, the most spectacular one of the century, completely destroyed the main building and only the twin towers at either end were left standing. The current rumour was that the Palace had been deliberately fired, as offering a too prominent landmark for German bombers.

On December 3rd the crisis was for the first time aired in the Press. The *Daily Herald* went much further in its opposition to the King's plan than most of the pro-Government papers. This was because the Labour Party was supported in ex-Liberal constituencies by a large number of Nonconformists: in the north of England particularly they were shocked at the idea that the King proposed to marry not only a commoner, but also a foreigner and a divorced woman. (British public characters, especially politicians, had to live very careful private lives to pass the scrutiny of the Nonconformists: how careful, was shown in the early Twenties when Asquith succeeded in picking a Derby winner by careful comparison of pedigrees—and had to protect himself with a public statement that he had not backed his judgement by so much as a sixpenny bet.) Discussion led nowhere, however, and still nobody told the public what to think. Baldwin took his customary refuge in the silence of 'sealed lips'; and the country and the Empire were left to the mercy of rumour.

Most ordinary people were for the King; most important people were against him. Churchill expressed the ordinary point of view when he accused the Prime Minister in the House of betraying both the King and Parliament. The Beaverbrook Press followed the same line, its aim being as much to get rid of Baldwin as to support the King. Intrigues became complicated: it was rumoured that Beaverbrook and Churchill were pressing the King not to give way to the Cabinet. Churchill was mentioned as an alternative Prime Minister; if he were gainsaid in the Commons, it was felt, he could carry the country with him in a general election. Sixty M.P.s were supposed to have written to the King, pledging their support. Nevertheless, nobody could tell how a general election would go, nor how the Dominions would react if Churchill were successful. The risk was not run.

On December 4th Baldwin took a firm line: he announced that the Government must refuse the King's wish, since legislation could not be introduced to permit such a special kind of marriage—the King's wife must automatically be Queen and her offspring heirs to the Throne. The feeling that the King was getting a raw deal from his Ministers was openly expressed. That night diners rose at restaurants and addressed the tables, proposing a loyal toast which nobody could refuse; and crowds paraded the streets shouting 'God save the King from Mr. Baldwin!'

For the next few days the newspapers were full of the 'Grave Constitutional Crisis', but it could not be foreseen what would happen. A black gloom spread throughout the country, with a most depressing effect on trade. Rumours now went round that the King was seeing more of Mrs. Simpson than was proper for a woman with a decree *nisi*, and a Common Informer complicated matters by lodging a statement which, if investigated by the King's Proctor, and proved true, would have prevented the divorce from being made absolute. The King was said to be consulting with Queen Mary and the Royal Family; and to believe that his subjects would not let him be overruled by the Cabinet in his choice of a wife. Whatever the feelings of Queen Mary and other members of the Royal Family may have been, there was certainly strong opposition among the officials at Buckingham Palace. They had resented the King's departure from the rigid standard of church-going behaviour which his father had set, and criticized his habit of spending week-ends at his estate in Fort Belvedere, where one of his favourite occupations, said to have been encouraged by Mrs. Simpson, was pottering about the gardens in shabby flannels. They were even more indignant that the King had dismissed some of their own number and replaced them with upstart youngsters. It was also alleged that he was impatient of dull functions and had even on occasion, by ordering the drastic curtailment of a musical programme, hurt the feelings of the loyal performers. And how insensate an act it had been to remove from Windsor Great Park the herd of Royal Goats that had pastured there for generations and confine the poor creatures to a pen at the Zoo!

After hurried conferences with the Royal Family and with his Ministers, the King left London to stay at Fort Belvedere; and Mrs. Simpson, to preserve herself and the King from further scandal, went to France. She was said to have begged him not to give up his throne for her. Baldwin's lips, meanwhile, were again sealed. In the Commons he was greeted with cheering, but when asked by Attlee to make a statement, replied that it was inexpedient. The suspense continued. At a mass meeting in the Albert Hall crowds cheered Churchill and fervently sang 'God Save the King'. The Press, however, was dropping hints of the way things were going: the *Daily Mail* even dared to mention the word Abdication. On the morning of December 8th there was a confident rumour that the King, who in a recruiting speech during the war had urged the men of Britain to put their Country before their womenfolk, would show his patriotism by giving up Mrs. Simpson; that afternoon it was rumoured, just as confidently, that he would not. An advertisement appeared in the *Bradford Telegraph and Argus*: 'The King may abdicate, but with the love for Dixon's jams and pickles the family sticks together like the Empire.'

The Times urged the King to make up his mind, and put the blame on him for the excited and puzzled state of public opinion. Harry Pollitt, the Communist leader, in a speech at Cambridge, denounced the Government: 'The spectacle of the National Government laying down a code of morals and behaviour for the King is indeed a sight. . . . There is no crisis in all this business for the working class. Let the King marry whom he likes. That is his personal business.' But it would have taken more than a Communist to persuade people to be indifferent. In London crowds packed Downing Street, chanting 'We want our King', and at Woolworth's the Edward VIII Coronation mugs were rapidly sold out. Unlike Pollitt, Mosley set himself and his Blackshirts on the side of Royalty. He had thousands of leaflets distributed which declared that the British Union of Fascists stood firmly behind the King. This was a disservice to the King's cause. It gave the conservative-minded the opportunity to utter warnings against the country's being split into two factions—Parliament and the King's Friends; public opinion was already bitterly divided by the Spanish problem, and if the constitutional crisis were to aggravate the division it might mean civil war for Britain too. Further pressure was put on the King to make up his mind, and his resentful silence was taken advantage of by his enemies to set a strong rumour going that he had drunk himself insensible and was only saved from death by the timely use of a stomach pump.

The end came on December 10th. At 3.35 Baldwin entered the House of Commons and read the Royal message of Abdication. The House received the news in silence; the country felt stunned. The strongest rumour of the week then ran around that the Duke of York would refuse the Throne, from fraternal loyalty, and that it would pass to the Princess Elizabeth, with Queen Mary as Regent. These were the two most popular members of the Royal Family and with the rumour went the observation that England had never been so well off as when it was ruled by women. Everyone felt suddenly cheerful again. In the evening the King, now Prince Edward, introduced by Sir John Reith himself, broadcast his farewell speech to the nation in an angry, tragic, harsh voice. He gave up his Throne, he said, because he could not be happy without the woman he loved, and he commended to his former subjects his brother, King George VI: 'God bless you, and God save the King.' Next morning he left England in the destroyer *Fury*, and went to stay in Austria with Baron Rothschild. His reign had lasted for 325 days. The upper-class Conservatives were deeply relieved when the Duke of York succeeded; he was known to conform to the conventional type of constitutional monarch. The Stock Exchange rallied, trade revived, and the Common Informer obligingly withdrew his statement, admitting that he had been mistaken.

The ex-King, now the Duke of Windsor, was not allowed to pass into retirement without recrimination. The Archbishop of Canterbury censured him immediately after his departure for

having had tastes not consonant with the dignity of a constitutional monarch, and for having neglected his duty to the Church.
This attack caused a strong recrudescence of feeling in favour of
the Duke. He had been through a difficult time, it was felt, and
it was 'bad form to kick a man when he's down'. The campaign
which the Archbishop had hoped to inaugurate for a revival of
church-going failed ignominiously.

The Press, for the next six months, printed little news about
the Duke, except occasional photographs of him in Austria and
of Mrs. Simpson in the south of France. He was pushed out of
the limelight, so that the personality of his brother, hitherto
scarcely known to the public, could be slowly and tactfully built
up to kingly dimensions. Most people believed that they could
never have the same feelings for King George VI as for his
father, or his brother. The Left rejoiced that the Abdication had
at last served to break down the atmosphere of hysterical mysticism with which the Royal Family had been surrounded. No
more, they said, would kings be looked upon as anything but
human.

The *Daily Telegraph* summed up the year 1936 on December
31st with:

'Certain years in history seem to have been desperately
charged with Fate. Of their number is the year whose last
hours are now passing. It is not that 1936 will be memorable
by the magnitude of its actual catastrophes. But it has abounded
in events which have seemed to bring catastrophe near. Serious
alarms at home, graver alarms abroad, a deepening sense of
gathering storm, feverish military, naval and aerial preparations, revolution and civil war have kept Europe continually on
tenterhooks. That there are more white stones in the British
record than in the general European is matter rather for thankfulness than for pride. Yet the British people have not escaped
affliction. Within a single twelvemonth three Kings have reigned
over us. . . .'

The Coronation of King George VI was fixed for the 12th
May 1937, the same date as had been fixed for King Edward
VIII's. The Coronation was to be a far grander and more impressive spectacle than the Jubilee of two years before. To the
splendid official street-decorations householders and shop-
owners added a bewildering variety of their own. A rare excep-

tion was Bond Street, the whole of which was worthily dressed by one architect. The large stores in London tried to outdo one another in the matter of Union Jacks, coloured banners, and bunting, boxes of red, white and blue flowers, huge placard portraits of the King and Queen, pictures of stirring scenes from Empire history, and gigantic plaster casts of symbolic statuary. By a common verdict, Selfridge's took first prize. There is a story that a policeman said to an old lady who had been staring at the decorations continuously for half an hour on Coronation Night: 'No, madam, Mr. Selfridge will not be appearing on the balcony to-night!' An Indian Rajah was so impressed by them that he bought them as they stood for re-erection on his own palace. Vast crowds came to Town: one thousand special trains arrived on Coronation Day alone, and fleets of charabancs. The newspapers printed full descriptions of the complicated ceremony to take place in Westminster Abbey. The rejoicing was more formal and less spontaneous than at the Jubilee. The Abdication had shaken people; also there was a general belief that the King's health was bad and that he suffered from a serious speech defect. This the newspapers roundly denied. They tried hard to associate George VI with George V in popular sympathy. The *Daily Express* wrote on Coronation Day: 'We have not known him long, but long enough to discover in him some of the steady, sterling stuff that made his father the most beloved Englishman of his generation.' He was to carry on the tradition of kindly kingship—non-political, non-social and, in general behaviour, above criticism. The wits even said that his chin was already showing signs of a beard. References to the Duke of Windsor were officially taboo. Some slum-dwellers in East London, however, hung up banners which read: 'God bless our King and Queen AND the Duke of Windsor.' A Roman Catholic publisher's advertisement referred obliquely to recent events in a quotation from Shakespeare: 'Now is the winter of our discontent made glorious by this summer sun of York.'

Huge crowds waited all night along the route that the procession was to take on Coronation Day, some even setting up camp-beds in the street. Seats in buildings, in stands, and in hotels overlooking the route had been sold long in advance often at profiteering prices. The night was fine, and so, fortun-

ately, was the morning. Peers wearing their coronets and ceremonial robes and M.P.s in hired costumes were crammed
together into a special Underground train which carried them
from Kensington High Street to Westminster. There were eight
hundred of them, and the fare was threepence a head.

The Crowned Heads of Europe were most of them present, or
represented by their Heir Apparents, but the complicated international situation was reflected in the absence of any member of
the House of Savoy—the King of Italy's new title as Emperor of
Abyssinia went unrecognized—in the representation of Germany
not by a Nazi but by an Army officer, and in the ironical presence of a Spanish Republican Minister. The Press concentrated
its descriptive reporting on the impressive robes of African chiefs
such as the Nigerian Alake of Abeokuta, and the Paramount
Chief of Barotseland; and on the soldierly bearing of the Canadian contingent that mounted guard at Buckingham Palace
for the first time in history, and of the other Imperial troops.
The great golden Coronation Coach itself, first used by George
III in 1762, trundled archaically down smooth parquetted
streets between high, grimy Portland stone buildings. It was
drawn by the famous team of Windsor greys. Reporters, looking
for the human touch, were pleased to notice Peers sneaking out
of the Abbey for a smoke during the ceremony, and bored pages
teasing one another. They also remarked that the Bible provided
for the rehearsal had proved too heavy for the aged Bishop of
Norwich, whose task it was to carry it, and that a lighter one
had been substituted. The American touch was provided by
Neile Vanderbilt, the millionaire's son. He had secured a ticket
for the Abbey, and during the ceremony was seen to be praying
constantly into his waistcoat: where he was broadcasting a commentary through a pocket radio transmitter. This was picked
up by his trailer, parked a few hundred yards away, and from
there transmitted direct to the United States—a magnificent
scoop, for no broadcasting but the B.B.C.'s had been allowed
from the Abbey.

After the ceremony a crowd of one hundred thousand gathered outside Buckingham Palace and cheered; the Royal Family
appeared four times in all to greet it—the first time they were
wearing their Coronation robes, crowns, and coronets. That
evening the King made a broadcast speech, in which he dedi-

cated himself to National Service. It was noted with relief that his voice, though hesitant, carried well and that he only showed one slight trace of a stammer. Later there were half-hearted attempts at dancing in the streets, but rain put an early end to them; and in any case most people were in a hurry to start for home, because there was a London bus-strike in progress. At one time it had been feared that the Underground railwaymen would come out in sympathy, but this danger was averted. Rather than cast a gloom on the Coronation proceedings, the Press had played down the bus-strike and contented itself with publishing pictures of people walking cheerfully to work. On the whole the public felt no grudge against the busmen. It was easy to sympathize with them over their long hours of heavy driving in crowded streets with speeded-up time-tables. The expectation of life for Metropolitan bus-drivers was said to be the shortest in any ordinary trade or calling—the country clergy had the highest. The trouble was ulcers of the stomach, due to nervous strain, hasty meals, and fumes from exhausts.

The organization of the Coronation traffic was so flawless that almost the only fatal street accident recorded was the death in Bird Cage Walk of an elderly Australian V.C., knocked down by a boy on a bicycle a day or two beforehand. When all was over, requests for souvenirs of the official decorations came in at the rate of eight thousand a day. The crowns from the masts erected in the Mall fetched £1 each; Abbey stools 25s. The succession of Royal events, the Jubilee, Accession of King Edward VIII, Abdication, and Coronation had also caused a boom in philately. On the day of the Abdication, the stocks of Edward VIII stamps were completely sold out in many post offices. By the end of 1937 Jubilee stamps of Great Britain and the Empire were fetching £20 a set. Coronation stamps were equally popular, and not only among stamp-collectors—ordinary people wanted them as souvenirs. The commonest attitude to the Coronation was to regard it as a solemn historical pageant, to be seen and stored in the memory: not an enjoyable entertainment but a dividing line between two periods—for most people still liked to think of periods in terms of Kings' reigns. They were not far out. Behind lay nearly nineteen years of difficult peace-time development; ahead lay the two crisis years that preceded the new war. There was no factious or disloyal manifestation anywhere in the British

Commonwealth of Nations except in Ireland: one was made at Dublin by the Irish Republican Army, the recalcitrant rump of the old I.R.A., which had repudiated the compromises of Cosgrave and de Valera with the British authorities and persisted in demanding complete Republican independence for Ireland. On Coronation Day the I.R.A. blew up the statue of George II, as a symbolic act.

On the day after the Coronation there was a State Banquet at the Palace, more cheering crowds outside, another balcony appearance. On May 19th a drive to the Guildhall for lunch with the Lord Mayor of London. Later in the month, a review of the Fleet at Spithead, at which eighteen foreign nations were represented by their warships. The King sailed around the Fleet in his yacht on a tour of inspection and boarded the flagship, where he sent out an order for the 'main brace to be spliced'. This occasion was remarkable for a commentary on the nighttime illuminations of the Fleet by the B.B.C. The commentator, who was himself a naval officer, began to speak at 10.45. He was so overcome by emotion and the sudden dizzying effect of the night air after drinking the King's health below, that all he could say was: 'The Fleet's lit up. . . . I mean with fairy lights. . . . When I say lit up, I mean outlined with tiny lights. . . .' When the lights of the Fleet went out he added incoherently: 'Now the whole ruddy Fleet is gone. . . . Nothing between me but sea and sky. . . . Nothing between me but sea and sky. . . .' The B.B.C. faded him out, and on the next day published the laconic announcement that the commentary had proved unsatisfactory. The newspapers made as much as they could of the incident in a guarded way.

The Coronation festivities in country villages were celebrated in traditional style. A Coronation Committee would usually be chosen at a parish meeting and convened in the parlour of the principal inn. Often, a commentator noted, there was a vacant chair at the top of the long oak table. 'In former days this would have been awaiting the Squire; to-day all too frequently the big house stands empty. The prime mover now is the resident clergyman or doctor, or the senior retired officer of the neighbourhood.' At one typical village the proposals debated were: 'a fancy-dress procession, the planting of a tree, a May Queen, fireworks, etc.' It was first decided to plant a tree in the centre of the Village Green. The gardener to the local retired Colonel then wrote to the Vicar as Chairman of the Committee:

Reverend Sir:

To plant a tree at the Coronation of our King and Queen in May is very pathetic, as it is the wrong time of year to plant trees.

Yours obediently,

JOHN BROWN, MR.

The Committee ignored the letter but decided to ask permission for the planting from the Parish Council; which after deliberation reported that it could find no title deeds to the Green—it belonged to the village only by immemorial tradition —and refused to do anything out of order on so solemn an occasion! No tree was therefore planted. However, a May Queen was chosen from among the village schoolgirls, and a Ladies' Committee appointed to discuss the material and length of the train of her dress and those of the Maids of Honour. Some-one remembered that the old maypole from the 1911 Coronation was still lying about in the tithe barn. It was hauled out and re-erected in the middle of the Green, title deeds or none. The children were taught to dance round it, holding red, white, and blue ribbons, plaiting them as they danced to the tune of 'Come, Lassies and Lads!' The British Legion of ex-Servicemen provided marshals, wearing red silk sashes, for the festivities and undertook to give, as a main feature of the day, a tableau: 'The Army down the Ages'. The Procession, headed by the May Queen, would include trade turn-outs, decorated perambulators, the Silver Band. Also it was arranged that the local bus-proprietor, 'in one of his father's great box-coats flung wide, a beaver hat, top-boots, and a Union Jack waistcoat, would drive, as John Bull, a wagonette-party dressed symbolically as the League of Nations'. A prize was also offered for the best decorated house.

On Coronation morning an ambitious peal was rung on the church bells and most of the village went to church. The local brewery company had brewed a specially strong Coronation ale which was drunk to the King's and Queen's health after the service, with three hearty cheers led by the vicar. Then the Maypole Dance, and the tableau. In the afternoon there were village sports: these included a race for veterans handicapped according to their age, a Band race in which the performers had to play their instruments as they ran, a fifty-yards race for children under seven, a tug-of-war between married and single. A Tip-and-run cricket match was also played, and a free repast provided for all the children in a great marquee, with seed-cake, buns, and tea out of Coronation mugs. In the evening, a torch-light procession, fireworks, and a great bonfire on the church hill. The men of the village, perfectly sober on all other occasions, were by now rolling drunk under the renewed influence of the Coronation ale, but showed this only in their extraordinary friendliness and in their insistence on telling the same story again and again.

After the Coronation festivities the King followed the normal routine of constitutional monarchs, his official appearances being limited to the inspection of factories, regiments, camps and hospitals, and opening new buildings. But in July 1938, with the Queen, he paid a week's State visit to Paris, which was celebrated in French and British newspapers as a sign of close Franco-British co-operation. In March 1939 President Lebrun and his wife returned the visit, and spent some festive days in London. Among other functions they attended a grand gala performance at the Royal Opera House at Covent Garden. A B.B.C. commentator on this event—the daughter-in-law of an ex-Lord Mayor of London—drew attention to Mme Lebrun's homely appearance by saying enthusiastically that 'she did not look a *bit* out of place!' In May 1939 began the six weeks' Royal tour of Canada, which included a brief visit to Washington and to New York. Canadian loyalty was stirred by the cheerful assiduity of the King and Queen in attending the numerous public functions arranged for them, and American pride and curiosity tickled to welcome the first British King to set foot in the New World. The French and Canadian and American visits proved the King's capacity to play the public rôle of his father without apparent impatience; but it was the Queen who roused the crowds' greatest admiration. In Paris and in Washington she was proclaimed charming, graceful, and regally dressed; and that she could make a simple, moving speech she showed at the launching of the liner *Queen Elizabeth* at Glasgow on September 27th, the day before the Munich conference was announced.

The King and Queen and the Princesses were made a symbol of simple, well-regulated family life. 'As used in the Royal Nursery' was a sure-selling recommendation for teething biscuits, baby soap, perambulator accessories, and the like. The King's genuine interest in Boy Scouts was also approved. The most popular act that the Royal Family ever performed was 'Under the Spreading Chestnut Tree', a song with gestures, at the Duke of York's Camp for Boys. It was recorded on a news reel. The King wore an open-necked shirt, the Queen had no hat on and the two Princesses were dressed in simple blouses and skirts. The King, as song leader, spread out his hands for 'spreading', touched his chest for 'chest' and his head for 'nut', and branched his arms for 'tree'. It was fine!

The Duke of Windsor came back into the news after the Coronation. His departure from Austria to join Mrs. Simpson in France as soon as her decree *nisi* was made absolute, and their quiet wedding at Candé on the 3rd June 1937, were both decently featured in the popular Press, though *The Times* and the *Daily Telegraph* almost ignored them. Official news-sources in England during the next three years continued to divert public attention from the Duke and Duchess: the vehemence of several books on the subject of the Abdication—violently pro-Duke, anti-Baldwin, and anti-Church—suggested this as a wise course. Compton Mackenzie, the novelist and Scottish Nationalist, was a leading King's Friend: he took up the cause of the 'King across the Water' with Jacobite intensity. As late as May 1939 the B.B.C. refused to transmit the Duke's speech at Verdun, which was therefore broadcast only to the United States; and about the same time a penny mazagine was hawked in the London streets by the Octavian Society, founded to 'combat all ungenerous treatment of the Duke of Windsor and to assure fit recognition of his long and able service to the British peoples'.

The Duke, however, almost invited ungenerous treatment. He decided to study social services in Germany and in the United States, and unfortunately chose to visit Germany first and meet Hitler in person. This meeting was misunderstood, and the Duke accused of having Nazi sympathies. The select Press contented itself with describing his visit as 'ill-advised' but contrived to imply that Britain was lucky to be rid of a King who was now showing totalitarian leanings. Some American news-papers expressed this view openly and in strong terms. They were indignant not only that the Duke had gone first to Germany but that one of his chief American friends and advisers was the exponent of an unpopular factory speed-up system. Warned that he would have a bad reception, the Duke cancelled his American visit, and abandoned all efforts to live a helpful public life. He passed the next years quietly and was seldom in the news even as a minor mention. The current rumour was that he would return to England only if his wife were granted the title of Royal Highness.

Perhaps the most curiously old-fashioned feature of the Windsor affair was the puritanical attitude to divorce which it revealed to be still widespread in Britain. This antagonism was aroused again in the summer of 1937, when A. P. Herbert, the novelist, dramatist, *Punch* jokester, and now a member of Parliament for Oxford University, succeeded in having passed what began as a most progressive Divorce Bill. There was so much opposition in both Houses to this 'assault on the sanctity of wedlock' that in the end it was doubtful whether the Bill as commended had been worth the trouble. Herbert had publicized his intentions beforehand in a best-selling novel, *Holy Deadlock*, which told of an ill-assorted couple's miserable experiences in trying to get unmarried. However, divorce for desertion was simplified, though one was only entitled to sue after three years of married life; and divorce after three years, also, where one's spouse was certified as incurably insane.

In Coronation year the Queen's taste was allowed to rule fashion: which implied 'feminine grace in colour, line, and style'. The Queen had had a good old-fashioned Scottish upbringing, and was almost as conservative in her tastes as Queen Mary. Evening skirts were long and flowing, bodices becomingly moulded, and necklines cut low. Day frocks and suits were slim and neatly tailored. Light powder-blue, the Queen's favourite colour, was loyally worn and for those who could afford it there was plum-coloured velvet trimmed with ermine. But as the 'next war' drew nearer, so did the end of the 'period'-period—it caught up with itself. Neo-Victorianism in fashion had run from the 1850–60 crinoline forward to the dress-styles of 1880–90. In the summer of 1938 the Duchess of Kent, who had moved with her father in the advanced artistic circles of Paris, and was always one stage ahead of Society, introduced the Edwardian mode. Frocks, suits, and hair-dressing styles were influenced by it: at the end of the year an Edwardian coiffure called 'The Bathtub Style' was worn, evening dresses had Gibson Girl silhouettes, and there were high-crowned, wide-brimmed hats and tiny top knots. But while fashionable women were whipping time on its second lap over the old course and leaving their rivals ten years behindhand in a week, there could no longer be a single fashion. Almost anything was worn, from the simply modern to the elaborately fancy-dress. 'Everyone' had quite different styles for successive days of the week; one evening a flowing, looped and knotted creation, and the next, perhaps, an informal print-frock in the Bali style. (Bali, in the Dutch East Indies, had recently become fashionable for its dances, music, clothes, climate, and beautiful girls. Rich British and Americans flocked there and came back with gaily coloured Bali-esque prints. Periodically certain islands exerted such a fashionable spell. Capri had been popularized by Norman Douglas's *South Wind* in the early Twenties, the Balearics by the lowness of the peseta in 1930-3. But when the Balearics could no longer be visited because of the Spanish War, or Capri because of the Mediterranean Crisis, Bali had its day. For the rich it had the advantage of being so far away from Europe that the middle-class tourist and the hungry painter could never afford to overrun it.)

Then there were trousers. When a woman got into 'slacks' now, it was not a sign of masculinity or bravado: it was merely to show that she was off duty for the moment, so far as fashion was concerned. 'Slacks' had been an Army term for trousers worn off duty instead of breeches or kilt. Most younger women had a pair or two, and the innovation evoked strangely little protest in any quarter. The newspapers printed benign warnings to outsize women that trousers did not suit their figures; but otherwise made no fuss. The Church withheld comment.

Women's shoes, which all these years had been the one fairly stable element in dress, had now also gone a little queer. The brightly coloured canvas and string sandal of 1935 and the abruptly square-toed walking shoe of 1936 were followed by a high-heeled fancy shoe with cut-away toe, and a wedge-heeled streamlined type. All these could be worn in town. At the very end of the period shoe-madness was concentrated in the heels: anything went, from monumental scrolls to golf-tees.

Royal influence on men's fashions was not so marked as on women's. The Duke of Windsor, when Prince of Wales, had popularized many unconventional modes—shorts, slacks, and open-necked shirts, for instance—and had once shocked the Navy by going hatless aboard a warship—which made it impossible for him to acknowledge the salute due to his rank. But King George VI, though he dressed well, was no *arbiter elegantiarum*. At the Royal Command Variety Show in 1938, he wore black 'patent-leather Oxford brogues' with formal evening dress; but it was not clear whether he was trying to set a new fashion or whether his valet had handed him the wrong pair of shoes by mistake—perhaps the latter, for he did not repeat the experiment.

However, Anthony Eden, the Foreign Secretary, had reintroduced the black Homburg hat, known as the 'Eden' in Savile Row—and as the 'Lord Eden' in Amsterdam—and the white linen waistcoat worn with a lounge suit. Men's hats, on the whole, had become less formal: provincial clerks still wore their bowlers and working-men their caps, but more and more London business men and salesmen were wearing soft-brimmed, variously coloured Homburgs with unbound edges. Low-crowned pork-pie hats were in fashion again and green Tyrolese hats, introduced by the Duke of Windsor, with feathers and cord bands instead of ribbon. Eden's moustache and those of such film stars as Ronald Colman, William Powell, and Clark Gable were imitated: the new moustache was small, short and carefully cut, sometimes slightly curved above the lip at either end, sometimes making a thin straight line.

New materials were being used for men's trousers—sackcloth for the summer and corduroy for the winter. Corduroys had hitherto been reserved for artists and working-men; but most working men in fact wore blue overalls over ordinary clothes. Trousers were cut close to the hips so as to stay up without braces or belt. Striped, checked and tartan shirts, in wool, cotton and linen had ceased to be merely holiday wear, and could be seen in every go-ahead City office. Overcoats, like hats and shirts, had become less formal; the single-breasted, loose-fitting Raglan was equally for town or country use. Elegant and moustached young men adopted an Army habit of carrying silk handkerchiefs tucked into their sleeves, one end carefully showing. Ties, too, had changed: the knitted silk kind had gone and plain bright colours were worn in wool, rayon and tussore as well as in silk. As in the United States, walking-sticks were no longer carried, except rough, knobbly ones for country use; neatly folded umbrellas had taken their place. Spats had completely gone. Greekish sandals for home and country wear were not thought eccentric. Yet in spite of these many small changes, most of them towards informality and comfort, male dress remained the same in essentials; the experiments made in the Twenties to devise completely new fashions for Western man had long since been abandoned.

CHAPTER TWENTY-TWO

Keeping Fit and Doing the Lambeth Walk

In 1934 the Press was agitating about the number of casualties on the roads due to car-accidents. For five years the death roll had averaged 7,000, and there had also been about 100,000 more or less seriously injured. Cottages near dangerous country cross-roads became unofficial dressing-stations—without pay or endowment—for sometimes dozens of cases in a single holiday season. Saturday and Sunday evenings—when cars from London and other big cities were hurrying home in an unbroken stream, trying to overtake one another on tricky, tortuous roads —and the work-day rush-hour in Town in foggy weather were the bloodiest times. There were also so many deaths, especially in tram-served areas, among children who had to cross main roads on their way to school that in some districts the parents went on strike: they would keep their children at home until the local Council either provided a school on the nearer side of the road, organized convoys for the crossing, or built overhead pedestrian bridges. The general use of traffic lights at main street-crossings had done little to cut down the casualty list.

That year the Ministry of Transport undertook a campaign to make the roads safer. New road-signs were introduced in January: 'Roundabout', 'Major Road Ahead', and 'One-Way Street'. Roundabouts were intended to prevent crashes and jams at traffic junctions, and one-way streets to avoid congestion in narrow areas. Oliver Stanley, then Minister of Transport, deplored road-deaths as 'a hideous and growing blot on our national life', and announced that the Ministry had further plans for traffic control. Authorized pedestrian crossings, traffic lanes, and speed-limits were to be introduced. Cyclists would have to use more visible rear-reflectors, and the surfaces of the roads were to be improved. In the course of 1934, however, Stanley was replaced as Minister by Leslie Hore-Belisha, and it was he who gave his name to the orange beacons that thereafter marked street-crossings, and to the steel-studded lines on the roadway that connected them. He also inaugurated silence-zones in London after 11.30 at night, in which headlight flashes were to be used as signals instead of hooting. They were such a success that soon all night-hooting was forbidden. It was during this period that the Anti-Noise League was active—protesting continually against electric road-drills, until more effective silencers were devised for them. As a result of Belisha's efforts, a thirty-miles-an-hour speed-limit was enforced in built-up areas—elsewhere there was now no speed-limit, but only a regulation against 'driving to the public danger'. The dimming of headlights as cars passed one another, and the use of wind-screen wipers and unsplinterable glass for windscreens became obligatory. More remarkable still, motorists were compelled to take driving tests before they were allowed to drive a car alone. Previously anyone had been allowed to get a licence, jump into a car and drive off without any experience whatever. But in fairness to the motorist 'jay-walking'—a term borrowed from the U.S.A. in 1927, meaning 'careless pedestrianism'—became a criminal offence. Next came the 'courtesy cops'-—policemen in cars with orders to warn drivers politely but firmly of any minor infringement of the rules of the road. They had microphones fitted in their cars, and the hollow courteous boom of their warnings reverberated down hundreds of yards of road. A courtesy cop once shouted to an erring woman driver through a microphone: '*Will the lady in the grey Ford V8 kindly pull in to the left of the road?*' The woman in the Ford V8 accelerated. The constable repeated: '*Speaking to the lady in the grey Ford V8. Will she be good enough, please, to pull in to the left of the road.*' The woman-driver tried to put a heavy lorry between her and her pursuers. '*Will the young lady in the Ford V8 kindly oblige us, please, by pulling in to the left of the road?*' The woman-driver shot across a major road, dodging a stream of fast traffic, and the courtesy cop, forgetting that his microphone was still in action, remarked in a terrific aside: '*Now for Christ Jesus' sake, what the bloody hell will the old cow do next?*'

These reforms did not pass without criticism. The *Spectator* objected to the Belisha beacons because they gave London the air of 'being prepared for a fifth-rate carnival'—many were deliberately destroyed by revellers—and motorists wrote angry letters to the Press when they were fined for only slightly exceeding the new speed-limit. But on the whole Hore-Belisha earned high praise, for by the end of the year there was a marked drop in the number of road-accidents in spite of the increase in the number of cars on the road. Beacons, pedestrian crossings, speed-limits, road-signs, and roundabouts made the public more traffic-conscious, and so more careful: it was really a success for judicious advertising. But the death-rate did not thereafter fall below 6,500. The gross casualties for the period were some 120,000 killed (equal to the strength of the original British Expeditionary Force to France) and some 1,500,000 who in wartime would have been dignified with a mention in the casualty list as 'wounded'.

Besides Belisha beacons, only one noticeable new change had brightened the appearance of towns; that was Neon signs—glass tubes containing incandescent neon gas. These allowed night advertisements, hitherto composed of rows of separate electric bulbs, to be designed in continuous coloured lines, and gave some streets the air not of a fifth-rate but a first-rate carnival. The usual incidental changes were going on: more and more new blocks of flats in Portland stone and red brick, more luxury cinemas, increased slum-clearance. In the outskirts, by-pass roads were being built to enable motorists to avoid congested traffic areas. Most of these were very soon lined with rows of suburban villas and shops, alternated with filling-stations, snack-bars, and 'road-houses'. Road-houses were large elaborate inns which provided meals, drinks, dancing, a night's lodging and no awkward questions asked, garage accommodation and, in summer, tennis, dancing, and even swimming. They were very popular around London, and especially on the Great West Road, where every few miles huge notices invited you in to 'Swim, Dine, and Dance.' One or two of them had a reputation of being '*bagnios*' in the Italian sense.

More than ever in the Thirties middle-class people went

abroad for their holidays; either on cruises or on the cut-rate European tours that the many travel agency services were offering: Scandinavia, the Danube countries, Holland, Dalmatia, even North Africa, were added to the list of holiday countries. Nor did dislike of Hitler greatly affect tourist traffic in Germany, except during the Czech crisis, or of Mussolini in Italy, except during the Sanctions period; and the 'tourist-mark' and the 'tourist-lira' were tempting. Most working-class families spent their short annual holiday at seaside resorts at home; but occasionally crossed the Channel for a day at Calais, Dieppe or Ostend, the passport regulations being waived. Visits to the seaside were being made easier for them by a movement for 'holidays with pay'. The Amalgamated Engineering Union in July 1937 arranged for its members to have a fortnight's holiday each year with pay. All engineering firms federated to the Union were to inaugurate holiday funds into which one-fifth of the value of each week's wages would be paid. Similar systems were introduced in other industries, but by no means all.

In the Thirties holiday camps on the American model came in. These were riverside or seaside establishments which combined the healthy pleasures of camping and aquatic sports with the advantages of a permanently organized community centre. The campers, who were chiefly shop-girls and salesmen, lived in wooden huts and had meals provided for them. Everything was organized by paid staffs: games, bathing, walks, dancing, and community singing. The camps were usually sited near funfairs and sometimes owned by the fun-fair proprietors themselves. Holiday camps were also organized for the serious-minded: Left camps, where people spent half their time in political argument; music camps, attended only by musicians; drama camps, where amateur actors got together to give open-air plays. The routine of the music camps was something of this sort. At daybreak physical jerks; then breakfast and cleaning up the camp; then members retired to different corners to practise on their instruments alone or in small groups. After lunch came organized games or an organized walk. Finally a tea-supper, and to conclude the day an impromptu concert in the twilight. This was typical of the health-and-culture movement.

Slimming had developed into 'Keeping Fit'. *The Times* in November 1936 had urged that 'a great national effort to improve the physique of the nation' should be undertaken. King Edward VIII was cited as an example of a truly 'fit' man. To help working-class boys to keep fit a fund was started in memory of King George V to provide them with playing fields. Women were expected to join the League of Health and Beauty, which organized classes in physical exercise. No special classes were provided for men, it being assumed that most of them did take exercise. Cabinet Ministers made speeches in favour of fitness. But though Neville Chamberlain fished, Sir Samuel Hoare skated and some junior Ministers even occasionally hunted, none of them offered to perform such 'total' feats as jumping over fixed bayonets, which Mussolini was enjoining on his Ministers. The early nineteenth-century origin of the phrase 'Keep fit' was a military one with the words 'for service' understood: this was how *The Times* had intended it. Only in the Thirties could the 'Keep Fit' movement have come into being without exciting mocking laughter from the 'intelligentsia' or suburban Left. But none went up. Keeping fit was as serious a problem as any other: one might not practise it, but at least one did not joke about it. The later Thirties were indeed no joking period. The current jokes were set to Victorian or Regency patterns: 'Knock-Knock, Who's There?' and 'She was only a Plumber's (Gardener's, Chauffeur's, Clergyman's, etc.) daughter', were based on the old-fashioned pun. 'Little Audrey laughed and laughed' was a series in the ceremonious Joe Miller vein. In 1937 there was a painstaking revival of the Limerick— the *Evening Standard* gave substantial weekly prizes to the best Holiday Limerick.

Working men could not afford to play golf, tennis, squash-rackets or badminton in their leisure time, or go motoring as did members of the middle and upper classes. The younger ones, especially those with girls, went to the pictures, or public baths, or cycling—tandem cycling was popular—and hiking; the older ones, and those without girls or allotments, usually went to pubs, or to football matches and greyhound races. But gambling was a chief distraction of both older and younger.

Two new gambling schemes were launched in the Thirties, designed especially for stay-at-home gamblers. First came the Irish Sweepstake, started in Dublin in 1930 by an ex-bookmaker and an ex-politician; they persuaded the Irish Government to sanction it on condition that they gave a large part of the proceeds to impoverished Irish hospitals. The first race on which the sweepstake was run was the Manchester Handicap, but in 1931 it was extended to three races: the Grand National, the Derby, and the Cesarewitch. Public lotteries were forbidden in England (though clubs legitimately organized sweepstakes among members), but the British postal authorities could not prevent people from buying tickets in Dublin without imposing a total censorship on the mail, which they hesitated to do. Hundreds of thousands of tickets were therefore sold to British and American gamblers, and smart publicity soon made the sweepstake the second greatest industry in Ireland—only Guinness's Brewery had a larger pay-roll. The huge drum, which mixed the tickets for the draw, stood in the Plaza Cinema hall in Dublin and became one of Ireland's sightseeing attractions for tourists. Three times a year the draw was held and the prettiest nurses in Dublin picked the winning tickets out of the drum's portholes. In the course of ten years the sweepstake collected over £60,000,000, of which it gave £14,000,000 to the Irish hospitals, and almost £200,000 a year to the Irish Government in taxes. Only the war brought an end to the organization. The British Government was constantly urged by the Press to keep this good money in the country by reintroducing State lotteries, which had been such useful money-makers in Georgian times, or at least to permit British hospitals to finance themselves in the same way as the Irish ones—most British hospitals, being supported by voluntary subscriptions, were in continuous financial difficulty. But the politicians did not wish to antagonize the Churches, especially the Nonconformist Church; also the British Medical Association was thoroughly set against State control of the hospitals and mistrustful of the Ministry of Health. To indulge the medical profession with a monopoly of public sweepstakes would stiffen them in their intransigeance. No action was taken.

The other gambling scheme, a more purely working-class one, was the Football Pools. They grew in popularity at the same time as the Irish Sweepstake, and in the last three or four years of the Peace they overtook it. In the Pools, lists were given of football matches to be played, and correct forecasts of the results won enormous prizes. Since correct forecasts, though largely a matter of luck, could be represented as arrived at by studying the form of the teams engaged, the Gaming Act did not apply to the Pools. The charges for entering the competitions varied from a shilling to a penny. The money subscribed to each Pool was lumped together, deductions were made for expenses and profits, and what was left was divided among the winners. On one occasion as much as £13,000 was won in a penny Pool, the winner claiming that it was his first attempt. Although such hauls were rare, the possibility of winning one attracted an enormous public. The Pools' promoters saw that the public got what it wanted by employing agents in almost every town, village, factory, and workshop: these distributed coupons and collected entrance fees and were paid about 25 per cent of their gross takings. But most of the business was done directly through the post, and on Mondays and Tuesdays, when the new week's coupons were delivered, extra postmen had to be employed in many working-class districts. A tremendous advertising campaign in Sunday newspapers and on the radio from Luxemburg, Normandie, and Poste Parisien helped to put the Pools over. Their growth was phenomenal: during the football season of 1934–5 they took a weekly average of £700,000. The season's total could not have been less than £20,000,000, and this figure was doubled in 1936. Responsible people began to feel worried by the great profits made by the Pools promoters, and by the waste of public purchasing power which the success of Pools' gambling implied. Legislation on the subject was being considered as the period ended.

Most pubs in England were divided into public bars and saloons, the saloons being patronized by people willing to pay an extra halfpenny a pint on beer for enjoying more select company and slightly more comfortable furnishings than in the public bars. The public bars were often bare and dirty, and usually their only ornament, beside advertisements, was a dartboard, not to be found in the saloons. Darts had therefore remained almost entirely a working-class game, only occasionally indulged in by middle-class commercial travellers, until in the middle Thirties it was taken up by Left undergraduates, slumming in search of 'actuality' in public bars. Advanced, Left-Wing gourmet clubs in London began to instal dartboards on their premises; soon the game spread to non-political society.

In 1937 a burglar was caught in one of the most lavishly appointed West End flats, making himself at home with beer and darts. Darts, with beer and sausages, became as upper class as bridge, with whisky and *pâté de foie gras* sandwiches. This upper-class incursion into low-life was Victorian too. As Mr Mountchesney had said in Disraeli's *Sybil*: 'J rather like bad wine; one gets so bored with good wine.' Dartboards were then made in refined colours, and with special unpierceable backcloths that could be attached to any drawing-room wall; and elm wood gave place to closely packed bristle. More boards and darts were sold in 1937 than in any year since the game began, and manufacturers complained that they had difficulty in keeping up with orders—especially when photographs were published in the Press which showed the Queen playing the game and giving the King a beating.

The indoor game of 'Monopoly' was now to the middle classes what Mah-Jong had been: it was first played in the United States in the depths of the Depression by Wall-Street brokers with time on their hands, and exported to the British Stock Exchange. Monopoly was not unlike the pre-war 'Pit', which had been based on bull and bear dealings in the Chicago wheat-pit; and consisted of mock deals in real estate, each player's aim being to buy up all the estate on the board and secure a monopoly.

Great Britain still relied almost wholly on America for her popular music and dances. Jazz since the Depression had developed two new forms: swing and crooning. The most celebrated crooner was Bing Crosby, who first sang in that way because of a defect in his vocal chords. For a time every popular band, in Britain as well as the United States, was expected to keep a crooner, who huddled up to the microphone, swaying and twisting his body voluptuously, tapping his feet, grimacing, and breathing out his suppressed syrupy wail. Bands with vocalists also often included tap-dancers and showgirls who put on an act during play. Music of this kind reached the wider public chiefly by way of the films. There were no British swing bands of any worth but occasionally famous coloured bandleaders, like Louis Armstrong and Duke Ellington, made a European tour. Swing was therefore best known through gramophone records. (Gramophones had maintained their popularity and were now often combined with wireless sets in vast, square, sideboard-like radiograms, built of ornamental woods.) Swing bands specialized in trumpets, clarinets and drums, the saxophone being no longer the star instrument. They were teams of virtuosos, each of whom had his solo turn to play in the course of every piece. The result was a roughly fugue-like movement, the main theme constantly recurring in different forms. Extempore playing by the soloists was one of the features of swing: entirely new things could happen each time a piece was performed. True swing was music to be listened to as much as danced to: it was a fine product of Jewish sweet-passion, negro relish of living and the stimulating climate of New York City. If there were lyrics to it, they were often noises integrated into the general sound rather than words with sentimental meanings.

British followers of true swing entered seriously into its spirit, showing for certain bands the intense enthusiasm of Spanish *aficionados* for particular bull-fighters, and using the complete swing technical vocabulary. The latest novelty to come over from the United States at the end of the period was 'swung popular classics': for instance, the Shakespearian 'It was a Lover and his Lass', and, to the disgust of all patriotic Scots, 'Loch Lomond'. The wider public heard only commercial swing, which lacked its creative spirit and its technical skill. The B.B.C. did not dare maintain a permanent band, nor would any have been found hardy enough to perform its exuberant feats in the staid soundproof halls of Broadcasting House, or desperate enough to put itself under the moral tutelage of the B.B.C. Council. Popular music in Great Britain was, in fact, not taken passionately, but expected to be either sentimental or humorous. Bands, especially in the north, played up to this view by dressing in extravagant uniforms or rigging themselves out as pierrots or pirates.

By the Thirties, radio had created new domestic habits. Regular seasons of symphony concerts, frequent recitals by prominent musicians, the annual 'proms', and talks by such speakers as Sir Walford Davies, Scott Goddard, and Dr. Malcolm Sargent trained the nation to appreciate educated as well as popular music; so that when 'This Symphony Business', a series in which a philistine grudgingly allowed himself to be enlightened by a serious musician, was broadcast in 1939, hundreds of people wrote to say that they postponed, or interrupted, their midday meal on Sunday to listen to it. In the later Thirties, twelve-instalment serial plays, such as *The Count of Monte Christo, Les Misérables,* and *The Cloister and the Hearth* were regularly broadcast on Sundays; the B.B.C. then learned that in thousands of homes week-end plans were altered to allow listeners to get near a radio-set when the performances were on. In certain cases these performances coincided with Evensong, and a clergyman complained to the *Radio Times* that not only was his congregation severely depleted, but that he himself regretfully missed every other instalment of the current serial through taking Evensong on alternate Sundays. Regular Saturday 'Music Hall' had for years brought a large number of men and women home early from the pubs; but this was nothing to the effect in the late Thirties of the popular 'Band Wagon' programme at 8.15 on Wednesday evenings. Cinema and theatre managers found that their Wednesday evening receipts fell in some cases by as much as one-third. Women's Institutes, Evening Classes, Clubs, Study Circles, that normally met on Wednesdays were forced to change their day to Tuesday or Thursday. 'Band Wagon Night' became one on which outside social engagements were refused. The chief catch-phrase of the show, 'I thank you'—pronounced in a heavily nasal manner—swept the country for a year. In trains, buses, and trams on Thursday mornings those who had been unfortunate enough to miss the previous evening's performance eagerly pressed for details from those who had not.

The practice of 'Group Listening', started by the B.B.C. in the cause of adult education, grew steadily under the superveillance of Local Education Authorities. The B.B.C. itself appointed Education Officers in various parts of the country whose duty it was to organize 'Discussion Groups' to assemble and listen to the various broadcast series. Many of these groups were quite large assemblies in Public Libraries, Institutes, or Church Halls, but the majority consisted of a few friends meeting in private houses. Listening attentively to particular programmes, instead of merely using radio as a noisy background for domestic life, became a natural habit; though small children complained that they could not get their homework done for the noise, and large families constantly quarrelled when different members wanted to listen to different programmes given simultaneously. The

B.B.C.'s official journal, the *Radio Times*, had reached a circulation of nearly three million copies weekly by the end of the period.

The suspicion of the newspaper proprietors that the B.B.C. damaged their interests was understandable. Early in its history the B.B.C. agreed with them that, in order not to discourage business people from buying morning or evening papers, it would not broadcast news between midnight and 6 p.m.; nor would it broadcast running commentaries on sporting events. Thus one heard the hoofs of the Derby race-horses pounding past Tattenham Corner, the shouts of the crowd and the yelling of bookmakers, but *not* the result of the race—one had to wait for the evening papers for that. When the B.B.C. became a public corporation in 1927, this ruling was relaxed and a few news commentaries were allowed. These gradually increased, until by 1939 practically every event of importance was covered by commentators. But news was still restricted to the 6 p.m. limit, except in circumstances of national importance. The rule, for example, was broken in the case of the crashing of the R101, because there were no Sunday evening papers to be considered; when King George V died; and at the height of the September crisis in 1939.

The entertainment world had the same jealousy of the B.B.C. as the Press. There was a long-standing conflict over the annual broadcast of the Royal Command Variety performance, which emptied music-halls, theatres, and cinemas all over the country. The B.B.C. eventually undertook to pay a large sum to charity in return for the right to broadcast the show, but this was robbing Peter to pay Paul, for houses of entertainment still continued to be half-empty on Royal Command nights. In 1938 the B.B.C. was forced to abandon the broadcast.

In many cases, however, broadcasting proved itself the ally rather than the enemy of the Stage. Theatre managers were delighted when the B.B.C. took to broadcasting fortnightly half-hour excerpts from their shows, most of which benefited by this gratuitous form of 'trailer'. Many people in the provinces selected the plays they wished to see on short visits to London entirely on the merits of these broadcasts. The most notable instance of B.B.C. assistance to the Stage was when it came to the rescue of 'Me and My Girl', the Christmas show at the

Chelsea Palace, in 1937. This was on the point of closing down
after a short run, when a broadcast from the theatre commended
it to the attention of some millions of listeners. The broadcast
contained 'The Lambeth Walk', sung by Lupino Lane in the
character of a Lambeth native who had inherited an earldom.
Lambeth retained the Victorian tradition of cheerful Cockney
behaviour, at music-halls, dance-halls, pubs, and boxing shows,
that had vanished elsewhere in London; so even in high Society
the new Earl preserved his Lambeth ways and at a high-class
dinner-party started 'doing the Lambeth Walk', with such
infectious gaiety that all the titled guests joined in. The original
words were:

> 'Any time you're Lambeth way,
> Any evening, any day,
> You'll find us all doin' the Lambeth Walk.
> Ev'ry little Lambeth gal
> With her little Lambeth pal,
> You'll find 'em all doin' the Lambeth Walk.
>
> Ev'rything free and easy,
> Do as you darn well pleasey,
> Why don't you make your way there,
> Go there, stay there,
> Once you get down Lambeth way,
> Ev'ry evening, ev'ry day,
> You'll find yourself doin' the Lambeth Walk.'

The tune was written by the composer of 'All the King's Horses'.
made famous by Cicely Courtneidge's rendering in the early
Thirties.

The broadcast turned 'Me and My Gal' into one of the greatest successes of the period, and a dance was at once invented to
suit the song. It included a jerky swagger, the 'thumbs-up'
gesture, and the hand-spreading Jewish 'Oi!' The dance version
of the Lambeth Walk swept the country, the B.B.C. plugging it
proudly.

More copies of the song were sold than of any other since
'Yes, we have no Bananas'. It provided a welcome change from
the eternal foxtrots, rumbas, and tangos, and even went down
well in the United States, which needed a sedative after 'the Big

Apple'. Journalists in Czechoslovakia in September 1938 reported that the Czechs were forgetting the crisis by doing the Lambeth Walk. In England its respectability was sealed when the Duke and Duchess of Kent were reported to have danced it in spite of protests against its vulgarity by the Blimps. ('Blimp' was a contemptuous term for every reactionary muddle-headed Conservative who feared a Red Revolution at home more than national humiliation by the Totalitarian Powers. Colonel Blimp in Low's *Evening Standard* cartoons was a bald, fat, walrus-moustached old man, usually depicted emerging from a Turkish bath with a towel round his middle, and preluding some fatuous Diehard remark with 'Gad, sir, Chamberlain—or Baldwin or Hitler or Mussolini—is right!' Low, who joined the *Evening Standard* in 1927 was far more Left-minded than the editorship, but so many people bought the paper only for his outrageous and beautifully drawn cartoons, that he could more or less make his own terms.)

The Lambeth Walk had its imitations: there was a dance-hall version of the Cockney song, 'Knees up, Mother Brown', the words of which ran:

> 'Knees up, Mother Brown,
> Knees up, Mother Brown,
> Under the table you must go,
> Ee aye, ee aye, ee aye oh,
> If we catch you bending
> We'll turn you upside down,
> Knees up, knees up, don't get the breeze up,
> Knees up, Mother Brown.'

'Mother Brown' never made the social grade; the lifting of skirts that went with the dance-version was a little too much. But in compliment to their Majesties 'Under the Spreading Chestnut Tree' was turned into a dance, an undistinguished foxtrot with formalized gestures, and was loyally and frequently performed.

The popularity of these cheerful, simple, miming dances began to decline in 1939. Jitterbugging had then just come over from the United States: this was an ecstatic mode of dancing to fast swing music in which the two partners could perform absolutely any tap or acrobatic feat they liked, provided they kept in time with each other and with the music. It demanded a capacity for idle nervous excess that the American climate might bestow, but not the English. Jitterbug competitions were held in some working-class dance-halls, but the fashion never ran wild in the Universities, as in the united States, nor was it tried out in Mayfair. All-in wrestling, however, which had long been practised in some British working-class districts under the name of Free-style wrestling was widely popularized by American fashion. The savage eighteenth-century 'nought barred' tradition of the Staffordshire mines and the Virginian mountains—where wrestlers were permitted to blind and castrate one another and bite off noses—had been gradually modified in both countries to the discouragement of actual mutilation; but 'All-in' still permitted blows and holds that were forbidden in official boxing and wrestling codes. Its attraction lay not only in the savagery and skill, but also in the humour of the proceedings. The crowd would cat-call blithely when the wrestlers were pinned down and nearly choked; it enjoyed seeing the light-weight referee slung out of the ring or crushed between two closely locked performers; and encouraged the performers themselves to do 'psychological' and dramatic clowning, of the sort that had made Max Baer more popular with the American masses than with strict lovers of boxing. 'All-in' enjoyed the approval of Mayfair, which imported East End wrestlers to perform at parties. Society people attended Wrestling Clubs and the daughter of the British Rajah of Sarawak put herself in the forefront of fashion by actually marrying a leading all-in wrestler, as her sister had done a season or two before by marrying a band-leader. But it was only a short fashion: for general opinion in Britain considered 'all-in' no less as vulgar than it was brutal.

Ordinary boxing was a sport followed chiefly by the industrial working class, though a few peers, social celebrities, and members of the Royal Family would attend major contests. Newspapers gave far less space to boxing news than to football, cricket, and racing, and the general public became interested only when British boxers made attempts at the World Heavyweight title, as Phil Scott did in the Twenties and Tommy Farr in the Thirties—both unsuccessfully. Sometimes a foreign boxer's personality would catch public attention. Jack Dempsey, for instance, was every small boy's hero in the Twenties, as Joe Beckett was too, while he lasted. Then the Italian giant, Primo

Carnera, came to England and caused great excitement because of his huge bulk, huge appetite, huge feet, and childlike disposition. For some reason or other, the lighter boxing weights did not attract so much popular interest as the heavy; though against the 'horizontal heavyweights' of Tom Webster's cartoons could be set the highly vertical light, bantam, feather, and fly-weights from South Wales, the East End, Birmingham, and Glasgow, who were a match for most American and Continental champions. Kid Berg, a Londoner, who carried on the Jimmy Wilde tradition of clean boxing and extraordinary courage, was one of the few little men whose names made news.

CHAPTER TWENTY-THREE

Social Consciences

Scientists towards the close of the Thirties were less occupied with the theoretical implications of their work, or with trying to give it religious and philosophical significance, than with asking themselves what was the place of science in the social system. They were beginning at last to have a social conscience. A twentieth-century system was developing, haphazardly and piecemeal; what form it would take and how England might fit into it was as much a scientist's business as anybody's. Some of them, of course, took the easiest path—to the Left; and were positive that science had no significance unless considered in Marxist terms: like everything else, it should be a handmaid of the dictatorship of the proletariat. A great deal of propaganda was published about the success of proletarian Russian scientists, and even the Conservative Press occasionally printed news stories of their remarkable experiments on dogs and rats.

The scientist now saw himself as the practical man who could reorganize democracy if only he were given a chance. Professor Lancelot Hogben followed up his best-selling *Mathematics for the Million* with *Science for the Citizen*: 'Science is no cosmic prophecy. True science, in the words of Robert Boyle, is "such knowledge as hath tendency to use". A scientific law embodies a recipe for doing something, and its final validification rests in the domain of action. . . . This is not the age of pamphleteers. It is the age of engineers. The spark-gap is mightier than the pen. Democracy will not be salvaged by men who talk fluently, debate forcefully and quote aptly.' Among the scientists who set about the work of salvage was J. B. S. Haldane. Just back from a visit to Republican Spain, he conducted a lively Left-Wing campaign for the provision of deep, underground air-raid shelters for the whole population, bringing forward scientific proof of their effectiveness—this, however, bore no relation to his own science of biology. It was, in fact, a characteristic of scientists to make recommendations on subjects far outside their own specialized fields; and the sociological vogue accentuated it.

The most notable practical achievement of science in the period was the development of synthetic products. German *ersatz* rubber, Buna, often sneered at in the British Press, had a British-American equivalent, Neoprene. Neither product was a slavish imitation of rubber: both claimed additional virtues—greater resistance to heat, light, and chemical action. They were largely used in the oil and chemical industries and for making printing rollers; and German Buna car-tyres were said to last half as long again as ordinary ones. By 1938 one-tenth of the world's rubber supply was produced synthetically.

Experiments in making artificial silk stronger and more durable continued; in 1939 the Americans were beginning commercial production of a kind called Nylon, which they claimed to be more elastic than real silk fibre and half as strong again. Patents were applied for in Great Britain. The new plastics, such as bakelite, were being put to countless new uses. Bakelite con-sisted of carbolic acid molecules linked together by formaldehyde and could be manufactured from coal-tar and milk: its chief use was as a substitute for wood and bone, because it did not warp, crack, or rot. Plastics of all kinds could be coloured in the making and moulded into any desired shape; thus the separate processes of sawing, planing, joining, turning, finishing and painting, through which wood had to go, were eliminated. Bakelite coffins, for instance, could be turned out all in one piece. For some purposes plastics took the place of metals: for plumbing, and even for bearings in machinery, which needed lubricating only with water. Their lightness also made them useful in aeroplane manufacture. Plastics became one of the main British industries: half a million workers were employed in it by 1939.

The effect of synthetic developments and of hydro-electric power was to free industry from its old dependence on iron and coal. Industry no longer needed to be strongly localized in areas where natural products occurred, nor to rely wholly on imported raw materials. Chile saltpetre could be made anywhere out of atmospheric nitrogen, aluminium alloys from clay, magnesium from sea-salt, and sugar by bacterial agency from waste vegetable matter. One result was that new 'light industries' were set up in the pleasanter Home Counties, with easy access to the gigantic London market, instead of in the gloomy districts of the industrial north. This drained away population and money from the north, as was sadly apparent in the number of shops to let in the main streets of its big cities.

The sociologists were justified in seeing these chemical triumphs as, ideally, a promise of the Golden Age of international goodwill—they would lessen competition for the possession of raw materials, a chief cause of international dispute. But, in effect, the success of synthetic products encouraged the nationalistic theory of 'economic autarchy'; and it was seen that if the totalitarian powers could make themselves independent of raw rubber, oil, cotton, nitrates, then economic boycott or blockade was no longer an effective weapon against an 'aggressor nation'. Rayon, again, was a most provocative invention. It threatened to make inroads on the cotton trade, and this encouraged the Japanese, whose national economy depended largely on exporting cheap cotton, to conquer China while they could still afford the necessary armaments.

As for Britain, for a century the national wealth had depended on the possession or financial control of raw materials, and on having heavy industries to convert them into goods and worldwide scope for export. But high tariffs and economic nationalism were shrinking the free world-market almost to nothing, and British heavy industries had to go through a period of disturbed and painful adaptation. The many new light industries that had successfully grown up did not compensate for all the distress caused by the breakdown of the nineteenth-century system. Everyone was aware that the world was changing, and that Britain had to change too. All sorts of plans were produced by every kind of theorist: but without any central clearing-house to sort them out.

Medical science was still concerned more with devising cures for particular diseases than with the general problem of raising the standard of national health. The study of malnutrition was not neglected, but there was no legislation to ensure that the millions of poor got the nutrition recommended by the specialists. The Government and the British Medical Association could not even agree on their estimates of minimum food requirements. The B.M.A. held that the weekly allowance of money to be spent on food should be considerably higher than that provided by Unemployment Relief. But the B.M.A. was a private body and unable to act even in fields where it was acknowledged as the highest authority. The average general practitioner had no time and little opportunity for prophylactic work: all that he could do was to mitigate the effects of often preventable illnesses and disorders. Excessive numbers of panel patients and excessive demands for medical certificates and returns of one kind or another reduced him to the position of an overworked prescription-agent and a licenser and registrar of sickness. His work was seldom in any way co-ordinated with Ministry of Health or with Home Office activities such as sanitation, street cleaning, and the working of the health clauses in the Factory Acts and Coal Mines Acts. The charge of national health was uncertainly divided between private enterprise and Government control. The confusion of this compromise was increased by the difference in the status of hospitals—hospitals run by local authorities and supported in whole or part by the rates, independent hospitals supported by voluntary subscriptions, private nursing-homes run for profit. All these were managed by separate committees, followed different methods, and fitted into no connected system.

Much research was being done into diseases which caused death or, like the common cold, a yearly loss of hundreds of millions of work-hours. The chief emphasis was on cure rather than prevention; medical research, like nearly all specialized scientific work, being largely unrelated to social problems. The Press encouraged this emphasis by headlining dramatic new developments—such as the radium and the Bendien cures for cancer, the insulin cure for diabetes, and the liver cure for pernicious anaemia—a cure being news in the journalistic sense, and prevention no news. (If it was news when a man bit a dog, rather than when a dog bit a man, still less newsworthy was the prevention of either incident by prudent action.) The period was also remarkable for the treatment of venereal diseases, and the insanity resulting from them, by induced fevers; the elimination of varicose veins by the injection of an irritant which caused them to dry up; and new cures for sleeping sickness, pneumonia, and peritonitis. A new drug was sulphanilamide, which was effective in cases of pneumonia, gonorrhea, and mental disorders; its disadvantage was that it left the patient's blood dangerously thinned. For that, however, there was now a remedy—blood transfusion. Blood was drawn off in half-pints from the arms of healthy volunteers and injected into the systems of the dangerously ill. It could be stored on ice for months until it was needed. A register was kept of voluntary blood-donors, to be called upon in emergencies. They were classified according to the newly discovered blood-groups.

Blood-groups made news in 1939, when it was found that children inherited the characteristics of the blood-group to which their parents belonged. If a child had blood-characteristics which neither parent possessed, some third party must be its real father. A man could not be proved by these means to be the father of his supposed child, but in some cases he could be proved not to be the father. Blood-tests would obviously be useful in determining paternity cases in the courts—and add a new relish to an old type of sensational newspaper story. In March 1939 the House of Lords was debating a Bill which would enable law courts to order blood-tests—though if either party refused, the case must be dismissed.

Advertisers were now exploiting the low level of national health, especially as it manifested itself in tiredness and lack of vitality. There was, for example, Horlick's 'Night-Starvation' campaign, which represented a night-cap of malted milk as an infallible aid to restful sleep. Daily doses of aperient salts ('enough to cover a sixpence') were recommended as a general cure-all: one firm advertised with the contrasting figures of 'Mr. Can and Mr. Can't', another with the elegant phrase 'Inner Cleanliness', another started a most successful whispering campaign which introduced the names of Royalty and a Royal physician-in-ordinary. The general medical opinion was that a daily dose of salts encouraged constipation, but the health-salt firms answered this by advertising their products as 'non-habit forming'. In a different field, but by the same school of copy-writers, soaps were sold as cures for 'Body Odour'.

A 'confidence-drug' which created an immense stir at the end of 1936 was benzedrine, an importation from the U.S.A. It was claimed that students under its influence could pass examinations that otherwise would baffle them; bar-tenders used it as an ingredient in pep-cocktails, and it was sold freely over chemists' counters. But in 1938, when coroners noted the increasing number of suicide cases in which the victim had relapsed into depression after taking benzedrine for some time, it was placed on the poisons-list, and manufacturers were warned that it should only be used under medical direction. Its widespread use in small inhalers was permitted, however, as a remedy for colds. The pathology of the common cold continued to puzzle research workers. They pronounced it to be the general name for perhaps a score of different minor diseases, each responding, if at all, to a different treatment.

By the middle Thirties the medical profession had become seriously concerned about the advertising of patent medicines—patent only in name, for few were actually patented. There was nothing in British law to prevent any firm from putting a medicine on the market, claiming therapeutical properties for it, and recommending it by means of bogus testimonials; so long as it did not contain a known poison or contravene the Adulteration of Food Act. Makers of these medicines were required by law to state their contents, but the analytic formula was usually quite unintelligible to the ordinary patient. The most that the law did was to prevent known poisons from being indiscriminately sold. There was no public protection against unlisted drugs which might prove poisonous, or against the advertisement of 'universally beneficial' compounds containing ingredients that in particular cases might cause death.

By the Thirties the advertising of patent medicines had grown enormously. They occupied about one-sixth of the advertising space in the daily Press, and about one-third of the space in the popular weeklies. The old type of advertisement story which showed a marvellous drug being given to some traveller by a grateful native in a particularly inaccessible part of the world was displaced by one which made it the culmination of a lifetime of laborious scientific research. One Sunday paper in 1938 was advertising in a single issue cures for epilepsy, varicose veins, piles, eczema, rheumatism and neuritis, a remedy which banished hay-fever, asthma, malaria, influenza and insomnia, and another which brought rapid relief to eleven different kinds of pain, including headaches, depression, insomnia, rheumatism, indigestion, constipation, and impure blood. In general, newspapers accepted patent-medicine advertisements without question, the fees charged for advertising space forming a large part of their revenue: the Yadil case was most exceptional. Most 'Tonic Wines' sold to the ailing poor at extortionate prices, to cover the expense of advertising, were in every way inferior in medicinal effect to ordinary cheap grocer's wine. A Bill to regulate the sale of these products had been introduced without success in 1931. A new Bill was brought forward in 1936, on the lines of one that had become law in the United States, to prohibit the advertisement of cures for blindness, cancer, consumption, epilepsy, paralysis, and Bright's disease. At the second Commons reading, however, in March, the House was counted out—the reason being that it was the day of the Grand National Steeplechase, which most members had gone to watch. The patent-medicine business continued. But at least individual members of the medical profession did not lend themselves to the fraud, the penalty for either advertising themselves or sponsoring proprietary goods being removal from the Medical Register.

There would have been no large market for these medicines, in spite of the advertisement copy-writers—part of whose profession was inventing new disorders from which people might imagine themselves to be suffering—if a large proportion of the population had not been in chronic ill-health. That this was so appeared during the Army recruiting drive in 1935 when no less than 62 per cent of the prospective recruits could not attain the comparatively low standard of physique required by the Army. The Pioneer Health Centre at Peckham, which was founded in 1928 to prevent sickness by regularly overhauling people, reported that 86 per cent of those examined were found to be suffering from some disorder, only 20 per cent were aware of it, and only 7 per cent receiving treatment. It was to remedy this state of affairs that the National Fitness Campaign was begun, but Low in a cartoon pointed out the absurdity of recommending physical jerks to citizens suffering from malnutrition and the effects of living in dilapidated houses in Special Areas. In December 1937 a social research group, named P.E.P. (Political and Economic Planning), published a fully documented report on Britain's health. They summed up the position thus: 'Perhaps the most fundamental defect in the existing system is that it is overwhelmingly preoccupied with manifest and advanced diseases or disabilities and is more interested in enabling the sufferers to go on functioning in society somehow than in studying the nature of health and the means of producing and maintaining it. From this it naturally follows that millions of pounds are spent in looking after and trying to cure the victims of accidents and illnesses which need never have occurred if a fraction of this amount of intelligence and money had been devoted to tracing the social and economic causes of the trouble and making the necessary adjustments.' In fact, the real problem was twofold: how to co-ordinate health services and how to pay for medical research. Lord Nuffield was doing his best for medical research by endowing magnificent laboratories at Oxford, at the cost of millions of pounds, and giving away 'iron lungs' (artificial breathing apparatuses) to any hospital that needed them. But the other problem had to wait.

The P.E.P. group was one of several now engaged in social research. By the end of the Thirties the single plan to right all Britain's wrongs, for which the cry had gone up during the Depression, was no longer being expected. There were so many wrongs, and they were so complicated, that obviously no single plan could cover them all. Instead, private groups were making special studies and analyses of particular subjects and drawing recommendations from them. Besides P.E.P., there were the New Fabian Research Bureau, and Social Survey committees sponsored by universities. The several social surveys made were immense undertakings, published in many volumes; each thoroughly covered living and working conditions in a single area. The Merseyside Survey, for example, was carried out by Liverpool University. Neither these nor the single-volume reports of private research groups were intended for popular sale, but were works of reference, intended to guide local and national authorities on social questions.

In the United States, shorter social histories and social surveys had become popular among a wider public. There had been K. S. and H. M. Lynd's *Middletown*, which gave the history of living conditions in a small Middle-Western town. And F. L. Allen's *Only Yesterday*, which presented the social life of the American Twenties in terms of fashion and current topics as well as of public events. Both books sold well in England, and had imitators. This documenting of life as it had really been served more than an official purpose: it was entertainment—a dramatic crystallization of the news that flowed in a haphazard stream through the newspapers.

Also from the United States came public opinion investigation. It was asked: 'What do people think, feel, want, from day to day and from year to year? How does one know what they are thinking, feeling, wanting?' The answer was: 'Chiefly from newspapers, books, films, plays, the radio—the current topics, forms of entertainment and fashions.' But no organization existed for the accurate analysis of dumb public opinion even in totalitarian states—where the Ministries of Propaganda were more concerned with directing public opinion than with investigating it. The only investigation that had hitherto been done in the United States and in Britain was for commercial purposes. Advertising firms had been making increased use of 'market research'—that is, they had employed girls to go round and find out by door-to-door questioning what people wanted and what could be sold to them. Girls were used because it was found that they were more readily and courteously answered than men. Advertising firms were thus able to advise their clients as to what goods the public could be made to buy, and what advertising line would be most persuasive.

Public opinion investigation was first started on a large and permanent scale by the American Dr. Gallup. His American Institute of Public Opinion used fairly accurate methods of gauging opinion on particular topics by taking what were called 'straw-votes' because they showed which way the wind was blowing. Small samples only of the population were touched, classed according to age, sex, income, and locality groups. Changes of opinion could be measured by repeating the same question among the same small sample-group of people. In this way Dr. Gallup managed to be right—for example, in forecasting President Roosevelt's victory over Landon in the Presidential election of 1936, when other straw-votes taken at the same time, such as that of the *Literary Digest*, were either completely wrong or far out in their percentages. A branch of Dr. Gallup's organization was set up in England in 1938 under the name of the British Institute of Public Opinion. The *News Chronicle* bought the exclusive right to publish its results. The Institute confined itself chiefly to questions on political matters, to which a simple 'Yes' was an adequate answer.

Straw-votes indicating Yes-or-No attitudes were useful chiefly to politicians and newspaper editors, who had to reckon with public opinion and had so far been content merely to guess what it was. But a more ambitious scheme of social reporting was launched in England in 1936 under the name of Mass Observation by two young men: Charles Madge, a poet and journalist, and Tom Harrisson, an amateur anthropologist. They proposed to observe almost everything. In a 'Fact' pamphlet, issued in 1937, they described their work: 'Mass Observation intends to make use, besides the work of scientists, of the untrained observer, the man in the street. Ideally, it is the observation of everyone by everyone, including themselves. . . . More recent acquisitions to society—electricity, aeroplanes, radio—are so new that the process of adaptation to them is still going on. It is within the scope of the science of Mass Observation to watch the process taking place—perhaps to play some part in determining the adaptation of old superstitions to new conditions.'

It set out, in fact, to be the science of everyday life, an anthropology of civilized peoples. No need to go to the South Seas to study strange customs and queer habits; English customs and habits were equally strange and queer, and in greater need of documentation.

By good publicity work on the part of its organizers, most newspapers were drawn into taking notice of Mass Observation. It was, as might have been expected, unfavourable notice. William Hickey gave it a few paragraphs in the *Daily Express*, headed 'Pryers, Please——!' The *Sunday Times* described it as 'Mass Eavesdropping'. The *Spectator* criticized observers as 'Busybodies of the Left'—and, indeed, many of them were Left-inclined, attracted by the hope that fact-finding would bring to fruition the theory of socialist realism. Despite the support of the zoologist Julian Huxley, and the qualified approval of the anthropologist Malinowski, the greater part of the Press ridiculed Mass Observation's claim to be a science. As the *Spectator* declared: 'Scientifically they're about as valuable as a chimpanzee tea-party at the Zoo.'

From the point of view of publicity, a wide bad Press was better than a small good one, and Mass Observation became overnight a recognized social phenomenon. After spending some time on a rather haphazard collection of people's dream images, a survey of the behaviour of the crowds on Coronation Day, and an examination of social habits in Bolton and Blackpool—with the help of enthusiastic field-work parties—it came to concentrate more expertly on investigating public opinion and its sources.

The significance of Mass Observation and of Dr. Gallup's Institute was that they provided democracy with the skeleton of an opinion-sounding machine, which could serve as a guide to the opinion-forming influences. The most arresting phrase in which democracy has ever been described was Abraham Lincoln's 'Government of the people, by the people, for the people'. Yet everyone knew that it was not government by the people, but by representatives of particular interests—employers, workmen, the professions, and so on—who were supposed to take into account the people's general interests, and who succeeded confusedly in doing so simply by a compromise between their own conflicting views. The people's general interests consisted of two things: what they needed and what they thought. Social research and social survey work could help to direct attention to what they needed, and public opinion investigation to show what they thought and why. It began to be realized towards the end of the Thirties that a closer integration of community needs and feelings would make class-war unnecessary and even impossible; and because of this realization the Left was growing less interested in ideal anarchy or Red revolution, and applying more of its energies to research work that would assist in bringing about social integration.

Such research groups, however, were too small to exercise any great influence, and agitation remained the chief means by which strongly felt wrongs could be righted. There were in 1937 1,600,000 unemployed, in spite of the rearmament boom, and the Left was accusing the Conservatives of allowing rearmament

SOCIAL CONSCIENCES

problems and foreign crises to blind them to the continued poverty of the Special Areas. In 1938 the National Unemployed Workers' Movement, which had developed the technique of Hunger Marches, started a new campaign to wake up the Blimps. In August of that year they had already frightened the Government into passing the Winter Adjustments Regulations, which granted Unemployment Assistance Boards powers to award extra winter relief. The mass of the unemployed, however, was not eligible for such awards. As winter approached, Wal Hannington, the organizer of the N.U.W.M., decided to exploit the nuisance value of the unemployed in a series of stunt agitations. The technique was one that had been brilliantly developed before the war by Christabel Pankhurst, leader of the militant Suffragettes· and since improved by Gandhi—whose followers did not scream and struggle with policemen but just lay about in impassive and inert heaps.

One of the most successful of these stunts took place at 3.15 in the afternoon five days before Christmas, in Oxford Street, which was then crammed with Christmas shoppers. At a signal from their leader, two hundred unemployed men played the Indian *hartal* trick: lying down in front of the traffic at a moment when the red lights had halted it. They lay on their backs, head to toe, eight abreast, right across the road. The sight of their bodies, almost beneath the wheels of buses, vans, and cars, made many of the women shoppers on the pavements scream. Crowds then rushed to the scene, looking anxiously at the traffic lights and wondering what would happen when they turned green. When the lights did change, not a wheel moved. The men in the roadway had meanwhile spread posters over their bodies, which read 'Work or Bread', and had begun to chant in unison 'We want work or bread' and 'We want extra relief'. After half a dozen changes of lights the whole of Oxford Street was one vast traffic jam. The police rushed up, perplexed, shouting politely, 'Get up, you fellows, you're holding up the traffic.' At this some of the crowd burst into laughter, in which the demonstrators joined. More police arrived and began to drag the men individually on to the pavements, to the accompaniment of ironical cheers from the onlookers. Those dragged off immediately went back to their places in the roadway while their comrades were being similarly dealt with. The police called for volunteer help from the crowd, but no one stirred. Reinforcements from Scotland Yard were meanwhile themselves caught in the traffic jam. Only after a prolonged struggle and the immobilization of traffic over a huge area for an hour or so was order restored.

More stunts followed. One hundred unemployed invaded the Grill Room at the Ritz and asked for tea. When the police arrived, they dispersed in an orderly way, but their action drew feature articles from the popular Press contrasting the life of the unemployed with that of the habitués of the Ritz. Then came a petition to the King, and on Christmas Eve the picketting of the main railway stations with posters: 'A Square Deal—the Unemployed Want a Square Meal Now'. (The railways were then conducting an advertisement campaign for a 'Square Deal', chiefly directed against the motor transport companies.) On Christmas Day, 150 demonstrators assembled outside the house of the Chairman of the Unemployed Assistance Board and sang a carol to the tune of the 'Policeman's Holiday'. On New Year's Eve at 11 p.m., when crowds were collecting in Trafalgar Square, a procession of unemployed suddenly appeared, bearing a black coffin. They marched sombrely down the Strand and Fleet Street and on into Stepney, having frequent tussles with the police, who attempted in vain to impound the coffin. Three days later they tried to leave the coffin at No. 10 Downing Street. Here again there was trouble with the police, but they were allowed to deliver the message contained inside the coffin: 'Unemployed—No Appeasement!' (It was four months after the Munich Agreement, and Chamberlain was just preparing to visit Mussolini in Rome.)

The demonstrations continued throughout January, the coffin frequently reappearing. On another occasion a party of demonstrators, in Suffragette fashion, chained themselves to the railings outside the house of Ernest Brown, the Minister of Labour, and the police had to use hack-saws to free them. They were arrested and charged with 'using insulting words and behaviour'. During this winter the trenches and air-raid shelters, which had been hastily dug in the previous September, became completely waterlogged, and a subject of much newspaper fun. A party of eighty unemployed took advantage of this to occupy the trenches on Primrose Hill, overlooking the Zoo. They carried fishing rods, to which were attached huge eels, and posters which read: 'Bring Anderson to 'Eel—Give us Work on A.R.P.' (Sir John Anderson, a former Governor of Bengal, was now Lord President of the Council, appointed to supervise Air Raid Precautions.) The police ordered them to move on. They asked whether the trenches were not for public use. The police replied lamely: 'Yes, but you can't fish in them.'

The campaign did not succeed in exacting new concessions from the Government, but it won the attention of the Press and the amused sympathy of the public, which had indeed been blinded to the continuance of unemployment by local prosperity caused by the rearmament boom and the migration of industries to the south. The British Press now began to print consoling reports of what was being done for the unemployed. 'Occupational clubs' had been in operation since 1933: instead of standing listlessly at the street-corners men were finding a fresh object in life. The chief difficulty, it was reported, that the organizers of these clubs met, was non-co-operation on the part of the unemployed. They suspected a Government plot to train them into half-skilled carpenters or boot repairers and then turn them out to under-cut prices of fully trained men. At Lincoln, unemployed were running their own nursery school; at Brynmawr, they had turned a slag-heap into a public park and built a swimming pool; at Hebburn, they had converted an old power station into a magnificent community hall for dances, plays, whist drives, and meetings. It was reported that though allotments were popular in Sheffield and Ipswich, among other places, in many towns the unemployed could not be brought to see any virtue in them at all. (The allotment scheme, it may be added, was better run than any other; it was under the control of the Society of Friends.)

The financial depression was now officially over and an industrial recovery under way. The extent of the recovery may be judged by the quotations of industrial shares on the Stock Exchange; between 1932 and 1937 these nearly doubled in value. Industrial profits, which had averaged six per cent in 1932, had now risen to ten per cent—not much below the 1929 boom level and even this ten per cent did not represent the full advance, surplus profits being 'ploughed in' to avoid taxation. In some fields the recovery had been even more marked: the output of cars had more than doubled since 1931, so had the monthly output of steel, and the rate of production in electrical engineering and shipbuilding had almost quadrupled. Nor did 1938 and 1939 bring a recession.

CHAPTER TWENTY-FOUR

'Markets Close Firmer'

The National Government was allowed to take some of the honour for Recovery, though cynical economists pointed out that in the prevailing Capitalist system recovery, like depression, was almost beyond the power of governments to prevent. Some praise came even from the Left—G. D. H. Cole, for example, in a pamphlet, *Economic Prospects of 1938*: 'I hate the National Government as much as anyone hates it, but at the same time I am well aware that in certain matters it has shown plenty of competence. It was competent to bring down interest rates and to base upon them a boom in private house-building which for the time being saved the Government the expense of financing a housing programme of its own. And, on the whole, its banking policy has been competent—or, rather, it has worked in so well with the bankers that they have been prepared on its behalf to follow a sensible line, which they would certainly not follow voluntarily or on behalf of a Government of the Left.'

In spite of strong criticism of its Non-Intervention policy in Spain, and continued violent demonstrations against the Means Test, the National Government jogged along fairly comfortably. It was looked upon as reasonably progressive, the best that could be expected from a Government largely composed of Conservatives. Attempts were made from the Left Centre to start a B.M.G. campaign ('Baldwin Must Go'—on the analogy of the old 'Balfour Must Go' line). But Baldwin's personality was not one to excite strong feelings in any breast: he had none of the provocative brilliance of Lloyd George or Winston

Churchill and his only devoted personal following was in the Conservative Party central office. There a legend had been built up for him of being a plain, sound, trustworthy man— 'Honest Stan', in fact. It was said that his greatest asset—when he chose to exercise it—was tactical skill in managing his party: tactical skill, too, in surmounting crises, the Strike, the Depression, the Abdication, with the least possible disturbance to himself, his party, or the country. Finally, he was a past master at timing his occasional bursts of 'appalling frankness' to best political advantage.

Winston Churchill was 'in the wilderness'. He had spoken out against the Nazi régime soon after it came into power and, for the sake of peace, Baldwin had denied him office. On the 28th November 1934 he had made a very strong speech about the danger to Britain of the new German air force:

'Germany . . . is now equipping itself once again, 70,000,000 of people, with the technical apparatus of modern war, and at the same time is instilling into the hearts of its youths and manhood the most extreme patriotic, nationalist, and militarist conceptions. According to what we hear, according to what we are told, and what comes in from every quarter, though little is said about it in public, Germany has already a powerful, well-equipped army, with an excellent artillery, and an immense reserve of armed, trained men. The German munition factories are working practically under war conditions, and war material is flowing out from them, and has been for the last twelve months in an ever broadening stream. Much of this is undoubtedly in violation of the treaties which were signed. Germany is rearming on land; she is rearming also to some extent at sea; but what concerns us most of all is the rearmament of Germany in the air. . . . I shall be specially careful not to exaggerate. Indeed, I hope that every statement that I make will be admitted to be an understatement. . . . I therefore assert, first, that Germany already has a military air force . . . which only awaits an order to assemble in full open combination—and that this illegal air force is rapidly approaching equality with our own. . . . Secondly, the German air force will this time next year be in fact at least as strong as our own, and it may be even stronger. . . . Thirdly . . . two years from now . . . the German military air force will be nearly 50 per cent stronger, and in 1937 nearly double. All this is on the assumption . . . that there is no acceleration on the part of Germany, and no slowing down on our part. . . . Beware: Germany is a country fertile in military surprises!'

He went on to discuss the possibility of the German air force before long reaching 10,000 machines. Baldwin replied to this staggering piece of news:

'Even now, when things look at their blackest, I have not given up hope either for the limitation or for the restriction of some kind of arms. . . . I think it is correct to say that the Germans *are* engaged in creating an air force. . . . The figures we have range from a figure . . . of 600 aircraft to something not over 1,000. . . . The first-line strength . . . of the R.A.F. to-day, at home and overseas, is 880 aircraft. . . . We propose to form in the years 1935 and 1936, 22 squadrons for home defence and, in addition, 3 squadrons for the Fleet Air Arm. . . . That means that by 1936 our first-line strength will be increased by some 300 aircraft over its present figure. . . .

'As for the position this time next year . . . we estimate that we shall have a margin in Europe alone of nearly 50 per cent. I cannot look farther forward than the next two years. Such investigations as I have been able to make lead me to believe that the right honourable member for Epping's figures are considerably exaggerated.'

The *Daily Telegraph* supported Baldwin in a leader, typical of the general Conservative view. It revealed details of British air-expansion unknown to the general public: 'Eleven new sites for aerodromes have been selected, six have been acquired; plans for altering some forty of the older stations are in hand; one new training school for flying has been opened and another will be ready in April. Air estimates . . . money will be readily voted by a House that, except perhaps on the Socialist benches, showed itself genuinely concerned at recent revelations of the inferiority we have imposed on ourselves in the hitherto fruitless search for peace for the world, and not less at the speed with which Germany is rearming herself in the air as on land.'

There was not a single mention of Churchill in this leader. At the end of 1936 Churchill was still in the wilderness. In Robert Graves's diary for November 24th that year there is a note:

'Saw Winston by appointment at Morpeth Mansions this

evening. Told him that as a non-party ex-Serviceman, who had been living in Spain, I wished to stress the great danger of the situation in the western Mediterranean: where the Germans and Italians are threatening British strategical positions. He said angrily, referring to the Spanish war: "Both sides have imbrued their hands with blood—do you wish for intervention? The country wouldn't stand it." I replied: 'Not intervention in the sense of taking sides in the pretended 'ideological struggle' in Spain but of safeguarding British interests in the Mediterranean." He said: "Seven French Deputies have just been to see me, making frantic appeals to me to urge intervention—the best brains in France." I said: "They know you are about the only member in the House with any power as a speaker." He said, suddenly changing his tone: "The trouble is, we are so damned weak. It is Baldwin who has reduced us to this shameful condition. If we went to war now we should have equal chances of defeat and victory." He paced up and down the room: "Baldwin is in power and Parliament is lethargic." "You could rouse them," I said. "Speak out as you did in 1934 and you'll have an overwhelming popular following. Everyone is waiting for you." He spoke of the strength of the Press behind Baldwin. I said: "Press propaganda does not guide or represent the country's real feelings nowadays. Go to a news-cinema any night, and get a sense of the people's reaction to news-reels of the Dictators. And look at Roosevelt's victory—a 2—1 victory when the Press was 3—1 against him!" He agreed that if one put the issue to the country at a general election something might be done; but there was no chance of that, Baldwin being so firm in the saddle. He said that he would make a speech the next day that he hoped would please me. He was thoroughly worked up.'

Churchill nearly got his chance a few days later in the Abdication Crisis; but Baldwin won, and settled more firmly than ever in the saddle.

1937 was Baldwin's year of triumph. He saw crowned the King whom he had brought to the throne, and wisely decided to retire amid the glory that the Coronation brought him. In May he made last speeches to the House, to his constituents, and to a Youth Rally at the Albert Hall. 'The torch which I pass on to you,' he said benevolently to Youth, 'and ask you to pass from hand to hand and along the pathways of the Empire, is the great Christian truth rekindled anew in each ardent generation. I have had my hour and pass soon into the shade, but life lies before you.' The words echoed dimly through the auditorium, as if from far back in the nineteenth century; yet it was a dignified farewell. He became an earl and took up the life of a country worthy in Worcestershire, making only rare appearances in the House of Lords.

He did not, of course, pass on his torch to the youth of Britain, but to a man only two years younger than himself: Neville Chamberlain, the younger son of 'Joe' Chamberlain and brother of Nazi-hating and vigorous Sir Austen. He had begun life as a sisal-planter in the West Indies, then returned to England and become interested in the municipal politics of Birmingham—in 1915 he was that city's Lord Mayor. In 1916–17 he had been Director-General of National Service. In the Twenties he had occupied the not very illustrious posts of Postmaster-General and Minister of Health, and was regarded merely as the competent junior member of a famous political family. For the last six years, however, he had been Chancellor of the Exchequer and had gained a reputation for business-like bureaucratic orthodoxy. As soon as he became Prime Minister, so Conservative columnists reported, his Cabinet, his party, and the House immediately recognized his qualities of brisk leadership. Yet to the country in general during his first year of office he seemed an unremarkable figure: gaunt, with bushy eyebrows and an old-fashioned moustache, but no democratically endearing features.

In the Cabinet reshuffle which followed on Baldwin's retirement Sir John Simon became Chancellor of the Exchequer: though the Manchurian affair of 1932, when he was Foreign Secretary, had 'smudged his copybook'—as the clubmen phrased it. He proposed a National Defence Contribution, levied upon business, for financing rearmament. The City strongly objected: the levy would drive business away and so contribute rather to a new slump than to rearmament. The N.D.C. was modified so as not to bear too heavily on profits: this pleased the City—and also the Left, as a new proof of the Government's capitalistic wickedness.

Another ex-Foreign Secretary with a smudged copybook was appointed Home Secretary. This was Sir Samuel Hoare, whose plan to carve up Abyssinia had now been forgiven him by his colleagues. Alfred Duff Cooper took his place at the Admiralty, although he had not proved a great success at the War Office, despite his warm agreement with the Chief of the Imperial General Staff, General Sir Archibald Montgomery-Massingberd, that mechanization of the Army at the expense of the cavalry arm was both unnecessary and dangerous.

The new War Minister was Leslie Hore-Belisha, who immediately began to apply to the popularization of the Army the same brisk methods which had created such a stir in the Ministry of Transport. He listened to the advice of reliable military experts outside the military hierarchy, with the intention of making the Army as progressive and efficient, if possible, as the Navy. The chief of these experts was Captain Liddell Hart, who had already been asked by the new Minister for the Co-ordination of Defence (Sir Thomas Inskip) to study the question of Army Reorganization. Liddell Hart reported among other things that:

'The size of the British Army has been determined not on any scientific calculation of its needs, but simply on a post-war return to the pre-war standard; and the proportions of the different arms in the total are not based on any principle either.

'There has been no real change in arm-proportions since 1870—a time when the number of "bayonets", as opposed to "fire-units", was the natural way of calculating an army's strength. Army tactical training is still based on the slow-moving infantry battalion, the other arms being regarded as mere auxiliaries.

'The chief need now is for mobile mechanized divisions, an increase of anti-aircraft defences, and a motorized infantry.'

Hore-Belisha met with violent opposition to the reforms which he attempted to introduce in the spirit of this report—even when he had persuaded the Army Council to retire some of the elder generals. Active field-officers who saw the enormous possibilities of army mechanization had advocated it at the sacrifice of their careers: the five who successively became major-generals between 1930 and 1937 had each in turn, on promotion, either been given no further employment or removed to commands where they had no chance to put their views into practice. The 'bow-and-arrow-brigade', as General Crozier had named them, was still dominant in the Army. Liddell Hart's name was especially execrated in higher Army circles and the mischievous rumour was set going that, like Hore-Belisha, he was of Jewish blood—the Army contained a strong anti-Semitic element. The situation had been well expressed by General Sir Philip Chetwode in January 1935, when C.-in-C. in India. He had told graduates of the Quetta Staff College that he was horrified at the number of officers he found who allowed themselves to sink into a state of complete brain slackness. 'Their narrow interests are bounded by the morning parade, the game they happen to play, and purely local and unimportant matters. . . . War, and particularly successful war, is much more an affair of imagination than people think, but few officers of the Army allow much play to their imagination. It would almost seem that it was a crime to do so, or to be one inch outside "sealed pattern" and regulations. The longer I remain in the Service, the more wooden and the more regulation-bound do I find the average British officer to be.'

Hore-Belisha's regenerative task was therefore a next to impossible one. The root of the trouble was that 'the well-bred horse' was still considered the chief auxiliary of the infantryman, and the infantry remained the main arm both for offence and defence. In *Cavalry Training, 1937*, twenty-three pages of text were devoted to sword and lance exercises, illustrated by twenty drawings, and a further twelve 'plates' devoted to drill; a brief supplement to this was enough for armoured cars, in which it was laid down:

'The principle and system of Cavalry Training (Mechanized) will be as laid down in *Cavalry Training* (*Horsed*), with certain modifications laid down in this chapter.

'Mounted drill (in armoured cars) is based on the same principles as that of cavalry.

'The principles of training in field operations given in *Cavalry Training* (*Horsed*) are, in general, applicable to armoured car regiments.'

Ministers came and Ministers went, but the National Government remained the same: more national, however, in name than in representation. Home affairs were not offering any widely debatable problems; in London, at least, the Depression was forgotten. Indeed, a Twentyish spirit was beginning to crop up again—a beggar outside the Piccadilly Hotel wore the remnants of fine clothes and carried, instead of the usual beggar's cap, a frayed top-hat, with a notice saying: 'Hallelujah, I'm a failure'. But the economic recovery was tempting a great many people who had lived through anxious times to shout suddenly in their hearts: 'Hallelujah, I'm a success', and to disregard the omens of war.

Two wars were in progress: in Spain and in China. Spain still figured prominently in the news. Captain 'Potato' Jones, with old-world sea-doggishness, had insisted on running the Insurgent blockade and delivering his cargo of potatoes to the starving citizens of Bilbao. The historic Basque city of Guernica had been bombed almost out of existence by German planes in the service of General Franco; which roused humanitarian, anti-Fascist feelings in circles far beyond the Left, and tempted the Die-Hard Press to assert, in defiance of common sense, that 'Red' Basques had themselves blown the town to pieces with dynamite. Then followed the fall of the Basque and Asturian provinces, with violent repercussions in Britain because of the hospitality given to Basque refugee children, whom the Right denounced as 'Red hooligans' likely to corrupt 'our pure English youth', and the Left defended with aggressive sentimental pity. In Autumn 1937 there was 'piracy in the Mediterranean'; 'unknown' submarines were sinking merchant ships bound for Spanish Republican ports. This was felt by the Fleet as derogating from British naval prestige and the Government was stung into action. A conference was called at Nyon in Switzerland, and an agreement made with the French and Italians to patrol the coasts of Spain in order to protect shipping. The sinkings diminished, and even the Left congratulated the Government on having acted, for once, with promptitude: the honour went to Anthony Eden, the Foreign Secretary, on whose initiative the conference was said to have been called.

The other war had broken out in China in July 1937: by August the Japanese were in possession of Pekin. The same month they fired on and seriously injured the British ambassador to China as he was driving in his car; but diplomatic apologies covered up this incident. In September they were landing at Shanghai, in December they advanced on Nanking, the Chinese capital, and during 1938 they pushed on five hundred miles farther up the Yangtse River, past Hankow, and also occupied Canton in the south. The China war, however, was too far away to attract much attention in Britain, and the Spanish war had become such a permanent feature of the European scene that people took it for granted. Neither war seemed likely to spread. Mussolini, it was said, had plenty to occupy him in Abyssinia, and in the end the Spaniards would throw out the Italian troops and the German technicians and airmen, whichever side won; Britain could then cash in with reconstruction loans.

As for Germany: was there not the Anglo-German naval pact, which limited the German navy to 35 per cent of the British, to prove that Hitler could be conciliatory and intended no menace to the British Empire? Was not Lord Halifax, formerly Viceroy of India and now Lord President of the Council, conferring amicably with him in Berlin in November 1937? Had not Hitler himself said in May 1933: 'No fresh European war is capable of putting something better in place of the unsatisfactory conditions which exist to-day. On the contrary, neither politically nor economically could the use of any kind of force in Europe create a more favourable situation.'. . . And what about Russia? A series of mass trials of alleged Trotskyist 'wreckers' was alienating a great deal of British Left sympathy. The intelligent Marshal Tukachevsky, who had attended the Jubilee of King George V, was sentenced to be shot in July 1937 along with seven other generals. In spite of the newly introduced Russian constitution, claimed to be the most democratic in the world, people shook their heads doubtfully over Russia and spoke of ineradicable Asiatic tyranny. Even some of the Left felt discouraged and ceased to take the *Daily Worker*. Yet it was noted with relief that the Russian generals' crime had been discovered in good time—they had been having secret talks with their opposite numbers in the German Army!

Whatever happened in this country or that, it still seemed to the mass of people in Britain that peace would go on for ever: war was unthinkable. This peace-time mood showed itself in January 1938 in tremendous excitement in the Press over the fact that Princess Juliana of the Netherlands was about to have a baby. Would it be a boy or a girl? If it were a girl Holland might have a succession of Queens whose lives would span a century. As January drew to a close, tension increased: the Dutch were reported to have made all their arrangements for that month, including the manufacture of dated Royal birthday mugs. Would all these have to be scrapped? Providentially no: a girl was born on January 30th.

There was no lack of other newspaper topics to divert public interest from the international scene. For example the pick-a-back planes, *Maia* and *Mercury*, which made successful trials in February. In the previous July there had been two-way air-mail flights across the Atlantic: how soon, people were asking, would passengers also be carried? Next came the case of the 'Mayfair men', Harley, Wilmer, and their associates, who were sentenced to be flogged and to serve long terms of penal servitude for having committed a violent jewel robbery in a high-class London hotel. The crime was the more newsworthy because the criminals belonged to an upper-class social set. This was well-featured in the popular Press with a bright spotlight on the administration of the 'cat' and its effects. From this sprang a controversy upon the morality of flogging as a punishment and its efficacy as a deterrent, which led Sir Samuel Hoare, the Home Secretary, to abolish it. There was another welcome 'torso mystery'; the mutilated body of a professional dancing partner was found at the house of an ex-Army captain, who had himself disappeared.

Yet political events were moving quickly. Neville Chamberlain was already pursuing a policy of appeasing the Dictators: in February 1938, Mussolini was the object of his efforts. He met with opposition, however, even within his own party, and Anthony Eden resigned from the Government, declaring, 'We must not buy goodwill.' At the debate which followed on his resignation the Government's majority in the House fell to 162, chiefly because of a large number of Conservative abstentions. The party line was now being enforced so strictly in the House that Conservative M.P.s could only signify their disagreement with it by abstaining from voting—otherwise they ran the risk of losing party support in their constituencies. No longer free representatives of the people, M.P.s were thus dragooned into party loyalty, as in the days of the 'personal Government' of George III. Eden himself remained loyal to the old school tie, and did not, as some hoped, lend any support to the Left attempts to bring down the Government: he preserved a gentlemanly restraint.

In March came the first overt act of Nazi aggression outside Germany proper: the occupation of Austria. For many it was a complete surprise, for the Press had reported on February 12th that the Austrian Chancellor Schuschnigg had had a highly successful diplomatic conference with Hitler. But on the whole, the annexation of Austria was received quietly: the Austrians were really Germans, people remarked, and theirs was a small country—a head and stomach that had been lopped of its limbs —why should it not be united with the Reich? And the usual optimism was expressed by those who did not understand the thoroughness of the Nazi régime. It was said that the Austrians were temperamentally very different from the Germans: to incorporate them into the Reich would cause Hitler plenty of trouble. British politicians denounced Hitler's act in mild terms as a 'rape'—to be accused of rape in Britain subjected one to much less loss of respect than defalcation or bigamy—and only a few of the more advanced members of the Opposition prophesied correctly to what it would lead. Sir Stafford Cripps said: 'The independence of Austria has disappeared. . . . Germany's next act of aggression will be directed against Czechoslovakia, and then the people of Great Britain will find themselves back in the days of 1914.' But nobody listened to Sir Stafford.

One of the immediate effects of the Austrian coup was to inspire renewed confidence among British investors and business men. No counter-action had followed this act of aggression: the profitable rearmament campaign could proceed at leisure. The front page of the *Financial News* for the 10th March 1938 contained these items:

> Vickers' Good Profits.
> English Steel Pay 20 per cent.
> Cammell Laird Income Rises Sharply.
> Thomas Frith and John Brown Earn More.
> Markets Close Firmer.
> Royal Mail Lines Pay More
> Dunlop Pays 9 per cent.
> Stock Exchange More Confident.

The confidence of the Stock Exchange, reflected in the newspapers, spread to the public, which had no sense of the imminence of war or the real dangers of the military situation. It was known that new ships were being laid down for the Navy, and that the Royal Air Force was being trebled; Hore-Belisha's Army Reforms were also being well publicized. The *Sunday Express* reported at the beginning of summer that in the 'New Army' troops were no longer expected to go daily for long route marches or take part only in the endless formalities of drill; instead they were whisked rapidly round the country in lorries and tanks. The modern soldier, the *Express* said, had ceased to be of the old, tough, liquor-loving, brave but stupid type: he was intelligent, he smoked a lot, but he rarely drank, and he consumed great quantities of nourishing cream buns and chocolate. The Army was no longer advertised merely by the old adventure-appeal posters: 'Join the Army and See the World', but by 'Join the Modern Army', with pictures of tanks, searchlights, lorries, anti-aircraft guns—all calculated to attract the mechanically minded, modern young man. This publicity for what Hore-Belisha hoped to be able to effect, and some successful reforms in the status of the Territorial Army and in the living conditions of soldiers, encouraged recruiting. At the beginning of 1939 the cadres of the Regular and Territorial Armies were almost filled—though the *Spectator* noted that it was proving easier to find officers than men for the latter.

Much disgust was felt with Belisha's Army 'democratization' by regular Army officers, especially with his plan for awarding commissions to promising N.C.O.s. It was felt that this course might be a proper one in war-time when the 'right type of man' would at once be drafted into the ranks, but not in time of peace. The 'right type of man' meant the socially right type from the Officers' Mess point of view—the ex-public-schoolboy. It was admittedly true that there were a number of active, intelligent and forceful N.C.O.s who, as war-time officers, might well know better what to do in a tight corner than some graduates of Sandhurst; but that was not the point. The country was still at peace, and if there was one thing that the Army officer disliked it was a ranker officer who 'ate peas with his knife and did not know how to address a lady ; a number of these had continued to hold commissions after the war ended, until forced to resign or transfer by the studied coldness of their brothers-in-arms.

Mildly disquieting questions were occasionally raised in the House and in the Press. Were our rearmament plans already out of date? Was Air Force expansion behind schedule? What about Ground Defence? The last was a particularly sore subject. Barrage balloons had been suggested, but would enough be sent up to keep off raiders? And was Britain not short of anti-aircraft guns? Were part-time voluntary A.R.P. workers sufficient? What about fire-fighting services? And what were the functions and powers of those heroic busybodies, the Wardens? Then there were gas-masks—the Government intended to distribute them to everybody—yet would they be proof against the most poisonous gases or, indeed, against any?

The most controversial subject was air-raid shelters. The Government was planning, it was said, to provide blast-proof steel shelters for every house in the country—free to all below a certain income level—to be sunk in the garden and covered with a protective layer of earth. Many people, however, had no gardens in which shelters could be sunk. Besides, the efficacy of this type of shelter was derided both by engineers and by Leftists who had been to Barcelona and had seen the effect of modern bombing attacks. The Government came in for heavy criticism in a pamphlet called *Ten Cambridge Scientists and Air Raid Protection*. No cognizance, the scientists said, had been taken of high-explosive bombs. Compared with these, gas was a negligible danger, if it was used at all—which was unlikely, since it had not been used in Spain. They accused the Government of distributing masks and shelters only as confidence-propaganda. 'The proposed precautions would fail', they wrote, 'even in this respect, the moment war broke out, and the propaganda drive which is being used to popularize them is a tragic deception of the people of this country.' These ten from Cambridge had social consciences, and protested strongly against the expenditure of A.R.P. money solely on the protection of business and residential quarters, to the neglect of working-class districts. Some borough councils, such as Finsbury in London, on which there was a Labour majority, then brought forward grandiose plans for the construction of deep shelters for all, but they were too expensive to be proceeded with. It is not altogether remarkable that so much energy went into controversies over means of civilian defence, while the newspaper critics almost entirely ignored the question of whether the Fighting Forces were equipped with sufficient striking power to wage a modern war. For the British in general were so pacifically inclined that they could only think of war in terms of defence: counter-attack seemed as unholy as the aggression that might provoke it.

CHAPTER TWENTY-FIVE

Still at Peace

In the Thirties the number and popularity of News Cinemas greatly increased. The news-programme usually repeated itself every hour and a half, rather than every three hours, and the entrance fee was correspondingly reduced. They were News Cinemas precisely in the sense that the newspapers were newspapers. The programme consisted usually of two short news reels giving pictures of parades, disasters, sporting events, and so on; a Walt Disney film for the comic strip; for feature articles, short sequences on travel, fashion, natural history, industry, sport; often an interview; musical interludes.

The last years of the Thirties were notable for some real improvement in full-length British films. In 1938 there was 'Pygmalion', featuring Leslie Howard; Bernard Shaw himself adapted his play for filming and won the American Academy of Motion Pictures' Annual Award for the best scenario. There was also 'The Citadel', starring Robert Donat, and adapted from A. J. Cronin's realistic moral novel about a doctor's progress from a Welsh mining village to a practice in Harley Street. Alfred Hitchcock was the most skilful of British directors: in his thriller, 'The Lady Vanishes', a high spot was an apparently topical Crisis-conversation between two Englishmen in the restaurant-car of a train, illustrated by tactical exercises with lumps of sugar on the tablecloth. The talk turned out to refer to the precarious position of the English cricket eleven in a Test Match, which they were hurrying from abroad to attend. When the enthusiasts reached Victoria Station they were met with a poster: 'Rain Stops Play'.

Many of the most talented British actors and actresses were still drifting to Hollywood. Herbert Marshall, George Arliss, and Edna Best had gone long before; Charles Laughton and Diana Wynard more recently; now younger people, such as Vivien Leigh and Leslie Howard, were going too. Hollywood could offer chances to actors, and produce films, with which Elstree, Denham, Teddington, Ealing, and the other British studios could not compete.

The highbrow vogue for German and Russian films was over; French films were the most admired, for a witty quality which was lacking in those of all other nations. The wit lay more in the smooth, cynically sentimental treatment of situations, than in the words—for nothing could equal American wisecracks, and, in any case, few intellectuals understood French dialogue. 'La Kermesse Héroique' was perhaps the most appreciated French film of 1937: it showed how the women of a prosperous town in the Low Countries warded off the destruction of their homes—their husbands being too cowardly to defend them against the savage Spaniards—by giving the invaders (and themselves) a thoroughly good time. This elegant defeatism agreed with a strong current of contemporary opinion: that perhaps if one were nice to the Germans and Italians in an unofficial way they might prove to be gentlemen after all. In this sense the Chamberlain Government represented the cowardly husbands. Episodic films were a French speciality: Sacha Guitry's autobiography and 'Un Carnet de Bal', which followed up the very varied careers of several young men who had written their names on a girl's dance-card. This was the time when American hay-wire comedy was at its wildest: the heartless and unnatural antics of the Marx Brothers giving their numerous British fans the same sort of Surrealist *frisson* as Salvador Dali was then handing out to New York window-shoppers.

British humorous plays inclined to farce: typical was a week-end country-house setting with several different types of conventional characters who invariably misunderstood each other, made passes at one another's girls, got into difficulties with their Blimp-like parents, and were accidentally shut in one another's bedrooms. A variation on this type was Terence Rattigan's competent 'French Without Tears'. The country-house was a French college for young diplomats with a comic French tutor and his conventionally beautiful daughter. The lives of the three young men there—the dreaming idiot, the jolly-good-funster and the intelligent one—were disturbed by the arrival of a right-minded naval commander and a feather-brained siren. The end of the resultant love-tangle was conventionally ironical: the siren captured the intelligent one and the dreaming idiot was won by the tutor's daughter. 'French Without Tears' ran in London for over two years.

Parody and topical satire were provided by the small revues: the Little Revue and the Gate Revue, especially, which ran every season at the theatres from which they took their names, with occasional change of turns. Full-length plays were rarely satirical, the only one to make a hit being an American social drama, 'The Women' by Claire Boothe; it was also filmed and printed in serial form in a London evening newspaper. The popular Press debated whether women were so cruel and cynical as Miss Boothe showed them—in Britain at least.

The theatres were providing a bewildering variety of entertainment: farces, revues, suburban comedy, period pieces, so-called realistic dramas, religious plays, verse plays, revivals of classics, thrillers, musical shows. There was an emotional play about 'the next war': 'Idiot's Delight', in which the characters gave vent to the prevalent anti-war feeling. 'They're all talking about security. They're all jittery. So they get bigger cannons and sharper bayonets. And that makes them more jittery. It doesn't seem to make sense.' And: 'I'll tell you what else you can do in these tragic circumstances. You can refuse to fight. Have you ever thought of that possibility? You can refuse to use those weapons that they have sold you!' The Peace Pledge Union seized on such remarks and reprinted them in pamphlets.

The plays of the whimsical Czech Carel Capek were also popular in London: three of them, 'The Insect Play', 'The White Plague', and 'The Mothers' dealt with war themes. But it was very seldom that plays reflected serious contemporary currents of thought; nor was this to be expected. They were written purely as upper-middle-class entertainment. Producers played for safety. A 'difficult' play was unlikely to run for more than a week or two, however encouraging the critics. As the period advanced it became almost impossible to engage good companies for a play that did not have a sporting chance of success, even if financial backing could be found. Most productions were therefore lightweight stuff with a backward slant to the pre-1914 sentimental level. Few intelligent people went regularly to the theatres, except as a social habit hard to break. Successful stage plays were usually filmed after a time and could be seen more cheaply and more comfortably in the cinemas. Actors on the whole were coming to prefer cinema work to stage work: not only because it was better paid and made less demands on the memory but because the result was less evanescent and incorporated the best possible versions of each dramatic sequence. Occasionally an actor or actress who had made a name in the films returned temporarily to the stage, missing the thrill of personally dominating an audience with voice or gesture. But few or none returned for good. Except for small experimental groups who drew special audiences—intellectual, Left, or Trade Union—to small halls at cheap prices, and the keen provincial repertory companies, which were graduate schools of dramatic art, the British Theatre was as good as dead.

Managers of theatres and cinemas were even more alarmed by the threat of commercial television than they had been by broadcasting. Their hostility threw television back on its own resources. It had its own studios at Alexandra Palace and was financed out of B.B.C. revenue, but the number of viewers in 1939 was only about 50,000. As an entertainment it was still chiefly a novelty; though the successful relaying of public events, such as the Derby, the Cup Final, and the University Boat Race, showed it as a probable rival to news-reels. Gaumont-British prepared to meet this danger by equipping seventy of their cinemas with apparatus for rediffusing television programmes. A poll among viewers showed that the most popular television items were productions of plays, and the studios therefore concentrated on these. Sets were still expensive, reception still uncertain, and programmes still experimental when the new war broke out and the studios were closed down.

The book-market, meanwhile, was being flooded with political titles: *Searchlight on Spain, Our Debt to Spain, The Spanish Cockpit, Danger Spots of Europe, Europe in the Melting Pot, Between Two Wars?, Britain Looks at Germany, Germany—What Next?, Blackmail or War?, Britain and the Dictators, Czechs and Germans, Europe and the Czechs, What Hitler Wants, I Was Hitler's Prisoner,*

I Married a German, and so on. Some of these were sold in Penguin editions. Penguins were first published in 1936; they were excellently printed in the readable New Roman type, which *The Times* had developed, and bound in stiff paper covers. They sold at sixpence—it was the first time that the public had been able to get really cheap reprints of successful books still in copyright.

Penguins also sold upper-class books such as Ernest Hemingway's *A Farewell to Arms*, Aldous Huxley's *Crome Yellow*, Liam O'Flaherty's *The Informer*, E. M. Forster's *A Passage to India*, George Moore's *Esther Waters*, Norman Douglas's *South Wind*, André Maurois's *Ariel*, to a huge self-improving public. Penguins became a household word and the cheerful, orange-and-white covers of their fiction were to be seen on every bookstall and at every newsagents'. The booksellers feared that Penguins might diminish the sale of dearer books, though it was pointed out that they reached a public which had never dreamt of paying 7s. 6d. for a novel and disliked the lending library system, and that buyers of 7s. 6d. novels would buy Penguins too. This was true, and before three years had gone by one could scarcely find a bookshelf in Britain which did not contain at least half a dozen Penguins. Yet the fee that Penguin authors got was small; and though to be in the series was held to be a fine advertisement, ordinary book publishers and literary agents were of opinion that, whatever the social benefits of the Penguin system might be, financially it was bad for publishers, booksellers, and authors alike. It was the same verdict that manufacturers of small high-grade articles, particularly hardware, china and glass, made against Woolworth's cheap lines.

Penguin Books soon launched other ventures. They produced Pelicans, which were informative books on science, economics, history, arts, sociology, and archaeology. Among the first Pelicans were Bernard Shaw's *Intelligent Woman's Guide to Socialism*, Julian Huxley's *Essays in Popular Science*, Sir Leonard Woolley's *Digging Up the Past*, H. G. Wells's *Short History of the World*, Sir James Jeans's *The Mysterious Universe*, and Dr. Freud's *Psychotherapy of Everyday Life*. Penguin Books also began to commission writers to do 'Specials', described as 'books of topical importance published within as short a time as possible from the receipt of the manuscript. Some are reprints of famous books brought up to date, but usually they are entirely new books published for the first time'. Their subjects were chiefly international crises and the problems of war and peace. Their authors were expected to rush them off at top speed so that they would be on the market when the crisis was at its height. Besides these specials, Penguin Books produced illustrated classics—Jane Austen, Daniel Defoe, Herman Melville, etc., editions of Shakespeare's plays, and guides to the counties of England.

Penguins had many imitators, but none covered so wide a range of subjects. Finding Penguin Books in possession of the serious sixpenny market, they tended to concentrate on thrillers. The wide sale of the informative and educational Pelicans, like the success of the Left Book Club, showed that people wanted to understand and to learn about current problems and the general life of the world. Different aspects of contemporary life were also being factually presented by writers of various trades and professions. Journalists, doctors, and lawyers wrote autobiographies from the point of view of their professional rather than their private lives. Big successes in these years were *Coming, Sir*, a waiter's autobiography, and *It's Draughty in Front* by a London taxi-driver, both dealing primarily with working conditions, and two or three books by amateur housemaids—university and Society girls who entered domestic service in order to find out what it was like. Intelligent ex-convicts also wrote up their prison experiences. They described realistically the strict Victorian rules which still governed English prisons and the brutalizing effect on the prisoners, but without attempting to whip up hysterical feeling against the prison-system or to glorify the convicts as martyrs. The intelligent middle-class public far preferred such 'low-life' books, written by people who had actually gone through what they described, to romantic write-ups by professional journalists of the Lowell Thomas, Harold Begbie, and William Le Queux tradition.

Some 'low-life' fiction was read in these years, particularly the new American short story. The stories of the American-Armenian, William Saroyan, began to be popular in England in 1936 and those of the American sports-columnist Damon Runyon in 1937. Saroyan's were scarcely stories at all, but inconsequential monologues on life, love, and work by low-class American-Armenian characters. Runyon's were farcical, rather long-winded anecdotes, also told in the first person, about a group of gangsters, racing men, and business men who haunted one of the lower-grade saloons of New York. Both Saroyan and Runyon were admired for their completely amoral, wise-cracking, slang-ridden treatment of the well-worn themes of love, work, and crime. The slang especially created a stir. E. C. Bentley accounted for it in an introduction to one of Runyon's books: 'We produce little slang of our own to-day: what we have is of old standing. Our borrowing in this way is, I suppose, one of the results of the enormous impression made on us (whether we like it or not) by the vigour, the self-sufficiency, the drama and melodrama of American life.' (E. C. Bentley was the most English of contemporary writers, author of the well-known parody of the stilted type of detective novel, *Trent's Last Case*, and inventor of the only popular verse-form that rivalled the Limerick—the 'Clerihew'. Clerihews were originally chanted to psalm-tunes, hence their stanzaic irregularity; e.g.:

> 'Sir Christopher Wren
> Was dining with some men
> He said: If any one calls
> Tell him I'm designing St. Paul's.')

People were also wanting factual information on political matters, and feeling that they were not always getting it from the mass-produced, Business-controlled, profit-making daily and weekly Press. The hush-hush over Mrs. Simpson in the months preceding the Abdication had made many people realize for the first time that newspapers did not necessarily print the whole news. The Left had long since developed its own methods of countering the self-censorship of the Press by starting news-services of its own. Besides the sensational *Daily Worker*, there was also the six-page, cyclostyled *The Week*, which offered its subscribers cynically written 'inside' information on the week's international political manœuvres. It often proved uncannily well-informed upon the opinions, activities and importance of back-stage political leaders, and made a point of boasting of its unimpeachable connections. *The Week* had many imitators, issued by people who were alarmed that the only source of 'inside' information should lie in Communist hands. Commander Stephen King-Hall, the son of an Admiral, himself an

ex-naval officer and a well-known political writer and broad-
caster, began in 1938 to publish a weekly bulletin, the *K-H News
Letter*. This contained personal views in essay-like form, rather
than strictly factual information. Nevertheless, by the middle of
1939 it had a circulation of over 50,000. It was followed by
many other news-letters. For example, the *Arrow*, by a diplomatic correspondent; the *Broadsheet*, by a distinguished lawyer;
Father Desmond's Views Letter, by an Anglo-Catholic ecclesiastic;
In Plain English, by the medical correspondent of *The Times*,
who had views about finance as well as about medicine; the
Fleet Street News Letter; the *Diplomatic-Political Correspondent*; and
Empire sheets such as the *Hong-Kong News Letter* and the Australian *Considerations*. All these gave facts overlooked or suppressed
by the newspapers, and represented one man's personal interpretation of events or the views of some important minority.
They were a revival of the personal news-letters which had been
circulated among large groups of friends or business associates
in the seventeenth and eighteenth centuries. All were distributed
by post to subscribers and none publicly offered for sale on
bookstalls or in the streets; this emphasized their personal,
'inside' appeal, and also protected them from retaliatory action
by the newspapers or the public characters they maligned.

Newspaper editors began to see that the public liked to feel
that it was getting the 'inside facts'. Already in France Mme
Géneviève Tabouis of the anti-Fascist *L'Œuvre* enjoyed a great
reputation for knowing what was happening 'behind the scenes',
even though many of her statements and predictions proved
unfounded. Her articles were published in England by the
independent-minded *Sunday Referee*, which some people bought
solely for that reason. Just before the war began, even the
popular newspapers began to run 'Inside Information' and
'Secret Service' columns in which were presented special pieces
of political information and conjecture in a way which suggested secret prowling down the 'diplomatic corridors'. It
would be wrong to suggest that the British were suddenly
developing an overpowering desire to know nothing but the
facts. They were also looking for optimistic encouragement and
for acknowledged authority to rely on in everyday decisions and
points of view. Part of the success of news-letters was due to
their avoidance of newspaper tricks and rhetoric, which made

them seem reliable. Yet almost all but *The Week* kept up the same optimistic tones as the general Press.

A highly soothing influence was exercised by horoscopes. They gave daily advice to people born within certain dates on love matters, family matters, business matters, when to travel, when to propose, when to get married, when to invest money. They were forced by pressure of space to break away from 'scientific' astrology by paying no attention to the latitude and longitude, nor to the hour, day, or even year of the births for which their horoscopes were cast. They even ventured into political prediction. The horoscopes of political leaders were drawn, and the aspect and conjunctions of the stars on particular dates considered—from these, solemn conclusions were reached as to the date, the character, and the consequences of the next crisis.

Toward the end of the Thirties nearly all popular newspapers were publishing horoscopes. An exception was the *Daily Herald*, which even after its regeneration under Odham's management continued to regard them as Capitalist dope. Later, horoscopes were chiefly a feature of Sunday newspapers, all of which except the *Sunday Times* and the *Observer*, were publishing them by 1938. A great number of people from every class studied them with religious care—especially women. Men were more ashamed of confessing themselves superstitious. The *Spectator*, however, observed in January 1939: 'Business men of position are known to refuse to sign papers or to make important decisions, should a certain day be indicated as unlucky.' The most famous astrologer was R. H. Naylor of the *Sunday Express*, whose well-featured column, when it first appeared, was illustrated by a photograph of himself, middle-aged, bespectacled, quietly lighting his pipe, a box of matches in his left hand, looking as respectable and reliable as any bank manager. Naylor also wrote for a sixpenny monthly magazine *Prediction*, which contained articles on palmistry, phrenology, numerology, graphology, clairvoyance, spiritualism, and hypnotism. One Sunday newspaper boasted that it had obtained the services of the one and only Petulengro, the Gipsy Oracle; a rival countered this by announcing the engagement of no less an authority than Old Moore himself. *Old Moore's* was the best known annual almanack; it had made its reputation in Victorian times by correctly prophesying snow

on Derby Day. Unfortunately nine different and conflicting
Old Moore's were published, the name never having been copy-
righted. Each chose to regard itself as the only genuine and
original one. All sold well around Christmas-time. Sir Thomas
Overbury had written three centuries before:

> 'An Almanack Maker
> Is the worst part of an Astronomer.'

But as the *Spectator* sagely pointed out: 'Times of fear and doubt
and uncertainty make even educated men and women seek to
lift the veil off the future and find guidance and reassurance
concerning things to come.'

A new illustrated weekly magazine, *Picture Post*, was founded
in 1938. It was a British version of the American magazine *Life*,
which set out to give documentary photographs of American
and foreign life, accompanied by short, incisive comment. *Life's*
technique of photo-journalism was derived from German experiments, begun about 1926, when the miniature Leica camera
was put on the market. With the fast, accurate, and unobtrusive
Leica the news-photographer could take snapshots of altogether
unsuspecting sitters unposed studies of politicians and other
notabilities by Dr. Salomon at first created a sensation. As the
art magazine the *Studio* remarked some ten years later: 'His
unprecedentedly candid camera snapped the mounting cigar-
ash of conference tables, the dishevelled glasses of long drawn-
out banquets, the weary humanity of the great off their guard,
a smile, a gesture, the droop of a boiled shirt, that were not
posed, but actual and revealing.' The 'candid camera' was
turned upon events and situations as well as upon notabilities.
Stefan Lorant, the editor of the *Münchner Illustrierte Presse*, began
to publish series of photographs which presented whole situations and problems pictorially. Lorant believed that people
should be photographed as they really were, not as they would
want to appear, and that the camera should be used like a
reporter's notebook to record the lives of all kinds of men and
women. He came to England after the rise of the Nazi party
and helped to found *Picture Post*. This weekly, like the American *Life* and the French *Match*, was concerned with portraying
life realistically. The picture-pages in daily newspapers were
now similarly used: their photographs, largely contributed by

'minicam' amateurs, were no longer mere illustrations of the day's news, but had intrinsic news value. Even *The Times*—and later on the *Times Literary Supplement*—began to admit photographs, though *The Times* still preferred choice pictures of the English countryside and large country houses.

The British and French imitators of *Life*, not having the same financial backing, experience, or command of advertisements, fell as short of the original as did the imitators of *Time*. It was the *Time* company that had launched *Life*. *Time* itself had started on an absurdly small capital in the early Twenties, but was in a position to announce that it expected to publish *Life* at a considerable loss for the first year of issue. Its imitators could not afford the best copy-writers available, nor the quality of printing that would do justice to their photographs. *Picture Post* attempted at the start to cater for the intelligent populace, as *Life* did: but as had happened so often before to ambitious new periodicals in Britain, the response was discouraging. The dead-alive reactions of the common people to vital topics raised was reflected in *Picture Post's* weekly post-bag. They preferred pictorial vaudeville. Lorant soon provided this in his bright monthly, *Lilliput*, a refugee version of *Querschnitt*.

It was rather to *The Times*, *Daily Telegraph*, *Observer*, and *Sunday Times* that intelligent people sent letters. If these papers had impartially printed all the well-informed letters that came in, rather than a picked selection confirming the general editorial policy, political and national history, especially during the Abdication, Non-Intervention, and Munich Crises might have taken a very different course. This partiality was forced on the select Press by the knowledge that any opposition to the line taken by the Government would be considered by them as 'against the National Interest' and that, as a punishment, news from Governmental sources would be withheld from any offending journal. The Press was not censored; it was coerced.

There was a fairly active form of censorship for American periodicals. Postal subscribers did not have their copies tampered with in the mails, but on several occasions, during the Abdication crisis and after, people who bought copies of *Time* and other American news magazines from the bookstalls found whole pages torn out. Censorship of political films was an old story. Propaganda dramas that were thought likely to cause a breach of the peace, such as 'Battleship Potemkin' and other Russian dramas, had been forbidden public showing in the early Twenties; now in the Thirties there was a ban even on straight commentaries, such as the Spanish War picture, 'England Expects', which showed the bombing of British ships, and a couple of issues of the *March of Time*—they were held to present the European war-danger too realistically. The censorship often seemed biased in its view of what was likely to cause a breach of the peace, and what was not. In the early Twenties, though 'Battleship Potemkin' was banned, anti-Bolshevist propaganda films were allowed, as has been noted—one was even run through in the House of Commons to the assembled members. And at the same time as a *March of Time* on the subject of Nazi Germany was forbidden, by request of the German Embassy, a news-film edited by the historian, Professor G. P. Gooch, was shown at all news-theatres, giving a pro-Nazi version of Germany's claim to her lost Colonies. Photography was no longer merely a science or a trade: it was an art, and took itself very seriously, even claiming its 'Old Masters'—Daguerre, Lewis Carroll, Julia Cameron. The same potential aesthetic value was claimed for detailed close-ups of 'actuality' —gutters in the rain, cats in the garbage bin, or dirty crockery in a restaurant sink—as for romantic corn-wagons waiting at rustic mills, moon-scapes, and female nudes. Abstract and surrealist photographs were also in vogue, and camera portraits were no longer regarded as album items or silver-framed mantelpiece ornaments: they were now mounted and framed and hung on walls with artistic deliberation, like paintings. The Queen herself graciously honoured a Mayfair fashion by allowing herself to be photographed by Cecil Beaton, whose work was distinguished for its 'tasteful composition'; his sitters were arranged in relation to carefully composed backgrounds and a few choice neo-Victorian objects.

Photography as a science, and as an aid to science, made great advances. Chemicals were analysed by X-ray diffraction and spectroscopic methods. Infra-red photography was used in criminology, botany, and in the examination of documents and paintings; aerial photography in geographical surveys; microphotography in all kinds of delicate work. After the Depression of 1931 advertisers began to prefer illustrative photographs, for black and white reproduction, to original drawings by artists: they were both more effective and cheaper. Colour photography was coming only slowly into trade use; eyes trained to interpret colour in terms of black and white were shocked by what seemed the unnatural emphasis of the colour photograph, though in effect this did not radiate nearly the same amount of colour as the subject taken. American advertising carried far more photographs than British, both coloured and black and white, in proportion to letterpress. The *Studio* remarked on this point in 1937: 'As British advertising accepts the powerful influence of the U.S.A. practice, similar developments are to be expected here.' By this time it was taken for granted not only in business but in all departments of everyday life that the United States should set the course and the pace, and Great Britain follow.

Books were being far better illustrated, especially travel books. General panoramas had gone out of fashion but intensely detailed 'bled' photographs were used—printed to cover the whole of the page, without a margin or a surrounding black line. This gave an impression of generous and intimate reality. Much else had been happening in book production. Not long after the war there had been a revival of interest in typography and wood-cuts, which caused a boom in extravagantly got-up limited editions. Some of these were printed in adaptations of antique type, some in specially designed, simple, modern type; fine expensive hand-made paper was used, calf and vellum bindings, and lithographic illustrations. The Depression put an end to this boom and many of the recently founded printing presses went out of business. Some publishers, however, had meanwhile learned to take an intelligent interest in the selection of type and in the lay-out and decoration of pages. A director of one of the youngest and most successful publishing firms said: 'The publisher, in assuming full responsibility for his books, has discovered two virtues as a result of his personal efforts: the well-produced book that has character and, hardly less important, the "house-style" . . . he designs them all, either consciously or with a natural style that he cannot avoid, in such a way as to make them recognizable as members of one family.'

Another new feature in book production during the period was the use of book-jackets. As late as 1928 the *Studio* was refer-

ring to them as a 'novel feature that has already attained importance'. They soon showed a vast variety of colours and designs:
simple and complex, abstract and representational, aggressively
modern and sentimentally 'period'. More than anything else,
jackets served to brighten up bookshop windows; and were
found by publishers' travellers to exercise an increasing influence on sales.

The factual, realistic, Leftward march of prose-books continued, yet without arriving at any remarkably new landscape
in literature, or providing any notable new figures to people one
if found. The poets and politicians of a period usually give a
valuable clue to its character. The politicians have been presented in the last chapter. Our last backward glance at the
literature of the period will therefore be at the work of the poets.
Most of the prominent elder ones were now dead: Charles
Doughty, Sir William Watson, Robert Bridges, Thomas Hardy,
A. E. Housman, and W. B. Yeats. John Masefield was now
Poet Laureate, but writing chiefly in prose. The middle generation—T. S. Eliot, Walter de la Mare, W. H. Davies, the Sitwells
—had all either almost or wholly stopped writing poems. The
two chief 'creative' literary magazines had ceased publication:
the pontifical *London Mercury* and the learned *Criterion*. Most of
the small periodicals of more recent foundation, such as *New
Verse*, had likewise been put out of action by the end of 1939.
What was happening to the English literary world? Was it
dying, or merely in hibernation?

Some seemed to regard it as already dead. W. H. Auden, the
leading Left poet, had migrated to the United States; so had
Christopher Isherwood. Louis MacNeice soon followed. (In the
last two peace-years, Auden had collaborated with both of
these in boyish, informal travel scrapbooks, written partly in
light verse, partly in light prose, but all in saleable journalese.)
It was not only the youthful idols of the Thirties who were
going. Some established men of letters, such as Aldous Huxley,
went too. In the gathering storm of Europe's crises the United
States stood out as a safe and lively place of refuge. Vera Brittain, the Feminist and Pacifist leader, wrote a book, *Thrice a
Stranger*, in 1938, about her visits to the New World and her
changing attitudes to it. She concluded with these lyrical words
of hopeful admiration: 'Thirteen years ago America appeared

to me in the guise of an antagonist. Nine years later she became my friend; to-day she represents the beloved refuge to which I would gladly entrust the lives that I hold most dear. From the forward direction of her aspiring, invincible spirit, freed from the impulse of death that leads ancient cultures to compass their own destruction, arises one sure and certain hope that for those whom she shelters, the dawn of to-morrow will break.' This was a new feeling for an English writer to express: none in the Twenties, or even in the early Thirties, could possibly have brought himself to look upon the United States as the home of culture. Yet now it was a common feeling among the intelligent few—not shared, however, by the majority, who still regarded Americans with jealous, condescending and irritated, yet proudly admiring suspicion.

Among those who remained, another member of the much-publicized Left trio of the early Thirties, Cecil Day Lewis, had become rather novelist, reviewer, pamphleteer, lecturer, and platform-speaker than poet. Stephen Spender alone of the three was still keeping his flannel-textured Red flag of culture flying —but the colour had not proved fast. Baldwin in July 1936 had appealed to the Congress of British Empire Universities at Cambridge to produce more poets. New poets were always, of course, appearing, but most of these came to a dead end as soon as they left the universities, which were their breeding-places. One made literary news: the crabbed and dark-minded Welshman, Dylan Thomas, whose poems were strewn with wild, organic, telescoped images, underneath which perhaps ran a submerged stream of poetic thought. His poems were the subject of a Press controversy on 'difficult poetry'; Edith Sitwell came out as his champion. Advanced literary critics also pointed hopefully to the turbulent and ecstatic torrent of verse on such themes as dreams, love, and the fate of Spain which spurted from George Barker's pen. Then there was a slim volume by Charles Madge, co-founder of Mass Observation, which began with astrological and dream poems and ended with prose fragments like newspaper cuttings; and the punning, pseudo-scientific schoolboy work of William Empson, a 'synthetic' writer.

Poetry in England was not dead, but it was in a bad way. The experimental stage and the Left stage had both been passed some time before war broke out and nothing new had replaced them. Like everyone else in the last two peace-years, the poets in general were in a state of expectant, fearful, inactive confusion. A few, however, contributed to the big critical compendium *The World and Ourselves*, edited by Laura Riding in 1938, the conclusion of which was that the tragic absurdity of public events was due to a moral failure among the 'outside people'—the institutionally minded directors of affairs; but equally to a failure among independent minded and sensitive 'inside people'—who should include most women and all poets —to give the outside people a lead. The remedy suggested was a continual insistence by the inside people on personal integrity —an attitude to be communicated from friend to friend through the close network of real friendships that made up society. This minority report conflicted with the popular view which, lumping painters, sculptors, musicians, and poets together under the single category of 'artists', denied that to be a 'good artist' one needed necessarily to be a good person. The most admired poet of the time, W. B. Yeats, had in 1935 rejected the suggestion that he should incorporate in his *Oxford Book of Modern Verse* any of the poems of James Reeves, who with Norman Cameron was among the few who still maintained poetic sincerity and dignity. He commented on Reeves's *The Natural Need*: 'Too true, too sincere. The Muse prefers the liars, the gay and warty lads.' Yeats's younger colleagues of the Thirties had indeed not fallen short of this monstrous specification.

To be a poet was no longer a popular distinction, as it had been even in the early Twenties. Hardly a poet now earned enough by the sale of collected poems to keep him in tobacco. The crown had passed to the novelist, who was essayist, dramatist, pamphleteer, prose-poet, historian, all in one. The novel became industrialized: novels succeeded less on their literary merits than on the sales-power that author and publisher could exert by direct and indirect advertisement and 'pull'. Useful instruments to this end were the professional reviewers, whose chief gift was knowing whom it was wise to praise or safe to slam. Their names grew bloated from constant quotation in publishers' announcements. In 1936 the head of one of the largest British publishing-houses congratulated his shareholders on the valuable contracts secured that year 'not only with well-known novelists, but with novelists who are also reviewers'.

CHAPTER TWENTY-SIX

Rain Stops Play, 1939

By 1939 it was calculated that some 25,000 refugees had entered the country from Germany and Austria, some of them illegally, since 1933. The stupider elements of the Right worked up an agitation against the alleged competition of refugees for jobs which Englishmen could do just as well. Some sections of the professional classes were particularly indignant that German and Austrian doctors and dentists should be allowed to practise in Britain. Serious weeklies then rallied to the defence of the refugee, under the old cry of 'England, the asylum for the persecuted'. The *Spectator* observed that a great many of the refugees who reached Britain were either highly trained men or else had sufficient funds to be more of an asset than a liability to the country. The *Manchester Guardian* quoted the case of three Austrians who had opened a factory which was then employing two hundred British workmen, thus helping to solve the unemployment problem. It was contended that refugees were transferring whole new industries to Britain—the Leipzig fur trade, for example, almost entirely built up by Jews, had been brought to London. In north-eastern England refugee Jews were setting up a number of new factories for furnishing materials; and dresses which had formerly been bought by London department stores from foreign firms could now be bought from the same firms in Britain. But this accounted only for the richer refugees. Poorer ones had to huddle together in back rooms and kick their heels in the offices of Refugee Committees. There was little sympathy felt for these, especially when they fell foul of the law. In 1938 the magistrate of the Old Street police-court sentenced three refugees, one of them a pregnant woman, to six months' hard labour for entering the country without an official permit. He described the influx of refugees as an 'outrage'.

There had always been a certain amount of latent anti-foreign feeling in Britain: this was often strongly expressed among middle-class people in the districts where the refugees tended to settle—Hampstead, in London, for instance, where a joke was current that if colonies were to be given to Hitler a start should be made there, so many Germans having already taken up residence in the borough. Mosley's Fascists tried to exploit anti-Semitic feeling in the East End, but with the surprising effect, rather, of making heroes of 'the kikes'. They had been disliked for their terrible industriousness, their habit of spending a large proportion of their income on showy dress, and the low wages that they offered in their shops. The popular Press was on the whole sympathetic toward the Jews—rather for anti-Nazi than for pro-Semitic reasons.

What was to be done with the Jews was a much-debated question. Guerilla-warfare was in progress in Palestine, where the Arab Nationalists were strongly opposed to the partition of their country into Jewish and Arab states, as the Peel Commission had recommended. The Government could not make up its mind about Palestine: a second Commission reported in 1938 that partition was impracticable. Meanwhile the military were left to deal with well-organized marauding Arab bands as best they could, without either inflaming Arab feelings against British rule throughout the Near East or over-exciting the Jews. Before the outbreak of war the Italian-financed Arab revolt had been quelled, but the problem was still unsolved: the Jews formed a prosperous, industrialized modern community, the Arabs—of whom there were twice as many—a poor, scattered, chiefly agricultural and labouring class. No co-operation between them seemed possible. Jewish farms were a standing annoyance to the Arab: tractors, artesian wells, nitrates, selected seeds, Zionist zeal, raised enormous crops from the same soil that he scratched with his plough for the sake of a few stunted sheaves. Bare-kneed and bare-faced Jewish farm-girls disgusted him. One thing the Government had decided: Jewish emigration into Palestine was to be restricted. But where the flow of emigration should be directed instead, nobody knew. Plans had been discussed for settling 10,000 Jews in British Guiana, and more in Tanganyika, Madagascar, Ecuador, and other distant parts of the world, but no definite arrangements had been made. Zionists took a firm line in the matter: Balfour during the war had promised them 'a National Home in Palestine', and they chose to read this 'in' as meaning 'consisting of'. It must be Palestine or nothing.

The Jewish problem was a permanent topic, taken up only occasionally by the Press, when there was a dramatizable riot in Palestine. In 1939, for example, the *Sphere* observed, hardly in the Christian spirit: 'The Church of the Annunciation is one of the sights of Nazareth, the town that has suddenly leapt into the news with the murder of British officials.' A similar topic was the unrest among the negro population of the British West Indies, where a Government Commission was studying the social effects of the decline of the sugar-exporting industry. Accounts of strikes in Jamaica and of the exploits of the negro agitator Bustamente in Trinidad were all that the Press usually printed on the subject.

Home news occupied more space. It was front-page news, for example, when Oxford won the boat-race in April 1938 for the second time in succession after a thirteen-year series of defeats. Shortly afterwards, a Brighton clerk compelled his young son to hold red-hot coals in his hands in punishment for some trivial offence. A case was brought against him by the Royal Society for the Prevention of Cruelty to Children (soon to be renamed 'for the Protection and Care' of Children, in order to remove the grounds for Dr. Goebbels' accusation that the English were a cruel race)—and he was fined £25. This unusual incident won the clerk so much publicity that he lost his job, and had to move with his family to another district; the child received an enormous fan-mail. Then there was the case of Mrs. Elsie Borders, the 'Tenants' K.C.'. She was sued by a Building Society for refusing to pay instalments on a mortgage on her house. She defended the case herself on the ground that the condition of the house when she bought it had been misrepresented. Several Tenants' Defence Leagues then sprang up for protection against the Building Societies, which had now become a great power.

The most sensational political case was that of Duncan Sandys, a Conservative M.P. and son-in-law of Winston Churchill, in July 1938. In June he had produced figures showing that the state of the country's anti-aircraft defences was unsatisfactory, and had sent them in a memorandum to Hore-Belisha at the War Office. Hore-Belisha was embarrassed and called in the Attorney-General, asking him to warn Sandys, who was a Territorial officer, that he had rendered himself liable to a court martial and two years' imprisonment under the Official Secrets Act for being in possession of confidential data. Sandys asserted his rights as an M.P., and refused to disclose the source of his figures. A hushed-up inquiry was then held, but the case gave two handles for attacks upon the Government. Britain's anti-aircraft defences had been revealed to be in a dangerous state of unpreparedness, and the Government had been caught trying to suppress the truth. The Press attack, unlike that in the House, was not directed against Hore-Belisha, who was the most popular figure in the Ministry and was held to have acted as he did merely to call attention to the problem of 'the Service member'.

The summer of 1938 was passing with the usual news of holiday crowds and cricket matches, but by August the difficult-looking word 'Czechoslovakia' had begun to appear daily in the newspaper columns. Little was known of this place except as a country which apparently exported cheap gloves, glassware, and boots. Newspaper readers now learned with interest that it was a democratic country near Austria which had come into being as a result of the Peace of Versailles—while they were busy reading about Hawker's Atlantic flight, Sir Alec Black's 'The Panther', and Lady Diana Manners's wedding. Soon they learned more: the Sudeten German minority, encouraged by the Nazis, was claiming autonomy from the Czechoslovakian government, the Hungarians were rumoured to be pressing their claims for frontier revision, and the Slovaks were proving far from loyal to this composite state. So serious had the situation become that the British Government sent Lord Runciman, a former President of the Board of Trade and a big shipowner, as a neutral observer, to appease, if possible, both the Czechs and the Sudeten Germans and somehow prevent a European conflagration. Unfortunately it was not to be a simple matter of redrafting the constitution of the Czech state: Germany was involved, and Hitler was letting it be clearly understood that the future of the Sudeten Germans was the exclusive concern of the Third Reich.

Already people were thinking of the peace of Europe as hanging upon Hitler's words. Every speech that he made was given enormous publicity in the British Press: 'HITLER SPEAKS ON WEDNESDAY, HITLER SPEAKS TO-MORROW, HITLER SPEAKS, HITLER'S SPEECH.' Not that he was yet generally thought of as an enemy; he seemed only an unpleasantly dynamic element in the world, ultimately manageable if the proper tactics were adopted. But what were the proper tactics? Most Conservatives agreed that he was a menace to the *status quo*, but that Britain could not stop him, on the Continent at least, and that therefore he must be appeased. And, after all, why even preserve the *status quo*? Were not many of his claims justified? The Germans had been given a raw deal at Versailles by the French and that bounder Lloyd George—and they were a great people, so nearly akin to the British! The Left, on the other hand, persistently depreciated Hitler's power: his régime was far from firmly established, they thought, he was bluffing and his bluff should be called. If only the Government could be compelled to take a strong line, he would topple down at once. And many intelligent non-Left people felt the same way. It is difficult to say at what stage in the story they were still right.

Yet on the whole the British were encouraged by the Press to remain blindly optimistic. The *Sunday Express*, for example, on the 4th September 1938: 'Crisis off till a Week To-morrow. No Sensations Expected.' The country could pass its week-end in peace, and if it did have a sneaking feeling that perhaps the peace would not last for long, there was the Maginot Line in France to restore its confidence. All newspapers were insisting on the unconquerable strength of this bulwark of freedom and on the indissolubility of Franco-British unity, which had just been sealed by the visit of the King and Queen to Paris.

A week later events took a more serious turn. 'Who Stands With Me? Asks Hitler', was one headline; others were 'Hitler's Ambassadors Sound Doubtful Nations! New British Defence Measures Likely To-morrow. To-morrow's Fateful Nuremberg Speech.' For the British public Hitler had at last ceased to be the funny little liar with the Chaplin moustache and the drooping lock of hair: he was the leader of Europe's other camp, now

for the first time generally seen to be separated almost unbridge-
ably from the Franco-British camp.

Crowds were gathering anxiously in Downing Street, but the
newspapers preferred to treat of 'The Brighter Side'. The *Daily
Express*, for instance, reported: 'The crowd outside 10 Downing
Street was amused yesterday. Some time after the Ministers had
left, the door opened and a trim maid came out. After looking
round she proceeded to shine the door-knocker and the brass
plate. The crowd laughed and faded away.' Yet the leader in
the same issue admitted: 'In 1918 we were marching to victory,
our courage high. In 1938 we are disturbed and distressed,
asking each other whether there will be war and dreading the
answer.'

Nobody except the extreme Left felt quite sure why Britain
should go to war, if at all. 'Who are them *Sizzeks*, anyway?' as
country people asked. What right had 'Sizzeks' to rule over
Germans (it was overlooked that the Sudetens had never formed
part of Germany), and why should they not make concessions?
The Government itself was already taking this point of view.
Sir John Simon in a speech at Lanark declared that the Czechs
should be pressed to make concessions, their country divided
into cantons and put on a federal basis. *The Times* went even
further than this: it published a feeler, suggesting that the
Sudeten districts should be ceded outright to Germany. The
Daily Mail agreed, but democratically maintained that a plebiscite should be held first. The *Manchester Guardian*, on the other
hand, produced a plan for the transference of the Nazi-minded
population of Sudetenland to Germany, and for a joint guarantee of Czechoslovakia's frontiers by Britain, France, and Russia.
The *News Chronicle* was bellicose: a firm note should be sent to
Hitler to let him know in unequivocal terms that if Czechoslovakia were invaded Britain, France, and Russia would
march. The *Daily Express* asserted complete faith in Chamberlain and announced that it would endorse whatever he decided
to do. 'The policy of this journal is to be sympathetic with those
in trouble and at the same time to look after our own affairs.
. . . For us, in Britain, in the midst of these troubled times,
it is the duty of all, every man and woman, to stand behind the
Prime Minister, to support his deeds, to ratify his acts, to uphold
his position.' Yet few of its readers considered this view extra-

ordinary or unworthy of a paper that had always described itself as independent!

Chamberlain was playing up well to the rôle forced on him. When, on September 15th, he set off with Sir Horace Wilson, the head of the Civil Service, from Croydon airport to interview Hitler at Berchtesgaden, he felt himself to be the saviour of European peace; and the Press in almost every country presented him as such—umbrella for olive-branch. It was the first time that Chamberlain had flown in an aeroplane; also the first time that any British Prime Minister had gone to the Continent post-haste to sue for peace. After his return there followed a week of suspense: had he succeeded? Might he not even have 'pulled a fast one' on Hitler? Then for the second time he flew to Germany, this time to Godesberg, to draw up definite terms, pressure having meanwhile been put on the Czechs to ensure their acceptance. It was now quite clear that Hitler was winning the trick: the Left raged furiously against Chamberlain for having given way, and so did Eden, Churchill, and other dissident Conservatives. Churchill said: 'Acceptance of Herr Hitler's terms involves the prostration of Europe before the Nazi power, of which the fullest advantage will certainly be taken.' But *The Times* on the 19th tried to justify acceptance on moral and humanitarian grounds: 'The proposed modifications of the peace treaties, if they were now carried through with general consent, would illustrate and strengthen the principle of change achieved without violence.'

The Czech Government on the 21st made the sorrowful official observation: 'You shall to-day level no reproaches at those who have forsaken us in our hour of direst need. History will pass judgement on the events of these days.' But the British public did not think of itself as forsaking anybody. It prayed hard (literally, for there was a sudden revival of church-going) that the Czechs would not prove obstinate. The *Daily Express* on the 25th: 'New Hope Rises in Europe. Will the Czechs Accept Hitler's Ultimatum? What he Asks: the Evacuation of Sudetenland by October 1st. Czechs May Refuse Because the Time-Limit May Cost them Their Guns. Prague's Fear: Losing her Maginot Line.' The onus of deciding for peace or for war was thus laid wholly upon the Czechs. Many British, meanwhile, had been terrified by tales of the might of the German air force (corroborated by Colonel Lindbergh, then in London and just back from Germany), and knew only too well that their own rearmament plans were hopelessly inadequate. Frantic appeals were made through loudspeakers in cinemas, at social functions, and at swimming galas that people should go and have their gas-masks fitted. Trenches were hastily dug in the London parks and steel shelters hurriedly erected. The surprised and puzzled populace was keyed up unwillingly for war.

How grateful they were, then, that Chamberlain saved them! What a wonderful man he was! And at the age of sixty-nine! He played his hand superbly: as he was delivering a foreboding speech in the House of Commons a providential message from Hitler was handed him by an attendant, fixing the date for another conference. The meeting at Munich followed on the 29th; this time Mussolini was present, too, as a self-styled arbiter, and Daladier as an uncomfortable spectator. Terms were drawn up, stricter than those first sketched out at Godesberg, and forced upon the unconsulted Czechs. *The Times* admitted, with a show of sympathetic understanding: 'The general character of the terms submitted to the Czech Government for their consideration cannot in the nature of things be expected to make a strong *prima facie* appeal to them.' But few people were worrying about 'them Sizzeks'.

In Britain, Munich at first seemed a victory. Peace had been preserved. Appeasement had triumphed. The umbrella had been mightier than the sword. Had not Hitler given a solemn undertaking that these were his last territorial demands? All was well again. As Chamberlain himself said: 'I have no doubt, looking back, that my visit alone prevented an invasion for which everything was prepared.' 'Thanks to Chamberlain,' wrote the now middle-aged columnist Lord Castlerosse, 'thousands of young men will live. I shall live.' The *Spectator* declared enthusiastically that Chamberlain deserved the Nobel Peace Prize. When he arrived back from Munich he was greeted with heartfelt cheers, so the Press reported, at Croydon airport. An independent-minded observer, however, reported that he had never seen so shameful a sight in his life—the huge crowd seemed ready to roll on the ground like worshippers at the Juggernaut festival to let Chamberlain ride in glory over them. *The Week* reported that Chamberlain's dominating effect on his colleagues in the Cabinet was due to his tremendous sense of being a chosen vessel of the Deity; while they were confused and frightened.

The *Daily Telegraph* (lately amalgamated with the moribund *Morning Post*) and the *Daily Mirror*, which alone of the big Conservative dailies had taken the Churchill point of view during the Crisis, now fell into line with the rest of the Press. They loyally accepted the course that had been taken as the only possible one. But in October the British conscience began to prick. Hitler had now occupied the ceded regions, and more besides: and the Hungarians and the Poles were taking their share of the spoils. The Cabinet itself was rumoured to be dissatisfied with the agreement, and on October 2nd Duff Cooper resigned: 'I profoundly distrust our foreign policy,' he said. So did many others who had not had Duff Cooper's opportunity, first as War Minister and then as First Lord of the Admiralty, to give foreign policy a substantial backing of force. Then Lord Halifax, the Foreign Secretary, in a speech at Edinburgh declared that Chamberlain had had to choose between war and sacrificing the Czechs, and that he had chosen right. The Germans had won, he said, by an overwhelming show of force.

Why had Britain, too, not been able to make a show of overwhelming force? people asked. Why, in the forceful phrase of *The Week*, had Chamberlain 'turned all four cheeks' to Hitler? The clouds of war had indeed rolled away, but they left an uncomfortable, doubting, fearful nation. What would happen next? At the end of November, during a speech by the Italian Foreign Minister, Count Ciano, Italians began screaming for 'Corsica, Nice, Tunisia, Djibouti'. But of course that was ridiculous. At Lloyds the odds were 32 to 1 against war within a year.

The eleven months which came between the Munich Conference and the German invasion of Poland were a confused and inglorious period. Immediate sense of relief was followed by a feeling of humiliated anger, and then by a purblind apathy. The contemporary by-elections showed a constant fall in the Government's majority—due, however, more to this apathy than to any strong public disgust with the appeasement policy. Rearmament was reported to be proceeding at an accelerated rate, A.R.P. services to be expanding and the Ministry of Health working hard at plans for evacuating children from danger areas. The Press successfully dispelled the crisis atmosphere by dwelling on pleasantly trivial things, such as the arrival at the Zoo from Central Asia of the cuddly, particoloured Giant Panda, the first ever brought to England alive. The most warlike activities were those of the Irish Republican Army, which was now blowing up telephone boxes and plateglass windows in large British cities, and planting time-bombs in suitcases at left-luggage offices.

Christmas passed with its turkey and plum pudding and shopping rush, as always. But in January came news of the fall of Barcelona. General Franco's forces had already in April 1938 driven a wedge between Catalonia and the central Republican area of Madrid and Valencia. Now, after a terrific offensive with the aid of strong mechanized forces supplied by Germany and Italy, he burst through and routed the starved Catalan Army. Then began a painful, straggling exodus into France of hundreds of thousands of militiamen and refugees, many of them fighting a continuous rearguard action and all persistently bombed. The French unwillingly admitted them, herding the greater number like animals into insanitary concentration camps, where they were well guarded behind barbed wire by Senegalese troops. Britain recognized Franco Spain at the end of February and a month later Madrid was taken over by a group of Army officers. The Spanish Republican cabinet fled, and Madrid surrendered. Thus ended the Spanish War. The French were doing what they could by a merciless neglect of their uninvited guests to persuade as many of them as possible to throw themselves on Franco's mercy. The shocking story of the Spanish camps in France was not allowed to appear in the Conservative Press, lest Franco-British amity should be endangered.

The tragedy did not arouse nearly so much feeling in Britain as it might have done a year earlier. The Left said: 'We told you so', and accused the Government of presenting the totalitarian countries with one more ally for the impending war; but the Left had been saying that for years—Britain herself only a few months before had come so near catastrophe that more than the end of a foreign civil war was needed to shake her fatalistic paralysis. British military opinion, and Conservative opinion generally, saw the result as a triumph for professional armies

over an undisciplined Red rabble—not as the victory of a rather
clumsily handled mechanized army, supported by inferior infantry, over a superior infantry with no air or artillery support
worth mentioning. By the end of the war Italian forces in Spain
numbered 100,000; the Germans never had more than 10,000
there at a time, but these were all technicians, constantly withdrawn and replaced as soon as they had passed the course in
practical fighting which was to prepare them for the war with
France and Britain.

On January 30th Hitler made a speech demanding back the
lost German colonies; the next day Chamberlain pronounced it
'not the speech of a man who was preparing to throw Europe
into another crisis'. He was wrong. Hitler occupied what was
left of the Czech state on March 15th. The action, correctly
forecast ten days earlier by the *Daily Worker*, was to have been
expected after the events of the previous September. Only
Chamberlain and his associates were grievously shocked; Hitler
had deliberately broken his pledged word! 'Is this an attempt
to dominate the world by force?' Chamberlain asked in plain-
tive anger in the House. It was; but the mass of the people still
thought of it as a bluff. It would be called when the great,
strong, slow-minded British lion 'left his lair, and roared his
beauty through the hills'. And it really seemed as if the lion was
prepared to roar: Hore-Belisha announced that same month
that a British Expeditionary Force of nineteen divisions was to
be marshalled. He wisely did not refer to their composition or
armament, or confess that only two divisions were as yet ready
for service. Czech refugees were now added to the German,
Austrian, and Spanish ones that had poured into Britain.

Happily newsworthy was the death of the old Pope, Pius XI,
and the preparations for the election of a new one. The Press
told in picturesque detail how the cardinals sat in secret con-
clave, forbidden to speak to anyone outside, receiving their
meals through guarded wickets, and how the election of a new
Pope was announced to the people of Rome by the lighting of
a fire which sent a wisp of grey smoke mounting above the
Vatican. There was much speculation, too, on the political
bearings of this election: would the new occupant of St. Peter's
Chair have Fascist or Democratic leanings? The human touch
was provided by an aged American cardinal, who had arrived

too late for the two previous elections but was determined to reach this one, if necessary by flying the Atlantic. The elevation of Cardinal Pacelli, Pius XI's political secretary, to the Papal Throne as Pius XII was announced in the stop-press of British newspapers on March 2nd, sometimes in comic conjunction with sporting events, as in the *Evening Standard:*

NEW POPE ELECTED
Harlequin 1, Tough Guy 2, Steel Blade 3

Hitler did not stop at Prague, nor Mussolini at Barcelona. The former German city of Memel was surrendered by Lithuania on March 22nd, after a German ultimatum, and Hitler made the first sea-trip of his life in order to visit it. It made popular news that he was extremely seasick On April 5th the Italians began bombing Albanian towns without warning; three days later organized resistance had been overcome throughout Albania and King Zog had fled. His Queen, lying-in with the newly born heir to the Throne, had already been hurried away over bad roads to Greece and found temporary refuge in a hospital at Salonika. The alarmed Greek Government at once requested her to move on. Both mother and child survived, despite gloomy reports as to their desperate condition of health. The democracies also now began to pride themselves on action: first Poland, then Greece and Rumania received a Franco-British guarantee. But except in the case of Greece, which could be protected against Italian action by the Mediterranean Fleet, it was not clear how these guarantees could be implemented. In May an anti-aggression pact was concluded between Britain and Turkey. Diplomatic negotiations had also been opened with Russia—but unaccountably and mysteriously they dragged on for nearly five months; optimistic reports were published, but never an encouraging official communiqué. The Left suspected that Chamberlain had no real intention of coming to an agreement with Russia, for fear both of antagonizing Hitler and of provoking the Red Revolution in Britain, which business men of his generation still regarded as a greater danger than foreign invasion. It was known at least that the Conservative Party's cherished hope for a Four Power Pact between

Britain, France, Germany, and Italy, though cooling, was by no means stone-cold yet.

The B.B.C. began to broadcast news bulletins in foreign languages in an attempt to counter German propaganda. Commander King-Hall also crossed swords with Dr. Goebbels. He distributed in Germany thousands of copies of a personal letter to all Germans, similar in form to his British news-letter. It put before them the righteous aims of British policy and strove to refute the theory, which Hitler had revived at the beginning of April, that Britain was intent on encircling Germany. Dr. Goebbels himself replied by sending a translation of one of his articles in the *Voelkischer Beobachter* by post to a large number of important people in Britain. He concluded: 'Tomfoolery such as that contained in your letter can no longer bamboozle us. . . . You can tell those tales to the marines, you honest old British Jack Tar.' The important recipients of this letter regarded such personal action on the part of a German Minister of State as most undignified.

Though diplomatic tension was increasing, the public was kept in the dark: how far they were kept in the dark was revealed by the Stanhope Affair in April. Lord Stanhope, First Lord of the Admiralty and descendant of the Stanhope who captured Minorca in the eighteenth century, made a speech to naval ratings in the hangar of the aircraft-carrier *Ark Royal*; he remarked incidentally that the attendance was scanty because the crew was manning the anti-aircraft guns night and day. He himself passed this speech for publication in the Press, but the Prime Minister authorized a 'D' notice to be sent round to the newspapers, warning them not to print it on the grounds that it gave the impression that a state of emergency existed. All newspapers accepted the 'D' notice, except the *Daily Sketch*, which explained its defiance: 'Both patriotism and public spirit demanded from us not the withholding of such a speech, but its frank, unfettered publication, accompanied by strong, clear explanations of what it really signified . . . we had, so it appeared to us, a clear duty to allay public anxiety.' The Prime Minister believed that he was allaying anxiety by having the speech suppressed. Other newspapers made news of the suppression, but did not print the contents of the speech. The effect was to bewilder the public. They saw newspapers admitting for the first time that they were subject to coercion, in spite of the much-trumpeted British right of free speech, and realized with alarm that war was nearer than they were supposed to know.

The popular Press, in fact, was doing its best to persuade people that the Anxious Thirties were not to be followed by Fighting Forties. The *Daily Express* in the early months of 1939 was conducting a 'No War This Year or Next' campaign. The *Sunday Graphic* was even more hopeful: just before Prague was occupied it ran a headline: 'Hitler Gets The Jitters'. The popular Press could not very well help itself: to point out the real gravity of the situation would mean spoiling the market for the advertisers on whom its revenue largely depended. Even as late as May and June the general public knew nothing. The King and Queen were then touring North America, and this seemed proof that no war was expected for some months at least. In June angry letters began to appear in the Press accusing the B.B.C. of being alarmist because its bulletins contained purely factual accounts of fresh European threats, incidents, and mobilizations without any optimistic gloss. *Punch* produced a cartoon, showing a well-dressed middle-class Surbitonian furiously hurling a book at his Cassandra-like radio. The British should be allowed at least to take their summer holidays in peace.

The more serious dailies and weeklies were now harping on the problem of Danzig, which was under a League of Nations mandate: every week there was a new incident reported between Danzigers and Polish customs officers or between the Nazified Free Corps and the Jews, and fresh rumours that German arms were being poured into the city. Those in the know—journalists, B.B.C. officials, civil servants, and intelligent people who read the foreign Press either directly or as summarized in the *News Digest, Foreign Affairs*, and similar papers—were in a constant state of anxiety, which the uninformed remainder of the country condemned as unworthy panic. The cause of Danzig and Poland did not arouse the same enthusiasm among Leftists as Spain and Czechoslovakia: it was easy to accuse Poland of being Fascist, difficult to excuse her for having seized Teschen from the helpless Czechs. Why choose the egregious Colonel Beck and the militarist Marshal Smigly-Rydz to fight for, when the more popular democratic figures of Dr. Negrin of Spain and Dr.

Benes of Czechoslovakia had been let down? It was being said
on all sides: 'I don't want to fight for Danzig.' Danzig, after all,
had been regarded as a German city for centuries.

Among those in the know, dates were constantly flashed round
for the next coup: 'Next week-end', 'He always chooses a Sunday', 'June 15th', 'July 15th', 'August 15th'. Which country
would it be: Poland or Rumania, Hungary or Holland? It was
as though Britannia were sitting with fascinated eyes fixed on a
German time-bomb placed a few paces from her throne. The
length of the spluttering fuse could not be determined: how
soon would it explode? The cotton-wool of Munich protected
her ear drums, and she still held the Trident; but was her shield
blast-proof and her helmet splinter-proof? It was easy to trot
out the old saying: 'Another war will mean the end of Western
civilization', to discuss masochistically and suicidally the effects
of aerial bombing, and yet absurdly to believe or, at least, hope
that nothing would happen after all. So many incidents did
happen, and yet war did not break out. How could it? The
news, if taken seriously, was so appalling that people preferred
to be blasé about it. As the *Spectator* wrote: 'A week whose first
four days have been marked by no accentuation of crisis is by
common consent being described as a period of "lull" in international affairs.' A phrase was coined to describe this condition
of war-peace: the 'war of nerves'. The optimists assumed that
since British nerves were reputedly tougher than others this war
could eventually be won without striking a blow.

Events were piling up. A Ministry of Supply was created to
look after the production of war materials. Chamberlain on
April 26th announced in the House that conscription for all
young men of twenty and twenty-one was to be introduced
immediately. This was accepted without a murmur from the
mesmerized population, although it had been an axiom among
politicians of all parties that the liberty-loving British would
never stand for conscription in peace-time. The measure was
solemnly justified, not so much on military grounds as because
it would be physically good for young men—especially those
from the slums—to spend six months with the Army under
canvas in the country. The clause which made allowance for
genuine conscientious objectors was pointed to with pride as
evidence of British freedom. When the first batch of conscripts

was enrolled in June, seventeen out of every thousand declared themselves conscientious objectors.

At the end of April Hitler denounced the Anglo-German Naval Pact; in May news of the German-Italian military alliance was published; there were demonstration flights by R.A.F. squadrons over France, and trial black-outs in fifteen British counties. But greater excitement was caused by the loss of the brand-new submarine *Thetis* on June 2nd, when on her trials, unescorted, in Liverpool Bay. Although at low tide the stern of the *Thetis* could be seen stuck on a sand-bank, she was not located until too late. When rescue ships did arrive, they so mismanaged their business that 99 officers and men lost their lives. Only four were able to escape. Who was responsible for the fate of the rest?

The holiday season had begun, and streams of travellers were going abroad and to the seaside. A cautious old lady at a travel agency asked, amid pitying smiles from the clerks and the other intending travellers, whether it was true that in the event of war British subjects in France would be provided with enough petrol to drive their cars to the Channel ports. (Actually, it was true, though not publicized.) Things would not really be so bad as some people made out. As late as July 23rd Robert Hudson, the Secretary for Overseas Trade, admitted in the House that to the Nazis had been suggested a £5,000,000,000 loan to get Germany on her feet again economically. And the Bishop of Chester was making news by playing a barrel-organ in the chief city of his diocese for the benefit of local hospital funds. Towards the end of August came startling news: the Russo-German non-aggression pact. It was signed while a delegation of British and French admirals and generals was still at work in Moscow. They returned sadly, amid sympathy from some for having, as it seemed, been double-crossed, and bitter attacks from others for having bungled their business. The truth appears to have been that they were not empowered to conclude any definite or far-reaching agreement. A roaring diplomatic week followed. Gratuitous appeals for peace, calls for a world conference from King Leopold of the Belgians, President Roosevelt, and the Pope. Communiqués and counter-communiques and rumour upon rumour. Parliament met on August 29th in the middle of the summer recess. Chamberlain reasserted the British anti-aggression policy, and announced amid applause that the Government's obligations to foreign countries would be honoured in full. He had changed his point of view since the previous September. Then he had said: 'How horrible, fantastic, incredible it is that we should be digging trenches and trying on gas-masks here because of a quarrel in a far-away country between people of whom we know nothing!' And in August 1939: 'We shall not be fighting for the political future of a faraway city in a foreign land. We shall be fighting for the preservation of those principles the destruction of which would involve the destruction of peace and liberty for the peoples of the world.' He had been obliged by his own personal Canossa to agree with what anti-Fascists had been saying ever since Abyssinia was invaded.

Yet even up to the last minute there was optimism. This time Germany would have to back down; Hitler could not bluff again, and if he did choose to fight, the Poles would prove a tough nut to crack. The continued exchange of diplomatic notes seemed to indicate that discussion might still settle the problem. Then, on September 1st came the news that German troops had crossed the Polish frontiers at five o'clock in the morning and that Warsaw had had its first air-raid. In Britain there were two days of nightmarish lull. On September 2nd general mobilization began, and the evacuation of one million children from supposed danger-areas was set under way. Anxious crowds in Downing Street, but no official statement. At 11.15 in the morning on Sunday, September 3rd, Chamberlain was heard to declare in virtuously agonized tones over the radio that he had asked Germany to undertake to withdraw her troops from Poland. He added: 'I have to tell you that no such undertaking has been received and that consequently this country is at war with Germany.' Almost before he had finished speaking the first air-raid siren was sounded. (A false alarm, as it happened, like so many others in the Thirties.) People smiled wrily at one another. So that was that, eh? War. Total war.

But the country was still sound at heart, the staunch Conservatives felt, as they hurried on, a few minutes late, to Sunday service; and the social revolution, so long averted, would now be made altogether impossible by a new and sterner D.O.R.A. Besides, Britain always won the last battle.

RAIN STOPS PLAY, 1939

The Left did not know what to feel or where to go. They were left staring rather stupidly at the knobs of their radio-sets. Chamberlain had faced up to Hitlerism at last; but was this exactly what they had meant?

Index

INDEX

Neill, A. S., 210, 211
Neon signs, 380
New Fabian Research Bureau, the,
  259, 400
New Guinea, 81, 82, 87
New Statesman, 23, 24, 32, 43, 54,
  241, 243, 244
New Verse, 300, 435
New Writing, 339
New York, 86, 159, 228, 235, 247,
  255, 372, 386
New York Herald, 82
Newfoundland, 85, 86
News Chronicle, 326, 336, 360, 402,
  443
'News-Hawks', 282, 283
Newspaper Proprietors' Association,
  359
Nice, 34, 446
Nicholas of Rumania, Prince, 121
Nicholas II, Tsar, 22
Nichols, Beverley, 62, 269, 338
Nichols, Robert, 53
Nicholson, Ben, 193, 194, 351
Nicholson, William, 353
Nicolson, Harold, 254
Nield, Sir Herbert, 114, 117
Nigeria, 321
Night-clubs, 120, 122, 129, 226
Non-Intervention, 337
Norman, Montague, 256
Northcliffe, Lord, 14, 55, 58, 60, 61,
  62
Nottingham, 107, 214
Nova Scotia, 86
Novar, Viscount, 221
Novello, Ivor, 109, 144
Nudism, 273, 274
Nuffield, Lord, 400
Nyon Conference, 415

Observer, 145, 192, 195, 234, 318,
  324, 336, 341, 430, 432
O'Casey, Séan, 347
'Occupational Clubs', 406
Octavian Society, 373
Oddie, Mr. Ingleby, 103
Odets, Clifford, 339
Officers' Training Corps, 212, 215
Official Secrets Act, 441
O'Flaherty, Liam, 426
Oil, 221
Old Moore's Almanac, 430, 431

Olympic Winter Sports (Garmisch),
  327
O'Neill, Eugene, 143
Oppenheim, E. Phillips, 304
Orchard, Dr., 103
Orczy, Baroness, 303
Organization for Maintenance of
  Supplies, 163
Orpen, Sir William, 193
Ottawa Agreements, 261
Ouspensky, 203
Outlook, 241
Oxenham, John, 52
Oxford, 17, 28, 46, 62, 83, 105, 106,
  122, 123, 124, 127, 131, 152, 179,
  202, 206, 212, 305, 334, 374, 400,
  440
Oxford Preservation Trust, 185

Page, Handley, 238
Palestine, 13, 31, 70, 71, 439, 440
Panama, 93
Pankhurst, Christabel, 404
Paris, 40, 41, 88, 125, 148, 164, 168,
  188, 192, 193, 197, 199, 200, 227,
  228, 241, 255, 287, 348, 351, 356,
  372, 374
Parker, Sir Gilbert, 32
Passchaendaele, 196
Patent Medicines, Register of, 189,
  398
Paul, Brenda Dean, 121
Payne, Jack, 237
Peace Ballot, the, 324
Peace News, 329
Peace Pledge Union, 328, 329, 424
Pekin, 16, 58
Pelmanism, 64, 65
Pemberton, Sir Max, 61
Pershing, General, 13
'Peterborough', 62
Petrie, Professor Flinders, 125
Philips (wireless operator), 88
Philipson, Mrs. Hilton, 47
Phillpotts, Eden, 144
Photography, 433, 434
Photomatons, 232
Picasso, Pablo, 193, 195, 200
Pickford, Mary, 134
Picture Post, 431, 432
Pioneer Health Centre (Peckham),
  399
Piper, John, 354

INDEX

IN THE NORTON LIBRARY

Gash, Norman. *Politics in the Age of Peel.* N564

Gatzke, Hans W. *Stresemann and the Rearmament of Germany.* N486

Gay, Peter. *The Party of Humanity: Essays in the French Enlightenment.* N607

Graves, Robert and Alan Hodge. *The Long Week-end: A Social History of Great Britain, 1918–1939.* N217

Greene, Jack P. *The Quest for Power: The Lower Houses of Assembly in the Southern Royal Colonies, 1689–1776.* N591

Halperin, S. William. *Germany Tried Democracy.* N280

Hamilton, Holman. *Prologue to Conflict.* N345

Haring, C. H. *Empire in Brazil.* N386

Haskins, Charles Homer. *The Normans in European History.* N342

Hill, Christopher. *The Century of Revolution 1603–1714.* N365

Holmes, George. *The Later Middle Ages, 1272–1485.* N363

Huizinga, Jan. *In the Shadow of Tomorrow.* N484

Jolliffe, J. E. A. *The Constitutional History of Medieval England.* N417

Keir, David Lindsay. *The Constitutional History of Modern Britain Since 1485.* N405

Kendall, Paul Murray. *The Yorkist Age.* N558

Kendall, Paul Murray (editor) *Richard III: The Great Debate.* N310

Kolko, Gabriel. *Railroads and Regulation, 1877–1916.* N531

Lamar, Howard Roberts. *The Far Southwest, 1846–1912.* N522

Leach, Douglass E. *Flintlock and Tomahawk: New England in King Philip's War.* N340

McFeely, William S. *Yankee Stepfather: General O.O. Howard and the Freedmen.* N537

Madison, James. *Notes of Debates in the Federal Convention of 1787.* N485

Magrath, C. Peter. *Yazoo: The Case of Fletcher v. Peck.* N418

Marwick, Arthur. *The Deluge: British Society and the First World War.* N523

Mattingly, Harold. *The Man in the Roman Street.* N337

Mattingly, Harold. *Roman Imperial Civilization.* N572

May, Arthur J. *The Hapsburg Monarchy: 1867–1914.* N460

Mosse, Claude. *The Ancient World at Work.* N540

Neale, J. E. *Elizabeth I and Her Parliaments,* 2 vols. N359a & N359b

Noggle, Burl. *Teapot Dome: Oil and Politics in the 1920's.* N297

North, Douglass C. *The Economic Growth of the United States 1790–1860.* N346

Ogilvie, R. M. *The Romans and Their Gods in the Age of Augustus.* N543

Pelling, Henry. *Modern Britain, 1885–1955.* N368

Pirenne, Henri. *Early Democracies in the Low Countries.* N565

Pollack, Norman. *The Populist Response to Industrial America.* N295

Quirk, Robert E. *The Mexican Revolution, 1914–1915.* N507

Read, Conyers. *The Tudors.* N129

Remini, Robert V. *Martin Van Buren and the Making of the Democratic Party.* N527

Ritcheson, Charles. *Aftermath of Revolution: British Policy Toward the United States, 1783–1795.* N553

Robson, Eric. *The American Revolution, 1763–1783.* N382

Roth, Cecil. *The Spanish Inquisition.* N255

Rowse, A. L. *Appeasement.* N139

Ruiz, Ramon Eduardo. *Cuba: The Making of a Revolution.* N513

Sarton, George. *A History of Science, I: Ancient Science Through the Golden Age of Greece.* N525

Sarton, George. *A History of Science, II: Hellenistic Science and Culture in the Last Three Centuries B.C.* N526

Seton-Watson, R. W. *Disraeli, Gladstone, and the Eastern Question.* N594

Smith, Abbot E. *Colonists in Bondage: White Servitude and Convict Labor in America, 1607–1776.* N592

Sontag, Raymond J. *Germany and England: Background of Conflict, 1848–1894.* N180

Spanier, John W. *The Truman-MacArthur Controversy and the Korean War.* N279

Stansky, Peter and William Abrahams. *Journey to the Frontier: Two Roads to the Spanish Civil War.* N509

Tan, Chester C. *The Boxer Catastrophe.* N575

Tarbell, Ida M. *History of the Standard Oil Company.* N496

Taylor, A. J. P. *Germany's First Bid for Colonies, 1884–1885.* N530

Thompson, J. M. *Louis Napoleon and the Second Empire.* N403

Tolles, Frederick B. *Meeting House and Counting House.* N211

Tourtellot, Arthur Bernon. *Lexington and Concord.* N194

Waite, Robert G. L. *Vanguard of Nazism: The Free Corps Movement in Postwar Germany, 1918–1923.* N181

Warmington, B. H. *Nero: Reality and Legend.* N542

Warren, Harris Gaylord. *Herbert Hoover and the Great Depression.* N394

Wedgwood, C. V. *William the Silent.* N185

Wheeler-Bennett, John W. *Brest-Litovsk: The Forgotten Peace, March 1918.* N576

Wolfers, Arnold. *Britain and France between Two Wars.* N343

Wolff, Robert Lee. *The Balkans in Our Time.* N395

Wright, Benjamin Fletcher. *Consensus and Continuity, 1776–1787.* N402

Zeldin, Theodore. *The Political System of Napoleon III.* N580

Zinn, Howard. *LaGuardia in Congress.* N488

Zobel, Hiller B. *The Boston Massacre.* N606

NOMINATED FOR THE ANDREW CARNEGIE MEDAL FOR EXCELLENCE

ONE OF THE BEST BOOKS OF THE YEAR

The New York Times, NPR, *The Washington Post*, *USA Today*, *Glamour*, *Esquire*, Oprah Daily, Literary Hub, *The Globe and Mail*, and more

"I could write a thousand words about Emily St. John Mandel, and this book, and this moment but I won't dare spoil it. Truly soul-affirming."
—Emma Straub, bestselling author of *All Adults Here*

"Powerful. . . . A book brimming with a sense of wonder, a sense of humour, and a sense for the weirdness we've all been experiencing." —*Locus*

"Illustrates how hope and humanity are flames that can never be fully extinguished." —*Elle*

"A spiraling, transportive triumph of storytelling — sci-fi with soul."
—Kiran Millwood Hargrave, author of *The Mercies*

"A full-on mindblower. . . . Mandel has crafted an enthralling narrative puzzle."
—*Minneapolis Star Tribune*

"Generous with flashes of wry humor. . . . Readers will leave *Sea of Tranquility*, like *Station Eleven* before it, feeling hope for humanity."
—*St. Louis Post-Dispatch*

"This slim novel is written in a cool, elegant voice, like that of a singer who never wastes a note."
—*Milwaukee Journal Sentinel*

Praise for Emily St. John Mandel's

SEA *of* TRANQUILITY

"Emily St. John Mandel . . . like an ingenious origami artist, seems determined with each new work to add yet another fold to our perception of what is real and one further twist to what we think of as time. . . . Transcendent."

—*The Wall Street Journal*

"Masterfully plotted and deeply moving, this visionary novel folds back on itself like a hall of mirrors to explore just what connects us to one another, and how many extraordinary contingencies bring us to each ordinary day of our lives."

—*Esquire*

"This story is really about the characters, survival, and human nature. You almost forget about the dystopian backdrop and the fact that the world may be ending and instead you focus on the beauty of the storytelling, the absorbing landscape, and the way these seemingly interconnected characters living in different time periods weave together."   —BuzzFeed

"Mandel's swift storytelling and puncturing emotional truths will leave you wishing [*Sea of Tranquility*] was hundreds of pages longer. She remains an instant-buy writer." —*Glamour*

"Mandel's most ambitious novel yet (which is saying something). . . . Inventive and . . . mind-bending. . . . Her depiction of a future pandemic is recognisable and touching. . . . An illuminating study of survival and, in the words of one character, 'what makes a world real.'" —*The Economist*

"The paradoxes of Gaspery's adventure will be familiar to anyone who's studied Jean Baudrillard or seen *Back to the Future*. . . . Absent your own time portal to the 1990s, it's a chance to . . . wrestle with the mind-blowing possibility that what *is* may be entirely different from what we *see*." —*The Washington Post*

"There is both elegance and tenderness in Mandel's narrative design. . . . For her, science fiction allows us only enough escape from our context to let us regard it from a softening distance." —*The Nation*

"Lovely, life-affirming. . . . Mandel's prose is shot through with moments of unexpected lyricism . . . that take you by surprise with their limpid sweetness. . . . Nourishing and needed. The world is always ending, this book says, and there is always beauty to be found in it." —*Vox*

"A triumph of science fiction." —*Good Housekeeping*

Emily St. John Mandel

SEA *of* TRANQUILITY

Emily St. John Mandel's five previous novels include *The Glass Hotel*, which has been translated into twenty-five languages, and *Station Eleven*, which was a finalist for a National Book Award and the PEN/Faulkner Award for Fiction, was the basis of a limited series on HBO Max, and has been translated into thirty-seven languages. She lives in New York City and Los Angeles.

Emily St. John Mandel is available for select speaking engagements. To inquire about a possible speaking appearance, please contact Penguin Random House Speakers Bureau at speakers@penguinrandomhouse.com or visit prhspeakers.com.

emilymandel.com

SEA *of* TRANQUILITY

SEA

of

TRANQUILITY

Emily St. John Mandel

VINTAGE BOOKS

A Division of Penguin Random House LLC

New York

FIRST VINTAGE BOOKS EDITION 2023

A few sentences in this book appeared, in different form, in a short story
published in the anthology *Imaginary Oklahoma* in 2013, an article published
in *The New Republic* in 2014, and an essay published in *Humanities* in 2016.

The Library of Congress has cataloged the Knopf edition as follows:
Names: Mandel, Emily St. John, [date] author.
Title: Sea of Tranquility / Emily St. John Mandel.
Description: First edition. | New York : Alfred A. Knopf, 2022.
Identifiers: LCCN 2021022674 (print) | LCCN 2021022675 (ebook)
Subjects: GSAFD: Epic fiction. | Science fiction.
Classification: LCC PR9199.4.M3347 S43 2022 (print) |
LCC PR9199.4.M3347 (ebook) | DDC 813/.6—dc23
LC record available at https://lccn.loc.gov/2021022674
LC ebook record available at https://lccn.loc.gov/2021022675

Vintage Books Trade Paperback ISBN: 978-0-593-46673-5
eBook ISBN: 978-0-593-32145-4

Book design by Anna B. Knighton

vintagebooks.com

Printed in the United States of America
10 9 8 7 6 5 4 3 2

For Cassia

Contents

Remittance /

1912

1

Edwin St. John St. Andrew, eighteen years old, hauling the weight of his double-sainted name across the Atlantic by steamship, eyes narrowed against the wind on the upper deck: he holds the railing with gloved hands, impatient for a glimpse of the unknown, trying to discern something—anything!—beyond sea and sky, but all he sees are shades of endless gray. He's on his way to a different world. He's more or less at the halfway point between England and Canada. *I have been sent into exile,* he tells himself, and he knows he's being melodramatic, but nonetheless there's a ring of truth to it.

Edwin's ancestors include William the Conqueror. When Edwin's grandfather dies, his father will become an earl, and Edwin went to two of the best schools in the country. But there was never much of a future for him back in England. There are very few professions that a gentleman can take up, and none of them are of interest to Edwin. The family estate is destined to go to his oldest brother, Gilbert, so he stands to inherit nothing. (The middle brother, Niall, is in Australia already.) Edwin might have clung to England a little longer, but he holds secretly radical views which emerged unexpectedly at a dinner party, thus speeding up his fate.

In a flash of wild optimism, Edwin has his occupation recorded as "farmer" on the ship's manifest. It occurs to him later, in a contemplative moment out on deck, that he's never so much as touched a spade.

2

In Halifax he finds lodging by the port, a boardinghouse where he's able to secure a corner room on the second floor, overlooking the harbor. He wakes that first morning to a wonderfully lively scene outside his window. A large merchant ship has arrived, and he's close enough to hear the jovial curses of the men unloading barrels and sacks and crates. He spends much of that first day gazing out the window, like a cat. He planned to go west immediately, but it's so easy to linger in Halifax, where he falls prey to a personal weakness he's been aware of all his life: Edwin is capable of action but prone to inertia. He likes sitting by his window. There's a constant movement of people and ships. He doesn't want to leave, so he stays.

"Oh, just trying to puzzle out my next move, I suppose," he says to the proprietor, when she makes gentle inquiries. Her name is Mrs. Donnelly. She's from Newfoundland. Her accent confounds him. She sounds like she's from Bristol and also from Ireland, simultaneously, but then sometimes he hears Scotland. The rooms are clean and she's an excellent cook.

Sailors pass by his window in jostling waves. They rarely look up. He enjoys watching them but dares not make any movement toward them. Besides, they have each other. When drunk they put their arms around one another's shoulders and he feels a piercing envy.

(Could he go to sea? Of course not. He discards the idea as soon as it arises. He once heard of a remittance man who reinvented himself as a sailor, but Edwin's a man of leisure through and through.)

He loves watching the boats come in, steamships pulling into the harbor with an aura of Europe still clinging to their decks.

He takes walks in the mornings and again in the afternoons. Down to the harbor, out to quiet residential areas, in and out of little shops under the striped awnings on Barrington Street. He likes to ride the electric streetcar to the end of the line, and then come back, watching the shift from small houses to larger houses to the commercial buildings downtown. He likes buying things that he doesn't especially need: a loaf of bread, a postcard or two, a bouquet of flowers. This could be a life, he finds himself thinking. It could be as simple as this. No family, no job, just a few simple pleasures and clean sheets to fall into at the end of the day, a regular allowance from home. A life of solitude could be a very pleasant thing.

He begins buying flowers every few days, which he places on his dresser in a cheap vase. He spends a long time gazing at them. He wishes he were an artist, to draw them and in so doing to see them more clearly.

Could he learn to draw? He has time and money. It's as good an idea as any. He makes inquiries with Mrs. Donnelly, who makes inquiries with a friend, and a short time later Edwin is in the parlor of a woman who trained as a painter. He spends quiet hours sketching flowers and vases, learning the fundamentals of shading and proportion. The woman's name is Laetitia Russell. She wears a wedding ring, but the location of her husband is unclear. She lives in a tidy wooden house with three children and a widowed sister, an unobtrusive chaperone who knits endless scarves in a corner of the room, so that for the rest of his life Edwin associates drawing with the clicking of knitting needles.

He's been living at the boardinghouse for six months when Reginald arrives. Reginald, he can tell at once, is not prone to inertia. Reginald has immediate plans to go west. He's two years older than Edwin, a fellow old Etonian, third son of a viscount, and his eyes are beautiful, a deep grayish blue. Like Edwin, his plans involve establishing himself as a gentleman farmer, but unlike Edwin, he's actually taken steps to achieve this and has been corresponding with a man who wishes to sell a farm in Saskatchewan.

"Six months," Reginald repeats at breakfast, not quite believing it. He stops spreading jam on his toast for a moment, seemingly unsure if he heard correctly. "Six *months*? Six months *here*."

"Yes," Edwin says lightly. "Six very agreeable months, I might add." He tries to catch Mrs. Donnelly's eye, but she's focusing intently on pouring tea. She thinks he's a little touched, he can tell.

"Interesting." Reginald spreads jam on his toast. "I don't suppose we're hoping to be called home, are we? Clinging to the edge of the Atlantic, staying as close as we can to king and country?"

This stings a little, so when Reginald lights out for the west the following week, Edwin accepts an invitation to join him. There's pleasure in action, he decides, as the train leaves the city. They've booked first-class passage on a delightful train that features an onboard post office and barbershop, where Edwin writes a postcard to Gilbert and enjoys a hot shave and a haircut while watching the forests and lakes and small towns slip past the windows. When the train stops at Ottawa he doesn't disembark, just stays on board, sketching the lines of the station.

The forests and lakes and small towns subside into plains. The prairies are initially interesting, then tedious, then unsettling.

There's too much of them, that's the problem. The scale is wrong. The train crawls like a millipede through endless grass. He can see from horizon to horizon. He feels terribly overexposed.

"This is the life," Reginald says, when at last they arrive, standing in the doorway of his new farmhouse. The farm is a few miles outside Prince Albert. It is a sea of mud. Reginald purchased it, sight unseen, from a disconsolate Englishman in his late twenties—another remittance man, Edwin can't help but suspect—who's thoroughly failed to make a go of it here and is headed back east to take a desk job in Ottawa. Reginald is very carefully not thinking about this man, Edwin can see that.

Can a house be haunted by failure? When Edwin steps through the door of the farmhouse, he feels immediately ill at ease, so he lingers out on the front porch. It's a well-built house—the previous owner was well-funded once—but the place is unhappy in a way that Edwin can't entirely explain.

"There's . . . a lot of sky here, isn't there?" Edwin ventures. And a lot of mud. Really an astonishing amount of mud. It glitters under the sun as far as he can see.

"Just wide-open spaces and fresh air," Reginald says, gazing out at the horrifically featureless horizon. Edwin can see another farmhouse, far away, hazy with distance. The sky is aggressively blue. That night they dine on buttered eggs—the only thing

Reginald knows how to cook—and salt pork. Reginald seems subdued.

"I suppose it's quite hard work, farming?" he says, after a while. "Physically taxing."

"I suppose so." When Edwin imagined himself in the new world, he always saw himself in his own farm—a verdant landscape of, well, of some unspecified crop, tidy but also vast—but in truth he never thought much about what the work of farming might actually entail. Taking care of horses, he supposes. Doing a bit of gardening. Digging up fields. But then what? What do you actually do with the fields, once you've dug them up? What are you digging for?

He feels himself teetering on the edge of an abyss. "Reginald, my old friend," he says, "what does a fellow have to do to get a drink around here?"

"You *reap,*" Edwin says to himself, on his third glass. "That's the word for it. You dig up the fields, you sow things in the fields, then you reap." He sips his drink.

"You reap what?" Reginald has a pleasant way about him when he's drunk, as if nothing could possibly offend him. He's been leaning back in his chair, smiling into the empty air.

"Well, that's just it, isn't it," Edwin says, and pours himself another glass.

3

After a month of drinking, Edwin leaves Reginald on his new farm and continues west to meet up with his brother Niall's school friend Thomas, who entered the continent via New York City and sped west immediately. The train through the Rocky Mountains takes Edwin's breath away. He presses his forehead to the window, like a child, and openly gapes. The beauty is overwhelming. He maybe took the drinking a little far, back in Saskatchewan. He'll be a better man in British Columbia, he decides. The sunlight hurts his eyes.

After all that wild splendor, it's an odd jolt to find himself in Victoria, in those tamed and pretty streets. There are Englishmen everywhere; he steps out of the train and the accents of his homeland surround him. He could stay here for a while, he thinks.

. . .

Edwin finds Thomas in a tidy little hotel in the city center, where Thomas has taken the best room, and they order tea with scones in the restaurant downstairs. They haven't seen one another in three or four years, but Thomas has changed very little. He has the same reddish complexion he's had since childhood, that perpetual impression of just having stepped in off the rugby pitch. He's trying to become a member of the Victoria business community, but he's vague on what kind of business he wants to be in.

"And how's your brother?" Thomas asks, changing the subject. He means Niall.

"Making a go of it in Australia," Edwin says. "He seems happy enough, judging by his letters."

"Well, that's more than most of us can say," Thomas says. "No small thing, happiness. What's he doing down there?"

"Drinking away his remittance money, I'd imagine," Edwin says, which is ungentlemanly but also the probable truth. They have a table by the window, and his gaze keeps drifting to the street, the shop fronts, and—visible in the distance—the unfathomable wilderness, dark towering trees crowding in around the periphery. There's something ludicrous about the idea that the wilderness belongs to Britain, but he quickly suppresses this thought, because it reminds him of his last dinner party in England.

4

The last dinner party began smoothly enough, but trouble started when the conversation turned, as ever and always, to the unimaginable splendor of the Raj. Edwin's parents were born in India, Raj babies, English children raised by Indian nannies— "If I hear one more word about her goddamned ayah," Edwin's brother Gilbert muttered once, never finishing the thought—and raised on tales of an unseen Britain that, Edwin couldn't help but suspect, had been slightly disappointing when they first laid eyes on it in their early twenties. ("More rain than I'd expected," was all Edwin's father would say on the matter.)

There was another family at that last dinner party, the Barretts, of similar profile: John Barrett had been a commander in the Royal Navy, and Clara, his wife, had also spent her first few years in India. Their eldest son, Andrew, was with them. The

Barretts knew that British India was an inevitable detour in any evening spent with Edwin's mother, and as old friends, they understood that once Abigail got the Raj out of her system, conversation could move on.

"You know, I so often find myself thinking of the beauty of British India," his mother said. "The colors were remarkable."

"The heat *was* rather oppressive, though," Edwin's father said. "That's one thing I didn't miss, once we came here."

"Oh, I never found it *terribly* oppressive." Edwin's mother had a far-off look that Edwin and his brothers called her British India expression. There was a haziness about her that meant she was no longer with them; she was riding an elephant or strolling through a garden of verdant tropical flowers or being served cucumber sandwiches by her goddamned ayah or something, who knows.

"Nor did the natives," Gilbert said mildly, "but I suppose that climate's not for everyone."

What inspired Edwin to speak just then? He found himself dwelling on the matter years later, at war, in the terminal horror and boredom of the trenches. Sometimes you don't know you're going to throw a grenade until you've already pulled the pin.

"Evidence suggests they feel rather more oppressed by the British than by the heat," Edwin said. He glanced at his father, but his father seemed to have frozen, his glass halfway between the table and his lips.

"Darling," said his mother, "whatever can you mean?"

"They don't want us there," Edwin said. He glanced around

the table, at all the silent staring faces. "Not a great deal of ambiguity on that point, I'm afraid." He listened to his own voice as if from some distance away, with wonderment. Gilbert's mouth had fallen open.

"Young man," his father said, "we have brought nothing but civilization to these people—"

"And yet one can't help but notice," Edwin said, "that on balance, they rather seem to prefer their own. Their own civilization, that is. They managed quite well without us for some time, didn't they? Several thousand years, wasn't it?" It was like being strapped to the roof of a runaway train! He actually knew very little about India, but he remembered having been shocked as a boy by accounts of the 1857 rebellion. "Does anyone want us *anywhere*?" he heard himself ask. "Why do we assume these far-flung places are ours?"

"Because we *won* them, Eddie," Gilbert said, after a brief silence. "One assumes that the natives of England were perhaps not unanimously delighted by the arrival of our twenty-second great-grandfather, but, well, history belongs to the victors."

"William the Conqueror was a thousand years ago, Bert. Surely we might strive to be somewhat more civilized than the maniacal grandson of a Viking raider."

Edwin stopped talking then. Everyone at the table was staring at him.

"'The maniacal grandson of a Viking raider,'" Gilbert repeated softly.

"Although one should be grateful, I suppose, that we're a

Christian nation," Edwin said. "*Imagine* what a bloodbath the colonies would be if we weren't."

"Are you an atheist, Edwin?" Andrew Barrett inquired, with genuine interest.

"I don't quite know what I am," Edwin said.

The silence that followed was possibly the most excruciating of Edwin's life, but then his father began speaking, very quietly. When Edwin's father was furious, he had a trick of beginning speeches with a half-sentence, to catch everyone's attention. "Every advantage you've ever had in this life," his father said. Everyone looked at him. He began again, in trademark fashion, only slightly louder, and with deadly calm: "Every advantage you've ever had in this life, Edwin, has derived in some manner or another from the fact of your being descended from, as you so eloquently put it, the *maniacal grandson of a Viking raider.*"

"Of course," Edwin said. "It could be so much worse." He raised his glass. "To William the Bastard."

Gilbert laughed, in a nervous way. No one else made a sound.

"I do beg your pardon," Edwin's father said, to their guests. "One might reasonably mistake my youngest son for a grown man, but it seems he's still a child. To your room, Edwin. We've heard quite enough for one evening."

Edwin rose from the table with great formality, said, "Good night, everyone," went to the kitchen to request that a sandwich be delivered to his room—the main course hadn't yet been served—and then retired to await his sentence. It came before midnight, with a knock on the door.

"Come in," he said. He'd been standing by the window, staring fretfully out at the movements of a tree in the wind.

Gilbert came in, closed the door behind him, and sprawled into the ancient stained armchair that was among Edwin's most treasured possessions.

"Quite the performance, Eddie."

"I don't know what I was thinking," said Edwin. "Actually, no, that's not true. I do know. I am absolutely certain there was not a single thought in my head. It was like a kind of void."

"Are you unwell?"

"Not at all. Never better."

"It must have been rather thrilling," Gilbert said.

"It was, actually. I won't say I regret it."

Gilbert smiled. "You're to go to Canada," he said gently. "Father's making arrangements."

"I was always going to go to Canada," Edwin said. "It's planned for next year."

"Now you're to go a little sooner."

"How much sooner, Bert?"

"Next week."

Edwin nodded. He felt a touch of vertigo. There had been a subtle shift in the room's atmosphere. He was going to go forth into an incomprehensible world and the room was already receding into the past. "Well," Edwin said, after a moment, "at least I'll still be on a different continent to Niall."

"You're at it again," Gilbert said. "Do you just say whatever comes into your head now?"

"I recommend it."

"We can't all be so careless, you know. Some of us have responsibilities."

"By which you mean a title and an estate to inherit," Edwin said. "What a terrible fate. I'll weep for you later. Will I receive the same remittance as Niall?"

"A little more. Niall's is just meant to support him. Yours comes with conditions."

"Tell me."

"You're not to come back to England for a while," Gilbert said.

"Exile," Edwin said.

"Oh, don't be melodramatic. You were always going to go off to Canada, as you said."

"But how long's a while?" Edwin turned away from the window to stare at his brother. "I'd thought I could go to Canada for a time, establish myself somehow, and then come home at regular intervals for visits. What did Father say, exactly?"

"I'm afraid the phrase that sticks in memory is 'tell him he's to stay the hell out of England.'"

"Well, that's rather . . . unambiguous."

"You know how Father is. And of course Mother is going along with it." Gilbert stood, and paused for a moment by the door. "Just give them time, Eddie. I'd be astonished if your exile were permanent. I'll work on them."

5

The trouble with Victoria, in Edwin's eyes, is that it's too much like England without actually being England. It's a far-distant simulation of England, a watercolor superimposed unconvincingly on the landscape. On Edwin's second night in the city, Thomas takes him to the Union Club. It's enjoyable at first, a shot of home, pleasant hours slipping past in the company of a few other old boys from the homeland and some truly exceptional single-malt scotch. Some of the older men have been in Victoria for decades, and Thomas seeks out their company. He stays close, asks their opinions, listens seriously to them, flatters them. It's embarrassing to watch. Thomas is clearly hoping to establish himself as a steady kind of man with whom one might wish to go into business, but it's obvious to Edwin that the older men are only being polite. They're not interested in outsiders, even outsiders from the correct country, with the correct ancestors and the correct accent, who've gone to the correct school. It's a closed society that admits Thomas only on the periphery. How long will Thomas have to stay here, circling around inside this clubhouse, before they'll accept him? Five years? Ten? A millennium?

Edwin turns his back on Thomas and goes to the window. They're on the third floor, with a view of the harbor, and the last light is fading from the sky. He feels restless and ill at ease. Behind him, men are relating tales of sporting triumphs and uneventful voyages by steamship to Quebec City, Halifax, and New York. "Would you believe," an arrival at the latter port is saying, somewhere behind him, "my poor mother was under the impression that New York was still part of the Commonwealth?"

Time passes; night falls over the harbor; Edwin rejoins the other men.

"But the unfortunate truth of the matter," one says, in the depths of a conversation about the importance of being an adventuring sort, "is we've no real future back in England, have we?"

A pensive silence falls over the group. These men are second sons, one and all. They are ill-prepared for a working life and will inherit nothing. To his own great surprise, Edwin raises a glass.

"To exile," he says, and drinks. There are disapproving murmurs: "I would hardly call this *exile*," someone says.

"To building a new future, gentlemen, in a new and far-distant land," says Thomas, ever the diplomat.

. . .

Later, Thomas finds him standing by the window.

"You know," he says, "I may have heard something or other in passing about a dinner party, but I'm not sure I quite believed it till now."

"I'm afraid the Barretts are incorrigible gossips."

"I think I've had about enough of this place," Thomas says. "I thought I could make a go of it here, but if you're going to leave England, surely there's something to be said for actually leaving England." He turns to face Edwin. "I've been thinking about going north."

"How far north?" Edwin is beset by a worrisome vision of igloos on the frozen tundra.

"Not very far. Just up Vancouver Island a little."

"You have prospects there?"

"Specifically, my friend's uncle's timber company," Thomas says. "But in the abstract, wilderness. Isn't that why we're here? To leave a mark on wilderness?"

What if one wanted to disappear into wilderness instead? A strange thought on a northbound boat a week later, steaming up the broken coast of the west side of Vancouver's Island. A landscape of sharp beaches and forest, mountains rising up behind. Then all at once the broken rocks subside into a white-sand beach, the longest Edwin has ever seen. He sees villages on the shore, smoke rising, those wooden columns with wings and painted faces—totem poles, he remembers now—erected here and there. He doesn't understand them and therefore finds them menacing. After a long time the white sand subsides into rocky crags and narrow inlets again. Every so often he sees a canoe in the distance. What if one were to dissolve into the wilderness like salt into water. He wants to go home. For the first time, Edwin begins to worry about his sanity.

The passengers on the boat: three Chinese men going to work in the cannery, a very tense young woman of Norwegian origin traveling to join her husband, Thomas and Edwin, the captain and two Canadian crewmen, all in the company of barrels and sacks of supplies. The Chinese men talk and laugh in their own language. The Norwegian woman stays in her cabin except for meals, and never smiles. The captain and crew are cordial but uninterested in talking to Thomas and Edwin, so Thomas and Edwin spend most of their time together up on deck.

"What those utterly inert fellows in Victoria don't quite understand," Thomas says, "is that the entirety of this land is here for the taking." Edwin glances at him, and sees into the future: since Thomas was rejected by the Victoria business community, he'll spend the rest of his life railing against them. "They're ensconced in their very English city, and, look, I do understand the appeal, but we have an opportunity here. We can create our own world in this place." He drones on about empire and opportunity while Edwin gazes out over the water. The inlets and coves and little islands are on their starboard side, and just beyond them rises the immensity of Vancouver Island, its forests ascending into mountains whose summits are lost in low cloud. On the port side, where they're standing, the ocean extends uninterrupted until, as far as Edwin can figure it, the coast of Japan. He has the same queasy sense of overexposure that he felt on the prairies. It's a relief when the boat finally makes a slow right turn and begins traveling up an inlet.

They reach the settlement of Caiette in the early evening. There isn't much to it: a pier, a small white church, seven or eight houses, a rudimentary road that leads up to the cannery and the logging camp. Edwin stands by the pier with his steamer trunk beside him, at a loss. This place is precarious, that's the only word for it. It's the lightest sketch of civilizations, caught between the forest and the sea. He doesn't belong here.

"That bigger building up there's a boardinghouse," the captain says kindly to Edwin, "if you wanted to stay here for a spell, get your bearings."

It's troubling to realize he's so obviously lost. Thomas and Edwin walk up the hill together to the boardinghouse and secure rooms on the upper floor. In the morning Thomas departs for the logging camp, while Edwin slips immediately into the same stasis that overcame him in Halifax. It isn't quite listlessness. He makes a careful inventory of his thoughts and decides that he isn't unhappy. He just desires no further movement, for the time being. If there's pleasure in action, there's peace in stillness. He spends his days walking on the beach, sketching, contemplating the sea from the porch, reading, playing chess with other boarders. After a week or two, Thomas gives up trying to persuade him to come to the logging camp.

Edwin is astonished by the beauty of this place. He likes to sit on the beach, and just gaze out at the islands, little tufts of trees rising out of the water. Canoes pass by sometimes, on unknowable errands, and the men and women in the boats sometimes ignore him and sometimes stare. Larger boats come in at regular intervals, bringing men and supplies for the cannery and the camp. Some of them know how to play chess, which is one of Edwin's great pleasures. He's never been very good at chess, but he enjoys the sense of order in the game.

"What are you doing here?" they sometimes ask.

"Oh, just contemplating my next move, I suppose," he always replies, or words to that effect. He has a sense of waiting for something. But what?

6

On a sunny morning in September, he's out for a walk when he comes upon two indigenous women laughing on the beach. Sisters? Good friends? They speak in a rapid language unlike anything he's ever heard, a language punctuated by sounds he can't imagine being able to replicate, let alone render in the Roman alphabet. Their hair is long and dark, and when one of them turns her head, light glances off a pair of enormous shell earrings. The women are wrapped in blankets against a cold wind.

They fall silent and watch him as he approaches.

"Good morning," he says, and touches the brim of his hat.

"Good morning," one replies. Her accent has a beautiful lilt. Her earrings hold all the colors of the dawn sky. Her companion, whose face bears a scattering of smallpox scars, just looks at him and says nothing. This isn't out of keeping with Edwin's experience of Canada—if anything, he reflects, it would come as the shock of his life if after half a year in the New World he were to find himself suddenly able to charm the locals—but the flat uninterest of the women's gaze is unnerving. This is a moment, he realizes, when he could express his views on colonization to people on the other side of the equation, so to speak, but he can't think of anything to say that doesn't sound absurd under the circumstances—if he tells them he believes colonization to be abhorrent, surely the logical next question will be *Then what are you doing here?*—so he says nothing further, and then they're behind him and the moment has passed.

He keeps walking, and then at some distance, still feeling their eyes on his back and wishing to convey an impression of having some sort of important errand to attend to, he turns toward the wall of trees. He never goes into the forest, because he's afraid of bears and cougars, but now it holds a strange appeal. He'll step in a hundred paces, he decides, no more. Counting off a hundred paces might calm him—counting has always calmed him—and if he walks straight for the full hundred then surely he can't get lost. Getting lost is death, he can see that. No, this whole place is death. No, that's unfair—this place isn't death, this place is indifference. This place is utterly neutral on the question of whether he lives or dies; it doesn't care about his last name or where he went to school; it hasn't even noticed him. He feels somewhat deranged.

7

The gates of the forest. The phrase comes immediately to mind, but Edwin's not sure where he picked it up. It sounds like something from a book he might have read as a boy. The trees here are old, and enormous. It's like stepping into a cathedral, except the underbrush is so thick that he has to fight his way through. He stops a few paces in. He sees a maple tree just ahead, large enough that it's created its own clearing, and that seems like a pleasant destination—he'll walk to the maple tree, he decides, he'll step out of the underbrush and linger a moment, then he'll go back to the beach immediately and never enter the forest again. This is an adventure, he tells himself, but it doesn't feel like an adventure. Mostly it feels like being slapped in the face with salal branches.

He fights his way through to the maple. It's quiet here, and he has a sudden certainty that he's being watched. He turns, and there—as incongruous as an apparition—is a priest, standing no more than a dozen yards away. He's older than Edwin, perhaps in his early thirties, and has very short black hair.

"Good morning," Edwin says.

"Good morning," the priest says, "and forgive me, I didn't mean to startle you. I like to walk here on occasion." There's something about his accent that eludes Edwin—it's not quite British, but not quite anything else. He wonders if the man's from Newfoundland, like his landlady back in Halifax.

"It does seem a peaceful destination," Edwin says.

"Quite so. I won't intrude on your contemplation, I was just on my way back to the church. Perhaps you'll stop in later."

"The church at Caiette? But you're not the usual priest," Edwin says.

"I'm Roberts. Filling in for Father Pike."

"Edwin St. Andrew. Pleased to meet you."

"Likewise. Good day."

The priest seems no more practiced at walking through underbrush than Edwin. He crashes away between the trees, and within minutes Edwin is alone again, gazing up at the branches. He steps forward—

8

—into a flash of darkness, like sudden blindness or an eclipse. He has an impression of being in some vast interior, something like a train station or a cathedral, and there are notes of violin music, there are other people around him, and then an incomprehensible sound—

9

When he returns to his senses he's on the beach, kneeling on hard stones, vomiting. He has a vague memory of having fought his way out of the forest in a blind panic, a nightmare of shadow and blurred green, branches lashing his face. He rises shakily, and walks to the water's edge. He wades in up to his knees—the shock of cold is wonderful, it's the thing that will restore his sanity—and kneels to wash vomit from his face and shirt, then a wave knocks him over, so that by the time he stands he's choking on seawater and soaked through and through.

He's alone on the beach now, but he sees movement among the buildings of Caiette, in the middle distance. The priest disappearing into the white church on the hill.

10

When Edwin reaches the church, the door is ajar, and the room is empty. The door behind the altar is open too, and through it he sees a few gravestones in the green quiet of the tiny cemetery. He slips into the last row of pews, closes his eyes, and rests his head in his hands. The building is so new that the church still holds the fragrance of freshly cut wood.

"Did you fall in the ocean?"

The voice is gentle, the accent still indecipherable. The new priest—Roberts, he remembers—stands at the end of his pew.

"I knelt in the water. To wash vomit from my face."

"Are you unwell?"

"No. I . . ." It seems silly now, and a little unreal. "I thought I saw something in the forest. After I saw you. I heard something. I don't know. It seemed . . . supernatural." The details are already slipping away from him. He walked into the forest, and then what? He remembers darkness; notes of music; a sound he couldn't identify; all of it over in a heartbeat. Did it really happen?

"May I sit with you?"

"Of course."

The priest sits beside him. "Would it help to unburden yourself?"

"I'm not Catholic."

"I'm here to serve everyone who walks through those doors."

But the details are already fading. In the moment, the strangeness Edwin encountered in the forest was utterly destabilizing, but now he finds himself thinking of a particularly bad morning at school. He was nine, maybe ten, and he realized that he couldn't read the words in front of him, because the letters were wriggling into incoherence and there were spots swimming in his vision. He stood from his desk to ask to go see matron, and he fainted. Fainting was darkness, but also sound: a murmuring and chirping like a chorus of birds, a blank void followed rapidly by an impression of being comfortably at home in bed—wishful thinking on the part of his subconscious, presumably—and then he woke into utter silence. Sound returned gradually, like someone turning a dial, silence fading into clamor and racket, the exclamations of other boys and the rapid steps of the approaching teacher—"Stand up, St. Andrew, no more malingering"— and was the moment just now in the forest really so different?

There were sounds, he reasons, and darkness, just like in that first instance. Perhaps he just fainted.

"I thought I saw something," Edwin says slowly, "but as I say it, I realize that perhaps I didn't."

"If you did," Roberts says gently, "you wouldn't be the first."

"What do you mean?"

"It's just, I've heard stories," the priest says. "That is, one hears stories."

This clumsy amendment strikes Edwin as a kind of camouflage, Roberts changing his patterns of speech to sound more English. More like Edwin. There's a wrongness about the man that Edwin can't entirely pinpoint.

"If I may ask, Father, where are you from?"

"Far away," the priest says. "Very far away."

"Well, that's all of us, isn't it," Edwin says, a little irritably. "Excepting the natives, of course. When we met in the forest just now, you said you were filling in for Father Pike, didn't you?"

"His sister was taken sick. He left last night."

Edwin nods, but there's something about this that rings utterly false. "Odd that I didn't hear anything about a boat going out last night, though."

"I have a confession to make," Roberts says.

"I'm listening."

"When I saw you in the forest, and I said I was going back to the church, well, I turned back for just a moment, as I was walking away."

Edwin stares at him. "What did you see?"

"I saw you walk under a maple tree. You were looking up, into the branches of the tree, and then—well, I had the impression that you could see something I couldn't. Was there something there?"

"I saw . . . well, I *thought* I saw—"

But Roberts is watching him too intensely, and in the quiet of this one-room church, at the far edge of the Western world, Edwin is oddly spooked. He's still a little ill—he has a pounding headache—and colossally weary. He doesn't want to talk anymore. He wants only to lie down. Roberts's presence here doesn't make sense to him.

"If Pike left last night," Edwin says, "he must have swum."

"But he did leave," Roberts says, "I assure you."

"Do you know how starved this place is for news, Father, really any news whatsoever? I live in the boardinghouse. If a boat had gone out last night, I would have heard about it at breakfast." The obvious next thought occurs to him: "Speaking of things I should have heard about, how did you get here? No boat's arrived in the past day or two, so am I to assume you strolled in through the forest?"

"Well," Roberts says, "I'm not sure how my mode of transportation is strictly relevant—"

Edwin rises, which forces Roberts to rise too. The priest backs into the aisle, and Edwin brushes past him.

"Edwin," Roberts says, but Edwin's already at the door. Another priest is approaching, climbing the stairs that lead up from the road: Father Pike, just returning from a visit to the cannery or the logging camp, his shock of white hair all but shining in the sunlight.

Edwin looks over his shoulder, into an empty church with its back door hanging open. Roberts has fled.

Mirella and Vincent /

2020

1

"I'd like to show you something strange." The composer, who was famous in an extremely limited, niche kind of way, i.e., in zero danger of being recognized on the street but most people in a couple of smallish artistic subcultures knew his name, was obviously uncomfortable, sweating as he leaned in close to his mic. "My sister used to record videos. This next one is a video of hers that I found in storage, after her death, and it's got some kind of glitch in it that I can't explain." He was quiet for a moment, adjusting a knob on his keyboard. "I wrote some music to go with it, but right before the glitch, the music will go silent, so we can appreciate the beauty of technical imperfection."

The music began first, a dreamlike swelling of strings, suggestions of static just under the surface, and then the video: his sister had walked with her camera along a faint forest path, toward an old-growth maple tree. She stepped under the branches and angled her camera upward, into green leaves flashing in the sunlight, in the breeze, and the music stopped so abruptly that the silence seemed like the next beat. The beat after that was darkness: the screen went black, just for a second, and there was a brief confusion of overlapping sounds—a few notes of a violin, a dim cacophony like the interior of a metropolitan train station, a strange kind of *whoosh* that suggested hydraulic pressure— then in a heartbeat the moment was over, the tree was back, and there was some chaotic camerawork as the composer's sister seemingly looked around wildly, forgetting that she had the camera in her hand.

The composer's music resumed, that video shifting seamlessly into one of his newer works, this one involving a video that he'd shot himself, five or six minutes of an aggressively ugly street corner in Toronto, but with orchestral strings laboring to produce the idea of hidden beauty. The composer was working rapidly, playing sequences of notes on keyboards that emerged a beat later as violin music, building the music up in layers as the Toronto street corner ticked by on the screen over his head.

In the front row of the audience, Mirella Kessler was in tears. She'd been friends with the composer's sister—Vincent—and hadn't known that Vincent had died. She left the theater soon after, and spent some time in the ladies' lounge, trying to pull herself together. Deep breaths, a fortifying layer of makeup. "Steady," she said aloud, to her face in the mirror. "Steady."

. . .

She'd come to this concert in the hope of speaking to the composer, in order to find out Vincent's whereabouts. There were certain questions she'd wanted to ask. Because in a version of her life so distant that it seemed now like a fairy tale, Mirella had had a husband—Faisal—and she and Faisal had been friends with Vincent and with Vincent's husband, Jonathan. There were several magnificent years, years of travel and money, and then the lights went out. Jonathan's investment fund turned out to be a Ponzi scheme. Faisal, unable to live in the face of financial ruin, took his own life.

Mirella had never spoken with Vincent again after that, because how could Vincent not have known? But a decade after Faisal's death she was at a restaurant with Louisa, her girlfriend of a year, and the first shiver of doubt crept in.

They were having dinner at a noodle place in Chelsea, and Louisa had been telling her about an unexpected birthday card from her aunt Jacquie, whom Mirella had never met because at any given moment half of Louisa's family was feuding. "Jacquie's kind of awful most of the time," Louisa said, "but she came by it honestly, in my opinion."

"Why, what happened to her?"

"I never told you this story? It's epic. Her husband had a secret second family."

"Seriously? What a soap opera."

"It gets better." Louisa leaned forward to deliver the punch line: "He parked the second family *across the street*."

"What?"

"Yeah, it was amazing. Okay," Louisa said, "picture this scene. Hedge-fund guy, Park Avenue apartment, nonworking wife, two kids in private school. Peak Upper East Side. Then one day Aunt Jacquie checks the Amex statement, and there's a tuition payment to a private school that neither of her children attend. So she hands the statement to Uncle Mike, like, 'What's this crazy charge,' and apparently he almost has a heart attack on the spot."

"Go on."

"So my cousins, at the time they're in like eighth grade and ninth grade, something like that, but turns out Uncle Mike's also the father of the kindergartner across the street. He put the five-year-old's tuition payment on the wrong Amex."

"Wait, *literally* across the street?"

"Yeah, the buildings face each other. The doormen at both addresses probably knew for years."

"How could she not know?" Mirella asked, and just like that the past had swallowed her whole and she was talking about Vincent.

"A man who works long hours can hide anything," Louisa said. She was still talking about her aunt, and hadn't noticed that Mirella was elsewhere. "Lucky for you I don't work."

"Lucky for me," Mirella echoed, and kissed Louisa's hand. "What a crazy story."

"It's the across-the-street thing that gets me," Louisa said. "That geography was *brazen*."

"I can't decide if it's very lazy or very efficient." Mirella was pretending to still be there in the restaurant with Louisa, eating noodles, but she was far away. Vincent had sworn she hadn't known about her husband's crimes, in deleted voicemails and in a deposition.

"Mirella." Louisa's hand rested gently on Mirella's wrist. "Come back."

Mirella sighed, and set down her chopsticks.

"Did I ever tell you about my friend Vincent?"

"The wife of the Ponzi scheme guy?"

"Yeah. That story about your aunt made me think of her. Did I tell you I saw her once, after Faisal died?"

Louisa's eyes widened. "No."

"It was a little over a year after his death, so March or April of 2010. I went into a bar with some friends, and Vincent was the bartender."

"Oh my god. What did you say to her?"

"Nothing," Mirella said.

She hadn't recognized her at first. In the days of money, Vincent had had long wavy hair like all the other trophy wives, but in the bar her hair was cut very short, and she wore glasses and no makeup. In the moment the disguise had struck Mirella as vindication—*of* course *you're trying to hide, you monster*—but now a certain ambiguity had entered the scene: a reasonable alternate explanation for the short hair/glasses/no makeup was that one or another of her husband's defrauded investors could walk in at any moment. Manhattan was lousy with defrauded investors in those days.

"I pretended not to know her," she said now, to Louisa. "As revenge, I guess. It wasn't my best moment. She always said she didn't know what Jonathan had been doing, but I just thought, *Of course you knew. How could you possibly not have known. You knew and you let Faisal lose everything and now he's dead.* That was all I could think about in those days."

Louisa nodded. "Stands to reason that she'd know," she said.

"But what if she didn't?"

"Is it plausible that she didn't know?" Louisa asked.

"I didn't think so, at the time. But you're telling me this story about your poor Aunt Jacquie, and, well, if you can hide a five-year-old, you can hide a Ponzi scheme."

Louisa held Mirella's hands across the table. "You should talk to her."

"I have no idea how to find her."

"It's 2019," Louisa said. "No one's invisible."

But Vincent was. In those days Mirella was working as a receptionist at a high-end tile showroom near Union Square. It was the kind of place that required few customers, because when people spent money here, they spent tens of thousands of dollars. The morning after her dinner with Louisa, whiling away a silent hour behind a reception desk the size of a car, Mirella searched for Vincent. She tried Vincent's husband's surname first. A search for "Vincent Alkaitis" produced old society photos, some with Mirella in them—parties, galas, etc.—and also pages of Vincent at her husband's sentencing hearing, blank-faced, in a gray suit, and absolutely nothing else. The most recent images were from

2011. "Vincent Smith" turned up dozens of different people, mostly men, none of them the Vincent she was looking for. She couldn't find Vincent on social media, or anywhere else.

She leaned back in her chair, frustrated. High over her desk, a light was buzzing. Mirella wore a great deal of makeup at work, and when she was tired in the afternoons, sometimes her face felt heavy. Out on the white-tiled prairie of the sales floor, a lone sales rep was walking a customer through every conceivable color of the company's signature composite material, which looked like stone but wasn't.

Vincent's parents were long dead, but she'd had a brother. Dredging up the brother's name required a deep dive into memory, which was a place Mirella generally tried to avoid. She glanced at the door to make sure no customers were approaching, then closed her eyes, took two deep breaths, and typed "Paul Smith + composer" into Google.

This was how she found herself at the Brooklyn Academy of Music four months later, waiting outside the stage door for Paul James Smith. She'd been hoping he could tell her how to find Vincent. But now Vincent was dead, apparently, which meant it was going to be a very different conversation. The stage door was on a quiet residential street. Mirella paced while she waited, not far, just a few feet in either direction. It was late January but unseasonably warm, well above freezing. Only one other person waited with her: a man of about her own age, mid-thirties, in jeans and a nondescript blazer. His clothes were too big. He nodded to her, she nodded back, and they settled into an awkward wait. Some time passed. A couple of staffers left without looking at them.

Then finally Vincent's brother emerged, looking a little haggard, although in fairness no one looked especially healthy in the orange glow of the streetlights here.

"Paul—" Mirella said, at the same moment that the other man said, "Excuse me—" and then they exchanged apologetic glances and fell silent, Paul glancing back and forth between them. A third man was approaching rapidly, a pale guy in a fedora and trench coat.

"Hello," Paul said, in a general way, to all of them.

"Hello!" said the newcomer. He took off his hat and revealed himself to be mostly bald. "Daniel McConaghy. Huge fan. Great show."

Paul gained an inch of height and a few watts of radiance as he stepped forward to shake the man's hand. "Well, thank you," he said, "always great to meet a fan." He looked around expectantly at Mirella and the guy in the oversized clothes.

"Gaspery Roberts," the oversized-clothes guy said. "Wonderful show."

"Hope you're not offended," the man in the fedora said, "I don't think your hands are dirty or anything, I've just gotten really into Purell since this thing in Wuhan hit the news." He was rubbing his hands together, with an apologetic smile.

"Fomites aren't a major mode of transmission with Covid-19," Gaspery said. *Fomites? Covid-19?* Mirella had never heard either term, and the other two were frowning too. "Oh, right," Gaspery said, seemingly to himself, "it's only January." He snapped back into focus. "Paul, could I maybe buy you a drink and ask you a couple quick questions about your work?" He had a faint accent that Mirella couldn't place.

"That sounds awesome," Paul said. "I could definitely use a drink." He turned to Mirella.

"Mirella Kessler," she said. "I was friends with your sister."

"Vincent," he said quietly. She couldn't quite parse his expression. Sadness but also a flash of something furtive. For a moment no one spoke. "Hey," he said, with forced cheer, "should we *all* get a drink?"

They wound up at a little French restaurant a few blocks away, across the street from a park that looked from Mirella's vantage point like a hill barely contained by a high brick retaining wall. She didn't know Brooklyn at all so everything was mysterious here, no points of reference beyond a vague notion that if she were to step outside the restaurant door, the spires of Manhattan would be somewhere to the left. The initial shock of the news of Vincent's death had faded a little, replaced by a limitless exhaustion. She was sitting next to the guy in the fedora, whose name she had forgotten, and across from Gaspery, who sat next to Paul. The fedora was going on and on about Paul's brilliance, his obvious influences, artistic debt to Warhol, etc.; he'd loved Paul's work from the beginning, that groundbreaking experimental collaboration with the video artist—what was his name again?—at Miami Basel, what a leap it had been when Paul suddenly started using his own videos instead of collaborating with others, and so on and so forth. Paul was glowing. He loved being praised, but who doesn't. She was facing the window, and her gaze kept drifting over Gaspery's shoulder to the park. If there were an earthquake and the retaining wall broke, would the park spill across the street and bury the restaurant? She returned her attention to the table when she heard Vincent's name.

"So your sister, Vincent, she's the one who filmed that strange video in your performance tonight?" This was Gaspery, his name memorable because she hadn't heard it before.

Paul laughed. "Name one of my videos that *isn't* strange," he said. "I did an interview last year, with this guy who kept calling me *sui generis,* and at a certain point I was like, 'Guy, you can just say *strange. Strange, weird,* or *eccentric,* take your pick.' Interview went a whole lot better after that, let me tell you." He laughed loudly at his own anecdote, and the fedora laughed too.

Gaspery smiled. "I meant that video with the forest path," he persisted. "With the darkness, the strange sounds."

"Oh. Yeah. That was Vincent's. She said I could use it."

"Was it filmed near where you grew up?" Gaspery asked.

"You've done your research," Paul said approvingly.

Gaspery inclined his head. "You're from British Columbia, aren't you?"

"Yeah. Tiny little place called Caiette, northern Vancouver Island."

"Oh, near Prince Edward Island," the fedora said confidently.

"Didn't really grow up there, though," Paul said, apparently not hearing this. "Vincent grew up there. Same dad, different moms, so I was just there summers and every second Christmas. But yeah, that's where the video was filmed."

"That . . . that moment on the video," Gaspery said, "that anomaly, for lack of a better word. Did you ever see anything like it in person?"

"Only on LSD," Paul said.

"Oh," the fedora said, brightening suddenly, "I didn't realize there was a psychedelic influence on your work." He leaned forward, in a confiding way. "I went pretty deep with psychedelics, myself. Once you get into heroic doses, you start to have certain realizations about the world. So much is an illusion, right?"

Gaspery shot him a troubled look. Mirella watched him while she waited for an opportunity to ask about Vincent. Gaspery seemed foreign in a way that she couldn't quite parse.

"And then once you grasp *that*," the fedora was saying, "it all just falls into place, right? Buddy of mine, he was struggling to quit cigarettes. Guy must've tried six or eight times. Not happening. Couldn't do it. Then one day he takes LSD, and *bam*. He calls me up the next evening, says, 'Dan, it's a miracle, I haven't even *wanted* a cigarette today.' I tell you, it was—"

"What happened to her?" Mirella asked Paul. She knew she was being rude but she didn't care, she was sitting there growing older by the minute, sinking into grief, and she wanted to know what had happened to her friend so she could leave these people.

Paul blinked at her, as if he'd forgotten she was there.

"She fell off a ship," he said. "About a year and a half—no, two years ago. It was two years last month."

"What kind of ship? Was she on a cruise?"

The fedora was glowering at his drink, but Gaspery was listening to the conversation with great interest.

"No, she was . . . I don't know how much you know about what happened to her in New York," Paul said, "that crazy thing with her husband, where it turned out he was a crook—"

"My husband was an investor in his Ponzi scheme," Mirella said. "I know all about it."

"Jesus," Paul said. "Did he—"

"Wait," the fedora said, "are we talking about Jonathan Alkaitis?"

"Yes," Paul said. "You know the story?"

"That crime was *insane*," the fedora said. "What was the size of the fraud, twenty billion dollars? Thirty? I remember where I was when that story broke. Call comes in from my mom, turns out my dad's retirement savings were—"

"You were telling me about the boat," Mirella said.

Paul blinked. "Right. Yeah."

"You have a bit of an interrupting problem," the fedora said, to Mirella. "No offense."

"No one's talking to you," Mirella said. "I asked a question of Paul."

"Yeah, so Vincent and I, we were out of touch for a few years," Paul said, "but after Alkaitis abandoned her and fled the country,

I guess Vincent got some training and certifications and went to sea as a cook on a container ship."

"Oh," Mirella said. "Wow."

"Sounds like an interesting life, right?"

"What happened to her?"

"No one really knows," Paul said. "She just disappeared from the ship. Seems like it was an accident. No body."

Mirella didn't know she was going to cry until she felt tears spilling down her face. All of the men at the table looked acutely uncomfortable. Only Gaspery thought to pass her a napkin.

"She drowned," she said.

"Yeah. I mean, it seems like it. They were hundreds of miles from land. She disappeared in bad weather."

"Drowning was the thing she was most scared of." Mirella dabbed at her face with the napkin. In the quiet, the small noises of the restaurant swelled around them: a couple arguing softly in French at a nearby table, clattering from the kitchen, the restroom door closing.

"Well," Mirella said, "thanks for telling me. And thank you for the drink." She didn't know who was paying for the drink, but she knew it wasn't her. She rose and walked out of the restaurant without looking back.

Outside, she felt directionless. She knew she should get in an Uber and go home, just go home and sleep and not do anything stupid like go for a walk after dark in an unfamiliar borough, but Vincent was dead. Mirella would find somewhere to sit for a few minutes, she decided, just to collect her thoughts. The neighborhood seemed fairly tame to her and it wasn't that late, also she was afraid of nothing, so she crossed the street and entered the park.

The park was quiet, but by no means unoccupied. People moved through pools of light, couples with arms around one another's shoulders and small groups of friends, a woman singing to herself. She sensed free-floating menace in the air, but it wasn't directed toward her. How could Vincent be dead? It was impossible, everything about it. She found her way to a bench and put on her headphones so she could pretend not to hear if anyone spoke to her, and willed herself toward invisibility. She would sit here for a while, she would sit here and think about Vincent, or sit here until she could find a way to stop thinking about Vincent, then she would go home and go to bed. But her thoughts shifted toward Jonathan, Vincent's former husband, living out his life in a luxury hotel in Dubai. The thought of him being there, wherever he was, ordering room service and asking to have the sheets changed and swimming in the hotel pool—*while Vincent was dead*—was an abomination.

A man walked in front of her and sat on the bench. She turned and it was Gaspery, so she took off the headphones.

"Forgive me," he said, "I saw you go into the park, and it's not a bad neighborhood, but—" He didn't finish the thought, because he didn't have to. For a woman alone in a park after nightfall, every neighborhood is a bad neighborhood.

"Who are you?" Mirella asked.

"I'm a kind of investigator," Gaspery said. "You'll think I'm crazy if I get into the details."

There was something familiar about him, it seemed to her now, something about his profile that rang a distant bell, but she couldn't quite place him.

"What are you investigating?"

"Look, I'll be frank with you, I have no interest in Mr. Smith or his art," Gaspery said.

"That makes two of us."

"But I'm interested in, well, in a certain kind of anomaly, like that moment in the video when the screen goes black. I waited outside the stage door to ask him about it."

"It is a strange moment."

"Can I ask, did your friend ever talk about that moment? Since it was her video, after all."

"No," Mirella said, "not that I remember."

"Stands to reason," Gaspery said. "She would've been quite young when she shot that video. The things we see when we're young, sometimes they don't stay with us."

The things we see when we're young.

"I think I've seen you before," Mirella said. She was looking at his face in profile in the dim light. He turned to look at her, and she was certain of it. "In Ohio."

"You look like you've seen a ghost."

She rose from the bench. "You were under the overpass," she said. "In Ohio, when I was a kid. That was you, wasn't it?"

He frowned. "I think you're mistaking me for someone."

"No, I think it was you. You were under the overpass. Right before the police came, before you were arrested. You said my name."

But he looked genuinely confused. "Mirella, I—"

"I have to go." She fled, not quite running, but walking in the flying unstoppable way that she'd perfected over years in New York City, darting out of the park, back down to the street, where in the fishbowl glow of the French restaurant the fedora and Vincent's brother were still deep in conversation. Gaspery hadn't followed her. She was grateful that he was wearing a white shirt; he would all but shine in the dark. She plunged into the shadows of a residential street. She flew past old brownstones standing beautiful in the streetlights, iron fences, old trees; faster and faster, toward the bright lights of a commercial avenue up ahead, where a yellow cab was gliding across the intersection like a chariot, like some kind of miracle—a yellow cab in Brooklyn!— and she hailed it and climbed aboard. A moment later the taxi was speeding over the Brooklyn Bridge, Mirella crying quietly in the backseat. The driver glanced at her in the rearview mirror, but—oh, the grace of strangers in this crowded city!—said nothing.

2

When Mirella was a child, she lived with her mother and her older sister, Susanna, in a duplex in exurban Ohio. The housing development was located in a territory composed of strip malls and big-box stores. Farmland extended to the back of the Walmart parking lot. Some miles away, there was a prison. Mirella's mother worked two jobs and spent very little time at home. In the early mornings—well before dawn in the wintertime—Mirella and Susanna's mother rose after a few hours of sleep, poured milk over her daughters' cereal and did their hair while blearily drinking coffee, and drove them to school. She kissed her daughters goodbye and they were at school for the next ten hours—early drop-off, then school, then after-school programming—until at the end of the afternoon they boarded a bus that dropped them a half-mile from home.

It was a bad half-mile. They had to walk under an overpass.

The overpass scared Mirella, but in all the years she lived there, from when she was five until she dropped out of school and took a bus to New York City at sixteen, there was only one truly terrible incident. Mirella was nine, which made Susanna eleven, and they did hear the gunshots as the school bus pulled away, but the sounds were clear only in retrospect. In the moment, they looked at each other in the winter twilight and Susanna shrugged. "Probably just a car backfiring or something," she said, and Mirella, who would have believed anything Susanna told her, took her sister's hand and they walked together. Snow was falling. The mouth of the overpass was a dark cave waiting to swallow them. *It's fine,* Mirella told herself, *it's fine, it's fine,* because it was always fine, but this particular time it wasn't. As they stepped into the shadows, the sound came once more, impossibly loud now. They stopped.

Two men lay on the ground a few yards ahead of them. One was perfectly still; the other was twitching. In the dim light, at this distance, she couldn't see exactly what had happened to them. A third man was sitting slumped against the wall, a handgun dangling loose in his hand. A fourth was running away—his footsteps echoed—but Mirella glimpsed him for only an instant, scrambling up the embankment at the far end of the overpass and out of sight.

For a long time all of them—Mirella, Susanna, the man with the gun, the two dead or dying men on the ground—were frozen in a winter tableau. How much time? It felt like forever. Hours, days. The man with the gun had a sleepy, sedated look about him; his head nodded forward once or twice. Then came the police lights, blue and red washing over him, and this seemed to wake him up. He stared at the gun in his hand, as if unsure how it had arrived there, then he turned his head, and looked directly at the girls.

"Mirella," he said.

Then came shouting and confusion, a swarm of dark uniforms—*"Drop your weapon! Drop your weapon!"*—and although the event objectively happened, she and Susanna really were interviewed by the police, and there really was a story in the papers the next day ("Two Shot Dead Under Overpass: Suspect in Custody"), it was easy to convince herself in the years that followed that she'd only imagined this last part, that he hadn't really said her name. How could he have known her name? Susanna didn't remember hearing anything.

But all these years later, in the back of a Manhattan-bound taxi, safe in another life, here was a certainty she couldn't shake: the man in the tunnel was Gaspery Roberts.

She closed her eyes, trying to relax, but her phone vibrated in her hand. A text from her girlfriend: *Are you coming to Jess's party?*

It took a moment to remember. She texted back—*On my way*—and waved to catch the driver's eye in the rearview mirror.

"Excuse me."

"Ma'am?" he said, a little wary because she'd just been crying.

"May I give you a new destination? I need to get to Soho."

3

She had to walk all the way through the party before she found Louisa, smoking a cigarette on a terrace that was really just a tiny patch of blacktop roof. She kissed her and then sat awkwardly beside her on a narrow stone bench.

"How are you doing?" Louisa asked. They lived separately but spent a great deal of time together.

"Not bad at all," Mirella said, because she didn't want to talk about it. It was troublingly easy to lie to Louisa. She knew it was unfair to compare people, everyone knows that, but a difficulty she was having at this moment was that Louisa seemed infinitely less interesting to her than Vincent. Louisa had a kind of unspoiled quality, an air of having been cushioned from life's sharper edges, which was less appealing now than it had been. "I'm a little tired," Mirella said. "I didn't sleep that well."

"How come?"

"I don't know, just one of those random bad nights."

Another difficulty of the evening: this was Jess's party, and Jess was Mirella's friend, not Louisa's. In Mirella's old life, her long-ago life wherein everything was different, she'd been to this terrace with Faisal. Now, as then, the space was dressed up with fairy lights and potted palms, but still felt a little like the bottom of a hole. This was the downside to having retained a few friends from her time with Faisal—there were dangerous places here and there, places where she could get sucked into memories of another life, and this terrace was among them. On another night, at another party—fourteen years ago? Thirteen?—she and Vincent had stood out here, a little drunk, looking straight up at the tiny patch of dark sky because Vincent swore she could see the North Star.

"It's right there," Vincent said. "Look, follow my finger. It's not that bright."

"That's a satellite," Mirella said.

"*What's* a satellite?" Faisal asked, stepping out onto the balcony. They'd arrived separately, and this was the first time she'd seen him all day. She kissed him and didn't quite fail to see the way Vincent glanced in their direction before returning her gaze to the sky. A difference between Mirella and Vincent was that Mirella truly loved her husband.

"There," Mirella said, pointing. "It's moving, right?"

Faisal squinted. "I'll have to take your word for it," he said.

"I think I need new glasses." He glanced around the cramped space, his arm around her waist. "Wow," he said, "what a thrillingly boho firetrap."

It was true. Buildings rose up on all sides. Three walls belonged to other buildings, and the fourth held the door that led back into the party. All these years later, sitting out here with Louisa, Mirella closed her eyes momentarily in order to not see Faisal gazing up at the sky.

"What did you do all day?" Louisa asked.

There had been a time when Mirella liked Louisa's questions— what a gift, she'd once thought, to be with someone who was so *interested*, interested in everything she'd done all day, someone who cared enough to ask—but tonight it was an intrusion.

"Went for a walk. Did some laundry. Stared at Instagram, mostly." Gaspery Roberts couldn't possibly have been the man under the overpass, now that she thought about it, because that was decades ago and he hadn't aged.

"Was that satisfying?"

"Of course not," Mirella said, a little sharper than she'd intended, and Louisa gave her a surprised look.

"We should go somewhere," Louisa said. "Maybe rent a cottage, get out of the city for a few days."

"That sounds nice." But Mirella was startled by the unhappiness that flooded through her at the suggestion. She very much did not want to go to a cottage with Louisa, she realized.

"But first," Louisa said, "I need another drink." She went inside and Mirella was alone for a while, then a woman came over to ask for a light and offered to tell Mirella's fortune in return. Mirella held her hands out as instructed, palms up, embarrassed by the way they trembled. How could she have fallen out of love with Louisa so suddenly, so cleanly? How could the man in the tunnel in Ohio have surfaced all these years later in New York? How could Vincent be dead? The fortune-teller put her hands over Mirella's hands, their palms almost touching, and closed her eyes. Mirella liked being able to watch her unobserved. The fortune-teller was older than Mirella had thought at first, somewhere in her thirties, first lines visible on her face. She was wearing a complicated arrangement of scarves.

"Where are you from?" she asked.

"Ohio."

"No, I mean originally."

"Still Ohio."

"Oh. I thought maybe I heard an accent."

"The accent's from Ohio too."

The fortune-teller's eyes were still closed.

"You have a secret," she said.

"Doesn't everyone?"

Her eyes opened. "You tell me yours, I'll tell you mine, and we'll never see each other again," she said.

It was an attractive proposition. "Okay," Mirella said. "But you go first."

"My secret is, I hate people," the woman said, very sincerely, and for the first time Mirella liked her.

"All people?"

"All except maybe like three," she said. "Your turn."

"My secret is, I want to kill a man." Was this true? Mirella wasn't sure. It had a ring of truth about it.

The fortune-teller's eyes darted over Mirella's face, like she was trying to work out if this was some kind of joke. "A specific man?" she asked. She smiled tentatively—*You're kidding, right? Please tell me you're kidding?*—but Mirella didn't smile back.

"Yes," Mirella said. "A specific man." It became real as she said it.

"What's his name?"

"Jonathan Alkaitis." When had she last said the name out loud? She repeated it to herself, more quietly this time. "Actually, maybe I just want to talk to him. I don't know."

"Pretty big difference," the fortune-teller said.

"Yeah." Mirella closed her eyes against the dark of the sky, the tumult of the nearby party, the reek of cigarette smoke, the fortune-teller's face. "I guess I'll have to make up my mind."

"Okay," the fortune-teller said, "well, thanks for the light." She slid away from Mirella and vanished into the party, through an open door like a portal into a lost world. It was a cold night, and the moon was brilliant over New York City. Mirella stood looking at it for a moment, then returned to the party, which felt like a dream she'd had once, all abstract color and commotion and lights. Louisa was dancing in the living room. Mirella stood watching her for a moment, then waded through the crowd.

"I've got a headache," Mirella said. "I think I'm going to go."

Louisa kissed her, and Mirella knew it was over. She felt nothing. "Call me," Louisa said.

"Adieu," Mirella said, as she backed away through the crowd, and Louisa, who spoke no French and didn't understand the implication, blew her a kiss.

3

Last Book Tour on Earth /

2203

THE FIRST STOP ON THE BOOK TOUR WAS NEW YORK CITY, where Olive did signing events at two bookstores and then found an hour to walk in Central Park before the bookseller dinner. The Sheep Meadow at twilight: silvery light, wet leaves on the grass. The sky was crowded with low-altitude airships, and in the distance the falling-star lights of commuter aircraft streaked upward toward the colonies. Olive paused for a moment to orient herself, then walked toward the ancient double silhouette of the Dakota. Hundred-story towers rose up behind it.

The Dakota was where Olive's new publicist was waiting, Aretta, in charge of all events in the Atlantic Republic. Aretta was a little younger than Olive, and deferential in a way that made Olive nervous. When Olive walked into the lobby, Aretta stood quickly, and the hologram with whom she'd been speaking blinked out. "Did you have a nice walk in the park?" she asked, already smiling in anticipation of a positive reply.

"It was lovely, thank you," Olive said. She didn't add *It made me wish I could live on Earth*, because the last time she'd confided in a handler, it was repeated at dinner—"Do you know what Olive told me on the ride over?" a librarian in Montreal had reported breathlessly to a restaurant table full of waiting librarians, "She told me she was a little nervous before her talk!"—

so now as a matter of policy Olive didn't reveal anything even remotely personal to anyone ever.

"Well," Aretta said, "we should probably be getting to the venue. It's about six or seven blocks, should we maybe just . . . ?"

"I'd love to walk," Olive said, "if you don't mind." They walked out together into the silver city.

Did Olive actually wish she could live on Earth? She vacilated on the question. She'd lived all her life in the hundred and fifty square kilometers of the second moon colony, the imaginatively named Colony Two. She found it beautiful—Colony Two was a city of white stone, spired towers, tree-lined streets and small parks, alternating neighborhoods of tall buildings and little houses with miniature lawns, a river running under pedestrian archways—but there's something to be said for unplanned cities. Colony Two was soothing in its symmetry and its order. Sometimes order can be relentless.

In the signing line after the lecture in Manhattan that night, a young man knelt on his side of the table so that he was more or less at eye level with Olive, and said, "I have a book to sign"— his voice trembled a little—"but what I really wanted to tell you is that your work helped me through a bad patch last year. I'm grateful."

"Oh," Olive said. "Thank you. I'm honored." But in these moments *honored* always felt inadequate, which made it feel

like the wrong word, which made Olive feel somehow fraudulent, like an actor playing the role of Olive Llewellyn.

"Everyone feels like a fraud sometimes," Dad said the following
day, on the drive from the Denver airship terminal to the tiny
town where he lived with Olive's mother.

"Oh, I know," Olive said. "I'm not suggesting it's an actual
problem." Olive's understanding of her own life was that she
didn't have any actual problems.

"Right." Dad smiled. "I'd imagine your life's a little disorienting these days."

"Perhaps just a little." Olive had forty-eight hours to see her
parents before the tour resumed. They were passing through
an agricultural zone, enormous robots moving slowly over the
fields. The sunlight here was sharper than at home. "I'm grateful
for all of it," she said. "Disorienting or not."

"Sure. Must be hard to be away from Sylvie and Dion, though."

Now they were in the outskirts of the little town where her
parents lived, passing through a district of robot repair foundries.

"I just try not to think about it," Olive said. The gray of the
foundries was subsiding into brightly painted little shops and
houses. The clock in the town square glinted in the sunlight.

"The distance is unbearable if you let yourself dwell on it."
Her father's gaze was fixed on the road. "Here we are," he said.
They were turning onto her parents' street, and there, so close,
her mother stood in the doorway. Olive leaped down from the

hovercraft the moment it stopped, and ran into her mother's arms. *If the distance is unbearable,* she didn't ask, then or in the two days she stayed with her parents, *then why do you live so far from me?*

Olive's parents' house couldn't be called her childhood home— her childhood home had been sold a few weeks after she left for college, when her parents decided to retire on Earth—but there was peace here. "It was so good to see you," her mother whispered when she left. She held Olive for just a moment, and stroked her hair. "Come back soon?"

A hovercraft was waiting outside the house, the driver hired by one of Olive's North American publishers. She had an event at a bookstore in Colorado Springs that night, followed by an early-morning flight to a festival in Deseret.

"I'll bring Sylvie and Dion next time," Olive said, and stepped back into the tour.

A book tour paradox: Olive missed her husband and daughter with a desperate passion, but also she liked very much being alone in the empty streets of Salt Lake City at eight-thirty in the morning on a Saturday in the bright autumn air, birds wheeling in white light. There's something to be said for looking up at a clear blue sky and knowing that it isn't a dome.

In the Republic of Texas the next afternoon, she wanted to go for a walk again, because on the map, her hotel—a La Quinta that faced another La Quinta, a parking lot between them—was just across the road from a cluster of restaurants and shops, but what the map didn't show was that the road was an eight-lane expressway with no crosswalk and constant traffic, mostly modern hovercraft but also the occasional defiantly retro wheeled pickup truck, so she walked along the expressway for a while with the shops and the restaurants shining like a mirage on the other side. There was no way to cross without risking her life, so she didn't. When she got back to her hotel she felt something scratching her ankles, and when she looked down her socks were spiked with little burrs, astonishingly sharp black-brown stars like miniature weapons that had to be extracted very carefully. She set them on the desk and photographed them from every angle. They were so perfectly hard and shiny that they could've passed for biotech, but when she pulled one apart, she saw that it was real. No, *real* wasn't the word for it. Everything that can be touched is real. What she saw was it was a thing that grew, a castoff from some mysterious plant they didn't have in the moon colonies, so she wrapped a few of them in a sock and carefully stowed the sock away in her suitcase to give to her daughter, Sylvie, who was five and collected that kind of thing.

"I was so confused by your book," a woman in Dallas said. "There were all these strands, narratively speaking, all these characters, and I felt like I was waiting for them to connect, but they didn't, ultimately. The book just ended. I was like"—she was some distance away, in the darkened audience, but Olive saw that she was miming flipping through a book and running out of pages—"I was just like, *Huh? Is the book missing pages?* It just *ended.*"

"Okay," Olive said. "So just to clarify, your question is . . ."

"I was just, like, *what,*" the woman said. "My question is just . . ." She spread her hands, like *help me out here, I've run out of words.*

The hotel room that night was all black and white. Olive had dreams about playing chess with her mother.

Did the book end too abruptly? She fixated on the question for three days, from the Republic of Texas to western Canada.

"I'm trying not to be pessimistic," Olive said, on the phone to her husband, "but I've barely slept in three days and I doubt I'll be terribly impressive in my lecture tonight." This was in Red Deer. Outside the hotel room window, the lights of residential towers glimmered in the dark.

"Don't be pessimistic," Dion said. "Think of that quote I've got pinned up in my office."

" 'It's a great life if you don't weaken,' " Olive said. "How's work going, speaking of your office?"

He sighed. "I got assigned to the new project." Dion was an architect.

"The new university?"

"Yeah, kind of. A center for the study of physics, but also . . .

I signed an ironclad confidentiality agreement, so don't tell anyone?"

"Of course. I won't tell a soul. But what's so secret about the architecture of a university?"

"It's not quite . . . I'm not sure it's exactly a university." Dion sounded troubled. "There's some serious weirdness in the blueprints."

"What kind of weirdness?"

"Well, for starters, there's a tunnel under the street connecting the building to Security Headquarters," he said.

"Why would a university need a tunnel to the police?"

"Your guess is as good as mine. And the building backs up on the government building," Dion said, "which, I mean, at first I thought nothing of it. That's prime downtown real estate, so you know, why shouldn't the university build next to the government building, but the two buildings aren't separate. There are so many passageways between them that it's functionally the same building."

"You're right," Olive said, "that seems weird."

"Well, it's a good project for my portfolio, I guess."

Olive understood from his tone that he wanted to change the subject. "How's Sylvie?"

"Doing fine." Dion immediately pivoted the conversation to some trivial matter involving the grocery order and Sylvie's school lunches, from which she understood that Sylvie probably wasn't in fact doing particularly well in her absence, and she was grateful for his kindness in not telling her this.

. . .

In the morning she flew to a city in the far north for a day of interviews, and then she had an evening lecture, and then there was a long signing line and a late dinner, followed by three hours of sleep and a three-forty-five a.m. airport pickup.

"What do you do, Olive?" the driver asked.

"I'm a writer," Olive said. She closed her eyes and rested her head against the window, but the driver spoke again:

"What do you write?"

"Books."

"Tell me more."

"Well," Olive said, "I'm traveling because of a novel called *Marienbad*. It's about a pandemic."

"That's your most recent?"

"No, I've written two others since then. But *Marienbad*'s being made into a film, so I'm on tour for a new edition."

"That's so interesting," the driver said, and started talking about a book she wanted to write. It seemed to be some kind of sci-fi/fantasy epic, the modern world except with wizards, demons, and talking rats. The rats were good. They helped the wizards. They were rats because in all the books the driver had read that involved helpful talking animals, the animals were just too big. Horses and dragons and whatnot. But how do you discreetly move through the world with a dragon or a horse? It's untenable. Try taking a horse into a bar sometime. No, what you want, she said, is a pocket-sized animal sidekick, a rat for example.

"Yeah, I guess rats are more portable," Olive said. She was trying to keep her eyes open, but it was very difficult. The massive transport truck in front of them kept weaving over the center line. Human-driven, or a flaw in the software? Unsettling either way. The driver was talking about the possibilities of the multiverse: rats can't talk here, she pointed out, but does it logically follow that they can't talk *anywhere*? She seemed to be waiting for a reply.

"Well, I don't know much about rat anatomy," Olive said, "like if their voice boxes and vocal cords or whatever are up to the task of human speech, but I'll have to think about it, maybe rats in different universes could have different anatomy . . ." (She may have been mumbling by that point, or possibly not speaking at all. It was so hard to stay awake.) The back of the transport truck was beautiful, a diamond-patterned textured steel that glinted and shone in the headlights.

"I mean, for all we know," the driver was saying, "there's a universe where your book is real, I mean nonfictional!"

"I hope not," Olive said. She could only keep her eyes half-open, so the lights in her field of vision were streaked into vertical spikes, the dashboard, the taillights, the reflections off the back of the truck.

"So your book," the driver said, "it's about a pandemic?"

"Yes. A scientifically implausible flu." Olive couldn't keep her eyes open anymore, so she surrendered, she closed her eyes and let herself fall into the kind of half-sleep from which she knew she could be summoned by a voice—

"Have you been following the news about this new thing," the driver said, "this new virus in Australia?"

"Kind of," Olive said, with her eyes closed. "It seems like it's been fairly well contained."

"You know, in my book," the driver said, "there's a kind of apocalypse too." She talked for some time about a catastrophic rip in the space-time continuum, but Olive was too tired to follow.

"I've kept you up this whole time!" the driver said brightly, as the car pulled into the airport. "You didn't get to sleep at all!"

Twelve hours later, Olive was delivering her *Marienbad* lecture, which leaned heavily on her research into the history of pandemics. The lecture was so familiar at this point that it required very little in the way of conscious thought, and her mind was wandering. She kept thinking about the conversation with the driver, because she remembered saying *It seems like it's been fairly well contained,* but here's an epidemiological question: if you're talking about outbreaks of infectious disease, isn't *fairly well contained* essentially the same thing as *not contained at all*? *Focus,* she told herself, and pulled herself back to the reality of the podium, the hard bright light, the microphone.

"In the spring of 1792," she said, "Captain George Vancouver sailed northward up the coast of what would later become British Columbia, aboard the HMS *Discovery*. As he and his crew traveled northward, the men found themselves increasingly unsettled. Here was this temperate climate, this incredibly green landscape, and yet it seemed strangely empty. Vancouver wrote in his shipboard diary: 'We traveled nearly one hundred fifty miles of those shores, without seeing that number of inhabitants.'" A pause to let that sink in, while Olive took a sip of water. A virus is either contained or it isn't. It's a binary condition. She hadn't been sleeping enough. She set down her water glass.

"When they ventured ashore, they found villages that could have housed hundreds, but those villages were abandoned. When they ventured farther, they realized that the forest was a grave-yard." This was the part of the lecture that had been easy before giving birth to her daughter, and was now almost impossible. Olive paused to steady herself. "Canoes with human remains were strung three or four meters up in the trees," she said. *Human remains that were not Sylvie. Not Sylvie. Not Sylvie.* "Elsewhere, they found skeletons on the beach. Because small-pox had already arrived."

In the signing line after that night's lecture, signing her name over and over again, Olive's thoughts kept drifting toward disaster. *To Xander with best wishes Olive Llewellyn. To Claudio with best wishes Olive Llewellyn. To Sohail with best wishes Olive Llewellyn. To Hyeseung with best wishes Olive Llewellyn.* Was there going to be another pandemic? A new cluster of cases had appeared in New Zealand that morning.

The hotel room that night was mostly beige, with a painting of some extravagantly petaled pink Earth flower—a peony?—over the bed.

. . .

"A year earlier," Olive told another crowd, same lecture/different city, "in 1791, a trading ship, the *Columbia Rediviva,* had sailed those same waters. They were trading sea otter skins." What did a sea otter even look like? Olive had never seen one. She resolved to look this up later. "They had a similar experience. They found a depopulated land, and the very few survivors they encountered had terrible stories and terrible scars. ' 'Twas evident that these Natives had been visited by that scourge of mankind the small-pox,' wrote a crew member, John Boit. Another sailor, John Hoskins, was moved to outrage: 'Infamous Europeans, a scandal to the Christian name; is it you,' he wrote, 'who bring and leave in a country with people you deem savages the most loathsome diseases?' "

A sip of water. The audience was silent. (A passing thought that felt like triumph: *I am holding the room.*) "But of course," she said, "there's always a beginning. Before smallpox could be brought from Europe to the Americas, smallpox had to arrive in Europe."

She got out of bed that night and walked into a side table, because she'd been thinking about the layout of the previous night's hotel room.

The next morning, on a long drive between cities, the driver asked if Olive had kids back home.

"I have a daughter," Olive said.

"How old?"

"Five."

"What are you doing here, then?" the driver asked.

"Well, this is how I provide for her," she said, in her mildest voice, and didn't add *Fuck you, I know you would never ask a man that question,* because after all it was just the two of them alone in the car, this man and Olive. Watching the trees slip by outside the window; they were passing through a forest preserve. Imagining Sylvie was here beside her, imagining that if she wanted to she could reach out and hold that warm little hand.

"You grew up there? In the colonies?" he asked abruptly, after some time had passed. They'd been talking about the moon colonies earlier.

"Yes. My grandmother was one of the first settlers."

She liked to picture her grandmother sometimes, twenty years old, rising out of the Vancouver Airship Terminal in the first light of dawn, her ship streaking out into the dark.

"Always meant to go up there," the driver said. "Never made it."

Remember that you're lucky to get to travel. Remember that some people never leave this planet. Olive closed her eyes, in order to better imagine that Sylvie was sitting beside her.

"You smell nice, by the way," the driver said.

The next four hotel rooms were white and gray and had identical layouts, because all four hotels were part of the same chain.

"Is this your first time staying with us?" a woman at a reception desk for the third or fourth hotel said to her, and Olive wasn't sure how to answer, because if you've stayed in one Marriott, haven't you stayed in all of them?

Another city:

"Before smallpox could be brought from Europe to the Americas, smallpox had to arrive in Europe." Olive was regretting her decision to wear a sweater. The lights in Toronto were too hot. "In the middle of the second century, Roman soldiers returning from their siege of the Mesopotamian city of Seleucia brought a new illness back to the capital.

"Victims of the Antonine Plague, as it came to be called, developed fevers, vomiting, and diarrhea. A few days later, a terrible rash would appear on their skin. The population had no immunity." Olive had delivered the lecture so many times that she felt at this point like a neutral observer. She listened to the words and cadences from some distance away.

"When the Antonine Plague raged through the Roman Empire," Olive told the audience, "the army was decimated. There were parts of the empire where one in three people died. Here's something interesting: the Romans wondered if they'd brought this calamity upon themselves, by their actions in the city of Seleucia."

She was in that night's hotel room—mostly beige and blue, with pink accents—when Dion called. This was unusual: generally speaking, she called him. Dion sounded tired. He'd been working long hours, he said, and the new university project was creepy, and Sylvie was being difficult. When he'd picked Sylvie up at school today she hadn't wanted to leave and had made a scene and everyone had felt sorry for him, he could see it in their soft expressions. "Have you been following the news about this new illness in Australia?" he asked. "I'm kind of worried about it."

"Not really," Olive said. "To be honest, I've been too tired to think."

"I wish you could come home."

"I'll be home soon."

He was silent.

"I should go," she said. "Good night."

"Good night," he said, and hung up.

"In the city of Seleucia," Olive told a crowd at the Mercantile Library in Cincinnati, a day or two later, "the Roman army had destroyed the temple of Apollo. In that temple, the historian Ammianus Marcellinus wrote, Roman soldiers had discovered a narrow crevice. When the Romans opened this hole wider, in the hope that it might contain valuables, Marcellinus wrote that there 'issued a pestilence, loaded with the force of incurable disease, which . . . polluted the whole world from the borders of Persia to the Rhine and Gaul with contagion and death.'"

A beat. A sip of water. Pacing is everything.

"This explanation might seem a little silly to us now, but they were grasping wildly for an explanation for the nightmare that had befallen them, and I think that in its outlandishness, the explanation touches upon the root of our fear: illness still carries a terrible mystery."

She looked over the crowd and saw, as always at this point in the lecture, that particular look on the faces of some of the audience, a specific grief. In any given crowd, several people will inevitably be incurably sick, and several others will have recently lost someone they love to illness.

"Are you worried about the new virus?" Olive asked the library director in Cincinnati. They were sitting together in the director's office, which Olive had immediately ranked as possibly her favorite of all the offices she'd ever seen. It was located beneath the stacks, which were hundreds of years old and made of wrought iron.

"I'm trying not to be," the director said. "I'm hoping it'll just fizzle out."

"I suppose they usually do," Olive said. Was this true? She was unsure as she spoke.

The library director nodded, her eyes wandering. She clearly didn't want to talk about pandemics. "Let me tell you something magnificent about this place," she said.

"Oh, please do," Olive said. "It's been a while since anyone's told me anything magnificent."

"So we don't own the building," the director said, "but we hold a ten-thousand-year lease on the space."

"You're right. That's magnificent."

"Nineteenth-century hubris. Imagine thinking civilization

would still exist in ten thousand years. But there's more." She leaned forward, paused for effect. "The lease is renewable."

The window in that night's hotel room opened, which after a dozen rooms with nonopening windows felt like something of a miracle. Olive spent a long time reading a novel by the window, in the beautiful fresh air.

The next morning, leaving Cincinnati, Olive saw a sunrise from the airport lounge. Heat shimmering over the tarmac, the horizon cast in pink. *Paradox: I want to go home but I could watch Earth's sunrises forever.*

"The truth is," Olive said, behind a lectern in Paris, "even now, all these centuries later, for all our technological advances, all our scientific knowledge of illness, we still don't always know why one person gets sick and another doesn't, or why one patient survives and another dies. Illness frightens us because it's chaotic. There's an awful randomness about it."

At the reception that night, someone tapped her shoulder, and when she turned around it was Aretta, her publicist from the Atlantic Republic.

"Aretta!" she said. "What are you doing in Paris?"

"I'm off work," Aretta said, "but one of my best friends works for your French publisher and she got us tickets for the reception, so I thought I'd say hi."

"It's good to see you here," Olive said, and meant it, but someone was pulling her away to speak to a group of sponsors and booksellers, so for a while afterward Olive stood in a circle of people who wanted to know when her next book was coming out and whether she was enjoying France and where her family was.

"You must have a very kind husband," a woman said, "to look after your daughter while you do this."

"What do you mean?" Olive asked, but of course she knew what the woman meant.

"Well, he's looking after your daughter, while you do this," the woman said.

"Forgive me," Olive said, "I fear there's a problem with my translator bot. I thought you said he was kind to care for his own child." As she turned away, she realized that she was grinding her teeth. She looked for Aretta but couldn't find her.

The next four hotel rooms were beige, blue, beige again, then mostly white, but all four had silk flowers in a vase on the desk.

"What's it like?" the interviewer asked. It was difficult to stop thinking about the woman in Paris, but Olive was trying. *Keep moving.* Olive and the interviewer were onstage in Tallinn. The lights were very hot.

"What do you mean?" It was a strange opening question.

"What's it like writing such a successful book? What's it like being Olive Llewellyn?"

"Oh. It's surreal, actually. I wrote three books that no one noticed, no distribution beyond the moon colonies, and then . . . it's like slipping into a parallel universe," Olive said. "When I published *Marienbad,* I somehow fell into a bizarre upside-down world where people actually read my work. It's extraordinary. I hope I never get used to it."

The driver who took Olive to her hotel that night had a beautiful voice and sang an old jazz song as he drove. Olive opened the hovercraft window and closed her eyes in order to live more completely in the music, cool air in her face, and for several minutes she was perfectly happy.

"It's amazing how time slows when I'm traveling," Olive said, on the phone to Dion. She was lying on her back on the floor of another hotel room, staring up at the ceiling. The bed would have been more comfortable, but her back hurt and the hard floor was helping. "I feel like I've been on the road for six months. I'm not sure how it's still November."

"It's been three weeks."

"Like I said."

There was silence on the line.

"Look," Olive said, "the thing is, it's possible to be grateful for extraordinary circumstances and simultaneously long to be with the people you love."

She felt a softening between them before he spoke. "I know, love," Dion said gently. "We miss you too."

"I've been thinking about your project," she said. "Why a university would need an underground passageway to police headquarters and—"

But Dion's device was ringing. "I'm sorry," he said, "it's my boss. Talk soon?"

"Talk soon."

She'd been on an airship crossing the Atlantic when the answer to the puzzle came to her.

Research teams had been working on time travel for decades, both on Earth and in the colonies. In that context, a university for the study of physics, with an underground passageway to the police headquarters and countless literal back doors into government, made perfect sense. What is time travel if not a security problem?

She kept searching for the song the driver in Tallinn had been singing, but she couldn't find it. The lyrics evaded her. She kept entering search terms into her device (love + rain + death + money + lyrics + song) and getting nowhere.

In Lyon, at a festival dedicated to mystery fiction, Olive's French publicist brought her to a media room where the interviewer, a woman who worked for a magazine, was programming an array of hologram cameras. "Olive," the interviewer said, "I love your work."

"Thank you, that's really nice to hear."

"Will you sit in that chair, please?"

Olive sat. An assistant affixed a mic to her shirt.

"So this is a feature I'm doing with all of the authors at the festival," the interviewer said, "just a brief interview feature. It's a fun thing for our audience."

"A fun thing?" Olive was troubled. Her French publicist shot the interviewer a look of alarm.

"Shall we get started?"

"Sure." Ten holographic cameras floated through the air and surrounded Olive like a ring of stars, building their composite impression.

"So these questions," the interviewer said, "they have a mystery focus!"

"Because we're at a mystery festival," Olive said.

"Exactly. Okay. Number one: what's your favorite alibi?"

"My favorite . . . alibi?"

"Yes."

"I don't really . . . I just say I have other plans. When I don't want to do something."

"I understand you're married to a man," the interviewer said. "When you met your husband, what was your first clue that you loved him?"

"Well," Olive said, "I guess just a sense of recognition, if that makes sense. I remember the first time I saw him, I looked at him and I knew he'd be important in my life. Is that a clue, though?"

"What's your idea of the perfect murder?"

"I remember reading a story once where a guy got stabbed with an icicle," Olive said. "I guess that's sort of perfect, a crime where the murder weapon melts. Do you mind if I ask, though, do you have any questions that have to do with my work?"

"I just have one more. Okay, last question. Sex with or without handcuffs?"

Olive unclipped the mic from her shirt as she stood. She placed the mic carefully on the chair. "No comment," she said, and left the room before the interviewer could see the tears in her eyes.

In Shanghai, Olive spent a combined total of three hours talking about herself and about her book, which meant talking about the end of the world while trying not to imagine the world ending with her daughter in it, and then returned to her hotel, where she noticed in the corridor that she was having difficulty walking in a straight line. She never drank, but drunkenness and fatigue look the same sometimes. Olive weaved down the hallway and stumbled into her room. She closed the door behind her and stood just inside for a long time, her forehead resting on the cool wall above the light switch. After a while, she heard her own voice, repeating *It's too much. It's too much. It's too much.*

"Olive," the room's AI system said softly, when some time had passed, "do you desire assistance?" When Olive didn't answer, it repeated the inquiry in Mandarin and Cantonese.

"Olive, this is totally random, but I was your agent's babysitter," a woman told her, in a signing line in Singapore the next day.

. . .

"What message would you like your readers to take away from *Marienbad*?" another interviewer asked.

Olive and the interviewer were onstage together in Tokyo. The interviewer was a hologram, because for unspecified personal reasons he'd been unable to leave Nairobi. Olive suspected the personal reason was illness: the interviewer kept freezing up, but the sound had no lag, which meant the interviewer wasn't freezing due to a bad connection, he was freezing because he kept pressing the Cough button on his console.

"I was just trying to write an interesting book," Olive said. "There's no message."

"Are you sure?" the interviewer asked.

"Will you sign a used book?" a woman asked, in a signing line.

"Of course, I'd be happy to."

"Also," the woman said, "is this your handwriting?"

Someone, not Olive, had already written in this woman's copy of *Marienbad: Harold: I enjoyed last night. xoxoxoxo Olive Llewellyn.*

Olive stared at the message and felt just a touch of vertigo. "No," she said, "I don't know who wrote that."

(She was distracted for days afterward by the thought of a shadow Olive moving over the landscape, on a kind of parallel tour, writing uncharacteristic messages in Olive's books.)

· · ·

In Cape Town, Olive met an author who'd been out on the road with his husband for a year and a half, touring in the service of a book that had sold several times as many copies as *Marienbad*.

"We're trying to see how long we can travel until we have to go home," the author said. His name was Ibby, short for Ibrahim, and his husband was Jack. The three of them were sitting together in the evening on the rooftop terrace of the hotel, which was filled with authors attending a literary festival.

"Are you trying to avoid going home?" Olive asked. "Or you just like traveling?"

"Both," Jack said. "I like being on the road."

"And our apartment's mediocre," Ibby said, "but we haven't decided what to do about it. Move? Redecorate? Could go either way."

There were dozens of trees up here, in enormous planters, with little lights sparkling in the branches. Music was playing somewhere, a string quartet. Olive was wearing her designated fancy tour dress, which was silver and went to her ankles. *This is one of the glamorous moments,* Olive thought, filing it carefully away so she could draw on it for sustenance later. The breeze carried a scent of jasmine.

"*I* heard some good news today," Jack said.

"Tell me," Ibby said. "I've been in a kind of book festival tunnel all day. Inadvertent news blackout."

"Construction just began on the first of the Far Colonies," Jack said.

Olive smiled, and almost spoke, but she was momentarily wordless. Planning for the Far Colonies had begun when her grandparents were children. She would always remember this moment, she thought, this party, these people whom she very much liked and might never see again. She'd be able to tell Sylvie where she was when she heard the news. When had she last experienced true awe? It had been a while. Olive was flooded with happiness. She raised her glass.

"To Alpha Centauri," she said.

In Buenos Aires, Olive met a woman who wanted to show her a tattoo. "I hope this isn't weird," she said, and rolled up her sleeve to reveal a quote from the book: We *knew it was coming,* in a beautiful curly script on her left shoulder.

Olive's breath caught in her throat. It wasn't just a line from *Marienbad,* it was a tattoo in *Marienbad.* In the second half of the novel, her character Gaspery-Jacques had the line tattooed on his left arm. You write a book with a fictional tattoo and then the tattoo becomes real in the world and after that almost anything seems possible. She'd seen five of those tattoos, but that didn't make it less extraordinary, seeing the way fiction can bleed into the world and leave a mark on someone's skin.

"That's incredible," Olive said softly. "It's incredible to see that tattoo in the real world."

"It's my favorite line from your book," she said. "It's just true of so much, isn't it?"

. . .

But doesn't everything seem obvious in retrospect? Blue dusk over the prairies, gliding toward the Dakota Republic in a low-altitude airship. Olive stared out the window and tried to find some peace in the landscape. She had a new invitation for a festival on Titan. She hadn't been since she was a kid and retained only vague memories of crowds at the Dolphinarium and some oddly tasteless popcorn, the warm yellowish haze of the daytime sky—she'd been in a so-called Realist colony, one of the outposts whose settlers had decided on clear domes in order to experience the true colors of the Titanian atmosphere—and strange fashions, this thing all the teenagers were doing that involved painting their faces like pixels, big squares of color that were supposed to defeat the facial-recognition software but that had the side effect of making them look like deranged clowns. Should she go to Titan? *I want to go home.* Where was Sylvie at this moment? *This is easier than having a day job, though, just remember that.*

"I remember reading somewhere," an interviewer said, "that the title of your first book actually came from your last day job?"

"Yes," Olive said, "I came across it at work one day."

"Your first novel was, of course, *Swimming Stars with Gold-flitter.* Will you tell me about that title?"

"Sure, yes. I was working in AI training. So, you know, correcting awkward renderings from the translator bots. I remember sitting there by the hour in this cramped little office—"

"This was in Colony Two?"

"Yes, Colony Two. My job was to sit there all day, rewording unfortunate sentences. But there was one that stopped me cold, because it may have been awkward and error-ridden, but I loved it." Olive had told this story so often that it was like reciting lines from a play. "It was a description of votive candles with little poems on the candleholders. The description had somehow been rendered as *seven motives for verse,* and then one of the candle descriptions was *swimming stars with goldflitter.* The beauty of those phrases, I don't know, it just stopped me cold."

Stopped me cold. Two days later she was on a panel with another writer at a festival in the city-state of Los Angeles, and the implication of that phrase had just occurred to her. What stops you, and turns you cold? Death, obviously. Olive couldn't believe she'd never thought of this. Los Angeles was under a dome, but still the light through the windows was blinding. This meant she couldn't see the audience, which was frankly ideal. All those faces staring at her. No, at them: the other writer's name was Jessica Marley and Olive was glad Jessica was here with her, even though she didn't actually like her very much. Everything offended Jessica, which is inevitable when you move through the world in search of offense.

"Well, some of us don't have doctorates in literature, Jim," Jessica said to the interviewer, in response to some imperceptible provocation. The look on his face mirrored Olive's thought at that moment: *Well, that escalated quickly.* But a man in the audience was standing up with a question about *Marienbad.* Almost all of the questions were about *Marienbad,* which was awkward because Jessica was there too, Jessica with her book about coming of age in the moon colonies. Olive was pretending that she hadn't read *Moon/Rise,* because she'd hated it. Olive had lived the real thing, and it wasn't nearly as poetic as Jessica's book suggested. Growing up in a moon colony was fine. It was neither great nor dystopian. It was a little house in a pleasant neighborhood of tree-lined streets, a good but not extraordinary public school, life lived at a consistent 15° to 22° Celsius under carefully calibrated dome lighting, scheduled rainfalls. She didn't grow up *longing for Earth* or experience her life as *a continual displacement,* thank you.

"I wanted to ask Olive about the death of the prophet in *Marienbad,*" the man in the audience said. Jessica sighed and slumped a little in her chair. "It could have been a much bigger moment, but you decided to make it a relatively small, not-climactic event."

"Really? I thought of it as climactic," Olive said, as mildly as possible.

He smiled, humoring her. "But you chose to make it really small, almost inconsequential, when it could have been cinematic, something really big. Why is that?"

Jessica sat up straight, excited by the possibility of combat.

"Well," Olive said. "I suppose everyone has a different idea of what constitutes a big moment."

"You're a master of deflection," Jessica murmured, without looking at her. "You're like some kind of deflection ninja."

"Thank you," Olive said, although she knew it wasn't a compliment.

"Let's move on to the next question," the interviewer said.

"You know the phrase I keep thinking about?" a poet asked, on a different panel, at a festival in Copenhagen. "'The chickens are coming home to roost.' Because it's never good chickens. It's never 'You've been a good person and now your chickens are coming home to roost.' It's never good chickens. It's always bad chickens."

Scattered laughter and applause. A man in the audience was having a coughing fit. He left quickly, bent over in an apologetic way. Olive wrote *no good chickens* in the margin of her festival program.

Was the death of the prophet in *Marienbad* too anticlimactic? It seemed possible. Olive was sitting alone at a hotel bar near the Copenhagen festival, drinking tea and eating a wilted salad with too much cheese on it. On the one hand the prophet's death *was* dramatic, after all he'd been shot in the head, but maybe there should've been some kind of battle scene, maybe the death really was too casual, in the way he went from perfect health to death over the course of a paragraph and the story kept moving without him—

"May I get you anything else?" the bartender asked.

"Just the check, please," Olive said.

—but on the other hand, isn't that reality? Won't most of

us die in fairly unclimactic ways, our passing unremarked by almost everyone, our deaths becoming plot points in the narratives of the people around us? But obviously *Marienbad* was fiction, i.e., reality wasn't relevant to the question at hand, and maybe the death of the prophet really was a flaw. Now Olive was holding the pen over the check, but there was a difficulty: she'd forgotten her room number. She had to go to the front desk to retrieve it.

"It happens more often than you'd think," the clerk at the front desk said.

At the airship terminal the next morning, she sat next to a business traveler who wanted to tell her about his job, which had something to do with detecting counterfeit steel. Olive listened for a long time, because the monologue distracted her from how much she missed Sylvie. "And what do you do?" the other traveler asked finally.

"I write books," Olive said.

"For children?" he asked.

When Olive circled back to the Atlantic Republic, seeing her AR publicist again was like seeing an old friend. Aretta and Olive sat together at a dinner for booksellers in Jersey City.

"How's it been since I saw you last?" Aretta asked.

"Fine," Olive said, "it's all going fine. I have no complaints." And then, because she was tired and she knew Aretta a little by now, she broke her own rule about never revealing anything personal, and said, "It's just a lot of people."

Aretta smiled. "Publicists aren't supposed to be shy," she said, "but I get a little overwhelmed at these dinners sometimes."

"Me too," Olive said. "My face gets tired."

That night's hotel room was white and blue. The thing with being away from her husband and daughter was that every hotel room was emptier than the one before.

The last interview of the tour was the following afternoon in Philadelphia, where Olive met a man in a dark suit who was her age or a little younger, in a beautiful meeting room at a hotel. The room was on a high floor with a wall of glass, and the city rolled away beneath them.

"Here we are," said Aretta brightly. "Olive, this is Gaspery Roberts, *Contingencies Magazine*. I have to make a couple of quick calls, so I'll leave you two." She receded. Olive and the interviewer sat in matching green velvet chairs.

"Thank you for meeting with me," the man said.

"My pleasure. Do you mind if I ask about your name? I'm not sure I've ever met a Gaspery."

"I'll tell you something even stranger," he said. "My first name is actually Gaspery-Jacques."

"Seriously? I thought I'd made up the name for that character in *Marienbad*."

He smiled. "My mother was astonished when she came across the name in your book. She thought she'd made it up too."

"Perhaps I came across your name somewhere and didn't consciously remember it."

"Anything's possible. It's hard to know what we know sometimes, isn't it?" He had a gentle way of speaking that Olive liked, and a faint accent that she couldn't quite place. "Have you been in interviews all day?"

"Half the day. You're my fifth."

"Ouch. I'll keep this brief, then. I'd like to ask you about a specific scene in *Marienbad,* if I may."

"Okay. Sure."

"The scene in the spaceport," he said. "Where your character Willis hears the violin and he's . . . transported."

"It's an odd passage," Olive said. "I get a lot of questions about it."

"I'd like to ask you something." Gaspery hesitated. "This might seem a bit—I don't mean to pry. But is there an element of—I'm wondering if that bit of the book was inspired by a personal experience."

"I've never been interested in auto-fiction," Olive said, but it was difficult to meet his eyes now. She'd always found something steadying in looking at her own clasped hands, but she didn't know if it was the hands or the shirt, the impeccable white cuffs. Clothes are armor.

"Listen," Gaspery said, "I don't mean to make you uncomfortable or put you on the spot. But I'm curious if you experienced something strange in the Oklahoma City Airship Terminal."

In the quiet, Olive could hear the soft hum of the building, the sounds of ventilation and plumbing. Perhaps she wouldn't have admitted it if he hadn't caught her toward the end of the tour, if she hadn't been so tired.

"I don't mind talking about this," she said, "but I'm afraid I'll seem too eccentric if it makes it into the final version of the interview. Could we go off the record for a moment?"

"Yes," he said.

4

Bad Chickens /

2401

1

No star burns forever. You can say "It's the end of the world" and mean it, but what gets lost in that kind of careless usage is that the world will eventually literally end. Not "civilization," whatever that is, but the actual planet.

Which is not to say that those smaller endings aren't annihilating. A year before I began my training at the Time Institute, I went to a dinner party at my friend Ephrem's place. He was just back from a vacation on Earth, and he had a story about going on a walk in a cemetery with his daughter, Meiying, who was four at the time. Ephrem was an arborist. He liked to go to old cemeteries to look at the trees. But then they found the grave of another four-year-old girl, Ephrem told me, and he just wanted to leave after that. He was used to graveyards, he sought them out, he'd always said he didn't find them depressing, just peaceful, but that one grave just got to him. He looked at it and was unbearably sad. Also it was the worst kind of Earth summer day, impossibly humid, and he felt like he couldn't get enough air. The drone of the cicadas was oppressive. Sweat ran down his back. He told his daughter it was time to go, but she lingered by the gravestone for a moment.

"If her parents loved her," Meiying said, "it would have felt like the end of the world."

It was such an eerily astute observation, Ephrem told me, that he stood there staring at her and found himself thinking, *Where did you come from?* They got out of the cemetery with difficulty—"She had to stop and inspect every goddamn flower and pinecone," he said—and never went back.

Those are the worlds that end in our day-to-day lives, these stopped children, these annihilating losses, but at the end of Earth there will be actual, literal annihilation, hence the colonies. The first colony on the moon was intended as a prototype, a practice run for establishing a presence in other solar systems in the coming centuries. "Because we'll have to," the president of China said, at the press conference where construction on the first colony was announced, "eventually, whether we want to or not, unless we want all of human history and achievement to get sucked into a supernova a few million years down the line."

I watched footage of that press conference in my sister Zoey's office, three hundred years after the fact. The president behind the lectern with her officials arrayed around her, a crowd of reporters below the stage. One of them raised his hand: "Are we sure it's going to be a supernova?"

"Of course not," the president said. "It could be anything. Rogue planet, asteroid storm, you name it. The point is that we're orbiting a star, and all stars eventually die."

"But if the star dies," I said to Zoey, "obviously the Earth's moon goes with it."

"Sure," she said, "but we're just the prototype, Gaspery. We're just proof of concept. The Far Colonies have been populated for a hundred and eighty years."

2

The first moon colony was built on the silent flatlands of the Sea of Tranquility, near where the Apollo 11 astronauts had landed in a long-ago century. Their flag was still there, in the distance, a fragile little statue on the windless surface.

There was substantial interest in immigration to the colony. Earth was so crowded by then, and such swaths of it had been rendered uninhabitable by flooding or heat. The colony's architects had set aside space for substantial residential development, which sold out quickly. The developers lobbied successfully for a second colony when they ran out of space in Colony One. But Colony Two was built a little too hastily, and within a century the lighting system on the main dome had failed. The lighting system was meant to mimic the appearance of the sky as viewed from Earth—it was nice to look up and see blue, as opposed to looking up into the void—and when it failed there was no more false atmosphere, no more shifting pixelations to give the impression of clouds, no more carefully calibrated preprogrammed sunrises and sunsets, no more blue. Which is not to suggest that there wasn't light, but that light was extremely un-Earthlike: on a bright day, the colonists looked up into space. The juxtaposition of utter darkness with bright light made some people dizzy, although whether this was physical or psychological was up for debate. More seriously, the failure of the dome lighting removed the illusion of the twenty-four-hour day. Now the sun rose rapidly and spent two weeks crossing the sky, after which there were two straight weeks of night.

The cost of repair was deemed prohibitive. There was a degree of adaptation—bedroom windows were outfitted with shutters, so people could sleep during the nights when the sun was out, and street lighting was improved for the days without sunlight—but property values declined, and most people who could afford it moved to Colony One or the recently completed Colony Three. "Colony Two" drifted out of common parlance; everyone called it the Night City. It was the place where the sky was always black.

I grew up in the Night City. My walk to school took me past the childhood home of Olive Llewellyn, an author who'd walked those same streets two hundred years ago, not too far out from the moon's first settlers. It was a little house on a tree-lined street, and I could tell that it had been pretty once, but the neighborhood had gone downhill since Olive Llewellyn had been a child there. The house was a wreck now, half the windows covered up and graffiti everywhere, but the plaque by the front door remained. I paid the house no attention, until my mother told me she'd named me after a peripheral character in *Marienbad*, Llewellyn's most famous book. I didn't read the book—I didn't like books—but my sister Zoey did and reported back: the Gaspery-Jacques in the book wasn't anything like me.

I decided not to ask her what she meant. I was eleven when she read it, which would have made her thirteen or fourteen. By then she was already a serious, driven kind of person who was obviously going to excel at everything she attempted, whereas by eleven I already had the first suspicions that I might not be exactly the kind of person I wanted to be, and it would be awful if she were to tell me that the other Gaspery-Jacques were, say, a strikingly handsome and generally impressive person who was extremely focused on his schoolwork and never committed petty theft. But nonetheless I began to secretly regard Olive Llewellyn's childhood home with a degree of respect. I felt connected to it.

There was a family living there, a boy and a girl and their parents, pale, miserable-looking people who possessed this weird talent for conveying an impression that they were up to no good. They had an air of having gone to seed, the whole family. Their last name was Anderson. The parents spent a lot of time on the porch, arguing quietly or staring into space. The boy was surly and got into fights at school. The girl, who was about my age, liked to play with a hologram in the front yard, an old-fashioned mirror hologram who danced with her sometimes, and that was actually the only time I saw the Anderson girl smile anywhere near her house, when she was spinning and leaping and her holographic double was spinning and leaping too.

When I was twelve, the Anderson girl was in the same class as me, and I learned her name was Talia. Who was Talia Anderson? She loved to draw. She did backflips on the field. She looked much happier at school than she did at home.

"I know you," she said abruptly one day, when we were in the cafeteria line together. "You're always walking by my house."

"It's on my way," I said.

"On your way to what?"

"Well, on my way to everywhere. I live at the end of the cul-de-sac."

"I know," she said.

"How do you know where I live?"

"I walk by your house too," she said. "I cut through your neighbor's lawn to get to the Periphery."

At the end of our lawn there was a screen of leaves. Push through them and you'd get to the Periphery Road, which circled the interior of the Night City dome. Cross the road and there was a strange, wild area, no more than fifty feet deep, a strip of wilderness between the road and the dome. Scrub brush, dust, stray plants, garbage. It was a forgotten kind of place. Our mother didn't like us playing there, so Zoey never ventured across the Periphery Road—she always did as she was told, which I found maddening—but I liked the wildness of it, the mild sense of danger inherent in a forgotten kingdom. That day after school

I crossed the empty road for the first time in a few weeks, and stood for a while with my hands pressed to the dome, looking out. The composite glass was so thick that everything on the other side looked like a dream, distant in a muffled kind of way, but I saw craters here and there, meteors, gray. The opaque dome of Colony One glowed in the near distance. I found myself wondering what Talia Anderson's thoughts were when she gazed out at the moonscape.

Talia Anderson transferred out of my class and left the neighborhood halfway through the year. I didn't see her again until my mid-thirties, when we were both employed by the Grand Luna Hotel in Colony One.

I started work at the hotel about a month after my mother died. She'd been sick for a long time, years, and at the end Zoey and I all but lived at the hospital. That last week we were there every day and every night, exhausted comrades keeping watch, while our mother murmured and slept. Death was imminent and remained imminent, for much longer than the doctors predicted. Our mother had worked at the post office since we were very young, but in her last hours she thought she was doing post-doctoral work in a physics lab again, murmuring in a confused way about equations and the simulation hypothesis.

"Do you understand what she's talking about?" I asked Zoey at one point.

"Most of it," Zoey said. In those hours Zoey sat by the bed

with her eyes closed, listening to our mother's words as if listening to music.

"Can you explain it to me?" It was like being on the outside of a secret club, nose pressed to the glass.

"The simulation hypothesis? Yeah." She didn't open her eyes. "Think of how holograms and virtual reality have evolved, even just in the past few years. If we can run fairly convincing simulations of reality now, think of what those simulations will be like in a century or two. The idea with the simulation hypothesis is, we can't rule out the possibility that all of reality is a simulation."

I'd been awake for two days and felt like I was dreaming. "Okay, but if we're living in a computer," I said, "whose computer is it?"

"Who knows? Humans, a few hundred years into the future? An alien intelligence? It's not a mainstream theory, but it comes up every so often at the Time Institute." She opened her eyes. "Oh god, pretend I didn't say that. I'm tired. I shouldn't have."

"Pretend you didn't say what?"

"The Time Institute part."

"Okay," I said, and her eyes closed again. I closed my eyes too. Our mother had stopped murmuring, and now there were just her ragged breaths, with too much time between each one.

When at last the end came, Zoey and I were sleeping. She woke me in the exhausted gray light of early morning, and we sat together for a long time in silence, in reverence, before the stilled figure of our mother on the bed. We dealt with the formalities, hugged goodbye, went our separate ways. I returned home to my cramped apartment, and several days passed where I spoke only with my cat. There was the funeral, then more stillness. I needed a new job—I'd been without one for some time, and was burning through my savings—and so a month after the funeral I found myself in the basement office of a hotel Human Resources officer, a vaguely familiar-looking woman with blond hair, accepting a position that had been advertised as "hotel detective" but whose exact parameters were unclear.

"To be absolutely honest," I told her, "I'm not entirely clear on what a hotel detective position might entail."

"It's just hotel security," she said. I realized I'd forgotten her name. Natalie? Natasha? "The job title wasn't my idea. You won't actually be a detective. Just a security presence, as it were."

"I want to be sure I'm not misrepresenting myself," I said. "I left school a few months shy of my criminal justice degree."

"Can we be honest here, Gaspery?" There was definitely something familiar about her.

"Please."

"Your entire job is to pay attention to what goes on around you and call the police if you see anything suspicious."

"I can do that."

"You sound doubtful," she said.

"I'm not doubtful for myself. I mean, I don't doubt I could do it. It's just, I'm—couldn't anyone do this job?"

"You'd be surprised. It's the attention part that's hard to hire for," she said. "Distraction is a problem, generally speaking. You remember that test you had to take on your first interview?"

"Sure."

"That was to measure attentiveness. Your score was high. Tell me, do you agree with your test results? Can you pay attention?"

"Yes," I said. I was pleased as I said this, because I'd never really thought of myself in this way before, but it seemed to me that I'd been paying close attention my entire life. I hadn't been successful at very many things, but I'd always been good at watching. That was how I knew my ex-wife had fallen in love with someone else, just by being attentive. There were no obvious clues, just a subtle shift in— but the HR person was talking again, so I reeled myself in from the past.

"Wait," I said. "I know you."

"From before this meeting, you mean?"

"Talia," I said.

Something changed in her face. A mask dropped. Her voice was different when she spoke again, less amused by the world. "I go by Natalia now, but yes." She was quiet for a moment, looking at me. "We went to school together, didn't we?"

"End of the cul-de-sac," I said, and for the first time in the interview, she gave me a genuine smile.

"I used to stand at the Periphery for hours," she said, "looking out through the glass."

"You ever go back there? To the Night City?"

"Never," she said.

3

Never to the Night City. The phrase had a rhythm that pleased me, so it lodged itself in my head. I thought of it often in my first weeks on the job, because the job was terminally boring. The hotel had retro pretensions, so I wore a suit cut in an antique style and a peculiarly shaped hat called a fedora. I walked the halls and stood watch in the lobby. I paid attention to everyone and everything, as instructed. I've always enjoyed watching other people, but people in hotels turned out to be surprisingly boring. They checked in and checked out. They appeared in the lobby at odd hours, asking for coffee. They were drunk, or they weren't. They were businesspeople, or they were with their families on vacation. They were tired and frazzled from their journeys. People tried to sneak in dogs. In the first six months I had to summon the police only once, when I heard a woman scream in a hotel room, and even then I wasn't the one who did the calling;

I called the night manager, who called the police for me. I wasn't there when the woman was carried out by paramedics.

The job was quiet. My mind wandered. *Never to the Night City*. What had Talia's life been like there? Not great, obviously, any idiot could see that. Some families are better than others. When her family moved out of the Olive Llewellyn house, some other family moved in, but I found I couldn't remember this other family beyond a general impression of dereliction. At the hotel I saw Talia only occasionally, passing through the lobby on her way home from work.

In those days I lived in a bland little apartment in a block of other bland little apartments on the far edge of Colony One, close enough to the Periphery that the dome barely cleared the roof of the apartment complex. Sometimes on dark nights I liked to cross the street to the Periphery, to look through the composite glass at Colony Two glittering in the distance. My life in those days was as bland and limited as my apartment. I tried not to think about my mother too much. I slept through the days. My cat always woke me in the late afternoons. Around sunset I ate a meal that could reasonably be called either dinner or breakfast, put on my uniform, and went to the hotel to stare at people for seven hours.

I'd been at the hotel for about six months when my sister turned thirty-seven. Zoey was a physicist at the university, and her area of expertise had something to do with quantum blockchain technology, which I was never able to understand although she'd made several good-faith efforts to explain it to me. I called to wish her a happy birthday, and realized in the beat before she picked up that I hadn't congratulated her on receiving tenure. Which was when, a month ago? I felt a familiar variety of guilt.

"Happy Birthday," I said. "And also congratulations."

"Thank you, Gaspery." She never dwelt on my lapses, and I couldn't entirely parse why this made me feel so awful. There's a low-level, specific pain in having to accept that putting up with you requires a certain generosity of spirit in your loved ones.

"What's it like?"

"Being thirty-seven?" She sounded tired.

"No, being tenured. Does it feel different?"

"It feels like stability," she said.

"So what are your birthday plans?"

She was quiet for a moment. "Gaspery," she said, "is there any way you could come to my office this evening?"

"Of course," I said. "Of course."

When had she ever asked me to her office? Just once, years ago, when she first started there. The university wasn't that far away from my apartment, but also it was fundamentally a different universe. When had I even seen her last? It had been a few months, I realized.

I called in sick to work and then lay on the sofa for a while to bask in my sudden freedom. Marvin, my cat, climbed heavily onto my chest, where he stretched out his legs and fell asleep purring. The night extended before me, all those magnificently empty hours shining with possibility. I dislodged Marvin, show-ered and put on nice clothes, stopped by a bakery for four cupcakes—red velvet, which I hoped was still Zoey's favorite—and by seven p.m. the sun was setting in a wash of oranges and pinks on the far side of the dome. I'd lived for a year in Colony One and the dome lighting still looked like theater to me. Were cupcakes enough? Should I buy flowers? I bought a bouquet of something unflashy and yellow, and was at the Time Institute gate by seven thirty. I took off my dark glasses for the iris scan and was still holding the glasses awkwardly in my hand six iris scans later, when I found Zoey pacing in her office. She didn't look like a woman celebrating a birthday. She took my flowers with a distracted air, and I could tell from the way she set them on her desk that she'd forgotten about them by the time they left her hand. I wondered if someone had just broken up with her, but Zoey's romantic life had always been a forbidden topic.

"Oh, thank god," she said, when I held out a cupcake. "I completely forgot dinner."

"You seem agitated."

"Can I show you something?"

"Sure."

She touched a discreet console on her office wall, and a projection filled half the room. There was a man on a stage, surrounded by bulky antique machines of some kind, inscrutable instruments. Above his head was an old-fashioned screen, a rectangle of white floating there in the dim light. It seemed to me that the scene we were looking at was quite old.

"A friend sent this to me," Zoey said. "She works in the art history department."

"Who is he? The guy in the projection."

"Paul James Smith. Twenty-first-century composer and video artist."

She pressed play, and the room filled with three-hundred-year-old music in a vague, shifting genre. Ambient, I supposed. I didn't know much about music, but found this guy's composition faintly annoying.

"Okay," she said, "now pay attention to the white screen above him."

"What am I looking for? It's blank."

"Watch."

The screen came to life. The video had been shot in a forest on Earth. The quality was a little jerky; the videographer had been walking on a forest path, toward an enormous leafy tree, some Earth species that didn't grow in the colonies. The music stopped, and the man looked up at the screen above him. The screen went dark. There was a strange cacophony of noise— notes of a violin, the indistinct murmur of a crowd, the hydraulic *whoosh* of an airship taking off—and then it was over, the forest was back, and for a moment the image was dizzying, as if the videographer had forgotten that they were holding a camera. The forest faded out, but the music continued.

"Listen carefully," Zoey said. "Listen to the way the music's changed. You hear how the violin notes from the video are there in Smith's music? That same motif, that five-note pattern?"

I couldn't hear it, and then I could. "Yes. Why is that important?"

"Because it means that . . . that weirdness, that glitch, whatever it was, it was part of the performance. It's not a technical problem." She stopped the recording. She looked troubled in a way I didn't understand. "It goes on," she said, "but the rest of the performance is uninteresting."

"You brought me here to show me that," I said, just checking.

"I need to talk this through with someone I trust." She picked up her device, and I heard my own device chime with an incoming document.

She'd sent me a book: *Marienbad,* by Olive Llewellyn.

"Mom's favorite novel," I said. I was thinking of our mother, reading on the porch at twilight.

"Have you read it, Gaspery?"

"I've never been much of a reader."

"Just jump to the highlighted passage and tell me if you notice anything."

It was disorienting, leaping into the middle of a book I'd never read. I started a few paragraphs before the passage she'd highlighted:

We knew it was coming.

We knew it was coming and we prepared accordingly, or at least that's what we told our children—and ourselves—in the decades that followed.

We knew it was coming but we didn't quite believe it, so we prepared in low-key, unobtrusive ways—"Why do we have a whole shelf of canned fish?" Willis asked his husband, who said something vague about emergency preparedness—

—Because of that ancient horror, too embarrassingly irrational to be articulated aloud: if you say the name of the thing you fear, might you attract that thing's attention? This is difficult to admit, but in those early weeks we were vague about our fears because saying the word *pandemic* might bend the pandemic toward us.

We knew it was coming and we were breezy about it. We deflected the fear with careless bravado. On the day reports broke of a cluster in Vancouver, which was three days after the British prime minister announced that the initial outbreak in London was fully contained, Willis and Dov went to work as usual, their sons Isaac and Sam went to school, and then they all met up for dinner at their favorite restaurant, which was crowded that night. (Bit of a horror movie in retrospect: imagine clouds of invisible pathogens drifting through the air, floating from table to table, swirling in the wake of passing servers.) "If it's in Vancouver it's obviously here," Dov said to Willis, who said, "I'd bet money on it," and refilled Dov's water glass.

"If what's in Vancouver?" Isaac asked. He was nine.

"Nothing," they said in unison, and felt no guilt at all because it didn't feel like a lie. Pandemics don't approach like wars, with the distant thud of artillery growing louder every day and flashes of bombs on the horizon. They arrive in *retrospect*, essentially. It's disorienting. The pandemic is far away and then it's all around you, with seemingly no intermediate step.

Dov, practicing his lines in front of the bedroom mirror after the community theater closed: "Is this the promised end?"

We knew it was coming but we behaved inconsistently. We stocked up on supplies—just in case—but sent our children to school, because how do you get any work done with the kids at home?

(We were still thinking in terms of getting work done. The most shocking thing in retrospect was the degree to which all of us completely missed the point.)

"God," Willis said, a few days before the schools closed, but after the news headlines had started, "this all seems so retro."

"I know," Dov said. They were both in their forties, which is to say they were old enough to remember Ebola X, but those sixty-four weeks of lockdown had faded to the hazy province of childhood memory, a span of time that was neither awful nor pleasant, months populated by cartoons and imaginary friends. You couldn't call it a lost year, because it did have nice moments. Their parents were competent enough at parenting to shield them from the horror, which meant it was lonely but not unbearable. There was a lot of ice cream and extra screen time. They'd been glad when it was over, but after a few years had passed they didn't think of it much.

"What does *retro* mean?" Sam asked.

As Willis glanced at his younger son, he did have the thought—he clung to this later—that perhaps school wasn't such a great idea. Nonetheless, the old world hadn't slipped away just yet, so in the morning he packed Sam's and Isaac's lunches and dropped them off at the academy, stepped back out into the bright sunlight and caught a transporter to the airship terminal. Just an ordinary morning under a harmless blue sky.

In the terminal he stopped to listen to a musician, a violinist playing for spare change in one of the cavernous entry corridors. The violinist was an old man who played with his eyes closed, coins accumulating in a hat by his feet. He played an ancient-looking violin—it looked like it was made of real wood—and Willis was by no means an expert in acoustics, but it seemed to him that there was a kind of warmth in the sound. Willis was listening to the music, to the way it rose up over the susurration of the morning commuter crowd, but then—

—a flash of darkness, weird sudden light—

—a fleeting hallucination of forest, fresh air, trees rising around him, a summer's day—

—and then he was back in the Oklahoma City Airship Terminal, in the cool white of the west entry corridor, blinking and disoriented. *Something just came over me,* he found himself thinking, but this was inadequate as an explanation, because *what* had just come over him? That flash of darkness, then the forest rising around him, what was that?

It hit him all at once: an afterlife.

The darkness was death, he told himself. The forest was the after.

Willis didn't believe in an actual afterlife, but he did believe in the subconscious, he believed in knowing without consciously knowing, and almost without thought he was walking away in the wrong direction, away from his commute. He didn't know where he was going until he found himself on the doorstep of his sons' school.

"But why are you pulling your boys out of school?" the principal asked. "I've been following the news closely, Willis, and there's just that tiny cluster of cases in Vancouver."

I closed the file and put my device in my pocket, unsettled in a way I couldn't explain.

"Do you see it?" Zoey asked. "The way the video mirrors the passage in the book?"

I did see it. A person in a forest in the twenty-first century sees a flash of darkness and hears noises from an airship terminal two centuries later. A person in an airship terminal in the twenty-third century sees a flash of darkness and is struck by the overwhelming sensation that he's standing in a forest.

"She could have seen the video," I suggested. "Olive Llewellyn, I mean. She could've seen it and worked it into her fiction." I was pleased with myself for this suggestion.

"I thought of that," Zoey said. *Of course you did,* I didn't say aloud. That was a major difference between us: Zoey always thought of everything. "There's something else, though. My team's spent the last month researching the region where the composer grew up, and this afternoon we found a letter." She was scrolling through files on her projection, but it was set to privacy mode, so it appeared from my angle that she was moving her hand through clouds. "Here," she said.

A projection snapped into place in the air between us. It was a handwritten document in a foreign alphabet.

"What is this?"

"I think it might be supporting evidence. It's a letter," she said. "From 1912."

"What alphabet's this?" I asked.

"Seriously?"

"What, should I be able to read it?" I peered closer, and recognized a word. No, two. It was almost English, but warped and slanted; there was a certain beauty to it, but the letters were misformed. Some kind of proto-English?

"Gaspery, that's cursive," she said.

"I don't know what that is."

"Right," she said, with that maddening patience I'd come to expect from her. "Let me switch to audio."

She toggled something in the clouds, and a man's voice filled the room.

Bert,

Thank you for your kind letter of 25th April, which made its way across the Atlantic and across Canada at a snail's pace and arrived in my hands only this evening.

How am I, you ask? The honest answer, brother, is that I'm unsure. This comes to you from a candlelit room in Victoria— you'll forgive, I hope, the dash of melodrama, but I feel that I've earned it—where I've taken up lodging in a pleasant boarding- house. I have given up all thought of establishing myself in busi- ness and wish only to return home, but this is a comfortable exile and my remittance provides for my day-to-day necessities.

I've had a very strange time here. No, that's not quite it. I've had a somewhat dull time here—my fault, not Canada's—except for a strange interlude in the wilderness, which I shall attempt to recount. I had travelled north from Victoria with Niall's old friend from school, Thomas Maillot, whose surname I'm possibly mis- spelling. For two or three days we moved north up the coast on a tidy little steamboat, weighed down with provisions, until at last we arrived at Caiette, a village consisting of a church, a pier, a one- room schoolhouse, and a handful of houses. Thomas continued on to a logging camp, a short distance up the coast. I elected to remain for the moment in the boardinghouse in Caiette, for the sake of enjoying the beauty of that place.

One morning in early September, I ventured into the forest, for reasons too tedious to relate, and a few paces in, I came upon a maple tree. I stopped there a moment, to catch my breath, and then there occurred an incident that struck me at the time as some kind of supernatural event, but seems to me in retrospect to have been perhaps some kind of fit.

I was standing there in the forest in the sunlight, and then all at once there was darkness, as abruptly as a candle snuffed out in a room, and in the darkness I heard the notes of a violin, an inscrutable noise, and with this a strange impression of being somehow fleetingly indoors, in some echoing cavernous space like a train station. Then it was over and I stood in the forest. It was as though nothing had happened. I staggered back out to the beach and was violently sick on the rocks. The following morning, concerned for my well-being and determined to quit that place and return to some semblance of civilization, I began the return journey to the little city of Victoria, where I remain.

I have a perfectly adequate room at a boardinghouse by the harbour, and amuse myself with walks, books, chess, and the occasional bit of watercolour painting. As you know, I've always adored gardens, and there's a public garden here in which I've found great solace. Not to trouble anyone, but I did consult a doctor, who is confident in his diagnosis of migraine. Seems a peculiar sort of

migraine that doesn't involve any pain in one's head, but I suppose
I'll accept it in lieu of an alternate explanation. I cannot forget it,
however, and the memory unsettles me.

I hope you are well, Bert. Please convey my affection and respect
to Mother and Father as well.

Yours,

Edwin

The audio stopped. Zoey swiped the projection into the wall
and came to sit with me. There was a heaviness about her that
I'd never seen before.

"Zoey," I said, "you seem more upset than . . . I'm not sure I
completely understand."

"Which operating system do you use on your device?"

"Zephyr," I said.

"Same. You remember that weird Zephyr bug a couple years
ago, this only lasted a day or two, but sometimes you'd open
a text file on your device and you'd hear whatever music you'd
been listening to last?"

"Sure. That was annoying." I only vaguely remembered it.

"It was file corruption."

I sensed something vast and terrible, swimming just outside
of my grasp.

"You're saying . . ."

Zoey's elbows were on the table, and as she spoke, she rested
her forehead in her hands.

"If moments from different centuries are bleeding into one another, then, well, one way you could think of those moments, Gaspery, is you could think of them as corrupted files."

"How is a moment the same as a file?"

She was very still. "Just imagine that they are."

I tried. A series of corrupted files; a series of corrupted moments; a series of discrete things bleeding into one another when they shouldn't.

"But if moments are files . . ." I couldn't finish the sentence. The room we were in seemed much less real than it had only a moment ago. *The desk is real,* I told myself. *The wilted flowers on the desk are real. The blue paint on the walls. Zoey's hair. My hands. The carpet.*

"You see why I didn't go out to celebrate my birthday," she said.

"It's just . . . Look, I agree that it's weird, but we're talking about Mom's thing, aren't we? The simulation thing?"

She sighed. "Believe me, the thought's occurred to me. It's very possible that my thinking is clouded. You know she's the reason I became a scientist."

I nodded.

"And look," she continued, "I know it's all circumstantial, I'm not crazy. It's just a series of descriptions of some kind of bizarre experience. But the *coincidence,* Gaspery, the way these moments seem to bleed into one another, I can't help but see it as some kind of evidence."

4

If we were living in a simulation, how would we know it was a simulation? I took the trolley home from the university at three in the morning. In the warm light of the moving car, I closed my eyes and marveled at the detail. The gentle vibration of the trolley on its cushion of air. The sounds—the barely perceptible whisper of movement, the soft conversations here and there in the car, the tinny notes of a game escaping from a device somewhere. *We are living in a simulation,* I told myself, testing the idea, but it still seemed improbable to me, because I could smell the bouquet of yellow roses that the woman sitting beside me held carefully in both hands. *We are living in a simulation,* but I'm hungry and am I supposed to believe that that's a simulation too?

"I'm not saying these things add up to any kind of definite proof that we're living in a simulation," Zoey had said, an hour ago in her office. "I'm saying I think there's enough here to justify an investigation."

How do you investigate reality? My hunger is a simulation, I told myself, but I wanted a cheeseburger. Cheeseburgers are a simulation. Beef is a simulation. (Actually, that was literally true. Killing an animal for food would get you arrested both on Earth and in the colonies.) I opened my eyes and thought, *The roses are a simulation. The scent of roses is a simulation.*

"What would an investigation look like?" I'd asked her.

"I think you'd want to visit all those points in time," Zoey said. "You'd want to speak with the letter writer in 1912, the video artist in 2019 or 2020, and the novelist in 2203."

I remembered the news stories when time travel was invented and then immediately made illegal outside of government facilities. I remembered a chapter from a criminology textbook dedicated to the near-annihilating nightmare of the so-called Rose Loop, when history had changed twenty-seven times before the rogue traveler was taken out of commission and his damage undone. I knew that one hundred forty-one of the two hundred and five people serving life sentences on the moon were there because they'd attempted time travel. It didn't matter if they'd been successful or not; the attempt was enough to send you away for life.

"Gaspery," Zoey had said, "I'm not sure why you look so shocked. What does the sign on the building say?"

"Time Institute," I admitted.

She looked at me.

"I thought you were a physicist," I said.

"Well . . . yes," she said. There was a knowledge-and-achievement gap the size of the solar system in that pause between words. I heard that old kindness, that familiar sense that she was extending generosity toward me. We can't all be geniuses, I wanted to tell her, but we'd had that conversation when we were teenagers and it had gone poorly, so I didn't.

We are living in a simulation, I told myself, as the trolley stopped a block from my apartment, but this fell so far short of, well, of the *reality,* for lack of a better word. I couldn't convince myself. I didn't believe it. There was a scheduled rainfall in— I glanced at my watch—two minutes. I stepped out of the trolley and walked very slowly, on purpose. I've always loved rain, and knowing that it isn't coming from clouds doesn't make me love it less.

5

In the weeks that followed, I tried to reacclimatize to the rhythms of my life. I rose at five in the afternoon in my tiny apartment, listened to music while I cooked, fed my cat, walked or took the trolley to work. I was at the hotel by seven p.m., gazing out at the lobby from behind dark glasses—most staffers didn't wear dark glasses, but as a light-sensitive native of the Night City who couldn't tolerate the diffuse glare of the dome, I had special dispensation from HR—and I stood there thinking of all of the things around me that might not be real. The stone of the lobby floor. The fabric of my clothes. My hands. My glasses. The footsteps of a woman crossing the lobby.

"Evening, Gaspery," the woman said.

"Talia. Hi."

"You were taking a very concentrated interest in the lobby floor."

"Can I ask you an extremely random question?"

"Please do," she said. "I've had a boring day."

"Do you ever catch yourself thinking about the simulation hypothesis?" It seemed worth asking. It was all I could think about.

She raised her eyebrows. "That's the idea that we're possibly living in a simulation, isn't it?"

"Yeah."

"Actually, yes. I have thought about it. I don't believe we're living in a simulation." Talia was gazing past me, past the lobby, to the street. "I don't know, maybe this is naïve of me, but I feel like a simulation should be better, you know? I mean, if you were going to the trouble to simulate that street, for example, couldn't all of the streetlights work?"

The streetlight across the street had been flickering for a number of weeks.

"I see your point."

"Well, anyway," Talia said, "good night."

"Good night." I returned to the exercise of noticing everything and telling myself that none of the things I noticed were real, but now I was distracted by her point. Something no one ever talked about in those days was the shabbiness of the moon colonies. I think we were all a little embarrassed by it.

"Yeah, I think it's fair to say the glamour's worn off," Zoey said, when I saw her later that night. My shift ended at two a.m., so I'd called to ask if I could come over and see her. I'd known she'd be up—she'd never fully transitioned out of the Night City either, and, like me, she preferred to stay up all night—and she was taking a couple of days off work, so I took the trolley to her apartment. I'd been to this apartment only a handful of times, and had forgotten how dark it was. She'd painted the walls in a deep shade of gray. She had a collection of old-fashioned paper books—mostly history—and a framed painting on the wall that we'd made together when we were children. I was moved by it. We'd been about four and six, something like that, and we'd painted ourselves: a boy and a girl holding hands under a tree in exuberant colors.

"Where did the glamour go?" I asked. She'd poured me a generous glass of whiskey, which I was sipping very slowly because I've never had much of an alcohol tolerance. She was already on her second drink.

"To the newer colonies, I suppose. Titan, I guess. Europa. The Far Colonies." We were at her kitchen table. She lived across the street from the Time Institute, which I'd known intellectually without fully absorbing. What did Zoey have? She'd been very close with our mother, and now that Mom was gone, what Zoey had was her work. Her work and almost nothing else, to all appearances, but who was I to judge. I leaned back in my chair, gazing over the Time Institute rooftops at the luminescent spires of beyond. Could I immigrate to the Far Colonies? Fantastical thought. But of course the thought that followed was *If we're living in a simulation, it's not like the Far Colonies are real either.*

"What happened to them?" I asked. "The letter writer back in the twentieth century, Edwin whatever his name was, and Olive Llewellyn?"

Zoey had somehow finished her second glass—I was still only halfway through my first—and poured herself a third.

"The letter writer went to war, returned home to England a broken man, and died in an insane asylum. Olive Llewellyn died on Earth. A pandemic broke out while she was on a book tour."

"Zoey," I said, "has your investigation started yet?"

"Sort of. Preliminary discussions are under way. The bureaucracy around travel is intense."

"Will you get to . . . Will you be the one to travel?"

"I almost left the Time Institute a few years ago," she said. "I agreed to stay on condition that I never have to travel again."

"You've traveled through *time*," I said, and my awe at my sister was boundless in that moment. "Where did you go?"

"I can't talk about it." Her expression was grim.

"Can you at least tell me why you don't want to do it anymore? I'd think it'd be . . ."

"You'd think it'd be interesting," she said. "It is. At first it's fascinating. It's a portal to a different world."

"Right, that's how I imagined it."

"But before you go, Gaspery, you might spend two years engaged in research. When you're going to a given point in time, you're there to investigate some specific thing, and you read up on everyone you expect to encounter. There are people at the Time Institute, hundreds of staff, whose entire job is researching long-dead people to compile dossiers for travelers, and your job is to study those dossiers until you know everything in them." She stopped to drink. "So, Gaspery, picture this scene. You step into a party, at some long-ago point in time, and you know exactly how and when each and every person in that room is going to die."

"That's pretty creepy," I admitted.

"And some of them are going to die in the most preventable ways, Gaspery. You might be talking to a woman, let's say she has young children, and you know she's going to drown at a picnic next Tuesday, and because you can't mess with the time line, the one thing you absolutely cannot say to her is 'Don't go swimming next week.' You have to let her die."

"You can't pull her from the water."

"Right."

For a while I wasn't sure what to say, so I gazed out the window at the rooftops and spires and wondered if letting someone die for the sake of the time line was something I could do. Zoey drank quietly.

"The job requires an almost inhuman level of detachment," she said finally. "Did I say *almost*? Not *almost* inhuman, *actually* inhuman."

"So someone will have to travel through time to investigate this," I said, "but it won't be you."

"It will be several people, but I don't know who. It's not exactly a popular job."

"Send me," I said. Because what I was thinking in that moment was that the theoretical woman who was going to drown next Tuesday was going to drown anyway.

She looked at me, surprised. Two spots of pink had appeared on her cheeks, but otherwise she seemed perfectly sober.

"Absolutely not."

"Why not?"

"One, it's a horrifically dangerous job. Two, you're not qualified."

"What kind of background would you have to have, to travel back in time and talk to people? That's what it is, isn't it? I mean, what are the qualifications?"

"There's a barrage of psychological testing, followed by years of training."

"I could do that," I said. "I could go back to school, I could do whatever training was required. You know I almost finished my criminology degree. I know how to conduct an interview."

She was quiet.

"You want to keep the circle small here," I said, "don't you? Imagine the panic if word got out that we're living in a simulation."

"We don't know that we're living in a simulation, and I don't know that *panic* is quite the word. More like terminal ennui."

I decided to look up *ennui* later. There are words you encounter all your life without knowing what they mean.

"Zoey," I said, "I'm not doing anything with my life."

"Don't say that," she said, too quickly.

"This is just . . . this situation," I said, "this thing, whatever it is, this possibility I guess, it's the most interested I've been about anything in maybe my entire life."

"Then get a hobby, Gaspery. Take up calligraphy or archery or something."

"Can you just think about it, Zoey? Talk to whoever you have to talk to? Can I be considered? If we're talking about traveling through time here, then there's no real rush, is there? I'd have time to prepare, I could do whatever you want, go back to school, psychological training, whatever—" I realized I was babbling, so I stopped.

"No," she said. "Absolutely not." She drained her glass. "When I say it's a dangerous job, Gaspery, I mean I wouldn't want anyone I love to do it."

6

I didn't see Zoey again for three weeks after that, and there was an away message on her device. I went to work, I came home from work, I paced my apartment and talked to the cat. Finally, on a day off from the hotel, I left her a voicemail to say I was coming to her office. She didn't respond, but I boarded a trolley to the Time Institute in the late afternoon. She'd told me her schedule. I knew she'd be there. I watched the pale streets slipping past, the old stone buildings with missing pieces of masonry and the ramshackle illegal dwellings pressed close against them—the influence of the Night City seeping in, a whiff of disorder that I found invigorating—and I had a strange, wild notion that she might be dead. She worked too much and drank too much. In that first year after our mother died, my thoughts often veered toward disaster.

I stood outside the Time Institute, white stone monolith, and called her one more time. Nothing. It was around six o'clock. A few people emerged from the building, singly or in pairs. I found myself studying their faces, wondering what it might be like to have a job with stakes attached to it, and then one of the faces was Ephrem's.

"Eph," I said.

He looked up, startled.

"Gaspery! What are you doing here?"

I'd talked to Ephrem at my mother's funeral, briefly, but that day was a blur. We hadn't spoken at any length since the last dinner party I'd attended at his house, a year ago now. Perhaps it was just the dome lighting—dimming gently but also increasingly silvery, in a rough approximation of an Earth twilight—but Ephrem looked older than I remembered, older and more careworn.

"I was about to ask you the same thing," I said. "What's an arborist doing at the Time Institute?" He hesitated, and in that beat, I saw an opening. There was something he didn't want to tell me, and there was something I wasn't supposed to know. "You work here, don't you?"

He nodded. "Yes. For some time now."

"Then do you know about the project Zoey's working on? The simulation thing?"

"For god's sake, Gaspery, don't say another word." Ephrem was smiling, but I could tell he meant it. "It's been a while. Shall we grab a cup of tea?"

"Love to."

"Come see my office," he said. "I'll get some tea sent up."

We walked together in silence through the atrium, past Security, into an elevator and through successive white corridors that all looked the same to me, a maze of blank doors and opaque glass.

"Here we are," he said.

His office was identical to Zoey's, but had a bonsai tree in the window. A tea service was waiting for us on the table, with three cups. I'd known Ephrem half my life, but had I ever really asked him about his work? He'd told me he was an arborist, I'd asked him the occasional question about a tree, but apparently I knew much less about my friend than I'd thought. His office was on a high floor, overlooking the spires of Colony One. In the distance, I saw the Grand Luna Hotel.

"How long have you been here?" I asked.

"About a decade." He was pouring tea, but he paused for a moment, considering. "No, seven years. It only feels like a decade."

"I thought you were an arborist."

"I miss that job, to be honest. I'm afraid trees are just a hobby now. Will you join me?"

I moved over to his meeting table, which was exactly like Zoey's. I was overcome by the strangeness of the moment, the disorienting sense of one reality slipping away and being replaced by another. *But I've known you for years,* I wanted to say, *and you're an arborist, not a suit at the Time Institute. We graduated high school together.*

"Were trees easier?" I asked.

"Than my current job? Yes. Very much so." His device vibrated. He glanced at the screen and winced.

"Why didn't you tell me you worked here?"

"It's just . . . it's awkward," he said. "By *awkward,* I mean classified. The thing is, I can't really answer questions about my job, so I don't like to talk about it."

"Must be strange," I said, "doing something secret." By *strange,* I meant wonderful.

"I try not to lie about it. If you'd asked where I was working, I'd have said I was doing some work with the Time Institute, and let you assume it was somehow tree-related."

"Okay," I said. The silence extended around us. I didn't know how to ask for what I wanted. *Hire me, let me in, let me be a part of whatever it is you people are doing here.* "Ephrem," I began, but the door opened just then, and Zoey came in. Her expression was set in a way I hadn't seen since childhood. Zoey was furious. She sat across from me, ignored her tea, and stared into my eyes until I was forced to look away.

"I've been losing staring contests with my sister since I was five," I said to Ephrem. "Maybe four." He rewarded me with a weak smile. No one spoke. My gaze drifted back to the bonsai tree.

Finally, mercifully, Ephrem cleared his throat.

"Listen," he said. "No one's broken any rules here. When

Zoey spoke with you about the anomaly, Gaspery, it hadn't been classified yet."

Zoey looked at her tea.

"Of course," Ephrem said, "that doesn't mean you should be standing outside the Time Institute repeating the things she told you."

"I'm sorry," I said. "Ephrem, can I ask, is it real?"

"What do you mean?"

"The things Zoey told me about seemed like a pattern, but, well, it was our mom's thing," I said. "Simulation hypothesis."

"I remember her talking about it," he said gently.

"I think that when you lose someone, it's easy to see patterns that aren't there."

Ephrem nodded. "True. I don't know if there's anything there," he said. "But I wasn't close with your mother, which makes me a somewhat neutral party in this question, and I think there's enough to make it worth investigating."

"Can I help?" I asked.

"No," Zoey muttered, barely audible.

"Zoey did tell me that you wanted to work here." I noticed that Ephrem was very carefully not looking at Zoey.

"Yes," I said, "I would."

"Gaspery," Zoey said.

"Why do you want to work here?" Ephrem asked.

"Because it's interesting," I said. "I'm more interested in this than—well, than anything I can remember, honestly. I hope that doesn't make me seem desperate."

"Not at all," Ephrem said. "It just makes you sound interested. All of us are interested, or we wouldn't be here. Do you know what we do here?"

"Not really," I said.

"We safeguard the integrity of our time line," he said. "We investigate anomalies."

"Have there been others?"

"Usually it turns out to be nothing," Ephrem said. "My first case at the Institute involved a doppelgänger. According to our best facial-recognition software, the same woman appeared in photographs and video footage taken in 1925 and 2093. I was able to collect DNA and establish that they were two different women."

"You said *usually*," I said.

"On a few occasions," Ephrem said, "we haven't been able to make a determination one way or the other." I could tell he was unsettled by this.

"Is there something you're looking for?" I asked.

"There are several things we're looking for." He was quiet for a moment. "The aspect of our work that relates to the anomaly," he said, "is a continuing investigation into whether we're living in a simulation."

"Do you think we are?"

"There's a faction," he said carefully, "myself among them, that believes time travel works better than it should."

"What do you mean?"

"I mean that there are fewer loops than one might reasonably expect. I mean that sometimes we change the time line and then the time line seems to *repair* itself, in a way that doesn't make sense to me. The course of history should be irrevocably altered every single time we travel back in the time line, but, well, it isn't. Sometimes events seemingly change to accommodate the time traveler's interference, so that a generation later it's as if the traveler were never there."

"None of which is proof of a simulation," Zoey said quickly.

"Right. For obvious reasons," Ephrem said, "it's difficult to confirm."

"But you could move a step closer to confirmation by identifying a glitch in the simulation," I said.

"Yes, exactly."

"Gaspery," Zoey said, "I know it's interesting, but it's a troubling line of work."

"Zoey and I have some disagreements regarding the Time Institute," Ephrem said. "I think it's fair to say that our experiences here have been different."

"Yeah, that's fair," Zoey said flatly.

"But what I can tell you," Ephrem said, "is that it's an interesting place to work."

"What *I* can tell you," Zoey said, "is that Ephrem missed his recruitment goals this year, last year, and the year before."

"The training and the job both require immense discretion," Ephrem said, ignoring her, "and a great deal of focus."

"I can focus," I said. "I can be discreet."

"Well," Ephrem said, "I'll set up a screening interview for you."

"Thank you," I said. "This will sound . . . look, I don't mean to sound pathetic, but I've literally never had an interesting job before."

Ephrem smiled. "I'm not worried about the screening interview. You'll pass easily. This calls for a celebration."

But if it called for a celebration, why was my sister speaking so little, why did she look so grim? *A troubling line of work.* Look, I wanted to tell her, as Ephrem ordered three glasses of champagne, I would rather do a dangerous job than a job that makes me comatose with boredom, but I was afraid if I said this she might start to cry.

A week later I arrived at the hotel fifteen minutes before my shift, and went to Talia's office.

"Gaspery," she said.

I started to close the door, but she shook her head and rose from behind her desk. "Let's go for a walk."

"I only have a few—"

"You know, it's interesting." She gestured for me to walk out ahead of her. "I studied the history of work in university, and if there's one historical constant over the centuries, it's that no one especially wants to mess with HR." She opened the side door and we emerged into daylight by the loading dock. "I told your supervisor that I needed to meet with you. No one will mind."

Today's weather programming called for clouds, so the daylight was dim and grayish. I found it unsettling.

"It's hard to get used to," Talia said. She'd seen me glance uneasily at the sky. We were walking toward the path that ran alongside the Colony One river. All three colonies had rivers, for mental health reasons, running along identical white stone riverbeds, with identical white stone bridges arcing across them. They were engineering marvels. They all sounded exactly the same. "Why did you leave the Night City?" she asked.

"Bad divorce," I said. "I just wanted a fresh start." There was comfort in the sameness of the river sound; if I didn't look up, if I didn't pay attention to the strange grayish fake-cloudy-day light, I could pretend I was home. "Why did you come here?"

"I'm from here," she said. "I didn't move to the Night City till I was nine."

"Oh."

We were approaching a bridge. In the Night City, the bridge would've had a selection of derelicts napping or getting high underneath, in the peace and shadows of the embankment, but here there was just an old man on a bench, sitting alone and staring at the water.

"You came to my office to give your notice," Talia said.

"How did you know?"

"Because my boss's boss's boss told me to speak with a couple of suits from the Time Institute three days ago. I could tell from their questions that they were vetting you for a position."

Is there an unease that's specific to the sense of an invisible bureaucracy in motion around you? Talia stopped walking, so I stopped too, and I gazed down at the water. When I was a kid I used to float little boats down the Night City river, but the Night City river was a dark and sparkling thing, reflecting both sunlight and the blackness of space. The Colony One river was pale and milky, reflecting the fake clouds on the dome.

"We used to live there," Talia said, pointing, and I looked up and across the river at one of the oldest and most splendid of the grand apartment buildings, a white cylinder of a tower with a garden on every balcony. "My parents worked for the Time Institute."

I wasn't sure what to say. There was no non-catastrophic reason I could think of why a family would go from one of the most fashionable addresses in Colony One to a falling-down house in the Night City.

"They were both travelers," Talia said. "Until a mission went wrong in some kind of awful way, after which my parents were unable to work, and within a year we were in that run-down neighborhood in the Night City."

"I'm sorry." I resented having to say this, because the thing was, I loved the Night City, and that run-down neighborhood was my home. My family—me, Zoey, our mom—weren't there because we *had* to be there, we were there because in my mother's words, "at least this place has some character to it, not like those sterile colonies with the fake lighting," although as I remembered this, I was also remembering that we couldn't afford to fix the roof when it leaked.

Talia was looking at me. "Drunks are indiscreet," she said.

"As I'm sure you're aware, if you've ever thought about the question for more than five minutes, sending someone back in time inevitably changes history. *The traveler's presence itself is a disruption,* that's the phrase I remember my dad using. There's no way to go back, engage with the past, and leave the time line perfectly unchanged."

"Right," I said. I wasn't sure what she was getting at, but listening to her made me so uneasy that I couldn't meet her eyes.

"Sometimes the Time Institute goes back in time and undoes the damage, ensures that the traveler doesn't do the thing that changes history. You know, the little thing, like you hold open the door for the woman who goes on to create a civilization-ending algorithm or whatever. Sometimes they go back and undo the damage, but not always. Do you want to know how they make that decision?"

"That sounds extremely classified," I said.

"Oh, it *is,* Gaspery, but I like you and also I've developed a reckless streak in my old age, so I'm going to tell you anyway." (She was, what, thirty-five? In that moment, I found her thrillingly jaded.) "Here's the metric: they only go back and undo the damage *if the damage affects the Time Institute.* What am I, Gaspery? How would you describe me?"

This felt like a trap. "I . . ."

"It's okay," she said, "you can say it. I'm a bureaucrat. HR is bureaucracy."

"Okay."

"As is the Time Institute. The premier research university on the moon, possessor of the only working time machine in existence, intimately enmeshed in government and in law enforcement. Even *one* of those things would imply a formidable bureaucracy, don't you think? What you have to understand is that bureaucracy is an organism, and the prime goal of every organism is self-protection. Bureaucracy exists to protect itself." She was gazing across the river again. "We lived on the third floor," she said, pointing. "The balcony with the vines and rosebushes."

"It's nice," I said.

"Isn't it? Look, I understand why you'd want to work with the Time Institute," she said. "It must seem like an exciting opportunity. It's not like you've got much of a career path at the hotel. But just know that when the Institute is done with you, they'll throw you away." She spoke so casually that I wasn't sure if I'd heard her correctly. "I have a meeting," she said. "You should probably start your shift in the next hour or so." She turned and left me there.

I looked back at the apartment building. I'd been to one of those apartments once, years ago, for a party, and I'd been fairly drunk at the time, but I remembered vaulted ceilings and spacious rooms. What I was thinking was that if anything went wrong with the Time Institute, I would never be able to say I hadn't been warned.

But I felt such impatience with my life. I turned back to the hotel, and found that I couldn't go in. The hotel was the past. I wanted the future. I called Ephrem.

"Could I start early?" I asked. "I know the plan was to give the hotel two weeks' notice, but could I just start the training now? Tonight?"

"Sure," he said. "Could you be here in an hour?"

8

"Would you like some tea?" Ephrem asked.

"Please."

He typed something into his device, and we sat together at the meeting table. A sudden memory: drinking chai tea with Ephrem and Ephrem's mother after school one day at Ephrem's apartment, which was nicer than mine. Ephrem's mother had a job she could do from home, I remembered; she'd been staring at a screen. Ephrem and I were both studying, so it must have been just before an exam, during a period when I'd been experimenting with (a) tea and (b) being a good student. I was about to bring up this moment—*Do you remember?*—when there was a soft chime at the door, and a young man came in with a tray, which he left on the table with a nod. *Chai tea is real,* I told myself, and then I realized: Ephrem must remember that long-ago moment too, because he'd only ever served me chai when I'd come here.

"Here you are." Ephrem passed me a steaming mug.

"Why didn't Zoey want me to work here?"

He sighed. "She had a bad experience a few years back. I don't know the details."

"Yes, you do."

"Yes, I do. Look, this is just a rumor, but I heard she was in love with a traveler, then the traveler went rogue and got lost in time. That's literally all I know."

"No, it isn't."

"Literally all I know that isn't classified," Ephrem said.

"How do you get lost in time?"

"Suppose you were to intentionally fuck with the time line. The Time Institute might decide not to bring you back to the present."

"Why would anyone intentionally fuck with the time line?"

"Exactly," Ephrem said. "Don't do that, and you'll be fine." He leaned over to touch a console on the wall, and a time line with photographs of people was suspended in the air between us. "I've been working on an investigation plan for you," he said. "We don't want to place you in the center of the anomaly, because we don't know what the anomaly is, or how dangerous it might be. We want you to interview people who we think have seen it."

He enlarged a very old photograph, black-and-white, of a worried-looking young man in military uniform. "This is Edwin

St. Andrew, who experienced something in the forest at Caiette. You'll visit him, and see if he'll talk about it."

"I didn't know he was a soldier."

"He won't be when you speak with him. You'll talk to him in 1912, and then later he'll go on to have a very bad time on the Western Front. More tea?"

"Thank you." I had no idea what the Western Front was and hoped it would be covered in my training.

He swiped the time line to the side, and I was looking at the composer from the footage Zoey had shown me. "In January 2020," Ephrem continued, "an artist named Paul James Smith gave a performance that involved a video, and it seems like that video maybe shows the anomaly that St. Andrew described a century earlier, but we don't know where exactly that video was taken. We don't have complete footage of his concert, just the clip Zoey showed you. You'll speak to him and see what you can learn."

Ephrem swiped again, and I saw another photograph, an old man playing a violin in an airship terminal, his eyes closed. "This is Alan Sami," Ephrem said. "He played the violin for several years in the Oklahoma City Airship Terminal, circa 2200, and we believe it's his music that Olive Llewellyn references in *Marienbad*. You'll interview him and find out more about the music. Really just find out anything you can." He moved on through the time line, and there was Olive Llewellyn, my mother's favorite author, long-ago resident of Talia Anderson's childhood home. "And here's Olive Llewellyn. I regret to report that absolutely no one keeps surveillance footage for two hundred years, so there's no record of whatever Olive Llewellyn may or may not have experienced there prior to writing *Marienbad*. You'll interview her on her last book tour."

"When was her last book tour?" I asked.

"November 2203. Early days of the SARS Twelve pandemic. Don't worry, you won't get sick."

"I've never heard of it."

"It was one of our childhood immunizations," Ephrem said.

"Will there be other investigators assigned to the case?"

"Several. They'll look at different angles, interview different people, or interview the same people in a different way. You may meet some of them, but if they're good at their jobs, you'll never know who they are. From your perspective, Gaspery, this is not a complicated assignment. You'll conduct a few interviews, and then hand off your findings to a more senior investigator, who will take over and make the final determination, and if all goes well, there will be other investigations for you. You could have an interesting career here." He was gazing at the time line. "Where I think you'll start," he said, "is by interviewing the violinist."

"Okay," I said. "When do I talk to him?"

"In about five years," Ephrem said. "You have some training to do first."

9

The training wasn't like immersing myself in a different world. It was like immersing myself in successive different worlds, these moments that had arisen one after another after another, worlds fading out so gradually that their loss was apparent only in retrospect. Years of private instruction in small rooms in the Institute, years of passing by people who may or may not have been my fellow students in the halls—no one wore name tags here—and years of studying quietly in the Time Institute library, or in my apartment late at night with my cat asleep on my lap. Five years after I left the hotel, I reported for the first time to the travel chamber.

It was a midsize room made entirely of some kind of composite stone. At one end was a bench, molded into a deep indentation in the wall. The bench faced an extremely ordinary-looking desk. Zoey was waiting there, with a device that looked unnervingly like a gun.

"I'm going to shoot a tracker into your arm," she said.

"Good morning, Zoey. I'm fine, thanks for asking. Nice to see you too."

"It's a microcomputer. It interacts with your device, which interacts with the machine."

"Okay," I said, giving up on pleasantries. "So the tracker sends information to my device?"

"Remember that time I gave you a cat?" she said.

"Of course. Marvin. He's napping at home as we speak."

"We sent an agent back to another century," Zoey said, "but the agent fell in love with someone and didn't want to come home, so she removed her own tracker, fed it to a cat, and then when we tried to forcibly return her to the present, the cat appeared in the travel chamber instead of her."

"Wait," I said, "my cat's from another century?"

"Your cat's from 1985," she said.

"What," I said, at a loss for words.

She took my hand—when was the last time we'd touched one another?—and I observed her grim concentration as she shot a silver pellet into my left arm. It hurt much more than I would've imagined. She opened a projection over the desk, and turned her attention to the floating screen.

"You should have told me," I said. "You should have told me my cat was a time traveler."

"Honestly, Gaspery, what difference would it make. A cat's a cat."

"You never were an animal person, were you."

Her mouth was set in a thin line. She wouldn't look at me.

"You should be happy for me," I said, while she was adjusting something in her projection. "This is the only thing I've ever really wanted to do, and I'm doing it."

"Oh, Gaspery," she said absently. "My poor little lamb. Device?"

"Here."

She took my device, held it close to the projection, and handed it back to me.

"Okay," she said. "Your first destination has been programmed. Go sit in the machine."

10

A transcript:

GASPERY ROBERTS: Okay, it's on. Thank you for taking the time to speak with me.

ALAN SAMI: You're welcome. Thank you for lunch.

GR: Now, just for the benefit of my recording, you're a violinist.

AS: I am. I play in the airship terminal.

GR: For spare change?

AS: For pleasure. I don't need the money, to be clear.

GR: But you do collect change, in that hat at your feet . . .

AS: Well, people were throwing change at me, so I did at one point decide to just turn my hat upside down in front of me, so that all the change would at least land in one place.

GR: May I ask, why do you do it, if you don't need the money?

AS: Well, because I love it, son. I love playing the violin, and I love seeing people.

GR: I'd like to play a short clip for you, if I may.

AS: Of music?

GR: Music with some ambient noises. I'll play it, and then I'm going to ask you to tell me anything you can about it. That sound all right?

AS: Sure. Go ahead.

[. . .]

GR: That was you, right?

AS: Yes, that's me in the airship terminal. Poor-quality recording, though.

GR: How can you be sure it's you?

AS: How can I . . . really? Well, son, because I know the music and I heard an airship. That *whoosh* just at the end.

GR: Let's focus on the music for a moment. That piece you were playing, can you tell me about it?

AS: My lullaby. I composed it, but I never gave it a title. It was something I made up for my wife, my late wife.

GR: Your late . . . I'm sorry.

AS: Thank you.

GR: Is there—did you ever record yourself playing it, or write down the score?

AS: Neither. Why?

GR: Well, as I mentioned, I'm an assistant to a music historian. I've been tasked with investigating similarities and differences between the music played at airship terminals in various regions on Earth.

AS: And your affiliation, what institution was that, again?

GR: University of British Columbia.

AS: That where your accent's from?

GR: My accent?

AS: It just shifted. I have an ear for accents.

GR: Oh. I'm from Colony Two.

AS: Interesting. My wife was from Colony One, but I wouldn't say she sounded anything like you. How long have you been doing this?

GR: Assisting in investigations? A few years.

AS: You go to school for that? How does a person get into that line of work?

GR: Fair question. I was spinning my wheels, if we're being honest here. I had a job in hotel security. It was fine. I just stood around a hotel lobby, staring at people. But then, well, I saw an opportunity. Something came up that really interested me, in a way I'd never been interested in anything. I spent five years in training, studying linguistics and psychology and history.

AS: I understand the history part, but why psychology and linguistics?

GR: Well, linguistics because people speak differently, at different points in history, and if you're dealing with old music that has a spoken-word element, it's helpful.

AS: Makes sense. And psychology?

GR: Personal interest. It wasn't relevant. It wasn't relevant at all. I don't know why I mentioned it.

AS: Methinks the lady doth protest too much.

GR: Wait, did you just call me a lady?

AS: That was Shakespeare, son. Come on, now. Didn't you go to school?

"Smooth," Zoey said, when she reviewed the recording. "Real sophisticate there."

Ephrem, who was sitting with us in her office, suppressed a smile.

"I know," I said. "Sorry."

"No, look," my sister said, "we didn't cover Shakespeare in your training."

"Zoey," I said, "Ephrem, what would happen, just theoretically, if I messed up?"

"Don't mess up." Ephrem glanced at his device. "I'm sorry," he said, "I have a meeting with my boss, but I'll see you in my office in an hour." He left us then, and I was alone with my sister.

"What were your impressions of the violinist?" Zoey asked.

"He was in his eighties," I said, "maybe even nineties. He had a slow way of talking, like his accent kind of dragged everything out. He'd done that thing to his eyes, that color-change thing? His eyes were this strange shade of purple. Violet, I guess."

"Probably all the rage in his youth."

She looked back at the transcript, rereading something. I rose and went to the window. It was night, and the dome had gone clear. Earth was rising on the horizon, a vision in green and blue.

"Zoey," I said, "can I ask you something?"

"Of course."

I turned back to her, and she looked up from the transcript.

"Do you remember Talia Anderson from the Night City?" I asked.

"No. No, I don't think so."

"She was in my grade for a while in elementary school. Her family lived in the Olive Llewellyn house, and then I ran into her again when she hired me for that hotel security job."

"Wait," Zoey said, "are we talking about Natalia Anderson at the Grand Luna Hotel?"

"Yes."

Zoey nodded. "She was on the list of people we interviewed when you were being cleared for this position."

"How do you remember a name on a list from five years ago?"

"I don't know," she said. "I just do."

"I wish I had your brain. Anyway. She kind of warned me off coming here, to be honest."

"So did I," Zoey said.

"I guess her parents worked here," I said, ignoring this. "A long time ago. She said her dad was indiscreet."

Zoey was watching me closely. "What did she say?"

"She said, *The traveler's presence itself is a disruption*—"

"Those exact words?"

"I think so. Why?"

"That's from a classified training manual that went out of circulation ten years ago. I wonder if she's telling anyone else about it. What else did she say?"

"She said that when the Institute was done with me, it would throw me away."

Zoey looked away. "It's not always the easiest place to work," she said. "Staff turnover is high. You'll remember that I tried to dissuade you."

"You were afraid I'd get thrown away?"

She was quiet for so long that I thought she wasn't going to answer. When she spoke again, she wouldn't look at me, and her voice was strained. "I was close with someone, a long time ago, another traveler who was investigating something else. She messed up."

"What happened to her?"

Her hand drifted to the necklace she always wore. It was a simple gold chain, and I'd never really noticed it before, but from the way she touched it, I understood that the lost traveler had given it to her.

"Here's what you have to understand," she said. "You don't have to be a terrible person to intentionally try to change the time line. You just have to have a moment of weakness. Really just a moment. When I say *weakness,* I might mean something more like *humanity.*"

"And if you intentionally change the time line . . ."

"It's not difficult to deliberately lose someone in time. Frame them for a crime they didn't commit, for example, or, in less serious cases, they can just be placed somewhere with no way home."

"Wouldn't framing a traveler for a crime have, well, some repercussions for the time line?"

"The Research department maintains a list of crimes," Zoey said. "Carefully selected, carefully vetted to avoid any major repercussions."

(*"Bureaucracy exists to protect itself,"* Talia said, gazing out over the river.)

Zoey cleared her throat. "Big day tomorrow," she said. "Remind me where you're going first?"

"1912," I said, "to talk to Edwin St. Andrew. I'm going to pretend to be a priest and see if he'll talk to me in the church."

"Right. And then?"

"Then I'm going to January 2020," I said, "to talk to the video artist, Paul James Smith, see what we can learn about that weird footage."

She nodded. "And you talk to Olive Llewellyn the next day?"

"Yeah." By now I'd read all of her books. I hadn't especially liked any of them, but it was hard to parse whether this was the fault of the books or the fault of the dread I felt when I thought of her, given the timing of the scheduled interview.

"You know you're meeting her in the last week of her life," Zoey said. "You'll interview her in Philadelphia, and she'll die three days later in a hotel room in New York."

"I know." I felt a little sick about it.

Zoey's face softened. "Remember how Mom used to quote *Marienbad* at us when we were kids?"

I nodded, and for a moment I was transported back to the hospital, the last days of our mother, the week outside of time and space when we never left her side.

"But you'll keep it together, right?" In the way my sister looked at me, I knew she saw a previous Gaspery, a shiftless version of myself who was prone to error, who lived aimlessly and hadn't spent the past five years in training and study and research.

"Of course. I'm a professional."

I knew the facts of the life, and of the death: Olive Llewellyn died in a pandemic that began during a book tour. She died in an Atlantic Republic hotel room. But of course the thought of breaking the protocol occurred to me, then and in the morning two days later when I reported to the travel chamber, when the coordinates were entered into my device, when I stepped into the machine to meet her.

5

Last Book Tour on Earth /

2203

"LISTEN," THE JOURNALIST SAID, "I DON'T MEAN TO MAKE you uncomfortable or put you on the spot. But I'm curious if you experienced something strange in the Oklahoma City Airship Terminal."

In the quiet, Olive could hear the soft hum of the building, the sounds of ventilation and plumbing. Perhaps she wouldn't have admitted it if he hadn't caught her toward the end of the tour, if she hadn't been so tired. The journalist, Gaspery-Jacques Roberts, was watching her closely. She felt he already knew what she was about to say.

"I don't mind talking about this," she said, "but I'm afraid I'll seem too eccentric if it makes it into the final version of the interview. Could we go off the record for a moment?"

"Yes," he said.

"I was in the terminal. I was walking toward my flight, and I remember I walked by a guy playing a violin. And then all of a sudden, everything went dark and I was in a forest. Just for a second. It was . . ."

"It was exactly like you described it in the book," Gaspery said.

"Yes."

"Can you tell me anything else?"

"There's not much else. It was so fast. I had an impression . . . This is going to sound crazy, but I was in two places at once. When I say I was in a forest, I was also still in the terminal."

"I knew it," he said.

"I'm not sure . . ." Olive didn't know how to ask the question. "Does it mean something?" she asked.

He looked at her, and seemed to grapple with what to say next. "This will sound silly," he said, in tones of forced lightness, "but my editor over at *Contingencies Magazine* likes me to end interviews with a fun question."

Olive clenched her hands together and nodded.

"Okay, so," he said, "this is kind of a question about destiny, I guess?" Olive noticed that he was sweating. "Barring some kind of unforeseen catastrophe, assuming that our technology continues to advance, we'll probably have time travel in the next century. If a time traveler appeared before you and told you to drop everything and go home immediately, would you do it?"

"How would I know they were a time traveler?"

The door was opening, and Olive's publicist was coming in.

"Well, let's say there was something about the person that couldn't be reconciled."

"For example."

Gaspery leaned forward, speaking softly and quickly. "Well, for example, suppose this person were an adult," he said. "Now suppose this person, this adult in his thirties, had a name you'd made up for a book that you only published five years ago."

"How's it going in here?" Aretta asked.

"Great," Gaspery said. "Your timing's perfect."

"You could've changed your name," Olive said.

"I could have." He held her gaze. "But I didn't." His tone brightened as he rose. "Olive, thanks so much for your time. Especially that last question. I know fun questions are the worst."

"Olive, you look tired," Aretta said. "You doing okay?"

"Just tired," Olive said, parroting the explanation.

"But you're going home right after this, aren't you?" Gaspery said smoothly. "Straight from here to the airship terminal, right? Well, anyway, goodbye, thank you!"

"No, she has another— Oh," Aretta said, "yes, goodbye!" Gaspery was gone. "He's a little odd, isn't he?"

"A little," Olive said.

"What was that about going home? You have another three days on Earth."

"Something's come up."

She frowned. "But—"

But Olive had never been more certain of anything. She'd never been warned more clearly in her life. "I'm sorry," she said, "I know this causes problems for everyone, but I need to go to the airship terminal. I'm going home on the next flight."

"What?"

"Aretta," Olive said, "you should go home to your family."

It's shocking to wake up in one world and find yourself in another by nightfall, but the situation isn't actually all that unusual. You wake up married, then your spouse dies over the course of the day; you wake in peacetime and by noon your country is at war; you wake in ignorance and by evening it's clear that a pandemic is already here. You wake on a book tour with several days left to go, and by evening you're racing toward home, your suitcase abandoned in a hotel room.

Olive called her husband from the car. It was a self-driven car, for which she was grateful; there was no driver to hear her and wonder if she'd lost her mind, which was something she was wondering herself. "Dion," she said, "I'm going to ask you to do something that's going to sound kind of extreme."

"Okay," he said.

"We need to pull Sylvie out of school."

"Like, not bring her in tomorrow? I have to work."

"Could you go and pick her up now?"

"Olive, what's this about?"

Outside the window, the Philadelphia suburbs were a blur of apartment towers. You can have an excellent marriage and still be unable to tell your spouse absolutely everything. "It's about this new virus," Olive said. "I met someone at the hotel with some inside knowledge."

"What kind of inside knowledge?"

"It's bad, Dion, it's spreading out of control."

"In the colonies too?"

"How many flights are there every day between Earth and the moon?"

He drew in his breath. "Okay," he said. "Okay. I'll go get her."

"Thank you. I'm on my way home."

"What? I know it's serious if you're cutting a book tour short."

"It's serious, Dion, it seems like it's really serious," and Olive realized she was beginning to cry.

"Don't cry," he said softly. "Don't cry. I'm heading to the school now. I'll bring her home."

In the departure lounge, Olive found a corner far from anyone else and took out her device. There was no new news of the pandemic, but she ordered three months' worth of pharmaceutical supplies, then bottled water for good measure, then a mountain of new toys for Sylvie. By the time she boarded the flight she had spent a small fortune and felt mildly insane.

What it was like to leave Earth:

A rapid ascent over the green-and-blue world, then the world was blotted out all at once by clouds. The atmosphere turned thin and blue, the blue shaded into indigo, and then—it was like slipping through the skin of a bubble—there was black space. Six hours to the moon. Olive had bought a package of surgical masks at the airport—sold to travelers who'd picked up colds on the road—and she was wearing three of them, which made it difficult to breathe. She had a window seat and was all but curled around her armrest, trying to stay as far from other people as possible. The surface of the moon rose out of blackness, bright from a distance and gray up close, the opaque bubbles of Colonies One, Two, and Three gleaming in the sunlight.

Her device lit up with a soft chime. She frowned at the new

appointment alert, because she couldn't remember having scheduled a doctor's appointment, and then she understood: Dion had scheduled the appointment for her. He'd seen how much money she'd just spent on canned goods. He thought she was losing her grip.

Then the landing, so gentle after that hurtling speed between Earth and the moon. Olive put on dark glasses to hide her tears. But it wasn't unreasonable, actually, the doctor's appointment. If Dion had called from a business trip to say that a plague was coming and she should pull their child out of school, if she'd seen those massive charges go through on their shared credit account, she would've feared for his sanity too. She waited as long as possible before disembarking, in order to create some distance between herself and other people, and stayed as far away as possible from everyone in the spaceport and on the platform for the Colony Two train. In the train car she stared out the window at the passing tunnel lights, through the composite glass to the moon's bright surface. She disembarked on a platform, where she kept reaching for her suitcase and then remembering that she was never going to see it again.

Olive had a moment of passing regret for the strange star-weapon burrs that she'd pulled from her socks in the Republic of Texas—she'd looked forward to showing them to Sylvie—but beyond that there was nothing of any real value in that suitcase, she told herself. (But she felt bereft: she'd been traveling with the suitcase for years now and it was almost a friend.) The trolley arrived. Olive sat close to the doors, for increased airflow—it was all coming back to her now, all of her research into pandemics— and the trolley glided through the streets and boulevards of this city of white stone, which had never looked more beautiful to her. The bridges arching over the street were possessed of uncommon architectural grace; the trees lining the boulevards and softening the tower balconies were almost unnaturally verdant, oversaturated in their green; and then there were the countless little shops with people walking in and out—unmasked, ungloved, oblivious, blind to the imminent catastrophe—and the sight of them was too much, actually, she could bear no more but of course she had to. Olive was weeping quietly, so no one came near her.

She disembarked early, and walked the last ten blocks in the sunlight. The Colony Two dome was displaying her favorite kind of sky, white skittering clouds on a background of deep blue. What was missing was the sound of suitcase wheels on cobblestones.

Olive turned the corner and there was the complex where she lived, a line of square white buildings with staircases leading down from the second and third floors to the sidewalk. She took the stairs to the second floor with a sense of unreality. How could she be home so soon? Without her suitcase? And why, because a journalist had said something strange about time travel? She raised her hand to knock—her keys were in her suitcase, on Earth—but froze. What if the contagion were on her clothes? She took off her jacket, her shoes, and then—after only a moment of hesitation—her pants and shirt. She looked down at the street and a passerby looked quickly away.

She called Dion.

"Olive, where are you?"

"Could you unlock the door, and then take Sylvie into the bedroom, and stay in there till I come into the room?"

"Olive . . ."

"I'm afraid of the contagion," Olive said. "I'm outside the front door, but I want to take a shower before either of you hug me. It could be on my clothes." Her clothes were puddled around her feet.

"Olive," he said, and she heard the pain in his voice. He thought she was terribly, desperately unwell, but not from the approaching pandemic.

"Please."

"Okay," he said. "I'll do it."

The lock clicked open. Olive waited for a slow count of ten, then let herself in, dropped her device and underwear into a heap on the floor, and went straight to the shower room. She scrubbed herself with soap, then found the cleaning alcohol, retraced her footsteps, and disinfected every surface she'd touched, then turned on the air purifier to its highest setting and opened all the windows, then used her towel to lift her underwear from the floor and dropped both underwear and towel into the garbage disposal, then disinfected her device, then disinfected the floor where the device had been, then disinfected her hands again.

This will be our lives now, she thought dully, *memorizing which surfaces we've touched.* Olive took a deep breath, and arranged her face into a semblance of calm. She opened the door to the bedroom, naked and deranged, and her daughter flew across the room and leaped into her arms. Olive fell to her knees, tears running hot down her face and onto Sylvie's shoulder.

"Mama," Sylvie said, "why are you crying?"

Because I was supposed to die in the pandemic but I was warned by a time traveler. Because a lot of people are going to die soon and there's nothing I can do to prevent it. Because nothing makes sense and I might be insane.

"I just missed you so much," Olive said.

"You missed me so much you had to come home early?" Sylvie asked.

"Yes," Olive said. "I missed you so much I had to come home early."

A strange alarm filled the room: Dion's device was blaring with a public alert. Over Sylvie's shoulder, Olive watched Dion staring at the screen. He looked up and saw her watching him.

"You were right," he said. "I'm sorry for doubting you. The virus is here."

For the first one hundred days of lockdown, Olive closed herself into her office every morning and sat at her desk, but it was easier to stare out the window than to write. Sometimes she just took notes on the soundscape.

Siren

Quiet; birds

Siren

Another siren

A third? Overlapping, from at least two directions

All quiet

Birds

Siren

The blur of passing days: Olive woke at four a.m. to work for two hours while Sylvie slept, then Dion worked from six a.m. to noon while Olive made an attempt to be a schoolteacher and to keep their daughter reasonably sane, then Olive worked for two hours while Dion and Sylvie played, then Sylvie got an hour of hologram time while both her parents worked, then Dion worked while Olive played with Sylvie, then somehow it was time to make dinner and then dinner blurred into the bedtime hour, then by eight p.m. Sylvie was asleep and Olive went to bed not long after, then Olive's alarm rang because it was once again four a.m., etc.

"We could think of it as an opportunity," Dion said, on the seventy-third night of lockdown. Olive and Dion were sitting together in the kitchen, eating ice cream. Sylvie was sleeping.

"An opportunity for what?" Olive asked. Even on Day 73, she still felt a little stunned. There was an element of incredulity— a pandemic? *Seriously?*—that hadn't quite faded.

"To think about how to re-enter the world," Dion said, "when re-entry is possible." There were certain friends he didn't miss, he said. He was quietly applying for new jobs.

"Let's pretend this seltzer bottle is a friend," Sylvie said, at dinner on Day 85. "Make it talk to me."

"Hello, Sylvie!" Olive said. She moved the glass bottle closer to Sylvie.

"Hi, bottle," Sylvie said.

In lockdown, there was a new kind of travel, but that didn't seem the right word. There was a new kind of anti-travel. In the evenings Olive keyed a series of codes into her device, donned a headset that covered her eyes, and entered the holospace. Holographic meetings had once been hailed as the way of the future—why go to the time and expense of physical travel, when one could transport oneself into a strange silvery-blank digital room and converse there with flickering simulations of one's colleagues?—but the unreality was painfully flat. Dion's job required a great many meetings, so he was in the holospace six hours a day and was dazed with exhaustion in the evenings.

"I don't know why it's so tiring," he said. "So much more tiring than normal meetings, I mean."

"I think it's because it isn't real." It was very late, and they were standing by the living room windows together, looking down at the deserted street.

"Maybe you're right. Turns out reality is more important than we thought," Dion said.

The thing with the tour—the thing with all the tours—is that there was no moment when she wasn't grateful, but also it was always too many faces. She'd always been shy. On tour all those faces kept appearing before her, face after face after face, and most of them were kind but all of them were the wrong faces, because after a few days on the road the only people Olive wanted to see were Sylvie and Dion.

But when the world shrank to the size of the interior of the apartment, and to a population of three, the people were what she missed. Where was the driver who was writing the book about the talking rats? She'd never even known the woman's name. Where was Aretta—the out-of-office message on Aretta's device was weeks out of date, which was worrying—and the other authors she'd met on that last tour, Ibby Mohammed and Jessica Marley? Where was the driver who sang an old jazz song as they drove through Tallinn, and the woman in Buenos Aires with the tattoo?

In lockdown, Colony Two was a strange, frozen place, silent except for the ambulance sirens and the soft *whir* of passing trolleys with their freight of masked medical workers. No one was supposed to go outside except for medical appointments and essential work, but on the one-hundredth night, while Sylvie was sleeping, Olive slipped out of the kitchen door and into the outside world. She moved swiftly and silently down the stairs to the garden, where she sat on the grass, under a small tree shaped like an umbrella. She was inches from the sidewalk but hidden by leaves. Being out of the apartment was disorienting. She was certain that the air here hadn't changed, but after her time on Earth it seemed wrong to her, flat and overly filtered. She stayed outdoors for an hour, then slipped back in with a sense of revelation. After that she went out every night to sit under the umbrella tree.

It was on one of those nights that the journalist appeared. The last journalist, as she'd always think of him, Gaspery-Jacques Roberts of *Contingencies Magazine*. On the night he appeared, she was under the umbrella tree, cross-legged on the grass, trying not to think of the day's numbers—752 dead today in Colony Two, with 3,458 new cases—and trying to let go of conscious thought, when she heard soft footsteps approaching. She didn't think it could be a patrol officer—they walked in pairs—but the fines for being outside in lockdown were steep, so she stayed very still and tried to breathe as quietly as possible.

The footsteps stopped, so close that she could see the person's shadow angled over the sidewalk. Could they have sensed her? It didn't seem possible. Someone else—another set of footsteps—was approaching, from the opposite direction.

"Zoey? What are you doing here?" Olive recognized the man's voice immediately, and her breath caught in her chest.

"I could ask you the same thing," a woman said. She had his accent.

"I told you in the travel chamber five minutes ago," Gaspery said. "I want to interview a literary scholar who interviewed Olive Llewellyn. One more layer of confirmation."

"I thought it was strange that you wanted to leave again after your interview with her, on an unscheduled trip," she said.

Gaspery didn't speak for a moment. "I thought you didn't travel anymore," he said finally.

"Yes, well, I felt the circumstances warranted an exception. Gaspery, how could you?"

"I was going to just talk to her," Gaspery said. "I was going to stick to the plan, but Zoey, I couldn't do it. I couldn't just let her die."

There was a moment of silence, during which both of these incomprehensible people were, Olive imagined, staring directly into her living room window. She looked up, but from her angle she could see only patches of the living room ceiling, mostly obscured by leaves.

"It's like you warned me," he said quietly. "You said the job required a lack of humanity, and it did. It does."

"You shouldn't come back to the present," Zoey said.

What?

"Of course I'll come back to the present," Gaspery said. "I believe in facing consequences."

"But the consequences will be terrible," Zoey said. "I've seen it happen before."

There was silence then. Gaspery didn't respond.

"The Night City's beautiful in this era," he said finally.

"I know." She was crying, Olive could hear it in her voice. "It isn't the Night City yet."

"You're right," he said. "The dome lighting still works. Are we standing on cobblestones?"

"Yes," she said, "I believe we are."

"There's a patrol coming," Gaspery said suddenly, and they were gone, walking quickly away together.

Olive stayed there for a long time in the shadows, in the strangeness. She was supposed to die in the pandemic, as she understood it, but then Gaspery had saved her. Hadn't he even told her what he was? *If a time traveler appeared before you . . .*

That night she looked up Gaspery-Jacques Roberts and the results were flooded with references to her own work, the book and the screen adaptation of *Marienbad*. She looked up *Contingencies Magazine,* and found a website with a few dozen articles, but the more she searched, the more it seemed like a front. It hadn't been updated in a long time, and its social media accounts were dormant.

She heard a small noise and started, but it was only Sylvie, standing in the doorway in unicorn pajamas.

"Oh, sweetie," Olive said, "it's the middle of the night. Let me tuck you in."

"I have an insomnia," Sylvie said.

"I'll sit with you for a bit."

Olive lifted her daughter, this warm weight in her arms, and carried her back to her bedroom. Everything in the room was blue. Olive tucked her in under an indigo duvet and sat beside her. *I was supposed to die in the pandemic.*

"Could we play Enchanted Forest?" Sylvie asked.

"Of course," Olive said. "Let's play for a few minutes, till you feel sleepy." Sylvie shivered with delight. The Enchanted Forest was a new invention: Sylvie had never gone in for imaginary friends, but in lockdown she had an entire kingdom filled with them, and she was their queen.

"When I feel sleepy we'll stop," Sylvie said agreeably. "We'll stop before I fall asleep."

"The portal door opens," Olive said, because that was how the game always began. Sylvie's bedroom was quieter than Olive's office, being at the back of the building, but Olive still heard the faint wail of an ambulance siren.

"Who comes through?" Sylvie asked.

"Magic Foxy leaps through the portal. 'Queen Sylvie,' says Magic Foxy, 'come quickly! There's a problem in the Enchanted Forest!'"

Sylvie laughed, delighted. Magic Foxy was her favorite friend. "And only I can help, Magic Foxy?"

"'Yes, Queen Sylvie,' says Magic Foxy, 'only you can help.'"

Another lecture, this one virtual. No, the same lecture, just performed now in the holospace. (In non-space. Nowhere.) Olive was a hologram in a room of holograms, a sea of dim lights flickering before her, all of them gathered in a minimalistic suggestion of a room. She gazed out at several hundred slightly luminescent facsimiles of people, their actual bodies in individual rooms all over Earth and in the colonies, and had the unhinged thought that she was speaking directly to a congregation of souls.

"An interesting question," Olive said, "which I'd like to consider in these last few minutes, is why there's been such interest in postapocalyptic literature over this past decade or so. I've had the tremendous good fortune of getting to travel a great deal in the service of *Marienbad*—"

Blue sky over Salt Lake City, birds wheeling overhead
The rooftop of a hotel in Cape Town, lights sparkling in the trees
Wind rippling over a field of long grass by a train station in northern
England
"Can I show you my tattoo?" the woman in Buenos Aires said

"—which is to say I've had the opportunity to speak with a great many people about postapocalyptic literature. I've heard a great many theories about why there's such interest in the genre. One person suggested to me that it had to do with economic inequality, that in a world that can seem fundamentally unfair, perhaps we long to just blow everything up and start over—"

"That's just how it seems to me," the bookseller had said,
in an old shop in Vancouver, while Olive admired his pink glasses

"—and I'm not sure I agree with that, but it's an intriguing thought." The holograms shifted and stared. She liked the idea that she could still hold a room, even if now the room was just in the holospace, even if the room wasn't really a room. "Someone suggested to me that it has to do with a secret longing for heroism, which I found interesting. Perhaps we believe on some level that if the world were to end and be remade, if some unthinkable catastrophe were to occur, then perhaps we might be remade too, perhaps into better, more heroic, more honorable people."

"Doesn't it seem possible?" the librarian in Brazzaville asked,
her eyes shining, and outside on the street
someone was playing a trumpet,
"I mean, no one wants this to happen, obviously,
but think of the opportunity for heroism . . ."

"Some people have suggested to me that it's about the catastrophes on Earth, the decision to build domes over countless cities, the tragedy of being forced to abandon entire countries due to rising water or rising heat, but—"

A memory: waking in an airship between cities,
looking down at the dome over Dubai,
and believing for a wildly disorienting moment that she'd left Earth

"—that doesn't ring true to me. Our anxiety is warranted, and it's not unreasonable to suggest that we might channel that anxiety into fiction, but the problem with that theory is, our anxiety is nothing new. When have we ever believed that the world *wasn't* ending?

"I had a fascinating conversation with my mother once, where she talked about the guilt she and her friends had felt about bringing children into the universe. This was in the mid-2160s, in Colony Two. It's hard to imagine a more tranquil time or place, but they were concerned about asteroid storms, and if life on the moon became untenable, about the continued viability of life on Earth—"

Olive's mother drinking coffee in Olive's childhood home:
yellow flowered tablecloth
hands clasped around a blue coffee mug
her smile

"—and my point is, there's always something. I think, as a species, we have a desire to believe that we're living at the climax of the story. It's a kind of narcissism. We want to believe that we're uniquely important, that we're living at the end of history, that *now,* after all these millennia of false alarms, *now* is finally the worst that it's ever been, that finally we have reached the end of the world."

In a world that no longer exists but whose exact end date is unclear,
Captain George Vancouver stands on the deck of the HMS Discovery,
gazing anxiously out at a landscape with no people in it

"But all of this raises an interesting question," Olive said. "What if it always *is* the end of the world?"

She paused for effect. Before her, the holographic audience was almost perfectly still. "Because we might reasonably think of the end of the world," Olive said, "as a continuous and never-ending process."

An hour later, Olive removed her headset and was once again alone in her office. She wasn't sure if she'd ever been so tired. She sat still for a while, absorbing the details of the physical world: the bookshelves, the framed drawings by Sylvie, the painting of a garden that her parents had given her as a wedding present, the odd piece of metal she'd once found on Earth that she'd hung on the wall because she loved the shape of it. She rose and went to the window to look out at the city. White street, white buildings, green trees, ambulance lights. It was midnight, and so the ambulances had no need of sirens. Lights flashed blue and red up the street and then receded.

I was supposed to die in the pandemic. She didn't entirely understand what that meant, and yet it was the point around which all of her thoughts revolved. A trolley passed, carrying medical workers, then another ambulance, then the stillness returned. Movement in the air: an owl flying silently through the dark.

"When we consider the question of why *now*," Olive said, before a different audience of holograms the following evening, "I mean why there's been this increased interest in postapocalyptic fiction over the past decade, I think we have to consider what's changed in the world in that timeframe, and that line of thinking leads me inevitably to our technology." A hologram in the front row was shimmering oddly, which meant the attendee had an unstable connection. "My personal belief is that we turn to postapocalyptic fiction not because we're drawn to disaster, per se, but because we're drawn to what we imagine might come next. We long secretly for a world with less technology in it."

"So I'm guessing I'm not the first to ask you what it's like to be the author of a pandemic novel during a pandemic," another journalist said.

"You might not be the very first."

Olive was standing by the window, staring up at the sky. The Colony Two dome had the same pixelations as Colonies One and Three, a shifting pattern of blue sky and clouds, but it seemed to her that there was a glitchy patch on the horizon, a section that flickered just slightly so that a square of black space showed through. It was hard to tell.

"What are you working on these days? Are you able to work?"

"I'm writing this crazy sci-fi thing," Olive said.

"Interesting. Can you tell me about it?"

"I don't know much about it myself, to be honest. I don't even know if it's a novel or a novella. It's actually kind of deranged."

"I suppose anything written this year is likely to be deranged," the journalist said, and Olive decided she liked her. "What drew you to sci-fi?"

That patch of sky had definitely just flickered. What would it look like if the dome lighting failed? It was a strange thought. She'd always taken the illusion of an atmosphere for granted.

"I've been in lockdown for one hundred and nine days," Olive said. "I think I just wanted to write something set as far away as possible from my apartment."

"Is that all it is?" the journalist asked. "Physical distance, a way of traveling during lockdown?"

"No, I guess not." An ambulance siren was approaching, and then the ambulance stopped in front of the building across the street. Olive turned her back to the window. "There's just . . . Look," Olive said, "I don't mean to be melodramatic, and I know it's like this in a lot of places now, but there's just, there is so much death. There's death all around us. I don't want to write about anything real."

The journalist was quiet.

"And I know it's like this for everyone else too. I know how fortunate I am. I know how much worse it could be. I'm not complaining. But my parents live on Earth, and I don't know if . . ." She had to stop and take a breath to compose herself. "I don't know when I'll see them again."

Two ambulances passed, one after the other, then silence. Olive looked over her shoulder. The ambulance across the street was still there.

"Are you there?" Olive asked.

"I'm sorry," the journalist said. Her voice was choked.

"What's your situation?" Olive asked softly. It occurred to her that the journalist sounded very young. She glanced at her calendar. The journalist's name was Annabel Escobar, and she worked in the city of Charlotte, which Olive dimly recalled visiting on a long-ago tour of United Carolina.

"I live alone," Annabel said. "We're not supposed to leave our houses, and it's just . . ." But she was crying now, truly weeping.

"I'm sorry," Olive said. "That sounds so lonely." She was staring out the window. The ambulance hadn't moved.

"I just haven't been in a room with anyone in a very long time," Annabel said.

On another night of searching, a centuries-old academic journal yielded a reference to a Gaspery J. Roberts. The journal had been devoted to prison reform. The hit sent Olive down a rabbit hole, at the end of which she found prison records from Earth: Gaspery J. Roberts had been sentenced to fifty years for a double homicide in Ohio in the late twentieth century. But there was no picture, so Olive couldn't be sure it was the same man.

"So, Olive," another journalist said. They were holograms in a silvery holospace room, along with two other authors who'd also written books whose plots involved pandemics. The four of them flickered like ghosts. "How many copies of *Marienbad* have you sold since the pandemic began?"

"Oh," Olive said. "I'm not sure. A lot."

"I know you've sold a lot," he said. "It's been on bestseller lists in a dozen Earth countries, all three moon colonies, and two of the three colonies on Titan. I'm asking you to be more specific."

"I'm afraid I don't have my sales numbers in front of me," Olive said. All of the holograms were staring at her.

"Really?" the journalist asked.

"It didn't occur to me to bring my royalty statements to this interview," Olive said.

An hour later, when the interview was over, she removed her headset and sat for a while with her eyes closed. She'd been home from Earth for long enough that when she opened the window, the night air of the Second Colony seemed fresh again. The air might be filtered, but there were plants, there was running water, there was a world outside her window as real as any world that anyone had ever lived in. Olive found herself thinking of Jessica Marley, for the first time in a while, and Jessica Marley's insufferable little coming-of-age-on-the-moon novel. Look, she wanted to tell her, there's no *pain in unreality* happening here. A life lived under a dome, in an artificially generated atmosphere, is still a life. A siren wailed and receded. Olive picked up her device, ran a search on Jessica's name, and discovered that she'd died two months ago in Spain.

"Mama?" Sylvie was in the doorway. "Is your interview over?"

"Hi, sweetie. Yes. It ended early." Jessica Marley was thirty-seven years old.

"Do you have another interview?"

"No." Olive knelt before her daughter, and then hugged her quickly. "No more till tomorrow."

"Then can we play Enchanted Forest?"

"Of course."

Sylvie wriggled a little in anticipation. *I was supposed to die in the pandemic.* Olive knew now that she was going to spend the rest of her life trying to understand that fact. But her effervescent five-year-old sat before her, grinning, and what she found at that moment, as the lights of yet another ambulance flickered over the ceiling, was that it was possible to smile back. This is the strange lesson of living in a pandemic: life can be tranquil in the face of death.

"Mama? Let's play Enchanted Forest."

"Okay," Olive said. "The portal door opens . . ."

6

Mirella and Vincent /

file corruption

1

Follow the evidence. In Gaspery's years of training, from the night he called Zoey to wish her a happy birthday through the present moment, that mantra had been a compass. *Present moment* was beginning to seem like a nonsensical term, but every moment can be distilled to a date, so let's call it November 30, 2203, in Colony Two, this city in the grip of a pandemic that would eventually kill 5 percent of its residents, this place that wasn't yet Gaspery's home and not yet the Night City, walking rapidly through the streets with Zoey to evade a lockdown-enforcement patrol.

"Here," Zoey said, and pulled him into a doorway. Gaspery peered through the glass door beside him, into a room of shadowy tables and chairs. This place was a restaurant, or had been. All of the restaurants in Colony Two were closed now.

They stood close together in the shadows, listening. All Gaspery could hear were sirens.

"You know you broke the most important protocol," Zoey said quietly. "Why did you do it?"

"I couldn't not warn her," Gaspery said.

"Okay," she said, "here's your situation. I've only done a preliminary analysis, but as far as I can tell, your decision to save Olive Llewellyn had no recognizable effect on the Time Institute."

"Does that mean I'll be okay?"

"No," she said, "it means you weren't immediately lost in time. It means your travel privileges haven't been revoked yet, because we sank five years of training into you and you still might be useful to the Time Institute, for at least the duration of this investigation. But if I were you, I'd get that tracker out of my arm and I wouldn't come back." She held up her device. "I have to go," she said. "Stay here, in this time, and I'll try to visit."

"Wait. Please."

She was still, watching him.

"I know you would never do what I did," he said. "But suppose you had done it. If you were in my position, Zoey, what would you do?"

"It's hard for me to imagine things that aren't real," she said.

"Can you try?"

Zoey sighed and closed her eyes. What occurred to Gaspery in that moment, watching her, was that he was her only person. Their parents were gone. She had never married. If she had friends or romantic interests, they'd never come up in conversation. He felt a fathomless guilt. Zoey opened her eyes.

"I might try to solve the anomaly," she said.

"How?"

Zoey was quiet for so long that he thought she wasn't going to answer. "Hold on," she said. "It took our best research teams a year to figure out these coordinates." She typed something into her device, and he heard his own device chime softly in his pocket.

"I sent you a new destination," Zoey said. "We don't know the time, we only know the day and the place, so you'll have to wait in the forest." She entered another code into her device and blinked out.

Gaspery was alone in the doorway, in the right city but the wrong time. He closed his eyes and considered the course of the investigation, because that was preferable to thinking about his sister, or thinking of what awaited him if he returned to his own time. He had a new destination. He entered the codes into his device, and he left.

2

He was on the beach at Caiette. He could see from the coordinates that he'd landed in the summer of 1994, but at first it seemed like a mistake, because the place hadn't changed at all over the past eight decades. He was staring at two little islands, tufts of trees across the water, and for a disorienting moment he thought he was back in 1912, dressed in the costume of an early-twentieth-century priest, preparing to meet Edwin St. Andrew in the church.

The little white church on the hillside was unchanged since the last time he'd been here—it must have recently been repainted—but the houses around it were different. He turned his back on the settlement, and his gaze fell on the ocean. The sun was rising, shades of blue and pink rippling over the water. He liked the way it moved, the gentle repetition of waves. He found himself thinking of his mother now, for the first time in a while. She'd spent time on Earth as a child. She'd kept a framed photo of an Earth ocean in the kitchen of his childhood home, a small rectangle of waves on the wall near the stove. He remembered her gazing at it while she stirred soup. And yet for himself, he realized, the ocean carried no weight in his heart, it featured in none of his childhood memories and none of the important moments of his life; it was just a place he'd seen in movies and visited for work, so he couldn't summon much feeling for it, and after a moment he turned and walked away down the beach, following the coordinates that flashed softly on his device. He walked beyond the last house, then into the forest.

Walking through this forest was easier now than when he'd been wearing a priest's robe, but he still had no talent for it. The ground was too soft; branches caught at his clothes; he felt assailed from all sides. It was a sunny afternoon, but it must have rained that morning. Ferns pulled wetly at his legs. His shoes were less waterproof than he'd thought. His device pulsed softly in his hand, with a message that he was very close to the place he sought; he let go of the branch he'd been holding to study the screen, and the branch slapped him across the face.

Here was the maple tree, eighty-two years older than the last time he'd seen it. It had gained less in height than in breadth and magnificence. The clearing around it had widened with the passage of time. He walked under the canopy of its branches, to look up at the sunlight shifting through leaves, and for the first time in memory, he felt true reverence.

When would Vincent Smith come here? There was no way to

know. Gaspery stepped just outside the clearing, and fought his way into a thicket of dense leaves, where he knelt on the cool, wet earth, and waited.

He was very still, listening. Another thing he didn't like about forests was the constant sound. It wasn't the steady white noise of the moon cities, the distant mechanicals that increased the gravity to Earth levels and kept the air inside the domes breathable and created the illusion of a breeze. There was no pattern to the white noise of a forest, and the randomness put Gaspery on edge. Time passed, hours. His muscles cramped. He was desperately thirsty. He stood a few times, to stretch, then crouched low again. It was impossible to hear anything coming, until it wasn't. A little after four in the afternoon, he heard the girl's soft footsteps on the path.

Vincent Smith at thirteen: she looked like she'd cut her own hair with blunt scissors before she'd dyed it bright blue. Her eyes were ringed in black. She radiated neglect. She walked slowly, looking through the viewfinder of her camera, and from his hiding place Gaspery recognized the scene: once he'd sat in a theater in New York City and watched a somewhat tedious musical performance accompanied by the footage that Vincent was creating at this moment. She stopped under the tree, angled the camera upward—

—and reality broke: Gaspery and Vincent were in the cavernous echoing cathedral of the Oklahoma City Airship Terminal, where Olive Llewellyn was walking just ahead of them and notes were rising from a nearby violin. And here too, impossibly, *was Edwin St. Andrew, face upturned toward the branches/the terminal ceiling—*

Vincent staggered and all but dropped her camera. Gaspery's hands were clasped over his mouth, because he wanted to scream, and the terminal was gone. It's one thing to know in the abstract that one moment might corrupt another moment; it's another to experience both moments at once; it's something else again to suspect what it might mean. Vincent was staring around wildly, but Gaspery was crouched low and she didn't see him. He closed his eyes, sank his hands into the mud, and tried to convince himself that the cold water seeping through the knees of his pants was real.

3

But what makes a world real?

Gaspery was lying on his back in the mud, staring up at leaves silhouetted against a darkening sky, and it seemed to him that he'd been there for some time. Night was falling in the forest. Vincent was gone. He sat up, with some effort—his back was stiff; how long had he been lying there unmoving?—and sent a message through his device: *I saw it! I saw the file corruption! It's real, Zoey.*

There was no reply. He knew what he'd done, he knew he'd broken the most important rule by saving Olive Llewellyn, but he retained a sliver of hope that the message might save him.

4

Gaspery returned to the moment he'd left, to Travel Room Eight in the third sub-basement of the Time Institute, Zoey sitting before him at the control desk.

"I saw it," Gaspery said. "I saw the anomaly."

"I got your message." Zoey was staring at him, and he saw that she'd been crying. "I just spoke with Ephrem," she said. "You're being taken out of commission."

"What will happen to me?"

"Nothing good."

"I know what I did," Gaspery said. "But if I finish the investigation, maybe they'll . . ."

"I don't think there's anything you can do to save yourself now."

"But there *might* be. Look. I just want another level of confirmation, another witness. I need two more destinations." Gaspery stepped out of the machine, and handed over his device.

She looked at it and frowned. "1918?"

"I have follow-up questions for Edwin St. Andrew."

"In 1918? He experienced the anomaly in 1912. And what's in 2007?"

"A party Vincent Smith attended," he said. "Or I guess she's Vincent Alkaitis by that point. The party was on a list of secondary destinations."

"But your device and your tracker are out of commission," she said.

"Zoey," Gaspery said. "Please."

She closed her eyes for just a moment, and then took his device. She was typing something that he couldn't see, then she leaned close to the projection for an iris scan. "I'm overriding the decommissioning order," she said. Her voice was strangely flat, and he saw terror in her eyes. "Ephrem will be here any minute, probably with security forces. I won't stop you from going, Gaspery, but I can't protect you if you come back."

"I understand," he said. "Thank you."

Gaspery heard the knock on the door just as he was leaving.

5

Gaspery stepped out of a New York City men's room in the winter of 2007, into the warmth and light of a party in an art gallery. He moved slowly through the crowd, trying to orient himself. He was looking for Vincent Smith. He knew she'd be here—her presence had been entered into the historical record, because somewhere in this room was a society photographer—but what that meant, in 2007, was that Mirella Kessler was here too, and after his strange encounter with her in 2020, Gaspery hoped to avoid her.

He saw them together at the far end of the room, admiring a large-scale oil painting. He plucked a glass of red wine from a little round tray and went to stare at a different painting and plot his next move. He was utterly unnerved by the crowd. They were shaking hands, which even after all of his cultural-sensitivity training seemed like a bizarre thing to do in flu season, and kissing one another on the cheek. These people have no direct experience of pandemics, he reminded himself. None of them were old enough to remember the winter of 1918–1919; Ebola was a few years out and would mostly be confined to the other side of the Atlantic; Covid-19 would not arrive for another thirteen years. Gaspery began moving slowly around the periphery of the room, sidling toward Vincent.

In 2007, Vincent was wealthy, and possessed of a sheen of elegance and self-confidence that he wouldn't have expected of the blue-haired waif he'd just encountered in Caiette. Her arm was looped through Mirella's, and they were standing in front of a painting, but, he saw now, not really looking at it. They were speaking in a conspiratorial way. Mirella laughed softly. They had a look of inseparability that brought him close to despair. But then Vincent extricated herself to say hello to someone else, while Mirella turned to find her husband, and Gaspery saw his chance.

"Vincent?"

"Hello." She had a warm smile, and he found that he liked her immediately.

"I'm sorry to bother you. I'm conducting an investigation on behalf of an art collector, and I wondered if I might ask you a quick question about your brother Paul's videos."

He had her attention. Her eyes widened. "My brother? But I didn't think—I didn't know he did videos. He's a musician. Or a composer, I guess."

"That's my suspicion," he said. "I don't think he shot those videos. I think someone else did."

She frowned. "Can you describe them?"

"Well, there's one in particular," Gaspery said. "The videographer was walking through a forest. British Columbia, I think. It was a sunny day. Judging by the quality of the footage, I'd say probably sometime in the mid-nineties."

Her gaze softened. Gaspery had a sense of performing some kind of hypnosis. "The videographer walked along a path," he continued, "toward a maple tree."

She nodded. "I used to record on that path all the time," she said.

"On this particular video, something strange happens. There's this weird flash of something," Gaspery said, "like it all goes dark for a second, probably just some kind of glitch on the tape—"

"It seemed like a glitch," Vincent said, "but it wasn't on the tape."

"You saw it?"

"I heard these weird noises, and everything went dark."

"What did you hear?"

"Violin music. Then a noise like hydraulics. It was inexplicable." Her eyes focused suddenly. "I'm sorry," she said, "what did you say your name was?"

Her husband was moving through the crowd toward them, he was handing Vincent a glass of wine, and Gaspery took advantage of this momentary distraction to slip away from them. He felt a strange elation that was equal parts exhaustion and joy. He had a corroborating interview, recorded on his device. He had his own observations. For the first time since his interview with Olive Llewellyn, on the morning of this strange and seemingly infinite day, he felt he might not be doomed.

But Gaspery hesitated by the men's room door for a moment, watching the party, and his happiness faded. Here was the awfulness that Zoey had warned him of, the utterly miserable knowledge of how everyone else's stories would end. He looked out over the room, and for the first time in his life, Gaspery felt old.

Vincent and her husband clinked their glasses together. In fourteen months Alkaitis would be arrested for running a massive Ponzi scheme, then released on bail, at which point he would flee to Dubai—abandoning Vincent—and live out the rest of his long life in a series of hotels.

Vincent would live for another twelve years, and then disappear under mysterious circumstances from the deck of a container ship.

Nearby was Mirella, talking with her husband, Faisal. Faisal was an investor in Jonathan's fraud scheme, and when the scheme collapsed in a year he would lose everything, as would the family members who'd invested at his urging. Faisal would die of suicide.

Mirella would find the body, and the note. Then she would remain for more than a decade in New York City, until in March 2020 she would travel to Dubai for unknown reasons, arriving just in time to be stranded by the Covid-19 pandemic.

There she would meet Himesh Chiang, a guest at the same hotel where she was staying, and after some time the two of them would return to his native London, where they would survive the pandemic, marry, and live out the rest of their lives together; she would give birth to three children, have a successful career in retail management, and die of pneumonia at eighty-five, a year after her husband's death in a car accident.

But so much is inevitably left out of any biography, any accounting of any life. Before all of that, before Mirella lost Faisal, before this party in this city by the sea, she'd been a child in Ohio. Gaspery shivered. He was thinking of the way she'd looked at him in the park, in January 2020. *You were under the overpass,* she'd said to him, with terrible certainty, *in Ohio, when I was a kid.* Not just that. She'd said he was arrested there.

He'd been thinking of 1918 as his final trip. He had made every effort to save himself, and after 1918 he was going home to face the consequences. But what he realized now, watching Mirella, was that it was too late. He was going to go to 1918, but there would be one more destination after that.

7

Remittance /

1918, 1990, 2008

1

In 1918 Edwin had no more brothers, and only one foot. He lived with his parents on the family estate. He walked constantly, ostensibly because he was trying to improve his gait—he'd been fitted with a prosthetic and walked in a lurching way—but really because if he stopped moving, the enemy might get him. He walked at all hours of the day and night. Sleep transported him reliably back to the trenches, so he avoided sleep, which meant it ambushed him unexpectedly: while reading in the library, while sitting in the garden, once or twice at dinner.

His parents weren't sure how to speak to him, or how to look at him even. They couldn't accuse him of shiftlessness anymore, because he was a war hero but also something of an invalid. It was obvious to everyone that he wasn't well. "You've changed so much, darling," his mother said gently, and he wasn't sure whether this was a compliment, an accusation, or pure observation. He'd never been good at reading people and now he was worse.

"Well," he said, "I saw some things I wish I hadn't."

Understatement of the goddamned twentieth century.

He felt more empathy for his mother than previously, though. When Abigail floated off at the dinner table, when talk turned to the colonies and the look that her sons had once unkindly termed her British India expression came over her face, Edwin understood more vividly now that she was mourning a loss. He still found the Raj indefensible, but that didn't mean she hadn't lost an entire world. It wasn't her fault that the world she'd grown up in had ceased to exist.

Sometimes in the garden, he liked to talk to Gilbert, although Gilbert was dead. Gilbert and Niall had both died in the Battle of the Somme, a day apart, while Edwin had survived Passchendaele. No, *survived* was the wrong word. Edwin's animate body had returned from Passchendaele. He thought of his body now in strictly mechanical terms. His heart flapped deathlessly. He continued to breathe. He was in good physical health, except for the missing foot, but he was fundamentally unsound. It was difficult to be alive in the world.

"It's not uncommon," he heard the doctor say in the corridor outside his room, in the earliest weeks, when all he did was lie in bed. "The boys who went over there and wound up in the trenches, well, some of them saw things none of us should."

He hadn't entirely surrendered. He was making an effort. He rose and dressed in the mornings now, he ate the food that appeared in front of him at the table, and then, his strength exhausted, he spent most of the remaining day in the garden. He liked to sit out there on a bench under a tree and talk to Gilbert. He knew Gilbert wasn't there—he wasn't *that* far gone—but there was no one else to talk to. He'd had friends here, once, but now one friend was in China and all the others were dead.

"Now that you and Niall are dead," he confided, to Gilbert, "I'll inherit the title and the estate." He was surprised by how little he cared.

It came as an odd jolt when he walked out into the walled garden one morning and saw a man waiting on the bench. For just a heartbeat he thought it was Gilbert—at this point anything seemed possible—but then he came closer and the man's true identity was almost as strange: he was the impostor from that tiny church on the westernmost edge of British Columbia, the strange man in the clothes of a priest whom no one else in that place had ever seen or heard of.

"Please," the man said. "Sit." That same unplaceable foreign accent.

Edwin sat beside him on the bench.

"I thought you were a hallucination," Edwin said. "When I

saw Father Pike and asked him about the new priest I'd just been speaking to, Pike looked at me like I had two heads."

"My name is Gaspery-Jacques Roberts," the stranger said. "I'm afraid I only have a few minutes, but I wanted to see you."

"A few minutes until what?"

"An appointment. You'll think I'm a lunatic if I tell you the details."

"I'm afraid I'm in no position to judge anyone else's lunacy, just at present, but why are you lurking around my garden?"

Gaspery hesitated. "You were on the Western Front, weren't you?"

Mud. Cold rain. An explosion, blinding light, things raining down around him, then one of those things hit him in the chest and when he looked down he recognized his best friend's arm—

"Belgium," Edwin confirmed, through gritted teeth.

Friend wasn't really the word for what that man was to him, actually. The thing that hit his jacket and fell to his feet was the arm of his beloved. His beloved's head landed nearby in the mud, eyes still wide with amazement.

"And now you fear for your sanity," Gaspery said carefully.

"It was always a little fragile, in all honesty," Edwin said.

"Do you remember what you saw in the forest at Caiette? It was years ago now."

"Vividly, but it was a hallucination. The first of many, I'm afraid."

Gaspery was quiet for a moment. "I can't explain the mechanics here," he said. "My sister probably could, but it's still beyond me. But whatever happened to you afterward, whatever you saw in Belgium, it's possible you're saner than you think. I can assure you that what you saw in Caiette was real."

"How do I know that you're real?" Edwin asked.

Gaspery reached out his hand, and touched Edwin's shoulder. They stayed like that for a moment, Edwin staring at the hand on his shoulder, then Gaspery removed his hand and Edwin cleared his throat.

"What I experienced in Caiette couldn't possibly have been real," Edwin said. "It was a derangement of the senses."

"Was it? I believe you heard a few notes of violin music, played by a musician in an airship terminal in the year 2195."

"An airship . . . the year twenty-one-*what*?"

"Followed by a sound that must have seemed quite strange to you. A sort of *whoosh*, wasn't it?"

Edwin stared at him. "How did you know?"

"Because that's the sound that airships make," Gaspery said. "They won't be invented for some time. As for the violin music . . . a kind of lullaby, wasn't it?" He was quiet for a beat, then hummed a few notes. Edwin gripped the armrest of the bench. "The man who composed that song won't be born for another hundred and eighty-nine years."

"None of this is possible," Edwin said.

Gaspery sighed. "Think of it in terms of . . . well, in terms of corruption. Moments in time can corrupt one another. There was a derangement, but it had nothing to do with you. You're just a man who saw it. You were helpful in my investigation, and

I believe you're in a somewhat delicate state, and I thought perhaps it might ease your mind just a little to know that you might be saner than you think. At that moment, at least, you were not hallucinating. You were experiencing a moment from elsewhere in time."

Edwin's gaze drifted away from the man's face, to the mild decrepitude of the September garden. The salvias were bare now, for the most part, brown stalks and dried leaves, a few last blooms wisping blue and violet in the failing light. He was struck by an understanding of what his life could be from this moment: he could live here quietly, and care for the garden, and that might eventually be enough.

"Thank you for telling me," Edwin said.

"Don't tell anyone else." Gaspery rose, brushing a fallen leaf from his jacket. "You'll get committed to an asylum."

"Where are you going?" Edwin asked.

"I've an appointment in Ohio," Gaspery said. "Good luck."

"Ohio?"

But Gaspery was already walking away from him, disappearing around the side of the house. Edwin watched him go and then remained on his bench for a long time, hours, watching the way the garden faded into twilight.

2

Gaspery walked around the side of the house, and in the shadows at the base of a weeping willow, he stood staring at his device for a moment. A message pulsed softly on the screen: *Return*. He had exhausted the limits of his itinerary. The only possible destination was home. For just a moment he entertained a wild notion of staying here in 1918, burying his device in the garden and cutting his tracker out of his arm, taking his chances in the flu pandemic and trying to find some kind of life for himself in a foreign world, but even as he thought this he was already entering the code, he was already leaving, and when he opened his eyes in the harsh light of the Time Institute, he was unsurprised to see the figures gathered there, the men and women in black uniforms waiting with weapons drawn. What was surprising, though, was that Olive Llewellyn's publicist was standing next to Ephrem. They were the only two out of uniform.

"Aretta?"

"Hello, Gaspery," she said.

"Stay where you are, please," Ephrem said. "There's no need to leave the machine." His hands were clasped behind his back. Gaspery stayed where he was. At the back of the room—he had to crane his neck to see around the black uniforms—Zoey was being restrained by two men.

"I never guessed," Gaspery said, to Aretta.

"That's because I'm competent at my job," Aretta said. "I don't go around telling people I'm a time traveler."

"That's fair." Gaspery felt a little unhinged. "I'm sorry," he said to Zoey. "I'm sorry I tricked you." But she was already being escorted from the room, the door closing behind her.

"You tricked her?" Ephrem asked.

"I told her I was going to 1918 as part of the investigation. I was really there to try to save Edwin St. Andrew from dying in an insane asylum."

"Seriously, Gaspery? Yet another crime? Does someone have an updated bio?"

Aretta was frowning at her device. "Updated bio," she said. "Thirty-five days after Gaspery's visit, Edwin St. Andrew died in the 1918 flu pandemic."

"Isn't that the same bio?" Ephrem reached for her device, read for a moment, then handed it back with a sigh. "If you hadn't changed the time line," he said to Gaspery, "he still would've died of the flu, just forty-eight hours later and in an insane asylum. You see how *pointless* that was?"

"You're missing the point," Gaspery said.

"That's very possible." Were there tears in Ephrem's eyes? He looked tired and strained. A man who'd preferred being an arborist; a man in a difficult position, doing a difficult job. "Is there anything you'd like to say?"

"Are we at last words already, Ephrem?"

"Well, last words in this century," Ephrem said. "Last words on the moon. I'm afraid you'll be traveling some distance and not returning."

"Can you take care of my cat?" Gaspery asked.

Ephrem blinked.

"Yes, Gaspery, I'll take care of your cat."

"Thank you."

"Is there anything else?"

"I'd do it again," Gaspery said. "I wouldn't even hesitate."

Ephrem sighed. "Good to know." He'd been holding a glass bottle behind his back. He raised it now, and misted something in Gaspery's face. There was a sweet scent, a dimming of the lights, then Gaspery's legs were giving way—

3

—as he faded out, he had an impression that Ephrem had stepped
into the machine behind him—

4

—Two gunshots, in quick succession—

Footsteps, a man running away—

Gaspery was in a tunnel. Light at either end, not just light but snow—

No, not a tunnel, an overpass. He could smell the exhaust of twentieth-century cars. He was very sleepy, from whatever he'd just been misted with. His back was to the embankment.

Ephrem was there too, calm and efficient in his dark suit. "I'm sorry, Gaspery," he said softly, his breath warm in Gaspery's ear. "I really am." He plucked Gaspery's device from his hand and replaced it with something hard and cold and much heavier—

A gun. Gaspery looked at it, curious, and the running man—the shooter, he realized dimly—disappeared, scrambling away and out of sight. Ephrem was gone too, a passing ghost. The air was cold.

He heard a soft groan near his feet. It was difficult for Gaspery to stay awake. His eyes kept closing. But he saw two men lying nearby, two men whose blood was seeping across the concrete, and one of them was staring directly at him. There was clear confusion in the man's stare—*Who are you? Where did you come from?*—but he'd passed beyond speaking, and as Gaspery watched, the light left his eyes. Gaspery was alone under an expressway with two dead men. He nodded off, just for a moment. When he opened his eyes, he was staring at the gun in his hand, and the pieces of the puzzle were drifting together. *It's possible to get lost in time,* Zoey had said, in a different century. Why go to the bother of incarcerating a man for life on the moon, when that man can be sent elsewhere, framed, and imprisoned at someone else's expense?

He sensed movement to his left. He turned his head, very slowly, and saw the children. Two girls, aged perhaps nine and eleven, holding hands. They'd been walking under the overpass, but now they'd stopped some distance away, staring. He saw their backpacks, and realized they were on their way home from school.

Gaspery let the gun fall from his hand, and it clattered away like a harmless thing. There were lights washing over him now, red and blue. The girls were staring at the two dead men, then the younger girl looked at him, and he recognized her.

"Mirella," he said.

5

No star burns forever. Gaspery scratched the words on a wall in prison some years later, so delicately that from any distance at all it looked like a flaw in the paint. You had to get close to see it, and you had to have lived in the twenty-second century or later to know what it meant. You had to have seen that twenty-second-century press conference, the president of China on a podium with a half-dozen of her favorite world leaders arrayed behind her, flags snapping against a brilliant blue sky.

There was time in prison, infinite time, so Gaspery spent a lot of it thinking about the past, no, the future, the point in time in which he'd walked into Zoey's office on her birthday with cupcakes and flowers, and everything that had followed. What had happened now was terrible, he was in prison in the wrong century and he was going to die here, but as months slipped into years, he found his regrets were very few. Warning Olive Llewellyn of the approaching pandemic was not, no matter how he turned the moment over in his mind, the wrong thing to do. If someone's about to drown, you have a duty to pull them from the water. His conscience was clear.

"What's that you wrote there, Roberts?" Hazelton asked. Hazelton was his cellmate, a much younger man who paced and talked incessantly. Gaspery didn't mind him.

"No star burns forever," Gaspery said.

Hazelton nodded. "I like that," he said. "Power of positive thinking, right? You're in prison, but that's not forever, because nothing is *forever*, right? Me, every time I start feeling a little down about my life, I—" He kept talking, but Gaspery stopped listening. He was calm these days, in a way he wouldn't have expected. In the early evenings Gaspery liked to sit on the farthest possible edge of his bunk, almost falling off the end, because from that angle there was a sliver of sky visible through the window, and through it he could see the moon.

8

Anomaly

1

Is this the promised end?

A line from Olive Llewellyn's novel *Marienbad,* but really a quote from Shakespeare. I found it in the prison library five or six years in, in a paperback with a missing cover.

2

No star burns forever.

3

Not long after my sixtieth birthday I developed some heart trouble, the kind of thing that could have been easily fixed in my
own century but was dangerous in this time and place, and I was
transferred to the prison hospital. I couldn't see the moon from
my bed, so there was nothing for it now but to close my eyes and
play old movies:

walking to school in the Night City, past Olive Llewellyn's childhood home
with its boarded-up front window and plaque;
standing in the church in Caiette in 1912 in my priest costume,
waiting for Edwin St. Andrew to stagger in;
chasing squirrels when I was five in the strip of wilderness
between the Night City dome and the Periphery Road;
drinking with Ephrem behind the school on an afternoon without

sunlight when we were fifteen or so, one of those afternoons that felt a
little dangerous,
even though all we were doing was getting slightly drunk and
trading dumb jokes;
holding hands and laughing with my mother on a
sunlit day in the Night City when I was six or seven,
stopping to look down at the river from a
pedestrian bridge, the river dark and sparkling below—

"Gaspery."

I felt a sharp pain in my arm. I gasped and almost cried out, but a hand was over my mouth.

"Shh," Zoey whispered. She looked like she was in her early forties, she was wearing a nurse's uniform, and she had just cut the tracker out of my arm. I stared at her, uncomprehending.

"I'm going to place this under your tongue," she said. She held it up for me to see: a new tracker, to correspond with the new device that she was pressing into my hand. She had drawn the curtain around my bed. She held her device against mine for a second or two, until the devices flashed in a quick coordinated pattern. I stared at those lights—

4

—and we were in a different room, in a different place.

I was lying on my back on a wood floor, in a bedroom, in what seemed to me to be an old-fashioned kind of house. My arm was bleeding; I held it reflexively to my chest. Sunlight poured in through a window. I sat up. There was wallpaper with roses, wooden furniture, and through a doorway I saw a room with a shower and a toilet.

"What is this place?"

"This is a farm on the outskirts of Oklahoma City," she said. "I've paid a great deal of money to the owners, and you can stay here indefinitely, as a boarder. The year is 2172."

"2172," I said. "So in twenty-three years, I'll visit Oklahoma City to interview the violinist."

"Yes."

"How are you here? Surely the Time Institute didn't approve this trip."

"I was arrested that day," she said. "The day you were sent to Ohio. I had tenure and an otherwise sterling record, so I wasn't lost in time, but I spent a year in prison and then immigrated to the Far Colonies. The Time Institute thinks they have the only functional time machine in existence. They don't."

"There's a time machine in the Far Colonies? And you just, what, get to use it?"

"I'm employed by . . . another organization there," she said.

"Even with your record?"

"Gaspery," she said, "no one's better than me at what I do." She spoke matter-of-factly; she wasn't boasting.

"You know, I still don't know what that is."

She ignored this. "I made this mission a condition of my agreeing to take the job in the Far Colonies," she said. "I'm sorry I couldn't come sooner. I mean to an earlier point in time."

"It's okay. I mean, thank you. Thank you for coming for me."

"I think it's safe here, Gaspery. I built a paper trail for you. You should settle in. Meet the neighbors."

"Zoey, I can't thank you enough."

"You'd do the same for me." (Unspoken between us: I *couldn't* do the same for her. She was of a different order from me, and always had been.) "I don't know if we'll see each other again," Zoey said.

Had we ever hugged before? I couldn't remember. She clasped me close for just a moment, stepped back, and was gone.

I was alone in the room, but *alone* wasn't a strong enough word for it. I knew no one in this century, and the fact of having been through this before did nothing to assuage my loneliness. I had a deranged moment of wondering how Hazelton was doing, then remembered that my cellmate would have died of old age by now.

I went to the window, in a daze, and looked out at a sea of green. The farm reached almost to the horizon, field upon field with agricultural robots moving slowly in the sunlight. In the far distance, I saw the spires of Oklahoma City. The sky was a dazzling blue.

5

The farm was owned and run by an older couple, Clara and Mariam. They were in their late eighties and had been here all their lives. They were pleased to have a well-paying boarder, they told me that first night, over a dinner of quiche and the freshest salad I'd tasted in decades, and they would ask me no questions. They respected privacy above all.

"Thank you," I said.

"Your sister left us some identity paperwork for you," Clara said. "Birth certificate and such. Shall we call you by the name on the paperwork?"

"Call me Gaspery," I said. "Please."

"Well, Gaspery," Clara said, "should you ever have need of your documents, it's all in that blue cabinet by the hallway door."

I didn't leave the farm at all those first few years, but I feared that eventually I'd have to. When Mariam fell ill, Clara drove her to the hospital, but who would drive Clara? They were nearing ninety. *My first case at the Institute involved a doppelgänger,* Ephrem had told me once, in another, unfathomable life. *According to our best facial-recognition software, the same woman appeared in photographs and video footage taken in 1925 and 2093.* Whenever I imagined leaving the farm, I imagined surveillance cameras picking up my face and setting off alarms through the centuries, a Time Institute agent arriving to investigate, a cascade of horrors. I spoke with Clara, who made discreet inquiries with a neighbor, who had a friend with useful contacts, and a short time later I was lying on my back on the farmhouse kitchen table, undergoing laser facial resculpting and iris recoloring.

When the sedation wore off and I sat up, the surgeon was gone.

"Whiskey?" Mariam asked.

"Please," I said.

"You look completely different," Clara said. She passed me a mirror, and I gasped.

I did look completely different. But I recognized my face.

6

Later that month, I found the violin. It was very old, and in a box at the very back of the hall closet; Mariam hadn't played it in years. Clara arranged for lessons from a neighbor.

"She goes by Lina," Clara said, on the drive over. "She's been playing violin all her life, in my understanding. Came here in much the same manner as you, if you get my drift."

I glanced at her. She was ninety-two that year, but her profile was still strong. Her eyes were unreadable.

"I had no idea," I said. There must have been a note of reproach in this, because Clara fixed me for a beat or two in her calm gaze.

"You know I believe in privacy," she said. "So does she, by all appearances. She's barely left that farm in thirty years."

We pulled up at the neighboring farmhouse—a gray cubist monstrosity that could have served as a hotel—and I was think-

ing of Zoey's words when she left me here, four years ago now—
You should settle in. Meet the neighbors—and wondering why
I'd never been able to properly apprehend anything she'd ever
said. I stepped out of the truck into glaring sunlight.

The front door opened, and the woman who stepped out was
around my age, early sixties.

"Good morning, Gaspery," Talia said.

7

"Your sister probably got me out just in time," Talia told me. "She came to the hotel one night, must have been right after she got out of prison, and told me the police had opened a file on me, something about repeating classified information."

"Well, in fairness, you did have a habit of repeating classified information." We were sitting on the porch of the farmhouse where she lived, our violins resting between us.

"I was reckless. Tempting fate, I suppose. She said she was about to move to the Far Colonies, and strongly suggested I come with her, but the Far Colonies have an extradition treaty with the moon, so she suggested once we got there that perhaps that shouldn't be my final destination."

"And that was thirty years ago?"

"Twenty-six."

I could see it when I looked at her, that quarter-century of living on this farm. Her skin was darkened by the sun and she had a peacefulness about her.

"What are they like?" I asked. "The Far Colonies?"

"They're beautiful," she said, "but I didn't like living underground."

8

We were married within a year, Talia and I, and when Clara and Mariam died, they left the farm to us.

This, I found myself thinking in the years that followed, on nights when my wife and I played the violin together, when we cooked together, when we walked in our fields watching the movements of the farm robots, when we sat on the porch watching the airships rise up like fireflies on the horizon over Oklahoma City, this is what the Time Institute never understood: if definitive proof emerges that we're living in a simulation, the correct response to that news will be *So what*. A life lived in a simulation is still a life.

9

A countdown had begun. I sensed it in the background of all my days. Sometime soon, I knew, I would move to Oklahoma City. I was scheduled to begin playing the violin in the airship terminal by 2195. I knew, because I remembered the interview, that my wife was going to die first.

10

Quietly
in the night
of an aneurysm
when she was seventy-five.

11

When Talia was gone I sat alone on the porch every night for a while, watching the airships rising over the distant city. My dog, Odie, lay beside me, head on his paws. At first I thought I was putting off moving to the city because I loved the farm, but one night it hit me: I *longed* for those lights. After all this time, I wanted to be around people again.

"I'll take you with me," I told Odie, who wagged his tail.

12

What someone—anyone!—at the Time Institute really should have caught, given how intelligent everyone was supposed to be over there, was that I was the anomaly. No, that's not fair. I *triggered* the anomaly. How did no one catch that I was interviewing myself? Because thanks to the documentation Zoey had created, on paper my name was Alan Sami and I'd been born and spent my life on a farm outside of Oklahoma City.

I watched the anomaly from the airship terminal. On an October day in 2195, I was playing the violin, my dog beside me, and I noticed two people almost at the same time.

Olive Llewellyn was walking along the corridor, pulling her silver suitcase. She didn't notice the man walking toward me a few meters ahead of her, but I did. The man had just stepped out of a utility closet.

As the man walked toward me, crossing Olive Llewellyn's path, the air seemed to ripple behind him. He didn't notice, because he was focused on me, and because he was a little anxious; this was, after all, his first interview for the Time Institute.

I kept playing, sweating now, holding on for dear life to my lullaby for Talia. The rippling intensified; the software, if that was the word for it, whatever unknowable engine kept our world intact, was struggling to reconcile the impossibility of both of us being here. But it wasn't just that the same person was in the same place twice; the engine, the intelligence, the software, whatever it was, it had detected a third Gaspery, somewhere else altogether in time and space, in the forest at Caiette, and now things were truly coming apart: this moment was corrupted, but so was *that place,* that point in the forest where in 1912 Edwin St. Andrew gazed up into the branches, where in 1994 I hid behind ferns and watched Vincent Smith. There was a strange wave of darkness behind the approaching man, light rippling away. Olive Llewellyn stopped as if struck. I saw myself kneeling in 1994, and Edwin St. Andrew in exactly the same spot—we were superimposed on one another—and nearby was Vincent Smith, thirteen years old with a camera in her hand.

An airship ascended at a nearby port, that unmistakable *whoosh,* and the specters were gone. Time was running smoothly again. The file corruption was repairing itself, the threads of the simulation knitting into place around us, and Gaspery-Jacques Roberts, my younger self, new recruit and distressingly inept investigator for the Time Institute, had noticed none of it. It had all transpired behind his back. He did glance over his shoulder, but—I remembered the moment—chalked up his overwhelming sense of wrongness to runaway nerves.

I closed my eyes. All this time, it had been me. Vincent and Edwin had seen the anomaly because I'd been with them in the forest. I must not have been close enough to Edwin to see it myself, that first time in 1912. I finished the lullaby, and heard Gaspery's applause.

He stood before me, clapping awkwardly. I was so embarrassed for him—for me? for us?—that it was difficult to meet his eyes, but I managed it. I was grateful that my dog had slept through my younger self's incompetence.

"Hello," he said brightly, in a jarringly imperfect accent. "My name's Gaspery-Jacques Roberts. I'm conducting some research on behalf of a music historian, and I wondered if I could possibly buy you some lunch."

13

"How would I describe my life?" I repeated, stalling. "Well, son, that's a big question. I don't know what I can tell you."

"Maybe you could tell me a little about what your days are like. If you don't mind. I haven't turned the recorder on yet, by the way. This is just us talking."

I nodded. I would keep him off-balance. I would quote Shakespeare at him because I knew he didn't know his Shakespeare yet. I would call him *son* because he hated being called son, and his irritation would distract him. I would bring up my dead wife because he was embarrassed by his own failed marriage. I would make him feel insecure about his accent, because accents and dialects were what he'd struggled with the most in his training. But first I would lull him with the quiet of my life.

"Well," I said. "I stand there for a few hours a day, playing the violin, while my dog naps at my feet, and the commuters dash by and throw change at me. They move with inhuman speed, the commuters. It took me some time to get used to this."

"Are you from around here?" the investigator asked.

"A farm just outside the city. Lived there all my life. But listen, son, by the time I took over the farm, small-scale farming had become mostly a matter of watching. You watch the robots move over the fields. You tinker with their settings sometimes but they're well-made, they adjust themselves mostly, they don't need you for much. You play your violin in the field just to keep yourself occupied. In the distance the airships rise with the speed of fireflies, but they're faster up close."

When I played my violin at the airship terminal I sometimes thought it was as if the airships were falling upward, gravity reversed. They filled with a cargo of blank-faced commuters, then fell toward the sky. The commuters glanced at me sometimes as they passed, tossed coins into my hat. I watched their ships carry them up into the early morning, to jobs in Los Angeles, Nairobi, Edinburgh, Beijing. I thought of their souls moving fast through the morning sky.

"When my wife died," I told the investigator, "I kept up the farm for another year and then thought, to hell with it."

He was nodding, feigning interest, trying not to be nervous, trying to convince himself that he was doing a good job. What I didn't tell him: I felt that without Talia I might disappear into thin air, out there by myself. Just me and the dog and the farm robots, day after day. Loneliness wasn't a strong enough word for it. All that empty space. At night I sat on the porch with my dog, avoiding the silent house. Playing that game kids play, where you squint at the moon and half-convince yourself that you can see the brighter spots of the colonies on its surface. Distant over the fields, the lights of the city.

"Is it okay if I switch on the recorder?" the investigator asked.

"Go ahead."

"Okay, it's on. Thank you for taking the time to speak with me."

"You're welcome. Thank you for lunch."

"Now, just for the benefit of my recording, you're a violinist," my earlier self said.

I followed the script. "I am," I said. "I play in the airship terminal."

When I wasn't playing my violin in the airship terminal I liked to walk my dog in the streets between the towers. In those streets everyone moved faster than me, but what they didn't know was that I had already moved too fast, too far, and wished to travel no further. I've been thinking a great deal about time and motion lately, about being a still point in the ceaseless rush.

Notes and Acknowledgments

The quote referenced on page 72, "It's a great life if you don't weaken," is from John Buchan's 1919 novel *Mr. Standfast*.

The riff on page 95 re: chickens coming home to roost—"It's never good chickens"—is paraphrased from something the American poet Kay Ryan said when we were at a literary festival together in 2015.

The quote in the same chapter from the fourth-century Roman soldier and historian Ammianus Marcellinus, re: the Antonine Plague, is from Book XXIII of his writings, which are fascinating and available online.

I'm indebted to the books *Voyages of the* Columbia (ed. Frederic W. Howay) and *Scoundrels, Dreamers and Second Sons: British Remittance Men in the Canadian West*, by Mark Zuehlke.

With thanks to my agent, Katherine Fausset, and her colleagues at Curtis Brown; my editors—Jennifer Jackson at Knopf in New York City, Sophie Jonathan at Picador in London, and Jennifer Lambert at HarperCollins Canada in Toronto—and their colleagues; my U.K. agent, Anna Webber, and her colleagues at United Agents; Kevin Mandel, Rachel Fershleiser, and Semi Chellas, for reading and commenting on early drafts of this manuscript; and Michelle Jones, my daughter's nanny, for taking care of my daughter while I wrote this book.